DOMESTIC VIOLENCE, ABUSE, AND CHILD CUSTODY

Legal Strategies and Policy Issues

Edited by
Mo Therese Hannah, Ph.D.
and
Barry Goldstein, J.D.

CRI
Civic Research Institute

4478 U.S. Route 27 • P.O. Box 585 • Kingston, NJ 08528

Printed in the United States of America

Library of Congress Cataloging in Publication Data
Domestic Violence, Abuse, and Child Custody: Legal Strategies and Policy Issues/ Mo Therese Hannah, Ph.D., and Barry Goldstein, J.D.

ISBN 1-887554-76-9

Library of Congress Control Number: 2010920249

We dedicate this book to

Monique Therese Hannah
1987–2007

*"She has taught me more
in the time she's been gone
than I taught her in
the twenty years she was with me."*
–MTH

Table of Contents

PART 1: PARAMETERS OF THE PROBLEM

Chapter 1: Child Custody Practices of the Family Courts in Cases Involving Domestic Violence
Joan Zorza, J.D.

Chapter 2: Recognizing Domestic Violence: How to Know It When You See It and How to Provide Appropriate Representation
Lois Schwaeber, J.D.

Chapter 3: Historical Legal Context in Domestic Violence Custody Cases
Marvin Timothy Gray, J.D., M.A., C.D.S.V.R.P.

Chapter 4: Historical Origins of the Fathers' Rights Movement
Jan Kurth, M.U.P.

Chapter 5: Gender Bias in the Courts: Implications for Battered Mothers and Their Children
Molly Dragiewicz, Ph.D.

Chapter 6: Domestic Violence, Contested Child Custody, and the Courts: Findings From Five Studies
Sharon K. Araji, M.Ed., Ph.D., and Rebecca L. Bosek, Ph.D., L.M.F.T., L.P.C.

Chapter 7: Do Judges Adequately Address the Causes and Impact of Violence in Children's Lives in Deciding Contested Child Custody Cases?
Thomas E. Hornsby, J.D.

Chapter 8: Truth Commission: Findings and Recommendations
Mo Therese Hannah, Ph.D.

PART 2: SURVIVORS' STORIES

Chapter 9: Courageous Kids: Abused Children Sharing Their Experiences
Karen Anderson

Chapter 10: From the Mouths of Mothers
Wendy Titelman, Annette Zender, Paige Hodson, B.A.,
and Larissa Pollica, R.N., B.S.

PART 3: CAUSES OF AND CONTRIBUTORS TO THE PROBLEM

Chapter 11: Reframing Child Custody Decisions in the Context of Coercive Control
Evan Stark, Ph.D., M.S.W.

Chapter 12: Parental Alienation Syndrome
Paul Jay Fink, M.D.

Chapter 13: Why Do Judges Do That?
Mike Brigner, J.D.

Chapter 14: Batterer Manipulation and Retaliation Compounded by Denial and Complicity in the Family Courts
Joan Zorza, J.D.

Chapter 15: The Yuck Factor, the Oprah Factor, and the "Stickiness" Factor: Why the Mainstream Media Has Failed to Expose the Custody Court Scandal
Garland Waller, M.S.

PART 4: SOLUTIONS AND STRATEGIES

Chapter 16: Leveling the Landscape: Family Court Auxiliaries and How to Counter Them
Michael Lesher, M.A., J.D.

Chapter 17: Organizing in Defense of Protective Mothers: The Custody Rights Movement
Lundy Bancroft

Chapter 18: Recognizing and Overcoming Abusers' Legal Tactics
Barry Goldstein, J.D.

Chapter 19: DV Case Preparation and Trial Examination: A Heavy Burden
Marjory D. Fields. J.D.

Chapter 20: Fighting False Allegations of Parental Alienation Raised as Defenses to Valid Claims of Abuse
Nancy S. Erickson, J.D., L.L.M., M.A.

Chapter 21: Urgent Need for Quality Control in Child Custody Psychological Evaluations
Robin Yeamans, J.D.

Chapter 22: Factoring in the Effects of Children's Exposure to Domestic Violence in Determining Appropriate Postseparation Parenting Plans
Claire V. Crooks, Ph.D., C. Psych., Peter G. Jaffe, P.h.D., C. Psych., and Nicholas Bala, J.D.

Chapter 23: Court-Appointed Parenting Evaluators and Guardians Ad Litem: Practical Realities and an Argument for Abolition
Margaret K. Dore, J.D.

Chapter 24: American Law Institute Principles: A Tool for Accessing Justice for Battered Mothers and Children
Erika A. Sussman, J.D., LL.M.

Chapter 25: Covering the Crisis in the Custody Courts
Anne Grant, M.A., M.Div.

Acknowledgements

The editors would like to acknowledge the help and assistance of many dedicated individuals who have contributed to the preparation of this book. The writers of this book brought incredible expertise, hard work, and caring to this work. They are dedicated to making sure children will be protected from abusive parents. Without exception, these experts were cooperative and easy to work with. We look forward to working with them in the future to present trainings and other educational opportunities so the latest research can be available to professionals working in the child custody system.

We have worked with protective mothers as part of the Battered Mothers Custody Conference (BMCC) for the past seven years. They have brought us tears and inspiration as we watched and hopefully sometimes helped their attempts to protect their children. We will know the custody court system is reformed when these women are viewed not as disgruntled litigants but as the heroes they are.

The truth commission, held at the fourth BMCC, launched the beginning of this book project. We would like to thank the sixteen protective mothers who found the courage to testify in public about their experiences. We also deeply appreciate the truth commission members whose expertise and hard work created the *Truth Commission Report* with so many useful recommendations for reforming the system.

The editors wish to thank Deborah J. Launer for her support, encouragement, and cooperation in bringing this project to fruition. This book would not have been possible without her help.

Maxine Idakus has performed her work as line editor of this book with a professionalism and dedication the editors have come to respect and admire. She has made the information in the book clearer and more accessible.

Barbara Hart and Billie Lee Dunford Jackson helped us with suggestions for potential contributors to the book.

Mo Hannah wishes to thank the following additional individuals:

First, I would like to thank the countless battered mothers who had the courage to share with me what happened to them and their children. They are the major reason why this book has come to fruition. My appreciation also goes to a growing network of mothers' custody advocates, many of whom have been laboring for this cause far longer than I have. Among these fellow activists are Liliane Miller, who cofounded the BMCC with me, Robin Yeamans, Esq., Amy Neustein, Ph.D., Garland Waller, Ben Atherton-Zeman, and the Hofheimers' legal team of Virginia Beach, VA. I also want to express my sincere thanks to the students at Siena College who assisted me in editing this volume: Jennifer Bart, Nora Boyle, Heather Delong, Kelley Harvey, J. J. Hibbs, Courtney Hibbs, Meaghan Johnson, Lauren Morere, Annette Morere, Babette Peach, Meaghan Young, and Mary Richmond.

Finally, I'd like to offer my loving thanks to my three living children—Will, Alexis, and Jesse—who are, and have always been, my primary source of inspiration.

Barry Goldstein wishes to thank the following additional individuals:

I am deeply grateful Mo Hannah invited me to participate in this project. I have had the privilege of working with Mo as my expert witness, presenting at conferences, trying to help protective mothers, and now coediting this book. I deeply admire her courage, dedication, caring, and talent.

I have had the distinct privilege and opportunity to work with and learn from Phyllis B. Frank during the last ten years in my role as an instructor and supervisor in a New York Model Batterer Program led by Phyllis. From Phyllis, I have learned to recognize my sexism and hopefully avoid acting on my male privilege. She taught me about oppression, domestic violence, and clarity of thinking. This is a better book because of what I learned from Phyllis.

Many of the lessons I have shared in this book have come from the clients I have tried to help. Too often, in this broken system, I have failed. Nevertheless, their wisdom, courage, caring, and tears are with me every day.

During the preparation of this book, I have been subjected to an effort to take my legal license in retaliation for my work to help protective mothers and expose a system that is broken. Nancy Erickson, Dr. Mo Hannah, Judge Mary Anne Scattaretico-Naber, Phyllis B. Frank, Dr. Sharon Goldstein, and others had the courage to stand up to those who sought to silence their critics by the misuse of the disciplinary system.

The pain of watching children lose their safe, protective mothers has been accentuated because of the love and support I have received my entire life from my mom, Judith Goldstein. I understand what the courts are taking from these children.

My wife, Dr. Sharon Goldstein is the love of my life. I owe her my life, my happiness, and my opportunity to work to change the world.

Editors' Note

After this volume was written, the New York Appellate Division Second Department, in an unprincipled decision suspended Barry Goldstein's license in retaliation for pointing out the problematic responses of one of its colleagues to his zealous advocacy of a client.

Foreword

by Jay G. Silverman, Ph.D.

Although great strides have been made in raising awareness of violence against women, and despite the significant changes made to institutional practices (e.g., within health care and criminal courts) to promote the safety of abused women and their children, the family courts remain a dark and terrifying gauntlet through which battered mothers must pass in their attempts to protect both themselves and their children from the violence of their ex-husbands.

In creating this historic volume, Mo Hannah and Barry Goldstein have brought together a powerful cast of scholars, activists, and legal professionals to tell the full story of how and why the risks to the safety and well-being of battered mothers and their children from abusive men are too often seen as irrelevant or are grossly mischaracterized by family courts across the United States. The result of this failure is the endangerment of tens of thousands of children every year.

The importance of the problem cannot be overstated: there are approximately 100,000 contested child custody cases each year in the United States, with studies indicating that two-thirds of them likely involve domestic violence. Conservatively estimating that 90 percent of such cases involve violence by fathers towards mothers, these statistics imply that the fate of 90,000 children and adolescents who have been exposed to violence against their mothers is placed in the hands of the family courts every year.

What is central to understanding how critical a role the family courts play in these cases is the very real risk of both physical and sexual abuse of these children from their fathers. In the author's own recent research (unpublished), men who perpetrated violence against their female partners were six times more likely to physically abuse a child and twenty times more likely to sexually abuse a child in comparison with men who did not use violence against their girlfriends and wives. As obvious as this risk ought to be to professionals who are mandated to safeguard children embroiled in these cases, historic notions of fathers' rights over their family members, misguided public policy, inadequate judicial guidelines, the perversion of scientific evidence and, finally, the reluctance of many to even contemplate such horrific risks from men who claim to be fighting for the right to be a father, have led to a crisis in which the courts of virtually every state in the nation have increased the desperation of protective mothers and become complicit in the continuing victimization of thousands of children.

This groundbreaking collection first presents an historical examination of this problem. Following is a presentation of the major causes of family court malpractice. Finally, a comprehensive discussion of avenues for positive change, both inside and outside the family court system, is presented. Collectively, the chapters of this book provide professional and lay readers, including those directly affected by the family courts, with a critical guide to both understanding and taking action regarding what is, perhaps, the greatest single barrier to the safety of battered women and their children.

Introduction

by Barry Goldstein, J.D., and Mo Therese Hannah, Ph.D.

NEED FOR A SAFER RESPONSE TO CUSTODY
ISSUES IN DOMESTIC VIOLENCE CASES

As coeditors, we are pleased to present this comprehensive analysis of our nation's busiest civil court system, alternatively referred to as the "divorce courts," "custody courts," or more frequently, the "family courts." This book may very well contain the closest examination done to date of how fairly and justly these courts are as far as handling child custody and visitation disputes involving domestic abuse. Insuring an objective assessment of this matter has thus far been hindered by a list of factors, beginning with the thick layer of confidentiality under which the courts operate and, next on the list, the judicial or quasi-judicial immunity that covers virtually all officers of the court and, therefore, each and every court agent who handles these cases. We believe we have created, in this collection of twenty-five chapters, this rare type of assessment.

We believe you will be as impressed as we are by the breadth and depth of knowledge and experience our contributors brought to the task. A sizable number are or have been agents of the court—judges, attorneys, law clerks, and so forth—who therefore have a high stake in its reputation, since it is the system in which they themselves work and make a living. We view these authors, especially, as standing shoulders above their peers, not only because of the very good work they do, but also because of the honesty and courage they have shown in criticizing the club to which they also belong.

Domestic violence (DV) has been a public issue only since the mid to late 1970s. Much of the information and research we have now did not exist when the custody court system was first asked to respond to DV custody cases. At that time, the general belief was that DV entailed physical abuse and nothing else. The substantial proportion of abuse involving nonphysical means was ignored. Too, children were believed to be unaffected by DV unless it was perpetrated directly against them, and not by their mere observation of it.

Research has since proven these assumptions wrong. But the custody courts have been slow to notice: from all reports, the findings of up-to-date research on the impact of DV rarely make their way into judicial decisions. However, institutions outside of the legal system have had a greater degree of success in making good use of such research. In the past, the standard practice of police when responding to DV calls was to separate the parties and to perhaps ask the abuser to walk around the block to cool off. In studying these practices, we discovered that, in most DV homicides, the police had previously been called to the parties' home, often multiple times. Findings such as these drove home the fact that "standard practice" did not work. As a result, police departments shifted to the pro-arrest policy that has contributed to the reduction we have seen in DV homicides.

The editors' reason and purpose for preparing this book is to apply up-to-date research and information to DV custody cases. The purpose was not to promote a particular outcome (other than to best protect children), but rather to apply the most up-to-date research and information to understanding the custody court system and supporting any changes this research requires.

As one would expect of a diverse group of experts coming from many different disciplinary and practice fields, our contributors do not agree on every issue or approach. Nevertheless, they show an overwhelming consensus that the custody court system as presently constituted is broken and that the courts' failure to apply current research findings to court practices has placed the lives and well-being of thousands of children and protective mothers in jeopardy.

We have sought to consider how the use of up-to-date research and information can help the custody court system respond better to these disputes. There are professionals who seek to defend the status quo or even complain that fathers are mistreated by the courts. We have not included the perspective of this group of professionals because, simply put, their position generally is based upon myths, stereotypes, and misconceptions about gender, DV, and child abuse rather than the body of credible research on which our authors rely.

At a men's conference in Utah, for example, a professor and proponent of "fathers' rights" (FRs) made a presentation on what he claimed was new research to support his perspective. The "research" was based upon interviews with alleged abusers. Periodically, popular publications report on research claiming that men are abused by women as often as women are abused by men. A closer look at these findings reveals that the authors failed to consider rape, failed to consider how hard someone was hit or the injuries that were caused, and failed to differentiate between assaults and self-defense. In one Queens County, New York, custody case, the court appointed a FRs psychologist to perform an evaluation. This particular psychologist had recently been quoted in a *New York Times* article. At trial, during cross-examination, he could not provide a single research citation to support his views. Instead, he said he had discussed the subject with some of his friends (presumably other psychologists). This is typical of mental health professionals who do not have the knowledge, training, or experience to accurately assess the presence of DV and other forms of abuse. Whether through misinterpreting the research or ignoring it altogether, using gender bias in formulating their opinions, or relying on inappropriate and invalid psychological tests, such professionals mislead the courts into believing that they have a scientific basis for their opinions.

This book was never meant to be just a tome by lawyers for lawyers. We are, after all, well aware that a fairly broad swath of the population has, or ought to have, serious concerns about the malfunctioning of our courts. This includes family court judges and family lawyers, of course, but also members of mental health and related professions who play a role in these cases, along with anyone who potentially could end up in the midst of a custody or visitation dispute with an ex-partner. They include psychiatrists, DV advocates, researchers, educators, journalists, and activists who have witnessed up close the myriad of harms resulting from system malfunctioning. Among these are DV professionals who have devoted entire careers to these issues and DV workers who, for little or no pay, sit day after day beside litigating mothers in family courtrooms, which they call the "final frontier" of domestic abuse.

Any critique that claims to be objective will include the observations of outsiders who—as in the present case—studied the system from the outside looking in. Along this same vein, three chapters are by investigative journalists who, while covering a related topic, stumbled onto the dark terrain of the family courts. Moved by the outrages they uncovered, and deluged by mothers begging for publicity for their cases, they took up the torch for exposing the legal injustices suffered by battered mothers. In service to this cause, they have developed a growing collection of newspaper articles, blogs, editorials, chapters, documentaries, and conference presentations, collectively shedding considerable light on what is often referred to as the dirtiest little secret in America.

As often occurs when governments refuse to remedy the harms for which citizens seek redress, the injustices meted out by the family courts have triggered waves of grassroots activism. To flesh out our analysis, therefore, we include reports from several activists who have led the campaign for family court reform. Last but not least, we present brief testimonials of several mothers who share what they and their children went through during their harrowing journey through custody litigation.

The news, as they say, is not good. If this were a report of findings from a medical workup, the diagnosis would be serious. Perhaps "Massive Systemic Dysfunction," a progressive and debilitating disorder in which a societal entity designed to dispense justice becomes, instead, an instrument of oppression, would be the best-fitting label.

Given this diagnosis, what might be the cure? What has been done so far to improve the system's handling of cases involving DV and child abuse? What, if anything, has worked? Is the system, as it is structured, reparable, or is it irretrievably broken? How do we get rid of the expediency, cronyism, and profit motive that seems to drive many cases? How can we transform a harmful system into a helpful one? What can readers do to facilitate family court reform? These questions call out for answers; these problems demand solutions. That is precisely what this book is meant to provide.

Before we begin, we present a word about pronoun usage in this book. Generally, the chapters in this book refer to abusers as male (he) and victims as female (she). This is consistent with the majority of heterosexual cases, although assaults can be committed by either sex.

PURPOSE OF THIS BOOK

This book is designed to deliver something for everybody, particularly judges, attorneys, and court auxiliaries, but also for legislators, social workers, law students, DV staff, school counselors, litigating mothers, and, especially, citizens who have not yet learned about the serious malfunctioning going on in today's family court system.

We hope the book will accomplish the following modest goals:

1. *Convince legal actors of the harm caused by all types of abusive behavior, whether physical, verbal, financial, legal, or other forms.*

2. *Establish the paramount importance of children's safety beyond all other priorities that may emerge in a child custody case.*

3. *Alert attorneys to be sensitive to the many issues facing battered mothers.* Attorneys should be aware of the profound trust issues their clients may have toward them, due, in many cases, to the betrayals they have suffered at the hands of their abusers and the court system. Attorneys should use the information in this book to guide their representation of protective mothers and to help them locate additional research, case law, and consultation to improve their case outcomes.

4. *Provide judges with new insight into the dynamics of violence, so that they refrain from blaming the victim or painting both parties with the same brush.* We hope it will help judges to recognize when experts and other types of witnesses are providing testimony based on myths, stereotypes, and discredited theories. We also hope it will lead them to issue orders emphasizing the safety of protective mothers and the accountability of batterers.

5. *Encourage journalists and others working in the media to do their job by exposing these problems.* For too long, reporting on the crisis in our nation's family courts has been stymied by the focus on "fair and balanced reporting." Of course, there are two sides to every case, just as a story about a murder trial would include the defendant's side. However, some people deny that the Holocaust occurred; some argue that whites are superior to blacks; and others argue that the earth is flat. Yet no one argues for the need to write "balanced" stories on these kinds of topics. Every state, province, and court in the United States and Canada has a policy against DV. The debate should be about the best ways to prevent DV and not whether abusive behavior is justified.

6. *Inform professionals from all fields about the risks facing women and children who approach the family courts for protection.* We believe that professionals of all stripes, along with many other concerned constituencies, have the wherewithal to turn this crisis around.

There is no justification for forcing one more child to cry himself/herself to sleep because of the flawed custody decision of a family court judge. For the sake of just that one child, we are proud to present this cutting-edge work that, we hope, will alter the legal landscape for battered mothers and their children.

ORGANIZATION OF THIS BOOK

Opinions vary regarding what caused the current crisis and what must be done about it, but there is generally agreement on at least one point: the problems we are seeing in our family courts have complex causes that require complex solutions. As a way of drawing the big picture, we broke the problem down into four areas, assigning the chapters to one of four parts:

- Part 1. Parameters of the Problem

- Part 2. Survivors' Stories

- Part 3. Causes of and Contributors to the Problem

- Part 4. Solutions and Strategies

We will now review the chapters in their order of appearance.

Part 1: Parameters of the Problem

Joan Zorza's contribution, *Child Custody Practices of the Family Courts in Cases Involving Domestic Violence,* is appropriately placed as the first chapter of the book. An eminent attorney and prolific writer, Ms. Zorza's work is informed by her decades of working as a legal advocate for battered women, beginning in the earliest years of the DV movement. In discussing how today's harmful court practices have evolved, she identifies the legal theories (e.g., Parental Alienation Syndrome (PAS) and "friendly parent" statutes) that coalesced to form the toxic landscape facing litigating mothers throughout the past two decades or so.

In Chapter 2, *Recognizing Domestic Violence: How to Know It When You See It and How to Provide Appropriate Representation,* Lois Schwaeber, J.D., outlines the essential information that court agents and their auxiliaries must know in order to accurately discern whether or not DV is affecting a custody case. She strongly cautions against discrediting women's allegations of DV on the basis of equivocal factors. For example, professionals often misinterpret the absence of police reports, 911 calls, or emergency room visits as proof that a woman is making false allegations of DV. But, in fact, research demonstrates that victims often fail to report abuse out of fear for their own and their children's safety. This chapter is critical as courts often make harmful decisions because they fail to recognize the abuser's DV.

Chapter 3, *Historical Legal Context in Domestic Violence Custody Cases,* by Marvin Timothy Gray, J.D., traces the historical lineage of modern legal theories and practices to their roots in ancient Greece, the Roman Empire, the Catholic Church, and other societal codes. Mr. Gray, with his own lengthy experience as a legal advocate for battered women, provides rich discussion of the impact of these historical precedents on how today's courts view and handle women's allegations of DV in their custody petitions.

In Chapter 4, *Historical Origins of the Fathers' Rights Movement*, Jan Kurth, M.U.P., outlines the origins and development of the male supremacist movement. She explains the tactics used, often successfully, by male supremacists to gain custody of their children for the precise purpose of punishing the mother for leaving him or to force her to return. Inadequately trained professionals often fail to recognize these tactics for what they are, assuming, instead, that the father's quest for custody is motivated by love for his children, whom he claims he must rescue from their "crazy" (or "drug-addicted," "promiscuous," "narcissistic," etc.) mother. For example, in the Shockome child custody case of Dutchess County, New York, the abuser actually provided evidence of his own ulterior motive: in a statement he wrote to his wife, he said that he had brought her to this country (she was a Russian citizen at the time) and that, therefore, she had no right to leave him. He further warned that she would "never get away from him." The family court judge nonetheless ignored this evidence and ruled against the mother who, at this writing, has not seen her children for five years.[1]

Molly Dragiewicz, Ph.D., in Chapter 5, *Gender Bias in the Courts: Implications for Battered Mothers and Their Children,* eloquently summarizes what has been learned about the extent to which females are treated in a discriminatory manner, in comparison with males, by court agents. As discussed by Dr. Dragiewicz, gender bias studies commissioned by at least forty states, along with many local court districts, have unanimously confirmed the existence of pervasive bias against protective mothers vis-á-vis litigating fathers.

Next, in Chapter 6 (*Domestic Violence, Contested Child Custody, and the Courts: Findings From Five Studies*), Drs. Sharon K. Araji and Rebecca L. Bosek provide a concise review of previous literature on battered women's experiences with the legal

---

[1] This information is contained in the transcripts of *Shockome v. Shockome* and is on file with the coeditors.

system. The authors combine these earlier findings with their own research in developing a classification of factors that contribute to bad outcomes in battered women's custody cases. Citing from surveys of battered mothers in Massachusetts, Arizona, Pennsylvania, California, their own state of Alaska, and elsewhere, these authors draw a bright outline around the legal landscape facing battered mothers in today's family court system.

In Chapter 7 (*Do Judges Adequately Address the Causes and Impact of Violence in Children's Lives in Deciding Contested Child Custody Cases?*), Judge Thomas E. Hornsby discusses the role of judges in recognizing and responding to DV in child custody cases. He writes,

> During the nineteenth year of my twenty-three-year tenure as a circuit court judge in the 15th judicial circuit of the state of Illinois, my negative attitude toward female DV victims who sought orders of protection after I had granted them previous orders dramatically changed.

In the mid to late 1970s, when the modern DV movement began, little had been published about these problems. As research began to accumulate, early assumptions about DV, its causes, and remedies, were eventually proven wrong, if not outright dangerous. Nonetheless, many professionals continue to use discredited theories that blame either the victim or both partners for the abuse perpetrated by one against the other. We are aware of cases in which judges refused to listen to the testimony of DV experts, claiming that after being on the bench for many years, they did not need to learn anything more about DV. Some of these same judges proceeded to place children into the custody of abusive parents—and solely on the basis of myths, misconceptions, and stereotypes about DV. Judge Hornsby's chapter, therefore, is an especially valuable resource for family court judges and other court agents whose understanding (or misunderstanding) of DV may have profound implications for the future lives of battered mothers and their children.

In January 2007, a group of nationally recognized experts assembled in the form of a truth commission at the Fourth Battered Mothers Custody Conference (BMCC IV). As described in Chapter 8 by Mo Therese Hannah (*Truth Commission: Findings and Recommendations),* the truth commission was modeled after those developed in Latin American countries, South Africa, and elsewhere to give voice to citizens who had been victimized by agents of their own governments. During the BMCC IV, sixteen protective mothers from across the country testified publicly in front of the commission about the family courts' failure to protect them and their children. After these hearings, commission members met together to deliberate; they then summarized their findings, conclusions, and recommendations in the form of a written report, which is published verbatim and discussed in Dr. Hannah's chapter. It was the BMCC IV Truth Commission report that sparked the idea and development of this book.

Part 2: Survivors' Stories

In this relatively brief part, we hear from several extraordinary women—mothers whose own custody travails led them to extend a helping hand to other mothers going through similar fights. Among the most notable of these figures is Karen Anderson who, in Chapter 9 (*Courageous Kids: Abused Children Sharing Their Experiences*) describes the unique organization she cofounded (in collaboration with fellow activist

Connie Valentine). The Courageous Kids (CK) Network is a loose collection of older adolescents and adult children who, having been court-ordered to live with their abusive parent, are speaking out about their experiences. The CK Network provides a platform through which young people can express their thoughts and feelings about being raised by the courts. This powerful, life-affirming chapter will touch the most callous reader and create demands for the reform of the current broken system.

In Chapter 10 (*From the Mouths of Mothers*), four formerly battered mothers give a brief synopsis of their navigation of the family court system. Their stories, as shocking as they may be, are similar to those we have heard from mothers across the country. As of this writing, three of these four mothers never regained custody of their children, while two have not laid eyes on their children in years.

Part 3: Causes of and Contributors to the Problem

In this part, professionals from a variety of disciplines, including psychiatry, law, sociology, and the media assemble a sizable segment of the puzzle of court malfunction. The discussion begins with a cutting-edge analysis by Evan Stark, Ph.D. (Chapter 11: *Reframing Child Custody Decisions in the Context of Coercive Control*). Dr. Stark is a sociologist and expert witness whose treatise, *Coercive Control: How Men Entrap Women in Personal Life,*[2] marked a watershed in understanding the control dynamics driving woman abuse.

Next, the highly regarded Dr. Paul Jay Fink, a past president of the American Psychiatric Association, dissects the notorious phenomenon known as Parental Alienation Syndrome (PAS). As he explains in Chapter 12, *Parental Alienation Syndrome* (and, we would add, offshoots like the absurd "future alienation") has been the primary justification used to extract thousands of children from the custody and care of their protective mothers. Dr. Fink exposes the fatal flaws of alienation theories, arguing for their banishment from the courtroom.

In Chapter 13, *Why Do Judges Do That?* Judge Mike Brigner clearly articulates what fellow judges tend to miss when evaluating the veracity of abuse allegations in child custody cases. With unusually deep insight into the dilemma faced by battered mothers, he notes,

> Women trapped in relationships with abusers come to expect horrendous misbehavior from their partners. What they cannot fathom is the maddening reinforcement commonly provided to abusive men by the justice system and the public at large. . . . That key abuse collaborator is the custody judge. Of all of the actors in a battered woman's life, none wield more power over her children and financial future. It is beyond infuriating when women discover that their custody judges lack understanding of DV and are colluding with abusers to take away women's financial resources and, even worse, their children.

Joan Zorza returns in Chapter 14, to write about a mounting problem, in *Batterer Manipulation and Retaliation Compounded by Denial and Complicity in the Family Courts.* Ms. Zorza demonstrates how abusers are manipulating courts to help them

---

[2] E. Stark, *Coercive Control: How Men Entrap Women in Personal Life* (2007).

control their ex-partners and punish them for leaving. Although the courts frequently fail to recognize domestic violence or minimize its importance, they frequently retaliate against mothers who continue to complain about their partners' abuse despite the courts' determinations. The author recommends that courts look for patterns of behavior to better understand domestic violence and consult with genuine domestic violence experts rather than the inadequately trained mental health providers the courts often rely on.

In Chapter 15, *The Yuck Factor, the Oprah Factor, and the "Stickiness" Factor: Why the Mainstream Media Has Failed to Expose the Custody Court Scandal,* Garland Waller, M.S., speaks from her expertise as a journalist, documentary producer, and communications professor. As she points out in her chapter, a major roadblock to improving the court system is the media's reluctance to cover this unpleasant issue. Professor Waller notes that with a few exceptions—most notably, the PBS documentary *Breaking the Silence: Children's Stories,*[3] *Newsweek*'s "Fighting Over the Kids,"[4] and scattered newspaper stories and magazine articles—the media's limited resources, fear of lawsuits, and perhaps simple laziness have culminated in a virtual brownout, if not blackout, of media coverage of this important public health issue.

Part 4: Solutions and Strategies

If the book ended prior to this final part, readers would likely be left feeling outraged and without any direction for channeling their outrage into action. Thanks to the collective genius of our last group of knowledgeable contributors, we are left, instead, with voluminous possibilities for restoring sanity and justice to the system.

Attorney Michael Lesher (with Dr. Amy Neustein) studied over 1,000 custody cases involving claims of child sexual abuse. Among the pair's disturbing findings are that courts often disbelieve valid abuse claims and further decline to fully investigate some of these cases. Consequently, as Mr. Lesher observes in Chapter 16: *Leveling the Landscape: Family Court Auxiliaries and How to Counter Them*, sexually abused children and their protective mothers are not only refused protection but also are, in many cases, revictimized by court auxiliaries like custody evaluators and law guardians. The implications for our children and our society are obvious and frightening.

A sought-after speaker and prolific author, Lundy Bancroft, B.A., is perhaps best known for his landmark book (with Dr. Jay Silverman), *The Batterer as Parent.* Mr. Bancroft combines the insights of a court insider, gained through years of experience as an expert witness and custody evaluator, with the passion of a revolutionary. His contribution (Chapter 17, *Organizing in Defense of Protective Mothers: The Custody Rights Movement*) argues for what he considers a much-needed paradigm shift in our efforts for reform. Mr. Bancroft maintains that the profligacy of the system will not be

---

[3] *Breaking the Silence: Children's Stories,* a documentary produced by Catherine Tatge and Dominique Lasseur (http://www.tatgelasseur.com) was broadcast on most PBS stations in October 2005. It is among the very few to publicize these injustices through the victims' own voices. Before the video had even aired, FRs groups launched a ferocious backlash, bombarding PBS stations with calls and e-mails criticizing the documentary for being antifather and demanding it not be shown. Their efforts were met by an intense countercampaign on the part of women's custody advocates, who encouraged viewers to e-mail PBS to praise the documentary and to thank them for airing it.

[4] Sarah Childress, "Fighting Over the Kids," *Newsweek,* Sept. 26, 2006.

eradicated by the system itself; that is just another example of asking the fox to watch over the henhouse. Rather, change can and will come only when masses of informed and organized citizens insist on it.

By the time he published his 2002 book, *Scared to Leave, Afraid to Stay*, Barry Goldstein (Chapter 18, *Recognizing and Overcoming Abusers' Legal Tactics*) had already devoted nineteen years to the movement to end DV. He had served on the board and as chairperson for a DV organization, My Sisters' Place; he also had represented hundreds of women who had been partnered with abusers, and he taught classes for men convicted of DV. Because initial reviews of the book were glowing, he was taken aback when one reviewer, attorney Joan Zorza, provided a more equivocal response. Mr. Goldstein came to realize that Joan Zorza was right and that he had much more to learn. He also came to appreciate the great deal he learned from her and many others working along with him in the DV movement. His chapter demonstrates how professionals can learn to recognize common abuser legal tactics and use this knowledge to understand their motivation.

Next, we gain the hard-earned insights of retired judge Marjory D. Fields, whose many years on the bench makes her uniquely qualified to speak to these issues. In Chapter 19, *Lawyer Skills Training for Domestic Violence Representation: Tips From a Retired Judge,* Ms. Fields wisely directs her advice toward family law attorneys, especially those who lack the training and insights needed to competently and vigorously represent battered mothers in complicated cases.

Along a similar vein, Nancy S. Erickson, J.D., brings her uncommonly rich knowledge base to her recommendations to lawyers handling PAS allegations. After toiling for years as an attorney for battered women, she took the courageous step of returning to school midcareer to earn a master's degree in forensic psychology. In her contribution to this book (Chapter 20, *Fighting False Allegations of Parental Alienation Raised as Defenses to Valid Claims of Abuse*), Ms. Erickson brings a rare combination of legal and psychological expertise to advise attorneys on how to counter the use of pseudoscience and flawed practices by mental health professionals who perform evaluations and provide testimony in family court cases.

In writing Chapter 21, *Urgent Need for Quality Control in Child Custody Psychological Evaluations,* Robin Yeamans, J.D., applies the experience gained through her many years spent dissecting child custody reports and cross-examining child custody evaluators who testify in California courts. Ms. Yeamans is an especially unique figure among legal advocates: she has not only served as an attorney on complex custody cases in the northern counties of California, but also demonstrated gifted leadership skills in organizing California mothers to engage in protests and rallies against corrupt court practices in her state.

In Chapter 22, *Factoring in the Effects of Children's Exposure to Domestic Violence in Determining Appropriate Postseparation Parenting Plans,* Claire V. Crooks, Peter G. Jaffe, and Nicholas Bala, widely respected researchers on topics related to family violence, give readers a tour of children's developmental journeys, pointing out their particular needs and risk factors at different stages of development. Against this backdrop, they identify the developmental harms faced by children who are exposed to DV. Accordingly, they urge courts to rely on nothing less than credible and robust research findings in making custody and visitation decisions involving domestic abuse.

Attorney Margaret K. Dore, in Chapter 23, *Court-Appointed Parenting Evaluators and Guardians Ad Litem: Practical Realities and an Argument for Abolition*, cogently outlines her case against permitting custody evaluators, parenting coordinators, and, especially, guardians ad litem, to usurp the decision-making role of judges in contested child custody cases. Her call to eliminate these extrajudicial actors has considerable support among observers inside and outside the court system.

In her chapter, Erika A. Sussman, J.D., LL.M., offers a refreshing alternative to the best interests of the child (BIC) legal standard that guides child custody determinations in the courts of virtually every state. In *American Law Institute Principles: A Tool for Accessing Justice for Battered Mothers and Children* (Chapter 24), she provides compelling rationales for replacing the BIC standard with those developed by the American Law Institute (ALI). Experts have criticized the BIC standard because it often is subject to vagueness, subjectivity, and gender bias. Issues critical to the welfare of children—such as primary attachment and safety—are given less weight. This puts protective mothers at an unfair disadvantage. Less important factors, like economic superiority, employment stability, and remarriage, are given greater weight. The subjectivity of the BIC standard often combines with the lack of adequate training and gender bias (usually unconscious) to advantage abusive fathers over protective mothers.

Finally, journalist Anne Grant, in *Covering the Crisis in the Custody Courts* (Chapter 25), caps this final part with her eye-opening rendition of cases she covered in her published work on the family courts. Ms. Grant is one of the few journalists who have invested their time, talents, and even reputations toward exposing and correcting what she, and countless others, considers an egregious social injustice.

About the Editors and Contributors

Mo Therese Hannah, Ph.D., is professor of psychology at Siena College in Loudonville, New York. She cofounded and serves as chair of the annual Battered Mothers Custody Conference, now in planning for its seventh year, to be held in January 2010. This conference hosts the nation's leading attorneys, experts, authors, and advocates working in the area of battered mothers' custody problems in presenting their cutting-edge knowledge and experience to litigating mothers, to other experts, and to the general public. A clinical psychologist specializing in relationship dynamics, Dr. Hannah has a practice working with couples and individuals. She was named an academic faculty member of Imago Relationships International, the professional training organization for Imago (couples) Therapy. In 2008, she was honored as one of the "30 Leaders in 30 Years" by the New York State Coalition Against Domestic Violence. She has published five books and produced numerous articles and presentations on issues revolving around interpersonal relationships.

Barry Goldstein, J.D., practiced law in New York for thirty years and frequently represented protective mothers. He served on the board of My Sisters' Place for fourteen years, including four years as chairperson. He has been an instructor and is now supervisor in the VCS Domestic Violence Program for Men, one of the New York Model Batterer Programs. Mr. Goldstein is the author of *Scared to Leave Afraid to Stay: Paths From Family Violence to Safety* (2002). He has been qualified as an expert witness in domestic violence and the courts' response to domestic violence in New York, North Dakota, New Jersey, and California. Mr. Goldstein is the author of several articles, including "Custody-Visitation Scandal Cases," published in *The Voice by the National Coalition Against Domestic Violence* (Fall 2006). He has presented at numerous judicial trainings and workshops for the National Coalition Against Domestic Violence, Battered Mothers Custody Conference, Oklahoma Attorney General's Office, Safespace (Tennessee), Rockland Family Shelter, Catholic Charities (Buffalo, New York), Fairleigh Dickinson University, and The Retreat. Mr. Goldstein served on the truth commission held at the Fourth Battered Mothers' Custody Conference (2007). A member of the Family Court Reform Coalition, he received his B.A. (political science) from George Washington University (1974) and J.D. from New York Law School.

Karen Anderson is the cofounder and director of California Protective Parents Association (CPPA), incorporated in 1998. In 2004, she assisted a core group of teens in forming the Courageous Kids Network, a division of CPPA. In addition to her work with CPPA, Karen worked for eight years as a domestic violence and sexual assault counselor for a violence prevention agency, the Center for Violence Free Relationships, in Placerville, CA. In that capacity, Karen provided local high school students with on-sight counseling services for child sexual abuse, teen dating violence, and witnessing domestic violence in the home, as well as providing sexual assault and domestic violence counseling services for adults in the agency office. She has been active in initiating, drafting, and lobbying for family court reform and child protection statutes. Karen is currently working in a private capacity as a court advocate and paralegal, providing services to victims of domestic violence and child abuse who arc unable to access services from public agencies. She also plans to work in the area of family violence tort law.

Sharon K. Araji, M.Ed., Ph.D., is a professor of sociology and chair of the Department of Sociology at the University of Colorado, Denver, and recently retired from the same positions at the University of Alaska Anchorage. She has conducted research and published in the areas of domestic violence, child abuse, and women's issues, developed educational documentaries and training materials, and presented at professional meetings and community workshops. She frequently serves as an expert witness in domestic violence cases, including those involving contested custody. Her interest in these areas peaked while completing a National Institute of Mental Health postdoctoral fellowship at the University of New Hampshire, working with Drs. Murray Straus and David Finkelhor. Currently, she is primarily focusing on the issue of domestic violence and its relationship to contested custody and sexual abuse perpetrated by preadolescent children.

Nicholas Bala, J.D., has been a professor at the faculty of law at Queen's University in Kingston, Canada, since 1980, and he has taught in the law schools of Duke, McGill, and York University. His primary area of teaching and research interest is family and children's law, focusing on such issues as child welfare law, child abuse, and child witnesses in the criminal justice system; family violence; the best interests of children; parental rights and responsibilities after divorce; the legal definition of the family; the Canadian Charter of Rights and the family; juvenile justice; and child and spousal support obligations. Much of Professor Bala's research has an interdisciplinary approach, as he recognizes the importance of understanding not only what the law says, but also the actual functioning and impact of the justice system, in particular on those who are most vulnerable.

Lundy Bancroft, has twenty years of experience specializing in interventions for abusive men. He is the author of three books in the field, including *Why Does He Do That*, *When Dad Hurts Mom,* and the national prize winner *The Batterer as Parent*. He has worked with over a thousand abusers directly as an intervention counselor, and has served as clinical supervisor on another thousand cases. He has also served extensively as a custody evaluator, child abuse investigator, and expert witness in domestic violence and child abuse cases. Lundy appears across the United States as a presenter for judges and other court personnel, child protective workers, therapists, law enforcement officials, and other audiences. His current training and writing work focuses on the impact on children of exposure to men who batter women and how professionals can best support children's recovery.

Rebecca L. Bosek, Ph.D., L.M.F.T., L.P.C., is an assistant term professor at the University of Alaska, Anchorage, where she teaches courses on gender issues, human sexuality, lifespan development, and community psychology. She is the former clinical director of the Center for Psychological Development, a specialized clinic that serves people with intellectual disabilities who are crime victims or offenders. She has published on treatment issues for people with intellectual disabilities who are victims and offenders and, also, on sexually aggressive children. In addition to her teaching duties, she conducts child custody evaluations and has been an expert witness in contested child custody cases where domestic violence has been present.

Mike Brigner, J.D., is one of Ohio's leading experts in the field of domestic violence. He authored two editions of the *Ohio Domestic Violence Benchbook for Judges and Magistrates* and consulted on similar projects for several other states. He is the immediate past chair of the Ohio Supreme Court Domestic Violence Advisory Committee that created standard statewide protection order forms, and he has testified repeatedly before the Ohio General Assembly on domestic violence legislation. In his legal career, he has authored over 100 articles on legal topics, most of them regarding family law and domestic violence. Professor Brigner served a decade as an Ohio domestic relations court judge whose duties included exclusive jurisdiction over divorces and civil protection order cases. He is experienced in training judges, lawyers, police departments, prosecutors, and other professionals across the United States on domestic violence issues.

Claire V. Crooks, Ph.D., C.Psych., is a registered clinical psychologist. She is the associate director of the Centre for Addiction and Mental Health (CAMH) Centre for Prevention Science and an assistant professor at the Centre for Research and Education on Violence Against Women and Children (University of Western Ontario). Dr. Crooks is an external consultant to the Centre for Children and Families in the Justice System of the London Family Court Clinic, where she conducts custody assessments with the London Custody and Access Project. She frequently conducts training on a wide range of topics related to family violence and serves as faculty for the National Council for Juvenile and Family Court Judges in this regard. Dr. Crooks is a cofounder of the Caring Dads program, a parenting intervention for men who have maltreated their children. Dr. Crooks has written numerous articles and chapters on topics, including children's exposure to domestic violence, child custody, adolescent dating violence and risk behavior, intervening with fathers who maltreat their children, and trauma.

Margaret K. Dore, **J.D.,** is an attorney in private practice in Seattle, Washington. Her published decisions include *In re Guardianship of Stamm*, 91 P.3d 126, 133 (Wash. Ct. App. 2004) (reversing due to the improper admission of guardian ad litem testimony), and *Lawrence v. Lawrence*, 20 P.3d 972, 974 (Wash. Ct. App. 2001) (use of the "friendly parent" concept in a child custody case "would be an abuse of discretion"). *Lawrence* was nationally recognized. See, for example, Wendy N. Davis, "Family Values in Flux," 87 *ABA Journal* 26 (October 2001). Ms. Dore is a former law clerk to the Washington State Supreme Court and the Washington State Court of Appeals. She worked for the U.S. Department of Justice. She is the chair of the Elder Law Committee of the ABA Family Law Section. She was nominated for the 2005 Butch Blum/Law & Politics Award of Excellence. She is a graduate of the University of Washington School of Law. She has an M.B.A. in finance and a B.A. in accounting. She passed the C.P.A. examination in 1982. Further information about Ms. Dore and her practice can be viewed at http://www.margaretdore.com.

Molly Dragiewicz, Ph.D., is assistant professor on the Faculty of Criminology, Justice, and Policy Studies at the University of Institute of Technology in Ontario, Canada. Dr. Dragiewicz's research interests include violence and gender, domestic violence and child custody, the antifeminist fathers' rights movement, and human trafficking policy. She is a founding member on the advisory board for the Communities Against Violence Network (CAVNET) and is a member of the American Society of

Criminology and the National Women's Studies Association. Dr. Dragiewicz holds a Ph.D. in Cultural Studies from George Mason University and an M.Phil. in Women's Studies from the University of Western Australia.

Nancy S. Erickson, J.D., LL.M., M.A., attended Brooklyn Law School and Yale Law School and earned a master's in forensic psychology from John Jay College of Criminal Justice. She is an author and consultant on family law and matrimonial issues, including custody evaluations, especially those involving abused children and children of abuse victims. She was a senior attorney at Legal Services for New York City, Brooklyn Branch, representing low-income clients—primarily battered women—in divorce and other family cases for eight years. For over ten years, she was a professor of law, teaching at New York Law School, Cornell University, Ohio State, New York University, and Seton Hall Law School. She also has had positions in government and has been in private practice. She has written books and articles on family law and forensic psychology, including domestic violence, child support, custody, marital property, attorneys for children, custody evaluations, and adoption. She has lectured to judges, attorneys, mental health practitioners, and others throughout the country.

Marjory D. Fields, J.D., is a retired New York State Supreme Court justice and a retired family court judge. She is an attorney licensed to practice law in New York State. She is counsel to Beldock Levine Hoffman in New York City and International Family Law Chambers in London. Fields works on public policy issues addressing legal remedies and protection for women victims of family violence, abuse, and sex crimes. She represents litigants in family law and divorce cases. On September 1, 2002, she retired after sixteen years on the bench to resume working to combat violence against women. Fields continues to be a member of the New York State Courts Family Court Advisory and Rules Committee and Family Violence Task Force. In 2002, Fields was awarded an Abe Fellowship by the Japan Foundation Center for Global Partnership and the Social Sciences Research Council. The fellowship supported Fields' work with Japanese women's organizations throughout Japan. Fields' many articles on civil remedies and procedures and criminal justice responses to domestic violence and sexual assault are published in scholarly journals and books in the United States, the United Kingdom, and Japan. Fields chaired the New York State Commission on Domestic Violence from 1976 to 1986. She began her legal work at South Brooklyn Legal Services representing victims of domestic violence in divorce actions for fifteen years, prior to being appointed to the New York State Family Court bench in March 1986. She was a member of the six-lawyer team that brought a law suit, which was settled successfully in 1978, whereby the New York Police Department consented to the first mandatory arrest policy for violations of protection orders and serious domestic violence assaults. During her years at South Brooklyn Legal Services, Fields traveled throughout the United States training legal services lawyers representing domestic violence victims and testifying before state legislatures and the U.S. Congress in support of new laws to protect victims of domestic violence and marital rape.

Paul Jay Fink, M.D., a prominent psychiatrist, psychoanalyst, and public health officer with a strong interest in youth violence and youth murder, is a professor of psychiatry at Temple University School of Medicine. Dr. Fink has extensive managerial, educational, planning, and clinical experience. He is the director of the Blueprint for a Safer Philadelphia, a consultant to the School District of Philadelphia, and is on the boards of Philadelphia Anti-Drug/Anti-Violence Network (PAAN), Institute for the Development of African American Youth (IDAAY), Joseph J. Peters Institute (JJPI), and CeaseFire

PA. Dr. Fink is a past president of the American Psychiatric Association, the American College of Psychiatrists, and the Philadelphia County Medical Society. He has over 210 articles published and has given over 900 lectures throughout the world.

Anne Grant, M.A., M.Div., won two Emmy Awards as a television writer and producer in the 1970s before becoming a United Methodist minister. In the 1980s and 1990s, she was executive director of the Women's Center of Rhode Island, the state's largest shelter for battered women and their children. There she documented practices at Rhode Island's Family Court and the Department of Children, Youth, and Families that endanger victims of domestic violence and sexual abuse. She wrote the column, "Overcoming Abuse," for the *Providence Journal* (1990–1996) and formed the Parenting Project at Mathewson Street United Methodist Church to assist children and protective parents. She produces several blogs, including http://www.littlehostages.blogspot.com and http://www.writing-truthtopower.blogspot.com. She is now writing screenplays and nonfiction based on her research into custody cases that illustrate the trauma of adversarial litigation.

Marvin Timothy Gray, J.D., M.A., C.D.S.V.R.P., is an attorney in private practice in northern Oklahoma and represents primarily survivors of domestic violence, sexual assault, and stalking in protective order, divorce, custody, and other family law and survivor-related and general law practice matters. He frequently advises domestic violence services agencies and many other agencies concerning domestic violence-related issues. Mr. Gray was the policy director and staff attorney to the Oklahoma Coalition Against Domestic Violence and Sexual Assault (OCADVSA), a coalition consisting of most of the domestic violence and sexual assault services providers in Oklahoma for nearly two years. In this position, Mr. Gray provided legal and policy analysis and technical assistance to OCADVSA, OCADVSA member programs, state agencies, national entities, legislators, and others. Mr. Gray also provided (and continues to provide pro bono) legal counsel, advice, and limited referral services to individual survivors in Oklahoma and elsewhere. Mr. Gray has been a designee to the Oklahoma Child Death Review Board, the Oklahoma Domestic Violence Fatality Review Board, and the Oklahoma Child Abuse Training and Coordination Council of the Oklahoma Department of Health. Mr. Gray provides numerous trainings throughout Oklahoma and nationally on subjects relating to Oklahoma legislation, domestic violence, sexual assault, stalking, dating violence, pro bono legal assistance and programs, custody issues, court watch, and court procedures for the layman as well as teaching college-level classes on subjects related to domestic violence, sexual assault, and related issues. Mr. Gray has worked with adult and child survivors of domestic violence and sexual assault for more than ten years in varying capacities including policy director and staff attorney for OCADVSA (the Oklahoma Coalition Against Domestic Violence and Sexual Assault), director of legal services and general counsel for Domestic Violence Intervention Services and Call Rape in Tulsa, Oklahoma, supervising attorney of the Tulsa Presidents Family Safety Center Civil Legal Assistance Office, and Americorps domestic violence attorney in rural Appalachian southeastern Ohio. Mr. Gray received his juris doctorate from the University of Tulsa College of Law with a certificate in international and comparative law in 1998, a master's degree in liberal arts from St. John's College in Santa Fe, New Mexico, a certificate in Chinese law from the East China University of Politics and Law in Shanghai, People' s Republic of China, and is an Oklahoma Certified Domestic and Sexual Violence Response Professional.

Paige Hodson, B.A., is a life-long resident of Anchorage, Alaska, a real estate appraiser and business owner, a single mother of two children, and a domestic violence survivor. She graduated from Washington State University with a B.A. in Business Administration with a real estate emphasis. Paige is the creator of the educational Web site http://www.custodyprepformoms.org, a valuable national resource for domestic violence victims. She is the editor of the *Alaska Moms for Custodial Justice* newsletter and an invited member of the National Network on Family Law Policy and the Family Court Reform Coalition. She cowrote and lobbied to pass state legislation that provides better protections for abused women and children during contested child custody proceedings. Paige has presented at various workshops and conferences on the topics of domestic violence, child custody, child abuse, court reforms, activism, and advocacy in the state of Alaska and around the country. She most recently served as consultant to the University of Alaska Anchorage on a study of battered mothers and the Alaska courts as well as a film documentary on the subject.

Thomas E. Hornsby, J.D., is a professor of professional skills at the Florida Coastal School of Law, in Jacksonville, Florida. He teaches the courses of Family Law, Domestic Violence, and Juvenile Law. He practiced law from 1964 to 1972, and in December of 1972 he was appointed by the Illinois Supreme Court to the office of circuit court judge in the Fifteenth Judicial Circuit. He retired from the bench in December of 1995. He is a regular member of the faculty of the National Council of Juvenile and Family Court Judges (NCJFCJ) and presents nationwide on the subjects of the Interstate Compact on the Placement of Children, Judicial Ethics, Judicial Responsibility in Assuring Fairness in the Courts, Ethical Issues in Dependency Court and has served as a consultant on those subjects and domestic violence. He is a past president of the NCJFCJ, a former member of the Board of Fellows of the National Center of Juvenile Justice and a board member emeritus of the National Court Special Advocates (CASA). He currently serves as a member of the Conduct Committee of the NCJFCJ and is a past president of the board of directors of the Betty Griffin House, a domestic violence shelter in St. Johns County, Florida. In 1994, he was elected as an honorary fellow of the Illinois Bar Foundation, "In recognition of a legal career exemplified by outstanding legal ability, devotion to the public welfare, the advancement of the legal profession and the objectives of the Illinois Bar Foundation."

Peter G. Jaffe, Ph.D., C.Psych., is a professor in the faculty of education at the University of Western Ontario and the academic director of the Centre for Research on Violence Against Women & Children. He is the director emeritus for the Centre for Children and Families in the Justice System in London, Ontario. He currently sits on Ontario's Chief Coroner's Domestic Violence Death Review Committee. He has coauthored nine books, twenty-five chapters, and over seventy-five articles related to children, families, and the justice system, including *Children of Battered Women*, *Working Together to End Domestic Violence* and *Child Custody & Domestic Violence: A Call for Safety & Accountability*. He has presented workshops across the United States and Canada, as well as in Australia, New Zealand, Costa Rica, and Europe to various groups, including judges, lawyers, mental health professionals, and educators. Since 1997, he has been a faculty member for the U.S. National Council of Juvenile and Family Court Judges.

Jan Kurth, **M.U.P.,** is a freelance writer and former columnist for the Jamestown, N.Y. *Post-Journal*. She is also a protective parent and veteran of the family court system. She has a B.A. from Vassar College and a masters in urban planning (M.U.P.) from the State University of New York at Buffalo. Her first novel, *Broken Angels,* was published in 2008.

Michael Lesher, **M.A., J.D.,** writer, journalist, and attorney, has devoted years to fighting for mothers who have lost custody of their children for trying to protect them from alleged sexual abuse. His legal work for mothers and children has appeared in states all over the country, including Arizona, California, Colorado, Idaho, Maryland, Michigan, New Jersey, and New York. He has also handled major federal civil rights cases, including a pending suit seeking equal protection under the law for a child who contends her alleged rapist was not prosecuted because he was her father. Mr. Lesher is coauthor, with Dr. Amy Neustein, of *From Madness to Mutiny: Why Mothers Are Running From the Family Courts—And What Can Be Done About It* (University Press of New England/ Northeastern, 2005) and several academic articles for publications such as the *Journal of Child Sexual Abuse*. As a legal writer, Mr. Lesher has contributed to *Moore's Federal Practice*, *Weinstein's Evidence*, and *The Federal Litigation Guide Reporter*. His journalism has appeared in the *Village Voice*, the *Jewish Week*, *Forward*, *Canadian Jewish News*, and *North Jersey Herald & News*; he has also published short fiction and poetry. He has received extensive media coverage for his advocacy for child sex abuse victims within the Orthodox Jewish community, which has recently resulted in the Israeli government ordering the extradition of two alleged abusers to the United States for trial. Mr. Lesher holds postgraduate degrees from the University of Virginia and Brooklyn Law School.

Larissa Pollica, **R.N., B.S.,** is a protective mother who testified before the BMCC IV Truth Commission. She is cofounder of the Tompkins County Family Court Reform Group. She is a critical care emergency nurse.

Lois Schwaeber, **J.D.,** is the Director of Legal Services for the Nassau County Coalition Against Domestic Violence. She is also cochair of the Domestic Violence Committee of the Women's Bar Association of the state of New York and chair of the Domestic Violence Committee of the Women's Bar Association of Nassau County. She is a member of the County Executive's Family Violence Task Force. She has authored several articles on domestic violence and on representing victims of abuse and the impact of domestic violence on custody/visitation. She is an active board member and participant on coalitions, task forces, and advisory committees on domestic violence, custody, and women's issues, and has organized and presented workshops on these issues to both the legal and lay communities. She is also a frequent lecturer on these topics to schools and community groups, and professionals.

Jay G. Silverman, **Ph.D.,** is a developmental psychologist and public health researcher whose work focuses on the etiology, health effects, and prevention of gender-based violence against adolescent and adult women (e.g., intimate partner violence, sexual assault, sex trafficking) in the United States and internationally. Dr. Silverman's research has included examinations of prevalence and health correlates of adolescent dating violence, social contextual influences on the etiology of intimate partner violence (IPV) perpetration among men, health and help-seeking of battered immigrant women in the United States, school-based primary prevention of IPV, health-care–based intervention for IPV and sexual assault in the United States and India, health-related behaviors of adolescent and adult battered women, HIV/STI prevalence and risk associated with IPV, IPV and pregnancy-related health and pregnancy outcomes in the United Slates and India, overlap of IPV and child abuse, the role of IPV in spousal heterosexual transmission of HIV in India, HIV among South and Southeast Asian sex trafficking victims, and proximal mechanisms related to trafficking of women and girls for sexual exploitation. He is currently collaborating with a range of UN agencies as well as the U.S. Department of State to move a broad public health agenda on understanding and preventing sex trafficking forward. Dr. Silverman's work has been broadly published in premier scientific journals and includes coauthorship with Lundy Bancroft of the award-winning practitioner guidebook, *The Batterer as Parent* (Sage, 2002). He is currently an associate professor of society, human development and health and Director of Violence Against Women Prevention Research at the Harvard School of Public Health.

Rita Smith, B.A., is the executive director of the National Coalition Against Domestic Violence. Rita began working as a crisis line advocate in a shelter for battered women and their children in Colorado in 1981. Since then, she has held numerous positions in Colorado and Florida at local programs and state coalitions, including program supervisor and director. She has been interviewed by hundreds of newspaper reporters, appeared on many local and national radio and television news shows, including *Good Morning America* and *Oprah Winfrey,* and in print media, such as the *Washington Post* and *USA Today.* She coauthored a legal manual for attorneys working with domestic violence victims in Colorado. She also coauthored an article on child custody and domestic violence that was published in the *Judges' Journal,* in 1997.

Evan Stark, Ph.D, M.S.W., is a forensic social worker who is internationally known for his research on domestic violence and his advocacy on behalf of battered women and their children. A founder of one of the first shelters for abused women in the United States, in the 1980s, Evan Stark conducted path-breaking research with Anne Flitcraft, M.D., which demonstrated the significance of domestic violence for female injury and a range of other medical, behavioral, and psychosocial problems, including child abuse. Dr. Stark has served as an expert in more than 100 criminal and civil cases involving battered women and their children, consulted with numerous federal and state agencies, and won a number prestigious awards for his research, advocacy, and policy work, including the Trend Setter Award from the National Health Council. Dr. Stark was the lead witness for the plaintiff mothers and children in the landmark federal class action suit, *Nicholson v. Williamson* and served on the Nicholson Review Panel (2002-2005) appointed to monitor compliance by the Administration of Children's Services in New York City with the federal injunction. The American Publishers' Association named his recent book, *Coercive Control: The Entrapment of Women in Personal Life* (Oxford University Press) the best book in sociology and social work for 2007. Dr. Stark is a professor at the School of Public Affairs and Administration at Rutgers University-Newark and at the University of Medicine and Dentistry of New Jersey's School of Public Health.

Erika A. Sussman, J.D., LL.M., is the executive director of the Center for Survivor Agency and Justice, a national organization dedicated to enhancing advocacy for survivors of oppression-based intimate partner violence. For four years, she served as an adjunct professor at Cornell Law School where she taught a class on law and violence against women. She was previously a teaching fellow and women's law and public policy fellow at Georgetown University Law Center's Domestic Violence Clinic, where she supervised law students and litigated cases on behalf of domestic violence survivors in the District of Columbia. Prior to that, she was a litigation associate at Swidler Berlin Sherreff Friedman, LLP, where she provided pro bono representation to domestic violence survivors in conjunction with Women Empowered Against Violence (WEAVE) and cocounseled a race-profiling class action suit against the Maryland State Police Department. She has published several articles and served as faculty for various academic and practitioner workshops related to violence against women. She obtained her B.S. from Cornell University, her J.D. from Cornell Law School, and her LL.M. from Georgetown University Law Center.

Wendy Titelman is the author of *A Mother's Journal, Let My Children Go!,* which was published in 2003. In 2004, she kicked off her advocacy organization, "Kourts for Kids," with a 518-mile walk on the historical Trail of Tears, which she organized to publicize the revictimization of abused children by the family court system. As one of the nation's most prominent activists on this issue, Wendy has made invited presentations at conferences and seminars across the country. Having enjoyed a successful career in marketing and management as well as with the airlines, over the past decade Wendy's greatest challenge and overriding priority in life has been as a mother trying to protect her children from abuse by their father and by the courts. After living most of her life in Atlanta, Georgia, and then moving away from her home in New Orleans due to Hurricane Katrina, Wendy now lives in Cincinnati, Ohio.

Garland Waller, M.S., is an assistant professor in the department of television and film at Boston University's College of Communication. She teaches Producing for TV, Childhood and Television, the Branded American Child, and Hothouse Productions. Before becoming a professor, she produced and wrote over ten documentaries and specials at WBZ-TV in Boston. Her awards include more than five New England Emmys, the Iris Award for Best Entertainment Special, the Grand Prize at the International Film Festival of New York, and the American Women in Radio and Television Merit Award. *Small Justice: Little Justice in America's Family Courts* (distributed by Intermedia, Inc.) was her first independent documentary. It won Best Social Documentary at the New York International Independent Film and Video Festival in 2001 and the Award for Excellence in Media by the Eighth International Conference on Family Violence. It was selected for screenings at the Key West Indies Film Festival, GirlFest, and the Museum of Fine Arts in Boston. She recently produced the educational video, *Debating Richard Gardner.* She has appeared on FOX NEWS, Court TV, WBUR/NPR, WNYC/NPR, and the Comcast Network.

Robin Yeamans, J.D., is one of only three California attorneys who have been certified by the California State Bar Board of Legal Specialization as a specialist in both family and appellate law. Robin became a certified family law specialist in 1980. She graduated from Stanford Law School, where she was on the *Stanford Law Review.* Her undergraduate work was at the University of Southern California, where she majored in philosophy and graduated Phi Beta Kappa. Robin has published large amounts of material to help self-represented litigants, including *"Here's How You Get a Divorce in Santa Clara County* and *How to Do a Contested Divorce in California,* by Nolo Press. Her Web site, http://www.divorcecal.com, features many videos useful to self-represented litigants nationwide such as *Trial in a Box* and *Dissecting Custody Psychological Evaluations.*

Annette Zender is a protective parent, licensed Illinois foster parent, and adoptive parent. She cofounded the Illinois Coalition for Family Court Reform, and she speaks regularly at conferences for the prevention of child abuse and protection for battered mothers.

Joan Zorza, J.D., is the founding editor of both *Domestic Violence Report* and *Sexual Assault Report,* and she has been working to end violence against women and children for forty years. A member of the bars of Massachusetts, New York, and the District of Columbia, she has written extensively on child custody, domestic violence, stalking, and sexual assault matters, and she is the author of the three-volume set of books, *Violence Against Women* (2002, 2004, and 2006), and *Guide to Interstate Custody: A Manual for Domestic Violence Advocates* (1992, 1995). She was awarded for her work on custody by the Department of Justice in 1998, by the City of New York Human Resources Administration for her work on behalf of victims of domestic violence in 2000, and by the Sunshine Lady Foundation for her work on violence against women in 2002. Since 1995, she has been a liason or a member of the board of the American Bar Association's Commission on Domestic Violence and represented or supervised lawyers and law students in cases on behalf of more than 2,000 battered women and almost 200 sexually abused children as an attorney at Greater Boston Legal Services and at the National Battered Women's Law Project of the now defunct National Center on Women and Family Law. She no longer represents clients but remains involved with many organizations and, through her writings and presentations, helps to increase the safety of women and children.

Part 1
Parameters of the Problem

Chapter 1

Child Custody Practices of the Family Courts in Cases Involving Domestic Violence

by Joan Zorza, J.D.

INTRODUCTION

This chapter examines some of the laws and practices, which currently influence child custody determinations in divorce and family courts,[1] in disputes between the parents, particularly in cases involving domestic violence (DV). It covers where the laws and practices originated and how they often disadvantage women and children. The chapter also explores why battered women continue to fare so badly in custody disputes.

EVOLUTION OF THE LAWS GOVERNING DOMESTIC VIOLENCE AND CUSTODY

As awareness has grown of the negative impact that DV has on children, even when they do not see or hear it in person,[2] legislatures and courts have increasingly made DV a consideration in child custody decisions. However, until very recently it was not a listed factor, let alone a permissible criterion, for courts to use in custody determinations. For much of America's history, even the best mothers had no right to custody of their children. The first custody laws in the colonies, and later in the states, followed those of British common law and the laws in European countries. Those laws automatically granted custody to the father[3] unless he was clearly unfit, unavailable, or consented to his wife having custody. In the latter half of the nineteenth century, largely in response to industrialization, fewer fathers working at home, and the

---

[1] States differ widely in which of their courts decide divorce and custody matters. This chapter will refer to the family courts to designate all courts making divorce and custody decisions, even though the designation might not be correct in a particular state.

[2] *See, e.g.,* Liz Pawelko & Catherine Koverola, "Exposed—The Developmental Impact of Domestic Violence on Children," in *Intimate Partner Violence* 2-7 (K.A. Kendall-Tackett & Sarah. M. Giacomoni eds., 2007); Lorraine Radford & Marianne Hester, *Mothering Through Domestic Violence* (2006); Robert A. Geffner, Robyn Spurling Ingleman & Jennifer Zellner, *The Effects of Intimate Partner Violence on Children* (2003); Sandra A. Graham-Bermann & Jeffrey L. Edleson, *Domestic Violence in The Lives of Children: The Future of Research, Intervention, and Social Policy* (2001); Caroline McGee, *Childhood Experiences of Domestic Violence* (2000); B.B. Robbie Rossman, Honore M. Hughes & Mindy S. Rosenberg, *Children and Interpersonal Violence; Impact of Exposure* (2000); Robert A. Geffner, Peter G. Jaffe & Mariles Suderman, *Children Exposed to Domestic Violence: Current Issues in Research, Intervention, Prevention and Policy Development* (2000); George W. Holden, Robert Geffner & Ernest N. Jouriles, *Children Exposed to Marital Violence: Theory, Research, and Applied Issues* (1998); Einat Peled, Peter G. Jaffe & Jeffrey L. Edleson, *Ending the Cycle of Violence: Community Responses to Children of Battered Women* (1995); Peter G. Jaffe, David A. Wolfe & Susan Kaye Wilson, *Children of Battered Women* (1990); Maria Roy, *Children in the Cossfire: Violence in the Home—How Does It Affect Our Children* (1988).

[3] Elizabeth Pleck, *Domestic Tyranny* 49-50 (1987); Leora N. Rosen & Michelle Etlin, *The Hostage Child* 137-38 (1996); Marianne Takas, *Child Custody A Complete Guide for Concerned Mothers* 10-11 (1987).

recognition that the nurturing children need is best provided by mothers, the legislatures in almost all states[4] adopted the "tender years presumption." This presumption gave custody of young children (generally those under age seven, or the age when children started school or began apprenticeships) to the mother unless she was unfit. After the tender age, the father was entitled to reclaim custody, although few did; however, fathers were still entitled to the wages of their children even when raised by their mothers.[5] When custody was challenged, family courts began carefully scrutinizing the mother to see if she was "fit," a trend that continues to the present. Because standards have always been much higher for women, a mother's misbehavior (e.g., adultery or drinking), or her inability to support her child justified denying her custody, reasons seldom used against a man. Many laws penalized her for misbehaving; for example, an adulterous woman was disqualified from receiving any alimony,[6] which both directly and indirectly affected her likelihood of gaining custody.

Best Interests of the Child Standard

During the last sixty years, states abandoned the tender years presumption in favor of a best interests of the child (BIC) standard,[7] for the first time officially permitting courts to consider both parents as possible caretakers throughout the child's minority. To determine which parent should get custody under a BIC standard, a judge must consider many factors set forth in the laws and court decisions of the state involved. In practice, this standard is very unclear and elusive, leaving it to the judge's discretion as to how to weigh the relevant factors, with the result that these laws are often criticized, particularly in cases when one parent is committing DV.[8] While the BIC standard "sounds enlightened and child centered," it is neither. It often "offers no recognition of the developmental needs of a child; . . . the wishes and feelings of the child; and perhaps most damningly, its vagueness opens the door to almost complete judicial discretion . . . and actually 'encourages parents to fight over custody, because the outcome is unpredictable,' although custody fights are highly detrimental to the child."[9]

Mental Health Input

In the 1960s, California started using mental health professionals (MHPs) as mediators, guardians ad litem (GALs), custody evaluators, and more often as expert witnesses in their family courts, particularly in custody cases, a trend that spread over the next twenty-five years throughout the country, with legislators enacting statutes and increasing court budgets to enable these changes. The use of MHPs and how

---

[4] Ruth I. Abrams & John M. Greaney, *Report of the Gender Bias Study of the [Massachusetts] Supreme Judicial Court* 60 (1989) (noting that Massachusetts law never recognized maternal preference even for children of tender years, holding since 1855 that the rights of both parents to custody were equal).

[5] Rosen & Etlin, *supra* note 3, at 138.

[6] Homer H. Clark, Jr., *The Law of Domestic Relations in the United States* § 16.4.6 (2d ed. 1988).

[7] Diane Boyd Rauber, *A Judge's Guide: Making Child-Centered Decisions in Custody Cases* (2001).

[8] Mary Ann Mason, *The Custody Wars* 19 (1999).

[9] Id.

these professionals rarely help battered women or their children will be discussed at greater length later in this chapter (see "Two Approaches Governing Custody of Determnations").

Joint Custody

Starting in the late 1970s but gaining much strength in the 1980s, a new push was made for joint custody awards. This was strongly encouraged by fathers' rights (FRs) advocates, in large part to reduce the amount of child support they had to pay. It took off with lightening speed,[10] and most states in the 1980s enacted laws permitting or even encouraging joint custody awards, something that was not a legal possibility and was even prohibited in the 1960s. However, it is still recognized that joint custody is not appropriate when parents are antagonistic or hostile to each other, as is the case in families with DV,[11] although mothers opposing joint custody are often denied all custody, as will be discussed later in this chapter (see "First Approach: Family Systems Dynamic"). Yet joint custody awards, whether legal (for sharing decision making about the child) and/or physical (for where the child will reside), are currently favored by judges in the United States and Canada (although they cost more), lead to lower child support awards, do not increase men's willingness to pay child support, increase parental conflict, are not better for the children, and result in little extra time spent by children with their fathers.[12]

Recognition of Domestic Violence in Custody Laws

Even before there was any official recognition of DV in the mid to late 1970s, when Del Martin[13] and Lenore Walker[14] started writing about the subject, all states permitted some kind of protection to battered women during the pendency of a divorce or legal separation or as a ground for divorce. All states had criminal laws that could be used to punish serious DV incidents,[15] although it was not until the mid 1970s (Pennsylvania is generally credited for having the first law in 1976) through the end of the 1980s that every state enacted civil order of protection laws.[16] Although 30 to 60 percent of perpetrators of DV are known to have also perpetrated abuse against their children,[17] many legislatures were slow to see the children as victims of this same abuse. Even when legislatures did enact laws to protect child witnesses, many

---

[10] Peter G. Jaffe, Nancy K.D. Lemon & Samantha E. Poisson, *Child Custody & Domestic Violence: A Call for Safety and Accountability* 13, 65 (2003).

[11] Clark, *supra* note 6, at § 19.5.

[12] Mason, *supra* note 8, at 55-58, 60-61.

[13] Del Martin, *Battered Wives* (1976).

[14] Lenore E. Walker, *The Battered Woman* (1979).

[15] Contrary to assertion, the British "rule of thumb" decriminalizing all but the most severe interspousal assaults was adopted only in Mississippi, although effectively practiced in North Carolina under the guise of protecting the privacy of the couple. Ann Jones, *Women Who Kill* 301-02 (1980); Pleck, *supra* note 3 (noting on pages 4 and 21 that the Puritans in colonial Massachusetts enacted the first laws in the world against wife and child beating).

[16] Andrew R. Klein, *The Criminal Justice Response to Domestic Violence* 68 (2004).

[17] Graham-Bermann & Edleson, *supra* note 2, at 9; Jaffe, Lemon & Poisson, *supra* note 10, at 30.

unsympathetic judges failed to protect them, incorrectly assuming that women exaggerate abuse for tactical gain in custody cases or that husbands who abused their wives were good fathers or merely stressed out by the divorce. A common misperception, often encouraged by the MHPs advising judges, was that the abuse would end once the divorce was final.[18]

In 1994, the National Council on Juvenile and Family Court Judges released its Model Code on Domestic Violence (Model Code).[19] It encouraged all states to enact statutes establishing a rebuttable presumption against giving sole or joint custody to abusive parents,[20] which at least six states had already enacted.[21] All states now require courts to at least consider DV as a "factor" in custody determinations (factor laws), and approximately half of the states have enacted a rebuttable presumption law.[22] Undermining the somewhat outdated Model Code, many presumption and even some factor laws impose extra requirements before a judge can consider the DV. Some count only documented incidents of DV; some require several incidents, count only recent incidents, or require a higher standard of proof (e.g., clear and convincing evidence or a criminal conviction) for abuse allegations as compared with any other matter involving custody determinations.[23] In addition, by law (e.g., in New York) or practice, orders of protection granted by consent of the parties *usually* are not recognized in other proceedings, although this may be at variance with the federal full faith and credit mandate requiring that every other state, territory, and tribe recognize and enforce (i.e., give full faith and credit to) the protective orders issued in other jurisdictions.[24]

Systematic collusions that trivialize abuse further undermine the legislative intent that DV be considered in custody decisions. These include, for example, widespread practices by prosecutors and criminal courts such as plea bargaining down to a trivial offense that will not affect the custody decision, pretrial diversion (typically by referring the batterer to a batterer intervention program), continuing cases without a finding, automatically dismissing the case after a certain amount of time or when the abuser completes the program, or vacating the judgment upon motion of the abuser. Similar measures are used in civil courts, along with many judges' common practice of failing to either record admissions or make findings that the abusers perpetrated the offenses.[25] After cases have gone to court, it seldom occurs to victims that they still need to safeguard evidence to relitigate these same issues in a family law custody

---

[18] Jaffe, Lemon & Poisson, *supra* note 10, at 11, 17; Lundy Bancroft & Jay G. Silverman, *The Batterer as Parent: Addressing the Impact of Domestic Violence on Family Dynamics* 119-20 (2002).

[19] National Council of Juvenile and Family Court Judges, *Model Code on Domestic and Family Violence* (1994) [hereinafter, Model Code]. (The Model Code was created with input from several organizations, including legislators, the American Bar Association, the American Medical Association, domestic violence experts, prosecutors, and defense counsel. Most of its recommendations, particularly those involving custody, are still good models, although it is currently being revised.)

[20] Id. at § 401.

[21] Joan Zorza, *Guide to Interstate Custody: A Manual for Domestic Violence Advocates* Appendix F (2d ed. 1995).

[22] Jannette Tucker, "Model Code Retrospective," 8(2) *Synergy* 6, 8 (2004) (noting that forty-nine states had such laws; and, since then, the remaining state, Connecticut, enacted a law).

[23] Jaffe, Lemon & Poisson, *supra* note 10, at 89-94; Bancroft & Silverman, *supra* note 18, at 121.

[24] 18 U.S.C. §§ 2265-2266.

[25] Klein, *supra* note 16, at 133-48.

dispute because there was no final judgment they can rely on. Also prejudicing abuse victims is the fact that many cases never get into the system because police fail to respond, never arrest the perpetrator or document the incident, arrest the victim instead of or in addition to the perpetrator, or fail to serve the defendant.[26] Further, prosecutors may fail to bring or prosecute charges. Such problems happen throughout the system but are endemic in rural regions.[27]

Even when the system responds appropriately, many abusers falsely accuse their victims of abuse or make it difficult or dangerous for victims to litigate the case. Consequently, many women are incorrectly held to be abuse perpetrators, never dare to bring or follow through with any of their own charges, or find that the abusers' charges against them effectively wash out their charges against the abusers.[28] Thus, abusers often sabotage the intent of these DV advantage laws, even in states that have enacted primary aggressor laws to encourage courts to punish the true perpetrator.

Financial Implications of Litigation

The cost of custody and divorce litigation has risen dramatically in the past few decades, so that even 80 percent of attorneys admit it "has become prohibitive in recent years."[29] This trend primarily impacts women, who tend to be poorer, particularly when they are battered.[30] Many states report that litigants in more than half of divorce or family law cases are self-represented, that the rates are even higher in larger counties, that they have risen dramatically (e.g., 77 percent of those filing divorces in San Diego in 2000, compared to 46 percent only eight years before), and that women (particularly African American and Hispanic women), are disproportionately more likely to have no attorney.[31] Many women who start with representation end up having to represent themselves—and eventually having to file for bankruptcy, which is not surprising; one survey found that the average contested custody cost for battered women in the United States was over $90,000.[32] While legal fees have generated the most attention, the reality is that the combined fees of all of the court agents (e.g., GALs, mediators, custody evaluators, custody supervisors, parent educators, and parent coordinators) who may become involved in a case has dramatically escalated. Many of these expenses go on for years after the initial divorce or custody dispute; yet, they are often not factored into estimates of the ultimate costs of litigation. Furthermore, many court systems have no mechanism or fees to pay these costs even for indigent parties, so the parents must pay them.[33]

---

[26] Id. at 108-10.

[27] Id. at 91.

[28] Bancroft & Silverman, *supra* note 18, at 17.

[29] Stephanie Francis Ward, "Pulse of the Legal Profession," 30 *A.B.A. J.* 31 (Oct. 2007).

[30] Penelope Eileen Bryan, *Constructive Divorce: Procedural Justice and Sociolegal Reform* 28 (2006).

[31] Madelynn Herman, *Self-Representation: Pro Se Statistics,* http://www.scsconline.org/WC/Publications/Memos/ProSeStats Memo.htm.

[32] Geraldine Butts Stahly, *Protective Mothers in Child Custody Disputes: A Study of Judicial Abuse,* Presentation at Battered Mothers' Custody Conference, Albany, NY, Jan. 14, 2007.

[33] Requiring indigent parties to pay these costs may violate *Boddie v. Connecticut,* 401 U.S. 371 (1971) (holding that states cannot require indigent divorce litigants to pay filing fees).

Criminalization of Domestic Violence When Children Are Present

Laws that criminalize or increase the penalties for DV committed in the presence of children are an unfortunate consequence of the medical profession's delayed recognition of the detrimental effects of DV on children. Rather than helping victims, these laws deter many battered women from seeking help. They have been used primarily to require children to testify as witnesses of the abuse, to file child abuse and neglect or failure to protect charges against mothers, or to charge mothers as accessories to crimes for engaging in DV.[34] New York's highest court, the only one to rule on this to date, has held that child protection agencies cannot remove children from the home solely because of witnessing DV, particularly since being put in foster care is extremely harmful to children.[35]

Gender Bias Backlash

As discussed elsewhere in this text (see Chapter 5 in this volume), a large number of gender bias studies of the courts were conducted during the last quarter of the twentieth century. These studies generally found that courts trivialize women's concerns, particularly in custody and DV cases, and that, compared to men, women are disbelieved more often, held to much higher standards, and judged far more punitively for failings such as drinking, use of drugs, adultery, or hostility to their partners. Such behaviors are readily seen as grounds for giving the father custody.[36] The gender bias studies found judicial bias was greatest, and nowhere more devastating than, in cases involving DV.[37] Over the last half century, mothering has been increasingly devalued as a basis for awarding custody. While in 1960, mothering was the most-cited factor for awarding custody, in the 1990s, it was cited in just 10.6 percent of cases. It is rarely mentioned today.[38] Courts also require a much higher standard of proof for abuse allegations made by mothers than for those made by fathers.[39] Although few courts still automatically deny custody to mothers who have committed adultery, much custody litigation still involves a mother's sexual conduct.[40] Since appellate courts generally reverse family law cases only if the trial judge abused his/her discretion, trial judges are seldom reversed after awarding custody to a father, especially as it is assumed that the paternal grandmother or the father's girlfriend will be caring for the child, rather than a day care center, although his employment needs are deemed to justify him placing the children in day care.

---

[34] Billie Lee Dunford-Jackson, "The Role of Family Courts in Domestic Violence: The U.S. Experience," in *Protecting Children from Domestic Violence: Strategies for Community Intervention* 188, 192-93 (Peter G. Jaffe, Linda L. Baker & Alison J. Cunningham eds., 2004).

[35] Nicholson v. Scoppetta, 820 N.E.2d 840, 787 N.Y.S.2d 196 (2004).

[36] *See, e.g.* Rosen & Etlin, *supra* note 3, at 134-43, Abrams & Greaney, *supra* note 4, at 59-77 (also citing gender bias studies from many other states); Klein, *supra*, note 16, at 173-74.

[37] Klein, *supra* note 16, at 172.

[38] Mason, *supra* note 8 at 21.

[39] Jaffe, Lemon & Poisson, *supra* note 10, at 89-94; Bancroft & Silverman, *supra* note 18, at 121.

[40] Clark, *supra* note 6, at § 19.4.

Resentful of the findings of the gender bias studies, the enactment of DV statutes, and the federal Violence Against Women Act[41] funding, FRs groups have pushed to dilute these laws by covincing legislatures to enact "friendly parent" provisions and presumptions of joint custody, eliminating "custody" language in favor of shared parenting concepts and other laws more favorable to men.[42] The result is that while all states now make DV a consideration in custody determinations, with the intent that battered women have a strong advantage in being awarded custody of their children, in practice, the DV history often is ignored, so that these laws have not worked to the advantage of battered women and are even used against them.[43] Batterers today are at least as likely, if not more likely, to win custody as are nonviolent fathers,[44] a finding that matches those of the gender bias studies conducted during the last quarter of the twentieth century before there was any awareness of DV.

TWO APPROACHES GOVERNING CUSTODY DETERMINATIONS

This section will introduce the two approaches that courts currently use in determining custody. The first is based on a family systems approach (FSA). The second, which assumes abuse allegations are largely trumped up, silences and punishes mothers for seeking to protect themselves or their children from their abusive partners. Both approaches (see "First Approach: Family Systems Dynamic" and "Second Approach: Richard Gardner's Two Theories") resonate with FRs activists in their minimization or discounting of family violence, their empowerment of abusers, and their disempowerment of battered women, all of which ultimately harm children.

Starting in 1963 when the Association of Family and Conciliation Courts was founded to promote mediation in California,[45] there has been a marked increase in the involvement of MHPs in the divorce and family courts, whether as custody evaluators, GALs, mediators, parent educators, parent coordinators (who act to enforce custody/visitation orders), or therapists for one or more members of the family, often mandated by the court. For largely political and self-preservation reasons,[46] and consistent with the backlash against women later documented by gender bias studies, the MHPs have

---

[41] 18 U.S.C. § 2265 (1994).

[42] Joan S. Meier,"Domestic Violence, Child Custody and Child Protection: Understanding Judicial Resistance and Imagining the Solutions," 11 *Am. U. J. Gender, Soc. Pol'y & L.* 657, 677-78 (2003).

[43] Allison C. Morrill et al., "Child Custody and Visitation Decisions When the Father Has Perpetrated Violence Against the Mother," 11(8) *Violence Against Women* 1076 (2005); Mary A. Kernick et al., "Children in the Crossfire: Child Custody Determinations Among Couples With a History of Intimate Partner Violence," 11(8) *Violence Against Women* 991 (2005); *see also* Abrams & Greaney, *supra* note 4, especially pages 59-73.

[44] Nancy E. Johnson, Dennis P. Saccuzzo & Wendy J. Koen, "Child Custody Mediation in Cases of Domestic Violence: Empirical Evidence of a Failure to Protect," 11(8) *Violence Against Women* 1022 (2005); Bancroft & Silverman, *supra* note 18, at 115-16.

[45] Association of Family and Conciliation Courts, http://www.afccnet.org/about/history.asp.

[46] Mental health professionals are primarily involved in cases where child custody or visitation is in dispute and hence have a self-interest in increasing the number of custody/visitation disputes. To hold themselves out as able to offer fathers something in custody/visitation cases, most mediators quickly learned that shared custody arrangements are the best (and perhaps only) way to do this.

selectively been promoting joint custody and father custody.[47] At the same time, the MHPs have largely ignored the mother-infant and attachment studies that favor mother custody,[48] along with the far greater role that mothers play in rearing children. (For example, parent gender accounts for 95 percent of the variance in parents' involvement with their adolescent children, with nonresidential mothers having much more involvement with their children than even residential fathers.[49])

Within the framework used by these MHPs, so undervalued is the importance of mothers that virtually all social science studies (and funding for them) attempt to document the importance of fathers' involvement with their children, ignoring that of mothers. Typical of the minimization of the mother's role is that the MHPs and judges involved in influencing or making custody determinations, who usually have little sympathy for the parent who fails to send or return the child's favorite comfy toy to or from visitation, virtually always ignore that the comfy object is itself a substitute for the child's primary custodial parent. Many of these MHPs helped the FRs movements articulate demands and expectations for fathers, which helped these organizations develop and gain credibility. The FRs organizations are relatively new, with one of the oldest national groups, the Children's Rights Council, having been formed in 1985 as the National Council for Children's Rights.[50] It is also one of the first groups to attempt to hide its agenda by purporting to advocate on behalf of children rather than for fathers.[51] Both the MHPs and FRs advocates have been highly successful in deflecting women's and children's needs, despite DV laws meant to advantage them and the recommendations in the Model Code[52] discouraging use of mediation, mutual orders of protection, and couples counseling in cases of family violence.

Bias Against Battered Mothers

The two approaches that family courts use to decide most custody and visitation cases interject philosophical belief systems that disadvantage all women, especially battered women. Both approaches further confuse their adherents, the courts, and the police because they are based on an incorrect understanding of DV. The first approach, which is derived from the "family systems" theoretical perspective, often results in the use of mediation or other types of alternate dispute resolution, couples counseling, parent education, or parent coordinators for divorcing couples, along with mutual orders of protection. The second approach is based on Richard Gardner's theory of Parental Alienation Syndrome (PAS), which alleges that mothers alienate their children from their fathers and thus deserve to be punished by depriving them of custody and, in some cases, even visitation. The American Psychological Association characterized PAS as having no scientific basis,[53] which renders it junk

---

[47] Abrams & Greaney, *supra* note 4, especially pages 59-73; Johnson, Saccuzzo & Koen, *supra* note 44.

[48] Mason, *supra* note 8, at 243.

[49] D.N. Hawkins, P.R. Amato & V. King, "Parent-Adolescent Involvement: The Relative Influence of Parent Gender and Residence," 68 *J. Marriage & Fam.* 125, esp. 126 (2006).

[50] Children's Rights Council, http://www.crckids.org.

[51] Many FRs groups also have token women involved who are often the second wives of the men.

[52] Model Code, *supra* note 19.

[53] American Psychological Association, *Violence and the Family: Report of the American Psychological Association Presidential Task Force on Violence and the Family* 40 (1996) [hereinafter APA].

science and therefore a concept that has no audience except in the family court system.[54] The favorable response by the courts to PAS and similar "alienation" theories and to the friendly parent concept–another of Richard Gardner's theories[55]—logically stems from the long-standing discrediting of women's concerns and creditability in comparison with those of men. Gag orders, which are the ultimate silencing of an aggrieved party, are also more likely to be imposed when either theory is used.

Proponents of these approaches (many of whom subscribe to both) believe in and apply these theories in ways that probably meet the U.S. Supreme Court's definition of religion.[56] Since they are believed on faith, have little or no scientific basis, and strongly favor fathers over mothers, serious constitutional problems arise when these approaches are used, particularly for mothers, who often have no option but to submit to the divorce and family courts for the protection and relief they need. While both approaches superficially seem benevolent, which might explain why decent people have so readily accepted them, the reality is they are neither fair nor helpful, but instead have enabled a serious backlash against women and children, especially in cases where the mother's intimate partner has been abusive toward her or the children. These approaches effectively silence or punish women for seeking protection from abuse, the exact opposite of what the legislatures intended in enacting DV laws. Both approaches tend to impress their adherents with the apparent logic of their position, further confusing court agents and endangering victims of DV. In applying such theories to child custody cases involving abuse, their proponents are, in effect, colluding with abusive fathers (who are quick to discredit and blame their victims[57]), which explains why they are basic to the agendas of FRs groups. They also encourage further abuse.

Neither Approach Will Stop the Abuse

In order to make an abuser stop abusing, it is necessary, but not sufficient, for the abuser to admit his wrongdoing, apologize, and accept responsibility for his abuse. He also has to change his ways, something that is not easy since abusive behavior is so rewarding in a society that largely fails to hold abusers accountable.[58] Psychotherapy, even when combined with psychotropic drugs, rarely helps batterers, and even the few helped seldom sustain the results for long.[59] Because batterers are not out of control, anger management programs cannot help them.[60] Those failing to require batterers to go through the entire process, be they MHPs, clergy, probation officers, or courts, encourage the status quo and the batterers' repeated victimization of their intimate partners. Furthermore, professionals focusing on changing the family system, instead of changing the batterer, increase the risk that he will further harm her while

---

[54] Amy Neustein & Michael Lesher, *From Madness to Mutiny: Why Mothers Are Running From the Family Courts—And What Can Be Done About It,* xxiii, 26 (2005).

[55] Joan Zorza, "The 'Friendly Parent' Concept—Another Gender Biased Legacy From Richard Gardner," 12 *Domestic Violence Rep.* 65, 75-80 (2007).

[56] *See, e.g.,* United States v. Seeger, 380 U.S. 163, 85 S. Ct. 850; Welsh v. United States, 389 U.S. 333, 90 S. Ct. 1792 (1970).

[57] Bancroft & Silverman, *supra* note 18, at 18-19.

[58] Id. at 49; Lundy Bancroft, *Why Does He Do That? Inside the Minds of Angry and Controlling Men* 151-58, 170, 197 (2002).

[59] Bancroft & Silverman, *supra* note 18, at 22.

[60] Id. at 183-84; Edward W. Gondolf & David Russell, "The Case Against Anger Control Treatment for Batterers," 9(3) *Response* 2 (1986).

simultaneously putting the onus on her to change.[61] Increasing numbers of scientifically designed studies show that batterer intervention programs make no, or at best a 5 percent, difference in ending men's violence and more than double the rearrest rate for unemployed men who attend them.[62] The fact that these programs are the main court-imposed sanctions for wife beating is another indication that the system fails to protect women and children and still trivializes the violence against them. In the criminal courts, the move towards restorative justice, an approach highly encouraged by public defenders who know how effective it is in keeping their abusive clients out of jail, has also helped to keep the system from holding abusers accountable and keeping women and children safe. FRs activists, who would like to see all DV laws removed from the books, are supportive of both approaches, which minimize the consequences of DV and the likelihood that offenders will face serious sanctions.

FIRST APPROACH: FAMILY SYSTEMS DYNAMIC

The FSA is a psychological theory that believes that one family member's behavior can only be understood in the context of the entire family, rather than being explained by factors inherent in that one individual. It believes that faulty communication is the root of most family problems and seeks to correct the communication problems by opening up dialogue between the parties to teach them to better cooperate—goals that sound positive, at least in theory. The FSA also sees the family unit as enduring even after a divorce, with both parents, and particularly the father—even if violent—remaining involved with the children.[63] When applied to DV cases, this approach is seriously flawed. Criminal behavior is the sole choice of the perpetrator; it is not a social or family dynamic problem, and it is seldom the result of mental illness.[64] The laws of every state make DV and incest crimes; yet, the family courts, at most, see them as a dynamic between both parties. This is reflected in the supposed truism that the criminal courts see bad people at their best, but the family courts see good people at their worst—stressed out because of the divorce or separation. Yet, when judges in Massachusetts were required to examine both parties' probation records in any case involving abuse, they found that the vast majority of the abusers, in contrast to their victims, had long involvement with the criminal courts, often in cases not involving their current victim. This means that the supposedly good men stressed out by divorce were actually the same bad ones often known for many years by

---

[61] Carol E. Jordan et al., *Intimate Partner Violence: A Clinical Training Guide for Mental Health Professionals* 124 (2004); Jeanne King, "Shining the Light on Casting a Shadow: A Psychologists' Personal Perspective on Certification," *The Voice: The Journal of the Domestic Violence Movement* 23-28 (2004); Lenore E.A. Walker, *The Battered Woman Syndrome* 18 (2d ed. 2000).

[62] Bernard Auchter, "Guest Editor's Introduction: Special Issue: Intervening With Domestic Violence Offenders," 14 *Violence Against Women* 131 (2008); Greg Berman & John Feinblatt, *Good Courts: The Case for Problem Solving Justice* 160 (2005); Casey Gwinn, *Keeping the Promise: Victim Safety and Batterer Accountability: Report to the California Attorney General from the Task Force on Local Criminal Justice Response to Domestic Violence* (2005), *available at* http://safestate.org/index.cfm?navid=386.

[63] Mason, *supra* note 8, at 152.

[64] Marjory D. Fields, "Getting Beyond: 'What Did She Do to Provoke Him?': Comments by a Retired Judge on the Special Issue on Child Custody and Domestic Violence," 14 *Violence Against Women* 93, 95-78 (2008); Bancroft & Silverman, *supra* note 18, at 19-23.

the criminal courts.[65] Yet, family court judges and MHPs persist in believing the myth that the divorce and poor communication cause the DV, leading them to conclude that his abuse will end after the divorce.

Violence in the family and between intimate partners also does not happen because the parties are not communicating well. Many couples with communication problems are nonviolent, and most perpetrators have no trouble communicating with other people.[66] Rather, the DV perpetrator deliberately creates a climate of fear and intimidation, coercively terrorizing and controlling his victim. He chooses when, where, and whom to attack, which is why most abusers have no trouble controlling their anger and resentment against their bosses, the police, or others who are more powerful. Similarly, most do not lash out against their secretaries, even though secretaries, like wives, typically have lower status and can be cause for frustration and annoyance. Choosing when to batter also explains why battering almost always happens in private without witnesses. Not only does his battering rarely extend outside of the family, but his lack of assertiveness, poor communications, and poor impulse control are also usually limited to within the family.[67] In addition, it is highly unusual for women to be violent or for the violence to be mutual, something only realized when one looks at who is the dominant or primary aggressor, who is fearful of the other, and who may be acting in a self-protective way or to protect the children or others.[68]

Except when victims are within the family, society does not expect victims and perpetrators to get along. Courts that would never order bank owners and bank robbers to attend couples counseling to improve their communication skills and cooperativeness frequently order abusive husbands and their victim partners to go together to mediation and/or couples or family counseling, especially when they have children in common. While communication is generally poor in families where one member is abusive, the poor communication is usually the result of, or at least exacerbated by, the fearful environment, which leaves the victim afraid to speak and feeling resentful. Those sensing her anger and frustration often blame her. Compared to him, she seems "untogether." Many psychological instruments regularly used to assess women incorrectly diagnose them as having various psychological problems, all of which are explainable from the partner's abuse. It is only if one is aware of his abusiveness that one can appreciate how amazingly together the woman is in the face of what he is putting her through every day and how manipulative, narcissistic, arrogant, disrespectful, egotistical, and abusive he is.[69]

With courts and the MHPs who inform the courts having a flawed and biased understanding of DV and a belief in the FSA, it is not surprising that abusive fathers are still winning custody more often than are mothers, as found, for example, by four recent federally funded studies about child custody determinations in DV cases.[70] In addition, a study in Canada also found widespread gender and racial bias, particularly against aboriginal and immigrant women.[71]

---

[65] Klein, *supra* note 16, at 80.

[66] Bancroft & Silverman, *supra* note 18, at 22-23.

[67] Id. at 23.

[68] APA, *supra* note 53, at 14, 36; Patricia R. Salber & Ellen Taliaferro, *The Physician's Guide to Intimate Partner Violence and Abuse: A Reference for All Health Care Professionals* 23-24 (2006); Pamela J. Jenkins & Barbara Parmer Davidson, *Stopping Domestic Violence: How a Community Can Prevent Spousal Abuse* 43 (2001).

[69] Edward W. Gondolf, *Assessing Woman Battering in Mental Health Services* 77, 132-33 (1998); Bancroft, *supra* note 58, at 34-36, 49; Salber & Taliaferro, *supra* note 68, at 20-21.

[70] Joan Zorza & Leora Rosen eds., " Special Issue on Child Custody and Domestic Violence," 11(8) *Violence Against Women* 983 (2005).

[71] Georgina Taylor, Jan Barnsley & Penny Goldsmith, *Women and Children Last: Custody Disputes and the Family "Justice" System* 3-4 (1996).

Mediation

Of all the approaches used in the family courts, mediation is probably the one that most encouraged the FRs movement. Mediators, more than other court actors, are supposed to interact impartially with both parties, encouraging them to speak their concerns and ideally reaching a settlement. Mediation began in the California family courts in the early 1960s before the FRs movement had taken hold, and, as previously noted, many of their beliefs and practices encouraged men to demand more rights.

In contrast to clergy who tend to focus on forgiveness and moving on,[72] mediators and family systems-oriented MHPs skip the forgiveness step, believing that what happened in the past is largely irrelevant, since they will teach both parties new communication skills that will free them from the dysfunction. Mediators' beliefs, like those of other MHP court players, are based on a number of disproved myths about DV, such as that DV seldom happens, and, when it does, it is not that severe; that both parties are to blame for the DV; that it is often mutual; and that it generally ends once the parties separate.[73] In actuality, the violence escalates, and sometimes only begins, postseparation, which is also when batterers are most likely to injure or kill their partners[74] or physically or sexually abuse their children.[75] Since most family systems advocates are blind to the abuse issues, their approach cannot end the abuse; to the contrary, the approach colludes in it by failing to hold abusers accountable.[76] Although over half of women filing for divorce do so because of DV, and even mediators admit that DV is present in at least half of divorce cases, mediators detect fewer than 5 percent of the cases, even in states that forbid mediation in abuse cases, rather than the more than 50 percent that they should screen out.[77] Mediation can be highly gratifying psychologically for the mediators,[78] and, in any case, it is their livelihood, providing them with a strong incentive to overlook the abuse or rationalize that it is not serious. A few mediators do acknowledge the abuse but genuinely believe the skills that they teach to couples will put an end to it.

Few Mediators Trained in Family Violence. Few MHPs—which includes the vast majority of mediators, custody evaluators, and many GALs—understand domestic or family violence and its dangers to its victims; most are not even trained to look for or assess for family violence, making them dangerous.[79] Two-fifths of MHPs

---

[72] Marie M. Fortune, "Pastoral Responses to Sexual Assault and Abuse: Laying a Foundation," 3(3/4) *J. Religion & Abuse* 91 (2001).

[73] Marsha B. Liss & Geraldine Butts Stahly, "Domestic Violence and Child Custody," in *Battering and Family Therapy: A Feminist Perspective* 175, 184 (M. Hansen & M. Harway eds., 1993); Bancroft, *supra* note 58, at 180-81; Bancroft & Silverman, *supra* note 18, at 119, 199; Jordan et al., *supra*, note 61, at 147.

[74] Caroline Wolf Harlow, *Female Victims of Violent Crime*, Bureau of Justice Statistics, NCJ 126826 (1991); Jordan et al., *supra* note 61, at 18-19; Jaffe, Lemon & Poisson, *supra* note 10, at 29.

[75] Bancroft & Silverman, *supra* note 18, at 85 and 127; Bancroft, *supra* note 58, at 245-46.

[76] Gus Kaufman, Jr., Wendy Lipshutz & Drorah O'Donnell Setel, "Responding to Domestic Violence," in *Jewish Pastoral Care: A Practical Handbook from Traditional & Contemporary Sources* 237, 238 (Dayle A. Friedman ed., 2001).

[77] Trina Grillo, "The Mediation Alternative: Process Dangers for Women," 100(6) *Yale L.J.* 1545, 1584, n.184 (1991); Jessica Pearson, *Divorce and Domestic Violence* 3, 48 (1997).

[78] *See, e.g.,* Grillo, *supra* note 77, at 1550.

[79] APA, *supra* note 53, at 13, 40, 100, 103.

have never had any training at any time in their careers on intimate partner violence, and, while this is changing, the National Institute of Medicine found that virtually none of those trained had more than two hours of DV training throughout their careers.[80] Not only is the content of most training seldom monitored for accuracy, but its efficacy is often diminished because of the bias that most MHPs have against family violence. Most of those doing mediation, couples counseling, parent programs, and custody evaluations are among the least well trained in DV; over 90 percent of psychologists are unable to identify DV and consider DV irrelevant in custody determinations.[81] With so little, and such inadequate training, these MHPs are unlikely to realize that DV tends to escalate greatly when the parties separate or divorce and that after separation abusers shift their abuse to the children. Over a third of abusive fathers threaten to kidnap their children, and 11 percent actually do abduct them; many batterers do not pay child support, and they are at least twice as likely to bitterly contest custody—particularly of sons[82]—although such custody fights are highly detrimental to the children.[83] In addition, 25 percent of abusive men threaten to hurt their children during visitation, 25 percent threaten to kill their children's mothers at visitation exchanges,[84] and many more physically hurt the mothers. In fact, the 10 percent of women who are separated or divorced are battered fourteen times as often as women still living with their abusers, and they account for 75 percent of all battered women injured by their past or present intimate partners.[85] Furthermore, studies find that men who batter women are 6.5 to 19 times as likely to sexually abuse their children as fathers who do not batter women and are more likely to do so postseparation. The more self-centered they are and the worse they abuse their intimate partners, the higher the chance they will be child molesters,[86] indicating that an alleged cooccurrence of DV and incest, rather than suggesting fraudulent allegations, is more likely to be true and indicative of a much more dangerous abusive situation.

Mediators and other MHPs are unlikely to recognize just how manipulative and deceptive abusers are and that they themselves are likely to be manipulated into siding with the abuser.[87] Mediators also have a strong shared custody bias, making few of them willing to protect either battered women victims or their children. Aggravating their bias, mediators have total immunity when they are court employees (as many are) or when the courts refer the parties to them, although it may be possible to file professional ethics charges against them or other MHPs, or have them prosecuted for failing to make a mandatory abuse report.

---

[80] Felicia Cohn, Marla E. Salmon & John D. Stobo, *Confronting Chronic Neglect: The Education and Training of Health Professionals on Family Violence* 50 (2002). (Hours of training data came from the press conference releasing the results of the report in Washington, DC, on September 11, 2001.)

[81] Bancroft & Silverman, *supra* note 18, at 119; Mason, *supra* note 8, at 164.

[82] Liss & Stahly, *supra* note 73, at 181-83.

[83] APA, *supra* note 53, at 40.

[84] Jaffe, Lemon & Poisson, *supra* note 10, at 29.

[85] Harlow, *supra* note 74, at 4.

[86] Bancroft & Silverman, *supra* note 18, at 85, 127; Lundy Bancroft & Jay G. Silverman, "Assessing Abusers' Risks to the Children," in *Protecting Children From Domestic Violence: Strategies for Community Intervention* 101, 103, 106, 109 (Peter G. Jaffe, Linda L. Baker & Alison J. Cunningham eds., 2004).

[87] Gondolf, *supra* note 69, at 77, 132-33; Bancroft & Silverman, *supra* note 18, at 125 and 203; APA, *supra* note 53, at 81.

Joint custody fosters continuing conflict for parents and children, particularly in families where there is any abuse,[88] and it is detrimental for children to shuttle between two homes, especially as there is no social scientific basis to support their assumption that children do better with frequent or continuing contact with their noncustodial parent.[89] Yet, most mediators and family systems proponents push for shared custody arrangements and for preventing mothers from relocating with the children. For example, 90.6 percent of psychologist custody evaluators, many of whom also act as mediators, admit they do not consider DV as grounds for recommending custody to the nonabusive parent, even though the laws of all states make the DV relevant in custody determinations.[90] Mediation is just not appropriate when there is violence[91] and does not protect victims of DV, as the next sections discuss.

Disadvantages to Battered Women. Mediation assumes that parties know what they want and are able to articulate it. Yet, battered women are often living moment to moment or are so frightened of their abusers that they cannot think through or articulate what they want. Mediation also assumes that both parties have roughly equal bargaining power, something that is simply not the case when one person subjects the other to domestic tyranny. It also assumes that the pool of what is up for grabs is large enough that both parties can come away with fairly equal shares of what they desire, something artificially accomplished by pushing joint custody on the parties. However, since many in the court system take men's concerns far more seriously, their real concerns—the division of property and alimony, and sometimes even child support—are often left outside of the mediation process so the parties can have input from lawyers.[92] Yet, as many as 85 to 90 percent of people going to family court are unrepresented because they cannot afford lawyers, and women, particularly battered women, are more adversely affected as they are poorer.[93] Batterers make it even less likely that their victims will have access to money, so battered women are even less likely to have lawyers than other women, but even when abused women have lawyers, their batterers dominate the litigation and exhaust them emotionally and financially, often resulting in their lawyers withdrawing or selling them out.[94]

Most battered women, and indeed most mothers, primarily want custody of the children, and if their children's fathers abuse the children, they probably want to restrict the fathers' visitations to protect the children. Yet, women are often forced to give up valuable property rights to protect themselves and their children, partly because many

---

[88] APA, *supra*, note 53, at 101; Jaffe, Lemon & Poisson, *supra* note 10, at 14-15, Model Code, *supra* note 19, at § 401.

[89] Judith S. Wallerstein & Tony J. Tanke, "To Move or Not to Move: Psychological and Legal Considerations in the Relocation of Children Following Divorce," 30 *Fam. L.Q.* 311 (1996).

[90] Marc J. Ackerman & Melissa C. Ackerman, "Child Custody Evaluation Practices: A 1996 Survey of Psychologists," 30 *Fam. L Q.* 565 (1996); Tucker, *supra* note 22.

[91] APA, *supra* note 53, at 100, 109.

[92] Abrams & Greaney, *supra* note 4, 24-25.

[93] Carol Tracy, Terry Fromson & Dabney Miller, "Justice in the Domestic Relations Division of Philadelphia Family Court: A Report to the Community," 8 *Domestic Violence Rep.* 81 (2003); Demie Kurz, *For Richer, For Poorer: Mothers Confront Divorce* 3-4, 23-24 (1995); Mason, *supra* note 8, at 154.

[94] Carl L. Tishler et al., "Is Domestic Violence Relevant? An Exploratory Analysis of Couples Referred for Mediation in Family Court," 19 *J. Interpersonal Violence* 1042, 1057 (2004); Taylor, Barnsely & Goldsmith, *supra* note 71, at 44-45, 51-53; Jaffe, Lemon & Poisson, *supra* note 10, at 32.

professionals are blind to the abuse and often encourage men to use custody fights as blackmail to pay lower child support and gain better financial results.[95] Mediators, like many others in the court system, while quick to accuse mothers alleging abuse of seeking tactical gain, ignore that virtually all of the three-quarters of fathers who threaten or seek custody do so for tactical gain, that most fathers win custody fights they seriously wage, and that noncustodial fathers are ordered to pay less than half of their children's needs through child support.[96]

In addition, many laws and court practices disadvantage women, even if not deliberately gender biased.[97] In an effort to reach settlement, mediators are permitted to mislead the parties about what the other said or how a court will react to their wishes. These questionable practices are all the easier to use against battered women in shuttle mediation, where the parties are separated for their protection and the mediator shuttles between them. Property division decisions are permanent judgments of the court, not generally subject to further modification especially when reached by agreement (including mediated ones), and only half of women are awarded any property, and, of those, only half ever get what the court ordered.[98] In contrast, custody, visitation, and usually child support orders are treated as only temporary orders, subject to modification upon a material change in circumstances. Since few abusers mediate fairly and are little inclined to abide by court orders however reached, the "final" agreement is highly likely to break down. Abusive fathers are three times more likely than other fathers to be in arrears in child support.[99] If his victim does not give him what he wants, he often takes or forces her back to court, and the court again sends the case back to mediation, now treating the prior mediated agreement as the status quo—but one that did not work. Nobody is willing to say the agreement did not work because the abuser had no intention of living up to it, or that the power dynamic made mediation inappropriate for this couple. Instead, the mediator starts with the apparently unworkable agreement and tries to mediate something that will work. Almost always, this means that the victim experiences court like a ratchet wheel, one that moves in only one direction, almost always giving the abuser a more favorable result each time the case returns to court. Rather than admitting that this ratchet wheel dynamic is happening, the mediator and the court pretend that the parties have reached another "fair" mediated agreement, never noticing that the victims are progressively drained of what little they were able to get from the process the prior time.[100] The dynamic is so rewarding that batterers are likely to keep forcing the case to return to court. It is also a strategy that many FRs groups advocate and one that is likely to be successful for fathers, particularly since mediation is a process that systemically disadvantages women, forcing them to bargain away property and support rights for safety.[101]

---

[95] Walker, *supra* note 61, at 170-71.

[96] Kurz, *supra* note 93, at 151.

[97] *See, e.g.,* id. at 24, 26-27.

[98] Id.

[99] APA, *supra* note 53, at 40.

[100] Joan Zorza, "What Is Wrong With Mediation?" 9 *Domestic Violence Rep.* 81, 92 (2004); Bancroft & Silverman, *supra* note 18, at 125; Taylor, Barnsely & Goldsmith, *supra* note 71, at 60.

[101] Zorza, *supra* note 100; Penelope Bryan, "Killing Us Softly: Divorce Mediation and the Politics of Power," 40 *Buffalo L. Rev.* 441, 458 (1992); Abrams & Greaney, *supra* note 4, at 24-25.

It is true that some women, even some battered women, do have positive experiences in mediation. Yet the batterers' claim that mothers win custody all the time is simply not true in either Canada or the United States, as shown by the studies in the special issue on child custody and DV in *Violence Against Women* in both mediated and adjudicated cases.[102] Citing similar findings from Arizona, California, Colorado, Florida, Maryland, Michigan, and New Jersey, the Massachusetts' gender bias study found that fathers seeking custody against mothers won sole or joint custody in 70 percent of cases, partly because women were held to a much higher standard and were disbelieved far more often than were men.[103]

Lawyers' Failure to Zealously Represent Battered Women. Mediation also disadvantages women because of deficiencies in their legal representation, with lawyers being unwilling to risk antagonizing judges, particularly judges before whom they often appear. Yet, the cannons of ethics for lawyers require that they zealously represent their clients. Objecting to mediation, as is permitted in many states, is seldom done, and constitutional arguments are virtually unheard of. The few times that I raised constitutional arguments against mediation during my practice, the court quickly exempted the parties from mediation or permitted me to represent my client at the mediation. Two judges explicitly said that they dared not risk an appellate court decision striking down the practice knowing how unpopular it would be with other judges.[104]

If a party has a lawyer, mandatory mediation usually violates that party's rights under the Sixth Amendment to the U.S. Constitution, which guarantees everyone the right to be represented by an attorney. (However, there is generally no right to a *free* lawyer in *civil* matters, such as, divorce and custody cases,[105] although New York State grants such a right to poor people when custody is an issue.) Mediation involves the very issues inherent in legal practice, including understanding one's case, what one's legal options are, what strategies and rationalizations will optimize obtaining desired results, what is the likelihood of the success for each option, and any disadvantages inherent in what one does. Even in the relatively rare instances where attorneys are permitted to attend or give input in the mediation process, mediation seeks to eliminate attorney influence on the assumption that mediation is a fairer, less combative approach and reaches better results from hearing only from the parties. Most mediators involve lawyers, if at all, mainly to write up or approve the mediated agreement. Since most parties, and particularly battered women, do not have the money for protracted litigation, and many family lawyers have little litigation experience, most lawyers readily advise their clients to accept the agreement they presumably thought was fair on the grounds that the client might get a far worse result if the case were to go to trial. Mediators also claim that adjudicated cases end with worse outcomes for the parties. Since many courts hear from the mediator that a party refused to mediate or ultimately rejected the mediated agreement, it is quite

---

[102] Zorza & Rosen, *supra* note 70, at 983-1107; Taylor, Barnsely & Goldsmith, *supra* note 71, at 3-4.

[103] Abrams & Greaney, *supra* note 4, at 62-63.

[104] In one case, the lawyers for both parties had already given the judge a complete agreement worked out with counsel. Knowing that the mediator would favor the father, I objected on Sixth Amendment right to counsel grounds. The judge, known for being sympathetic to men, backed down, admitting he would lose on appeal. That this case was ordered to mediation showed that getting a mutual agreement was not the judge's motive, since he already had a full agreement signed by both parties and their attorneys in his hand when he made the referral.

[105] Mason, *supra* note 8, at 158.

common for the court to treat those parties as less cooperative and to assume that this impacts their ability to parent well. Even in states where abuse victims are permitted to opt out of mediation, courts seldom infer that this was an abused mother acting to protect herself or her children. Again, the system is gender biased against women, making adverse inferences that are seldom made against men. In mediation, most battered women are forced to reveal to their abusers the whole theory of their case: what they want, how badly they want it, why they want it, and why they think it is fair. Ironically, although the man is considered entitled to at least shared custody just because he fathered a child, the more the mother tells of her need to protect herself and her children, the more she is likely to have her allegations turned against her. If no agreement is reached, the mediator is likely to recommend that custody not be given to her, even in jurisdictions where mediators are not supposed to make recommendations.[106]

As previously noted, judges can permit the attorney to attend and participate in the mediation as a way to eliminate any Sixth Amendment challenge. However, mediation also may violate a party's First Amendment rights, since it is based on a religious or at least philosophical approach, one to which the person may well not subscribe. Its approach incorporates the concept of forgiving and forgetting what happened in the past, as well as blaming the victim as much as the perpetrator, an approach completely foreign to both Judaism and Christianity. "In Judaism, the burden rests with the one who causes harm," which requires "confession, taking responsibility, repentance and restitution to the one harmed" before one's sins can be pardoned.[107] The words or concept of "forgive and forget" appear neither in the Old nor the New Testament, but rather in Shakespeare's *King Lear,* Act IV, Scene vii.[108] In Christianity, forgiveness is given by Jesus or God, not by a weaker person in response to the transgressions of a more powerful one. Even Jesus, as he suffered on the cross, did not forgive those crucifying him, but rather asked God to do so.[109]

Requiring a party in the United States to mediate family violence matters, when that person sincerely objects to it on religious grounds, violates that person's First Amendment rights. This is true even if the party's pastor or church does not understand or share that person's beliefs about this issue, since the issue is what the *individual* sincerely believes. While it is true that mediation and restorative justice are a part of the Native American religious tradition, they are not part of the religious traditions of either Christians or Jews, who comprise the vast majority of people in the United States. Many battered women (and undoubtedly many other people) feel uncomfortable with mediation, even if they do not fully understand why. Lawyers and advocates should explore whether their clients object to mediation on religious grounds.

Impeded Healing. Mediation and many other FSAs blame both parties for past behaviors and assume any abuse will stop in the future. In doing so, they further confuse and silence the victim, making it harder for her to name and validate the abuse she has experienced, which would allow her to heal. It also protects the perpetrator from having to take responsibility for his abuse, making it less likely that he will ever stop being abusive. This dynamic reinforces the abuser's belief that he will escape from any consequences for his abuse, increasing the likelihood that he will continue to use coercive tactics, knowing they work and have no negative consequences. Failing to name the abuse and hold the abuser accountable also makes it less likely that the children will heal, since

---

[106] Bancroft & Silverman, *supra* note 18, at 125.
[107] Fortune, *supra* note 72, at 109.
[108] Id. at 109-10.
[109] Id. at 111.

it conveys to them that abusers get away with, and may even be rewarded for, their abuse. Children, especially sons, often replicate what they see as winning behavior.[110]

FRs activists not only like that the abusers get more in mediation, but that it further hurts their victims by impeding their healing. Many men who did not start out with FRs inclinations were effectively, if inadvertently, encouraged to do so by mediators and other MHPs. Seeing the power of these MHPs, the lack of sanctions for men who fail to abide by mediated agreements, and pro-abuser court decisions bolsters the FRs movement's agenda, as well as many men individually.

Increased Danger to Victims. In mediation, couples counseling, or when meeting together with custody evaluators, the abuser is typically happy to listen to what his victim is saying, since he knows how to uncover her vulnerabilities and use them against her when it suits him. The victim usually participates in good faith, hoping that the approach will succeed, and hence reveals just what she and the children need and desire, which is what matters most to her. The abuser may or may not use this information against her immediately, but he is adept at storing such information for later use to psychologically hurt, isolate, or discredit her. If she disagrees with him or reveals anything that he has forbidden her to discuss, such as his abuse, he may well batter her later or retaliate in some other way.[111]

Litigants are told there is confidentiality in mediation and couples counseling. While confidentiality is not supposed to apply to threats and abusive conduct (e.g., the abuser actually attacking her or threatening to do so), the proscription against violating confidentiality is used as an excuse by many courts not to hear evidence about threats or abuse that occurred during mediation. Further, many prosecutors will not bring criminal actions for crimes committed during mediation. Victims who have no lawyers are even less able to persuade courts and prosecutors to protect them in such situations. Ironically, even when mediators do report threatened or actual abuse against the victim, the same courts that often refuse to punish the perpetrator or even grant the victim a protective order are often quite willing to hear that the victim did not want to bargain or give him unsupervised access to the children and to then use it against her. This is particularly true where court mediators are part of the courthouse staff or are paid by the county or state.

Mediators (and couple or family therapists), under the guise of being impartial and believing that any wrongdoing is because of the couple dynamic, often refuse to take a stand against the abuser's wrongful behaviors. This, as noted above (see "Impeded Healing"), colludes with and reinforces the abuser. This also makes it harder for each member of the family to understand what happened—a critical step toward healing. But when the mediator or therapist does take a stand against his abuse, the abuser often accuses the MHP of having lost all impartiality. In some cases, the abuser retaliates against his intimate partner, the children, or even the mediator, therapist, or other court players.[112] Showing their real lack of impartiality, some mediators not only fail to take a protective stance against the abuser's threats and abuse, but refuse to mediate unless the battered woman drops any preexisting order of protection or pending claims against the abuser. Being forced into this position violates the victim's civil rights and access to justice, leaving her with no protection and less credibility should she later seek a new order.

---

[110] Jaffe, Lemon & Poisson, *supra* note 10, at 30-31; Bancroft & Silverman, *supra* note 18, at 61, 125, 205.

[111] Bancroft, *supra* note 58, at 58, 124-30.

[112] Id.; Mary Pat Treuthart & Laurie Woods, *Mediation—A Guide for Advocates and Attorneys Representing Battered Women* 14-15 (1990); D. Weber, "Police Say Angry Father Gunned Down Investigator After He Lost Custody," *Boston Herald*, Sept. 15, 2004, at 22.

Higher Cost for Battered Women. One of the most common justifications for media-tion is that it is cheaper than going to trial. Often the expense of mediation is compared to the expense of litigating a case. This comparison does not take into consideration the fact that, in jurisdictions that do not use mediation, the same high percentage of cases are settled and that settled cases are far less expensive than the tiny percentage of litigated ones. Even in nonabuse cases, the savings gained through mediation are minimal, and in actuality, most women would gain more through attorney negotiated settlements.[113] This is because women tend to believe that they deserve less than men, and so they further bargain away what the law entitles them to receive.[114] Cases that do not settle in mediation are the slowest moving cases in the court and, therefore, are the most expensive.[115] In addition, since abusers seldom abide by the mediated agree-ment, mediated abuse cases that settle end up costing battered women much more than mediated nonabuse cases that are settled. While some battered women, realizing that the legal process is hostile to them, do not dare to return to court, many do go back. As a result, they often experience the ratchet wheel effect (see "Disadvantages to Battered Women"), with the abuser typically getting more and more of what he wants and the victim growing successively poorer. If mothers lose custody, it defies the intent of leg-islation proclaiming that it is not in the BIC for abusive fathers to get custody or unsu-pervised or overnight visitations. Many abusers use the mediation process to cause delay, with the case eventually forced to go to trial anyway. Unrepresented men gener-ally receive better assistance from court employees than do unrepresented women,[116] which again disadvantages battered women and often causes them extra expense.

Given all of the problematic dynamics and real dangers that women face in media-tion, not surprisingly, men feel better with the mediation process. Women, however, end up more depressed than when they use the adversarial process.[117]

Couples Counseling

Similar dynamics arise in couples counseling. The American Psychological Association warns that mediation and parent coordination are controversial and inadvisable in DV cases, at least before all of the violence has ended.[118] The American Medical Association explic-itly states that "[c]ouples counseling or family intervention is generally contraindicated in the presence of domestic violence . . . [and] may increase the risk of serious harm. *The first concern must be for the safety of the woman and her children*" (emphasis in original).[119] For victims, couples counseling is not safe unless and until the victim feels comfortable and the abuser has stopped all forms of abuse, including physical abuse, sexual abuse, and coercive control. Many battered women's attorneys and DV advocates direct clients who

---

[113] Treuthart & Woods, *supra* note 112, at 68-71.

[114] Bryan, *supra* note 101, at 477.

[115] Jessica Pearson & Nancy Thoennes, "Divorce Mediation: An Overview of Research Results," 19 *Colum. J.L. & Soc. Probs.* 463-64 (1985).

[116] For example, the Divorce Unit at Greater Boston Legal Services received periodic requests from court employees to represent fathers in custody cases whom they knew to be abusers of women, children, alcohol and/or drugs, always praising the fathers' parenting skills. Not once in over ten years did we ever receive a court request that we represent a mother.

[117] Grillo, *supra* note 77, at 1578.

[118] APA, *supra* note 53, at 100.

[119] American Medical Association, *Diagnostic and Treatment Guidelines on Domestic Violence* 12 (1992).

are living in shelters or safe houses to engage in couples counseling with their abusers. The victims often dare not tell their therapists that the abuse is continuing or even escalating, in hopes that the therapy will end the abuse, although it is likely to empower the abusers and exacerbate their abuse. Those advocating for and doing couples counseling admit that further violence is to be expected, hardly a result that is ethical or fair for them to be making on behalf of the victim,[120] and certainly not one that would be considered acceptable in treating a bank robber with his victims. Yet, many victims report never being beaten again when their brothers or sons tell their abusers that they will "beat you up if you ever touch her again." (It has been widely reported, for example, that President Clinton's stepfather stopped all abuse of his mother when young Clinton made such a threat.) This shows that abusers do indeed do a cost-benefit analysis and can control themselves permanently when "the game's up," something seldom conveyed in conjoint counseling or believed by those adopting a FSA theory.

Mutual Orders of Protection

Mutual orders of protection are often issued on the theory that both parties must have contributed to the abuse. Mutual orders of protection usually violate the victim's constitutional due process rights because the judge, mediator, abuser, or his attorney often insists that the mutual order of protection be issued even when the abuser never filed any petition or pleading against the victim, gave her no advance notice of the filing, or never informed her of her alleged wrongdoing, which thereby prevents her from being able to defend against the allegations.[121]

Based on the FSA, many people assume that mutual orders of protection are fairer and will keep both parties from further harming each other. But mutual orders actually further empower the abuser and disempower the victim,[122] with the result that they are more dangerous than the victim having no order at all. The abuser can now call the police and use the court order against her, and often does so to retaliate, turning the police and courts into his agents to use against her.[123] Whether his allegations are based on truth or completely fabricated, as they often are,[124] she must expend enormous amounts of energy and often financial resources attempting to minimize the damage he has done to her credibility, her case, her self-respect, and her trust in the police and courts.

As with mediation, mutual orders of protection give everybody the wrong message. Such orders convey to the abuser that he can continue being abusive, that the court system believes his victim was also (or solely) at fault, and that he need not accept responsibility for his abuse. They tell the victim that she bears at least some of the responsibility for what happened, reinforcing the abuser's messages to her that she is to blame for making him abuse her. Mutual orders do not convey to the children that the abuser's tactics are wrong, encouraging them to regard their father's abuse as socially acceptable behavior. When the abuser tells the children that their mother is stupid, that she is unworthy of respect, or that nobody will believe her, it encourages them to disrespect their mother and conclude that their father is

---

[120] Jordan et al., *supra* note 61, at 124.
[121] Joan Zorza, "What Is Wrong With Mutual Orders of Protection," 4(5) *Domestic Violence Rep.* 67-68, 78 (1999), *available at* http://www.scvan.org/mutual_orders.html.
[122] Walker, *supra* note 61, at 165.
[123] Id.; Zorza, *supra* note 121.
[124] Bancroft, *supra* note 58; Jaffe, Lemon & Poisson, *supra* note 10, at 247.

right;[125] this increases the likelihood that the sons will grow up to be abusers.[126] These wrong messages make it far less likely that anyone in the family will heal, since understanding the wrongdoing and who was responsible are the first steps to healing.

Mutual orders give the neighbors, the police, and the public the message that both of the parties were to blame. Without guidance on how to enforce mutual orders, the police either do nothing to protect the victim the next time she calls, or they threaten to or arrest both parties. Both responses reinforce the notion that the victim is to blame or that the abuse is mutual. When both parties are arrested, it is far more likely that the victim will stay in jail much longer than the abuser; batterers usually control the family's finances and isolate their victims from friends and family, so that few battered women are able to meet bail. If the children have not already been put in foster care, the batterer usually gets out of jail very quickly and picks them up. Arrested victims get worse legal advice because attorneys fail to think their cases might involve complexities and because they are far less likely to spend much, if any, time with their female clients preparing for court. Women tend to be held in facilities further away from the courthouse than are male inmates, and attorneys' offices are usually located near courthouses and not jails. The result is that, by the time a victim with children appears before a judge, she will likely plead guilty, just to get home to the children. Yet, she may find that her abuser already has custody of them. Once the victim is typed as an abuser, she is far more likely to end up being convicted. Terrified by her abuser into dropping her charges against him lest he further hurt her or the children, she loses the custody advantage that the legislature intended. These dynamics are so rewarding to the abuser that he is likely to keep calling the police against the victim, further disempowering her, and confusing the police and courts as to who the real abuser is.[127]

Because the system does not work for victims when there are mutual orders of protection, the victim is discouraged from using the system again. This leaves the violence free to escalate unchecked, increasing the risk of serious injury and homicide. Because mutual orders encourage abusers to call the police for real and even fabricated allegations against the victim, he has been made far more powerful, turning the police and courts into tools to use against her. Mutual orders are thus far more destructive and harmful than having no order at all.[128] Like other FSAs, they also confuse the professionals, who assume that the abuser's continued allegations about the victim's wrongdoing show that the abuse is mutual, increasing the chance that their mutual abuse theory may become a self-fulfilling prophesy.[129] FRs activists support mutual orders of protection because they provide men with more tools to use against the victims and less incentive to acknowledge men's violence.

SECOND APPROACH: RICHARD GARDNER'S TWO THEORIES

The second approach used by family courts in custody disputes are two theories (PAS and the friendly parent concept) created by Richard Gardner. They appear gender

---

[125] Lundy Bancroft, When Dad Hurts Mom: Helping Your Children Heal the Wounds of Witnessing Abuse 24, 29-33 (2004).

[126] Bancroft & Silverman, *supra* note 86. *See also* Jaffe, Lemon & Poisson, *supra* note 10, at 30–31; Banrcroft & Silverman, *supra* note 18, at 61, 125, 205.

[127] Zorza, *supra* note 121.

[128] Id.

[129] Rockford Register Staff, "Man, Wife Dead in Murder-Suicide [After Mutual Protection Orders Issued]." *Rockford Register Star.* July 3, 2003, at 1A.

neutral and responsive to what is in the child's best interest, but they are actually highly gender biased and not even based on any scientific research. They are virtually always used to punish mothers and often children, particularly those seeking protection from abuse. It is surprising that either theory ever caught on, given that Gardner also advocated many deviant sexual behaviors, including sexual sadism, child sexual abuse, necrophilia, and sex involving animals, enemas, or urination as supposedly beneficial, normal behaviors. He also blamed the Jews for laws criminalizing child sexual abuse, and he killed himself by repeatedly plunging a knife deep into his chest and neck while overdosing on drugs.[130]

Furthermore, contrary to Gardner's assertions, women seldom make false allegations and do not gain any tactical advantage by making such reports.[131] Although incest allegations are rare in divorce cases, arising in only 2 to 3 percent of cases, when they are impartially investigated, they are sustained or founded as often as when there is no divorce or custody dispute.[132] Canadian statistics show that fathers are sixteen times as likely as mothers to make maliciously fabricated allegations of child sexual abuse, even though mothers make 71 percent of the allegations and fathers only 17 percent of them.[133]

Despite the flaws in the PAS theory (see "Parental Alienation Syndrome and Its Progeny") and Gardner's bizarre beliefs, many MHPs subscribe to his theories for discrediting mothers' incest and DV allegations,[134] some believing PAS "on faith" and others to please the judges who appoint them, presuming that the judges believe it, or having been taught from other unknowledgeable people that PAS is valid.[135]

Parental Alienation Syndrome and Its Progeny

PAS is Richard Gardner's pseudoscience theory that gives accused fathers a defense against incest allegations.[136] It has never been peer reviewed but has been widely promoted in books that Gardner self-published.[137] It blames the mothers for any hostility that the children feel towards their fathers, maintaining that children normally always love and respect their fathers unless their mothers poison the children against them,

---

[130] Stephanie J. Dallam, "Dr. Richard Gardner: A Review of His Theories and Opinions on Atypical Sexuality, Pedophilia, and Treatment Issues," 8(1) *Treating Abuse Today* 15, 15, 16, 22 (1998); *Richard Gardner's Complete Autopsy Report, available at* http://cincinnatipas.com/dr-richardgardnerautopsy.html.

[131] Jaffe, Lemon & Poisson, *supra* note 10, at 1, 17; Bancroft & Silverman, *supra* note 18, at 119-20; Zorza Rosen, *supra* note 70, at 983-1107.

[132] APA, *supra* note 53, at 12.

[133] Nicolas M.C. Bala, Joanne J. Paetsch, Nico Trocmé, John Schuman, Sherri L. Tanchak & Joseph P. Hornick, *Allegations of Child Abuse in the Context of Parental Separation: A Discussion Paper* (Department of Justice, Canada, 2001), *available* at http://www.justice-canada.ca/eng/pi/pad-rpad/rep-rap/2001_4.html.

[134] Bancroft, *supra* note 58, at 258.

[135] *See, e.g.,* I. David Turkat, "Divorce Related Malicious Mother Syndrome," 10(3) *J. Fam. Violence* 253 (1995); I. David Turkat, "Divorce-Related Malicious Parent Syndrome," 14(1) *J. Fam. Violence* 95 (1999) (the *Journal of Family Violence* printed both, even while acknowledging that no research backed up PAS).

[136] Meier, *supra* note 42, at 689, n.105, citing Richard Ducote, "Guardians Ad Litem in Private Custody Litigation: The Case for Abolition," 3 *Loy. J. Pub. Int. L.*.106, 140, n. 158 (2002).

[137] Jaffe, Lemon & Poisson, *supra* note 10, at 34, 53; Dallam, *supra* note 130, at 15, 22.

even when the fathers beat or sexually abuse the mothers and/or children.[138] PAS has no scientific basis and has never been recognized within the mental health profession,[139] as some of its proponents admit.[140] At different times, when Gardner or PAS have been discredited (e.g., after his instrument to measure the truthfulness of maternal incest accusations was discredited or when he was caught advocating pedophilia as an honorable lifestyle choice),[141] the theory has risen again with other names, including Sexual Abuse in Divorce (SAID) Syndrome, Malicious Mother Syndrome, and, after that theory was attacked for being gender biased, as Malicious Parent Syndrome, on the theory that a tiny number of alienating fathers also exist.[142] These theories recommend "treating" the seriously alienating parent by imprisoning her, and/or giving custody to the other parent, even if he is a batterer or pedophile and, if she protests in any way, cutting off all of her visitation. They also recommend making the parents attend couples counseling together, an approach that obviously serves abusive fathers well, providing a chance for further contact to monitor and harass their female intimate partners. Gardner eventually acknowledged that PAS should not apply if the father really is perpetrating incest or battering the mother, but he never retracted his claim that such allegations in custody disputes are virtually always false and raised solely for tactical advantage. However, so biased was he against mothers that even when he was unable to find that a mother ever alienated a child, he still urged courts to give custody to the father because she was at risk of alienating the child in the future. PAS proponents seldom check if there is any basis for the abuse allegations, presuming them to be false and that the mother should lose custody. Hence, if a mother knows that she risks losing not only custody but even the possibility of ever seeing her children again, no matter how abused she or her child is, she will probably not dare to raise the abuse allegations or seek needed safety.

Friendly Parent Concept

Even when courts understand that PAS is a bogus theory, the notion that many mothers alienate their children from their fathers, a concept unique to the family courts,[143] still persists. At least thirty-two states[144] have incorporated the milder sounding friendly parent concept into their custody laws. This concept was also created by Richard Gardner for the purpose of giving custody to the parent who will encourage more contact and a better relationship between the children and the other parent. Even when there is no statute authorizing the

---

[138] Even Gardner was forced to retract that abuse never justifies children feeling estranged from the abuser in a March 1991 addendum to his book, *The Parental Alienation Syndrome* (1988).

[139] Jaffe, Lemon & Poisson, *supra* note 10, at 34; Dallam, *supra* note 130, at 22; APA, *supra* note 53, at 40 and 100.

[140] Turkat (1995), *supra* note 135.

[141] Lucy Berliner & John R. Conte, "Sexual Abuse Allegations: Conceptual and Empirical Obstacles," 17 *Child Abuse & Neglect* 111 (1993); Rita Smith & Pamela Coukos, "Fairness and Accuracy in Evaluations of Domestic Violence and Child Abuse in Custody Determinations," 36(4) *Judges' J.* 38, 41 n.34 (1997) (noting that Turkat's statistics on visitation interference from the Children's Rights Council were only a "guesstimate").

[142] Turkat (1995), *supra* note 135; Turkat (1999), *supra* note 135, at 95-97; Smith & Coukos, *supra* note 141, at 38-42, 54-56.

[143] Peter G. Jaffe, The Personal Costs of Dispensing Justice. Plenary, Family Violence and the Courts: 10th Anniversary Conference, San Francisco, CA (Sept. 9, 2004).

[144] AL, AK, AZ, AR, CA, CO, DC, FL, ID, IL, IA, KS, LA, ME, MI, MN, MO, MT, NV, NH, NJ, NM, OH, OR, PA, TN, TX, UT, VT, VA, WI, and WY.

friendly parent concept, most mediators, custody evaluators, parent educators, parent coordinators, GALs, and judges use the concept anyway. FRs advocates and those favoring PAS also like the friendly parent concept, because it discourages exploration of why a custodial mother might be unfriendly toward the father, thus assuming that her unfriendly behavior is unjustified. The friendly parent concept purports to be gender neutral and to help ease the burden on children postseparation.[145] Yet, after an initial custody decision, only the custodial parent (most often the mother) can be hurt by the friendly parent concept, since it is a scheme to deprive custodial parents of custody if they are "unfriendly" to the other parent. Far from helping families, it generates expensive, protracted custody litigation that benefits only the lawyers and MHPs involved in the case.[146] Further, the unfriendly behavior of noncustodial parents (usually the father), such as not paying child support, physically or verbally abusing the mother, or stalking her, is not considered as meeting the definition of unfriendly. This is true even though fewer than 20 percent of divorced fathers make support payments three years after their divorces,[147] and men who batter their intimate partners are three times more likely than other fathers to be in arrears.[148] Even refusing to legitimate an undocumented alien wife is not considered unfriendly, even though it may result in her being permanently deported and never seeing her children again. The friendly parent concept encourages and facilitates the abusive father to have access to his victim by assuming his monitoring and stalking contacts are to see the children or are done to foster more cooperative parenting.

Relatively few mothers actually speak badly of their former partners or complain about their intimate partners' behavior in front of the children, but men do both,[149] so that courts overwhelmingly hear fathers' complaints, both true and false, about mothers' alleged wrongdoings. These complaints are used to label mothers as the unfriendly or alienating parent, thereby depriving them of custody. Amazingly, the system misses the fact that a father, who complains of a mother's unfriendliness, is being unfriendly himself and is probably doing so solely for tactical gain.

Courts are also fooled by fathers who make themselves look good by devaluing and criticizing only the mother of his children while idealizing his current partner. In contrast, the mother, having suffered months or years of abuse, often seems angry and hostile, making the father's criticisms appear more credible.[150] As a result, the court rewards him for making unfriendly allegations, encouraging him to keep returning to court with more unfriendly allegations as a way to keep the children and mother in a constant state of anxiety and disruption. By minimizing the importance of the children's bond with their primary custodial parent, which is typically the mother, and by seeing caretaking as a fungible activity, most courts transfer custody of the children from the mother to the father punitively, to teach the allegedly unfriendly mother a lesson. Some courts even jail unfriendly mothers or remove their right to ever see or speak to their children again.

---

[145] Zorza, *supra* note 55; Margaret Dore, "The 'Friendly Parent' Concept: A Flawed Factor for Child Custody," 6 *Loy. J. Pub. Int. L.* 41 (2004).

[146] Dore, *supra* note 145, at 53-54 (noting that some combined fees exceed $200,000 and bankruptcy is common).

[147] William F. Hodges, *Interventions for Children of Divorce: Custody, Access, Psychotherapy* (2d ed. 1991).

[148] APA, *supra* note 53, at 40; Tishler et al., *supra* note 94, at 1057.

[149] Kurz, *supra* note 93, at 181. Furthermore, no long-term data shows that children are negatively impacted when mothers use alienating behaviors. Joan S. Meier, "A Historical Perspective on Parental Alienation Syndrome and Parental Alienation," 6 *J. Child Custody* 232, 249 (2009).

[150] David Schuldberg & S. Guisinger, *Divorced Fathers Describe Their Former Wives; Devaluation and Contrast, in Women and Divorce/Men and Divorce* (Sandra S. Volgy ed., 1991).

The friendly parent concept also harms the children affected by domestic or family violence because it is diametrically opposed to the research, which concludes that what makes children most resilient and able to heal is having a stable close bond with their nonabusive parent.[151] Children are actually "in terror during court proceedings, especially those proceedings that involve evaluation of the child, separation from custodial parents, and disruption of the family unit," which, like other disruptions involving a divorce, increases the "potential for not only creating more suffering, but for doing lasting psychological damage to a child."[152]

Despite its harm to the children, judges love the friendly parent concept because it enables them to decide custody disputes so easily. Instead of analyzing all of the custody factors they are supposed to consider, judges need only to decide if the custodial parent has been unfriendly in order to justify switching custody. While some judges use the friendly parent concept out of laziness, more benevolent ones justify using the concept to affirm that both parents are fit and are maybe even good parents, but since both are good parents, it comes down to giving custody to the more friendly parent.

The friendly parent concept almost always favors fathers over mothers. It actually results in the worse parent winning, that is, the parent who is abusive and who therefore abusively criticizes the custodial parent as unfriendly. As the gender bias studies have shown, even legitimate complaints by women against men are trivialized or ignored by courts.[153] Accordingly, and in contrast to men, noncustodial mothers virtually never win custody by alleging unfriendly behaviors against their intimate partners.

The friendly parent concept has several other problems that make it anything but a contributor to a good relationship between parents. Friendly parent provisions (whether statutory, case law, or just used by practice of the court or custody evaluators, investigators, GALs, or other MHPs who advise the court) make it almost impossible and highly dangerous for mothers to complain of any legitimate problems for fear that they will be labeled as unfriendly. The mother is seen as having no credibility, especially if custody is contested and especially if she alleges incest.[154] Further, many child protective service agencies never investigate child sexual abuse allegations when there is a custody dispute, either because they think the mother is already protecting the child by filing for divorce or custody, or because they assume that the mother made false allegations for tactical advantage when custody is being litigated.[155] Unaware of this dubious practice, courts assume that the agency found no basis for the allegation and conclude that the mother was being unfriendly and made a false accusation for tactical advantage.

As previously noted, only rarely do women make false allegations; when they do, they do not gain any tactical advantage by making such reports.[156] But battered women and mothers of children who are being sexually abused by their fathers often lose custody just because they raise such allegations, in large part because MHPs are even less knowledgeable about

---

[151] Jaffe, Lemon & Poisson, *supra* note 10, at 27-28; Bancroft & Silverman, *supra* note 18, at 42, 104, 140.

[152] Wallerstein & Tanke, *supra* note 89, at 311.

[153] Abrams & Greaney, *supra*, note 4, at 59-98.

[154] John E.B. Myers, *A Mother's Nightmare—Incest; A Practical Legal Guide for Parents and Professionals* 126, 133 (1997).

[155] 3 Joan Zorza, *Why Courts Are Reluctant to Believe and Respond to Allegations of Incest, in The Sex Offender: Theoretical Advances, Treating Special Populations and Legal Development* 33-2 to 33-3 (Barbara K. Schwartz ed., 1999); Abrams & Greaney, *supra* note 4, at 69; J. Melbourne McGraw & Holly A. Smith, "Child Sexual Abuse Allegations Amidst Divorce and Custody Proceedings: Refining the Valuation Process," 1(1) *J. Child Sexual Abuse* 49 (1992).

[156] Jaffe, Lemon & Poisson, *supra* note 10, at 11, 17; Bancroft & Silverman, *supra* note 18, at 119-20; Zorza & Rosen, *supra* note 70, at 983-1107.

child sexual abuse than they are about DV.[157] These professionals have a long history of being unwilling to credit incest allegations no matter how valid the proof.[158]

By awarding custody to the so-called friendly parent (in actuality, the abusive parent), the friendly parent concept not only punishes the unfriendly parent, but also punishes the children by forcing them to live with a parent who has poor parenting skills and may even abuse them. Because the friendly parent concept is not in the BIC, Washington State has repeatedly rejected it, both legislatively and in some state appellate decisions, as have some other courts.[159]

When a woman's intimate partner abuses her or her children, she is put in a Catch 22 position: if she complains about the abuse, she risks being labeled unfriendly, and, consequently, losing custody to her abuser; if she does not do everything possible to protect herself and her children, she risks being harmed by her abuser or losing custody to a child protective agency for "failure to protect."[160]

Severely abusive fathers may deliberately escalate their abuse to force the women to complain, flee, or bargain away valuable marital assets, alimony, or child support. They then retaliate by filing for custody, knowing they will likely be able to deprive the mothers of the children. Even after the divorce, more than three-quarters of men threaten to go back to court for custody.[161] Yet, men's threats and actions are not interpreted as unfriendly, even though protracted litigation is extremely harmful, both economically and emotionally, to the children.[162] Other abusive fathers use the friendly parent concept to force the mother to pay them child support and to deprive her of any visitation. Some actual friendly parent examples follow:

Case 1: Sue[163] always had to pay for all of the gifts for the children on her own. One December, after she and the children were threatened with eviction because the father, David, bought a new car instead of paying any child support, Sue put her name only on the children's Christmas gifts. In response, the court switched custody to the father, faulting Sue for not putting David's name also on the gifts, meanwhile ignoring the fact that he beat her up, had a serious drinking problem, and often neglected the children.

Case 2: Upon learning that Rick had never revealed that he was HIV positive, despite his having known this for the past five years, and fearful that he might have

---

[157] Myers, *supra* note 154, at 40, 79; Cohn, Salmon & Stobo, *supra* note 80, at 41-43, and 50 (noting that only 3 of 258 bachelor of social worker programs had a course on intimate partner violence, and 90 percent of psychology professional schools have no course on any aspect of child abuse).

[158] Myers, *supra*, note 154, at 133; Zorza, *supra*, note 155, at 33-2.

[159] Dore, *supra* note 145, at 41-51; Tekester B.M. v. Zeineba H., 2007 N.Y. Slip Op. 00902 (App. Div., 4th Dept. 2007); John A. v. Bridget M., 791 N.Y.S.2d 421 (App. Div., 1st Dept. 2005); Hayes v. Gama, 67 P.3d 965 (Ariz. 2003); Lawrence v. Lawrence, 20 P.3d 972 (Wash. Ct. App. 2001).

[160] Martha Shaffer & Nicholas Bala, "The Role of Family Courts in Domestic Violence: The Canadian Experience," in *Protecting Children From Domestic Violence: Strategies for Community Intervention* 171, 184 (Peter G. Jaffe, Linda L. Baker & Alison J. Cunningham, eds., 2004); Zorza, *supra*, note 155, at 33-3; Bancroft & Silverman, *supra* note 18, at 96.

[161] Kurz, *supra* note 93, at 161.

[162] Dore, *supra* note 145, at 53-54; Linda D. Elrod, "Reforming the System to Protect the Children in High-Conflict Cases," 28 *Wm. Mitchell L. Rev.* 495 (2001); Wallerstein & Tanke, *supra* note 89, at 311.

[163] Names and some identifying information have been changed to protect the individuals in these examples.

infected her, Lois called Rick an "SOB" within earshot of the children. He reacted by cursing at her in another language, justifying his infidelity by calling her lousy in bed, and mentioning the names of several women (one of them Sue's close friend) with whom he had cheated on her during their marriage. He then struck her, breaking her jaw. Nonetheless, the judge awarded Rick custody because her swearing at him (despite her fear that he might have infected her with a fatal disease) was seen as unjustified. The custody evaluator actually praised Rick for using another language in front of the children when he lashed out verbally at her. The fact that the children were terrified by their father's tone, if not his actual words, and that they saw him fracture their mother's jaw was considered irrelevant. (At least tests later showed that Lois had not been infected with HIV.)

Case 3: Other mothers whose husbands' affairs have broken up their marriages have lost custody for taking their children to churches or synagogues that teach the children that adultery is wrong. The husband's affairs are not viewed as alienating the children, but the mother's practicing of her religion is seen as alienating if anything that is preached can be inferred as critical of the father's conduct.[164]

The friendly parent concept reinforces learned helplessness in the victimized, non-abusive parent by forcing her to suppress her legitimate grievances for fear of losing custody should she deny him visitation or complain about his abusiveness to the police or court.[165] Like PAS, the friendly parent concept is a perfect tool for FRs adherents.

Legislation Incorporating Gardner's Punitive Theories

Despite its rhetoric of encouraging frequent contact between the parents, the punitive approach taken by PAS and the friendly parent concept are the exact opposite of the stated approach advocated by FSA proponents: to maximize the involvement of both parents with their children. Until recently, no state had incorporated PAS or any of the punitive measures advocated by Gardner, although a majority, as noted, have incorporated the friendly parent concept into their laws. However, at least Washington and Rhode Island have incorporated child removal language in statutes governing custody modifications and contempt findings against visitation denials, respectively.[166]

Gag Orders

Gag orders are the ultimate means used by family courts to silence and control an aggrieved party. Courts sometimes go as far as forbidding a party to raise abuse allegations in court, preventing the court from ever deciding whether the complaints were valid.[167] Gag orders are used mainly against women and can result from either the FSA or the junk science, misogynistic theory of PAS or the related friendly

---

[164] Joel Belz, "Live With the Consequences: Custody Issues, Like Divorce, Are Too Complicated for Our Courts," *World Mag.,* Sept. 21, 2002; *see also* Dore, *supra* note 145, at 48-49.

[165] Joan Zorza, "'Friendly Parent' Provisions in Custody Determinations," 26 *Clearinghouse Rev.* 921-65 (1992).

[166] *See* Wash. Rev. Code Ann. § 26.09.260(2)(d), (3); R.I. Gen. Laws § 15-5-16(d).

[167] Ford v. Ford, 700 So. 2d 191 (Fla. Dist. Ct. App. 1997).

parent concept. Gagging an abused party from speaking out prevents that party from validating her experience, obtaining support, or achieving healing. While gag orders are officially justified as vindicating the court's orders and protecting the privacy of the family, and especially that of the children, in actuality they protect the court and abuser from being publicly shamed while reinforcing the victim's feelings of desperation, isolation, self-blame, and shame. Some courts have used gag orders to prevent the victim or children from seeking therapy, medical treatment, or help from a clergy member, DV program, sexual assault program, child protection agency, or even from the police and criminal courts. Gag orders are the ultimate weapon in preventing each member of the family from ever understanding that the abuse was wrong, illegal, and extremely harmful, which makes them a favorite tactic of FRs proponents.[168] When gag orders prohibit victims from seeking help, they not only impede the victims' healing, but may also violate their civil rights and possibly international human rights law. If orders prevent victims from talking to a pastor, they violate the First Amendment's constitutional right to practice religion.[169]

More often, a lesser version of a gag order is put in place, which orders both parents to never speak disparagingly about the other parent in front of the children. Since fathers are judged more leniently, and since women seldom dare to complain when fathers disparage them, such orders serve as vehicles for further empowering abusive fathers and disempowering nonabusive mothers.

Closing hearings to the public has a similar effect on those involved, isolating them and making the abuse seem more shameful to its victims. A perhaps unintended consequence of closed hearings is that lawyers have few opportunities to hear other lawyers argue motions or cases involving abuse allegations, which impedes their learning how to effectively argue such cases. Some speculate that closed hearings make the judicial system more vulnerable to corruption.

Although gag orders are seldom appealed, a Florida intermediate appellate court struck down a gag order, holding that it was beyond a Florida court's authority to issue it. The order, issued in a termination of parental rights case, directed the parties and participants and an attorney not to discuss the underlying facts of their case "with any third party or counsel not participants in this action." Even though the Florida law provides that court records in parental termination and dependency cases are confidential, the appellate court held that the trial court had no authority to enter an injunction gagging relatives not to address anyone, including the press. It specifically stated that a "court cannot prohibit citizens from exercising their First Amendment right to publicly discuss knowledge that they have gained independent of court documents," even if the same information appears in court documents.[170]

Just as the secrecy in settlements of clergy sexual abuse cases has colluded with and protected pedophile pastors at the expense of their victims, gag orders do the same to mothers. Gagging is the ultimate weapon in a gender biased war.

Vicarious Traumatization

Not only are battered women and their children traumatized by the abuse they have experienced, but those who work with them and hear about the abuse also may be vicariously

---

[168] Walker, *supra* note 61, at 175.

[169] Zorza, *supra* note 165.

[170] Stanfield v. Florida Dep't Children & Families, 698 So. 2d 231 (Fla. 3d Dist. Ct. App. 1997).

traumatized. Undoubtedly, some of the minimization and denial of battering and child abuse noted in this chapter may be attempts by professionals involved with such cases to avoid or minimize vicarious traumatization. While MHPs often have mechanisms for dealing with this, lawyers and judges generally have no clue about the nature of this problem, nor do they know how to minimize its effects. This issue must be included in the training of lawyers and judges if they are ever to handle abuse cases fairly and effectively.[171]

CONCLUSION: WHAT SHOULD BE DONE

For all of the gains that battered women have made in the criminal justice system and in many legislatures, they and their children are still losing custody disputes in our family courts. Concern for their children's safety is the strongest motivator for battered women to leave their batterers. Yet, the efforts of large numbers of battered women to protect themselves and their children are being sabotaged in the family courts by those with a family systems or other gender biased approach, preventing the victims from safely extricating themselves and protecting their children from the parent who abuses them. Battered women and their children can heal only if they understand the injustices they have endured, which normally is followed by a period of angry feelings. Attempts to silence or punish battered mothers for displaying anger toward their abusers denies the validity of their experience and impedes, if not arrests, the healing process for them and their children.

Forbidding battered mothers to protect and help children heal after witnessing DV is diametrically opposed to what we know these children need, which is to have strong, stable, long-term relationships with their nonabusive mothers, even though this may mean stopping all contact with their abusive fathers, at least until they have healed.

Since mothers rarely make false reports of DV or child abuse, it is time for the divorce and family courts to abandon all ill-advised, misogynistic theories and approaches that assume, without basis, that allegations of DV and child abuse are fraudulent. To that end, the many MHPs who advise the courts need to state that these theories are either without any scientific basis or are at best have only weak support. In any event, these practitioners should recognize that these approaches clearly are not in the BIC and only exacerbate abusive situations.

Courts should not permit those who are biased against women to be used as mediators, GALs, custody evaluators, or court-referred couples counselors, particularly in cases where abuse has been alleged. This prohibition must include any case involving an abuser and his victim, and not just cases seeking orders of protection. Although more education would be desirable and is certainly urged, it remains doubtful that education alone could fix this problem: California's exceptionally well-trained mediators and custody evaluators, normally seen as the model for the rest of the nation, are still failing to protect battered women and their children, even in the much praised San Diego courts.[172] It is also time to bar misogynist, junk science theories from use in courts and for legislatures to repeal

---

[171] Peter G. Jaffe, The Personal Costs of Dispensing Justice. Plenary, Family Violence and the Courts: 10th Anniversary Conference, San Francisco, CA (Sept. 9, 2004); Peter G. Jaffe et al., "Vicarious Trauma in Judges: The Personal Challenge of Dispensing Justice," 54(4) *Juv. & Fam. Ct. J.* 1-9 (2003).

[172] *See* Johnson, Succuzzo & Koen, *supra* note 44; Jaffe, Lemon & Poisson, *supra* note 10, at 138-39 (noting that although California is the only state to mandate training—at least 16 hours on domestic violence—before custody evaluators can even begin their first evaluation, many of them still ignore or minimize the violence).

friendly parent provisions, particularly in cases where one family member is abusing another, or at least when there is DV, as Minnesota does.[173] Whether the victim is a child, a disabled adult, or an elder living in the household, the intimate partner who is trying to protect the victim is subject to the same effects of the abuser's coercive control tactics.

It also may be time to tackle a topic that the battered women's movement has feared addressing, which is to redefine DV as incorporating coercive control, a type of abuse that many victims find the worst.[174] A redefinition of DV should also include components such as which partner fears the other and whether a perpetrator of violence acted as a primary aggressor, in self-defense, or for the purpose of defending another person. The advantage of incorporating these concepts into the definition of DV is that everyone in the criminal and civil court system (i.e., police, prosecutors, child protection, judges, and all of the court players) would have to take them into account before arresting, charging, prosecuting, determining guilt or innocence, sentencing, and issuing orders of protection. A disadvantage would arise if those who are biased against women construe her legitimate requests (e.g., for him to stop being abusive, get a job, or bring home some of the money) as examples of her coercive control of him.

To counter the devaluing of the primary custodial parent, legislatures should explicitly include the parent's resilience and willingness to promote children's healing as factors in any custody determination. Further, courts should be required to be trained about these issues. States in which divorce and custody hearings are closed should consider opening them to the public. States should also craft legislation that would ban gag orders prohibiting the raising of abuse allegations or that would at least permit speedy interlocutory appeals of any gag orders.

Above all, if violence within the family is to end, everyone must be willing to believe and offer emotional support to victims of violence. Court agents must stop colluding with abusers, especially in the form of making negative, baseless assumptions about women's credibility or trivializing the violence. This will not happen unless all professionals involved in the family court system are trained and knowledgeable about the realities of DV, child abuse, and incest, about what makes children resilient and helps them to heal, about vicarious traumatization and how to minimize its effects, and, most importantly, about circumventing the biased and inappropriate approaches discussed in this chapter. Most medical schools provide minimal training on DV,[175] but they and all professional schools for MHPs and lawyers should also incorporate such training into their curriculums.[176] Legislatures should help influence this process by, for example, ensuring that none of the misguided, misogynistic approaches discussed here are proclaimed to be valid or as admissible in court. These approaches should also not be allowed entry into the criminal courts, as some now unwisely suggest[177] (e.g., using a pretrial diversion to force both the victim and perpetrator, under penalty of arrest into "Intimate Abuse Circles" couples counseling, which assumes that both partners are at fault).

---

[173] Minn. Stat. § 518.17.1.

[174] Evan Stark, *Coercive Control: How Men Entrap Women in Personal Life* 5-6, 11-14 (2007).

[175] Cohn, Salmon & Stobo, *supra* note 80, at 35-36; Bancroft, *supra* note 58, at 280 (noting he was unable to find in any psychology graduate school catalogue a course on or reference to domestic violence or child abuse).

[176] Id.; American Bar Association, Commission on Domestic Violence, *Teach Your Students Well: Incorporating Domestic Violence Into Law School Curricular: A Law School Report* (2003), *available at* http://www.abanet.org/domviol/pubs.html. Linda Mills, *Insult to Injury: Rethinking Our Response to Intimate Violence* 137-38 (2003).

[177] Id. at 140-41.

Represent Victims Responsibly

The approaches discussed in this chapter discredit women and children while bolstering fathers in custody disputes. As Gardner's PAS theory was never peer reviewed, is not recognized professionally, and is gender biased against women, it should be judged unequivocally as a theory without scientific basis. Victims' lawyers, therefore, should always challenge it (in whatever guise it might be raised) as not meeting their state's evidentiary standard for admissibility. Lawyers also should object to the friendly parent concept on gender bias grounds, particularly in states with equal rights amendments. In objecting to laws and practices that are gender biased and operate only against custodial parents, they should cite the language their state uses to establish the equal rights of both parents. Sadly, few lawyers are knowledgeable about the inadequacies of Gardner's theories or are willing to antagonize a judge by zealously representing their clients, as is required by the attorneys' canons of professional responsibility.

Recognize Need for Children's Bond With Mothers

Gender biased approaches are violations of the civil and possibly human rights of those harmed. Since not even judges are immune from civil rights suits, it is crucial that judges and all others who work within the court system stop subjecting battered women and their children to these gross injustices. Only when it is recognized that the FRs movement is motivated primarily by the goal of reducing child support obligations and that children are best served by maintaining a strong bond with their mothers will these injustices end.

Chapter 2

Recognizing Domestic Violence: How to Know It When You See It and How to Provide Appropriate Representation

by Lois Schwaeber, J.D.

INTRODUCTION

Despite numerous studies showing that domestic violence (DV) is very common even in society today, many people deny or minimize its existence. However, a 1998 Commonwealth Fund survey shows that "[n]early one-third of American women (31%) report being physically or sexually assaulted by a husband or boyfriend at some point in their lives."[1] "In 2001, intimate partner violence made up 20% of violent crime against women."[2] The same year, female intimate partners committed only 3 percent of the crimes against men.[3] A woman is four times as likely as a man to fear for her life, and three and one-half times as likely to be murdered by a male spouse than vice versa.

Canada's 2000 Report on Family Violence[4] noted that women are five times as likely to require medical attention as a result of men's violence.

In 2005, the Corporate Alliance to End Partner Violence conducted a national telephone survey, which found that 21 percent of full-time employed adults were victims of DV.[5] Studies have shown that one in four women will experience DV during their lifetime.[6]

This chapter will delve into the many facets of DV, the reasons that many people find the existence of DV "unbelievable," and how they can find ways to identify its victims and help them to seek safety for themselves and their children.

WHAT IS DOMESTIC VIOLENCE?

"Domestic violence is a pattern of behavior in which one intimate partner uses physical violence, coercion, threats, intimidation, isolation or emotional, sexual or economic abuse to control the other partner in the relationship."[7] "Domestic violence

---

[1] The Commonwealth Fund, *Health Concerns Across a Woman's Lifespan: 1998 Survey of Woman's Health* (May 1999). *See also* Family Violence Prevention Fund, *The Facts on Domestic Violence,* http://www.endabuse.org/resources/facts.

[2] Bureau of Justice Statistics Crime Data Brief, *Intimate Partner Violence 1993-2001* (Feb. 2003), http://www.endabuse.org/resources/facts.

[3] Id.

[4] *See* http://www.statcan.gc.ca/daily-quotidien/000725/dq000725b-eng.htm.

[5] Group SJR, Corporate Alliance to End Partner Violence, *National Telephone Benchmarking Survey* (Oct. 2005), *available at* http://www.caepv.org/about/program_detail.php?refID=5.

[6] Patricia Tjaden & Nancy Thoennes, *Extent, Nature and Consequences of Intimate Partner Violence: Findings From the National Violence Against Women Survey, available at* http://www.ncjrs.gov/pdffiles1/nij/181867.pdf.

[7] J.D. v. N.D., 170 Misc. 2d 877, 652 N.Y.S.2d 468 (Westchester Cty. Fam. Ct., 1996) (husband's psychological, sexual, and economic abuse of the wife during their nine-year marriage constituted DV).

does not necessarily involve physical violence and it equally affects all aspects of our society, rich or poor, regardless of race, ethnicity, religion, or national origin."[8] Others describe battering and DV as power and control.

DV is not just physical,[9] not merely a slap, a punch, or a kick. It is a pattern of coercive control that may be primarily psychological, economic, or sexual,[10] and is consistently reinforced by one or more acts of frightening physical violence or threats thereof. This physical violence may not necessarily be directed against a spouse or intimate partner, but may be used against animals,[11] other people, or inanimate objects. It entails a credible or actual threat of physical or sexual assault.[12] The pattern of control and intimidation may be predominantly psychological,[13] economic, or sexual in nature, or may rely primarily on the use of physical violence.[14]

Intimate partner violence takes place between people of all ages, racial, ethnic, social, religious, and economic backgrounds. It is present in same sex[15] as well as heterosexual relationships. It occurs between people who are married, who are living together, simply dating, or are in intimate relationships.

DV is not a one-time uncharacteristic loss of control, but rather a mechanism of ongoing power and control. It is not one drink too many, caused by "provocation," or even an outburst of anger fueled by a "bad day," but rather it is a consistent pattern of abuse.[16] DV is not caused by alcohol abuse, substance abuse, or mental health illnesses, but it exists with them, and in spite of them, and they are simply used as excuses by both the victim as well as the abuser as justification for his abuse.

[D]omestic violence can affect anyone, regardless of age, race, economic background, religious beliefs, marital status, or sexual preference. Abusive

---

[8] Lundy Bancroft & Jay G. Silverman, *The Batterer as Parent: Addressing the Impact of Domestic Violence on Family Dynamics* 3 (2002). *Tool for Attorneys to Screen for Domestic Violence,* http://www.abanet.org/domviol/screeningtoolcdv.pdf .

[9] Peter G. Jaffe & Claire V. Crooks, "Assessing the Best Interests of the Child: Visitation and Custody in Cases of Domestic Violence," in *Parenting By Men Who Batter; New Directions for Assessment and Intervention,* 45, 46 (Jeffrey L. Edelson & Oliver J. Williams eds., 2007).

[10] Bancroft & Silverman, *supra* note 8, at 3.

[11] "Golden Retriever Given Order of Protection," *N.Y. Times,* Oct. 2, 2007, at B6, col. 1. *See, also* Frank R. Ascione, "Emerging Research on Animal Abuse as a Risk Factor for Intimate Partner Violence, in *Intimate Partner* 3-1–3-17 (K. Kendall-Rackett & S. Giacomoni eds., 2007) (independent surveys reported that 18 to 48 percent of battered women delayed leaving their homes or returned to their batterer out of fear for the welfare of their animals).

[12] Marital rape as a form of control—sex on demand as a marital obligation; Clare Dalton, S. Carbon & N. Olesen, "High Conflict Divorce, Violence and Abuse: Implications for Custody and Visitation Decisions," 54 *Juv. & Fam. Ct. J.* 15 (2003).

[13] *See, e.g.,* A.F. v. N.F., 156 A.D.2d 750, 549 N.Y.S.2d 511 (2d Dept. 1989) (one of the first New York State decisions to include psychological abuse as DV); J.D. v. N.D., 170 Misc. 2d 877, 652 N.Y.S.2d 468 (Westchester Cty. Fam. Ct. 1996) (the court held that nonphysical abuse can be as devastating and harmful as physical abuse); and *In re* Marriage of Stewart, 137 P.3d 25 (Wash. 2006) (psychological harm is considered DV in Washington and may be the basis of a protective order against a father).

[14] Bancroft & Silverman, *supra* note 8.

[15] Eric Houston & David J. McKirnan, "Intimate Partner Abuse Among Gay and Bisexual Men: Risk Correlates and Health Outcomes," 84 *J. Urban Health: Bulletin of the N.Y. Academy of Medicine* 681 (2007) (32 percent of gay and bisexual men are victims of intimate partner abuse).

[16] Margaret B. Drew et al., *The Impact of Domestic Violence on Your Practice: A Lawyer's Handbook* ch. 1 (2d ed. 2004).

behaviors include verbal, emotional, sexual, physical, psychological, and economic abuse and typically get worse and more frequent over time. Any behavior that intimidates, manipulates, humiliates, isolates, frightens, terrorizes, coerces, threatens, blames, hurts, injures, or wounds someone is abuse.[17]

The batterer may deprive the victim of bodily integrity and the right to make decisions for herself and her children. The abuser may isolate her from her friends and family.[18] In some cases, the abuser will demand sex or threaten to withhold money for groceries, gas, fees for the children's activities, or other necessities if he is not obeyed. DV is dangerous and can be fatal. It affects the entire community and should not be considered a private family matter.[19]

"I didn't know it was abuse." This statement is made by numerous abuse victims during consultations, because DV is not only a physical attack such as broken bones, bruises, and black eyes. It includes slaps, shoves, and threats to kill and maim, with or without a weapon, and even embraces uncomfortable, violent, or unwanted sex. In addition, the abuser uses threats, intimidation, dominating behaviors, denigrating language, and other forms of coercion to maintain his coercive control. The abuser maintains tyrannical control over the household and uses the children to control and manipulate his partner. He may also undermine and belittle her parenting abilities not only to her, but to their children, friends, and families.

DV may also include the following behaviors:

- Isolating the victim from family and friends;
- Injuring pets;
- Insistence on following certain rules;
- Damaging personal property;
- Controlling financial matters;
- Forcing a partner to engage in unwanted or uncomfortable sex;[20]
- Engaging in excessive criticism, denigration, and belittling;
- Name calling;

---

[17] *See* J.D. v. N.D., 170 Misc. 2d 877, 878 (The court stated "[d]omestic violence is not limited to overt acts of violence which cause physical injury." The court found that the father's pattern of power and control, economic and verbal abuse, and frequent threats of intimidation, to be as much evidence of DV as outright physical abuse. "Indeed, whether an abuser physically injures his victim, or whether an abuser engages in psychological assault, the wounds are deep, long lasting, and far-reaching." Id.).

[18] Often he does this by degrading her friends, calling them "sluts and whores," and making the victim choose between "me and them." The abuser uses the same strategy with her family. ("They never liked me. Your family is trying to poison you against me.") Similarly, if they have seen the batterer act violently, her friends and family might discontinue contact with her because they are afraid of retribution from the batterer.

[19] *See* http://enditnow.gov/dv/am_tipsheet.html.

[20] Marty Roper, Anne H. Flitcraft & William Frazier, *Rape and Battering: An Assessment of 100 Cases,* unpublished paper, Dept. of Surgery, Yale Medical School, at 246-47 (1979), *cited in* Evan Stark, *Coercive Control: How Men Entrap Women in Personal Life* 128 (2007).

- Controlling financial decisions;

- Controlling what the person wears, says, and does;

- Enforcing the way the household is maintained;[21]

- Destroying walls and furniture;

- Imprisoning the victim;

- Prohibiting the victim from going places without the abuser;

- Monitoring the victim's whereabouts and checking the car's mileage;

- Making frequent telephone calls to the victim's home and business;

- Questioning the children about the victim's activities;[22]

- Undermining a woman's capacity to parent;

- Denigrating a mother's parenting abilities; and

- Stalking.[23]

In fact, many battered women report that emotional and psychological abuse has a greater traumatic impact on them than does physical abuse.[24]

HISTORICAL, RELIGIOUS, SOCIAL, AND CULTURAL FOUNDATIONS

History of Women as Chattel

Considering the age of the earth, humans are relative newcomers. We can postulate that some intimate relationships existed at least four to six million years ago, based on the dating of fossils,[25] and that DV has been a recurring phenomenon. However, DV has been a public policy issue only for a relatively short period of time.

"Laws of chastisement" existed even in the "Roman Empire and medieval times."[26] Before the late nineteenth century, the use of physical force was an accepted manner for a husband to fulfill his marital obligation to control and chastise his wife. Indeed,

---

[21] For example, the obsessive alphabetical order maintained in the household spice cabinet, as illustrated in the 1991 movie thriller *Sleeping With the Enemy* starring Julia Roberts (20th Century Fox).

[22] *See* Bancroft & Silverman, *supra* note 8, for an excellent overview of the effects of DV on children and families.

[23] Lois Schwaeber, "Representing Victims of Domestic Violence," in *Wiley Family Law Update* ch. 6, at 163,165–66, (Eric Pierson ed., 1999).

[24] Peter Jaffe, Michelle Zerwer & Samantha Poisson, *Access Denied: The Barriers of Violence and Poverty for Abused Women and Their Children After Separation* 1, 2 (2002).

[25] The fossil of the first man was dated to have existed about 6 million years ago, and the fossil of the first child at 4.4 million years ago. *See* http://www.pbs.org/wgbh/evolution/library/faq/cat06.html.

[26] Anson Shupe, William A. Stacy & Lonnie R. Hazelwood, *Violent Men, Violent Couples: The Dynamics of Domestic Violence* 11 (1987), citing R.E. Dobash & R.P. Dobash, "Wives: The Appropriate Victims of Marital Violence," 2(3/4) *Victimology, an Int'l J*. 426 (1977–78).

the duty to control and chastise a wife was considered a necessary aspect of marriage. Through the contract concept, the husband's property included his wife and children. Husband and wife were considered one person.[27] A husband was considered the king of his castle (a term even sometimes used today). The male sense of entitlement arose from this historical perspective and persists even today.

It was not until 1856, in England, that the term "wife-beating" appeared during a divorce reform campaign.[28] The famous "rule of thumb," an early common law concept in England, became part of common law in the United States as well. The rule of thumb recognized the premise that a man could beat his wife with a switch, provided that it was no thicker than his thumb.[29]

Evolution of U.S. Law

Very slowly, the law evolved. In 1824, Mississippi granted wives some legal protections; several other states provided some punishments for spousal abuse by 1870.[30] Nonetheless, DV was still generally considered "a family affair" or "private matter." In 1874, the North Carolina Supreme Court stated that "if no permanent injury has been inflicted, nor malice, cruelty nor dangerous violence shown by the husband, shut out the public gaze, and leave the parties to forget and forgive."[31]

DV advocacy was developed by survivors reaching out to other victims of abuse. Prior to the 1970s, there were no shelters for abused families.[32] DV shelters arose out of a grassroots movement by survivors to provide safe housing for the victims of DV and their children who needed a secure environment free from violence as well as a place where an abuser could not pursue his victim. By the 1990s, the federal government had enacted the Violence Against Women Act,[33] and most states had passed civil legislation giving protections to victims of DV.[34]

Today over 2,000 DV shelter and service programs exist nationwide. These agencies provide advocacy for victims of abuse, existing in every state in the union.[35] By

---

[27] George Levinger, "Patterns of Violence Between Spouses and Kin," in *Violence and the Family* 85, 89 (Suzanne K. Steinmetz & Murray Strauss eds., 1974).

[28] Evan Stark, "From Battered Women Syndrome to Coercive Control," 58 *Albany L. Rev.* 987 (1995), citing Elizabeth Pleck, *Domestic Tyranny: The Making of Social Policy Against Family Violence From Colonial Times to the Present* (1987).

[29] Id. (It seems to be questionable whether this was actually English law or just a myth.)

[30] Kathleen O'Connell Corcoran & James C. Melamed, "From Coercion to Empowerment: Spousal Abuse and Mediation," 4 *Mediation Q.* 304 (Summer 1990).

[31] Del Martin, "Historical Roots of Domestic Violence," in *Domestic Violence on Trial: Psychological and Legal Dimensions of Family Violence* (Daniel Jay Sonkin ed., 1987) citing R. Calvert, "Criminal and Civil Liability in Husband-Wife Assaults," in Levinger, *supra* note 27, at 89. For other historical cases recognizing a husband's right to enforce subjugation of his wife, see State v. Black, 60 N.C. 262, 263, 86 Am. Dec. 436 (1864) and Commonwealth of Massachusetts v. McAfee, 108 Mass. 468, 22 Am. Rep. 383 (1871).

[32] National Coalition Against Domestic Violence and Soroptimist International of the Americas, *Every Home a Safe Home: General Information Packet* 1 (1998).

[33] 18 U.S.C. § 2265 (1994).

[34] *See* also http://www.abanet.org/domviol/statutorysummarycharts.html for charts that summarize statutes regarding DV, sexual assault, stalking, dating violence, and trafficking.

[35] *See, e.g.,* American Bar Association, Commission on Domestic Violence, http://www.abanet.org/domviol/home.html; Battered Women's Justice Project, http://bwjp.org; Family Violence Prevention Fund, http://www.endabuse.org; National Council of Juvenile and Family Court

2005, concerned about the effects of DV on children, most states had enacted legislation requiring consideration of DV in custody/visitation cases and denying the award of sole or joint custody to an abuser.[36]

As recently as the late 1980s and early 1990s, the police, not wanting to interfere in family matters, commonly took an abuser for a walk around the block to "cool off" rather than making an arrest or filing a domestic incidence report. Police rarely arrested an abuser unless the victim insisted that an arrest take place, or the victim was bleeding and seriously hurt. Lacking severe injury, victims were told to go to the local family court because this was a "private family matter,"[37] leading victims to believe they had no recourse. The advent of mandatory arrest policies in the mid-1990s[38] changed the police procedure of asking the victim whether she wanted her abuser arrested. Many victims of DV hesitate to request an arrest, fearing retribution when the abuser is released.

Cultural Context

The American melting pot has become increasingly diverse in recent years. Even today, women in most foreign countries are denied the human rights that are available to women in the United States.[39] Violence against women is global and pervasive.[40] According to a 2002 demographic and health survey,[41] 87 percent of Jordanian women believe their husbands are justified in using physical or verbal abuse. It is estimated that this year in Bangladesh, 200 women will be injured and horribly disfigured by the spurned husbands or suitors who burn them.[42] Acid burnings, which occur in many Southeast Asian countries, are used as revenge for a woman's refusal to be subjugated to her in-laws.[43]

A woman suspected of having a sexual relationship with anyone other than her husband, even if she was raped, may be murdered by her male relatives in an "honor killing."[44] "Under Syrian law, an honor killing is not murder, and the man who commits

---

Judges, http://www.ncjfcj.org; and U. S. Department of Justice, Office on Violence Against Women, http://www.ojp.usdoj.gov/vawo.

[36] Annette M. Gonzalez & Linda M. Rio Reichmann, "Representing Children in Cases Involving Domestic Violence," 39 *Fam. L.Q.* 197, 198 (2005).

[37] *See* Schwaeber, *supra* note 23, at 177.

[38] *See, e.g.,* N.Y. Crim. Proc. L. § 140.10 (Mckinney's 1997) (requiring arrests if police have reasonable cause to believe that a felony, other than grand larceny in the fourth degree, has been committed against a family member, and, in cases where an order of protection, issued in supreme or family court, has been violated. This act also creates a presumption in favor of arrest in misdemeanor family offenses, "unless the victim requests otherwise." The police are directed not to ask victims whether an arrest is to be made and not to attempt to mediate or reconcile the parties.).

[39] Schwaeber, *supra* note 23.

[40] Matt Malinowski, *Thousands of Chileans to March Against Femicide* (Nov. 4, 2007)*, available at* http://www.womensenews.org/article.cfm?aid=3372.

[41] "Cheers and Jeers of the Week," Sept. 15, 2007. On September 10, 2007, the Associated Press reported that Jordan's Queen Rania launched a $1 million project to fight violence against women. This project intends to provide medical assistance and counseling to abused women and to raise public awareness. *See* http://www.womensenews.org/article.cfm/dyn/aid/3316/context/archive.

[42] *See* http://www.amnestyusa.org/Womens_Human_Rights/Violence/page.do?id=1108440&n1=3&n2=39&n3=739.

[43] Id.; for example, countries such as India, Pakistan, Syria, and Bangladesh.

[44] Id.

it is not a murderer. As in many other Arab countries, even if the killer is convicted on the lesser charge of a 'crime of honor,' he is usually set free within months."[45] Battered women fleeing their abusers come to the United States seeking asylum and safety because their home countries cannot, or will not, protect them from DV.[46]

Many immigrants come to the United States after an arranged marriage to an American citizen. Threats of deportation by the abuser, refusal to assist the wife in obtaining permanent residency status, and isolation from her family and cultural community become additional tools in his arsenal of abuse. In some immigrant communities, the family dynamics require that the newly married woman live with her husband's family. The new bride is expected to obey her in-laws as well as her husband and is abused by both for failing to obey their rules. Often, she is treated as little more than a slave: not allowed to eat with the family whom she serves and expected to sleep on the floor beside her husband's bed. Unable to speak English and fearing that they will be ostracized by their ethnic communities, these victims of DV lack the resources to reach out for safety.

Religious Roots

DV occurs in every religion. Traditionally people have turned to their spiritual leaders for guidance and support. A woman who sought help from her spiritual leader was told that it was her responsibility to "stay in the marriage," "to keep the family together," and to remember her vows, "for better or for worse . . . till death do us part." Most leaders sent an abused woman home to pray and told her to be a better wife. "Misinterpretation and misuse of Jewish, Islamic, and Christian traditions have often had a detrimental effect on families dealing with family violence."[47] The North American Council for Muslim Women reported that approximately 10 percent of Muslim women are abused emotionally, physically, and sexually by their husbands.[48] The Jewish concepts of *bayit shalom* ("keeping peace in the home") and *"shalom bayis"* ("peace at any price") were considered a Jewish woman's responsibility. The concept that DV does not happen in Jewish homes added to her shame and kept her from seeking help.[49]

Scriptures from the New and Old Testaments and the Koran were used to keep wives submissive,[50] and women were advised to pray to end the abuse. Husbands and

---

[45] Katherine Zoepf, "A Dishonorable Affair," *N.Y. Times Magazine*, Sept. 23, 2007.

[46] *See,* Alex Kotlowitz, "Asylum for the World's Battered Women," *N.Y. Times*, Feb. 11, 2007; *see also* the case of Rodi Alvarado, who, after ten years, is still awaiting a decision on her case by the Board of Immigration Appeals, http://www.commondreams.org/headlines06/0427-04.htm.

[47] Rev. Marie M. Fortune, *A Commentary on Religious Issues in Family Violence* 71 (1991).

[48] Information obtained from Muslim leaders and social workers in Kamran Memon, *Wife Abuse in the Muslim Community* (2008). *See also* Nada Stotland, "Tug of War: Domestic Abuse and the Misuse of Religion," 157 *Am. J. Psychiatry* 696 (May 2000).

[49] "Domestic Violence occurs in Jewish families at about the same rate as it does in families of other religions—about 15–25%. Domestic violence is found in every kind of Jewish home. Reform, Conservative, Orthodox, Reconstructionist, and unaffiliated." Tammy Goldberg, *Do Jewish Men Really Do That?: Domestic Violence in the Jewish Community,* http://tmt.urj.net/archives/5jewishworld/101207.htm.

[50] *Ephesians* 5:22–24 ("Wives be the subject to your husbands, as to the Lord . . . As the church is subject to Christ, so let wives be subject in everything to their husbands."); *Qu'ran, al-Nisa*:34 ("Men have authority over women . . . good women are obedient, humble and submissive . . . As for those from whom you fear disobedience, admonish them and expel them to beds apart and beat them.").

religious leaders quoted religious scriptures, such as, "[Y]our husband shall rule over [the woman],"[51] which seemed to condone male dominance and domestic abuse. "For the most part clergy have hindered rather than helped women break free from their abusive partners. Our apathy, denial, exhortations, ignorance, and misinterpretations of the Bible have added to women's pain and suffering and placed them in even greater danger."[52]

Modern theologians are taking a more contemporary stance and are being educated to counsel victims of DV without placing the responsibility for the abuse on them. The clergy are working with victim assistance providers in their local communities to provide resources and support to the victims. Religious leaders are now counseling the abuser that his behavior is not acceptable in either the social or religious community.

In 2002, the U.S. Conference of Catholic Bishops stated, "Violence against women, inside or outside the home, is never justified. Violence in any form—physical, sexual, psychological, or verbal—is sinful; often, it is a crime as well."[53] They recognized that victims of abuse may ask questions like, "How do these violent acts relate to my promise to take my spouse for better or for worse?" "The person being assaulted needs to know that acting to end the abuse does not violate the marriage promises." The conference also made recommendations for the clergy to follow when counseling both victims and abusers. The Muslim community instituted a DV forum to reach out to parishioners and clergy.[54] Jewish Women International[55] began a campaign to break the silence about DV in the Jewish community. Currently there are many resources available for spiritual leaders on counseling victims and their abusers.[56]

Importance of Language

People have traditionally used sexist language, jokes, and attitudes that degrade women and perpetuate DV. Women are portrayed as objects, not people. Some people talk about "abusive homes" or "violent relationships." This language does not describe intimate partner violence. Homes and/or relationships are not violent; it is the people in those homes who are abusive and responsible for the violence.[57] Violence is perpetrated by one person against another. The use of language and pictures that describe women as sexual commodities perpetuates the misogyny of women. Use of sexist language that degrades women condones violence, provides a negative role model, and helps perpetuate DV.

In response to the realization that violence against women had become an ingrained part of international culture, the White Ribbon Campaign was created in 1991 by a group of men in Canada who decided they had a responsibility to urge men

---

[51] *Genesis* 3:16.

[52] Rev. Al Miles, *Domestic Violence: What Every Pastor Needs to Know* (2000).

[53] U.S. Catholic Bishops, *When I Call for Help*: *A Pastoral Response to Domestic Violence Against Women* (2002). *See also* Faith Trust Institute, http://www.faithtrustinstitute.org.

[54] *See* http://www.isna.com/Services/pages/Domestic-Violence-Forum.aspx.

[55] *See* http://www.jwi.org/site/c.okLWJ3MPKtH/b.2213779/k.BFB9/Home.htm.

[56] *See, e.g.,* Faith Institute, http://www.faithtrustinstitute.org/; *An Abuse, Rape and Domestic Violence Aid and Resource Collection,* http://www.aardvarc.org/dv/religion.shtml; Eastside Domestic Violence Program, http://www.edvp.com/AboutDV/religion_and_dv.htm.

[57] "When I was young, people said I came from a violent home. But that wasn't true. My family wasn't violent. Only my father was." From an address by Ann Jones, author of *Next Time She'll Be Dead* (2000), at a seminar sponsored by Lawyer's Against Domestic Violence, Fordham Law School, November 1995.

to speak out against violence against women. They encourage men to talk in schools, workplaces, and places of worship about the problem of violence and wear a white ribbon as a personal pledge never to commit, condone, or remain silent about violence against women.[58]

Another contemporary movement embodying the principle that violence against women is a man's problem is the Founding Fathers.[59] It was begun on Father's Day in 2003 with the publication of the Founding Fathers Declaration in the *New York Times*. Its goal is to teach boys "that violence does not equal strength and where men stand with courage, lead with conviction and speak with one voice to say "No More.""[60]

Despite statutory changes in the law and some social movement, it is apparent, as one looks at contemporary social interactions, that core beliefs regarding gender roles and sexual autonomy still linger. Societal attitudes and actions have simply not reflected the public policy concerns.[61]

MYTHS, MISCONCEPTIONS, AND STEREOTYPES THAT HAMPER IDENTIFICATION OF THE PROBLEM

Many women fail to self-identify as victims of DV, sexual assault, dating violence, or stalking because of embarrassment or shame, fear that they will not be believed, fear of more serious assaults, or fear of further abuse by their intimate partner. Because of threats by their partners to kill or seriously harm them and their families and to deny them custody of their children, many women silently remain with their abusive partners. And, indeed, that may be the safest place for many of them. Many victims are murdered or seriously assaulted when they attempt to leave the relationships, despite having obtained prior civil orders of protection.[62] Anyone who reads our newspapers can frequently find articles that report the murder of a woman and her children at the hands of the woman's abuser. Sometimes the abuser murders only his female victim, sometimes only his children, and, at other times, both mother and children are murdered. In many cases, the abuser commits suicide after the murders rather than facing society's punishment.[63]

---

[58] *See* http://www.whiteribbon.ca/.

[59] *See* http://www.founding-fathers.org/.

[60] Id.

[61] People still laugh at the reruns of television comedy shows like *I Love Lucy* (Desi spanking Lucy) and *The Honeymooners* (in every program Ralph Kramden raised his fist at Alice and promised to send her "to the moon.").

[62] *See* Martha R, Mahoney, "Legal Images of Battered Women: Redefining the Issue of Separation," 90 *Mich. L. Rev.* 1, 5–6 (1991) (one-third of all female homicide victims in the United States are killed by a husband or boyfriend after leaving their abusers, and coining the term "separation assault" to explain these attacks on women).

[63] *See, e.g.,* "Death In the Chair, Step by Remorseless Step," *N.Y. Times*, Sept. 16, 2007, at A3 (murderer confessed to killing his children ten years ago); "Child Sees Mom Gunned Down and Shooter Kills Self," *Newsday*, Sept. 16, 2007 ("man with history of abusing his girlfriend tries to burn down their home early yesterday before fatally shooting her—barely missing the women's 4-year-old daughter—and then himself"); Associated Press, *"Breakup & Rage: Argument with Girlfriend Spurred Wisc. Slayings,"* *Newsday*, Oct., 9, 2007, at A27; "Man Charged in Fatal Stabbing," *N.Y. Times*, Oct. 15, 2007, at Metro Briefing (Stamford man stabs girlfriend after she broke up their relationship); "Police Captain Sentenced," *N.Y. Times*, Oct. 19, 2007, at Metro Briefing (police officer convicted of third-degree assault of female officer with whom he was having an extramarital affair

"Women who are separated from their husbands are 25 times more likely to be victimized by spouses than are married women. . . . Sixty-five percent of DV homicide victims had separated from their abusers prior to their deaths."[64] In an effort to help reduce homicides, some police departments are now working with DV activists to identify victims of DV who are most at risk of being killed by their abusers.[65]

Women with abusive partners frequently feel "coerced" to have "unwanted sex" with their partners.[66] Under the misconception that women have a marital duty to provide sex on demand to their spouses, women often fail to report marital rape or even identify it as sexual assault. This continues today, despite the fact that marital rape has been recognized by most states as a crime.[67] Many police officers and prosecutors still fail to provide a positive response to marital rape due to gender biases and societal conceptions of what a woman's duty to her husband requires.[68] Even women in non-marital intimate relationships regularly feel that they have a duty to provide sex to their intimate partners anytime and in any way that they demand it.

Intimate Partner Abuse Is Counterintuitive

DV is simply beyond the ken of people who grew up in loving and nurturing households. People who are unfamiliar with the dynamics of DV may have difficulty believing that any violence exists in intimate partner relationships for many reasons. Intimate partner abuse is complicated and complex.[69]

1. Society believes that these intimate partner relationships are loving, and the couples "will live happily ever after."

2. We are accustomed to seeing evidence of alleged crimes. Evidence of intimate partner violence, however, rarely exists. Most incidents occur in the privacy of the families' homes. There are rarely any witnesses besides the children.

3. Previous incidents may not have been documented. There may be no police reports and no medical evidence, even if medical treatment was necessary.

---

because he thought she was flirting. He dragged her outside to her car where he beat and kicked her.); "Woman Charged in Fatal Stabbing," *N.Y. Times*, Nov. 12, 2007, at Metro Briefing (Brooklyn woman fatally stabs man in his torso during a domestic dispute).

[64] National Council of Juvenile and Family Court Judges, *A Guide for Effective Issuance & Enforcement of Protection Orders* 1 (2005).

[65] Donna St. George, *"Police Tool Assesses Abuse Lethality,"* *Wash. Post*, Oct. 2, 2007.

[66] Id.

[67] *See* National Clearinghouse on Marital and Date Rape, *State Law Chart Outlining Marital Exemption Status of Each State,* http://ncmdr.org.

[68] Raquel Kennedy Bergen, *Marital Rape: New Research and Directions* (Feb. 2006), http://www.wcsap.org/maritalraperevised.pdf, citing K.C. Basile, "Prevalence of Wife Rape and Other Intimate Partner Sexual Coercion in a Nationally Representative Sampling of Women," 17(5) *Violence and Victim* 511 (2002).

[69] Loretta Frederick, Battered Woman's Justice Project, *Context Is Everything* (2001), *available at* http://data.ipharos.com/bwjp/website/index.html ("In order to effectively intervene in these cases, it is important to understand the complex issues of violence within intimate relationships, including the intent of the offender, the meaning of the act to the victim, and the effect of the violence on the victim.").

Victims of DV frequently lie to medical providers, either because their abusers are with them when they are seeking treatment, or because of shame and embarrassment at their situations.

4. The abusive relationship may have lasted many years, and it may be counter-intuitive to find that the victim is still living with the abuser. Many women return to their abusers multiple times before they can obtain the necessary economic, social, and external emotional supports and resources to maintain a healthy, safe, and independent life with their children.[70]

5. Victims tend to minimize the abuse and attribute too much power to the abusers because they have always controlled the situation. In addition, emotional battering, such as "crazy making"[71] behaviors may result in victim reactions that are difficult to understand by the average onlooker.

Who Is a Batterer? Who Is a Victim?

The general public, as well as those in the civil and criminal justice systems who work with victims of abuse, falls prey to the many myths and misconceptions about DV and its victims. These copious myths, fallacious allegations, and misconceptions work to undermine and devalue the credibility of victims of DV. Some are used by abusers as evidence that they are not the perpetrators of abuse that their victims claim they are. Victims of DV are often forced to defend themselves against these accusations. This is one reason why it is important to believe a victim's claims, because generally "[h]er description of the violence is only the tip of the iceberg."[72]

Research suggesting that both sexes use violence on an equal basis fails to differentiate between violence used in self-defense and violence used by the primary aggressor. This research also fails to account for bias in the reporting.[73] In fact, men use "severe acts" of violence more frequently than women and also "injure their partners more seriously."[74]

Some common misconceptions, stereotypes, and myths are as follows:

- DV is rare;

- DV is not serious;

---

[70] American Bar Association, Division of Public Education, *Why Abuse Victims Stay* (2001), http://www.abanet.org/publiced/domviol.html.

[71] Such behaviors, which increase confusion and insecurity in the victim, have been demonstrated in classic movies such as *A Clockwork Orange* (directed by Stanley Kubrick, Warner Bros., 1972), and *Gaslight* (MGM, 1994), with Ingrid Bergman and Charles Boyer).

[72] *See* "Guidelines for the Clergy," in *An Abuse, Rape and Domestic Violence Aid and Resource Collection,* http://www.aardvarc.org/dv/religion.shtml.

[73] *See, e.g.,* Daniel G. Saunders, "Wife Abuse, Husband Abuse, or Mutual Combat? A Feminist Perspective on Empirical Findings," in *Feminist Perspectives of Wife Abuse,* 90, 101 (Kersti Yllo & Michele Bograd eds., 1986).

[74] Mary Ann Dutton, "Understanding the Women's Responses to Domestic Violence: A Redefinition of Battered Women's Syndrome," 21 *Hofstra L.Rev.* 1191 (1993) citing Angela Browne & Kirk R. Williams, "Exploring the Effects of Resource Availability and the Likelihood of Female-Perpetrated Homicides," 23 *Law & Soc'y Rev.* 75, 78 (1989). (explaining and citing Lenore Walker's definition of the battered women's syndrome with elements of posttraumatic stress syndrome and learned helplessness).

- DV is mutual violence and the fault of both parties;

- The victim provoked her abuser;[75]

- DV is caused by the lack of communication;

- The problem is simply a dysfunctional family;

- Mothers raise the issue for tactical gain in divorce or custody proceedings;

- DV ends after separation or divorce;

- DV only happens in "those" families;[76] and

- Child sexual abuse is caused by strangers.

Repeatedly, victims of DV are accused of fabricating allegations of child sexual abuse to win custody. In fact, actual allegations of child sexual abuse in custody cases are "rare (about 6%) and the majority of allegations are substantiated (⅔)."[77] Research has also shown that "fathers are far more likely than mothers to make intentionally false allegations (21% compared to 1.3%)."[78] Other research found that about half of the allegations were believed to be true, and approximately one-third were unsubstantiated but "believed to have been made in good faith and based on genuine suspicions."[79]

Furthermore, a considerable overlap between child abuse and DV exists. In one study, 73 percent of mothers reported that their abusers also sexually abused their children.[80] Another study showed 44 percent of incest victims' mothers had been physically abused by the fathers.[81] These myths, misconceptions, and fallacious allegations must be vigorously and strenuously defended against if we are to protect victims of DV and their children.

There is no single profile of either the batterer or the victim. Both abusers and victims come from every demographic group. Their ethnic, national origin, religious, income, and educational backgrounds are as varied and diverse as our population.

---

[75] Sandra Tam, "Images Vivid to Open Trial in Domestic Abuse Case: Videotape by Son,13, Offers Dramatic Detail," *Buffalo News*, Oct. 15, 2004, at D1 ("You just stood there to provoke me," husband tells wife as he forces their 13-year-old son to videotape him verbally and physically abusing her for almost one hour.).

[76] Depending on the speaker "those" will mean anyone but "me and my kind." The author is often asked if her clients are only lower class, belong to minority groups, or are not of the speakers' religion. She always answers, "Our statistics show that our clients and their abusers are reflective of the demographics of the geographical location of the county in which I practice."

[77] American Bar Association, Commission on Domestic Violence, *10 Myths About Custody and Domestic Violence and How to Counter Them,* http://www.abanet.org/domviol/custody_myths.pdf, citing Nancy Thoennes & Patricia Tjaden, "The Extent, Nature and Validity of Sexual Abuse Allegations in Custody and Visitation Disputes," 14(2) *Child Sexual Abuse and Neglect* 151 (1990).

[78] Nicolas M.C. Bala, Joanne J. Paetsch, Nico Trocmé, John Schuman, Sherri L. Tanchak & Joseph P. Hornick, *Allegations of Child Abuse in the Context of Parental Separation: A Discussion Paper* (Department of Justice, Canada, 2001), *available* at http://www.justicecanada.ca/eng/pi/pad-rpad/rep-rap/2001_4.html; Bancroft & Silverman, *supra* note 8, at 97.

[79] S.J. Dallam & J.L. Silverberg, "Myths That Place Children at Risk During Custody Litigation," 9(3) *Sexual Assault Report* 33–47 (Jan/Feb 2006), *available at* http://www.leadership-council.org/1/res/cust_myths.html.

[80] D.L. Truesdell, "Incidence of Wife Abuse in Incestuous Families," 31 *Social Work* 138 (1986).

[81] Elizabeth A. Sirles & Pamela J. Franke, "Factors Influencing Mothers' Reactions to Intrafamily Sexual Abuse," 13 *Child Sexual Abuse and Neglect* 131 (1989).

Women who have been exposed to, or witnessed, DV in their childhood homes seem to be at greater risk of DV in their own relationships but do not seem to share any other common characteristics. Researchers estimate that between 30 percent and 80 percent of the women reporting battering had witnessed DV in their childhood homes.[82]

The abuser[83] may be a responsible community member, professional, police officer, or even a judge. He may be a billionaire or a pauper. He may be of any religion, belong to any race, or be of any national origin. He may be an undocumented immigrant or a descendant of the Mayflower. He may be illiterate or have multiple degrees from well-respected universities. The offender may seem kind and considerate in his public and professional life.

Studies based on psychological testing indicate that male batterers do, however, have certain characteristics in common.[84] "They have high degrees of suspiciousness and jealousy, depression, dependency, dysfunctional thinking, and poor social skills."[85] They are often self-interested and self-centered. They also believe that men have a natural superiority.

The one factor that overwhelmingly places a male at the greatest risk of becoming a batterer is having witnessed DV in his childhood home.[86] Witnessing DV is a significant factor in the intergenerational transmission of DV. Boys who witness their fathers' violence have a 1,000 percent greater chance of abusing their partners when they reach adulthood than boys who had not witnessed any violence in their childhood homes. [87]

Things are seldom what they seem. Abusers generally make a very good presentation in public. They can be charismatic and charming.[88] Many abusers are familiar with the criminal and civil justice systems and so are adept at convincing professionals who work in those systems that they are the victims.[89] Batterers tend to "rationalize, minimize, or outright deny their very real violence."[90] Nevertheless, the batterer may have other relevant history, such as a previous abuse toward a former intimate partner or member of his family, most frequently his mother or other female relatives. The abuser may also have a criminal record involving other violent crimes. He may be unable to hold a job because of his aggressive actions in the workplace.[91]

DV has been regarded as evidence of the abuser's poor mental health. The batterer, however, is capable of behaving in a very functional way, in the sense that his violent

---

[82] David Pelkovitz & Sandra J. Kaplan, "Child Witnesses of Violence Between Parents," 3(4) *Child & Adolescent Psychiatric Clinics of N. Am.* 745 (Oct. 1994).

[83] For an extensive explanation of abusive men, see Lundy Bancroft, *Why Does He Do That?: Inside the Minds of Angry and Controlling Men* (2004).

[84] S*ee* Bancroft & Silverman, *supra* note 8, ch. 1.

[85] "Violence and the Family," *Report of the American Psychological Association Presidential Task Force on Violence and the Family* 3 (1996).

[86] *See, e.g.,* G.T. Hotaling & D.B. Sugerman, "An Analysis of Risk Markers in Husband to Wife Violence: The Current State of Knowledge," 1 *Violence & Victims* 101 (1986).

[87] *See* Pelkovitz & Kaplan, *supra* note 82.

[88] Dalton, Carbon & Olesen, *supra* note 12.

[89] Bancroft & Silverman, *supra* note 8, at 15.

[90] William A. Stacy, Lonnie R. Hazlewood & Anson Shupe, *The Violent Couple* 50 (1994). *See also* Sharon Moshavi, "Domestic Violence in Israel," *Newsday*, Apr. 6, 1998 at A17 ("Everyone blamed the woman.").

[91] *See, e.g., In re* Marriage of Houtens, 233 Mont. 266, 760 P.2d 71 (Mont. 1988). Between 10 percent and 20 percent of the men arrested for DV have committed other crimes. *Violence and the Family; A Report of the American Psychological Association Professional Task Force on Violence and the Family* (2002).

and coercive behavior gets him what he wants. The abuser makes choices about how to behave, choices that are supported by societal attitudes and lack of accountability. The abuser uses violence to control his partner. He uses the social and sexual prejudices that are prevalent in our society to maintain control and justify his behaviors.

The batterer uses various tactics to maintain control and domination. Anger and violence are his weapons of choice. He may engage in rule making,[92] which is enforced on whim. He relies on cultural mores for male dominance and female subservience. He may be very manipulative and have a sense of entitlement. The abuser blames the victim for provoking him by not adhering to his rules or complaining that she is "not doing what society expects," even though such required behavior may be illegal,[93] immoral,[94] or unfair. Enforcement of the abuser's rules may also endanger the child or prevent the mother from providing needed care to the child.[95]

The abuser also has a sense of entitlement. The perpetrator has learned to think of women as inferior and as possessions, often due to witnessing DV as a child. Abusers tend to objectify their victims, calling them derogatory names during abusive incidents and in front of their children. One mother reported to me that her husband would tell the children, "Bring the fat bitch in here." Another recalled her husband telling the children, "Your mother is a fat pig."[96] This was in addition to the obscene name-calling that went on daily.

RECOGNIZING THE TRUTH ABOUT DOMESTIC VIOLENCE

Therapy Is Not the Answer

There are many myths and misconceptions regarding DV. It is critical to understand what is really happening. DV is not an illness. Victims and their children, therefore, need support—not therapy. Victims need to attain safety and healing from the effects of the abuse. They need services that provide support and self-empowerment. Therefore, victims should be referred to local community DV agencies.

Likewise, counseling and therapy cannot cure abusers. Battering is not caused by mental illness, although some batterers also have mental health problems. Along the same lines, DV is not caused by alcohol or substance abuse, although some batterers who abuse their partners also abuse alcohol and/or controlled substances. Batterers need educational programs to help them understand the harm that they are causing their partners, their children, and society. Batterers need to accept responsibility for choosing to use violence and to, instead, learn to behave in a noncoercive, nonabusive manner.

Leaving the Relationship Is Not Always Possible

A frequently asked question is, "Why didn't she just leave?" Victims often have no choice. Resistance to the abuse and separating from the abuser often precipitates increased

---

[92] As demonstrated in *Sleeping With the Enemy, supra* note 21.

[93] Buying drugs or forging checks for him.

[94] Engaging in unwanted sex with another person to please him.

[95] Barbara Hart, *Coercion, Intimidation, Degradation, Violence and Exploitation*, quoting Beth Sipe & Evelyn J. Hall, "Rule Making and Enforcement/Rule Compliance and Resistance," in *I Am Not Your Victim: Anatomy of Domestic Violence* 258–63 (1996).

[96] Statements made to the author during a consultation with a client. Another client reported that her husband would call a family meeting and tell the children what a bad wife and mother she was if she did not follow his rules exactly.

violence.[97] Some victims are held captive by their abusers by the use of threats. Victims are often trapped in their intimate relationships by fear and lack of outside support. They are continually engaging in adaptive strategies in an attempt to protect themselves and their children. The longer a victim has been abused by a partner, the more likely she is to be engaged in actively seeking help. Leaving is often a difficult choice requiring an act of courage. Victims need to achieve economic security for themselves and their children to be able to live independently in a safe, nurturing, and healthy environment.

Mutual Orders of Protection Are Dangerous

Mutual orders of protection are another weapon in the batterer's arsenal of harassment. Offenders frequently file retaliatory, frivolous, or fraudulent orders of protection to intimidate the victims into dropping their petitions for orders of protection or to ensure that mutual orders of protection are issued. The issuance of mutual orders of protection gives the mixed message that both parties are violent. The issuance of mutual orders of protection can be potentially dangerous to the victim in the following ways:

- The victim is at risk of being arrested by a false allegation of violating the abuser's order of protection;

- The victim is at risk of falsely being labeled an abuser or mutual offender;

- The victim is at risk of having her children sent to foster care in case of mutual arrests or if she is arrested on fallacious allegations that she violated the order of protection;

- A mutual order of protection persuades the victim that no one will help her;

- A mutual order of protection convinces the victim that she cannot get legal redress; and

- A mutual order of protection further empowers the abuser by allowing him to deny his responsibility for the abuse.[98]

In the recent past, mutual orders of protection were often given simply at the request of the abuser when he appeared in court to oppose the victim's order of protection. Mutual orders of protection, which are issued *sua sponte,* violate the due process rights of the party who it is issued against.[99] However, since the passage of the Violence Against Women Act,[100] every state has changed its laws to conform to the Violence Against Women Act requirements for full faith and credit acceptance.[101]

---

[97] *See* Mahoney, *supra* note 62.

[98] Joan Zorza, "What Is Wrong With Mutual Orders of Protection," 4(5) *Domestic Violence Rep.* 67 (1999), *available at* http://www.scvan.org/mutual_orders.html.

[99] A mutual order of protection issued after a petition has been filed by the person seeking the protection does not violate the due process rights of the party against whom the protection order is sought.

[100] 18 U.S.C. § 2265 (1994) (provides that no order of protection is to be given full faith and credit if there was no cross-petition or pleading filed seeking such an order or if the court did not make specific findings that each party was entitled to receive that order). This provision was enacted to deter the issuance of mutual protective orders on consent.

[101] *See* American Bar Association, Commission on Domestic Violence Web site, http://www.abanet.org/domviol/docs/ProhibitingMutualProtectiveOrdersJuly2007.pdf.

As a retaliatory allegation in restraining order cases, abusers frequently allege that the victims attacked them. They claim that the defensive actions taken by the victims were offensive actions and fail to inform the court that they were the primary physical aggressor. The abuser actually considers himself a victim of his partner, believing that he was provoked and was therefore justified for reacting in such a way. The abuser also believes that he is a victim of society when his victim seeks safety, support, and assistance from the social services or civil and criminal justice systems. It is common for the abuser to allege that his victim abused their children, engaged in mutual violence, and denied him visitation in an effort to show that she is unfit, so that he can fulfill his threat that he will take the children away from her. Use of these illegitimate allegations is calculated to keep the mother on the defensive by always placing the blame on her behavior and deflecting it from the abuser. It is used as a way of denying the abuser's responsibility for the DV. This is simply another manifestation of the abuser's aggression, harassment, and need to control the situation. The victim of DV then finds herself defending against the bogus accusations instead of concentrating on presenting her evidence of his abuse.

Batterers Harm Children

Abusers often use other retaliatory tactics to keep victims in line. Often these tactics are detrimental to the children, like withholding spousal and/or child support. Foreseeable consequences of withdrawal of financial support "can include, hunger, homelessness, loss of utilities, illness, and adverse psychological consequences, and many other . . . life-threatening deprivations"[102] and work to distance the children from their father.

Men who batter are sometimes dangerous to their children as well. Recent research shows that child abuse also occurs in 30 to 60 percent of households where the mother is abused.[103] Daughters in homes where their fathers assaulted their mothers were more than six times at risk of being sexually abused than in homes where there was no DV.[104] Men who batter sometimes use their children as weapons against their children's mothers and seek custody more often.[105] Even men who were relatively uninvolved with their children preseparation used this tactic to further control and harass their intimate partners after separation. Abusive men in a 2003 study identified this strategy as one they used to continue their control of their partners.[106]

---

[102] Joan Zorza, " The Friendly Parent Concept—Another Gender-Biased Legacy from Richard Gardner" 12(5) *Domestic Violence Rep.* 75 (June/July 2007).

[103] *See* National Clearinghouse on Child Abuse & Neglect Info, *In Harm's Way: Domestic Violence and Child Maltreatment* 1 (1999). *See also* Jeffrey L. Edelson & Susan Schechter, *Effective Intervention in Domestic Violence and Maltreatment Cases: Guidelines for Policy and Practice* 9 (1999) (citing National Resource Council, *Understanding Child Abuse And Neglect* (1993)).

[104] Barbara J. Hart, *Children of Domestic Violence: Risks and Remedies,* http://www.mincava. umn.edu/documents/hart/hart/html.

[105] Peter Jaffe, Claire V. Crooks & Samantha Poisson, "Common Misconceptions in Addressing Domestic Violence in Child Custody Disputes," 54 *Juv. & Fam. Ct. J.* 57, 59–60 (2003).

[106] Id.

OVERCOMING THE PROBLEM OF BIASED OR UNQUALIFIED PROFESSIONALS

Require Extensive Training for Professionals

It is not only the general public but also many professionals who "don't get" DV. Although some professionals may have gotten some basic education on DV, they do not fully understand the complexity of DV, DV's effects on its victims, and its impact on children, especially within the context of contested custody cases.

Modern courts use many auxiliary professionals, such as lawyers, judges, psychotherapists, law guardians or guardians ad litem (GALs),[107] custody evaluators, parent coordinators, alternate dispute resolution systems, and mediators to help resolve a case. These professionals, many if not most of whom never experienced DV in their personal lives, often fail to grasp the dynamics of DV and the variety of power-and-control tactics used by offenders.[108] It is imperative that attorneys, law guardians, therapists, social workers, and forensic and custody evaluators develop a full comprehension of the dynamics of DV and of the variety of forms that DV takes.[109]

Recognizing the myriad complex issues surrounding DV, The American Law Institute, in *Principles of the Law of Family Dissolution: Analysis and Recommendations*,[110] states that when ordering a measure to protect the parent or child, "Courts should recognize that abusers often use access to the child as a way to continue abusive behavior against a parent."[111] However, many professionals fail to properly investigate and take into account allegations of DV, substance abuse, criminal histories, prior DV, threats of violence, and/or threats to kill the victim or members of her family, threats of suicide, or child sexual abuse and inappropriate touching.[112] Mental health

---

[107] Both law guardians and GALs represent children. The difference is defined by individual state laws. In some states, they must be attorneys and represent the child, not the child's best interests. In other states, they can be an attorney and/or a mental health professional and represent the child's best interests. See http://www.abanet.org and the individual state bar association sites for definitions, requirements, standards, and guidelines for law guardians and GALs.

[108] Lynn Hecht Schafran, "Evaluating the Evaluators: Problems With "Outside Neutrals," 42(1) *Judge's J.* 10 (Winter 2003); Bancroft & Silverman, *supra* note 8, at 119–21 (stating that when a victim of DV has left her abuser, "professionals often become suspicious of a mother's motives to protect her children").

[109] "By conservative estimates, 1.5 million women in the United States are assaulted by their partners every year. Nationally, one in three women will experience sexual violence in her lifetime, and one in twelve women will be stalked in her lifetime. Although women are the victims in the majority of these crimes, men are also victims: the same studies reveal that 835,000 men are physically assaulted by an intimate partner annually in the United States, one in five sexual assault victims are male, and one in forty-five men are stalked in his lifetime." *See* http://www.abanet.org/domviol/docs/StandardsCommentary.pdf. *See* Patricia Tjaden & Nancy Thoennes, *Full Report of the Prevalence, Incidence and Consequences of Intimate Partner Violence Against Women* (2000), *available at* http://www.ojp.usdoj.gov/nij/pubs-sum/183781.htm; Patricia Tjaden & Nancy Thoennes, *Stalking in America: Findings From the National Violence Against Women Survey,* (1998), *available at* http://www.ojp.usdoj.gov/nij/pubs-sum/169592.htm.

[110] *Principles of the Law of Family Dissolution: Analysis and Recommendations*, § 2.11, cmt. c. (2002).

[111] Id.

[112] Stark, *supra* note 20, at 246–47 ("controlling partners perceive events through a veil of primary narcissism that suggests that they are the real victims, not their partners"). *See also* Castle

evaluators must conduct fair-minded evaluations, have specialized mental health expertise, demonstrate an understanding of the safety risks and issues, and consider the range of options available for protecting victims and their children.[113]

Behaviors shown by abusive fathers that tend to be minimized or dismissed by the courts include the following:

1. Not visiting at appointed time and thus disappointing the children and requiring the mother to cancel work or other plans;

2. Withholding child and spousal support;

3. Failing to pay the utility, household, or credit card bills;

4. Letting the house go into foreclosure;

5. Evicting the mother and children because her name is not on the deed;

6. Threatening to take the children away, so the mother will never see them again;

7. Threatening to have the mother deported; and

8. Failing to legalize the mother's immigration status.

Certainly none of these behaviors are in the children's best interests, nor are they caused by how a mother behaves, talks, or acts. Nonetheless, courts tend to believe the father over the mother, ignore the father's role in the breakdown of visitation,[114] and hold a mother to higher parenting standards. Court professionals, such as law guardians, judges, and their law secretaries, have been heard to tell victims of DV to "move on" past the DV.[115] To reiterate, court professionals must be trained extensively on DV, its manifestations inside and outside of court, and its effects upon children.

Require Training for Law Guardians or Guardians Ad Litem

Guardians should learn and use proper interviewing methods and avoid the use of leading, suggestive, or otherwise improper questioning techniques.[116] It is more appropriate to use questions that are open-ended and require a narrative answer. Children are very perceptive and want to please adults.

Rock v. Gonzalez, 545 U.S. 748 (2005) (where the father made threats just preceding the murders of his daughters).

[113] American Bar Association, Family Law Section and the Johnson Wingspread Conference Center, *High Conflict Cases: Reforming the System for Children,* Conference Report and Action Plan (Sept. 8–10, 2000, Racine Wisconsin).

[114] Judith M. Reichler & Nancy S. Erickson, "Custody, Domestic Violence and a Child's Preference," *N.Y.L.J.,* Apr. 24, 2003, at 1, col. 1.

[115] A Colorado magistrate has ordered at least five women into counseling or classes with their abusers despite restraining orders that barred contact. "I think you two just need to get along," he told one victim. Lisa Ryckman, "Advocates for Abused Women Focus on Judges," *Rocky Mountain News,* Sept. 21, 2007, *available at* http://www.rockymountainnews.com/drmn/local/article/0,1299, DRMN_15_5703562,00.html.

[116] An improper question would be "Your father loves you and wants to see you. You don't want to disappoint him, do you?"

Law guardians should not assume that, because the child reports not having seen the abuse, the child is not in danger or has not been affected by the violence. Nor does this mean that the mother does not need an order of protection to be safe. Children are often embarrassed to reveal their family's secrets and are afraid of what would happen to them were the family to break up. Many children stay in their bedrooms when the screaming and violence occurs. They often hide in closets or under their beds, "closing" their ears to minimize their exposure to the violence. But they cannot hide from the evidence of the abuse, such as holes in the wall, black eyes, or broken doors and furniture, and so they become traumatized, regardless. Law guardians or GALs should follow the guidelines of their respective jurisdictions so that their clients are effectively represented.[117]

Recognize the Need for High-Quality Custody Evaluations

Recognizing the need for high-quality custody evaluations, The National Council of Juvenile and Family Court Judges, in 2006, published *Navigating Custody and Visitation Evaluations in Cases With Domestic Violence: A Judge's Guide* to assist judges in determining "whether ordering an evaluation is appropriate and, if so, to ensure that the evaluations are of high quality and properly attentive to the issues raised by domestic violence."[118]

The Honorable Betty Weinberg Ellerin, chair of the New York State Judicial Committee on Women in the Courts, as reported in *Women's News,* June 15, 2007, said,

> An overburdened family court system means that judges often lack the time to hear all details in a case, including potential abuse charges. . . . Families' futures,' she says, "are too often decided by under-trained judges, law guardians . . . and court officers, . . . Some judges are more suited to those courts than others."[119]

Improve Divorce Process Training

In 2006, the New York State Matrimonial Commission suggested improvements to the state's divorce process, including additional specialized training for judges and the regulation of law guardians. The New York State Matrimonial Commission also recommended that "forensic psychologists who evaluate families and children in custody/visitation cases and court-appointed children's law guardians would especially benefit by specialized instruction."[120] The forensic specialists should be educated to recognize their

---

[117] American Bar Association, *Standards of Practice for Lawyers Who Represent Children in Abuse and Neglect Cases* (Feb. 5, 1996), http://www.abanet.org/child/repstandwhole.pdf; N.Y.S. Bar Association, Committee on Children and the Law, *Law Guardian Representation Standards, Volume II: Custody Cases* (3d ed. June 7, 2005). The standards were approved by the Executive Committee of the N.Y.S. Bar Association on January 26, 2006, http://www.nysba. org/Content/ContentGroups/Children_and_the_Law/2005NYSBAchildcustodystandardsMay 132005_finaldraft.pdf; *A Challenge for Change: Implementation of the Michigan Lawyer-Guardian Ad Litem Statute: Final Report* (Nov. 2002), http://www.abanet.org/child/cipcatalog/pdf/mi-02-03.pdf.

[118] Available from the National Council of Juvenile and Family Court Judges, Reno, NV 89507.

[119] Judge Ellerin, *quoted in* Alison Brown, "N.Y. Bribery Case Casts Shadow on Divorce Court," June 15, 2007, http://www.womensenews.org/article.cfm/dyn/aid/3205/context/archive.

[120] Id.

own biases.[121] Even today, many forensic evaluators are gender biased. It is important that, as part of their training, mental health evaluators be required to attend many hours of intensive DV training and education to be competent to perform abuse analysis.

Evaluate Custody Awards in Cases With Domestic Violence

Matrimonial attorneys, judges, DV advocates, and other professionals and organizations have recognized a "disturbing trend" nationwide of awarding custody to abusive parents.[122] In April 2006, the American Academy of Matrimonial Lawyers, a Chicago-based group, reported that 22 percent of their responding members said that they had seen a rise in custody awards toward the fathers, while no one in a separate study reported an increase in custody awards for mothers. Sixty-one percent of the responders in the American Academy of Matrimonial Lawyers survey reported a shift from sole custody toward joint custody. The California chapter of the National Organization of Women (NOW) reported that fathers win sole or joint custody in 40 to 70 pecent of contested custody cases. The NOW survey of 212 women found that 86 percent reported DV and that, 69 percent of the time, their abusers were given unsupervised contact or custody of the child, despite evidence of the abuse.[123]

Too often courts ignore evidence of domestic violence or fail to even consider it.[124] In *Wissink v. Wissink,*[125] a New York State Second Appellate Department decision, Justice Sondra Miller held that when adjudicating a case, merely mentioning that DV was present is insufficient. She stated that the "consideration accorded the effects of DV in this case was, in our view, sorely inadequate."[126] The court found that the court-ordered evaluation of the parties was "clearly deficient."[127] Justice Miller said that the lower courts must conduct comprehensive psychological investigations in cases such as this. The trial courts must also specify the reasons why custody was awarded to the perpetrator.

Justice Miller further recognized that the courts may inadvertently contribute to the abuse during a custody dispute. "While one might naturally assume that a child who fears one parent would prefer to live with the other, such an assumption underestimates the effects of domestic terror on its victims."[128] And, as noted elsewhere, "The

---

[121] Id.

[122] Joan S. Meier, "Domestic Violence, Child Custody, and Child Protection: Understanding Judicial Resistance and Imagining Solutions," 11 *Am. U.J. Gender Soc. Pol'y & L.* 657, 661 (2003).

[123] M.T. Hannah, *Disorder in the Courts: Mothers and Their Allies Take on the Family Law System,* 2002, *available at* http://canow.org/documents/fam_report.pdf. *See also* L. Bancroft, with C. Cuthbert, K. Slote, J. Silverman, M.G. Driggers & C.Mesh, "Battered Mothers vs. U.S. Family Courts," *Human Rights Dialogue* Series 2, No. 10 (Fall 2003); *Battered Mothers Speak Out: A Human Rights Report on Domestic Violence and Child Custody in the Massachusetts Family Courts* (Nov. 2002); Women's Law Project, *Justice in the Domestic Relations Division of the Philadelphia Family Courts* (Apr. 2003) (concluded that there is a crisis in the Domestic Relations Division and that the courts cannot serve families in crisis); Arizona Coalition Against Domestic Violence, *Battered Women's Testimony Project: A Human Rights Approach to Custody and Domestic Violence* (June 2003).

[124] Id.

[125] 301 A.D.2d 36 (N.Y. 2d Dept. 2002).

[126] Id. at 39.

[127] Id.

[128] Id.

child may have the well-founded fear that the abusive father will harm the mother, if custody is awarded to the mother, or that the father will retaliate against the child if he finds out that the child wants to live with the mother."[129]

The District of Columbia Court of Appeals, in *Cassandra Wilkins v. Eugene Ferguson*,[130] reversed a lower court order granting the father unsupervised visitation, despite the lower court finding that the father committed a family offense against the mother by engaging in "substantial physical, verbal, and psychological abuse." None of the health professionals recommended unsupervised visitation, and the child had alleged that the father may have sexually abused her. The District Columbia Court of Appeals, in reversing, stated that the lower court failed to "explicitly follow the factors in D.C. Code §16–914 relevant to the best interest of the child determination" and "did not adhere to its mandate to consider evidence of an intrafamily offense and its effects on the emotional development of the child." The District of Columbia Court of Appeals found that the trial court simply ignored the findings of DV and child sexual abuse. They stated that the lower court "focused on hypothesizing the reasons why the child might make new allegations and doubting her veracity, instead of focusing on the domestic violence."[131]

HOW TO RECOGNIZE AND HELP A VICTIM OF DOMESTIC VIOLENCE

Whatever type of law is practiced,[132] or whatever the setting for the practice,[133] practitioners have a responsibility to society to assist victims of DV and their children to be safe. Every attorney should be prepared to assess DV. Victims and perpetrators appear in every legal setting, even partnerships and corporations.

There are several excellent tools available, and most are available without charge.[134] Every attorney should make use of the American Bar Association's Commission on Domestic Violence's Web site, which is available to the public, as well.[135] The Commission on Domestic Violence publishes a book[136] to assist attorneys in evaluating their clients for DV in the specialized area of their practice as well.

Representing Victims of Domestic Violence

Attorneys who work with victims of DV need to make accurate evaluations.[137] Recently, the Commission on Domestic Violence issued "Standards of Practice for

---

[129] Reichler & Erickson, *supra* note 114.

[130] 928 A.2d 655 (D.C. Ct. App. 2007).

[131] Id.

[132] That is, real estate, wills and trusts, family and matrimonial law, criminal law, elder law, partnerships, and corporations, etc.

[133] That is, courts, private practice, law guardians, unions, prepaid legal services, government or municipalities, legal aid, etc.

[134] A useful assessment tool for advocates, attorneys, mental health professionals, and even the general public is Domestic Abuse Intervention Project, *A Guide for Conducting Domestic Violence Assessments,* (2002), http://www.duluth-model.org.

[135] *See* http://www.abanet.org/domviol/.

[136] Drew et al., *supra* note 16.

[137] *See* American Bar Association., Division of Public Education, *Representing Victims of Domestic Violence: Breaking the Silence, Journeys of Hope: A Guide to Community Outreach* (2001), http://www.abanet.org/publiced/domviol.html.

Lawyers Representing Victims of Domestic Violence, Sexual Assault and Stalking in Civil Protection Order Cases."[138] Its aspirational guidelines recognize that "[a]ccess to justice is essential to ensuring that victims of DV, sexual assault and stalking receive the protection and remedies necessary to prevent and minimize the lifelong, devastating effects of these crimes."[139] The standards require that attorneys who represent victims of DV have competent knowledge of the issues.[140] Two excellent tools that can be used in assisting an attorney in recognizing a victim of DV are *A Guide for Conducting Domestic Violence Assessments*[141] and *Tool for Attorneys to Screen for Domestic Violence.*[142]

Client Interview

An attorney must recognize the necessity of using a qualified interpreter in cases where the client is not proficient in the English language or is hearing impaired. It is inadvisable to use a family member, friend, or child to interpret. The attorney must realize that if someone other than a qualified interpreter is used, he/she may not be getting the client's actual words but instead a synopsis or condensed description of what the interpreter feels the attorney should be told. The interpreter may be embarrassed by what is being said, may not be truly aligned with the client's position, or may try to downplay the abuse because of loyalty to the abuser. It is important to explain this to the client.[143] The attorney must also explain to both the interpreter and client the limits of confidentiality.

Client-Centered Lawyering. An attorney should provide client-centered lawyering by earning the client's trust and remembering that she has not been able to trust her intimate partner and has lost her expectations of a loving, trusting relationship. Attempting to confirm the client's story simply makes it a "he said, she said" situation. The client is best suited to determine what options may be safest for her and her children. Appropriate referrals should be provided. The victim should be linked to local community-based resources that are experts in DV and rape/sexual assault and can provide services and appropriate support groups. The client's immediate and long-term needs and concerns should be addressed.

---

[138] Adopted as American Bar Association Policy on August 13, 2007, *available at* http://www.abanet.org/domviol/.

[139] *Preface.* http://www.abanet.org/domviol/docs/StandardsofPracticeCommentary82407.pdf.

[140] Competent Knowledge of Domestic Violence, Sexual Assault and Stalking, id. at 17:

> Before representing a client . . . the lawyer should have competent knowledge of the dynamics of domestic violence, sexual assault, and/or stalking. In particular, the lawyer should understand the potential risk of escalated violence due to litigation, and how the experience of domestic violence, sexual assault and/or stalking may affect the client-lawyer relationship, including the process of establishing rapport with and gathering information, evidence and case direction from the client.

[141] Domestic Violence Intervention Project, *A Guide for Conducting Domestic Violence Assessments, available at* http://www.duluth-model.org.

[142] American Bar Association, Commission on Domestic Violence *Tool for Attorneys to Screen for Domestic Violence.* (2005), *available at* http://www.abanet.org/domviol/.

[143] Drew et al., *supra* note 16, at 73; *Lawyers Committee for Human Rights, Guidelines for Immigration Lawyers Working with Interpreters: Extending Legal Assistance Across Language Barriers* (June 1995).

Safety Plan. An attorney should help the client make a safety plan. Even at this point, she may be forgetting about, rationalizing, or minimizing the frequency of physical or other forms of abuse. These are typical coping mechanisms that victims of DV use to survive on a day-to-day basis. The attorney should take the time to listen and be nonjudgmental; he/she may be the first one to do so. Options should be clearly and perhaps repeatedly explained, if necessary. Decisions should not be made for the client and advice to enter into unfair or dangerous settlements and/or custody/visitation orders should not be provided. Advice to drop the order of protection "in the interests of settling the case" should not be given. The outcome should not be predicted. The legal risks of all decisions should be explained, and the client should be referred to the local DV agency for counseling and support for her and her children.

Risk Assessment. The presence of any of the following factors may indicate increased danger or lethality. While these may assist in assessing the protections needed immediately, any of these factors can change over time and so should be reassessed repeatedly.

- Escalating severity of the violence;
- Threats to kill the victim or her or the children, and/or threats or attempts at suicide;
- Access to weapons;
- Violations of court orders;
- The victim entering into a new relationship; and
- Increased use and/or abuse of alcohol or controlled substances.

There is, however, no sure predictor of lethality, and batterers can be unpredictable. Safety planning and risk assessment are ongoing processes that needs to be addressed each time the attorney talks to and meets with the client.

Before Court. The exact procedures that the client can expect should be explained. She should know what time to come to court and where to meet her attorney. If there is a safety issue, an escort should be arranged. How to dress for court and how to obtain suitable clothing, if none is available, should be explained.[144] What the client needs to bring to court should be spelled out (e.g., evidence, witnesses, perhaps even a book to read while waiting). What not to bring to court unless so ordered should also be explained. The client should not bring the children; if she has no child care and is unable to arrange any, she should be advised about the location, procedures, and policies for using the child care center at the courthouse. Who will be in the courtroom when her case is called and what their roles are should also be explained. The attorney should explain where he/she will be when not with the client. As well, the attorney should explain what he/she will be doing and how the client can contact him/her.

Relief and remedies that the client might want to request should he reviewed again. The various possibilities of relief the court can offer, the possibilities of negotiation, the pros and cons of each and all, and what she must do if the court makes an order should be explained.[145]

---

[144] If she separated from her abuser without his permission, she might not have had the opportunity to obtain all her clothes and personal possessions. The local community-based DV agency can assist her to obtain suitable clothing.

[145] If the decision is unfavorable, the appeal process should be explained, and unless and until the order is changed, the client must obey the order.

After Court. The actual court session often seems to go far too quickly after the long wait and anticipation. The client was probably overwhelmed by the court proceedings, intimidated by the courtroom surroundings, and ignorant of the legal terminology used, even if English is her first language. Undoubtedly, the client was traumatized by being in the same environment as the abuser, especially if he brought along his family and friends. She is likewise embarrassed by revealing her family secrets in public and especially mortified if she sees a neighbor or friend.

The attorney should repeat and recap what happened in the courtroom. The client must understand everything that occurred in the courtroom and what her obligations are now. How the proceedings will affect her and her children should be clarified. All questions should be answered. The client must understand how to comply with and enforce any orders that were issued. What happens next should be described, and her legal options and rights must be explained. The client should be asked what she wants to transpire next, and the attorney should explain how he/she can or cannot help make that become a reality. The safety plan should be reviewed again. When the client has to return to court and what steps she needs to take in the meantime should be explained. Her safety when she is leaving the courthouse should be assured.

WHAT TO KNOW WHEN REPRESENTING THE BATTERER

Attorneys who work with perpetrators of victims of DV need to make a proper assessment of what constitutes zealous representation in these cases. It is typical for most abusers to blame the victim and to minimize and deny the abuse. The perpetrator's attorney has a duty not to exacerbate the harm to the victim.[146] If the attorney is representing an abuser, Chapter 3-H of the American Bar Association's, *The Impact of Domestic Violence on Your Practice,* is a "must read."[147]

How can the attorney best represent the client without becoming his tool for continuing to harass his intimate partner? "Civility is an important obligation of a lawyer."[148] Throughout representation of the abuser, the attorney must ask himself/herself a series of questions:

- Am I allowing the abuser to use the courts to harass the victim?

- Am I harming a third person, the children, by placing them in a potentially dangerous situation?

- Should I be referring the abuser to a batterers' intervention program?

It is understood that attorneys have a duty to their clients. However, attorneys should provide zealous but ethical representation of abusers. They have a moral responsibility and so should not collude with abusers to prolong litigation, submit fallacious allegations and pleadings, secrete funds, or allow them to put a third person in danger. Zealous representation does not mean allowing the abuser to use the courts to continue the battle, harass his partner, or inflict injury on his spouse and children.[149] Attorneys should rely on collateral sources to assess his parenting abilities, because a

---

[146] Lisa Angel & Lee Rosen, "Zealous and Ethical Representation of Batterers," in American Bar Association, *The Impact of Domestic Violence on Your Practice* 83-86 (2d ed. 2004).

[147] Id.

[148] American Bar Association, Section of Family Law, "Civility Standards," 40(4) *Fam. L.Q.,* xv (Winter 2007).

[149] *See* NYS Lawyer's Code of Professional Responsibility, DR 2-110:

B. Mandatory withdrawal.

batterer's depiction of his parenting involvement or his capability to have a positive, healthy, relationship with his children cannot be trusted. The attorney should avoid giving the batterer inadvertent access to his victim.

If the court has ordered supervised visitation, the attorney should ask if the supervisor the client suggests is suitable. Will the proposed supervisor accept the responsibility or just be a "warm body"? Can the supervisor terminate visitation if the abuser is inappropriate or drives while under the influence of alcohol or controlled substances, or will the supervisor be present only when the children are exchanged? One cannot safely assume that an abuser would not harm his children or expose them to drugs. One can also not assume that a grandparent would not allow any harm to come to his/her grandchildren. Parents of abusers may be unable to control the abuser. Some abusers were abusive toward their parents, too. Some grandparents have evicted the victim and her children from their home, as requested by the abuser. By making her homeless, the abuser will be in a better position to obtain custody of the children.

Courts often order abusers into "anger management" under the mistaken belief that intimate partner violence is about anger. However, abusers are in control of their violence and use it strategically. They "appear to control their anger while simultaneously engaging in power and control and revictimizing their partners."[150] "One study has shown that convicted batterers who attend anger management or substance abuse programs are significantly more likely to re-offend than those who attend state-certified batterer intervention programs."[151]

Today, many criminal courts who work with abusers use batterer intervention programs as a condition of bail, and, indeed, most victims request that the abuser be ordered into a program in the hope of his stopping his abusive behavior. Research into batterers programs conducted by the Center for Court Innovation in March 2007[152] concluded that enrollment in batterer programs did not affect recidivism or reoffending rates. Courts continue to use these programs because of a lack of other alternatives and as a means of making the abuser "accountable."[153]

A lawyer representing a client before a tribunal, with its permission if required by its rules, shall withdraw from employment, and a lawyer representing a client in other matters shall withdraw from employment, if:

1. The lawyer knows or it is obvious that the client is bringing the legal action, conducting the defense, or asserting a position in the litigation, or is otherwise having steps taken, merely for the purpose of harassing or maliciously injuring any person.
2. The lawyer knows or it is obvious that continued employment will result in violation of a Disciplinary Rule.

The American Bar Association, Model Rules of Professional Conduct, Rule 1.16 (b) "[A] lawyer may withdraw from representing a client if: . . . (4) the client insists upon taking action that the lawyer considers repugnant or with which the lawyer has a fundamental disagreement."

[150] Marc Dubin, *Men as Victims of Domestic Violence* (June 29, 2003),, http:.// www.cavnet.org.

[151] David Adams, *Why Do They Kill? Men Who Murder Their Intimate Partners* 104 (2007), referring to pages 5–7 of S. Bocko et al., *Restraining Order Violators, Corrective Programming, and Recidivism* 5–7 (Boston: Massachusetts Trial Court, Office of the Commissioner of Probation 2004).

[152] Center for Court Innovation, Melissa Labriola et al., *Court Responses to Batterer Program Noncompliance: A National Perspective* (Mar. 2007). *See also* Melissa Labriola, Michael Rempel & Robert Davis, *Testing the Effectiveness of Batterer Programs and Judicial Monitoring: Results for a Randomized Trial at the Bronx Misdemeanor Domestic Violence Court* (Nov. 2005).

[153] Accountability may be difficult to define since it is used in different contexts. Accountability supports the premise that courts should impose meaningful consequences if an abuser does not complete a batterer program or if he reoffends.

ADDRESSING VIOLENCE IN THE WORKPLACE

Intimate partner abuse affects every part of the victim's life, even when the abuser is not by her side. Often, it follows her into the workplace.[154] According to two recent surveys,[155] one in four employees self-identify as a victim of DV, and 22 percent of employees report that they have worked with a colleague who is a victim of DV. It is important for an abused employee to keep her job.

Even if it does not follow her into the workplace, domestic abuse affects the workplace. Without her job, a victim of DV may be economically trapped. Her job provides economic security and social contact for her, especially if she has been isolated from friends and family by the abuser. Her job may also provide a "purpose in life."

DV leads to poor work performance. It causes lateness because the abuser may hide her car keys, rip her clothes, prevent her from getting the children ready for school on time, or keep her captive in a room while he continues his tirade about "breaking his rules." DV in the workplace also affects the "bottom line" because it affects performance and productivity. Some signs of DV in the workplace are as follows:

- Excessive or unexplained repeated lateness and absenteeism;

- Disruptive visits by the abuser;

- Clothing inappropriate for the season to cover bruises (like wearing long sleeves outside on a very warm day, or wearing sunglasses indoors);

- Repeated calling, faxing, or text messaging the victim at work;

- Frequent bruising caused by repeated "accidents" or "clumsiness";

- Poor concentration and inconsistent work quality;

- Frequent need to leave early especially after a telephone call;

- Signs of emotional distress and depression;

- Uncharacteristic signs of fear or anxiety; and

- Angry or nasty messages for the victim left with a secretary or a fellow employee.[156]

Since abusers frequently pursue and harass their victims in the workplace, every workplace should have a policy to assist victims of DV.[157] Employers are increasing their efforts to assist workers who are being abused by their intimate partners. Many workplaces use mandatory trainings. These trainings not only help an employee recognize that

---

[154] *See, e.g.,* Ellen Simon, "Helping an Abused Employee*," Newsday*, Sept. 2, 2007, at F6, col. 1 ("setting up programs to deal with domestic violence aids, workers, company"); Kelley Holland, "Under New Management: Strife at Home Affects the Office, Too," *N.Y. Times*, Oct. 28, 2007, at Job Market ("Employers are learning that victims of violence are often reluctant to seek help.").

[155] Corporate Leaders on Domestic Violence and America's Workforce on Domestic Violence surveys are available at http://www.caepv.org/about/program_detail.php?refID=34.

[156] *See* http://www.loveisnotabuse.com/pdf/230–001–05%20DV%20trifold.v2.pdf.

[157] *See* http://www.endabuse.org/workplace for information in instituting a program.

she is being abused, but may help relatives, friends, fellow employees, or supervisory personnel recognize that someone they know, they are related to, or work with is being abused. It also enables them to refer the victim to a local DV agency for support, safety planning, and appropriate services for her and her children.

How Employers Can Help

If an employer suspects that an employee is a victim of DV, there are some positive ways to offer help.

- Listen if the victim wants to talk;
- Be nonjudgmental. Do not say "How could you let that happen?" Also do not say, "You must get out immediately," because where the vicitm is may be the safest place for her at that given moment;[158]
- Do not make the victim feel badly;
- Encourage the victim to go to a local DV agency for support and services;
- Have an open-door policy so the victim feels free to talk to someone;
- Put materials about the local community DV agency in the restrooms;
- Display social-norming posters;[159]
- Provide educational programs and trainings at staff meetings;
- Require employees to abstain from using offensive, sexist, or racist language;
- Educate employees about the importance of standing up against the violence aimed at women and children;
- Give the message to prospective employees during the hiring process that abuse is not acceptable in your workplace;
- Support an environment of nonviolence; and
- Help the victim to be safe in the workplace.

If the Employee Is an Abuser

A batterer may be abusing another employee at the workplace or his intimate partner at home. Workplace resources should not be used to harass, stalk, or abuse victims. Employers should not condone or remain silent about abuse. If the abuser says something about how he keeps his intimate partner in line, he should be told that this is not acceptable behavior. Society has the power to change societal attitudes just as it did with smoking and drunk driving. Sexist jokes should be forbidden. If the abuser indicates that his employer does not have a sense of humor, he should be told that he is just making up excuses. Language that denigrates the

---

[158] *See* Mahoney, *supra* note 62.
[159] The local community DV agency or the Corporate Alliance to End Partner Violence (http://www.caepv.org) can provide appropriate posters.

opposite sex should not be allowed. Nonsexist, nonracist, and respectful language is all that should be accepted in the workplace. Abusers should not be allowed to harass anyone in the workplace. Batterers should be reminded that DV is not a woman's problem, since men are the perpetrators of 95 percent of the violence. If the abuser asks for help, he should be referred to a batterer's accountability program.

It should be an essential part of the workplace culture to ensure that every employee is safe. DV is a value issue, and people must be invested in having a violence-free workplace. The workplace needs ongoing enforcement of a nonviolence policy. Management and other personnel must be committed to this.

CONCLUSION

Anyone working with victims of DV, abusers, children who witnessed DV,[160] or litigants in cases involving DV must educate themselves about the complex issues of intimate partner abuse. Recognizing the true victims of DV can be a difficult but essential task for the protection of the most vulnerable members of our society—our women and children. Each and every one of us is entitled to live in a safe, nurturing environment. Society should aim to eradicate DV and work toward enforcing zero tolerance as public policy. "Freedom from DV is a human right that should be enjoyed by all."[161]

---

[160] An excellent book that addresses the issue is Lundy Bancroft's, *When Dad Hurts Mom: Helping Your Children Heal the Wounds of Witnessing Abuse* (2002).

[161] Andrea C. Farney & Roberta Valente, "Creating Justice through Balance: Integrating Domestic Violence Into Family Court Practice," 54 *Juv. & Fam. Ct. J.* 50 (Fall 2003).

Chapter 3

Historical Legal Context in Domestic Violence Custody Cases

by Marvin Timothy Gray, J.D., M.A., C.D.S.V.R.P.

INTRODUCTION

Scope and Premises of This Chapter

It is necessary, when introducing this chapter, to give due consideration to its scope and some basal premises upon which it is styled and written. First, this chapter does not cover any subject or topic definitively or dispositively and does not aim to do so: it is intended to touch briefly on over 4,000 years of history and jurisprudence. The brief considerations in this chapter are meant to create a reference that can aid us in navigating future experiences or even in changing systems that are dysfunctional or in need of enhancement.

Second, as this is but one chapter within the entire work, many topics briefly mentioned here will undoubtedly be covered more definitively in other chapters. Each of the chapters in this work will provide deeper tools in specific areas of law, jurisprudence, and activism that can be used to assist in family court cases throughout the nation.

Third, this chapter is written to create something of a framework or a lens. Through this framework, it is hoped that battered mothers and others (as well as their advocates, legal counsel, and others interested in improving and making safer our present system of jurisprudence in the family courts) who have suffered not only from domestic violence

(DV), sexual violence, stalking, child abuse, and other forms of abuse, but also from intentional or unintentional revictimization inherent in our legal system and most family court systems in operation in the United States today can see some historical comparisons with their own present-day situations and cases. It is further hoped these brief considerations of historical contributions to American legal history and the family court jurisprudence in effect in U.S. family courts will be made accessible within the chapter as real-time tools for seeking and promoting both understanding of the family court system and its present inherent limitations and promoting successful outcomes for battered mothers and their children.

As such, subsections titled "How About Women and Children" and "Relevance to Your Legal Case" are added to many sections to increase understanding of both the points of origin of the processes and jurisprudential underpinnings of the family courts and, to some small extent, how women and children were treated under the law. To consider the development of family law jurisprudence without consideration of the conditions of women and children at the times of those developments would be of little use to this work. Further, it is the express purpose of this author and of this chapter to open legal history and family court jurisprudence to battered mothers, their children, and those assisting them, to both increase understanding and to suggest real-life arguments, dangers, tools to be used, and potential techniques to consider in their family court cases. These will be drawn from history, from the law, and from the experiences of the author in both legally representing battered mothers/women and survivors of sexual assault and stalking in protective order, family law, and related cases, and in acting as a direct services and systems advocate for those same groups throughout legal, legislative, health services, and community advocacy systems.

Fourth, the materials in this chapter are necessarily brief and composite. While it is certainly important to provide citations and references to guide future study or academic debate, some of the information in this chapter is experiential, and some is so composite in nature as to resist specific references. References have been cited where the author feels they are of use; however, not everything alleged within the chapter is referenced to any specific source and are the assumptions (direct or composite), experiences, or allegations of the author.[1] In all cases, the subject of legal history related specifically to family courts and jurisprudence and the increased efficacious use thereof in present-day court cases, to seek justice and positive experiences for battered mothers and their children, is not only the subject of this chapter, but an often underutilized tool for understanding the sometimes seemingly mystical or nonsensical procedures and outcomes of family court cases today.

Other Introductory Matters

There are several other key concepts or warnings to keep in mind while reading this chapter. First, it is important to remember that history and practice teaches that despite

---

[1] Based on the author's experience as an advocate for, attorney and/or legal counsel for, and sounding board/support network participant for survivors of DV, sexual assault, stalking, dating violence, and related issues, as well as counsel to multiple DV and sexual assault services and support agencies serving survivors in day-to-day direct services, systems advocacy, coordinated community responses, legislative efforts, etc., and as a contact and resource locally and nationally for survivor issues.

statutes, controlling authority, case law, or widely accepted rules or practices, law and family courts not only vary from state to state and region to region, from judicial district to judicial district and from jurisdiction to jurisdiction, but often even differ from court building to court building and from courtroom to courtroom. Considerations or tools useful in one may be detrimental or dangerous in another. Neither battered mothers nor their lay advocates or legal counsel should go it alone. Developing knowledge of the court, its judge, the court's rules, the local bar's practices concerning certain issues and procedures, resources available to the battered mother in the community, and the community's response to issues of DV, sexual assault, stalking, child abuse, and similar issues is vital to consideration of a family court case even before anything is filed.

Second, this should not be undertaken alone. If nothing else, this chapter and other chapters in this work should clearly stand for the proposition that not only are family court cases exceedingly complex, but they can be extremely dangerous in terms of the lives and safety of battered mothers and their children, and the decisions made in court can affect numerous lives for a very long time. Battered mothers (and their advocates) who have interacted with the family court and other court systems for a significant length of time know this; but for those just beginning to interact with these systems, such warning deserves to be stressed for the safety and long-term maximization of positive results for all concerned. It is certainly in the best interests of battered mothers to find those in the advocacy and legal communities who can help them navigate this system. Whether the old adage that it takes a community to raise a child is true or not, it is undoubtedly true that it takes a cohesive and dedicated team, with the battered mother at the helm, making informed choices that are best for her and her children at each vital juncture in a case, to win a primarily positive outcome in a long-lasting custody battle in most family courts in the United States. Any person assisting the battered mother in such a case should attempt to muster the resources available nationally and in the local community on her behalf. Multiple support systems for the battered mother and her children are vital to her strength to continue and almost certainly will affect the eventual outcome of her family court custody case. A valuable player on the team can be that person who just spends time talking to the mother.

Third, with every single battered mother/woman whom this author has represented, provided assistance to, or advocated for in a family court case, the author has found that family court cases are, by nature and often with the full and (wittingly or unwittingly) supported intentional design of the batterer, *traumatic*. The battered mother, her children, and everyone assisting her must plan from the beginning with that in mind: and they all should make extra efforts to take care of themselves and, to the extent appropriate within their respective roles, each other. In many cases, the final custody battle goes not to the most deserving or the least harmful parent, but to the one who lasts the longest. The very nature of batterers makes it necessary to prepare for long-term engagement with the family court system.

Fourth, it should be clear in this chapter (and it is the clear and fundamental belief of this author) that law, which does not ultimately seek and serve the ends of justice, is of little value to a society that is progressing towards an inherent respect for human rights. In the *Oklahoma Rules of Professional Conduct* (the state in which this author generally practices and writes), the code of conduct, which is used to oversee the practice of law by attorneys, it says in relation to the scope of the rules,

> [16] Compliance with the Rules, as with all law in an open society, depends primarily upon understanding and voluntary compliance, secondarily upon reinforcement by peer and public opinion and finally, when necessary, upon

enforcement through disciplinary proceedings. The Rules do not, however, exhaust the moral and ethical considerations that should inform a lawyer, for no worthwhile human activity can be completely defined by legal rules. The Rules simply provide a framework for the ethical practice of law.[2]

In this set of rules is the inherent recognition that "no worthwhile human activity," including family court cases one would presume, "can be completely defined by legal rules." Despite the best attempts by advocates, attorneys, activists, and others to develope good laws for the benefit of battered mothers, and as courts are, to a great extent, a product of the legal profession, it should be clear that a balance should be struck in any case between the letter of the law and equitable or justice-related considerations. The rule makes clear what those familiar to family court systems already know: moral and ethical considerations (as interpreted by judges, attorneys, law enforcement officers, and others in the justice system), as well as public opinion, will almost undoubtedly play a part in the battered mother's family law case in some proportion to considerations under the written law and authorities. In a modern family court, for those assisting a battered mother and her children, it is imperative that public opinion, as well as ethical, human rights-related considerations and the written law and authorities, be considered in the context of that specific court and that case and its players, and be brought to bear upon the case (either in or out of the courtroom as suits the particular case best strategically and tactically), the family court system, and those functioning in a humanitarian and educated manner to provide maximum opportunity for justice to result. Failure to do so almost certainly, in many if not most cases, will see the bulk of the letter of the written law, the jurisprudence of the courts of law, and the local beliefs and practices of the jurisdiction and/or court personnel favor the male batterer and remain ripe for the manipulation of the system by the batterer and his counsel; said system has favored the male batterer's position for several thousand years of law and jurisprudence.

COLORING THE DEVELOPMENT OF WESTERN LAW AND JURISPRUDENCE RELATED TO THE FAMILY

Focus on Property

Various ancient and premodern codes of law are about property; they have always been about property, and we are just starting to make it *not* about property. The Code of Hammurabi, the Jewish law, the Roman Twelve Tables, and the later Corpus Juris Civilis, perhaps the oldest sets of written rules concerning legal behavior, which were generative in Western law and jurisprudence, were each exceedingly concerned with concepts of property, and the law was framed in property terms. In the second law of the Code of Hammurabi,[3] for instance, if an accused was guilty, the accuser took his house (possibly meant in the general sense to include his household and all property). If the accused was innocent, he took the accuser's house. In the third law, an accuser who brought a charge before the elders that he could not prove was to be put to death; however, in the fourth law, he could instead convince them to fine him in grain or money. In Law 203

---

[2] 5 Okla. Stat. app. 3-A, § 16, *available at* http://www.oscn.net (emphasis added).
[3] Richard Hooker ed., *The Code of Hammurabi, The Mesopotamian Reader, World Civilizations* (1996).

a free man who struck another free man had to pay a gold mina, and in Law 204, if a freed man struck another freed man, he had to pay ten shekels. Most of the provisions of Hammurabi's Code concerned property in one fashion or another and conceptualized human rights, human issues, etc., almost entirely as property rights or as crimes.

Roman law from the Twelve Tables forward was much the same. Property was of primary concern. Several types of harms against another were subject to fixed fines as the punishment. Early Jewish law was frequently similar, and though each of these legal traditions/systems differed in currency used, time frames for punishment, etc., each was clearly concerned with property and using property to recompense for crimes including most harms against a human being.

Battered mothers and others face a legal and jurisprudential system based, to a great extent, on property laws of one sort or another. When the main emphasis of law is the protection or organization of property and not concerned with addressing direct harms to another human being, as is the case with most American courts of law, it is difficult to address issues such as DV, sexual assault, stalking, and child abuse within that system. Only when society places its focus on justice, safety, and the well-considered construction of an actual viable solution for the person harmed, fully considering the behavioral, socioeconomic, and other pertinent factors involved and tailoring solutions thereto, will U.S. family court systems substantially and adequately serve the needs of battered mothers, their children, the batterer, and society.

Focus on People as Property

In the ancient law systems, not only was property a focus, but, to a large degree, each focused numerous laws and much attention on the issue of slavery or at least on people as property in one way or another. In most of these systems, women and children, while occasionally protected to some small degree by the letter of the law, were treated in much the same manner as property controlled by an owner—much like control and use of slaves (or at least servants). The United States has only recently (in a timeline of over 4,000 years of legal history, as set out below) begun to address slavery as an issue, and it is even more recent that U.S. Supreme Court decisions, in the mid 1900s, have paved the way for the much earlier nineteenth-century ban on slavery and declaration of rights for people of color to actually become any level of common practice or reality. Even with the ban on slavery, the concept that people can be valued somewhat as a piece of property is alive and well in U.S. legal systems.

One only needs to attend a personal injury case hearing, in which harms to a person and a person's ability to earn are given a value (much as the value of a slave or of harms to a person were determined historically), a social security disability hearing, in which the person's continued ability to earn is valuated, certain tort cases, where similar principles are considered to see how people and/or the harms done to them are valuated as property. Certainly some concepts of restitution are extremely valuable and even necessary in considering many types of cases and issues. However when the only or main emphasis is upon the property issues exclusively, problems occur, and the systems both fail justice and fail to construct safe, workable long-term solutions. In the family court systems, if the format for valuating and separating the values and rights of the marriage (or really the family), where each parent's earning potentials, net worth, debts, and "parental rights" to a child or children are parceled out exactly like the law school analogy of the "bundle of sticks," focuses on the "property" issues strictly and does not include sufficient consideration and valuation of "sticks" in various orders or proceedings that represent consideration of and carefully crafted safety measures for the abused parent and the children, does not include family dynamics as they really are in the case rather than as they are automatically or categorically valuated to be, the orders and proceedings of that family court will almost certainly fail the cause of justice and fail to create solutions promoting safety for the family/persons involved.

While it may be debated whether other substantial and preferable methods of consideration are adequately available within the jurisprudential systems acting upon these cases or, perhaps, even available within the experience of humanity to contrive, it is vital to anyone entering these systems to be cognizant that these sorts of valuations and types of thinking are occurring, perhaps even unbeknownst to the participants in those systems, and that such styles of consideration of a family law case will tend to make the court exercise its discretion toward decisions from a property division framework, even when determining the custody of children. After all, custody of a child, in almost any statute, is framed, to some extent, as a property right of a parent or custodian (a word first and still used regularly for one who watches or cares for property).

Inherent Human Rights

The concept (politically and in law) of inherent human rights, even for free adult men, is less than 250 years old. While philosophical discussions of "Natural Law" and "Natural Rights" (*ius naturale* in Latin) are age old, the U.S. Constitution with the Bill of Rights and the U.S. Declaration of Independence are two of the first and certainly two of the most well promulgated examples (derived from a Western law/society) to infuse the concept of inherent rights of an individual, beyond those legal rights given by a nation or government, onto the foundational legal structure of a modern nation. Suffragists in the mid to late 1800s began a more than fifty-year struggle to cause the U.S. government to grant them the right to vote. Children's rights, until the latter quarter of the 1900s, were (and frequently remain) even less well defined. Other chapters in this work will certainly discuss in greater detail the gender disparities that continue to disadvantage battered mothers in family courts and throughout the legal systems as well as almost universally render their children, even those of significant age, without a voice in family court proceedings even when (or especially when) a guardian ad litem or similar counsel is appointed.

Rape as Property Rights Issue and Tool of Subjugation

Rape is a premier tool of war that has colored cultures, law, and society since the dawn of time. Most of the earliest codes address rape in some form or other, though most often simply to require recompense for a property right and sometimes penalizing the woman raped. It is extremely likely that, to a greater or lesser extent, rape has been sanctioned as a tool of war or at least ignored by almost every government in history. It may be that there is no better tool for subjugating/gaining power over and maintaining control of a populace than systematic rape. Modern nations are no stranger to it either, and, in fact, it is frequently used today in many places (with the tacit or complicit consent or inaction of the United States and other Western nations) today as a tool of war and even for "ethnic cleansing." A 2007 Amnesty International fact sheet summarizes the use of rape as a tool of war:

In every armed conflict investigated by Amnesty International in 1999 and 2000, the torture of women was reported, most often in the form of sexual violence. Rape, when used as a weapon of war, is systematically employed for a variety of purposes, including intimidation, humiliation, political terror, extracting information, rewarding soldiers, and "ethnic cleansing." . . . Rape is not an accident of war, or an accidental adjunct to armed conflict. Its wide-spread use in times of conflict reflects the unique terror it holds for women, the unique power it gives the rapist over his victim, and the unique contempt he displays for its victims. The use of rape in conflict reflects the inequali-ties women face in their everyday lives in peacetime. Until governments take responsibility for their obligations to ensure equality, and end discrimination against women, rape will continue to be a favored weapon of the aggressor.[4]

The effects of rape on the community as well are serious and not limited to the family setting. When rape and other forms of sexual abuse are involved in a case that will enter the family courts, the battered mother and, either directly or indirectly, her children are at increased vulnerability from a family court jurisprudence that (espe-cially after the advent of no fault divorce concepts and rules) refuses to consider any fault or bad acts by a parent previous to the case and that operates knowingly or unknowingly on property principles and with frequent disregard for safety consider-ations. These property principles in the family court jurisprudence, unless carefully and judiciously balanced with equitable and safety considerations for the battered mother and her children, reflect to the battered mother and often to the children involved that it is all about property and what or who belongs to whom, much the same as the ownership and objectification the rapist/batterer has claimed and imposed upon the battered mother and the children. Rape is a premier tool of war that accosts the being of the person raped at the most basic core levels and is exceedingly effective at subjugating/gaining power over and maintaining control over whole populaces or nations. Thus, it is no surprise that sexual assault (and the techniques it utilizes) plays the same role in a batterer or rapist's repertoire, most frequently with the same lack of accountability or consideration it receives in the international arena.

Modern Customary Law, a Frequent Curse to Battered Mothers

"'The way we've always done it,' or customary/vulgar law, is the most pervasive legal tradition throughout history and the most damaging to battered women and their children." This statement is primarily experiential by this author, though evidence for it can be found throughout this chapter, most likely throughout this work, and certainly in great prevalence in the experiences of battered mothers, their children, and those who assist them in family courts. Similarly, the way things are done in any specific jurisdiction or courtroom or with a particular judge or attorney frequently plays a vital or even determinative roll in courtroom outcomes today. Much as local areas throughout history have had laws of a local flavor, courts today have both court and area rules and day-to-day practices or ways of handling business of that court, court clerk's office, prosecutor's office, etc. This sort of jurisprudence is largely unwritten,

---

[4] Amnesty International, *Stop Violence Against Women, Rape as a Tool of War: A Fact Sheet* (2007), http://www.amnestyusa.org/women/rapeinwartime.html.

but it is pervasive and frequently seen behind the terms "discretion" or "exercise of discretion," as unwritten effects of relationships between the court and those within the justice system, such as lawyers or state children's services organization workers, or even just a flat-out statement of "that's the way we handle things in this court." Unwritten rules of any family court must be understood as clearly as possible and can be both protective and helpful or harmful and discriminatory, as well as very difficult to quantify or prove.

Failure to understand the unwritten rules or practices of any family court will almost certainly have detrimental consequences on the custody case of any battered mother. Protective mothers and their advocates must account for the practices of a specific court or even the personality of a specific judge to avoid great detriment to a family law case even before it is filed.

Hope, Societal Intervention, and Activism

It is quite possible that, in looking at the foregoing discussion, one would begin to believe there is little or no hope for those who must enter family court to protect themselves and their children. In fact, though the battles that must be waged to create positive changes in cases, courts, and legal systems, are long, difficult, and very tiring, history is revealing that the process of creating those positive changes in society, in the law, and in the family courts, from a long-term historical viewpoint, has been increasingly successful. *Hope* is a critical factor in aiding a battered mother or those who would help her. This author is convinced that the legal history of our Western systems of law and jurisprudence, built as it were upon the backs of giants in the suffrage, civil rights, and other human rights-oriented movements offers real hope of positive changes to come—even in the family courts of the United States.

HOW EARLIER LEGAL CODES AFFECT WOMEN AND CHILDREN IN OUR MODERN LEGAL SYSTEM

Code of Hammurabi

The Babylonian Code of Hammurabi (the Code),[5] written in approximately 1780 BC, is perhaps the oldest known code of laws from a ruler to his people intended to comprehensively cover acceptable and unacceptable behaviors and actions. Hammurabi is widely considered the first ruler known to bring all of his subjects under one code of law in the form of statutes with judges to make decisions, although the Code may have been built upon previous codes as well. This Code is likely to have influenced the later Roman law, the legal thought of the Greeks, and, to some extent, the later Mohammedan Islamic law. Babylon was a superpower by modern terms for hundreds of years, and the laws of Babylon were undoubtedly promulgated widely. Property laws in the Code, including those for ownership of slaves, women, and children, are a far greater percentage of its bulk than crimes against persons.

---

[5] Hooker, *supra* note 3; 5 *New Encyclopaedia Britannica* 668-69 (15th ed., Macropaedia ed. 1988).

How About Women and Children? Marriages were likely arranged, but a wife was allowed to keep (and was required by law or custom to be given) her dowry even from her husband, and it was hers after his death.[6] While women retained some protections and some rights to own and manage property in various circumstances, they were also considered property to be owned and managed by their husbands.[7] Some protections were available for a married woman who was raped,[8] and several fairly strict incest laws are in the Code.[9]

Children were also generally property, and the fruits of their labor or their sale was their father's to manage as he wished. A few protections were in evidence in certain cases, but, for the most part, children were property of their father and subject to his will in almost all cases—even to their sale or possibly death.[10]

While the Code would not seem to have many protections or equitable treatment for women and children by modern standards, it was likely a very enlightened Code for its time with some intent to protect many classes of women and children. Through a modern lens, with a view to human rights, it was likely to have been somewhat more protective of various rights of women and children, at least in the letter of the law, than the later Roman law and the law and legal thought of the Greeks.

Relevance to Your Legal Case. Why would such a Code, with far less influence on legal systems today than the Roman law, be of significance to modern readers interested in the cases of battered mothers in family courts? It is important to see that, in the written law of ancient civilizations, women and children were generally treated as property in most if not all ways. Judges were employed to judge cases for the ruler, and laws were written to attempt to govern human activities and behaviors including marriage, divorce, and custody of children, and these procedures, laws, and customs have influenced the law used in U.S. courts, including the family courts, today in ways that are most often invisible to most participants in the court system.

It is important to see that, from the very inception of and throughout the development of these earliest available written laws, the law and society they were created for placed the fathers in clear positions of power over their wives, slaves, and children in the household and considered the fathers the general manager of the property and wealth of the family. In nearly 4,000 years of the development of law and jurisprudence, which influenced, to greater and lesser extents, the modern family court, equal or even extensive rights for women and certainly for children were not in existence or even contemplated. Laws that were conceived and developed under such circumstances and in such societies are unlikely to be deemed generally appropriate or efficacious through a modern human rights lens for application in modern family courts—however, there are scarce historical alternatives or authority in the law. Such authority is new, a product of approximately the last 200 years of history, and most such authority is even more recent than that. It is, however, important to observe that the modern written law has, at least in certain circumstances, related to women and children and, despite its many inadequacies, evolved positively.

---

[6] Hooker, *supra* note 3, at 137, 138–40.

[7] Hooker, *supra* note 3.

[8] Id. at 129–32.

[9] Id. at 154–58.

[10] Hooker, *supra* note 3.

Hebrew Mosaic Law

Much like the Roman law and the law of Babylon, the law of the Hebrews was taken largely from someone (in the person of Moses and then later prophets) considered a wise or inspired leader, believed to have been inspired by a god or gods, and then added to by scholars or leaders thereafter. The law of the Hebrews consisted of written laws, and judges were in place to make judgments according to those laws. However, the law of the Hebrews was undoubtedly of far greater influence upon the modern law than that of Babylon, though many provisions are similar—likely through a shared area of generation.[11]

Since the early centuries AD, the influence of the Roman Catholic Church has been immense in Rome, in Byzantium, in Greece, in the later Holy Roman Empire, and throughout the Western world. While that influence could be thought to be primarily religious in nature, the influence of the Hebrew laws, retained in the primary scriptural doctrines of the early, middle, and renaissance Christian world, and in the later Holy Roman Church (certainly during the development of the common law in England and the formation of the United States from Colonial America), had profound effects and influence upon the laws written for those societies. The influence of the Holy Roman Church in secular matters was immeasurable during various generative periods of history, and the canon law of that church formed alongside the civil law.[12]

Jewish people and communities existed in many metropolitan and other areas throughout the last nearly 3,000 years of Western history.[13] Jewish scholars have undoubtedly had varying levels of effect on the law (as well as custom and society) of many places and continue to do so (though primarily indirectly and through their effect on the generation of Western law traditions) in the United States and other Western nations today. The commandments in the first five books of the Torah or first five books of the Christian Old Testament, called Halakha, accompanied by Talmudic law and later rabbinical texts, comprised the bulk of the Hebrew law.[14] These first five books are utilized/referenced by Jews, Christians, and followers of Islam.

How About Women and Children? A marriage contract was required under the older Hebrew law, and divorce was allowed under certain circumstances. Some laws provide protections for women, but, again, other than the dowry, the woman and the children were, to greater or lesser extents, under the control of the male leader of the household. The "eye for an eye and a tooth for a tooth" concepts of the Mosaic law, the Code of Hammurabi, and the Roman Lex Talionis are common to the development of many aspects of modern criminal and property law as well as philosophies of incarceration, punishment for crimes, rehabilitation, etc. Similarly, how the laws of these ancient societies treated women and children, issues of marriage, custody, and divorce, during their development and later consideration or adoption, in whole or in part, by other nations is likely to have a continuing effect on the jurisprudence of the modern family court.

---

[11] 5 *New Encyclopaedia Britannica*, *supra* note 5, at 669.

[12] John Henry Merryman, David S. Clark & John O. Haley, *The Civil Law Tradition: Europe, Latin America, and East Asia* 294–97 (1994), referencing David S. Clark, "The Medieval Origins of Modern Legal Education: Between Church and State" 35 *Am. J. Comp. L.* 653, 675–78, 693–96 (1987).

[13] Merryman, Clark & Haley, *supra* note 12, at 8–9.

[14] 5 *New Encyclopaedia Britannica*, *supra* note 5, at 427–35.

Relevance to Your Legal Case. Between the influence of Judaism and that of Christianity, many modern school children are quite possibly more likely to be able to quote passages of the Mosaic law, especially the Ten Commandments, than any passages from the Declaration of Independence, the U.S. Constitution, or the U.S. Bill of Rights. Law has colored society throughout history, and society colors law. Judges in family courts today (as well as prosecutors, law enforcement, and others), while making decisions according to the law will often look to their own moral and ethical code to exercise discretion in instances where the law does not reach to equity or justice (as is undoubtedly needed in the consideration and adjudication of modern family court cases where issues of safety and equitable remedies are requisite to craft lasting, safe decisions) or, more problematically, replace the law entirely with such, usually to the detriment of the battered woman and her children.

While there is, of necessity, a place in the law, in society, and in the family courts for reliance on an ethical code in the exercise of discretion due to the absence of, or for assistance in, interpreting the law, confusion as to the proper utilization of such discretion or code exists in the modern family court and society. In many modern family courts, equitable remedies (such as protective orders, other safety-seeking mechanisms, and equitable attention to justice) are often few and far between (and somewhat outside the usual past practice of the court or the local bar in relation to such cases), and a property-driven jurisprudence and the interests of judicial economy seek to avoid the time-consuming but necessary task of untangling the difficult and complex behavior patterns and past actions of the parties before crafting a final decision. Again, this leads to unsafe and poorly crafted family court decisions and contributes to repeat appearances by parties in crowded courtrooms and to human pain and suffering in the form of continued abuse or even death at the hands of an abuser.

Athenian/Greek Philosophy, Plato, and the Logic-Reason of Aristotle

Various ethical and natural law concepts were expressed by the author Plato in numerous works through the character of the philosopher Socrates. Many of these concepts were generative to, as well as descriptive of, Greek ideas of the value of the individual and the beginning elements of democracy. Legal and other scholars have read and utilized the concepts popularized by Plato for centuries, and these writings, along with Plato's student Aristotle (considered to be a legal authority during the revisions of Roman law[15]), Tacitus, and other ancient writers were, until the last century or so, considered necessary reading for any educated person (man). Aristotle's ideas of logic and reason, of organization, of categorization of things by their natures, and other philosophical concepts played a great part in the organization of the law by glossators, canonists, and commentators in later history. Early professors of the law, intending to create or at least organize the law as a social science, paid great tribute to the elements and principles of reason such early philosophers set forth. Certainly Greek society has been heralded as formative of the early democratic principles of government.

How About Women and Children? Athenian and other Greek societies possessed some ideas of the inherent value of individuals including women and children. The consideration of reason and ethics in the creation and administration of law and of the appropriate ascendancy of justice can be attributed to Greek philosophers. However, Athenian Greek

---

Merryman, Clark & Haley, *supra* note 12, at 286–87, referencing Clark, *supra* note 12, –78, 693–96.

women were still only able to own certain types of personal property, and they were generally considered the property of their male relatives and were, according to Aristotle, completely secondary in actual nature to men, weak and feeble minded creatures. In the *Politics*, Aristotle, in examining the appropriate relationship between husband and wife, made comments such as "man is fitter by nature to command than the female just as the elder and the full grown is superior to the younger and the immature"[16] and "the courage of a man is shown in commanding, of a woman in obeying."[17]

Interestingly, Spartan Greek women may have been somewhat better situated and are reputed to have owned two-fifths of Sparta at one time, to have been educated and literate, and to have had some training at war. Athenian Greeks (Aristotle) stated that the Spartan men obeyed their women—citing this as one of two reasons the Spartan Constitution was not good. Aristotle went on to speak about the license of the Spartan women being adverse to the state and that the Spartans, like every warlike race (including the Celts), were prone to the love of their women.[18] To Aristotle, this was obviously not a trait to be desired. Such commentaries by Aristotle, perhaps more than other writings, make clear the position women were to hold in Athenian or, to Aristotle's way of thinking, any reasonable, desirable, functional, or just society.

Before coming to too great a belief in the greater liberties of Spartan women, Professor Michael Whitby, Professor of Classics and Ancient History at the University of Warwick, in his book titled simply *Sparta*, cautions modern persons to "hesitate before seeking to enlist the women of ancient Sparta as allies in the just cause of feminism."[19] He mentions that there were, or may have been, a number of positives, "an equal but separate education, their frankness of utterance, their liberating attire, their property rights, and control of their households," etc., but he cautions that there were other factors much less positive including Spartan women being forced to look and act like men, their restricted or nonexistent choice in acquiring a husband, the likely way they were "seized" and "had" as wives by their husbands, the fact that their husband could lend them out for extramarital procreation, etc.[20] If such was the case with the obviously far more liberated Spartan women, a picture of other Greek wives can be drawn to some extent, perhaps by contrast.

Relevance to Your Legal Case. Remember the influence Aristotle (and those like him) had on generations of scholars and lawmakers including (directly or indirectly) those representing the battered mother and those adjudicating her case. Aristotle's *Politics* was, in fact, a required reading of this author's master's degree program, and Aristotle was mentioned in more than one law school class. Consider Aristotle's respect as a philosopher, statesman, and scholar, and his influence on the generation of precedents of our modern law and jurisprudence. It seems unlikely, to say the least, that his ideas about the Spartan women's more equal participation in society, politics, property ownership, and possibly even war, as well as his inferences as to the appropriateness of the love of a spouse in relation to the love of the state, has failed to influence the jurisprudence that has descended to modern family law. Many persons, legal scholars and other scholars, highly respected by the legal profession, may have introduced these and

---

[16] Benjamin Jowett trans., *The Works of Aristotle, Great Books of the Western World* 1259b (1987).

[17] Id. at 1260a (20).

[18] Id. at 1269b (10) through 1271b (20).

[19] Michael Whitby, *Sparta* 160 (2002).

[20] Id.

similar influences to generations that, when examined under a lens of consideration of modern concepts of human rights, are potentially extremely detrimental to safety, empowerment, and positive outcomes for battered mothers.

Law and Practices of Rome

As the Romans developed gradually from an agrarian society to the subsequent forms of republic and then (for all intents in purposes) dominate, their laws transformed with them.[21] From the Roman Twelve Tables, an early Roman code of law frequently referred to throughout history and still today by legal scholars, the Roman law changed with the times and needs of that society and its leaders. Since it is from these laws that later generations of Western lawmakers drew their basis and further inspiration in developing civil law and common law traditions, which are the dominant legal traditions of Western nations today, it is important to recognize that these laws and the Roman society/empire generated both an amazing and valuable set of laws and legal precedent *and* that certain concepts, which were apparent and integral to these laws and the legal and social assumptions of Roman society, were also generated with beliefs and practices that are inimical to modern concepts of equality between sexes and of the inherent value of people.

> The concepts of Pater Familias (loosely Father/Head of the Family) and of Patria Potestas (loosely Law of the Father) serve to exemplify the first way in which the generation of laws was detrimental to modern concepts of equality between the sexes. These laws gave the father or grandfather who was head of the household complete control over his wife, servants, slaves, children, grandchildren, etc. Anyone who was not the Pater Familias was "in Potestas" and could not own any property (usually), were subject to nearly any level of paternal discipline including inflicting death (throughout much of the duration of the Roman Empire), and their acts were answered for by the Pater Familias who could surrender them (in a property sense) for any wrong doing to the alleged victim (until the Emperor Justinian's time well after the fall of the Western Roman Empire). The Roman Law of Persons was based on the property ownership of the head of Household over all of the family. Relationships were described in terms of property.[22]

The Romans themselves recognized that the patriarch had an amazing level of control over his family, even for the times—and from this culture much of our modern law developed.

The Corpus Juris Civilis (frequently referred to by modern legal scholars) was a compilation of earlier Roman law, from the Twelve Tables forward and was requested by the Eastern Roman Emperor Justinian. It was compiled under the auspices of a famous juris consult (a scholar in the Roman law who gave advice, wrote about and interpreted the law) and a wealthy Roman citizen named Tribonian with the help of other notable juris consults of the day. Roman law included legal opinions (of those considered the

[21] Merryman, Clark & Haley, *supra* note 12, at 213–81.
[22] Merryman, Clark & Haley, *supra* note 12, at 238–40, referencing 1 Samuel P. Scott, *The* · iii–iv, 64–65 (1932); Merryman, Clark & Haley, *supra* note 12, at 261–65, referenc- ıtson, *Society and Legal Change* 23–29 (1977).

wisest of the juris consults), imperial edicts (issued by the ruler), and court adjudications (outcomes of various trials at the law). The Corpus Juris Civilis took these as well as the codified law and attempted to make a "once and for all" final and definitive version of the laws of and for Rome. To emphasize, perhaps, the reverence with which the modern legal profession has held the Roman law, perhaps the most influential twentieth-century legal encyclopedia that nearly every U.S. law student is introduced to is called the *Corpus Juris Secundum* or "Body of the Law the Second," and it attempted to do for American court cases, as well as statutory and other laws, from the mid 1600s on and for twentieth-century American attorneys and judges what Justinian attempted to do for Rome with the Corpus Juris Civilis in the sixth century.

The Roman law also held the legal profession in great esteem. Much as wealthy men might have utilized a duel to settle an argument, so Roman culture viewed recourse to law and making learned use of it as sophisticated behavior. Of historical note is that frequently in Roman law, judgment winners had to either enforce their own judgment or appeal to a wealthy citizen to do so, and usually a juris consult argued the matter for them.[23] Also wealthy juris consults, such as Cicero, actually undertook some of the responsibility of the people they represented when they agreed to argue their cases. This changed later after the emergence/resurgence of legal science in Italy, but it is notable that rights to legal counsel did not develop for family law cases in the same manner as for other civil and criminal law cases. Also, in some Roman periods, the written opinions of respected juris consults were binding upon some courts and gave a certain level of legal protection to persons who engaged them to issue the opinion.[24] This would be equivalent to searching out a highly respected legal textbook writer or other highly acclaimed lawyer in modern America and engaging that attorney as one's counsel because that attorney's opinions would have binding value on the courts and protect the individual, to some extent, against an adverse court outcome. Anyone who has observed the actual interplay of modern courts at work has seen the immense influence that well-respected and influential/acclaimed counsel can have upon the outcomes of a court case.

How About Women and Children? The exact status of women and children varied with time, place, and social status during the course of the Roman Empire(s), but generally women and children were property and could be dealt with, in most instances, as the head of the family wished. The history/story of the Lex Oppia,[25] a Roman law mostly considered by legal scholars to be an early sumptuary law, that is, a law that controlled what someone could wear/spend, gives some insight to the condition of Roman women under the Roman law. The Lex Oppia was a Roman law instituted in the third century BC, and it placed limits upon the jewelry and clothing a woman could wear and what property she could own. It was to prevent huge expenditures of wealth (by women) on what were considered frivolities such as costly apparel and jewelry. Later, when Rome had defeated Carthage, wealth to the Roman Empire greatly increased and mores changed, some sought to repeal the Lex Oppia.

---

[23] Merryman, Clark & Haley, *supra* note 12, at 245–46, referencing Paul Veyne, "The Roman Empire," in 1 *A History of Private Life: From Pagan Rome to Byzantium* 5, 166–68 (Paul Veyne ed., Arthur Gold Hammer trans., (1987).

[24] Merryman, Clark & Haley, *supra* note 12, at 242–44, referencing Bruce W. Frier, "Autonomy of Law and The Origins of the Legal Profession," 11 *Cardozo L. Rev.* 259, 262–66 (1989).

[25] 3 Theodor Mommsen, *The Project Gutenberg Ebook The History of Rome* bk. 34, at 1–8, *available at* http://www.gutenberg.org/ebooks/10703.

Some argued against it saying that women could never manage money, and keeping all women wearing the same clothes and limited jewelry was an important social equalizer. Others argued it was wrong to keep the Roman women from wearing such jewelry, now easily afforded, when they had to see the wives of Rome's allies wearing such. It is said that Roman matrons crowded and blocked the streets outside the Forum where the arguments were taking place and beseeched the men to lift the laws. They were said to approach the Roman leadership the next day and kept up their beseeching until the law was repealed.

Having been involved with statutory changes for the benefit of battered women, this historical incident takes on a distinctly different context and character for this author. While it seems apparent that chroniclers of the time felt women would "storm the capitol" as it were to be allowed to wear fancy clothes and jewelry (this was likely considered to be a sign of female irrationality and of a desire on the part of women to live in inappropriate opulence, while ignoring the breadth of the damage of the law to Roman women), the activism of the Roman women involved in advocating the repeal of the Lex Oppia could be, and more likely was, of a very different character.

The Lex Oppia regulated a woman's access to and ability to own personal property (gold), not exclusively jewelry or clothing. The issues at stake were much greater than a frivolous desire to wear fancy jewelry or clothing. The Roman women were fighting for a right to own personal property, a right that not only made sense, but was a foundational right protected and given great importance by generally every legal code and every society of the time for the leading men of that society. The Roman women knew (as did the Roman men assuredly) that their access to property (such as easily accessible and stored gold) was essential to their survival and the survival of their children, and the protection or enforcement of any possible individual freedoms or rights the women may be allowed to exercise or possess were heavily contingent upon their access to property.

There were few protections under the Roman law for women and children, and it remains that equality of the sexes and the inherent value of a human being, other than as property, were generally not concepts within that law. Relationships of husband and wife were legally framed as property rights invested in the husband. Statutory laws similar to those in effect in Oklahoma today on many subjects existed in the Corpus Juris Civilis, especially in relationship to various types and concepts of property. While practice, due to societal pressures and activism by Roman women and others, such as with the Lex Oppia, may have blunted the absolute power of the husband over the wife and children in some cases, the primary recourse of the Roman woman and children under the law to redress a wrong was not the courts, but rather the male head of household.

Relevance to Your Legal Case. It is nearly impossible to emphasize strongly enough the effects that Roman law and culture have had on most every nation of the Western world and the laws of those nations—including the United States. The law that is utilized in the modern battered woman's family court case was developed for thousands of years in cultures utilizing laws that placed men clearly in control of the property as well as the persons of the wife and children, to greater or lesser degree, and in societies where concepts inimical to modern concepts of equality between the sexes and of the inherent value of people and thus harms to people, other than as a function of that person as property, were either nonexistent or minimal. An unfortunate reality is that, in some cases/places, the laws, jurisprudence, and practices may be only a little better in modern family courts. If a case is approached from this perspective, the battered mother, marshaling her resources for the protection of her children and/ or herself, must realize that the law has not even appeared to support her position of equality in custody, property division, and in respectful consideration of the case until very recent modern times, and it is still fraught with glaring biases against her in many cases. While some might cite the so-called tender years doctrine (where a young child needed to be placed with his or her mother, which once characterized some custody cases for a short period of time as a challenge to this allegation), even if that doctrine did empower the battered mother in past custody cases to some extent, it certainly does not, by statute in most states, do so now.

A battered woman undertaking a family court case might also consider the pattern of the events involved in the story of the Lex Oppia. The matrons of Rome were advocating for their right to own personal property, and it was seen (or at least cast) as a frivolous and wasteful desire on their part to live opulently and wear costly things. In much the same fashion, a battered woman who is fighting for the safety and security of herself and her children must consider the actual and possible perceptions of the court from before the case is even filed. If her batterer can cause the court to perceive her concerns as frivolous no matter the reality of her concerns or even the evidence to support those concerns, she will face an uphill battle against marginalization of her concerns by the court. Her batterer will almost certainly try to convince the court that her attempts to seek safety and security, to the extent she knows to be necessary for the protection of herself and her children, are frivolous, unnecessary, and a waste of the courts' time, and a conscious interference with the batterer's rights.

With knowledge of these likely possible perceptions and the batterer's almost assured attempts to marginalize the battered woman (this author has seen the shifting of the court's perception about the case and minimizing of the battered woman's respectability, her concerns for her safety and the safety of her children, and her worthiness of real consideration by the batterer in hundreds of court cases throughout his career and in fact in almost *every* such case) she can plan, from the beginning, to counteract these offenses and barriers.

Also, it is important to realize that most courts are far happier and usually feel themselves to be on far firmer ground legally and, for most judges in this author's experience, personally, considering the division of property in a case than in becoming involved in the difficult, time-consuming, and emotionally draining process of determining if domestic or sexual violence to the battered woman or her children has occurred, and thus extraordinary (for a family court case) measures need to be implemented. Most judges in most courts will almost inevitably try to take any and every opportunity to reframe the events involved in the divorce (such reframing gladly handed them by the batterer and his counsel), especially as it relates to custody, visitation, and safety, into property terms that are far easier to deal with and to marginalize or even ignore safety issues.

Many courts start out with this framework intentionally or unintentionally in place and are most often heavily supported by the law and by customary practice in doing so. Such courts will resist many if not almost any attempts to seek safety within the contexts of the divorce proceeding or to limit custody or visitation (which does not contain evidence that is unimpeachable and utterly shocks the conscience and perhaps not even then) and will be even more susceptible to being convinced by the batterer or his counsel that the battered woman's concerns are frivolous, of no merit, and generally obstructive to the proceedings. Such a forum is fertile grounds for assertions of "alienation" or "Parental Alienation Syndrome" on the part of the battered woman by the batterer and come to the view of the court and the judge (and others that may be involved such as social workers, child protective services, etc.) almost completely self-proven due to the paradigm of the usual family court model jurisprudence as well as the preferences and legal training of most judges and legal counsel.

This also serves to illustrate the extreme care that is necessary in the selection of counsel, though most battered mothers go forward with no counsel or have very little ability (due to resources, availability of counsel, or for other reasons) to choose said counsel. Choosing counsel who is, if possible, highly respected in the community and who recognizes the uphill battle the battered mother will face up front, or, if unable to choose her counsel, taking careful but consistent steps to educate the counsel she does have or respectfully educating (or finding those who will educate) the court, if no counsel is available, about the dynamics of DV, the need for safety, and the law that supports her positions *is vital* in most cases. While some jurisdictions are favored with judges who are educated in the dynamics of DV and willing to consider these dynamics in the context of family court proceedings, some jurisdictions may even consider training in DV dynamics to be bias. All sources of legal assistance from local legal aid services, advocacy programs, state coalitions, national level legal assistance groups, and other efforts should be carefully considered in addressing education of the court. Great attention should be paid to developing all possible positive binding or nonbinding but influential court opinions or other influential sources such as domestic-violence–related products of state agencies, national judicial groups, the American Bar Association, etc.

The battered mother also could be greatly benefited by knowing how the court her case will go to has proceeded in the past in similar cases and/or what the proclivities and preferences of the judge in the case are; but, as this is often not possible or extremely difficult to ascertain, she should gather all of the help she can, researching what resources are available at all levels and then marshal those forces from the beginning.

The battered mother must stand up, unrelentingly, for her own value as a human being, something extremely hard for many battered women who have been conditioned intentionally by their abusers to *not* see themselves as valuable. While, in some situations, perhaps as a witness in some criminal cases, a battered mother who seems not to value her own worth might, by some, be considered more convincing of her status as a battered woman, the modern family court, if it even recognizes the battering and harm, is more likely in most situations, over the course of the case, to equate any lack of self-worth on her part to be helplessness. Family courts seldom give great credence to the concerns and assertions of a battered woman who lacks self-worth, and they are unlikely to bestow custody on someone they consider "helpless." Thus, a vital part of every battered mother's team is one or more supportive persons (or support systems) who will support her sense of self and assist with empowering her to believe she is worthwhile. Local advocacy agencies may be of assistance in helping the battered mother.

Law and Practices of the Celts

The Celtic peoples sacked Rome (the Gauls) and were conquered intermittently by the Romans, but very little of their law and practices were embodied in the framework for later modern law systems.[26] The "brehon" or "brithem" laws (loosely "judge" laws)

---

[26] Due to the unwritten nature of most pre-Christian Celtic laws, and the conflicting allegations as to the nature and character of Celtic law in various places and sources, in-depth and authoritative consideration of the Celtic law systems is beyond the scope of this chapter.

of the various Celtic peoples (portions of which were in use in Ireland through the 1500s) appear to have been largely similar to Germanic laws in existence at the time. These laws, like the Germanic customary laws were also predominantly concerned with property and placed emphasis on the payment of compensation for a crime to the victim or the victim's kin rather than on punishment by the ruler. Crimes, even capitol crimes, were generally punished by fines, public censure, or religious censure (which may be the most unusual Celtic addition to law until the canon law of the Holy Roman Church was developed). Banning from religious ceremonies was considered (according to Ceasar) the greatest punishment—somewhat like excommunication in the later Holy Roman Church. Administration of law was mostly by local custom and involved customary law, that is, "the way we've always done it."

How About Women and Children? The status of women and children and their treatment under the law was likely area specific, as the customary law of various places held sway. It is clear that some early Celtic women fought alongside their husbands as did the early Germanic women. Boadicea, or Boudica, an Iceni Breton queen was recorded by Tacitus in the Annals of Rome as having fought around 50 and 60 AD and, for a time, won against the might of Rome.[27] She and her daughters had inherited her coruling husband's kingdom along with the Roman Emperor Nero in an attempt by her husband to appease Rome. The Roman leader there instead publicly scourged Boadicea and had her daughters (and other Iceni noble women) raped by Roman slaves. She fought back and drove the Romans back in several encounters before a final loss to Roman tactics, sheer numbers, and military prowess. Tacitus mentioned other Celtic women fighting as well, all the while apparently glorying in the might and right of Rome in killing them off. While women under the Celtic law may or may not have always fared well, they were certainly likely to have fared better under Celtic law and culture than under the law and might of Rome.

Relevance to Your Legal Case. While the Celtic law likely had little influence on the further development of the modern law used in U.S. family courts today, the events described above showed yet another highly quoted Roman author relating, with apparent relish, the destruction of a female leader. With such authors so widely read by many during the course of the development of Western law and jurisprudence, it again points out and exemplifies the biases inherent in the development of those systems towards women and the "proper" place for women in society. It may also be worth considering if societies, based on such laws and willing to take such steps against women, might not affect the women and men in those societies, over time, to accept these ways as correct and normal, much as a batterer, over time, through various methods of intimidation convinces his victim that she is of no worth and convinces her (or tries to) that obeying him is the correct and normal way of the world.

Information in this section derives from the author's own accumulated knowledge of Celtic legal issues as well as reference to multiple sources. For reference and inclusion of other sources, see "Celtic Law," in *Wikipedia—The Free Encyclopedia,* http://en.wikipedia.org/wiki/ Celtic_law, Raimund Karl, *A Short Summary,* http://draeconin.com/database/celtlaw.htm, and F. Kelly, *A Guide to Early Irish Law. Early Irish Law Series vol. III* (1988, 2d reprint 1995).

[27] Alfred John Church & William Jackson Brodribb trans., *The Works of Tacitus, Great Books of the Western World* bk. XIV, at 29–37 (1952, 29th printing 1987); *See also* H. Mattingly & S.A. Handford, *The Agricola and Germania,* "Tacitus, 16," at 66 (1948, rev. 1970).

Law and Practices of the Early Germanic Peoples

Early Germanic peoples sacked Rome several times and were the ancestors of the later Germanic rulers of the Western Holy Roman Empire.[28] As these peoples conquered, they brought their own systems of law with them, each grouping having their own laws. These laws were largely customary and seldom recorded. Recourse for a wrong was generally to a local moot or "thing," which stood in judgment on certain issues—mostly related to property and crimes against persons. In these cultures, a man was required to seek retribution for damages to himself or his family and the local things were likely set up to help arbitrate these disputes and avoid blood feuds. Money or "wergilt" was the mechanism by which a man or his life or his honor was valued and then paid by the offender to the man or his family. Things, composed of many people from local communities, made decisions according to local customary law and the values of the culture. The victorious party in a decision by a thing must enforce his or her own judgment entirely.

As the Germanic peoples mixed with the Roman conquered, they accepted some Roman law, and some Germanic/Gothic kings issued partial Roman law compilations. Generally and initially, however, Roman law was utilized for Romans, and German law for was utilized for the Germanic people. Payment of wergilt for crimes including murder of another, trial by combat/proof by battle (or wager of battle), and ordeals to prove guilt or innocence, representation by champions, and oath swearings by numerous witnesses in support of the accused were features of the Germanic laws that prompted medieval and later authors to consider it to have a "sensuous" or dramatic element. This, to later legal scholars, was considered to make these Germanic law systems inferior to the Roman law system; however, the modern system of law and jurisprudence in the United States likely partially derives modern tort issues, where money substitutes for human pain and suffering, from wergilt concepts, testimony by witnesses under oath for the accused and concepts of the weight of testimony from oath swearings, the jury of peers from having local persons hear the case, attorneys as champions for litigants with a duty to zealously represent their client in modern adversarial litigation from trial by combat, and the drama of cross-examination so beloved by modern television to determine the truth of the matter, from these dramatic or sensuous Germanic practices and concepts.

How About Women and Children? The treatment and legal recourses of women likely varied greatly as would be expected with customary law in many different places. Roman women living under the rule of Germanic kings, if married to a Roman man were still usually under Patria Potestas (see "Laws and Practices of Rome"). Early Germanic women were likely members of the things and could speak along with the men in the earlier periods. If Tacitus is to be believed, early German men revered and respected women and worked with them as two valued parts of a family unit far more extensively than did most other societies of the time.[29] Germanic women could own property in these earlier periods and may have been able to engage in commerce themselves. Merchant scales have been found in the graves of some Viking women,

---

[28] Merryman, Clark & Haley, *supra* note 12, at 265–73, referencing Paul Vinogradoff, *Roman Law in Medieval Europe* 13, 15–18, 24–29 (2d ed. 1929); Harold J. Berman, *Law and Revolution: The Formations of the Western Legal Tradition* 52–59, 76, 81, 297–98 (1983). *See also* 22 *New Encyclopaedia Britannica*, *supra* note 5, at 922–23.

[29] Mattingly & Handford, *supra* note 27, "Tacitus, 16," at 107–08.

Germanic women managed the home and farm while the men were away, and they held the keys to the family food stores. Evidence exists that they had greater influence in the homes than their non-Germanic counterparts at the time. Noble women in nomadic early Germanic households were held in high esteem, and women were consulted in many matters including battle.[30]

Relevance to Your Legal Case. Women's struggles to own property, to seek redress for injuries, and to obtain any form of equality have had a long and often bitter history. Though the law of the Germanic peoples had quite a large influence on the beginnings of modern Western law traditions, the Roman law had a greater influence and was largely incorporated over time to replace the more female reverent aspects of the early Germanic law and culture.

Battered mothers might wish to consider how the "sensual" and "dramatic" aspects of early Germanic law, so degraded by many legal scholars, have filtered down into our present legal system and can affect their cases. Family court judges, as with most of society, are conditioned by years of history, law, and jurisprudence to accept money as payment for injuries. In the family court case, some judges, trained in tort and most other property-oriented areas of the law, may, if they see the domestic or sexual abuse as worthy of merit at all, see payment of money by the batterer as the most appropriate way for the batterer to make recompense. Frequently these courts will shy away from what they may see as applying penalties in the areas of custody or visitation and find any recompense for the harms done to the battered mother or her children in the property issues of the case, which misses the point and continues the property paradigm for the case. Further, after such recompense is made, it is well established in legal training that the penalty has then been paid, and all is thus made right; there is no revisiting it. Shifting the paradigm from concentration on property to a paradigm balanced between safety, social justice, and property is, perhaps, one of the greatest battles battered mothers, their children, or their advocates will have with the family court.

The concept of weight of evidence should be given serious consideration. Though many judges will attest that they do not wish to see numerous witnesses and exhibits in a family court matter because of the time involved, many may still be, by the nature of their legal training, convinced to take more favorable action by witnesses who have testimonial evidence that can be presented on the matter, as well as by expert witnesses and other evidentiary exhibits of both a binding and merely influential nature, which support the battered mother's position. Knowing whom these witnesses are, what their relevant testimony will be, and what these pieces of evidence are, their relative value, and when/how they can be used in the battered mother's legal case is a vital step in the battered mother's attempt to marshal her forces and present her case.

Finally, the representation by champions, which clearly evolved into our modern system of utilizing attorneys as champions of the causes of each side of a legal conflict, bears serious consideration. While most courts will assure anyone that the courtroom and the judge is no respecter of persons, experience in many courtrooms has taught this author that the reputations of the attorneys involved in a case can have a great bearing on the outcome. Such champions who do not zealously advocate for their clients (because the battered mothers cannot pay their fees, or they see an uphill battle in court, or because they feel the case cannot be won in front of a particular judge, or they are just tired of the case) face few if any repercussions for not doing so. Another harsh reality for a battered mother is that, at

---

[30] O.B. Duane, *Chivalry* (1997).

the end of the legal court day, the abuser will likely have enjoyed the fight that drained her emotionally and spiritually and likely placed her and her children in increased danger from him, and the abuser may possibly still be allowed by the system to exercise great control over her life and the life of their children in the form of joint custody and/or visitation. The judge, tired of dealing with the case, will largely wash his/her hands of the matter and will sublet the day-to-day difficulties of dealing with any disagreements in the case to a largely highly paid, untrained person with his/her own prejudices and little knowledge of the parties and the matters. It is no cause for wonder that many battered mothers feel not only that they are revictimized again by the court system, but that they have fought a long and hard battle against incredible odds. They have!

Law and Practices of the Holy Roman (Germanic) Empire—The First Reich

From the coronation of Charlemagne in December of 800 and the extensive conquests of Germanic lands of a successor, Otto the Great (who received the title Holy Roman Emperor from the Pope after taking Rome) until the abdication of Francis II of France in 1806 during the Napoleonic Wars, the Holy Roman Empire existed, in one form or another, and heads of state of Europe would vie to be crowned Holy Roman Emperor. Many felt they thus would be the recipient of both the continuation of the great glory of the Old Roman Empire and the divine head of state through the Holy Roman Church. Some may have felt that, in doing so, they were literally continuing the glory of the Roman Empire, and religiously they were postponing or preventing the Christian Armageddon by postponing the prophecy of Daniel in the Hebrew/Christian Old Testament that the final battle of Armageddon would come after Rome fell.[31]

Two very different philosophies of what made law binding, one from Germanic, possibly Celtic and certainly indigenous roots and the other from Roman law concepts as adapted by the Holy Roman Empire of the day, struggled for supremacy. The first philosophy was that of customary, local, or indigenous law; a group's consent to a particular practice was needed to create a binding rule.[32] In this, perhaps the seeds of the later U.S. Declaration of Independence that, after describing the inalienable rights of life, liberty and the pursuit of happiness, declared "That to secure these rights, Governments are instituted amongst men, deriving their just powers from the consent of the governed."[33] The second philosophy was that the Holy Roman Emperor had inherited the glory of the Roman Empire (i.e., conquered it), that it and its functions were sacred, and that, as the emperor was by divine authority the supreme secular monarch of the world and the Pope of the Holy Roman Catholic Church, the divine religious ruler law derived its binding authority from that authority. The Holy Roman Emperor Constantine I clearly chose Roman law and the second philosophy and decreed that customary law could not deviate from the positive written law of the state.[34] Once again, concepts of individual rights and consent of the people in governance were buried for many centuries.

---

[31] Merryman, Clark & Haley, *supra* note 12, at 273–75, referencing Clark, *supra* note 12, at 653, 661–67.

[32] Merryman, Clark & Haley, *supra* note 12, at 274, referencing Clark, *supra* note 12, at 653, 661–67.

[33] The U.S. Declaration of Independence, *available at* http://www.archives.gov/exhibits/charters/declaration_transcript.html.

[34] Merryman, Clark & Haley, *supra* note 12, at 273–75, referencing Clark, *supra* note 12, at 653, 661–67.

During the tenth, eleventh, and twelfth centuries within the Holy Roman Empire, the Colleges of Law at Bologna elsewhere in Italy and later in France arose and began using and studying the Roman law of the Corpus Juris Civilis. Such law scholars were in great demand by the princes of the empire and elsewhere.[35] The Italian legal science of those called the glossators and the commentators had a huge impact on later law in both Europe and England. Glossators acted as law teachers primarily, but they also gave legal opinions, acted as advocates in lawsuits, and resolved disputes as judges. They created glosses, law treatises, and considered the Corpus Juris (or body of the law) to be a truly organic living body of the law. Main sources of secular law concepts were the Bible, Corpus Juris Civilis, other Roman law, and Aristotle. The commentators of legal science (and canonists of the Holy Roman Church) developed new law in criminal law, choice of law, matrimonial property, land utilization, commerce, and procedure. They also favored Aristotle's concepts of logic and reason in the law, religious and canonical works of Accursius, Gratian, and St. Thomas Aquinas, and the philosophies of Plato.

How About Women and Children? Generally law related to women, children, divorce, and marriage were almost exclusively within the province and jurisdiction of the Holy Roman Church (see "Law and Practices of the Holy Roman Church/Canon Law"). In the secular law, women and children had no property rights and were, to some extent, the property of the male heads of household,[36] as influenced by the Roman law. Sexual assault crimes in the Middle Ages were prosecuted as a loss of wealth to the father. A daughter's virginity and a wife's virtue were considered her most valued asset. A truly horrid but generally accurate analogy is that a daughter's virginity was treated as property much like the value of a new car still on the lot today. Once the car had been driven off the lot, it lost a great deal of its value. Once a girl lost her virginity, she also was believed to have lost much of her value. It was generally accepted that men would only want, or pay the highest price in political or money currency for a new car, that is, a virgin bride. So, secular punishments were for loss of wealth to the father, not damage to the girl's psyche or her pain and suffering.

Relevance to Your Legal Case. With the increasing appreciation for Roman law and reliance upon Roman and Greek authors concerning law and reason, it is likely the Roman/Athenian Greek lack of respect for women (by modern standards at least) became enmeshed ever more firmly in the laws and cultures of the times. During these times, the beginnings of the two great Western law traditions were born, the civil law tradition, present today in most of Europe, Louisiana, and taken to various other places over time, and the common law tradition (more appropriately viewed as judge-made law than necessarily as customary law) in use in present-day Britain and in most British Empire former holdings including the United States. The secular law jurisprudence that developed during the birth of legal science did not, generally, deal with family law matters except as, or in relation to, property concerns. If modern family courts are based to some extent on the jurisprudence and legal/social philosophies as they were developed through the secular law of this time and refined under the common law, it is of little surprise that modern U.S. family courts may not be, by their very genesis, good forums for dealing with social justice and safety-seeking issues as opposed to division and adjudication of property.

---

[35] Merryman, Clark & Haley, *supra* note 12, at 281–85, referencing Clark, *supra* note 12, at 653, 661–67

[36] Merryman, Clark & Haley, *supra* note 12, at 274, referencing Clark, *supra* note 12, at 298–300, referencing Berman, *supra* note 28, at 222–23, 226–34, 237–41, 245–48, 250–53.

Law and Practices of the Holy Roman Church/Canon Law

Simultaneous with the development of a *jus commune* (or community of the law) with the birth of Italian legal science in the secular world, Holy Roman Church scholars were developing canon law based on the Bible, St. Thomas Aquinas, the writings of Accursius and the monk Gratian, secular Roman law, and Platonic concepts.[37] Canon lawyers, mostly monks and priests, were considered as respectable as the up and coming members of the secular legal profession and were trained side by side with their secular counterparts in the colleges of Italy and later France. Canonists developed new law in criminal law, procedure, choice of law, matrimonial property, land utilization, commerce, and created corporate law entirely with the church having been declared by the secular rulers a corporate body.

While the secular rulers, from the Holy Roman Emperor on down, exercised rulership over the law in many instances, there were certain areas in which the Holy Roman Church and the canon law of the church were given exclusive or nearly exclusive dominance including personal jurisdiction over the poor, widows, orphans, students, clergy and their households, crusaders, Jews in legal conflict with Christians and travelers (including merchants and sailors), subject matter jurisdiction over all matters spiritual, and sacraments, testaments, benefices, pledges of faith, the Church itself, and sins. Family law initially developed under canon law as derived from the sacrament of marriage (which according to canon law could not be sundered but could be declared to have been void from the beginning. Inheritance, property law in the modern sense, contract law, criminal and tort law, and corporate law all developed from church jurisdictions over matters. Appeals could be made to church canon law when secular court's decisions resulted in "default of secular justice" allowing appeals based on justice/equitable principles. Gratian, a Church monk, clearly delineated a system in which divine law, as represented by the Bible was of primary significance; natural law, developed from reason, and human ethical considerations were secondary; secular human law derived from written human law; and the edicts of rulers was tertiary theoretically in importance and in binding legal power. Secular law, of course, frequently fought this paradigm.

Canonists also made many other contributions to modern law and practice only a few of which are mentioned here. Canonists developed the concept and practice of legal representation of another without assuming that person's legal position or assuring their obligations. Simplified procedures for the poor or the oppressed were integral to Holy Roman Church courts; these were original access to justice concepts. Canon law also developed (and later inspired the modern American concepts of) privilege and to some extent confidentiality, derived initially in part, if not wholly from church concepts of the sanctity of the confessional. The concept of sanctuary by the church within church premises, respected by most monarchs during these times, devolved, in much weakened form, into a place where a person, such as a battered mother and her children, can go to be safe, similar to a battered women's shelter, etc.

---

[37] Merryman, Clark & Haley, *supra* note 12, at 294–97, referencing Clark, *supra* note 12, at 294–97, referencing Clark, *supra* note 12, at 653, 661–667; *see also* Merryman, Clark & Haley, *supra* note 12, at 298–307, referencing Berman, *supra* note 28, at 222–23, 226–34, 237–41, 245–48, 250–53; 22 *New Encyclopaedia Britannica, supra* note 5, at 924.

How About Women and Children? Church promotion of monogamous marriage by free will of both parties seemed to be good; however, neither party could break the covenant of marriage thereafter, and arranged marriages continued, most likely without the consent of the woman or girl involved. On the other hand, before the 1500s and the Council of Trent, no priest was even required to create a valid marriage; crossing the threshold by both parties by mutual consent was enough, and a father's permission was not required by the Holy Roman Church to formalize a marriage. While the church required consent from both parties to formalize a marriage contract, in practice the consent of the husband sufficed for both in most instances.[38] Some protections were afforded under canon law to women, including the concept that marriage obligations were mutual. Unfortunately, that jurisprudence did not develop simultaneously in the secular law, and men were not held to the same standards as women.

Secular Middle Ages law severely restricted female ownership of property. The Holy Roman Church required a dowry (not to be depleted during marriage) to care for a widow or orphan, which property the church controlled as it chose in such instance. Canon law required the wife and legitimate children to be included in inheritances and allowed women (as could men) to tender their property by verbal wills to their confessor. Still, instances of graft and ignoring the law are synonymous with the secular and religious authorities of the times. Though canon law governed issues of marriage, canon lawyers were trained in the predominantly Roman law-influenced law schools and laws of the times complete with the built-in bias and objectification of women and children.

Relevance to Your Legal Case. Simply put, it is important to realize that canon law was developing the early jurisprudence on most subjects with which the modern family court is concerned. Due to later breaks from the Holy Roman Church by monarchs in England and lack of ecclesiastical courts in the early United States, little of the jurisprudence developed in canon law seemed to devolve into the secular common law (or into U.S. law at all),[39] with the possible exception of principles of taking "defaults of secular justice" or insufficiency of the law to the courts of equity and the modern U.S. concept of common law marriages. Many battered mothers are unable to afford the extreme expenses associated with long and complex family law cases in modern family courts, but the jurisprudence for applying to have fees waived for the court-specific costs of these actions (applications in *forma pauperis*) was developed in canon law predominantly.

Without recourse to canon law, access to justice issues becomes more difficult for family courts, and many such courts are loathe to grant such applications. The general philosophy in courts of law that each individual should pay his or her own way resists such measures as *pauperis* affidavits, pro se (or self) representation, and simplified procedures for those unable to afford attorney representation. Such measures are seldom available and even less likely to be granted in many family courts. Even measures that are or may be required by law, such as providing sign or foreign language interpreters, in many places may be sparingly provided or simply not enforced in some jurisdictions. The concepts and jurisprudence of making a court's proceedings accessible to the poor or the illiterate is in stark contrast to the jurisprudence of the courts of law from which our family courts are generally derived, which attempts to always apply the same procedure to everyone and highly discourages and penalizes failure to follow all required procedures.

---

[38] Merryman, Clark & Haley, *supra* note 12, at 299, referencing Berman, *supra* note 28, at 222–23, 226–34, 237–41, 245–48, 250–53.

[39] Lawrence M. Friedman, *A History of American Law* 140 (Rev. ed. 2005).

English Common Law and Early English and American Colonial Systems of Law and Jurisprudence

In the aftermath of conquest of the originally Germanic-based Saxons in England by the originally Germanic/Scandinavian-based Norman Harold the Conqueror, after the battle of Hastings in 1066, the Norman kings who came after him needed a way to deal with the property of the conquered and assure property succession by the conquerors. From that beginning, the feudal system of England and the generation of the common law tradition and its systems was based on property rights and instituted to insure the safety and security of land for the wealthy and nobility.[40]

Judges began to get paid to hear certain property cases and began to build up the law with their decisions. These courts were the safeguards of landholding and thus were the basis of the wealth of the noble and notable families as well as the churches. There was a native law, generally common to all of England, that was not as affected by the Romanization of the law traditions of the Continent.[41] This was the beginning of the English common law tradition. Judges could and did change the law much as judicial activism has sometimes changed the course of society in America in modern times.

To allow enforcement of laws against the high nobility, higher/appellate courts, came into being over time and allowed the less highly placed judges to resort to other high nobles, perhaps trained in the law, for ratification or nonratification of their decisions. Juries of peers were inherent to the common law process, but during the Renaissance, they were frequently thought to be "rigged and bought." Influence from the developing civil law tradition did come to England in the form of the ecclesiastical/church/canon law courts such as courts of chancery in which the chancellor was almost always a church bishop. The Star Chamber was another such court that developed from the king's Privy Council and became at first a well-loved court of recourse, especially for its expedited proceedings and avoidance of supposedly "rigged and bought" juries. The Star Chamber did not utilize juries in its decisions, and its deliberations were held "privily," that is, secretly to the general populace and even those accused.[42] Practices like those of the Star Chamber (in support of considerations of religious freedoms) were a root cause for the dissatisfaction of the early American colonists, as there was often no way for them to affect or often even to hear the deliberations of the court. The Star Chamber would hear issues with only judges and legal representatives present and were hated by many early American colonists, especially Puritans.

How About Women and Children? The law related to women and children was not, for the most part, greatly different under the English common law. While secular common law handled issues relating to women similarly to the law in Europe, common law did not have a direct counterpoint for canon law, until the English Court of Chancery came into existence. While such courts may have provided justice for some women and children in limited instances, it was clear in later times that the Court of Chancery was interested in preserving the father's rights only, at least in some arenas. A *New York Times* article published April 25, 1879, alludes to a decision of the court with the following quote.

---

[40] Merryman, Clark & Haley, *supra* note 12, at 347–50, referencing R.C. Van Caenegem, *Judges, Legislators and Professors: Chapters in European Legal History* 114–15, 118–22 (1987).

[41] Id.

[42] Id.

The father may be heathenish brutal and depraved, he may hold opinions atheistic and utterly subversive of moral and social order, and yet retain control over the education of his children. Though the mother is pious and exemplary and solicitous for the well-being of her offspring, she has no law or court to interfere for her. Both father and mother may bring up their children in blasphemy and iniquity, no Court of Chancery will intervene for their rescue. The law and the court become solicitous for the moral and religious welfare of children only in carrying out the wishes and purposes of a father, either living or dead. Against those wishes, or in their absence, it can do nothing, *and it has no regard for the feelings or the convictions of the mother, or even for the highest interests of the child, where they are in conflict with the paternal authority which the law regards as so sacred.*[43]

As the common law proceeded into the early U.S. colonial period, several sources, some much debated, might give further indication of the status of women as U.S. courts developed. Sir William Blackstone in the mid 1700s in his *Commentaries on the Laws of England* stated that "the husband might give his wife moderate correction"[44] and also went on to suggest that this was no longer the law in his day but was still tolerated in some cases. In a Mississippi court case in 1824, *Bradley v. State,* the court refers to Blackstone's comments and the comments of one Mr. Justice Raymond involving a right to chastise (the wife) with a "stick or a rattan, no bigger than my thumb."[45] The court in *Bradley* goes on to continue to allow a husband to "exert the right to moderately chastise his wife in causes of great emergency, without subjecting himself to vexatious prosecution for assault and battery."[46] Perhaps even more telling of the status of women, and far less argued, is another comment by Blackstone, where he says, "By marriage the husband and the wife are one person in the law: that is the very being or legal existence of the woman is suspended during the marriage, or at the least is incorporated and consolidated into that of the husband."[47] He goes on to state, "If the wife be injured in her person or her property, she can bring no action for redress without her husband's concurrence, and in his name as well as her own."[48] Such quotes should be sufficient to indicate the disadvantages with which a woman or child of those times approached the legal system period, no less when the perpetrator of the crimes against her person was her husband.

Relevance to Your Legal Case. Unfortunately, practices such as those engaged in by the Star Chamber can seem hauntingly similar to the frequent, in chambers, deliberations in some modern U.S. family courts where pro se or even represented litigants in family law matters have no idea what goes on in the judge's chambers and where, in some instances, it may be that only the attorneys and judges are allowed to go beyond certain boundaries to deliberate the merits and status of a case or enter judges' chambers

---

[43] "The Paternal Court of Chancery," *New York Times,* Apr. 25, 1879 (emphasis added), *available at* http://query.nytimes.com/gst/abstract.html?res=9905E0D6123EE63BBC4D51DF B2668382669FDE.

[44] 1 William Blackstone, *Commentaries on the Laws of England* ch. 15, at 432 (1st ed. 1765–69), *available at* http://www.yale.edu/lawweb/avalon/blackstone.

[45] Bradley v. State, 1 Miss. 156 (1824).

[46] Id. at 158.

[47] Blackstone, *supra* note 44, at 430.

[48] Id. at 431.

where much of the business of the case may be and often is handled in many courts.[49] Even if the battered mother is allowed to enter chambers, she may not know that she is allowed to do so. The battered mother who has to survive and hopefully secure a positive outcome in a legal battle in a family court should be ready to confront, to whatever extent it is, in her case, safe to do so, such tactics and system bias. If pro se, she might want to consider speaking to various legal assistance programs or even her local law school if such tactics are being used to limit her interaction in her own case.

As the law has moved from the Roman father's right to kill his wife, if he so chose, to Blackstone's commentary about "moderate correction" (which was clearly still tolerated in his day whether it was the status of the law or not) and of the subsumed person of a wife in his day, it is clear that progress in the law is, to a great extent, taking place over time, and many biases are deeply embedded in family law jurisprudence. As in the *New York Times* article about the English Court of Chancery above, in many ways courts have long been clearly biased to enforce the rights of a father over the mother or children. Further, courts of law, generally divorced from equitable remedies are frequently willing, as in *Bradley* above, to continue within the letter of the law rather than make equitable changes for the benefit of humanity (and battered mother's/women or children in particular), or to use law or equitable remedies available to the court that favor the battered mother or allow consideration of the harms she and her children have suffered. It should be no surprise then that the family court systems of today appear to hold biases against and barriers to the positions and cases of battered mothers as litigants. Of importance is to note that such biases are not restricted, as might be easily thought, to the personality of certain judges or legal officers or even to men in general. Such biases are built in to the family court system.

Combination of Law and Equity Courts in the Late 1800s and Early 1900s

Black's Law Dictionary defines a court of equity as

> a court which has jurisdiction in equity, which administers justice and decides controversies in accordance with the rules, principles and precedents of equity, and which follows the forms and procedure of chancery; as distinguished from a court having the jurisdiction, rules, principles and practice of the common law. Equity courts have been abolished in all states which have adopted the Rules of Civil Procedure; Law and equity actions have been merged procedurally into a single form of "civil action."[50]

In contrast, a court of law is defined as

> in a wide sense, any duly constituted tribunal administering the laws of the state or nation; in a narrower sense, a court proceeding according to the course of the common law and guided by its rules and principles, as contrasted with a "court of equity."[51]

---

[49] For example, a warning previously existed on doors within the Tulsa, Oklahoma, District Court Family Court, which generally stated that only attorneys with business before the court were allowed beyond that point, and all pertinent judges chambers were beyond that point. Further, it was, perhaps an unwritten practice, for attorneys to go to the judge's assistants' desk (beyond that point) to report that they were ready for the judicial/case appointment that day.

[50] *Black's Law Dictionary* 356 (6th ed. 1990).

[51] Id. at 358.

American courts of law and equity, previously separate courts in many places, combined in the late 1800s and early 1900s (except in Delaware) under the auspices of the courts of law for all practical purposes. To most legal scholars and practitioners, such a move made sense, and the resultant civil action was thought to be a more ready vehicle for utilization in U.S. courts. Courts of equity developed in the Chancery Courts of England and were intended to provide justice (originally in mercantile and property-related law but later also applied to family law) when the common law courts were insufficient to the task. (Notice that the definition of the court of equity has the word justice in its definition, and the definition for the court of law does not.)

Injunctive and other equitable relief was a swifter remedy than could be obtained in courts of law and could require that something be done or not done if it was necessary to prevent irreparable harms. Harms, and thus to some extent the concept, potentially, of seeking safety through the law was likely developed within the jurisprudence of the equity courts. Unfortunately, when courts of equity were subsumed into the courts of law in the United States, equitable concepts were subsumed into the jurisprudence of the courts of law, a jurisprudence almost entirely developed on concepts of property and money damages or criminal punishment and which concepts are far more related and devoted to a proper operation of the law and to adherence to procedure than to concepts of justice. A modern example of the difficulty of combining an equitable remedy with a family law court devised and jurisprudentially prepared to make decisions at law is seen in the issue of the difficulty of obtaining or retaining protective orders in some U.S. family and other courts, especially when a family court case is involved.

How About Women and Children? Subsumation of the courts of equity into the courts of law in the United States has been detrimental to women and children. Concentration on adjudication at law and strict adherence to procedure rather than constructing remedies to achieve safety and effectuate justice, characteristic of courts of law historically, have made many courts, judges, and attorneys reluctant to consider the value of protective orders and other laws that have been designed to provide safety and assistance to women and children. Though legislation, and other measures seeking to address the social and safety issues of women and children have been increasingly constructed, courts have been slow to support such legislation, and the Supreme Court of the United States has increasingly, in the last few years, made decisions that are detrimental to the safety of women and children and show a focus on procedure, strict application of law, and protection of the state rather than on justice and upholding measures designed to promote safety for those harmed by abusers.[52]

Relevance to Your Legal Case. Many of the equitable and justice concepts and remedies, including pro se representation and access to courts for the poor and oppressed, which have been developed over time in canonical, chancery, and other courts of equity, can be, and often are, lost in practice and procedure in modern U.S. family courts. The combination of protective orders with subsequent family law pits dubious arguments of judicial economy against increased danger to battered mothers and their children. Frequently, family courts and attorneys in such cases will attempt to substitute civil restraining orders (generally unenforceable by law enforcement in many places and often only enforceable in the same court by the same judge in a civil contempt proceeding after a long period of time and further filing and attorneys' fees by the battered mother) for protective orders (devised to be immediately or nearly

---

[52] *See, e.g.,* Castle Rock v. Gonzales, 545 U.S. 748 (2005).

immediately enforceable by law enforcement and usually carrying much more substantial penalties for violations of the order than do civil contempt proceedings) thus greatly increasing danger to the battered mother and her children.

One family court judge in the author's practice area had a clearly stated policy that removed children from protective orders, without hearing, as a general practice in all cases, when a protective order was in place while a family court custody or visitation proceeding was ongoing. The judge felt that it interfered with the parents "getting along" and "getting over" what had happened in the past. This judge was not a woman hater or uncaring as to the welfare of children. He simply believed that his duty in a family court custody case under the law and the general practice of the court was to require the parties to cooperate for the benefit of the children in all cases, and the safety concerns of the protective order had little or no place for children in most family court cases. While he could be brought to relax this position and keep some protection in place for children, in some cases, each case was an uphill battle for the battered mother and the children. His beliefs and practices, or similar ones, are not uncommon in family courts and, in fact, are often supported by practice and state legislation that guides family courts.

Battered mothers entering the family court system should consider, very early in the process, whether extraordinary arguments may need to be made to convince judicial officers that safety is a real concern. In fact, it may be better, strategically, to always be prepared to do so. Deprivation of useful equitable relief to women, children, and men is not infrequent in many family courts. Such actions, policies, and reliance on strict procedure and failure to exercise the inherent power of the family court ignores justice and suggests to future generations that the abuse in such situations and continued human suffering is of less importance than judicial economy or the convenience of U.S. family courts.

RISE OF THE CONCEPT OF HUMAN RIGHTS

From Early American Constitutionalism to Today

Most modern Americans are familiar with what many would consider awful human rights violations during the late medieval, Renaissance, and American colonial periods. Arranged marriages (the father's permission for marriage was often required), children were worked literally to death in many cases, and women were not only subject to physical and other forms of chastisement by their husbands, but were, for all intents and purposes, nonpersons under the law in many ways much as slaves were nonpersons under the law. Interestingly, however, history suggests that the very concept of human rights would have meant very little to most of those in almost any echelon of those societies at those times. Such concepts in the political and legal arenas are, in Western law, largely a product of the American colonial reversion to and enhancement of the concept (at least originally) of government and law deriving its consent from the people. The American Declaration of Independence, U.S. Constitution, the Bill of Rights (perhaps influenced by the Iroquois Constitution), and the later conversations, societal changes, and Supreme Court decisions invoked by those documents showed a society trying to make and embrace changes from the way things had always been or at least had historically been done for centuries.

The concepts of all men (not to mention women or children) being created equal and being endowed by a creator with unalienable rights separate from the state were not and (if ever truly existent in a political body) had not been, for some time, a concept of any popular or mass societal consideration or certainly a general objective of any Western state or ruler for centuries. Though concepts of natural right and natural law had been subjects for philosophical conversation and debate (usually among wealthy learned men and the clergy) for many years, embodying such into a document for a government was generally new to the Western mind. History shows us that law, especially law that changes the way people think, changes slowly when it changes at all. The women's suffrage movement of the mid to late 1800s, which culminated in the Nineteenth Amendment to the U.S. Constitution in 1920 after over sixty years of agonizing efforts, and which granted women the right to vote in the United States, is exemplarary of the significant time required to make or even begin such societal changes.

How About Women and Children? Numerous remarkable cases, politically driven and, in an advocate for social change's historical hindsight, seemingly long after the issues they addressed should have been addressed in a modern society, have shown judicial activism in the United States that affected the way society thinks about or at least discusses and publicly behaves towards various issues. *Brown v. Board of Education*[53] made huge ripples in the fabric of U.S. law and society that are still felt today and gave teeth to a principle of respect under the law for differences in race and various rights in America of people of color, which had been paved by the Fourteenth Amendment to the Constitution in 1868 nearly 100 years earlier (accompanied by the Thirteenth Amendment banning slavery itself as a practice and the Fifteenth Amendment banning race based voting qualifications), but was seldom enforced in practice in many places, and, in fact, heavily eroded in its potential full meaning in law and in practice until *Brown*. The civil rights movement sparked by *Brown* and other issues showed not a culture that was ready for such changes in philosophy across the board, but rather a culture that contained a philosophy that such changes *could be* good and, *if good*, should occur and contained legislative and judicial mechanisms under the law that allowed the law to begin to embrace such societally driven changes (i.e., the Supreme Court overturning previous holdings in *Plessy v. Ferguson*,[54] which supported the idea of separate but equal). Still, it seems unlikely that anyone who participated in the early civil rights movement would be likely to suggest that *Brown* effected a sudden change in the hearts of all Americans or in the status of the law in all related areas. Those doors, in the law and in the society, are still being slowly pushed open.

Another such decision, clearly related to the welfare and rights of women and, to some, children was the Supreme Court decision in *Roe v. Wade*,[55] concerning abortion. While many fine treatises from many viewpoints are available on the subject, it is enough to serve the purposes of this work to point out how the case reshaped the political panorama of the country (every candidate for political office is expected to take and is often scrutinized intensely as to whether he/she is "pro-choice" or "antiabortion") and highlighted the social fighting between numerous factions that continues over the case today (from legislation seeking to erode or support the decision to fist fights in picket lines). Clearly, such social change, whether it is made first in the law and then in society or first in society and then in the law, does not usually come about without great effort and a price tag of some sort attached.

---

[53] 347 U.S. 483 (1954).
[54] 163 U.S. 537 (1896).
[55] 410 U.S. 113 (1973).

Relevance to Your Legal Case. From the suffragists of the 1800s, seeking to allow women the right to vote (certainly a step towards women's inclusion into a broader concept of all men created equal), to the battered mother in a family court today, the effort to remove bias against women in many places in law and society is ongoing. Doors have been opened repeatedly and continue to be further opened in the law to remove bias and seek safety; however, practice has certainly not always followed principle in the family courts. Why?

To illustrate from a recent historical perspective, let us consider how generally effective social and legal changes have come about and utilize the issue of drunk drivers and their treatment by society and the law. During this author's childhood, there was no significant discussion about the concept of drinking and driving. The idea that someone would go to court for drinking and driving was not a cultural consideration, and the idea that there was anything unusual or inappropriate about driving drunk did not exist as a social discussion. It was not a question this author ever observed in society. Mothers Against Drunk Driving (MADD), for example, and others launched campaigns to change these views in society, started the conversation, and changed laws to hold those who drink and drive accountable. Many jurisdictions have bureaus within district attorneys' offices to prosecute the much-stricter laws related to drinking and driving offenses. Some jurisdictions have specialized courts to address the problem. Almost all jurisdictions have training programs designed to change the behavior of those committing what society now clearly considers crimes. Perhaps more importantly, almost any grade school child in the United States can recite a commercial ditty such as "stay alive—don't drink and drive," Many, if not almost all, of them would know, would understand, and could tell, if asked, that drinking and driving was a crime, and someone will get in trouble for doing so.

Why are there such apparent differences between two similar movements seeking safety and accountability in courts of law and society? Why are those who drink and drive (in this author's geographical area and in his experience, perpetrators of these crimes are certainly predominantly male as are perpetrators of DV and sexual assault) considered so much more of a risk to safety and held so much more accountable than many if not most batterers? One reason might be a perception by courts, prosecutors, legislators, and society members that a drunk driver is more likely to hit them or their loved ones—that is, something that could directly affect them. Another might be that drinking and driving is not shaded with the same level of protection by society or the law that the rights of a man in his home or the right to rule his family have been throughout most of Western history. Another reason might be the perception that the property destruction and damage caused by drunk drivers is far greater than that caused by batterers, and such destruction might affect anyone's property rather than the property of the battered woman making it her personal problem not the problem of society.

A last might be that, as recent Supreme Court cases have shown us,[56] the law and even the courts are generally willing to enforce protections for society as a whole or perhaps for individuals as a class, but they are not willing to do so, when the state itself provides legislation on the matter for individuals (perhaps especially battered mothers) who are harmed; and such a case clearly shows that the predominant social and legal opinion continues to be that DV is a private matter and places the burden of protection of the battered mother precisely where most family courts attempt to place it—on her shoulders. Greater inquiry may be called for certainly, but for the battered mother in the

---

[56] Castle Rock v. Gonzales, 545 U.S. 748 (2005).

family court, the potential conclusions serve to illustrate the underlying biases she may face in her case not only with a court, but with law enforcement, social workers, child protection agencies, and even her own support networks and society as a whole.

Demise of No Fault Divorce

Most jurisdictions have converted to a divorce process, unlike under the common law, where there are no or few fault or bad acts requirements to obtain a divorce. All that is generally needed to obtain the divorce are allegations of irreconcilable differences or incompatibility. In English history, courts did not have the authority, before 1857, to grant a divorce under any circumstances; that was reserved for the legislature. Many U.S. state courts followed this with occasional limited exceptions.[57] Afterwards, states started allowing occasional divorces, but grounds such as extreme cruelty, adultery, etc., were required. The demand for divorce increased. Some began to believe divorce was becoming a "woman's remedy." Divorce had not, however, necessarily improved the state of many women. As stated by Lawrence M. Friedman in *A History of American Law* speaking historically concerning this period, "The women in divorce cases were victims, not partners, dependants, not independent women—by and large. Often, they wanted divorce only because it was forced on them by a brutal, absent or philandering husband."[58] Then no fault divorces became the norm in U.S. family courts. No fault divorces were allowed for irreconcilable differences, etc., and have few if any requirements and no grounds needed for dissolving the marriage. Despite the thought that courts would still decide questions as to whether the marriage had broken down irrevocably, in fact, almost immediately, no fault came to mean "*no hearing, no fact finding, no judging at all . . .* The judge was a rubber stamp."[59]

While such freedom certainly has worked to make women freer to end harmful relationships, and while it is not the intent of this author to advocate for return to fault requirements for divorce procedures, the battered mother pays a price for this expedited procedure in many family courts. Despite all of its failings, the fault-required divorce proceedings prior to 1970 required a showing of fault on the part of the person not requesting the divorce. Thus, an environment existed in which the question of bad acts (though not necessarily that of safety) by the bad actor was usual. In modern no fault divorces, especially after the concept of high-conflict divorces became commonplace in the law, that environment either does not exist or is exceedingly difficult to raise in a family court proceeding.

For the battered mother and her children in family court cases, this frequently means the court does not want to hear (and has no legal requirement to hear) about any previous bad acts by the batterer (except possibly where those bad acts were to the children) or to take any action concerning those bad acts. Many courts seem to be telling battered mothers that if there are no fault issues involved with the divorce, ending the marriage is as simple as adjudicating a contract dispute. Many courts may see their role as divide the property, divide the debt, divide the children (custody and visitation), make the parents behave responsibly for the benefit of the children, and move on quickly to the next pressing matter on the overcrowded docket. Few places exist for a conversation about the father's abuse of the battered mother in this process.

---

[57] Friedman, *supra* note 39, at 142–45.
[58] Id. at 377–80.
[59] Id. at 578–80 (emphasis added).

Further, while the concepts of making the parents get along to take better care of their children may have some efficacy in a family dynamic where DV and coercive control do not exist, such tactics, usually the norm in many family courts, only serve to increase the danger for the battered mother, any children, and potentially the court and its officers themselves, when safety is ignored. The addition of a protective order, an equitable measure designed to protect and seek safety for the battered mother, into the family court mix, often meets with detrimental results, as the protective order and its equitable measures are not part of the no fault conversation and process happening in the family court. From the historical perspective, only when the jurisprudence, language, accepted norms, and daily practice of family courts include measures that readily allow safety for victims to be sought, swiftly places injunctive and protective measures in place, and encourages past coercive control and behaviors to be addressed, even if it means permanent sole custody to the battered mother and no or permanently limited visitation for the batterer, will safety be enhanced, children and survivors of violence be protected.

Modern Vulgar/Local Customary Law and Its Effects/Use on Women and Children

Throughout this chapter, mention has been made of customary law. Customary law refers to law developed locally from the society in which it is utilized. Customary law is in no less use and vogue, despite frequent protestations to the contrary by some law scholars, in many ways today in modern U.S. courts than it was in past cultures. While attorneys are trained in the U.S. systems of the law on a federal and state level, most learn, after leaving law school and entering practice, that each and every court before which they appear has its own way of doing things. This customary law (often referred to as "that's just the way we've always done it"), quietly underlying every individual jurisdiction remains, frequently, the law battered mothers and their children are most damaged by. It is also the type of law or procedure that is hardest to become familiar with or discover. It is, despite the statutory or case law binding in that jurisdiction, often *a,* if not *the,* controlling factor in the outcome of a battered mother's family law case. Such policies often survive intense scrutiny under the guises of judicial discretion and courtroom economy.

If the professionals working in the local judiciary are not well trained in equitable principles and the dynamics of DV, or choose not to utilize them, the suffering of battered women and their children is greatly increased, and safety is made practically impossible by the very system tasked to protect them. Many attorneys, including this author, can attest that courts have policies, collectively and by judges, of which an unrepresented battered mother is likely to have no knowledge but can seriously impact her case and the rest of her and her children's lives. Many family courts express a dislike of pro se litigants and will not inform unrepresented battered mothers of these hidden requirements or procedures but hold them strictly to such procedures despite the danger to their safety. The courts often use the phrase "ignorance of the law is no excuse" to absolve themselves of accountability for even extreme harms done to battered mothers and their children.

A few examples of such unwritten laws, which this author has experienced in his clients cases (or more frequently in nonclients' cases where his advice was sought in the midst of the case by unrepresented battered mothers), are given here. The list is by no means exhaustive.

1. Requirements to mediate even when the law in the jurisdiction does not require or even encourage such in DV cases (including penalties or attempts by the family court judge to impose penalties against the battered woman for not knowing she was required by that judge in that court to make attempts to mediate before coming to later stage case conferences but not holding such against the represented batterer);

2. Judges who had clearly stated policies of removing children from any protective order without hearing (certainly if there was no previously filed objection) if a family court case was filed and consolidated with that court either before or after the protective order was final;

3. Courts with signs disallowing anyone except attorneys to go back to judicial chambers and then holding conferences with the batterer's attorney and the judge alone (occasionally telling the batterer's attorney to tell the battered woman what had been decided as the attorney left);

4. Policies in which the judge would dismiss, without comment, all protective order petitions coming before them, which did not include certain statutorily unrequired allegations or which contained children in the protective order when no family court case had been filed; and

5. A judge whose policy was, when children were on a protective order petition, but the battered mother had not yet moved out of the residence where the abuser lived, or the abuser had not left the residence, to immediately call the Department of Human Services and have the children removed from the mother's custody in an expedited manner despite the petition's request that the batterer be removed.

Many more similar unwritten rules or procedures with the same effects as law for the battered mother exist.

Just as judges and other family court participants must go beyond the mere written law to look for equity, justice, and safety in family court cases (especially to provide longer-term solutions to family law cases and heal or safely disentangle complex family dynamics when patterns of DV, sexual assault, and stalking are involved), before the family courts will operate positively for battered mothers and their children, courts must clearly, define, post, and explain unwritten policies or procedures or utilize abbreviated or modified procedures equitably to achieve positive, safety seeking, long-term results. It is vital for battered mothers and their advocates to be aware that such policies may, and usually do, exist in any jurisdiction and with any judge, and they must take steps early in the case to ascertain their existence and to advocate any exceptions available, add such to their case strategies, and be prepared to take measures to seek interim appellate or advocacy measures to combat such detrimental policies. Local customary law can be extremely difficult to navigate for protective mothers.

Pain and Suffering, Human Rights, and the Almighty Property

How do battered mothers and their advocates move family courts away from a jurisprudence of strict adherence to law and procedure, failure to take measures to seek or consider safety, failure to apply available equitable remedies, failure to apply laws or remedies that favor battered mothers, and framing such issues in terms of social justice and valuing amelioration of human pain and suffering? Does the culture of the United States only truly recognize human pain and suffering as a dollar value? Do U.S. courts, family courts specifically, and U.S. laws do so? Torts of assault, battery, false imprisonment, intentional infliction of emotional distress, defamation, rape/sexual battery, etc., are still putting a price on human life, human dignity, and even on murder of women, children, and men. While such may, at times, be the only remedies or relief available to victims of these crimes, and they have value, are they sufficient? What do these remedies, historically developed from multiple sources of law, say about the values of society? Even utilization of property remedies to ameliorate or recompense human pain and suffering are under attack in the U.S legal system. Punitive damages for punishment of the bad behavior of offenders of various types, frequently for causing or contributing to human pain and suffering, face continued attempts, such as "tort reform," to severely limit recoveries when a person is willfully or negligently harmed by another and are looked down upon as remedies and infrequently imposed by courts. Even the right of self-defense is couched in terms of not having to allow damage to oneself in many places; it is couched in property terms not in terms related to the suffering of the individual or any requirements to protect the individual by the laws of the state.

DV is almost exclusively couched in terms of physical injury and harm in the law of most states. While many states allow protective orders to be utilized to protect from nonphysical harassment or stalking of a person eligible for a protective order, these bases are seldom used in many jurisdictions and are enforced far less vigorously, and some courts will not grant protective orders unless the physical harm to the abused person is immense and very recent, often ignoring the past history of domestic abuse and the mental and emotional distress that is often the most damaging in the experience of battered women and children.

District attorneys in many jurisdictions will only consider a domestic assault and battery charge to be a lesser offense when property crimes such as burglary, breaking and entering, etc., are also involved. Plea bargains for these offenses will usually subsume or possibly drop the domestic assault and battery charge, giving no penalty for the physical or emotional harm done to the victim (and possibly damaging a potential future tort claim) but only to the victim's property. The state in which the author lives and primarily practices, Oklahoma, as an example, incarcerates more women per capita than any (or almost any) state in the United States and thus anywhere in the world. Many of those women are incarcerated for bogus check charges (in Oklahoma it is misdemeanor or possibly a light felony for the batterer to beat the battered mother on the first charge and usually results in a suspended sentence, requirements to attend counseling, and occasionally court costs for the batterer, but it is a serious and vigorously prosecuted felony the first time for her to write a bad check to feed her children), for drug charges (again a felony should the battered woman self-medicate with drugs or alcohol and not a felony the first time her protective order is violated), for self-defense from her abuser (it is this author's experience as an attorney and a citizen that a woman in Oklahoma and in many other jurisdictions across the United States, who fights back against her abuser, is frequently prosecuted far more vigorously than her abuser or a man in a similar case), and for other property-related crimes. Property issues are prosecuted in most jurisdictions throughout the United States more vigorously and with less acrimony towards the victim than are most crimes causing pain and suffering to the individual including DV crimes and sexual assaults.

There are almost no reasons a family court would *not* treat children as property to be divided, since almost all of the jurisprudence historically treats them as exactly that. The jurisprudential tenets, which do not treat children as property, cannon courts, and courts of equity/equitable principles, are not in effect in modern family courts or do not receive a great deal of deference or consideration in many cases. Changes to statutory and even case law that make attempts to protect a battered mother or her children are, historically speaking, very new. In fact, some of the remedies available to address DV, sexual assault, and child abuse were not in existence when many family court judges were attending law school. For over 2,500 years, and quite likely much longer, Western societies and Western systems have treated almost all human pain and suffering as property issues.

EFFECTING CHANGE

How do we change the law, jurisprudence, and the practices of courts, law enforcement, prosecutors, and legal officers? Historically, the simplistic answer is "when society makes them do so." There are examples of heroism from the judiciary and from attorneys throughout the United States every day. There are men and women of the highest caliber of scholarship, professionalism, honor, and compassion amongst them in the family courts. The same is true for the legislature and law enforcement and for court clerks and other actors in the modern U.S. system of law. Why are things the way they are then? Why do advocates see what seem to be tragic amounts of harm and injustices accrue to victims and survivors of DV, sexual assault, stalking, and child abuse every day in U.S. family courts? Why, when there are many good laws on the statute books, are those laws regularly ignored or marginalized? Why are issues of "father's rights" and alienation or Parental Alienation Syndrome, refusal by the bench to give sufficient weight to evidence of domestic, sexual, and child abuse brought before it, failure by the bar to bring such evidence regularly before the bench so prevalent in U.S. family courts, and why do these issues cause so much continued pain and suffering to protective mothers and their children? Because more than 2,500 years of jurisprudence, law, societal norms, and accepted modes of behavior say to do it that way, and that that is the way it should be. Less than 250 years of Western political, societal, constitutional, and legal basis exists to say otherwise. Less than 100 years of Western political, societal, constitutional, and legal basis exists to *strongly* say that women and children are anything other than valued property to be treated as such by the property owners. For only about twenty-five years, protective orders designed to provide emergency safety and protection-based remedies to abused persons enforceable immediately by law enforcement have existed throughout the United States.

Changes have been made in this society. Two hundred and fifty years is only 10 percent of 2,500, and we see many people talking about inherent rights of the person, human rights as an international and domestic concept, the right in some jurisdictions (for men *and* women) to choose to elect judges, district attorneys, and legislators, and a belief that governments are instituted among men deriving their just powers from the consent of the governed. Twenty five years is only 10 percent of 250, and we have protective orders based on equitable principles of safety and justice to some extent in every state and legal requirements in some states that family courts consider evidence of domestic and sexual abuse brought before them, that custody of the children go to the nonabusive parent, that batterers should only get supervised visitation, and it is possible for a man to be convicted of raping his wife.

Every day, increased opportunities for the education of society are available. The opportunity to converse with others in society (including family court judges, prosecutors, attorneys, court clerks, counselors, advocates, law enforcement officers, social workers, legislators, court watch volunteers, public officials, businesspeople, and others) about issues of DV, sexual assault, stalking, and child abuse exist. Society can change law, policy, and practice if it is determined and moved to do so. History shows positive change is happening in U.S. family courts. Everyone concerned—battered mothers, their children, advocates, attorneys, community groups, court watchers, legislators, and others—needs to keep up the pressure and remember that this movement is not about finding and restoring what used to be better; it is about creating what has never been. Even in the face of the tides of the system and society backlash against battered women (from courts, fathers' rights groups, lack of press coverage, etc., this movement is creating something new: a new understanding and a new family court system of procedure and jurisprudence that has never collectively or extensively existed in any Western law tradition in more than 2,000 years. To quote Margaret Mead, "Never doubt that a small group of thoughtful, committed citizens can change the world. Indeed, it is the only thing that ever has."[60] Battered mothers and their allies have begun and can certainly, with determination, perserverance, and long suffering, successfully continue to make positive changes in the world and in the family courts.

---

[60] *See* http://www.interculturalstudies.org/resources.html.

Chapter 4

Historical Origins of the Fathers' Rights Movement

by Jan Kurth, M.U.P.

INTRODUCTION

To the casual observer, it can sometimes seem like the fathers' rights (FRs) movement (or the closely related men's rights movement) magically surfaced sometime in the 1980s, as traumatized men, robbed of their children or bankrupted by divorce and child support began to network and organize.[1] However, this view is far from the mark. Just as American civil rights did not begin in the 1950s with Martin Luther King, or feminism in the 1960s with Gloria Steinem, so too does the contemporary FRs movement have deeper roots.

Indeed, in taking the long-range historical view, it soon becomes evident that the FRs movement is actually quite old or, at any rate, much more than a Johnny-come-lately rights movement barking at the heels of larger and better-known rights movements. In fact, FRs have arguably been the norm for most of Western history, which distinctly sets this movement apart from other contemporary movements claiming to work towards some vision of social justice. As Phyllis Chesler broadly observes,

> For more than 5,000 years men (fathers) were legally entitled to sole custody of their children. Women (mothers) were obliged to bear, to rear, and economically support children. For more than 5,000 years, men (fathers) were legally *entitled* to sole custody of their children. Women (mothers) were *obliged* to bear, to rear, and economically support children. No mother was ever legally entitled to custody of her own child.[2]

Nevertheless, this generalization is also somewhat misleading, since for much of Western history, FRs was conceptualized very differently from how they are publicly presented and marketed today—as a beleaguered movement defending the rights of a heretofore unrecognized and oppressed social group, namely ordinary middle-class men and fathers victimized by the family courts. In contrast, for most of Western history, FRs—or "father rule"—reigned as part of a seldom questioned background ideology, as an intrinsic part of a deeply hierarchical world in which individual or civil rights had comparatively little meaning for the vast majority of people of either gender. Despite the plethora of generally misogynistic beliefs and social practices, during much of the premodern period, when women had very few legal or political rights, an articulated political movement defending the "rights" of men would have been something of an oxymoron.

In this stricter sense, the beginnings of a men's rights ideology as such would not come into being until the nineteenth century, when it was launched as a counterreaction to the first wave of organized feminist or women's rights activism. Historically, the FRs movement has a radically different impetus and origin than other reformist movements rooted in the nineteenth century, which were fundamentally opposed to father rule in orientation. As a result, the FRs movement has, at best, a problematic relationship to traditional father rule (with its essential indifference to democratic values and human rights). This presents a unique contradiction or challenge to its self-styled "grievance-based" politics.

Not surprisingly, this ambivalence is played out most prominently in the contemporary FRs movement positions on child custody and family violence.

---

[1] "Men's rights" here refers to antifeminist men's groups, not to the pro-feminist men's groups that are often derogatorily dismissed as "collaborationists" or "manginas" by the antifeminist groups. Men's rights and FRs are here used interchangeably, as they are basically represented by the same advocates.

[2] Phyllis Chesler, *Mothers on Trial: The Battle for Children and Custody* xii (1987) (emphasis in original).

SURVEY OF FATHERS' RIGHTS IN WESTERN HISTORY

The subject of FRs (or father rule) in Western history is an enormous one. Entire volumes have been devoted to the subject, so a comprehensive analysis cannot be attempted here. What will be presented is a cursory look at the rights of fathers under Roman and English common law and in American history, especially as those rights impacted the issues of child custody and the abuse of women and children.

Roman Law

Roman law laid the foundation for much of the Western legal tradition, including family law. Under early Roman law, the *familia* (from which *family* is derived) consisted of the *pater familias* (the oldest surviving male ascendant) and his male descendants. All persons within the household, including all "free" women, children (regardless of age), and slaves, were under the guardianship and direct control of the *pater familias*. Paternal power (*patria potestas*) was virtually complete and unquestioned until his death, with no legal avenue for contesting his decisions or his competency to make them. In fact, paternal power literally included the right to make life and death decisions about family members, that is, "the power to live or not" (*vitae necisque potestas*).

Not surprisingly, the *pater familias* not only had the power to arrange his daughters' marriages, but also the power to end marriages by divorce. Once married, a woman was not considered a slave per se, but she was essentially her husband's property, a person over whom he had total control. In addition, any money or property a woman possessed at the time of her marriage passed to the control of the *pater familias* of the new husband's family. As Lisa S. Morin notes in *Roman Family Law and Tradition,*

> The father of the Roman family had the power over everyone and everything in the home. This power was legally recognized. If any member of the family behaved in any way that he considered exceeding the boundaries of proper behavior, he had the power to punish the offender with harsh sentences, such as: banishment, slavery, and death. This power extended to the man's slaves and tenant farmers as well. Only the *pater familias* had the right before law to buy, sell, or hold property. He owned, as agent and trustee, all the property of the extended family and held absolute power over persons within his household. As long as the *pater familias* was alive, the sons could not own property or have legal authority over their own children.[3]

Not surprisingly, male children were strongly favored over females, although both were subject to infanticide or abandonment upon the whim of the *pater familias*:

> One old law states that fathers had to raise all of their sons but only their first daughter. . . . Right after a child was born it was laid at its father's feet and if the father took it into his arms, it was his and became part of the family. Otherwise the child would be disowned and left on the street to die or to be taken by slave traders.[4]

---

[3] Lisa S. Morin, *Roman Family Law and Traditions* (University of Alabama Department of Modern Languages and Classics), http://bama.ua.edu/~morin002/.

[4] Id.

However, this state of affairs did not always rest easily among Romans. No less than the historian Dionysus was appalled that "the atrocious power of putting his children to death, and of selling them three times in an open market, was invested in the father."[5] (This last comment regarding the selling of children is a reference to one of the "Rights of Fathers" spelled out in the Law of the Twelve Tables (circa 450 BC), the earliest code of Roman law. The "right" actually states, "If a father surrenders his son for sale three times, the son shall be free from his father.")

Needless to say, there was no concept of Roman mothers having any form of legal custody, much less any legal authority over their own children. In addition, there would have been no legal recourse for the *pater familias'* abuse of any family member—male or female, child or adult—not even if it resulted in death.

English Common Law

English common law, as summarized by the famous jurist Sir William Blackstone, reflected many of the tenets of Roman law, albeit with some moderation. In his *Commentaries on the Laws of England (1765-1769),* Blackstone makes it quite clear that married women (and by extension, married mothers) not only had no rights as such but also had no "legal existence":

> By marriage, the husband and the wife are one person in law: that is, the very being or legal existence of a woman is suspended during marriage, or at least incorporated and consolidated into that of the husband: under whose wing, protection and cover she performs everything; and is therefore called in our law-french a *feme-covert* [married woman]; is said to be *covert-baron,* or under the protection of her husband, her baron, or lord; and her condition during her marriage is called her coverture.[6]

Under such a system, domestic violence (DV) and child abuse (not to mention corporal punishment of laboring people) were essentially sanctioned by law. As Blackstone notes, the husband/master was legally entitled to exercise "moderate correction" or "restraint" of wives, children, and servants. Indeed, some wifely "misdemeanors" might permit more extreme measures:

> The husband also (by the old law) might give his wife moderate correction. For as he is to answer for her misbehavior, the law thought it reasonable to entrust him with this power of restraining her, by domestic chastisement in the same moderation that a man is allowed to correct his servants or children; for whom the master or parent is also liable to answer. But the power of correction was confined within legal bounds; and the husband was prohibited to use any violence to his wife *aliter quam ad virum, ex causa regiminis et castigionis uxoris suae, licite et rationabiliter pertiner* [other than lawfully and reasonably pertains to the husband for the rule and correction of his wife]. The civil law gave the husband the same, or a larger authority over his wife; allowing him,

---

[5] *Quoted in* Mary Ann Mason, *From Father's Property to Children's Rights: The History of Child Custody in the United States* 7 (1994).

[6] Sir William Blackstone, *Commentaries on the Laws of England (1765-1769), available at* http://www.lonang.com/exlibris/blackstone/.

for some misdemeanors, *flagellis et fustibus acriter vererare uxorem* [To beat his wife severely with whips and sticks], for others, only *modicum castigationem adhibere* [with moderate punishment].[7]

It goes without saying that all "correction" flowed in one direction: if the master's wife were to beat an apprentice or servant, it was considered "good cause for departure." In addition, "if any servant, workman, or laborer assaults his master or dame, he shall suffer one year's imprisonment, and other corporal punishment, not extending to life or limb."[8]

After reflecting on the powers of the Roman father, Blackstone concludes that the power of an English father "is much more moderate; but still sufficient to keep the child in order and obedience." Nevertheless, what powers parents did possess were situated solely in the father. The father was the only parent entitled to "benefit of his children's labor" or to bind out a child into an apprenticeship or position of indentured servitude. He was the only parent authorized to give permission for underage marriage. He was the only parent authorized to delegate his parental authority, namely to a tutor or school master. This person was thus placed in a position of *in loco parentis* (in place of a parent) and therefore entitled to restrain or correct a child. "A mother," Blackstone bluntly declares, "is entitled to no power, but only to reverence and respect."[9]

In fact, mothers did not necessarily gain power over their own minor children upon the death of the father: "The empire of the father continues even after his death; for he may by his will appoint a guardian to his children."[10]

Colonial America

Following English common law, colonial-era fathers "had almost unlimited authority of custody and control over their natural, legitimate children, leaving almost no room for maternal authority, at least during the father's lifetime."[11]

Part of the impetus for maintaining such control was that in labor-scarce America, the services or wages of children were considered a valuable economic asset. So, along with all rights of association (which included the right to ship off a child to a relative or another family), fathers alone were entitled to all of their children's wages if the children performed income-earning work. Indeed, it was common for fathers to apprentice or bind out their children—effectively separating them from either parent—at age ten. As a result, most children did not remain in the physical placement of either their mother or their father.[12] In fact, most court records of that era regarding child custody or control had to do with approving contracts for indenture or other conflicts regarding a child's labor and not with divorce, which was extremely rare.

The plight was even worse for children who were illegitimate or born to slave mothers: "Children born out of wedlock were routinely separated from their mothers upon weaning and 'bound out' to a master. Slave children, who comprised about one-fifth of all children by the end of the eighteenth century, could be sold away from their parents at any time."[13]

---

[7] Id.
[8] Id.
[9] Id.
[10] Id.
[11] Mason, *supra* note 5, at 6.
[12] Id. at 2.
[13] Id.

In essence, colonial America was a rigidly stratified society in which all economic advantages flowed back to the father/master—with little but barely enforceable social obligations to constrain him:

> The father/master, clearly at the pinnacle of the [production unit] hierarchy, was obliged to provide adequate sustenance, rudimentary education and religious training to all children (except the slave children) in his custody. The mother was obliged to help him in these tasks. Children were obliged to be obedient and to provide labor as fit their age and legal status. The labor of a child, even a non-slave, was a commodity that could be sold or hired out by fathers and assigned by masters. Slave children, like their natural parents, were sold as chattel. All children were looked upon as current or potential producers; in the labor-hungry colonies, small hands could not be idle.[14]

To summarize, "In the hierarchical structure of the colonial household the relationship between child and father overlapped the relationship between slave and master."[15] And needless to say, even a properly married woman had no legal right to interfere with or intervene in this arrangement, either through common law or in courts of equity. Divorce, which was not uniformly established in colonial America, obviously conferred no additional rights. Therefore, it is revealing that in the very few cases where women did file for divorce, the leading grounds were adultery *and* desertion. This might have allowed them to maintain de facto custody, since the father who "went west" seldom wanted children in tow.[16]

The vast majority of women, however—even relatively privileged or wealthy women—avoided divorce, partly out of custody concerns. One such woman was Nancy Shippen Livingston. As Mary Ann Mason explains,

> Nancy Shippen Livingston, from a prominent Philadelphia family, endured a loveless marriage in which her husband forced her to turn the baby over to his family to be brought up. Since she was living in New York, she could obtain a divorce only by private bill in the legislature, which was a notoriously difficult feat. She considered hiring the dashing lawyer, Aaron Burr, to plead her case with the legislature, but lost courage when she realized that if she won her divorce her husband would gain complete custody and she could be prevented from ever seeing her child again.[17]

As common law evolved, married mothers tended to be appointed the "natural guardian" of their children's person upon the death of the father. But the fathers still reserved the power to appoint someone else as guardian if they wished, and the courts were bound to respect the father's testamentary wishes. In addition, it was still fairly common for fathers to appoint a male guardian to control the children's estate. For many financially strapped mothers, this often resulted in the children being bound out by the authorities. In addition, if mothers remarried, they once again lost the ability to act as legal beings.

---

[14] Id. at 5–6.
[15] Id. at 3.
[16] Id. at 16–18.
[17] Id. at 17.

CONTEMPORARY MEN'S RIGHTS MOVEMENT AND ITS VIEWS ON PATRIARCHAL HISTORY

The historical record is fairly clear: traditional men's rights or FRs was linked incontrovertibly to a harsh social system. The system was typically identified by both the left and the right sides of the political spectrum as patriarchy, which did not recognize human rights as such. This system actually stripped most men of any meaningful authority or autonomy outside of their own homes, with the majority of men being subject to the dictates of a slave owner, master, feudal lord, or monarch. Even within the family or clan, younger adult men were frequently subject to the rule of the eldest male.

Of course, this same system stripped women and children of nearly all legal recognition and at various times legitimized infanticide, murder, violence against women and children, economic exploitation of the powerless (including indentured servitude and child labor), and chattel slavery for both sexes. Despite the shattering social changes brought forth by the rise of capitalism and liberal democracy, the established structure did not begin to erode until the rise of broad-based agitation and social reform during the nineteenth century. This occurred particularly in the areas of abolitionism, women's rights and suffrage, the labor movement, and general advocacy for the poor.

It is nearly impossible to briefly outline the explosion of reform movements that arose in nineteenth-century America or their mixed record of success. In terms of mothers' rights to their own children, however, certain other social changes set the stage for reform. For example, the development of larger-scale economic institutions began to shift husbands and fathers away from home-based workshops or farms. The birth rate gradually declined, perhaps because the relative economic value of children declined. A new emphasis on the value of mothering also accompanied these changes, as children (or at least middle-class children) came to be seen as both inherently deserving of and requiring nurturing and education to better function within an increasingly competitive urbanized world.

Nevertheless, the legal recognition of mothers' and children's rights did not flow smoothly. The Married Woman's Property Act, which was passed by the State of New York in 1848, was the pioneering piece of legislation leading to the gradual erosion of the common law concept of coverture. But the establishment of a married woman's rights to her own wages (in some states) was not accompanied by women's custody rights. While *Prather v. Prather*[18] was the first published decision in America awarding custody of a child to the mother, it was not until *Pennsylvania v. Addicks*[19] that the best interests of children was introduced as a factor in child custody decisions. In this same decision, the "tender years" doctrine marked the legal recognition of the custodial value of a fit, nurturing mother.

Despite these developments, the common law rights of fathers were defended well into the 1890s, especially regarding the custody of older children and boys. In addition, mothers were widely held to much higher moral standards than fathers, even when there was evidence of a husband's adultery, alcoholism, or violence. Fathers still won custody in many of these cases, while mothers were punished for "abandoning" their husbands without "just cause."[20]

---

[18] 4 S.C. Eq. 35 (1809).
[19] 1815 WL 1309 (1815).
[20] Mason, *supra* note 5, at 63–64.

Over time, "deserving" widowed mothers gradually won testamentary rights to their own children, or at least the physical custody of their children. By the end of the nineteenth century, only four states allowed a guardian to take physical custody away from a widowed mother without her consent.[21] However, most states continued to allow a father to testamentarily appoint anyone he liked to be the guardian of the estate of his minor children.

In addition, the evolution of inheritance laws gradually undermined the old bastardy laws, which allowed unmarried mothers the parental prerogatives normally reserved for fathers. Increasingly, illegitimate children were no longer legally shunned and were able to inherit the estates of their mothers. However, insofar as most of these children were poor, they were increasingly vulnerable to "placing out" by the new children's aid societies. These schemes typically involved the exchange of child farm labor for room and board—but without the legal constraints or monetary compensations of an indenture contract. Children of the immigrant poor and the newly freed slaves were also vulnerable to various "placing out" schemes.[22]

Over the course of the nineteenth century, the apprenticeship of young children to skilled tradesman came to an end—as much for economic reasons as for humanitarian ones. On the other hand, children from poor families rapidly filled the new factories as day workers, particularly in the textile industry. Within the mills and factories, any traditional lip service to employer "obligation" came to an end, although the abuse and exploitation of children within the workplace did not. In Lowell, Massachusetts, for example, mill girls as young as ten were subject to fourteen-hour days and then expected to hand over their wages to their families—typically (according to former mill girl Harriet Hanson Robinson) so that they might "make a *gentleman* of a brother or a son." Nevertheless, when wages were slashed in 1836, these same mill girls initiated one of the first labor strikes in the country. As Robinson recalls in her autobiography, "One of the girls stood on a pump and gave vent to the feelings of her companions in a neat speech, declaring that it was their duty to resist all attempts at cutting down the wages. This was the first time a woman had spoken in public in Lowell, and the event caused surprise and consternation among her audience."[23] Unfortunately, the strike was crushed—just like most attempts at organizing labor in the nineteenth century.

In summary, the patriarchal golden era represents an interesting challenge to contemporary men's rights and FRs advocates, with its long and extended history of institutionalized economic exploitation and violence. As will become clear, the historical record provokes a rather mixed response—from avoidance, amnesia, or half-hearted apologies by the more "mainstream" FRs advocates, to outright historical distortion or open defiant embrace by the hardliners.

Proponents' Views

Wendy Kaminer. For FRs apologist Wendy Kaminer, the premodern historical period is something of an embarrassment, a tricky piece of political quicksand best negotiated

---

[21] Id. at 66–67.

[22] Id. at 68–81.

[23] Harriet Hanson Robinson, "Early Factory Labor in New England," in *Massachusetts Bureau of Statistics and Labor, Fourteenth Annual Report* 38082, 38788, 39192 (1883), *available at* http://www.fordham.edu.Halsall/mod/robinson-lowell.html.

deftly. As she concedes, "It's often difficult for a feminist to garner much sympathy for the father's rights movement. At first glance it seems, at best, redundant. Fathers monopolized rights and power for much of our history."[24]After recounting some of the more prominent abuses, Kaminer concludes, "It's not surprising that the domestic subordination of women, under law, helped fuel the nineteenth- and twentieth-century women's movements."[25] Nevertheless, Kaminer makes a brave (if convoluted) attempt to sell the FRs cause to feminists and other progressives on the basis of "fairness and equal treatment."[26]

Wendy McElroy. Wendy McElroy, who is associated with "ifeminists," a pro-fathers' rights group, uses a more clever propaganda trick: she simply obliterates the actual historical context of FRs and then uses a sleight-of-hand to situate FRs advocates among their historical opponents. For example, in an article she wrote about Fathers 4 Justice (F4J), an English group infamous for their reactionary politics and confrontational (if not outwardly terroristic) tactics, McElroy tries to enhance the group's reputation by dressing them up within the historically progressive traditions of "civil disobedience or non-violent resistance." F4J, of course, has neither current nor historical linkages with either tradition. Nevertheless, McElroy attempts to convince her audience that F4J actually advocates "peaceful non-violent direct action based on the Greenpeace model with a dash of humour thrown in."[27]

Of course, to make such a generalization stick, McElroy finds it necessary to omit some of the more "humorous" details. Among these are some of F4J's direct actions, like the foiled attempt to kidnap the five-year old son of Prime Minister Tony Blair in January 2006, or the assault upon UK Education Secretary Ruth Kelly a month later, just as she was arriving at court to testify about an earlier F4J attempted assault against her in April 2004.[28] Nor does McElroy take into account the group's long history of "amusing" threats and intimidation directed at family court staff or family lawyers, such as the group's storming of a family law conference in October 2004 with smoke bombs and flares.[29] Needless to say, McElroy also ignores the "side-splitting" fact that many F4J activists and leaders have documented (and even self-confessed) histories of intimidation, harassment, and violence directed towards family members.[30]

---

[24] Wendy Kaminer, "Fathers at Court," 11(21) *American Prospect* 62 (Sept. 25, 2000), *available at* http://www.ancpr.org/fathers_in-court.htm.

[25] Id.

[26] Id.

[27] Wendy McElroy, *Father's Rights Movement to Get English Invasion,* May 18, 2005, http://www.ifeminists.net/introduction/editorials/2005/0518.html.

[28] For initial British coverage of these F4J "direct actions," see Simon Jeffery, "Fathers 4 Justice Founder Ends Campaign," *Guardian Unlimited,* Jan. 18, 2006, *available at* http://www.guardian.co.uk/uk/2006/jan/18/pressandpublishing.immigrationpolicy; Mark Oliver, "No. 10 Questions Coverage of Fathers 4 Justice," *Guardian Unlimited,* Jan. 18, 2006, *available at* http://www.guardian.co.uk/media/2006/jan/18/pressandpublishing.politics; "Protester Hits Kelly With Egg," *Guardian Unlimited,* Feb. 6, 2006, *available at* http://www.guardian.co.uk/education/2006/feb/06/schools.uk3.

[29] John Martin, "Fathers Arrested Over Conference Protest," *Society Guardian,* Oct. 29, 2004, *available at* http://www.guardian.co.uk/society/2004/oct/29/childrensservices.politics.

[30] As F4J founder Matt O'Connor freely tells an interviewer, "I've put my hands up in the past. I was a shit husband, I lived life to bacchanalian excess, and paid the price." *See* Hannah Poole, "A Parent Has 'Fewer Rights Than a Terrorist,' Says Fathers 4 Justice Founder Matt O'Connor. So Is Dressing Up as Spiderman The Answer?" *The Guardian,* Aug. 30, 2007,

More to the point, McElroy tosses in a historically misleading reference to nineteenth-century antislavery activists like William Lloyd Garrison, who "flouted the law by harboring runaways."[31] Here again, McElroy leaves out several incongruent details, for example, that Garrison himself was an active supporter of women's rights, that the antislavery movement was deeply antipatriarchal to the core, and that Garrison and his cohorts posed a direct threat to the power of the master/father to financially exploit and abuse his human chattel, his own biological children.

Needless to say, passing references to the modern civil rights movement and the antiwar movement of the 1960s are not particularly convincing pieces of window dressing either. Both are historically irrelevant or antithetical to the development of FRs politics.

Richard Doyle. Richard Doyle, generally credited as a founder of the modern FRs movement, takes an approach similar to Wendy McElroy's. In fact, in a 2007 essay published in *Men's News Daily*, he cites McElroy's essay and her reference to William Lloyd Garrison.[32] However, Doyle far outpaces McElroy in the way he juxtapositions FRs and earlier, legitimate rights movements. In what is perhaps his most outrageous and self-aggrandizing claim, he equates the "anger" of men's rights movement activists to "Jews [who] are angry about their treatment at the hands of Nazis."[33] Doyle goes on to name drop other bona fide resistance movements and freedom fighters—Shay's Rebellion, the nineteenth-century labor movement, Rosa Parks and the Montgomery bus boycott, Mahatmas Gandhi, Martin Luther King, Malcolm X, Bobby Sands and the Irish nationalist movement, the antiwar movement of the 1960s—as if to establish the "street credibility" of FRs by mind-numbing repetition alone.

In addition, Doyle is fond of stringing together random "inspirational" quotes from famous leaders, typically without any historical or political context, as if to further legitimize the FRs movement by sheer association. Perhaps the most astonishing of the quotes comes from Frederick Douglass, the famous African American orator, writer, and abolitionist. When Douglass spoke about the need for struggle in the pursuit of freedom, his life and political commitments suggest that he certainly did not have the modern FRs movement in mind:

---

available at http://www.guardian.co.uk/society/2007/aug/30/childrensservices.familyandrelationships. Ex-partners of F4J members have also reported abusive incidents: "Former wives and girlfriends who spoke to the Guardian described relationship break ups involving DV, being forced to live in refuges and incidents in which their children witnessed frightening aggression by their fathers." In addition, while F4J activist Conrad Campbell has admitted assaulting his ex-partner (which his ex-partner confirms), the ex-partner also reports that Campbell was still allowed contact with their son after their break up. *See* Sandra Laville, "Partners Condemn Protest Fathers," *The Guardian,* May 22, 2004, *available at* http://www.guardian.co.uk/society/2004/may/22/childrensservices.uknews. David Chick, another F4J activist, has also faced legal challenges for sending an abusive text message to a woman, blocking her car, and making obscene gestures at her. *See* "F4J 'Text Abusive'," *The Mirror,* June 30, 2005, *available at* http://www.mirror.co.uk/news/top-stories/2005/06/30/f4j-txt-abusive-115875–15681569/. Jason Hatch, yet another major F4J activist, also admits to "harassing" his second wife. *See* James Geary & Bobby Ghosh, "In the Name of the Fathers," *Time,* Sept. 19, 2004, *available at* http://www.time.com/time/Europe/html/04927/story.html.

[31] McElroy, *supra* note 27.

[32] Richard Doyle, "The Men's/Fathers' Movement: Fighting the Good Fight," *Men's News Daily,* June 13, 2007, *available at* http://mensnewsdaily.com/2007/06/13/the-mensfathers-movement-fighting-the-good-fight/.

[33] Id.

Those who profess to favor freedom and yet deprecate agitation, are people who want crops without plowing the ground; they want rain without thunder and lightning; they want the ocean without the roar of its many waters. The struggle may be a moral one, or it may be a physical one, or it may be both. But it must be a struggle. Power concedes nothing without a demand; it never has and it never will.[34]

On the contrary, Douglass's life can be interpreted as an open testimony to the evils of slavery and the abuses of patriarchal power. Aaron Anthony, Douglass's first master/owner (and very possibly his biological father), wrenched him from his mother, Harriet Bailey, when Douglass was still a baby. She later died when Douglass was only seven.

Douglass's few words about his mother, as recorded in his *Narrative of Frederick Douglass, An American Slave*, speak poignantly to the injustice and pain of his situation:

My mother and I were separated when I was but an infant—before I knew her as my mother. It is a common custom, in the part of Maryland from which I ran away, to part children from their mothers at a very early age, Frequently, before the child has reached its twelfth month, its mother is taken from it, and hired out on some farm a considerable distance off, and the child is placed under the care of an old woman, too old for field labor. For what this separation is done, I do not know, unless it be to hinder the development of the child toward its mother, and to blunt and destroy the natural affection of the mother for the child. This is the inevitable result.

I never saw my mother, to know her as such, more than four or five times in my life; and each of these times was very short in duration, and at night. She was hired by a Mr. Stewart, who lived about twelve miles from my home. She made her journeys to see me in the night, travelling the whole distance on foot, after the performance of her day's work. She was a field hand, and a whipping is the penalty of not being in the field at sunrise, unless a slave has special permission from his or her master to the contrary—a permission which they seldom get, and one that gives to him the proud name of being a kind master. I do not recollect of ever seeing my mother by the light of day. She was with me in the night. She would lie down with me, and get me to sleep, but long before I waked she was gone. Very little communication ever took place between us. Death soon ended what little we could have while she lived, and with it her hardships and suffering. She died when I was about seven years old, on one of my master's farms, near Lee's Mill. I was not allowed to be present during her illness, at her death, or burial. She was gone long before I knew anything about it. Never having enjoyed, to any considerable extent, her soothing presence, her tender and watchful care, I received the tidings of her death with much the same emotions I should have probably felt at the death of a stranger.[35]

---

[34] Frederick Douglass, *quoted in* Doyle, id.

[35] Frederick Douglass, *Narrative of the Life of Frederick Douglass, An American Slave Written by Himself* (1849), *available at* http://memory.loc.gov/cgin/query/r?ammem/lhbcb-bib:@field(NUMBER+@band(lhbcb+25385).

At the age of six, Douglass was once again forcibly separated from a caretaker, this time from the grandmother who had been raising him, Betsey Bailey. He was relocated to another plantation where he and the other slave children were forced to eat out of a common trough. After a series of other moves and dislocations, Douglass was finally sent at age sixteen to a "slave-breaker" who viciously beat him on a daily basis, which was perfectly legal and socially acceptable by the traditional standards of the time. Sometime after Douglass had finally managed to escape into freedom in 1838, he met the aforementioned William Lloyd Garrison, who encouraged him to become an antislavery orator. Throughout his life, Douglass adamantly supported the rights of all people, especially the poor and downtrodden, whether African American, Native American, or immigrant.

Douglass was also fully committed to the nascent women's rights movement and participated in the 1848 Seneca Falls convention, which is generally credited as the first women's rights movement convention in the United States. In addition, Douglas was a signatory of its Declaration of Sentiments. Significantly, among the sentiments included in that document was the following:

> He [Man] has so framed the laws of divorce, as to what shall be the proper causes of divorce, in case of separation, to whom the guardianship of the children shall be given; as to be wholly regardless of the happiness of the women—the law, in all cases, going upon a false supposition of the supremacy of man, and giving all power into his hands"[36]

So it seems quite clear that Frederick Douglass was (and is) no poster child for FRs; quite the contrary. To present him as such, if only by association or implication, smacks of utter dishonesty if not outright fraud.

Glenn Sacks. Glenn Sacks, a noted FRs media personality, employs a strategy similar to McElroy and Doyle's yet far more subtle. He simply lumps FRs with another "underdog" cause he describes at some length, namely the labor movement of the 1930s, and specifically the Minneapolis Teamsters Strike of 1934, or the "Battle of Deputies Run."[37] Unlike McElroy or Doyle, there is virtually no discussion or mention of FRs at all and no attempt to link, however feebly, the two movements historically or ideologically.

Needless to say, there is no connection between the FRs and labor movements, either in the past or at present. While the women's movement has had a sometimes tangled relationship to organized labor, there is no discernable evidence that the FRs movement has ever worked in any coalition with organized labor. Nor is there evidence that the FRs movement has advocated on behalf of any legislation that would benefit laboring people, such as laws defending or expanding the right to organize within the workplace, giving the right to collective bargaining, mandating the effective regulation of workplace conditions or hours, providing for the right to adequate health care, putting into place child labor restrictions, or increasing the minimum wage. The only possible exception to the

---

[36] Seneca Falls Declaration of Sentiments (1848), *available at* http://usinfo.state.gov/usa/infousa/facts/democrac/17.htm.

[37] Glenn Sacks, *The Fatherhood Movement & Underdog Social Movements in History (Part I: Labor Unions & the "Battle of Deputies Run"),* Oct. 16, 2007, *available at* http://fathersandfamiliesblog.org/?p=86.

FRs movement's overall disinterest in labor issues has been its general sniping at affirmative action or sexual harassment policies in the workplace.[38] In contrast, the National Organization for Women (NOW)—to cite one feminist organization—has taken broad public stances in support of the minimum wage while opposing the Central American Free Trade Agreement (CAFTA) and changes to the Fair Labor Standards Act that eliminated overtime pay for nonmanagement salaried workers.[39]

Daniel Amneus. The late Daniel Amneus joyfully wallowed in the premodern history of the FRs movement by proclaiming its "civilizing" effects. Neatly bypassing actual historical scholarship or research, Amneus proclaims that father rule (and specifically father custody) represents a necessary evolutionary advance: the beginnings of a "male kinship system" that marked a clear improvement upon the "female mammalian kinship system."[40] Without father custody, he warned, we are left with nothing but the promiscuity of the jungle or the modern American ghetto—both amounting to the same thing, according to Amneus.

> Fathers have to wake up to what is happening—*a change in the kinship system*. Fathers have to realize that if women are released from sexual loyalty to their husbands ("you don't own me!"), men must be released from their vow to provide for them ("you don't own me either!") and must accept the corollary by claiming custody of their children. The fathers' right movement will be helpless until it understands the necessity of this, of playing their Money Card, their only bargaining chip. Claiming joint custody won't do it—it will merely perpetuate the destruction of families and still leave fathers saddled with support obligations.[41]

Amneus also made clear that this kinship change was not some new act of feminist perfidy per se. On the contrary, he saw the damage as dating back to the nineteenth century's "first wave" of social reform:

> The FRs movement must stop what the legal system has been doing for a hundred dred years with dizzying acceleration for the last thirty years, using patriarchal

---

[38] *See, e.g.,*, Trudy W. Schuett, "What Is the Men's Movement?" *DesertLight Journal*, 2002, http://www.desertlightjournal.homestead.com/movement.html. Schuett promotes a "moderate" image for the men's rights movement—only a "tiny minority" of men's rights activists "would prefer women be forced into the submission," she claims, while "most men's groups are interested in gender equality." Nevertheless, the only relevant men's movement "workplace issues" that Schuett can identify are apparently feminist-inspired abuses of affirmative action and sexual harassment policies. It would seem that in that in the view of the men's movement, there are no male workers experiencing stagnant or declining wages, plant closures, mass layoffs, diversion of jobs to overseas contractors, or reduced health care coverage. This appears to be keeping to the men's rights movement's confinement to a narrow backlash reaction to a caricatured feminism, rather than in an honest appraisal of the issues facing American workers, male or female.

[39] National Organization for Women (NOW) positions on Economic Justice issues can be viewed at their Web site at http://www.now.org/issues/economic/index.html.

[40] Daniel Amneus, *The Case for Father Custody* (1999), *available at* http://www.fatheringmag.com/news/case_for_Father-Custody.pdf.

[41] Id. at 139–40.

marriage to subvert patriarchy, but letting women go through the marriage ceremony, then repudiating the marriage but taking custody of the children and claiming the benefits of marriage in their name.[42]

Although cynics might assume that Amneus was something of a marginal figure—the proverbial loony living in his mother's basement—he was actually a more-or-less respectable academic, a professor of English at California State University at Los Angeles, and an expert on Shakespearean textual criticism. (Amneus is notably silent on whether his resurrection of old-fashioned patriarchy would grant a thick hickory stick to university provosts and "correctional" powers over errant faculty.)

Also noteworthy is Amneus's regard as a hero or "patron saint" among many prominent FRs groups, including F4J, Father Mag, Dads Against Discrimination, the Christian Party, Fathers Rights of Western New York, Men's Defense Association, and others. In fact, as Richard Doyle declares, "Amneus is the leading theoretician and articulator of the Fathers Rights (and Men's Rights) movement."[43]

Fathers' Manifesto

Unfortunately, the quirky nostalgic appeal that patriarchy's "golden era" has had for men's rights groups has inspired some widely publicized efforts to accomplish a general resurrection. One of the most controversial was a Fathers' Manifesto that first surfaced in southern California in the mid-1990s. Among other things, the Fathers' Manifesto called for the repeal of women's right to vote and a restoration of full father rule, including father custody—"Recognizing patriarchy to be the greatest creator of wealth, prosperity, and stability civilization has ever known, we hereby demand that our children, homes, lives, liberty, and property be unconditionally restored to us."[44]

As Trish Wilson, a prominent critic of the FRs movement, has documented, signatories include leaders and members of many of the major FRs groups. According to Wilson, these groups include the American Fathers Coalition (a/k/a American Fathers Alliance), Fathers for Equal Rights, The Men's Internetwork, The Children's Rights Council, the Family Guardian Network, Fathers Rights and Equality Exchange, and the American Coalition for Fathers and Children. Wilson suggests that these groups represent not just the noisy radicals, but many organizations considered more or less mainstream:

> Lest anyone believes that signatories of Fathers' Manifesto represent the lunatic fringe of the movement, it should be noted that representatives of the groups listed (including specific signatories) testified at 1995 public hearings for the U. S. Commission on Child and Family Welfare. The World Wide Web site for KidsCampaigns, driven by the Benton Foundation and supported by the White

---

[42] Id. at 143.

[43] The Richard Doyle quote praising Daniel Amneus appears in several places, including the last page of Amneus's book and the Dads America Web site, http://www.dadsamerica.org/ffamneus.htm.

[44] Fathers' Manifesto "Reaffirmation and Declaration," *quoted in* Trish Wilson, "American Fathers: Equality or Patriarch?" 1(3) *Feminista!* (1997), *available at* http://www.feminista.com/archives/v1n3/wilson.html Wilson, "American Fathers: Equality or Patriarch? (no longer available).

House, cites the following FRs groups as participants: Children's Rights Council, Coalition of Parental Support, Dads Against Discrimination, Family Guardian Network, Fathers' Rights and Equality Exchange, My Child Says Daddy, National Congress for Fathers and Children, The American Fathers Alliance, and United Fathers of America. All of these groups have either leadership, membership, or both who are signatories of Fathers' Manifesto.[45]

Nevertheless, many of these groups tried to downplay or deny the manifesto's significance, or to repeal their signatures, when it surfaced on the World Wide Web in 1995.

As should be evident, then, the FRs movement is by no means situated within the progressive tradition of affirming the basic human rights of persons or groups who have historically experienced oppression or exploitation. The movement has never clearly repudiated or denounced the traditional antidemocratic social, racial, and economic hierarchies of power or privilege. In fact, more often than not, the FRs movement is about reasserting traditional privilege (much as the old-fashioned patriarch was determined to do) while sometimes playing dress up in liberal or even radical political clothing.

In this sense, the FRs and men's rights movements are not so much about rights as such, but about regaining or reestablishing some real or imagined supremacy for themselves. In this sense, they are more politically akin to movements that advance a "supremacist" ideology, like various white supremacist groups. This becomes increasingly clear when the nineteenth-century beginnings of modern FRs ideology are examined.

ANTIFEMINISM AND THE NINETEENTH CENTURY

The Right: The "Natural Order" and "Natural Rights"

Although there was not yet a full-fledged men's rights movement in the late nineteenth and early twentieth centuries, there were certainly inklings of a politically organized counterreaction to the progress that had been made by women's rights advocates and social reformers toward improving the status of women over the prior three decades.

As one might expect, many of these nineteenth-century opponents to women's rights were deeply conservative in the most traditional sense: their objections were borne from a faith in the "natural order" and its concomitant "natural rights" that can sound quite musty today. These objectors, the most eloquent of which were frequently clergyman, nursed an abiding loyalty to the old hierarchical order: God over man, man over woman, master over servant, and father over child. It was a worldview that was rooted in a stable, agrarian existence, and, in general, it was deeply distrustful of the disruptive, modern industrialized world as a whole. It especially distrusted modern "individualism" and its democratic emphasis on individual rights at the expense of the "family as a social organism." It held a worldview that was often deeply chivalrous (if naïve). As one plaintive reverend pled in 1884, women's suffrage was a "tacit declaration that the husband and father cannot be trusted to protect the interests of his wife and daughter in political as in domestic affairs, which is a sure method of relaxing his sense of responsibility and loosening the ties of family affection."[46]

---

[45] Id.

[46] H.M. Goodwin, "Women's Suffrage," 43(179) *New Englander & Yale Rev.* 193 (Mar. 1884), *available at* http://cdl.library.cornell.edu/cgi-bin/moa/moa-cgi?notisid=ABQ0722-0043-33.

Needless to say, this particular worldview did not allow for the articulation of a "men's rights" position and such, as it did not openly acknowledge the rights or grievances of any social group, including men. Rather, it was dependent on a seamlessly hierarchical (and antidemocratic) world in which—at least in principle—every group had its place, with its corresponding duties and obligations.

Contemporary Echoes

Peter Zohrab. One can still see glimmers of this worldview in certain contemporary men's right advocates such as Peter Zohrab, who is associated with the New Zealand Equality Education Foundation (and signer of the aforementioned Fathers' Manifesto). As Zohrab earnestly declares,

> Even though men ran the Western World (which I am not denying), they ran it for the benefit of families, not for the benefit of other men. . . . In fact, in some countries and sometimes women were not even legal persons in the sense of being responsible for their own actions! That is surely a privileged status, not a subordinate status. . . . Pre-Feminist, patriarchal society was based on a different model. It was not based on adult individuals as the basic unit. It was based on the family. Each family had a head, and that head was male. The male had the power, but he also had the responsibility. [47]

Will Malven. Will Malven, writing for *Men's News Daily*, recasts the same argument along religious lines.[48] While he assures his readers that he sympathizes "with those of you who have been victimized by a court system that the Left has succeeded in turning into an advocacy forum for the 'victimized group' of the year," Malven also suggests that certain men's rights obsessions are "whiny" and "a totally irresponsible crock of manure." Malven acknowledges that some of his more militant readers may dismiss him as a "mangina" or a "vaginalized man." But lest those readers take up arms in protest, Malven hastens to add that some of these obsessions are basically the fault of feminism and its rights-based thinking:

> The "Men's Rights Movement" is a lie. It is the same old song, just a different refrain. It is based upon the same false premises as "Women's Lib," "Gay rights," "Equal Rights," and whatever "Heinz 57 Right's Movement" has been.[49]

So what is the solution? For Malven, it is quite obviously "God's will":

> Any movement, any effort to achieve fulfillment outside of "God's will" is destined to fail. The ash-heap of history is replete with these "movements," each of which has promised that if you do things their way, you will have a happier, more successful life.

---

[47] Peter Zohrab, *A Revisionist History of Feminism,* http://nzmera.orcon.net.nz/revision.html.

[48] Will Malven, "God's Rights, Not Men's Rights," *Men's News Daily,* May 14, 2007, http://mensnewsdaily.com/2007/05/14/gods-rights-not-mens-rights/ (no longer available).

[49] Id.

A simple and highly relevant example: are women any happier now that they have dominated the social scene for the past several decades? Did "Women's Lib" achieve lasting happiness for those who so devoutly followed its dictates?

I doubt it.

Has the "right" to brutally murder our unborn children made us a better, happier, more compassionate society? Hardly.

The "Men's Movement" will end in precisely the same result, more frustration, more anger, and less happiness.[50]

Nevertheless, it is clear from the comments attached to Malven's piece that his arguments are too subtle, too old-fashioned, and too religious for many men's rights advocates. While the men's-rights-come-from-God school of thought clearly appealed to those who found it spiritual and natural, many others rebelled against the practical implications, that is, that they would have to subordinate their wills or egos to anyone or anything (including a mythical God of the Old Testament) or quit blaming women or feminism for all their frustrations in life. One critic commented that the premise was "trite" while another dismissed it as "hogwash." "It's 'blame the victim,' 'take it like a man' codswallop," stated another. A string of fresh and vehement attacks followed, including accusations of betrayal against "the movement."[51] Obviously, the mythos of the benevolent patriarch—with head bent, dutiful to God and bound to the needs of his earthly flock—did not fit their agenda.

In fact, outside the explicitly conservative or right-wing Christian organizations (such as Promise Keepers, which in its "Seven Promises" pays at least nominal attention to the commitments of men to family and church), such views are no longer popular or consistently adhered to in most men's rights or FRs groups.[52] In other words, while the idea of the traditional patriarch's wide-ranging power base was exciting and sexy, the idea that the patriarch was—if only in ideology—subject to the will of God (or some higher ethical code embodied by the idea of God) and utterly responsible for the well-being of those within his household (women, children, servants, and so forth) was not.

A "Rights" Rhetorical Framework. A "rights" rhetorical framework has come to predominate most men's rights or FRs writings, despite the fact that rights-based political theory is thoroughly liberal in origin. Any truly progressive style of political analysis is based on the assumption of basic, inalienable human rights and on the identification of the actual legal, political, and economic powers of various social actors as they are concretely situated, that is, within their real-life conditions. The beginnings of the men's rights ideology, however, deviate from this model in many significant ways, as was made clear earlier (see "Proponents' Views").

The Left

Despite a slow start, many of the central ideas and tenets associated with the contemporary FRs movement were in fact introduced and developed in the late nineteenth

---

[50] Id.

[51] Id.

[52] For information on Promises Keepers and their "Seven Promises," see http://www.promisekeepers.org/. Critiques of Promise Keepers can be found on the NOW Web site at http://www.now.org/issues/right/pk.html.

century, even though the successes of nineteenth-century feminism were still fairly modest by today's standards and divorce was comparatively rare.

Key to this effort were the writings of E. Belfort Bax, most prominently in *The Legal Subjection of Men*[53]—basically a denunciation of John Stuart Mill's *The Subjection of Women*[54]—and *The Fraud of Feminism.*[55] This latter volume, especially, has often been heralded as the first "masculinist text" and "secular response" to feminism.[56]

While many (if not most) antifeminist writers and theoreticians have been publicly identified with conservative or religious causes, Ernest Belfort Bax (1854-1926) was a notable British atheist and socialist intellectual of his day. Along with the Pre-Raphaelite artist and writer William Morris, Bax was closely associated with the Social Democratic Federation (SDF), a precursor of Britain's Labour Party. For a time, Bax served as the editor of the SDF's official party organ, *Justice.* (Perhaps not entirely coincidentally, Friedrich Engels, Karl Marx's famous collaborator and influential feminist-socialist theorist—most prominently in *The Origin of the Family, Private Property, and the State*[57]—had opposed the SDF's formation in 1881. Apparently, Engels' opposition had something to do with the questionable political commitments and authoritarian personality of party founder H.H. Hyndman.)

In a fashion similar to that of many contemporary men's rights academics and intellectuals, Bax's political writings tend to be characterized by many different styles. His monographs on Jean Paul Marat and on the ethics of socialism, for example, are fairly eloquent and even-handed.[58]

But when the topic shifts to women's rights, the tone turns vitriolic and wildly anecdotal, with frequent *ad hominem* (or *ad feminem*) attacks. In fact, at least one Bax scholar, Ted Crawford, has noted the contrast between Bax's mainstream journalistic work and his "increasingly eccentric views about feminism."[59]

Attack on "Bourgeois Idols." This tension is immediately evident in one of Bax's first forays into leftist antifeminism, "Some Bourgeois Idols; or Ideals, Reals, and Shams."[60] For most of the essay, Bax merely reiterates Marx's theory of reification

---

[53] E. Belfort Bax, *The Legal Subjection of Men* (1908), *available at* http://www.menstribune.com.

[54] John Stuart Mill, *The Subjection of Women* (1869), *available at* http://www.menstribune.com.

[55] E. Belfort Bax, *The Fraud of Feminism* (1913), *available at* http://www.menstribune.com.

[56] See, for example, the entry for "masculism" in Wikipedia, http://en.wikipedia.org/wiki/Masculism. Several other Web-based articles on "masculism" have repeated the same point regarding E. Belfort Bax almost verbatim.

[57] Frederick Engels, *The Origin of the Family, Private Property, and the State Frederick Engels* (1884), *available at* http://www.marxists.org/archive/marx/works/1884/origin-family/index.htm.

[58] *See* E. Belfort Bax, *Jean-Paul Marat: A Historico-Biographic Sketch* (1882); E. Belfort Bax, *The Ethics of Socialism* 1893). Unless otherwise noted, Bax's writings can be accessed through the Marxists Internet Archive Library, http://www.marxists.org/archive/index.htm.

[59] Ted Crawford, *Ernest Belfort Bax Biography,* http://www.marxists.org/archive/bax/bio/biography.htm.

[60] E. Belfort Bax, "Some Bourgeois Idols: Or Ideals, Reals, and Shams," *Commonweal,* Apr. 1886, at 25–26.

(or ideology) for an English-speaking audience, albeit in a rather colorful and lively fashion. With evident gusto, Bax attacks the "catchwords" and "idols" that lead us "out of the regions of mere argument and recognition of facts" and into the world of worship and "deified abstraction" as the "ultimate manifestation of goodness, beauty, and truth." Unsurprisingly, among these "bourgeois idols" are such familiar leftist shibboleths as "liberty of contract," "liberty of conscience," "rights of majorities," and "rights of property."

Anyone with any familiarity with Marx and the socialist writings of that era would not have been overtly startled by Bax's analysis of ideology or how particular ideologies associated with the rise of capitalist nation-states came to be severed from critical analysis or material reality. In fact, as far as leftist journalism goes, the writing is reasonably succinct.

What is startling—and contrary to the beliefs of both Marx and Engels—is that "equality between the sexes" is also rejected as a "bourgeois idol." As Bax declares, when we take on "equality between the sexes," we "tread on sacred ground indeed" if not an out-and-out "vampire."[61]

In deference to socialist orthodoxy, Bax does concede that in some vague, undefined "earlier state of social development" (presumably during the "female slavery of ancient times" or feudalism), women were undoubtedly placed in a "condition of social inferiority" relative to men. With the rise of the "modern middle-class world," however, the "cry of 'equality between the sexes' was raised," which led to the removal of certain undoubted grievances.[62]

As a result, women had not only achieved equality (even in 1886, before British women had the right to vote), but had elevated themselves into a quasi-privileged class with most dire results: the factitious exaltation of the woman at the expense of the man and the middle-class subjection of man to woman. In short, the cry for equality between the sexes has, in the course of its realization, become a sham, masking a de facto inequality.

Astonishingly, Bax fails to elaborate this point across obvious class lines, that is, the relative power of a woman of the capitalist class to a man of the working class. Instead, we are treated to a somewhat fantastic delusion: that a late nineteenth-century working-class woman now had more social and economic power than her husband:

> The inequality in question presses as usual, heaviest on working-man, whose wife, to all intents and purposes has him completely in her power. If dissolute or drunken, she can sell up his goods or break up his home at pleasure, and still compel him to keep her and live with her to her life's end. There is no law to protect him. On the other hand, let him but raise a finger in a moment of exasperation against this precious representative of the sacred principle of "womanhood," and straightway he is consigned to the treadmill for his six months.[63]

In response to this shocking state of affairs, Bax insists, the (hypothetical) "ordinary woman's rights advocate" now sings "paeans over the power of the 'law' to protect the innocent and helpless female," while the law now "jealously guards the earnings or property of the wife from possible spoliation."[64]

---

[61] Id.

[62] Id.

[63] Id.

[64] Id.

To a large extent, Bax's rather fanciful diatribe was a predictable if not entirely rational reaction to the fairly modest reforms that nineteenth-century British women's rights advocates and social reformers had won in the areas of marriage, divorce, and custody—topics that still remain as prickly areas of contention for contemporary men's rights advocates. Over the fifty years proceeding Bax's essay, laws that had automatically granted fathers nearly complete power over their wives and children had been gradually chipped away. Beginning with the Custody of Infants Act of 1839 (also known as the Talfourd Act),[65] British mothers of "unblemished character" were granted access (though not legal custody) to their children in the event of a separation or divorce. This access allowed children to reside with their mothers until the age of seven and for mothers to visit them at arranged times afterwards. It was not until 1873 that access was extended to all mothers, unblemished or not.

An 1857 amendment to the Matrimonial Causes Act[66] gave British wives some rights to divorce, although those rights were not equal to those of the husband (a husband had only to prove his wife's adultery, while the wife had to prove that her husband had not only committed adultery but also incest, bigamy, cruelty, and desertion). The Matrimonial Causes Act was finally amended in 1878, so that wives could secure a separation on the grounds of cruelty and perhaps claim legal right to the custody of their own children. For perhaps the first time, magistrates were authorized to issue protective orders for wives, although the husband had to have been previously convicted of aggravated assault.

It was not until 1884—a mere two years before Bax's essay was published—that the Married Woman's Property Act[67] was passed, guaranteeing married women a legal existence outside of marriage, such as the right to buy, sell, or own property. And it was not until 1886—the same year that Bax's essay was published—that a woman could be named sole guardian of her children upon the death of her husband.

In addition, at the time of Bax's essay, the Representation of the People Act of 1918,[68] which gave the vote to women over thirty years of age, was thirty-two years away. The Sex Disqualification (Removal) Act of 1919, which lifted other common law restrictions against women—such as the right of a married woman to hold a civil or judicial office or to enter a profession or vocation—was thirty-three years into the future. The Representation of the People Act of 1928, which provided equal suffrage for men and women, was still forty-two years away.

The social, political, and legal evidence hardly supported Bax's claim of legal equality, much less of female privilege or domination. But contrary to the painstaking sociological and historical research that Fredrick Engels had pioneered in *The Condition of the Working Class in England*,[69] Bax did not seem much interested in the actual material conditions of men and women. Nor did he seem interested in the actual power or autonomy that derived from those conditions. As a result, he could randomly allege that shrewish women were wantonly destroying hearth and home (though there is a slight nod to the alcoholic husband) while fattening themselves with the marital assets, not

---

[65] Custody of Infants Act of 1839, 2 & 3 Vict., c. 54.

[66] Matrimonial Causes Act, 1857, 20 & 21 Vict., c. 85.

[67] Married Woman's Property Act, 1882, 45 & 46 Vict., c. 75.

[68] Representation of the People Act, 1918, *available at* http://www.parliament.uk/documents/upload/1918%20Rep%20people%20Act.pdf.

[69] Frederick Engels, *The Condition of the Working Class in England* (1845), *available at* http://www.gutenberg.org/etext/17306.

to mention the hard-earned wages of their poor, oppressed husbands. And all this was apparently occurring in an era when divorce was still both very much socially and culturally stigmatized and relatively scarce, since most women had little or no means of self-support. Bax's writings, therefore, suggest that much of the impetus for the men's rights movement was, especially at its very beginning, lightly rooted in real-life conditions and far more reflective of a pervasive social or masculine anxiety.

Furthermore, we see another theme alluded to in Bax's essay, a theme that also was destined to become a central proposal within the men's rights belief system: the prevalence of presumably baseless accusations of DV, with women frequently using false allegations of DV (or child abuse) to achieve some personal advantage. In fact, Bax goes on to argue—by unsubstantiated anecdote—that women abuse children far more than men but are never held responsible for their crimes.

Later Writings on the "Woman Question." Beginning in the mid-1890s, Bax would dedicate entire essays to the harsh denunciation of women's rights, typically with ever-increasing venom and extremism.

For example, in an August 1895 critique of August Bebel's now classic *Woman and Socialism*,[70] Bax is notably dismissive and curt.[71] In still another essay from July 1895, "The Woman Question," it is clear that Bax has raised his antifeminist line to new bombastic highs: "the theory of 'woman the victim of man's oppression'" is now the "'conventional lie of modern civilization.'"[72] Not only were women not oppressed, but they had also effected "a revolution which has placed the whole judicial and administrative machinery of the country at the disposal of one sex." And what was the proof of his assertions? Once again, it is the "complete serfdom of the husband to the wife under our marriage laws."

Needless to say, Bax's so-called evidence is peevish and frenzied. That women should have any rights to their own children, much less a mere fraction of the household worth upon divorce, is clearly intolerable to Bax.

Bax undertook a major summary of his views in *The Legal Subjection of Men*.[73] A listing of some of the chapter titles fairly well reflects the book's contents: "Matrimonial Privileges of Women," "Non-Matrimonial Privileges of Women," "The Criminal Law," "The Civil Law," "The Actual Exercise of Women's Sex Privileges, "Muscular Inferiority and Sex Privilege," "A Sex Noblesse, Socialists and Feminists," and "The Oppressed Woman."

Similarly, in *The Fraud of Feminism*,[74] the chapter headings are indicative of the general direction of Bax's work during that era: "The Main Dogma of Modern Feminism," "The Anti-Man Crusade, Always the 'Injured Innocent'," "The 'Chivalry' Fake, Some Feminist Lies and Fallacies," "The Psychology of the Movement," and "The Indictment."

It is tempting to write Bax off as a cranky historical curiosity, a mere footnote to turn-of-the-century political infighting. However, it is important to realize that many if not most of the ideas promulgated by the men's rights activists of today's era—the distorted

---

[70] August Bebel, *Woman and Socialism* (Meta L. Stern trans., 1979 [1879]) (originally published as *Der Frau und derSocialismus*).

[71] E. Belfort Bax, "Bebel's Woman and Socialism," *Justice,* Aug. 17, 1895, at 2.

[72] E. Belfort Bax, "The Woman Question," *Justice,* July 27, 1895, at. 6.

[73] E. Belfort Bax, *The Legal Subjection of Men* (1908), *available at* http://www.menstribune.com/.

[74] E. Belfort Bax, *The Fraud of Feminism* (1913), *available at* http://www.menstribune.com/Belfort_Bax.html.

and obsessive attacks on feminism, the smug assumptions regarding father entitlement without personal or financial responsibility, and the contemptuous dismissal of violence against women and children—were first articulated and circulated in print by Bax. And further, those same beliefs are still being disseminated in the same confrontational style with the same flagrant disregard for solid sociological evidence or research.

BEGINNING OF THE MODERN TWENTIETH-CENTURY FATHERS' RIGHTS MOVEMENT

The fragmentation and disorganization that characterized the men's movement earlier in the twentieth century persisted even until the 1970s and 1980s. As even some FRs advocates concede, FRs was less a disciplined or collective movement than a collection of disgruntled individual men with a personal beef. As Richard Doyle freely confesses,

> Rival organizations and coalitions came and went throughout the 70s and 80s, reproducing like amoebas. A veritable alphabet soup of acronyms was spawned, theoretically all on the same side in the struggle against injustice, many of them just one man, a typewriter and followers. Meetings were, and still are, held across the country which accomplish little more than venting wrath at ex-wives, judges, and lawyers, now via internet.[75]

Although all social movements struggle with personality conflicts and ideological differences, the FRs movement seems to have had more than its fair share of problems in terms of coalescing around core concerns. This is perhaps because their members do not, in fact, share any common experience of systematic discrimination or oppression. Therefore, group cohesion, which is always an issue in any movement, is particularly problematic for FRs advocates who are often individualistic to the extreme. In general, outspoken and often egotistical spokesmen or stuntmen (like F4J) distinctly outnumber grassroots workers or community-based organizers.

As FRs advocate Richard Doyle concedes,

> In most movements, and especially this one, there have always been differing factions. Many tunnel vision reformers concentrate on a favorite aspect of reform, one that may have personal significance to them. But the philosophical differences are not nearly as great as the personal ones. Activists often act like crabs in a bucket, dragging back down any others climbing to the top. Some have egos the size of the Hindenburg, but without the intelligence to match. This type pursues private fantasies of being the Messiah who will bring us out of the wilderness. Each rooster is king on his own dung heap. The attendant ego blast overrules the greater good. Little did, or do, these 'leaders' seem to realize that lieutenants in a major organization are more important than generals in an unnoticed group.[76]

For someone like Doyle, this individualism seems to be a true source of frustration. It is apparently very aggravating for Doyle that a FRs advocate can go on a hunger strike

---

[75] Doyle, *supra* note 32.
[76] Id.

over his inability to see his children, only to have little movement or popular support rise up to back him. (No doubt, this public indifference is at least partly due to the fact that comparatively few fathers have actually been legally blocked from visitation with their children, even those with histories of DV and child abuse.[77])This reality is clearly at odds with Doyle's romanticized vision of Bobby Sands—who went on a prolonged hunger strike in 1981in an effort to obtain political prisoner status for Irish Republican Army (IRA) inmates—and the outpouring of support that Sands received from the Irish independence movement and the international community in general.

Needless to say, the lack of a real cause that resonates with an actual grassroots constituency is not an insurmountable barrier to political success, as any corporate trade group lobbyist could attest. So it should not come as any surprise that FRs has had some notable successes in unifying the movement.

Some of the major unification efforts from these years include Men's Equality Now International (M.E.N. International), which was founded by Charles Metz, Daniel Amneus, and Richard Doyle in Los Angeles in 1977. Other better-known groups from this period include Free Men, Inc. (later the National Coalition of Free Men), founded in Maryland in 1977, and the National Congress for Men (NCM)—later the National Congress for Fathers and Children (NCF)–which was founded in 1981. By 1984, the National Council for Children's Rights was formed (renamed the Children's Rights Council in 1992).

If there is any irony in this flurry of activism, it seems to be this: the FRs movement was essentially chasing social and legal reforms that had already been implemented or were in the process of being implemented. As Joan Kelly notes, the "maternal presumption" that had predominated over the first half of the twentieth century was already being phased out, just as the divorce rate was undergoing a dramatic rise in the 1960s:

> Spurred on by fathers' claims of sex discrimination in custody decisions, constitutional concerns for equal protection, the feminist movement, and the entry of large numbers of women into the workforce, which weakened the concept of a primary maternal caretaker, most states abandoned the maternal presumption by the mid 1970s in favor of gender-neutral laws. *The Uniform Marriage and Divorce Act*, approved in 1970, provided for a straight *best interests* standard, and was adopted in varying forms by the majority of states. For the first time in history, custody decisions were to be based on a consideration of the needs and interests of the child rather than on the gender or rights of the parent.[78]

---

[77] That fathers with histories of DV or child abuse have been granted visitation or even child custody has been documented extensively. *See, e.g.,* M.A. Kernic et al., "Children in the Crossfire: Child Custody Determinations Among Couples With a History of Intimate Partner Violence," 11(8) *Violence Against Women* 991 (2005). This particular study examined 800 Seattle-area couples who filed for divorce in 1998 and 1999. These included 324 cases with a history of DV and 532 cases without such a history. It was determined that although mothers in general were more likely than fathers to be awarded custody of children, mothers who were victims of domestic abuse were no more likely than other mothers to receive custody. In addition, fathers with a history of committing DV were no more likely than other fathers to be required by the court to have a third party supervise child visitations. Just 17 percent of fathers with a known history of DV were denied child visitation.

[78] Joan B. Kelly, "The Determination of Child Custody," 4(1) *Children and Divorce* 122 (1994), *available at* http://www.futureofchildren.org/usr_doc/vol4no1ART8.pdf.

Generally speaking, however, most children continued to reside with their mother after a divorce or separation—as long as the father concurred with the custody arrangement and did not contest it. However, it was becoming increasingly clear—even as early as the mid 1970s—that when fathers contested custody, they were frequently achieving their aims. In addition, a history of DV proved to be no barrier to a father's successful custody bid. On the contrary, there was a growing accumulation of evidence to suggest that fathers with a history of DV were just as successful—if not more successful—than fathers without a history of DV at securing custodial rights.

In an influential early study, Phyllis Chesler interviewed sixty white mothers who represented all of the geographical regions of the United States and Canada. All of the women had served as primary caretakers of their children before their divorces, and all of them were considered "good enough" mothers. In short, they were more or less demographically similar to the majority of divorced white mothers in America. All sixty mothers had also experienced "custodial challenges" between 1960 and 1980. Seventy percent of these "good enough" mothers lost custody of their children.[79]

Similar findings continued to surface in the 1980s. The Committee for Justice for Women examined custody awards in Orange County, North Carolina, over a five-year period between 1983 and 1987. According to their findings, "in all contested custody cases, 84% of the fathers in the study were granted sole or mandated joint custody. In all cases where sole custody was awarded, fathers were awarded custody in 79% of the cases. In 26% of the cases fathers were either proven or alleged to have physically and sexually abused their children."[80]

In addition, J. Suchanek and G.B. Stahly examined 150 randomly selected files of marital dissolution from a Southern California district courthouse between 1980 and 1989. They found that dissolution cases in which violence toward the woman had been asserted (usually in support of a restraining order) were significantly more likely to include custody disputes. In fact, when there were allegations of violence perpetrated by the father, he was twice as likely to seek sole physical and legal custody of the children and just as likely to win. Thus, violence did not appear to make a difference in how courts determined custody, since fathers who were alleged to be violent were no less likely to win custody than fathers with no allegations of violence.[81]

TWENTY-FIRST CENTURY AGENDA

Although fathers had largely won legal equality in the 1970s and 1980s, the FRs movement became much more publicly visible and militant in the 1990s and in the beginning years of the next century. And, indeed, as any random Internet search of FRs will show, a lot of the incentive behind this new activity was financial. This motive was spearheaded by the beefed-up efforts at child support collection that accompanied the Uniform Interstate Family Support Act of 1992 (UIFSA) and the Personal Responsibility and Work Reconciliation Act of 1996 (PRWORA).

---

[79] Chesler, *supra* note 2, at xiii.

[80] The Committee for Justice for Women and the Orange County, North Carolina, Women's Coalition, *Contested Custody Cases in Orange County, North Carolina, Trial Courts, 1983–1987: Gender Bias, the Family and the Law* (1991).

[81] J. Suchanek & G.B. Stahly, The Relationship Between Domestic Violence and Paternal Custody in Divorce, paper presented at the annual meeting of the Western Psychological Association (San Francisco, Apr. 1991).

Opposition to child support is particularly strong among fathers who have never married. These men now argue—in a direct appropriation of feminist language—that a "Choice for Men" movement is needed to "give 'coerced fathers' the right to relinquish their parental rights and responsibilities within a month of learning of a pregnancy, just as mothers do when they choose to place their children for adoption."[82] This resentful aspiration is reflected by the plethora of FRs and FRs-inspired legal Web sites that have sprung up to offer advice on how to legally (or not so legally) dodge child support. Recommendations often include the broad details of a slash-and-burn how-to guide for getting sole or joint custody.[83] Demands for increased visitation have also been used as a technique for minimizing the amount of child support imposed.

In addition, the U.S. Department of Health and Human Services, through its Fatherhood Initiative Access and Visitation program, has promoted the development of "safe," "neutral," and "supervised" drop-off centers and other similar programs as a way to promote visitation for fathers with histories of criminal activity or DV. Critics charge that these programs have also been utilized for various custody-switching scams, so that abusive or negligent fathers are released from child support obligations.[84]

The Bax legacy (see "The Left") has also flourished as far as its basic contempt or dismissal of violence towards women and children. In fact, the FRs movement's basic ideological indifference to DV and child abuse has mushroomed into an aggressive political agenda directed against mothers and children. Speaking from an Australian context, Michael Kimmel has identified five essential ways in which FRs groups within that country "have had a damaging impact on interpersonal violence":

1. By influencing changes in family law that privilege parental contact over safety, particularly through moves towards a presumption of children's joint residence;

2. By attempting to discredit female victims of violence;

3. By attempting to wind back the legal protections available to victims;

4. By attempting to wind back the legal sanctions imposed on perpetrators;

5. By attempting to undermine the services and institutions that work with the victims and survivors of violence.[85]

Overall, Kimmel's analysis is equally applicable to any number of countries, including the United States and Canada. Regardless of their home base, it is becoming increasingly common for FRs groups to directly insert their influence into the divorce

---

[82] National Fathers' Resource Center, *Shouldn't Men Have a Choice, Too?* http://www. fathers4kids.com/html/FathersRights.htm?article_id=38.

[83] For a particularly egregious example, see Intellectual Conservative, *Guide: How Fathers Can Win Child Custody,* http://www.intellectualconservative.com/how-fathers-can-win-child-custody-a-book-in-progress/. Among the topics discussed are "Perseverance—Money and Emotional Stress Will Wear Your Ex Down," "You Need to Build Up a Substantial Case Against Your Ex," "You Need an Aggressive Attorney," and "Watch Out for Domestic Violence and Restraining Orders (also known as Orders of Protection)."

[84] *See, e.g.,* Liz Richards, "Forum: The Other Side of Fathers' Rights Controversy," *Wash. Times,* Apr. 23, 2006.

[85] Michael Kimmel, *Fact Sheet #3: How the Father's Rights Movement Undermines the Protections Available to Victims of Domestic Violence and Protects the Perpetrators of Violence,* (Aug. 2005), http://www.xyonline.net/Protectingperpetrators.shtml.

and custody decision-making process, often in "extralegal" ways. Although examples could be gleaned from any number of American states or Canadian provinces, just a few examples from New York State will be provided here.

In at least one situation, FRs "influence" has bordered on "influence peddling." Amy Neustein and Michael Lesher recount a case in which a prominent attorney—who was then chief counsel to the Fathers' Rights Association of Metro New York and Long Island—defended Brooklyn Family Court Judge Leon Deutsch at a legislative hearing in 1989. Mothers who had charged Judge Deutsch with judicial misconduct—essentially for penalizing mothers who brought forth allegations of child sexual abuse—were smeared as "vindictive." Two years later, evidence surfaced that the attacks on the judge's victims had been prearranged with the judge himself. The evidence showed that the FRs chief counsel in question had pledged to the judge that he would discredit a particularly outspoken victim whenever and however possible, including attempted efforts to monitor her activities.[86]

Evidence of questionable FRs influence can also be found in areas quite removed from Brooklyn—even in the greener and ostensibly less corrupt regions of upstate New York. To cite one example, in Jamestown, New York, Family Services of Jamestown, at least in the mid-1990s, administered a Parent Education and Custody Effectiveness (PEACE) program that was marketed as a statewide "dispute resolution" program offering an "alternative approach to resolving the issues of custody and visitation." The New York State Office for the Prevention of Domestic Violence (OPDV)—to mention just one DV organization—strongly cautions against the use of counseling, alternative dispute resolution services, or mediation for persons who have been in relationships with abusers. Usually, such programs are found to pose significant safety concerns and to encourage victim-blaming and "compromise."[87] Given this, it is highly suggestive that the president of "I Love Being a Dad," a Jamestown FRs association affiliated with the Fathers' Rights Association of New York (FRANY), served on the board of Family Services of Jamestown and that "I Love Being a Dad" promoted its mediation services in its organizational literature.[88]

Fathers' Rights Spin

It also should be noted that when another board member of "I Love Being a Dad" (see "Twenty-First Century Agenda") was charged with aggravated harassment in the second degree and criminal trespassing in the second degree subsequent to an incident at his ex-wife's house, the FRs board member in question actually sent a letter to the *Jamestown Post-Journal* arguing that counseling or mediation (rather than his arrest) would represent "better ways of dealing with unresolved feelings and issues." Unfortunately, the board member in question was apparently incapable of following through on his own advice, as he was soon thereafter charged with harassment in yet another incident.[89]

---

[86] Amy Neustein & Michael Lesher, *From Madness to Mutiny: Why Mothers Are Running From the Family Courts—And What Can Be Done About It* 13–14 (2005).

[87] New York State Office for the Prevention of Domestic Violence, *Model Domestic Violence Policy for Counties* (Jan. 1999), http://www.opdv.state.ny.us/coordination/model_policy/guiding.html.

[88] Cheryl Mason, "Fathers Cope With Being Part-Time Parents," *Jamestown Post-Journal,* Oct. 26, 1997.

[89] *Jamestown Post-Journal,* Dec. 28, 2003; *Jamestown Post-Journal,* Jan. 11, 2004; *Jamestown Post-Journal,* Jan. 25, 2004.

Needless to say, the Jamestown example represents one of the milder (and perhaps more typical) attempts by a FRs leader to promote organizations, persons, or ideas that soft-pedal violence or minimize accountability for criminal behavior. In a more extreme vein, James Hays, the president of Coalition for Fathers and Families, a FRs group based in Clifton Park, New York, published a 2002 newspaper op-ed piece making excuses for convicted serial killers John Allen Muhammad and John Lee Malvo. In his piece, Hayes blamed "family dissolution and fatherlessness" and the "disenfranchisement of a father from his children and family" for the killers' actions.[90] Muhammad and Malvo were found guilty of murdering ten persons in the 2002 Beltway Sniper killings but were generally credited in the murders of sixteen, possibly seventeen, persons in eight states. Muhammad also had an extensive history of DV. Defense attorneys at their trials had argued that the ultimate goal of the murders was to kill Muhammad's ex-wife so he could regain custody of their children.

In but another incident involving the Coalition for Fathers and Families, this time in June 2006, Vice-President Randy Dickinson sent an e-mail to New York state legislators, just after a mandatory shared-parenting bill had died in committee. According to the *Albany Times Union*, the e-mail included a news clipping regarding the then recent shooting of a Nevada family court judge, Chuck Weller, which was being heralded by various FRs groups as an act of "political resistance." Dickinson also attached a quote from John F. Kennedy: "Those who make peaceful revolution impossible will make violent revolution inevitable." When questioned by the *Times Union*, Dickinson tried to backpedal on his e-mail's threatening between-the-lines connotations: "Dickinson said he was just trying to make a point the group has communicated in the past to legislative leaders, that 'they cannot continue to ignore our issues and refuse to provide any relief or accommodation, without encouraging violence from those more inclined to express their frustration and anger in that manner.'"[91] Needless to say, the communication alarmed staff members from the office of Assembly Speaker Sheldon Silver, who naturally interpreted it as a genuine threat, so Silver's counsel, Dan Conviser, contacted the state police. This particular incident followed reports from women activists in April 2006 involving being stalked and receiving violent threats, even death threats, from Dickinson and his organization.[92]

Other FRs organizations, particularly on the national level, target what they call the "domestic violence industry," typically with ever-escalating viciousness. In the United States, this has taken many forms, including efforts to repeal the Violence Against Women Act (VAWA) as "discriminatory." One group that has been particularly active in the battle to repeal VAWA—and generally spreading disinformation about DV—is a FRs organization called Respecting Accuracy in Domestic Violence Abuse Reporting (RADAR).[93]

In other cases, FRs activists target media that provides sympathetic coverage of DV issues. One prominent example was the avalanche of FRs-inspired criticism that followed the PBS showing of *Breaking the Silence: Children's Stories* in October 2005.[94] This seemingly benign and straightforward documentary, which reports on the family court system's failure

---

[90] James Hays, "Stopping Violence Begins at Home," *Jamestown Post-Journal,* Dec. 8, 2002.

[91] "Message Proves Unsettling," *Albany Times-Union,* June 26, 2006.

[92] Michelle Morgan Bolton, "Women's Groups Say They Are Being Threatened Over Their Stance on Legislation," *Albany Times-Union,* Apr. 21, 2006.

[93] *See* http://www.mediaradar.org/.

[94] *Breaking the Silence: Children's Stories*, a documentary produced by Catherine Tatge and Dominique Lasseur (http://www.tatgelasseur.com) was broadcast on most PBS stations in October 2005.

to protect children and their mothers from DV, prompted a campaign of utter distortion and misrepresentation by FRs groups ("An assault on fatherhood!") as well as smear campaigns directed at some of the mothers and legal experts who participated in the filming.[95]

"Men Are Battered, Too"

Other FRs groups have sued battered women's shelters directly in an effort to either force them to admit men—which is generally a ruse, since these groups make virtually no effort to fund or develop men-only shelters—or shut them down entirely. One such effort was initiated by the National Coalition of Free Men, which initially sued ten Southern California emergency shelters for homeless battered women and children in 2003, then lost on appeal in 2005. As Marci Fukuroda, a staff attorney with the California Women's Law Center, observed in 2004, "While this lawsuit purports to promote increased services for abused men, what it actually does is launch an unreasonable and harmful attack on what are already over-extended resources for battered women and their children." As evidence, Fukuroda reports that during the 2000-2001 fiscal year, DV shelters funded through the California Department of Health provided services to approximately 80,000 women and 20,000 children. However, more than 23,000 persons had to be turned away because the shelters were full. In addition, Fukuroda notes that women represented 74 percent of all intimate partner homicides in California in 2001.[96] In a similar move, the Maine Coalition to End Domestic Violence was also sued in 2004.[97]

On occasion, men's rights partisans apparently notice that many homeless persons are, in fact, men. But in no case is any empirical analysis brought to bear on the problem. Dr. Karl Glasson, Ph.D., writing for *Men's News Daily*, dogmatically asserts that homelessness and all other social problems can be blamed on fatherlessness, which, of course is blamed on family breakdown, which, of course, is blamed on pesky feminists: "In my view, the major cause of what seems to be a significant deterioration in the behaviors of men is quite simply, feminism."[98] George Rolph at *Divorced Dads' News* apparently occupies the same blinkered universe: men become "homeless drifters" because they are "raped in every way by a savage, feminized system."[99]

The National Center for Men simply plays tit for tat. As their Web site fumes, "while our government spends hundreds of millions of dollars on women's programs and services, these men sleep on park benches and in railroad stations."[100] Apparently, the center hasn't heard that federal and state funding for social services has been precarious for many years now, as organizations that work with the homeless or other at-risk clients well know. But the center is not alone in its ignorance. Denise Noe, also writing for *Men's News Daily*, echoes the same curious and misplaced envy:

---

[95] *See, e.g.,* Glenn Sacks, *PBS's Breaking the Silence: An Assault on Fatherhood,* http://www.glennsacks.com/pbs/index.php.

[96] Marci Fukuroda, "Men's Groups Threaten Women's Shelters through Litigation," *UCLA Center for the Study of Women (CSW) Newsletter* (Spring 2004), *available at* http://www.women.ucla.edu/Newsletter/Shelters.htm.

[97] *See* PRWeb Press Release (Feb. 9, 2005), http://www.prweb.com/newsbycategory/1430/2007-10-13/4360/index.htm.

[98] Karl Glasson, "Men Behaving Badly—Why?" *Men's News Daily,* July 23, 2003, http://mensnewsdaily.com/archive/g/glasson/03/glasson071503.htm.

[99] George Rolph, "Should Men Apologize for Being Angry?" *Divorced Dads' News,* Sept. 23, 2007, http://www.fathers-resources.com/Blog/tabid/581/EntryID/615/Default.aspx.

[100] National Center for Men, *Our Issues,* http://www.nationalcenterformen.org/page3.shtml.

But in discussions of the poorest of the poor, we must take gender into account and recognize that, in this area, men may be considered the disadvantaged sex. After all, one program aimed at helping the poor, WIC, is actually titled 'Women Infants Children.' Men can and do receive WIC if they have custody of a child under the age of 5. However, would modern America tolerate an anti-poverty agency that had "Men" in its name?[101]

Apparently Noe has not examined any White House budgets within the past decade or so; WIC is hardly some "queen bee" program sucking off resources from deserving low-income men. As the Children's Defense Fund noted at the beginning of the 2008 budget process, in February 2007,

the 2008 Budget . . . proposes to reduce quality services for infants, young children, and their low-income mothers who are nutritionally at risk. It would limit automatic eligibility of Medicaid recipients for the Special Supplemental Food Program for Women, Infants, and Children (WIC) and reduce funding for nutrition education and WIC services.[102]

Meanwhile, the Children's Defense Fund carefully documents the real winners in the federal budgetary process—and it was not low-income children or their mothers, or homeless men:

The President's 2008 Budget once again proposes the permanent extension of the individual tax cuts implemented in 2001 and beyond, which overwhelmingly benefit the wealthiest Americans. The Urban Institute-Brookings Institution Tax Policy Center reports that households in the top one percent of the population will receive tax cuts averaging $67,000 a year by 2012. Those with annual incomes over $1 million would average $162,000 a year in tax breaks. Making these tax breaks permanent would result in some $2 trillion in lost revenues over the next ten years and even more in later years—revenues that are urgently needed to address the still large unmet needs of low-income children and their families.[103]

But, as noted before, real-world issues are just not on the men's rights movement agenda—not unless they provide a quick and easy angle for trashing feminism. If an economic or social issue does not involve "he-man" worship of labor union strikers from seventy years ago, or a fast jab at affirmative action or sexual harassment laws, the movement has no interest. Regressive taxation, structural unemployment, the loss of well-paying manufacturing jobs, a stagnant minimum wage, the decline of the American labor movement, housing costs increasing faster than inflation, the lack of universal and affordable health care—none of these things register on the men's rights radar screen. That is because, since before Bax's day until the present, real-world facts have no relevance at all, as far as the FRs movement is concerned.

---

[101] Denise Noe, "Why Homelessness Is a Man Thing," *Men's News Daily,* Oct. 9, 2005, http://mensnewsdaily.com/blog/2005/10/why-homelessness-is-man-thing.htm.

[102] Children's Defense Fund, *Children and Low-Income Families Continue to Be Left Behind: A Look at the President's 2008 Budget and Children* (Feb. 15, 2007), *available at* http://www.childrensdefense.org/child-research-data-publications/data/2008-Presidents-fy-Budget-Analysis.pdf.

[103] Id.

Chapter 5

Gender Bias in the Courts: Implications for Battered Mothers and Their Children

by Molly Dragiewicz, Ph.D.

Although the work on substantive areas of law is preliminary in nature, much of it is remarkably consistent. Our data came from many sources and in many forms. Across subject matters and districts, we heard overlapping and corroborating reports. We heard that gender counts, that in adjudication, whether you are a woman or a man affects the courtroom, the chambers conference, the perception of your credibility, the amount of damages you may receive, or the view of the importance of your claim.[1]

---

[1] Judith Resnik, "Gender Bias: From Classes to Courts," 45 *Stan. L. Rev.* 2195, 2206 (1993).

INTRODUCTION

Battered women face a number of challenges when trying to leave an abuser. These problems are multiplied, complicated, and exacerbated for battered mothers. Contradictory laws, policies, and cultural beliefs put battered mothers in an especially untenable situation as they attempt to implement separation. The economic costs for primary or exclusive care giving of children adds to these challenges, making it difficult for mothers to start over financially after leaving a relationship with an abuser. Recent changes in custody practice and policy have also begun to make it even more difficult for battered women to make a break from their abusers. Although every state is required to consider domestic violence (DV) as a factor for custody determinations, and many states have a presumption against granting custody to abusers, men's violence against women is often marginalized when considered alongside other factors. In combination with efforts to promote father involvement after divorce, mandates intended to increase safety and financial survival for battered women following divorce are increasingly being compromised.

Domestic Violence Defined

DV refers to a pattern of abusive, coercive, and controlling behavior by one partner against the other that includes violence. DV is comprised of multiple forms of psychological, economic, sexual, and physical abuse, and is often referred to as battering. These terms will be used interchangeably in this chapter in order to make clear that the author is talking about ongoing, dangerous forms of abuse and not minor disagreements or "conflict tactics." Conflating mere conflict with DV is misleading and irresponsible given the well-documented imbalances in power and outcomes in battering relationships as well as the inadequate resources currently available to deal with battering. Physical abuse varies in frequency from relationship to relationship, but the use and credible threat of physical harm including homicide intensifies the other forms of abuse. Battering in heterosexual relationships is overwhelmingly male against female, and women face a disproportionate risk of harm including homicide from intimate partners relative to men.[2] Cultural factors that condone men's use of violence against women in response to gendered transgressions, despite putative exhortations not to "hit a girl," contribute to the sex differences in battering and domestic homicide.[3]

---

[2] James Alan Fox & Marianne W. Zawitz, *Homicide Trends in the United States: 2002 Update* (U.S. Department of Justice: Bureau of Justice Statistics, 2004); Bureau of Justice Statistics, *Homicide Trends in the U.S.: Intimate Homicide* (U.S. Department of Justice, 2007); James A. Mercy & Linda E. Saltzman, "Fatal Violence among Spouses in the United States, 1976-85," 79(5) *Am. J. Pub. Health* 595 (1989); Margo Wilson & Martin Daly, "Spousal Homicide Risk and Estrangement," 8(1) *Violence & Victims* 3 (1993).

[3] Walter S. DeKeseredy, Martin D. Schwartz, Danielle Fagan & Mandy Hall, "Separation/ Divorce Sexual Assault: The Contribution of Male Peer Support," 1(3) *Feminist Criminology* 228 (2006) [hereinafter DeKeseredy et al., "Separation/Divorce Sexual Assault"]; Kate Cavanagh et al., "'Remedial Work': Men's Strategic Responses to Their Violence Against Intimate Female Partners," 35(3) *Sociology* 695 (2001); Russell P. Dobash et al., "Separate and Intersecting Realities: A Comparison of Men's and Women's Accounts of Violence Against Women," 4(4) *Violence Against Women* 382 (1998); Walter DeKeseredy, Alberto Godenzi & Martin Schwartz, "Toward an Integrated Gendered Social Bond/Male Peer Support Theory of University Woman Abuse," *Critical Criminology* 10 (2001); Jay G. Silverman & G.M.

One of the most insidious factors aggravating battered women's problems upon separation is persistent and pervasive gender bias in the courts. This chapter reviews the research on gender bias in the courts, with special attention to the impact of bias on battered mothers. First, it reviews the history of efforts to address gender bias in the courts. Next, the findings of the gender bias task forces that are most relevant to battered mothers are discussed. The chapter concludes with a discussion of the ways that social demands for equality interact with persistent and pervasive forms of bias to penalize battered mothers in custody disputes.

Gender Bias Defined

Gender bias is defined by the National Judicial Education Program (NJEP) to Promote Equality for Women and Men in the Courts, as "(1) stereotyped thinking about the nature and roles of women; (2) how society values women and what is perceived as women's work; and (3) myths and misconceptions about the social and economic realities of women and men's lives."[4] Although the terms "sex" and "gender" are often used interchangeably, it is important to recognize the distinction between the two. Sex generally refers to the category female or male and is ostensibly linked to biological differences. Gender, on the other hand, refers to femininity and masculinity, the normative socially and historically specific characteristics ascribed to the sexes.

Gender Versus Sex

Gender implies not only different stereotypical characteristics for women and men, but also hierarchy. Masculine characteristics are generally seen as more valuable than feminine ones. At the same time, masculinity is also considered neutral, the ungendered standard to which feminine behavior and characteristics are compared.[5] For example, legal understandings of self-defense have historically been based on what a "reasonable man" would do in a particular situation.[6]

The invisibility, centrality, and taken-for-grantedness of men's gendered experiences are revealed in the relative ease with which courts understand and identify with men's perspectives and actions. Judges often explicitly identify even with violent men (see "Minimization of Violence Against Women").[7] The other side of this coin is the incomprehensibility of battered mothers' experiences in court. Battered women experience denial of the validity of their experiences and needs, even in the face of copious evidence that they are both common and reasonable.

Williamson, "Social Ecology and Entitlements Involved in Battering by Heterosexual College Males: Contributions of Family and Peers," 12(2) *Violence and Victims* 147 (1997); Neil Websdale, *Understanding Domestic Homicide* (1999).

[4] Lynn Hecht Schafran, "Overwhelming Evidence: Gender and Race Bias in the Courts," in *The Criminal Justice System and Women: Offenders, Prisoners, Victims and Workers* 457, 459. (Barbara Raffel Price & Natalie J. Sokoloff eds., 2004).

[5] Allan G. Johnson, *The Gender Knot: Unraveling Our Patriarchal Legacy* (2005).

[6] Elizabeth Schneider, *Battered Women and Feminist Lawmaking* (2000).

[7] Peter G. Jaffe, Nancy K. Lemon & Samantha E. Poisson, *Child Custody and Domestic Violence: A Call for Safety and Accountability* (2003); James Ptacek, *Battered Women in the Courtroom: The Power of Judicial Responses* (1999); Schneider, *supra* note 6.

It is easy to think of multiple ways that each of the three types of gender bias might apply to battered mothers in court. Stereotyped thinking about the nature and roles of women has been documented in women's lack of credibility relative to men in the courts, especially around rape and other forms of men's violence against women.[8] The devaluation of women's work is relevant to mothers at divorce because women continue to bear primary responsibility for child care and housework, damaging their earning power and limiting the financial assets to which women have access at divorce. Myths and misconceptions about the social and economic realities of women and men's lives serve to inhibit the mostly male judiciary's ability to understand women's entrapment in violent relationships as well as their economic difficulties following divorce. They also create a rosier picture than is justified of the level of social and economic equality that women have attained and the proportion of child care that fathers currently provide.

The three forms of gender bias described by NJEP are manifested in conflicting policies, practices, and attitudes that too easily combine to coerce battered mothers and their children into contact with abusers even after separation. This is true despite the well-documented risks to mother and children, despite social expectations that battered women "just leave" abusers, and despite child protective policies that continue to punish women for "failure to protect" when they do not leave an abuser. In other words, battered women are blamed for the violence and abuse they and their children experience if they do not leave, and they may even lose custody of their children for exposing the children to DV if they stay with an abuser. But when battered mothers do leave, family law and the courts may well force them and their children into frequent and ongoing contact with their abusers even when there is a high risk of continued physical and emotional abuse, including risk of homicide.[9]

The practice of forcing battered mothers into visitation and joint custody arrangements with their abusers, or even awarding the abusers with sole custody, is on the increase following the expansion of "fatherhood promotion" funding, programs, and ideology.[10] For example, states with "friendly parent" provisions do not take violence against women as seriously as states without such provisions, weighing each parent's willingness to promote contact with the other parent more heavily than safety and therapeutic considerations related to violence and abuse.[11] Although the harm to battered women may not be intentional, such "friendly parent" provisions have obvious negative implications for battered women who seek to protect themselves and their children from an abuser. It is imperative that lawyers, judges, and others be aware of the impact of gender bias on battered women negotiating custody arrangements, regardless of the intention of the court actors involved. Gender bias studies help to shed light on why and how courts disadvantage battered mothers at divorce despite the juridical injunction for objectivity and justice.

---

[8] Leigh Goodmark, "Telling Stories, Saving Lives: The Battered Mothers' Testimony Project, Women's Narratives, and Court Reform," 37(3) *Ariz. St. L.J.* 709 (2005); Schafran *supra* note 4; Schneider *supra* note 6.

[9] Schneider *supra* note 6.

[10] Allison C. Morrill et al., "Child Custody and Visitation Decisions When the Father Has Perpetrated Violence Against the Mother," 11(8) *Violence Against Women* 1076 (2006); Peter G. Jaffe & Claire V. Crooks, "Partner Violence and Child Custody Cases: A Cross-National Comparison of Legal Reforms and Issues," 10(8) *Violence Against Women* 917 (2004).

[11] Morrill et al., *supra* note 10.

EFFORTS TO ADDRESS GENDER BIAS IN THE COURTS

Background

NJEP was formed by the National Organization for Women Legal Defense and Education Fund (NOW LDEF) in 1980. NOW LDEF had been formed by feminist lawyers and activists to "further women's legal rights and to end the gender bias women faced in the courts. The impetus for the focus on the courts was the way judges were applying, or failing to apply, new laws intended to end gender bias in situations that ranged from hiring decisions to rape trials."[12] NOW LDEF reasoned, that "there is no point in passing remedial legislation if the judges who interpret, apply, and enforce these laws are themselves biased."[13]

NOW LDEF invited the newly formed National Association of Women Judges (NAWJ) to partner in an effort to address gender bias in the courts. NOW LDEF chose to partner with NAWJ because its members knew that judges would be most likely to listen to other judges and that it was important to establish the project as about improving the administration of justice according to judicial standards rather than as a feminist political cause.[14] NAWJ was formed just a year earlier, in 1979, by Justice Joan Dempsey Klein, Justice Vaino Spencer, and 100 other women judges. The judges established the organization to work toward equal justice in the courts on a variety of fronts including advocacy for "women, youth, the elderly, minorities, the underprivileged, and people with disabilities."[15]

Documentation

Before it undertook to address the impact of gender bias in the courts, NJEP set out to document the existence of bias state by state. Since the most explicit forms of discriminatory legal practice, such as the exclusion of women from juries, the bench, and law schools, had already been eliminated, NJEP knew that it would have to unequivocally demonstrate the continued existence of gender bias before it could demand training for judges.[16] Members of NJEP correctly anticipated that courts would resist acknowledging the existence of bias in their own jurisdictions, necessitating the state-by-state approach. More than forty states have conducted gender bias self-studies to date. After many of the states had completed their assessments, circuit courts undertook self-studies as well, beginning with the Ninth Circuit Court. The majority of the circuit courts have now also completed self-assessments for bias.

The gender bias task forces utilized a number of qualitative and quantitative methods to assess bias-related factors, from the representation of women in the courts to the perceptions of those appearing in court. Many courts administered surveys to judges, lawyers, court personnel, plaintiffs, and defendants. Others took data from court watch

---

[12] Schafran *supra* note 4, at 458–59.

[13] Id.

[14] Dorothy W. Nelson, "Introduction to the Effects of Gender in the Federal Courts: The Final Report of the Ninth Circuit Gender Bias Task Force," 67 *S. Cal. L. Rev.* 731 (1994).

[15] National Association of Women Judges, *History,* http://www.nawj.org/history.asp.

[16] Linda K. Kerber, *No Constitutional Right to Be Ladies: Women and the Obligations of Citizenship* (1998); Schafran, *supra* note 4.

projects, employment records, focus groups, and interviews.[17] Levels of enthusiasm about the gender bias studies were mixed. Some gender bias task forces presented their findings tentatively, pointing out the many weaknesses of their approach.[18] Others seemed more convinced of the importance and validity of their studies' findings, asserting "the task force concluded 'gender counts' and can have an effect on litigants, witnesses, lawyers, employees, and judges."[19]

Participation of the Courts

The biggest accomplishment of the gender bias task forces may have been that so many of the courts participated, creating an atmosphere where the existence of perceptions of bias were at least acknowledged.[20] States varied widely in the amount of resources and energy that they offered to assist the task forces at the research and implementation phases. For example, New York's report concluded that "more was found in this examination of gender bias in the courts than bruised feelings resulting from rude or callous behavior. Real hardships are borne by women. An exacting price is ultimately paid by our entire society."[21] In response to this finding, New York established a standing Judicial Committee on Women in the Courts, which continues efforts to study and address gender bias.

The Fourth Circuit showed considerably less enthusiasm and reported, "In the summer of 1994, two students from the College of William and Mary, serving as interns in the office of the Circuit Executive, were assigned the task of preparing a report on the issue of gender bias in the courts."[22] Following the students' report, the Fourth Circuit declined to spend time or resources on a study of their circuit, citing the derogatory comments of Senators Grassley and Hatch about gender bias studies and their refusal to provide funding for the studies as justification.[23]

Overall, the state and circuit court gender bias task forces unearthed similar problems. The repetition of the findings across the various courts indicates that regardless of specific methodological shortcomings, the results are valid, having been effectively triangulated across the courts and with similar findings unearthed by multiple methods. Despite more than twenty-five years of work on the gender bias uncovered, issues persist.

FINDINGS OF GENDER BIAS TASK FORCES

The state gender bias task forces were led by New Jersey, which produced the first report at the request of Chief Justice of the New Jersey Supreme Court Robert

---

[17] Richard C. Kearney & Holly Sellers, "Sex on the Docket: Reports of the State Task Forces," 56(6) *Pub. Admin. Rev.* 587 (1996).

[18] Bruce M. Selya, "First Circuit: A Study of Gender Bias in and Around Courts," 32 *Univ. Richmond L. Rev.* 647 (1998).

[19] Procter Hug, Marilyn L. Huff & John C. Coughenour, "Ninth Circuit: The Gender Bias Task Force," 32 *Univ. Richmond L. Rev.* 735, 735 (1998).

[20] Lynn Hecht Schafran, *Gender Bias Task Forces: Findings and Recommendations, available at* http://www.nowldef.org/html/njep/findings.shtml.

[21] New York State Judicial Committee on Women in the Courts, *Women in the Courts: A Work in Progress: 15 Years after the Report of the New York Task Force* (2002), *available at* http://nysl.nysed.gov/Archimages/80218.PDF.

[22] Samuel W. Phillips, "Fourth Circuit: The Judicial Council's Review of the Need for a Gender Bias Study," 32 *Univ. Richmond L. Rev.* 721, 722 (1998).

[23] Judith Resnik, "Asking About Gender in the Courts," 21 *Signs* 952 (1996).

N. Wilentz in 1982.[24] State task forces continued to collect data through the 1990s and were met with remarkably divergent responses.[25] Accordingly, the reports take a variety of tones, from denying the seriousness of gender bias because of claims that the "nature of federal law" made such inquiry unnecessary, to boasting that "we were not asked simply to determine if gender bias exists in Florida, because this question already had been resolved."[26]

Despite the varying levels of enthusiasm for the study process or implementation, the courts' findings were remarkably similar. The results show that gender bias is pervasive and has serious consequences, and it "permeates the decision making, operations, and environment of state court systems."[27] The reports found both, "gender bias in the courtroom and under the law" and "gender bias in court administration and the legal profession."[28] The studies indicated that while gender bias sometimes affects men, its impact is overwhelmingly and disproportionately against women. They also consistently found that men are much less likely to see gender bias as a problem or to acknowledge its existence.

Some of the state and circuit reports express the belief that problems with gender bias will naturally fade, as the next generation of court staff take their places, and archaic ways of thinking change over time. Others assume that judges are insulated from gender bias because they are supposed to be objective. Neither is the case. Judith Resnik notes that "neither age nor professional role explains differences in perceptions of the existence and frequency of gender bias. Whether older or younger members of the bar or bench, men saw the world one way, women another."[29]

Those involved in the studies have remarked about the frequency with which participants in the studies objected to their existence and asserted that they were unnecessary since bias was not an issue, with many respondents writing comments in the margins to this effect.[30] The Delaware report noted that "the finding of virtually every task force has been that the refusal of some lawyers and judges to acknowledge this fact is one of the primary mechanisms by which gender bias is perpetuated."[31] Delaware's report recounted the negative reaction their study received from many male respondents.

> Some members of the legal community emphatically told the Task Force that the project was a "waste of time and money." For example, one attorney wrote that the survey portion was "(1) nonsense, (2) ideologically biased, (3) a waste of taxpayers' funds, and (4) certain to come to a 'politically correct' conclusion that there is gender bias in Delaware's courts–though there isn't." Another attorney questioned the survey saying, "Where did the money come

---

[24] Id.

[25] Lynn Hecht Schafran, "Will Inquiry Produce Action? Studying the Effects of Gender Bias in the Federal Courts," 32 *Univ. Richmond L. Rev.* 615 (1998).

[26] Id.; Florida Supreme Court, *Report of the Florida Supreme Court Gender Bias Study Commission* (1990).

[27] Kearney & Sellers, *supra* note 17, at 587.

[28] Id. at 588.

[29] Resnik *supra* note 1, at 2206.

[30] Deborah R. Hensler, "Studying Gender Bias in the Courts: Stories and Statistics," 45 *Stan. L. Rev.* 2187 (1993).

[31] Delaware Gender Bias Task Force, *The Delaware Gender Bias Task Force: Executive Summary*, at 2–3 (1995).

from for this and why did anyone think the money needed to be spent?," while a judge told the Task Force that the study was "totally unnecessary." One court employee referred to the survey as a "witch hunt" and another dismissed gender bias as frequently being merely an excuse for those who do not succeed. Reflecting the view of some respondents who told the Task Force that, though gender bias may have once existed, it is no longer a factor, one attorney stated: "I have completed your survey and herewith returned it despite the fact that I have concluded it is no longer relevant. Ten years ago maybe, twenty years ago certainly, five years ago possibly, but today gender discrimination, if it exists, cannot possibly be measured by an instrument as crude as the one I just completed."[32]

But it did measure gender discrimination. Another respondent to the same study remarked, "It absolutely confounds me that any male could have the arrogance to declare that there is no problem, based simply on his limited experience."[33] For example, a significant number of female respondents noted that they were subject to address by diminutive terms of "endearment," not being recognized as attorneys, and "rude and otherwise unprofessional behavior, including sexual comments and advances" in court.[34] The reports also frequently noted that racism magnifies the bias against women of color.[35] Some of the reports sought to examine both forms of bias, and many states later developed bodies to address race and gender bias, but most of the first reports tried to isolate gender bias from that based on race. Respondents talked about how forms of bias intersect anyway.

Gender Bias Issues Affecting Battered Mothers in the Courts

DV, child custody, and child support featured prominently in the gender bias reports produced throughout the 1980s and 1990s. The issues raised were remarkably consistent, and almost all of the gender bias reports devoted substantial sections to these areas of law. Key among the issues raised were women's credibility in court, double standards around parenting, inequitable distribution of resources, and the courts' lack of appreciation of the seriousness of violence and abuse against women by male intimates. Divorce cases involving battered mothers are a location where prejudices against women and mothers coalesce. Since "gender bias was not born in the court system[,] . . . it reflects the prevailing attitudes and conditions of our society," policies that may not be biased on their face are often applied in ways that systematically disadvantage women.[36]

Questioning of Women's Credibility. The issue of women's credibility in the court, especially around cases of men's violence against women they know, has been repeatedly documented.[37] The gender bias reports found that "women litigants are assumed

---

[32] Id. at 6.

[33] Id.

[34] Id. at 11.

[35] Hecht Schafran *supra* note 20; Kearney & Sellers *supra* note 17.

[36] Massachusetts Supreme Judicial Court, "Gender Bias Study of the Court System in Massachusetts," 24 *New Eng. L. Rev.* 745, 746 (Spring 1990).

[37] Schneider *supra* note 6.

to be less credible or their problems less important than those of men," and that "women's testimony may simply be thought to be complaints about life rather than as legally cognizable harms, and that even when believed, women's injuries may be trivialized or viewed as not 'worth much' in monetary terms."[38] In other words, state and circuit court studies found that "women are often disbelieved because they are women."[39] Courts that set out to aggressively address this issue, for example by advocating "reasonable woman" standards to ameliorate this form of gender bias, were among the most highly criticized, indicating the persistence of sexism.[40] Recent follow-up gender bias reports indicate that women's credibility is still a concern. North Dakota's ten year follow-up study found "continuing concerns related to victim blaming, lack of respect for victim concerns, and skepticism about the credibility of women in domestic violence proceedings."[41]

Elizabeth Schneider has written extensively about the contradictory legal position of battered women and the challenges this poses to their credibility.[42] In order to be "credible" as battered women, women have often been called upon to present themselves as incapacitated rather than as acting reasonably and justifiably in self-defense. Because violence committed against women by men known to them is so trivialized, and because the courts have been so slow to recognize the seriousness of violence against women as a crime, women's self-defense pleas were not comprehensible in the same way that men's have always been.

Credibility problems are also manifested in the higher standards for evidence required from abused women, whether they are seeking orders for protection, reporting violence by a spouse, or demonstrating that they are a good enough mother. According to the Massachusetts gender bias report, attorneys believe that juries require more corroborating evidence from women in sexual assault cases than for other serious felonies. And, "although half of those surveyed agreed that judges accord sexual assault victims the same credibility as victims of other serious felonies, the responses of the rest of the attorneys differed depending on the sex of the respondent."[43] The New York report found similar perceptions of rape victims' lack of credibility in court.[44] The gender bias reports hypothesized that this lower credibility was based on negative stereotypes about women's integrity as well as an unwillingness to hold men accountable for violence against women they know.

Although the above comments were not necessarily about marital rape and other forms of sexual assault in marriage, it is not uncommon to hear claims that women fabricate reports of sexual violence against them and their children in order to "get a leg up" in the divorce property settlement or custody determination.[45] The few studies

---

[38] Resnik, *supra* note 1, at 2205.

[39] Id.

[40] Id..

[41] North Dakota Commission on Gender Fairness in the Courts, *Gender Fairness in North Dakota's Courts: A Ten Year Assessment, available at* http://www.ndcourts.gov/court/committees/gender/gficreport.htm#p1.

[42] Schneider, *supra* note 6.

[43] Massachusetts Supreme Judicial Court, *supra* note 36, at 751.

[44] New York Task Force on Women in the Courts, "Report of the New York Task Force on Women in the Courts," 11 *Ford. Urb. L.J.* 15, 52–54 (1987).

[45] Janet R. Johnston et al., "Allegations and Substantiations of Abuse in Custody-Disputing Families," 43(2) *Fam. Ct. Rev.* 283 (2005); Eleanor E. Maccoby & Robert H. Mnookin, *Dividing the Child: Social and Legal Dilemmas of Custody* (1992).

available on this issue do not support this assumption.[46] In fact, studies have found that many women are willing to agree to unfair and inadequate property division and support arrangements in order to retain primary custody of their children.[47] Nonetheless, the idea that women fabricate reports of sexual assault and other forms of violence for personal gain is present in battered mothers' court cases just as in other contexts.[48]

Disregard of Evidence in Custody Determinations. Women's lack of credibility in court is also visible when courts simply ignore evidence of abuse in the context of custody determinations. Despite laws in every state mandating the consideration of DV, in practice, custody determinations often bracket evidence of violence and abuse in favor of formally equal arrangements that fail to account for family history, safety, and justice.[49] In sharp contrast to the well-documented harm to children from exposure to men's violence against women, and child protective services' use of this documentation to justify punishing women for failure to protect when they live with a batterer, family courts often ignore violence against women and focus only on men's direct abuse of children when it is time to allocate custody.[50]

Impact on Children. The impact on children of exposure to men's violence against women includes, but is not limited to, increased risk of physical, sexual, and psychological abuse; physical harm incidental to assaults against the mother; aggressive and noncompliant behavior; emotional and internalizing problems; effects on social and academic development; posttraumatic stress disorder; and traumatic bonding to the abuser. Effects also include the internalization of negative attitudes about women, feelings of guilt about causing the abuse, victim blaming, learning the appropriateness of using violence to get what you want, and the appropriateness of violence against women and intimates.[51] The negative impacts on children of witnessing men's violence against women are mediated by a variety of factors including the severity and duration of the abuse, the nature of children's exposure, whether the children are also directly abused, personality and other protective factors, the children's sex, whether the children maintain a close relationship with their mothers or peers, whether the children are believed at disclosure, and whether they are

---

[46] Carrie Cuthbert et al., *Battered Mothers Speak Out: A Human Rights Report on Domestic Violence and Child Custody in the Massachusetts Courts* (Wellesley Center for Women 2002); Johnston et al., *supra* note 45.

[47] Johnston et al., *supra* note 45; Maccoby & Mnookin, *supra* note 45.

[48] Massachusetts Supreme Judicial Court, *supra* note 36.

[49] Cuthbert et al., *supra* note 46.

[50] Lundy Bancroft & Jay G. Silverman, *The Batterer as Parent: Addressing the Impact of Domestic Violence on Family Dynamics* (2002) [hereinafter Bancroft & Silverman, *Batterer as Parent*]; Lundy Bancroft & Jay G. Silverman, A*ssessing the Risk to Children From Batterers, available at* http://www.lundybancroft.com/pages/articles_sub/JAFFE.htm; Cuthbert et al., *supra* note 46; Jaffe & Crooks, *supra* note 10; Peter G. Jaffe, Claire V. Crooks & Samantha E. Poisson, "Common Misconceptions in Addressing Domestic Violence in Child Custody Disputes," 54 *Juv. & Fam. Ct. J.* 57 (2003); Jaffe, Lemon & Poisson, *supra* note 7; Peter G. Jaffe, Michelle Zerwer & Samantha E. Poisson, *Access Denied: The Barriers of Violence and Poverty for Abused Women and Their Children's Search for Justice and Community Services After Separation* (2002), http://www.lfcc.on.ca/access_denied_full.pdf; Jay G. Silverman et al., "Child Custody Determinations in Cases Involving Intimate Partner Violence: A Human Rights Analysis," 94 (6) *Am. J. Pub. Health* 951 (2004).

[51] Bancroft & Silverman, *Batterer as Parent, supra* note 50; Jaffe, Lemon & Poisson, *supra* note 7.

protected from further exposure to abuse after separation.[52] Custody arrangements therefore have a significant impact on both potential harm to children and the availability of factors that can promote healing following the mother's separation from an abuser.

Significantly, the effects of exposure to adult DV on children include many of the behaviors and characteristics often described as negative "divorce outcomes." Family studies scholars are only just beginning to consider that the quality of family relationships prior to divorce may have an impact on outcomes for children after divorce.[53] That is to say, what the research terms "divorce outcomes" may have contributing factors in addition to experiencing divorce or "father absence." Unfortunately, almost all of the extant family studies literature still fails to investigate or even explicitly address violence and abuse of either mothers or children.

The available literature on "high conflict" divorce cases often minimizes the importance of men's violence against women, emphasizing instead the notion of conflict as mutual or the result of a communication problem.[54] This construction of "mutuality" obscures the marked and pervasive sex and gender differences in violence and abuse and their contributing factors, characterizing "conflict" as rooted in interpersonal dynamics. This framing of conflict does not accurately reflect the nature of DV and distorts the motives, meaning, and outcomes of abusive, protective, and defensive behavior. Significantly, in a court setting that is prone to underestimate the seriousness of men's violence against known women and children, this framing can be used to punish mothers who seek to protect themselves or their children from further harm and to blame victims for the violence used against them.

Even when men's violence against children has been reported, children's disclosures may be dismissed as "coached" by the mother, or children's objections to being around an abusive parent may be dismissed as the results of mothers' "alienation" rather than the child's justified and rational response to abuse. Alternatively, mothers' reports of abuse are simply ignored as irrelevant now that separation is under way.[55] This results in the exclusion of evidence of violence and abuse from evaluators' reports and judges' refusal to hear evidence of abuse.[56]

Notably, research has found that those responsible for considering violence and abuse at custody determinations often articulate very different priorities than they enact.[57] Perhaps this is due to courts and their proxies such as guardians ad litem (GALs) relying on the unfounded assumption that violence ends at separation or misguided efforts at allocating the children's time equitably as if they were property to which each parent was entitled a fair share. The problem with such formally equal arrangements is that they profoundly distort the realities of life and risk due to violence and abuse before and after separation.

---

[52] Bancroft & Silverman, *Batterer as Parent, supra* note 50; Margareta Hyden & Imelda Colgan McCarthy, "Woman Battering and Father-Daughter Incest Disclosure: Discourses of Denial and Acknowledgement," 5(4) *Discourse & Soc'y* 543 (1994); Jaffe, Lemon & Poisson, *supra* note 7; Audrey Mullender, Liz Kelly, Gill Hague, Ellen Malos & Umme Imam, *Children's Perspectives on Domestic Violence* (2002); Sally E. Palmer et al., "Responding to Children's Disclosure of Familial Abuse: What Survivors Tell Us," 78(2) *Child Welfare League of Am.* 259 (1999).

[53] Jaffe, Lemon & Poisson, *supra* note 7.

[54] Bancroft & Silverman, *Batterer as Parent, supra* note 50.

[55] Id.; Cuthbert et al., *supra* note 46; Joan Zorza, "The "Friendly Parent" Concept: Another Gender Biased Legacy From Richard Gardner," 12(5) *Domestic Violence Rep.* 65 (2007).

[56] Cuthbert et al., *supra* note 46.

[57] Id.

Minimization of Violence Against Women. DV is consistently remarked upon as a location of gender bias in studies of courts.[58] Lynn Hecht Schafran has noted that DV is located "at the intersection of two of the most pernicious tendencies in the law: the devaluation of violence against women and the devaluation of family law."[59] The gender bias reports affirm this observation.[60] Many of the reports comment on judges' dislike for hearing family law and DV, as do other studies.[61] Comments trivializing violence and abuse, and communicating judges' feeling that family matters were beneath them and a waste of the court's time, were common.

Schafran recounts comments from a judge who expressed his identification with a man who killed his wife because of her infidelity. The judge levied a minimal sentence, likening the man's killing of his wife to a drunk driving accident, and letting loose a string of comments about his doubts "that many married men . . . would have the strength to walk away, but without inflicting some corporal punishment . . . I shudder to think what I would do."[62] The judge further reflected that he was free to impose a lenient sentence because only the defendant's allies were in court, and women killed by their husbands did not have court watchers there to see what he was doing. The judge also required the perpetrator to work at a DV agency as part of his punishment. Schafran documents many cases like this where judges' identification with the perpetrator appears to drive their failure to protect victims. More than one of these cases has ended in homicide.[63]

Schafran relates additional examples of judges trivializing violence against women. The Missouri gender bias report notes that a member of the state's antiviolence coalition stated that "inappropriate comments and belittling behaviors" are often directed at women from the bench. One Missouri judge reportedly asked women if they enjoyed being beaten.[64] A Florida judge sang "you light up my wife" in court when he heard about a woman whose abuser had covered her with lighter fluid and set her on fire.[65] Many of the state reports recounted similar complaints that DV was not taken seriously by the courts and that court personnel were inadequately trained or sensitive to this area. In addition to minimizing the seriousness of violence against women, these disrespectful comments are also abusive and dangerous because they affirm abusers' perceptions that their violence is not a big deal and that even if they are penalized, it is just a formality.

The assumption that reports of abuse are often false is also an example of minimization.[66] The minimization of violence against women is also evident in the failure to take restraining orders or violations of them seriously. Despite the fact that only about half of all temporary orders are converted to more permanent ones, GALs often dismiss "permanent" protective orders (in reality normally valid for a year or two)

---

[58] Lynn Hecht Schafran & Norma J. Wikler, *Gender Fairness in the Courts: Action in the New Millennium* (2007), *available at* http://womenlaw.stanford.edu/genderfairness-strategiesproject.pdf.

[59] Lynn Hecht Schafran, "There's No Accounting for Judges," 58(4) *Alb. L. Rev.* 1063, 1077 (1995).

[60] Delaware Gender Bias Task Force, *supra* note 31, at 195.

[61] Kearney & Sellers, *supra* note 17; Schneider, *supra* note 6.

[62] Schafran, *supra* note 59, at 1064.

[63] Id. at 1066.

[64] Id. at 1065.

[65] Id.

[66] Cuthbert et al., *supra* note 46.

and their violation altogether since they are based on women's testimony. Judges often characterize restraining order violations as "inadvertent," in contrast to their own insistence that they take violence against women seriously.[67] This characterization of restraining order violation contradicts the research on batterers and battered women that describes postseparation stalking, harassment, terrorism, and violence including homicide, homicide/suicide, and familicide.[68]

A related problem exists where "many family court judges routinely enter mutual orders of protection in family-offense proceedings upon the mere oral request of respondents" or when the respondent has not even made such a request.[69] This characterizes battered women seeking protection as responsible for the violence done to them, effectively undermining the purpose of restraining orders to protect victims from further harm.

Double Standards for Parenting. At custody determinations, women face the combination of continued expectation of maternal responsibility for child and home care with the idealization of father involvement. This combination means that in family court women are held to a very high standard of parenting while men's expression of intent to parents is sufficient. Mothers' records of past care provide many opportunities to point out places where their mothering has fallen short of perfection: "I had the feeling that . . . every part of my parenting was criticized. Whereas he was a father who . . . moved from place to place and left the town . . . but not only did he not lose custody, I couldn't get sole custody. I felt the judges were blaming me for the kids' bad behavior or academic problems."[70] Men, on the other hand, have much less experience on average of day-to-day child care and are often judged to be potentially great fathers, regardless of their past conduct.[71] Men benefit from the idealization of "involved fathering," while entrenched and highly gendered stereotypes set a low threshold for the achievement of this goal. One battered mother commented, "I had to prove myself over all those years. He was just, you know, the perfect dad. The judge had no concerns over him. And it's like they wanted me to do so many things, they wanted me to go to school, they wanted me to do this and that, but they weren't asking him to do anything."[72] Another battered mother remarked, "[My ex-partner] doesn't pay child support . . . he hasn't seen my son in three years. . . . But now he wants to be a father. Everybody's like . . . now he's decided he wants to be a father, God forbid we don't give him the chance."[73] Women may also be punished by judges who determine that working outside the home

---

[67] Lori A. Zoellner et al., "Factors Associated With Completion of the Restraining Order Process in Female Victims of Partner Violence," 15(10) *J. Interpersonal Violence* 1081 (2007); Cuthbert et al., *supra* note 46.

[68] David Adams, *Why Do They Kill? Men Who Murder Their Intimate Partners* (2007); Walter S. DeKeseredy, McKenzie Rogness & Martin Schwartz, "Separation and Divorce Assault: The Current State of Social Scientific Knowledge," 9 *Aggression & Violent Behav.* 675 (2004) [hereinafter DeKeseredy et al., "Separation and Divorce Assault"]; Websdale, *supra* note 3; Wilson & Daly *supra* note 2.

[69] New York Task Force on Women in the Courts, *supra* note 44, at 38.

[70] Cuthbert et al., *supra* note 46, at 35.

[71] Lynne M. Casper, *My Daddy Takes Care of Me! Fathers as Care Providers* (1997). U.S. Department of Commerce, Economics, and Statistics Administration, *Current Population Reports* (U.S. Census Bureau, Jan. 23, 2007).

[72] Cuthbert et al., *supra* note 46, at 35.

[73] Id. at 36.

makes them bad mothers.[74] Alternatively, judges may treat women as if they are out to gain resources that they are not entitled to at divorce if they have stayed away from work to raise the children.[75] Despite some improvements, the financial and moral worth of women's contributions continue to be minimized in divorce settlements. In fact, mothers' greater provision of care during the marriage may be used against them at divorce, when the courts have sometimes decided that the fathers' greater income qualifies them as better able to provide for the best interests of the children.

Related to the double standard for women's parenting compared to men's is the assumption, common to many of the family studies scholars who have produced studies that largely ignore violence, abuse, and parenting patterns prior to divorce, that "everything changes at divorce." This assumption is unfortunate for three primary reasons. First, the research on battering and child abuse strongly contradicts this assumption. Many batterers and, significantly, many of those who kill women or children when they are attempting to leave, continue violent and abusive behavior at separation or escalate their efforts to regain control of or punish the women for leaving.[76] Yet some courts ignore this risk:

> Unless the battering has been directed at the children themselves, the courts will generally not deny custody or limit visitation solely on the basis of the father's violence against the mother. . . . [Frequently] courts will believe that wife beating will end with divorce and that supervised visitation . . . [is] unnecessary.[77]

Given the tenacity of the most dangerous batterers, the minimal "protection" offered by supervised visitation looks like a cruel joke. Regardless of whether or not the woman and man are separated in the building where supervised visitation takes place, regular contact offers an opportunity for motivated batterers to stalk, follow, threaten, or harm battered mothers and their children. One advocate noted that "even where pickup and dropoff [for visitation] is at the police station, women get harassed, followed, and threatened by ex-partners."[78] The serious risk to battered women at even supervised visitations receives little notice in the literature on custody and visitation. Supervised visitations are not risk-free ways to reconcile parents' demands for access to their children and battering.

Punishment of Women Who Report Abuse at Divorce. Not only is violence against women sometimes minimized and denied at divorce and custody determinations, but battered mothers appear to be increasingly likely to be punished for raising the issue of violence and abuse at divorce. This may take the form of punishing women who mention

---

[74] R. Abrams & J. Greaney, *Report of the Gender Bias Study of the Supreme Judicial Court of the Commonwealth of Massachusetts* (1998).

[75] Cuthbert et al., *supra* note 46; Schneider, *supra* note 6.

[76] Michael A. Anderson, Paulette Marie Gillig, Marilyn Sitaker, Marilyn McCloskey, Kathleen Malloy & Nancy Grigsby, "'Why Doesn't She Just Leave?': A Descriptive Study of Victim Reported Impediments to Her Safety," 18(3) *J. Fam. Violence* 151 (2003); DeKeseredy et al., "Separation/Divorce Sexual Assault," *supra* note 3; DeKeseredy et al., "Separation and Divorce Assault," *supra* note 68; Jennifer L. Hardesty, "Separation Assault in the Context of Postdivorce Parenting: An Integrative Review of the Literature," 8(5) *Violence Against Women* 597 (2005); Jaffe, Zerwer & Poisson, *supra* note 50.

[77] Abrams & Greaney, *supra* note 74, at 42.

[78] Cuthbert et al., *supra* note 46, at 17.

violence and abuse under "friendly parent" assumptions, punishing women who insist on the relevance of a history of violence and abuse when they are pushed into participating in mediation, or being pressured to drop restraining orders to move things along more quickly in court. One battered mother described the pressure to act as if the history of abuse was not relevant to the custody and divorce arrangements this way:

> We had to sit in a room, without our attorneys, with her [the probate probation officer] in the room, and I was made to look like the bad guy. Because I kept saying that's not acceptable. What about the domestic [assault and battery]? What about the history? It was totally disregarded. . . . I felt [the partner abuse] was not taken seriously, and I felt it was held against me.[79]

Another battered mother was pressured into visitation with a batterer who had just gotten out of prison after threatening to kill his new wife and her child. The probation officer assigned to the case argued that this was irrelevant since the visitation would be supervised and admonished the battered mother that "you need to help build the bridge here."[80]

The Massachusetts report noted that judges both minimize the risk related to battering around custody and punish mothers for bringing it up, quoting an attorney who said,

> Battered women are losing custody because courts refuse to consider a batterer's violence as evidence of his parental unfitness. . . . Many battered women are threatened with loss of custody or contempt if they take precautions to protect themselves from access by the batterer.[81]

In this context, women's reports of violence are unfairly presumed to be false and frivolous, and they are prevented for protecting themselves from further violence.

Unfair Financial Settlements. The gender bias studies found that discrimination against women at divorce was manifested in unfairness in financial settlements. Women often receive unfair financial settlements when their unpaid labor in the home, in family-owned businesses, and in child care are ignored in the division of marital assets. The original New York gender bias report found that

> male perspectives on family life has [sic] skewed decisions in equitable distribution cases. The perception of most men- and the judiciary is mostly male- is that care of the house and children can be done with one hand tied behind the back. Send the kids out to school, put them to bed, and the rest of the time free to play tennis and bridge. They think any woman- no matter her age or lack of training- can find a nice little job and a nice little apartment and conduct her later years as she might have done at age [twenty-five].[82]

Judges apparently failed to consider the impact of women's contributions to the family on their earning potential following divorce, the cost of child care, and the loss of earnings by women who have paid jobs but who have nonetheless subordinated their

---

[79] Id. at 51.
[80] Id. at 52.
[81] Abrams & Greaney *supra* note 74, at 42.
[82] Schafran, *supra* note 20.

careers to the needs of their husbands and children. Judges did not account for ongoing pay inequity between women and men. Other judges apparently assumed that since women would remarry, they would not need support from their ex-husbands. Courts usually did not award alimony, and, when they did, it was temporary.[83] Adding to the inequity of asset distribution, the gender bias reports noted that child support payment was often not enforced.[84]

These are all examples of the ways that the devaluation of women's work and the persistence of myths and misconceptions about the social and economic realities of women's lives disadvantage women at divorce. The financial implications of divorce become even clearer when what is known about the dynamics of DV is considered. Women often remain with abusers or reconcile with abusers because they lack the financial resources that would enable them to leave. Women with children are even more financially dependent.[85] Batterers often forbid women's employment or deliberately interfere with their work in ways that cause them to lose jobs.[86] In addition to the implications of poverty for women and children's survival following divorce, women's lack of assets often contributes to them not having legal representation at divorce.[87]

Is Gender Bias Gender Neutral?

In addition to the evidence of bias affecting battered mothers in court, some gender bias reports also remarked on perceptions of gender bias against men. Often this took the form of perceptions of favoritism to women. For example, according to some respondents, women's advancement on the bench or bar was attributed to affirmative action, and female defendants were seen as being treated more leniently than male defendants.[88] One of the places that gender bias task forces reported perceptions of bias against men was in family law cases around child custody and child support. These findings sometimes received pride of place in the final report by committees that chose to present gender bias as an equal opportunity problem, so it is important to consider these representations of bias.[89]

Other gender bias reports obscured differences by gender and race. For example, a report from the Second Circuit indicated that

> while an attorney survey reported occasional conduct by judges and more by lawyers that to the observer seemed to reflect bias, virtually no incidents of deliberate bias were reported or found. . . . [O]n the whole, attorneys think that the judges and the courts of the Second Circuit are fair, and that they enjoy practicing in the federal system. . . . In short, most lawyers, most of the time, think that the federal courts are fair and good institutions."[90]

---

[83] Delaware Gender Bias Task Force, *supra* note 31.

[84] Schafran, *supra* note 20; Kearney & Sellers, *supra* note 17.

[85] Jaffe, Zerwer & Poisson, *supra* note 50.

[86] Susan Lloyd, "The Effects of Domestic Violence on Women's Employment," 19(2) *Law & Pol'y* 139 (1997).

[87] Kearney & Sellers, *supra* note 17.

[88] Indiana Supreme Court Commission on Race and Gender Fairness, *Honored to Serve: Indiana Supreme Court Commission on Race and Gender Fairness Executive Report and Recommendations* (2007).

[89] Id. at 28.

[90] George Lange III, "Second Circuit: Study of Gender, Race, and Ethnicity," 32 *Univ. Richmond L. Rev.* 703, 704 (1998).

This kind of writing uses "neutral" language to obscure gender differences. However, the fact that some members of all groups noted instances of bias does not mean that the problem is simply one of neuter incivility. The task forces that reported perceptions of bias against men also found perceptions of bias against women in the same areas. Rather than indicating that bias is not really a systemic problem, close examination of these complaints indicates that sexism and patriarchal gender stereotypes are harmful to women *and* men.

As is often the case, looking at numbers out of context can lead to misleading conclusions Resnik has pointed out that complaints of favoritism to women in sentencing and custody decisions must be considered in the context of the realities of the courts' trivialization and marginalization of women and actual differences in women's and men's behavior. Women really do most of the child care. Men really do most of the violence.[91] In looking at the areas where women were sometimes perceived to have an advantage in the courts (custody, divorce, and sentencing), the context clearly is important to the disparities. The studies that included consideration of the factors affecting the award of custody rather than just counting who got custody the most, in fact, found that "the interests of fathers are given more weight than the interests of mothers and children."[92]

Sex differences in the history of care and parental preferences in particular are relevant to the disposition of custody cases. Certainly these factors are affected by ongoing sex and gender disparities in areas like assumptions about who is responsible for child care and women's lower wages than men, but this does not mean that gender bias against men caused the outcome of more women than men having primary custody. Instead, most divorcing couples agree to continue some form of the child care arrangements that existed prior to divorce (mothers doing most of the care and almost always being primarily responsible for it).[93]

Perceptions of bias against men must also be considered in the context in which the gender bias studies took place. The reports that framed gender bias as an equal opportunity problem were among the last ones to be completed, in some cases twenty years behind the others, and were conducted well into the backlash against feminist work to secure women's rights.[94] North Dakota's report remarked on the "risk of misperceptions when gender neutral legal doctrine [sic] are perceived as biased because of disparate impact in case results,"[95] apparently dismissing gender disparity as accidental. Perceptions about bias against men are not surprising given what is known about privilege, challenges to it, and how they are perceived. Assertion of "equality with a vengeance" is a hallmark of resistance to feminism and other movements for social justice. This is one way to resist challenges to current power relations that are perceived accurately by those in power as potential threats to their privilege, power, and prerogative.

As with any other facet of human behavior, it is essential to consider the context and effects of bias in addition to perceptions of it. Significantly, the areas in which men report being disadvantaged exist because of rigid patriarchal gender roles: men have to pay more support because they make more money. They are less likely to be

---

[91] Resnik, *supra* note 1.

[92] Abrams & Greaney, *supra* note 74, at 826.

[93] Maccoby & Mnookin, *supra* note 45.

[94] Susan Faludi, *Backlash: The Undeclared War Against American Women* (1991).

[95] North Dakota Commission on Gender Fairness in the Courts, *Gender Fairness in North Dakota's Courts: A Ten Year Assessment, available at* http://www.ndcourts.gov/court/committees/gender/gfireport.htm#p1.

seen as the best parent because women continue to do the vast majority of child care and household labor. In the interest of justice, courts need to work to eliminate the unconscious and intentional influence of stereotypes that are not just gendered but patriarchal; not just affected by race but white supremacy.

One of the most troublesome realities for battered mothers is the combination of persistent and pervasive impacts of sexism or gender bias alongside inaccurate assumptions that sexism is no longer a factor in women's lives. The gender bias studies made very clear that sex and race shaped very different perspectives on and experiences in the court. Across the board, women reported more gender bias than men and evaluated what they did see more seriously. Men, on the other hand, reported much less bias or none at all.

UNEVEN PROGRESS: EFFECTS OF THE GENDER BIAS STUDIES

Several positive outcomes resulted from the gender bias studies and the national conversation on gender bias in the courts. First, the very participation of the majority of the states and circuits in self-study represents a major achievement. At the very least, the hegemonic position shifted from denial that gender bias could exist to the recognition that at least perceptions of bias are pervasive and significant. Second, the fact that gender bias can be grounds for appeal is a major advancement. The recognition that gender bias can compromise the court's ability to do its job is perhaps the most powerful example of how the gender bias study results have been institutionalized. Third, the continued work of antibias task forces is a major accomplishment. While some states and circuits abandoned their investigation of bias as soon as federal funding was eliminated, many localities have established permanent bodies to study and work to ameliorate ongoing bias. Fourth, the availability of training on bias issues, from sexual harassment prevention for court personnel to education on DV, is a significant indication of progress. Finally, increased awareness of the realities of battered women's experiences in the courts is a major achievement. The stories collected by the battered mothers' testimony projects show that these are substantive problems for a significant number of women. Recognition is the first step toward action.

CONCLUSION: DIRECTIONS FOR FUTURE RESEARCH AND ADVOCACY

There is more to do. As the research on battered mothers' experiences in the courts demonstrates, resistance to, and reaction against, the implementation of efforts to eliminate bias may be increasing as the most blatant forms of gender bias decrease. Battered mothers are seeing a backlash against efforts to address DV as well as a backlash against child support enforcement from both mainstream "fatherhood initiatives" and more radical fathers' rights groups as they push to reduce the penalties against abusers and enforce ongoing contact between abusers, mothers, and their children.

As many of the gender bias task forces and battered mothers' testimony projects have made clear, there is a paucity of data on issues related to the courts in general and the disposition of custody cases involving battered mothers in particular. The continued efforts of state and federal courts to track and address bias by gender and race are contributing to a growing body of data on the issue, but there is no large-scale uniform data collection effort under way at this time.

In addition, the social science research that is used to justify custody disposi-tion in contested custody cases is inadequate and inappropriate for that use since it overwhelmingly ignores violence and abuse. Even worse, what we do know about violence against mothers and children is largely ignored at custody determination. The ongoing risk of violence, including homicide, is downplayed, and minimal efforts like supervised visitation and batterer intervention programs are assumed to take care of the problem. What we know about the therapeutic value of separation from the abuse and acknowledgement that the abuse was wrong are also largely ignored by current practices.[96] Clearly, there is a need for more research in this area. Research on the outcomes of custody arrangements and other divorce outcomes must take battering into account.

Violence against women is well documented and prevalent. Courts need to rec-oncile the prevalence of violence and abuse with the practice of the courts in divorce and child custody disputes so that the safety of battered women and the best interests of their children are protected. Given that battering requires such a large percentage of state and private resources, the serious consideration of abuse should be seen as a form of prevention for the public good. The gender bias reports have helped to lay the foundation for progress on this issue.

---

[96] Palmer et al., *supra* note 52; Zorza, *supra* note 55.

Chapter 6

Domestic Violence, Contested Child Custody, and the Courts: Findings From Five Studies

by Sharon K. Araji, M.Ed., Ph.D., and Rebecca L. Bosek, Ph.D., L.M.F.T., L.P.C

INTRODUCTION

Today, wife/partner abuse and child abuse are publicly recognized as social problems[1]—recognition that occurred through the process of social constructionism.[2] From this perspective, individuals, religious groups, advocacy groups, social movement organizations, political interest groups, researchers, and the media voice concerns about social injustices. Spector and Kitsuse call these individuals or groups claims makers.[3] When claims makers are recognized by society as having a legitimate grievance, the social condition is defined as a social problem.[4]

Over the past several decades, claims makers have been attempting to elevate another type of family violence to the status of a social problem.[5] This type of abuse occurs when victims of domestic violence (DV) leave relationships with abusers and become entangled in contested child custody issues with the abusive parent. Some success is evident at defining this as a social problem.[6] According to Jaffe, Crooks, and Poisson, judges are now being asked to consider family violence as a significant factor in making decisions about a violent spouse/partner becoming a custodial parent or having regular unsupervised visitation with children.[7] Levin and Mills

---

[1] Evan Stark, in chapter 2 of his book, *Coercive Control: How Men Entrap Women in Personal Life* (2007), discusses how the DV movement is stalled. He notes at the end of the chapter that the entrapment of women in personal life looks very similar to when the first shelters for battered women opened three decades ago, and asks, why. The information in this chapter provides some insight as to how the legal and court systems contribute to locking women and their children in abusive relationships.

[2] D.R. Loeske, *Thinking About Social Problems: An Introduction to Constructionist Perspectives* (2d ed. 2003); M. Spector & J.I. Kitsuse, *Constructing Social Problems* (1977).

[3] Spector & Kitsuse, *supra* note 2.

[4] We are aware that some readers will be interested in knowing the percentages of respondents in each study who reported the specific types of problems shown in Table 6.1 (see "Recent Studies: Findings"). We opted not to present the statistics as it would have complicated the presentation and discussion of information. The interested reader could request the data from each of the studies reviewed. In the case of our Alaska study (S.K. Araji, Demographics From a Sample of Women Who Have Experienced Domestic Volence and Child Custody Disputes (2006) (unpublished raw data on file with the authors), we looked for reoccurring problems mentioned by respondents to our survey that fit into different themes. Problems that seemed unique to only a few respondents were not included in our study.

[5] A. Neustein & M. Lesher, *From Madness to Mutiny: Why Mothers Are Running From the Family Courts—And What Can Be Done About It* (2005).

[6] *E.g.*, id.

[7] P.G. Jaffe, C.V. Crooks & S.E. Poisson, "Common Misconceptions in Addressing Domestic Violence in Child Custody Disputes, 54 *Juv. & Fam. Ct. J.* 57 (2003).

note that battered women's advocates have successfully lobbied in some states for rebuttal presumption statutes that instruct judges to deny sole or joint custody to abusive parents unless they can provide persuasive evidence that they are a suitable custodial parent.[8] Jaffe, Crooks, and Wolfe,[9] and attorney Allen Bailey[10] caution that these legislative changes are not always reflected in actual court practices. It is this gap, or lack of any legislation in many states, that elevates the importance of DV in contested custody cases and has very recently led to an increasing number of books, academic articles, documentaries, and movies that call attention to the plight of battered partners, mostly women, who are battling for their children in the court system. In May 2007, ten mothers, one victimized child (now an adult), and leading national organizations filed a complaint against the United States with the Inter-American Commission on Human Rights (IACHR). The complaint detailed several cases where there was documented medical evidence of child sexual abuse, but in each case the abusive father was given full custody of the children he abused.[11] Several years earlier, the American Civil Liberties Union (ACLU) had filed a petition against the United States with the IACHR for its failure to protect Jessica Gonzales' three children from their abusive father, who ended up murdering them. This petition was the first of its kind asserting that DV victims had the right to be protected by the state from the violent acts of their abusers.[12]

Following a social constructionist perspective, the research presented in this chapter seeks to increase awareness of the consequences that DV victims/survivors and their children encounter in the court system when they become engaged in child custody disputes with abusive partners. To achieve the study purpose, we reviewed relevant literature, conducted independent research in Alaska,[13] and gathered information from studies completed in Pennsylvania,[14] Arizona,[15] Massachusetts,[16] and California.[17] Information from these five studies was used to develop a schema that reflects problems victims/survivors of DV encounter when they become involved in contested child custody cases with abusive partners. At the end of the chapter, recommendations for addressing this emerging social problem are discussed.

---

[8] A. Levin & L.G. Mills, "Fighting for Child Custody When Domestic Violence Is at Issue: Survey of State Laws. 48 *Soc. Work* 463 (2003).

[9] P.G. Jaffe, C.V. Crooks & D.W. Wolfe, "Legal and Policy Responses to Children Exposed to Domestic Violence: The Need to Evaluate Intended and Unintended Consequences," 6 *Clinical Child & Fam. Psychol. Rev.* 205 (2003).

[10] A. Bailey, Comments About Domestic Violence and Child Custody, in Educational Videotape: S.K. Araji (executive producer), *Listen to Our Voices* (2007).

[11] M. Ellsborg & L. Heise, "Bearing Witness: Ethics in Domestic Violence Research," 359 *Lancet* 1599 (2002).

[12] Id.

[13] Araji, *supra* note 4.

[14] Women's Law Project, *Justice in the Domestic Relations Division of Philadelphia Family Court: A Report to the Community* (2003).

[15] Arizona Coalition Against Domestic Violence, *Battered Mothers' Testimony Project: A Human Rights Approach to Child Custody and Domestic Violence* (2003).

[16] C. Cuthbert, K. Slote, M.G. Driggers, C.J. Mesh, L. Bancroft & J. Silverman, *Battered Mothers Speak Out: A Human Rights Report on Domestic Violence and Child Custody in the Massachusetts Family Courts* (2002) [hereinafter Cuthbert et al.].

[17] S. Heim, H. Grieco, S. Di Paola & R. Allen, *California National Organization for Women: Family Court Report* (2002) [hereinafter Heim et al.].

LITERATURE REVIEW

In today's society, millions of children experience family breakups from divorce, separation, and desertion,[18] and many of these children witness and/or become victims of abuse while living with their parents.[19] A fairly recent body of literature reveals that if violence exists in relationships, and victims attempt to terminate a relationship, custody disputes may be employed by abusive partners to maintain control of victims.[20] In most cases, the perpetrator is a male, and the victim is his female partner.

According to Lundy Bancroft, abusive male partners are overrepresented in highly litigious custody cases, and the motive appears to be the extension of control and intimidation of their partners, wherein children are used as a means to an end.[21] Based on extensive experience with disputed custody cases, Jaffe, Lemon, and Poisson indicate that abusive husbands take pleasure from the "games playing" in adversarial court proceedings where there is always a winner and a loser.[22] This setting allows abusers to continue the power and control games they employed before the victims left the relationships. Part of winning the game may involve visitation or custody requests when they have no interest in, or time to spend, with children. The end goal is to show the victims that they still have the power and control. As a consequence, the children become pawns in the game. There are some specific examples of these games in later sections of this chapter.

While the abusers tend to win custody and/or visitation battles in the courts, when DV victims try to use the legal system for protection and redress of harm, instead of winning the battles, they frequently experience secondary victimization by such professionals as judges, attorneys, child custody and psychological evaluators, among others. As Erez and Tontodonato note, these women may be victimized by the very courts from which they sought protection and justice.[23] King refers to this as "systemic stalking."[24]

In the next five subsections of this section, we group into categories the major problems that DV victims face when they are involved in contested custody battles. The information emerged from a review of research studies, published articles, books, and reports from around the United States and Canada.

---

[18] J.R. Eshleman & R.A Bulcroft, *The Family* (11th ed. 2006).

[19] L. Bancroft & J.G. Silverman, *The Batterer as Parent: Addressing the Impact of Domestic Violence on Family Dynamics* (2002); S.E. Doyne et al., "Custody Disputes Involving Domestic Violence: Making Children's Needs a Priority," 50(2) *Juv. & Fam. Ct. J.* 1 (1999); R.J. Gelles, *Intimate Violence in Families* (3d ed. 1997); P.G. Jaffe, M. Sudermann & R. Geffner, "Emerging Issues for Children Exposed to Domestic Violence," in R. Geffner, P.G. Jaffe & M. Sudermann eds., *Children Exposed to Domestic Violence: Current Issues in Research, Intervention, Prevention, and Policy Development* 1-8 (2000); K.M. Kitzmann et al., "Child Witnesses to Domestic Violence: A Meta-Analytic Review," 71 *J. Counseling & Clinical Psychol.* 339 (2003); E. Peled, P.J. Jaffe & J.L. Edleson eds., *Ending the Cycle of Violence: Community Response to Children of Battered Women* (1995).

[20] M. McMahon, J. Neville-Sorvilles & L. Schubert, "Undoing Harm to Children: The Duluth Visitation Center," in M.F. Shepard & E.L. Pence eds., *Coordinating Community Responses to Domestic Violence: Lessons From Duluth and Beyond* 151–68 (1999).

[21] L. Bancroft, *When Dad Hurts Mom: Helping Your Children Heal the Wounds of Witnessing Abuse* (2004).

[22] P.G. Jaffe, N.K. Lemon, S.E. Poisson, *Child Custody and Domestic Violence: A Call for Safety and Accountability* (2002).

[23] E. Erez & P. Tontodonato, "The Effect of Victim Participation in Sentencing on Sentence Outcome, 28(3) *Criminology* 451 (1990).

[24] J. King, *Breaking the Cycle of Domestic Abuse and Healing the Harm of Relationship Violence* (2008), http://www.dr.jeanneking.com/needhelp.htm.

Importance of Finances/Resources to Custody Decisions

Women entering the court system regularly assume initial financial responsibility for children, have fewer available resources, and experience anxiety about child support. They often express concerns over the complex legal process and delays of the system, and lack adequate child care throughout the lengthy court process.[25] This is especially problematic if they are employed. Some experience ongoing manipulation and coercion by their partners when they feel pressured or are forced to cooperate with perpetrators due to fears of losing their children or needed child support.[26]

Abusive partners often have access to more resources and use these to obtain custody. Abusers may refuse to pay alimony or child support, which can result in women being evicted from their homes or having their homes sold. Women and children end up homeless.[27] Conversely, the perpetrators may have financial means to obtain a more attractive home and lifestyle in an effort to sway both custody evaluators and judges.[28]

Another strategy used by perpetrators is to deplete the financial resources of victims. Women describe financial abuse including partners or former partners not being forthright about assets, terminating their employment to avoid support payments, threatening the earning capacity of victims, and depleting joint bank accounts.[29]

The court system itself may be used to deplete the financial resources of victims. Perpetrators accomplish this through multiple court filings, depositions, and extended discovery practice. Perpetrators may attempt to get women who have few or no resources to pay expenses related to children and repeatedly bring their victims back to court to resolve disagreements. These practices force women to sink further into debt.[30] When court cases are lengthy and ongoing, the parent who is less financially capable (typically the mother) is less likely to gain custody due to her inability to retain an attorney.[31] Frequently women who lack the financial resources to pay the costs associated with legal representation experience financial devastation.[32]

When protective parents file claims contrary to the wishes of judges, they may incur excessive legal costs that perpetrators are not required to pay, be required to pay for their supervised visitations with children, and be threatened with loss of maintenance and child support for lack of compliance.[33]

A second problem faced by protective parents in contested custody cases that involve DV is a lack of knowledge by those involved in the case, including attorneys,

---

[25] S.C. Hare, "What Do Battered Women Want? Opinions on Prosecution, 21(5) *Violence & Victims* 611 (2006).

[26] D. Kurz, "Separation, Divorce, and Woman Abuse," 2(1) *Violence Against Women* 63 (2006).

[27] Bancroft, *supra* note 21.

[28] L. Bancroft, *Why Does He Do That? Inside the Minds of Angry and Controlling Men* (2002).

[29] Jaffe, Crooks & Poisson, *supra* note 7.

[30] J. Zorza, "How Abused Women Can Use the Law to Help Protect Their Children," in E. Peled, P.G. Jaffe & J.L. Edleson eds., *Ending the Cycle of Violence: Community Responses to Children of Battered Women* 147–69 (1995) [hereinafter Zorza 1995a]; J. Zorza, "Recognizing and Protecting the Privacy and Confidentiality Needs of Battered Women," 29 *Fam. L.Q.* 273 (1995) [hereinafter Zorza 1995b].

[31] Jaffe, Crooks & Poisson, *supra* note 7.

[32] Bancroft, *supra* note 28; Jaffe, Crooks & Poisson, *supra* note 7.

[33] Neustein & Lesher, *supra* note 5.

judges, child custody evaluators, and psychologists, among others. This problem is the focus of the next section.

Court Systems Lacking Knowledge About, or Consideration of, Domestic Violence in Custody/Visitation Decisions

Historically, DV has not been considered a relevant issue in child custody cases, as battering was considered a separate issue from parenting skills.[34] Whereas courts typically grant petitions for protective orders, they are often dismissed when women drop their cases or fail to continue the court process.[35] Some judges issue mutual restraining orders against both the victim and perpetrator. In the case of the victim, this is illegal and violates her right to due process. It also endangers the victim and her children.[36] When women either initiate or have contact with the perpetrators, they may be viewed and treated in a hostile or less sympathetic manner by the courts.[37]

Perpetrators who have protection orders against them may be denied custody but granted visitation. When this happens, women are placed in positions where they experience ongoing pressure, threats, and coercion, and children are placed at risk.[38] Now that a few successful civil suits have been filed on behalf of children harmed during child custody visits, there is increasing awareness that children raised in homes where DV occurs must be kept safe under general protective orders.[39]

Fear that abusive partners will get custody of children is a deterrent to women leaving battering relationships. Some women remain in battering relationships until they are sure the batterers will not gain custody, until children are old enough to protect younger siblings, or until children are old enough for the court to give weight to their preferences to remain with their mothers.[40] However, when women choose to remain in abusive relationships, this decision may be used against them in custody hearings. Ironically, they may be accused of child abuse for not attempting to remove the children from a dangerous situation.[41]

Women with children who attempt to receive assistance through the court system describe the overall process as intimidating, overwhelming, time consuming, and are often

---

[34] P.G. Jaffe & R. Geffner, "Child Custody Disputes and Domestic Violence: Critical Issues for Mental Health, Social Service, and Legal Professionals," in G.W. Holden, R. Geffner & E.N. Jouriles eds., *Children Exposed to Marital Violence: Theory, Research, and Applied Issues* 371–409 (1998).

[35] A.R. Roberts & K. Kurst-Swanger, "Court Responses to Battered Women and Their Children," in A.R. Roberts ed., *Handbook of Domestic Violence Intervention Strategies: Policies, Programs, and Legal Remedies* 127–46 (2002).

[36] J. Zorza, *What Is Wrong With Mutual Orders of Protection? Reprint From Domestic Violence Report* (1999).

[37] M.A. Dutton, *Empowering and Healing the Battered Woman: A Model for Assessment and Intervention* (1992); R. Gonzales, Interview on Domestic Violence, Child Custody, and the Legal System, in Educational Videotape: S.K. Araji (executive producer), *Listen to Our Voices* (2007).

[38] L.N. Rosen & C.S. O'Sullivan, "Outcomes of Custody and Visitation Petitions When Fathers Are Restrained by Protection Orders: The Case of The New York Family Courts," 11(8) *Violence Against Women* 1054 (2005).

[39] L.G. Mills, "Killing Her Softly: Intimate Abuse and the Violence of State Intervention, 113(2) *Harv. L. Rev.* 550 (1999).

[40] J.M. Davies, E. Lyon & D. Monti-Catania, *Safety Planning With Battered Women: Complex Lives/Difficult Choices* (1998).

[41] E.M. Schneider, *Battered Women & Feminist Lawmaking* (2000).

fearful that they will not receive needed protection.[42] Some women describe how the court-room atmosphere and the demeanor of judges who are condescending, patronizing, and demeaning results in women feeling frightened, degraded, humiliated, and embarrassed.[43]

Judges are often untrained and may have misconceptions and misunderstandings about the impact of DV on children.[44] Some women believe that the court minimizes harm to children, placing more importance on settling cases as fast as possible.[45] Judges with inadequate training may mistakenly believe that batterers should be awarded visitation or custody without realizing the best predictor of subsequent child adjustment is when the child is no longer exposed to violence.[46]

The fact that DV does not appear to be considered in awarding child custody or visitation is reported by Kernic, Monary-Ernsdorff, Koepsell, and Holt.[47] They found that women with a documented history of DV are no more likely than other women to be awarded legal custody, and perpetrators often receive unsupervised visitation. Even when judges have adequate training on DV, and women are awarded sole physical custody, perpetrators often are given unrestricted and unstructured visitation with children, thereby placing them at risk.[48]

When women perceive that the court system lacks knowledge of, or is insensitive to, issues regarding DV, they may choose not to use the available services.[49] Protective parents view judges as being most ineffective when they are tired, overworked, and lack knowledge of community resources, and these issues are compounded when the larger court system lacks access to translation services, advocacy, and relationships with local shelters.[50] Judges are seen as being supportive when they have thorough training on family violence issues.[51]

In addition to problems related to judges and the court system, many attorneys and mental health professionals may also be untrained or inadequately trained in DV. This results in judges not receiving sufficient evidence to recognize or favorably rule on the importance of DV issues.[52] Women generally consider their lawyers to be most effective when they have knowledge about DV, listen to their concerns, and inquire about their safety and their children's well-being.[53]

Similarly, women who perceive that police and prosecutors create unnecessary procedural obstacles and barriers and, moreover, believe that the court bureaucracy

---

[42] Roberts & Kurst-Swanger, *supra* note 35.

[43] J. Ptacek, *Battered Women in the Courtroom: The Power of Judicial Responses* (1999).

[44] L.S. Carter, L.A. Weithorn & R.E. Behrman, "Domestic Violence and Children: Analysis and Recommendations," 9(3) *Future of Children* 4 (1999); Jaffe & Geffner, *supra* note 34.

[45] Jaffe, Crooks & Poisson, *supra* note 7.

[46] Id.

[47] M.A. Kernic et al., "Children in the Crossfire: Child Custody Determinations Among Couples With a History of Intimate Partner Violence, 11(8) *Violence Against Women* 991 (2005).

[48] A.C. Morrill, J. Dai, S. Dunn, I. Sung & S. Smith, "Child Custody and Visitation Decisions When the Father Has Perpetrated Violence Against the Mother," 11(8) *Violence Against Women* 1076 (2005).

[49] Davies, Lyon & Monti-Catania, *supra* note 40.

[50] Ptacek, *supra* note 43.

[51] Jaffe & Geffner, *supra* note 34.

[52] M.D. Fields, "Getting Beyond 'What Did She Do to Provoke Him?' Comments by a Retired Judge on the Special Issue on Child Custody and Domestic Violence," 14(1) *Violence Against Women* 93 (2008).

[53] Jaffe, Crooks & Poisson, *supra* note 7.

is nonresponsive and impersonal, may drop their cases.[54] When prosecutors fail to prosecute DV cases, women may feel that they and their children will not be protected and, correspondingly, they may weigh the little relief they would receive from the court compared to further angering the perpetrators.[55]

Finally, battered women feel safest when they have choices about court intervention and are able to partner with the police, prosecutors, and medical personnel in the arrest and prosecution of DV crimes.[56]

Manipulative Strategies Used by Domestic Violence Perpetrators

In addition to problems protective parents face with the professionals (see "Court Systems Lacking Knowledge About, or Consideration of, Domestic Violence in Custody/Visitation Decisions"), perpetrators may find attorneys who will use legal strategies such as adjournments and delays until they are assigned judges who either lacks knowledge about DV or will render decisions favorable to their side.[57] Some strategies perpetrators use include presenting themselves as victims, claiming fear of or abuse by the victims, and setting up circumstances whereby court questioning revolves around whether the victims have mental health issues. Others manipulate new wives or partners into providing false information about the protective parents to the courts, in an effort to sway outcomes.[58] Perpetrators of DV appear to be quite good at shifting responsibility for their behavior to their victims.[59] Some perpetrators have the ability to present themselves as caring, concerned, and reasonable. This results in judges having difficulties believing accusations of DV,[60] and perpetrators are therefore often able to convince judges that they should be awarded custody.[61] These manipulative strategies serve as examples of the games playing techniques perpetrators use in the courtroom.

Changes in laws concerning what should be done in cases where DV is a factor do not always result in corresponding changes in the actual practice of the law.[62] When prosecutors and judges hold personal values that are contrary to the law, discretion may be used as a means to ignore laws. The result is that women are left with little recourse to contest the actions and decisions of the courts.[63]

---

[54] E. Buzawa, T.L. Austin & C.G. Buzawa, "Responding to Crimesof Violence Against Women: Gender Differences Versus Organizational Imperatives," 10(41) *Crime & Delinquency* 443 (1995).

[55] A. Gewirtz et al., " Domestic Violence Cases Involving Children: Effects of an Evidence-Based Prosecution Approach," 21(2) *Violence & Victims* 213 (2006).

[56] Mills, *supra* note 39.

[57] Jaffe, Crooks & Poisson, *supra* note 7.

[58] Bancroft, *supra* note 21.

[59] C. Dalton, S. Carbon & N. Olesen, "High Conflict Divorce, Violence, and Abuse: Implications for Custody and Visitation Decisions," 54 *Juv. & Fam. Ct. J.* 11 (2003).

[60] Bancroft, *supra* note 28; Dalton, Carbon & Olesen, *supra* note 59; D.M. Goelman, F.L. Lehrman & R.L. Valente eds., *The Impact of Domestic Violence on Your Legal Practice: A Lawyer's Handbook* (1996).

[61] P. Chesler, *Mothers on Trial: The Battle for Children and Custody* (1991); Zorza, 1995a, *supra* note 30; Zorza 1995b, *supra* note 30.

[62] Bailey, *supra* note 10; Bancroft, *supra* note 28; Jaffe, Crooks & Wolfe, *supra* note 9.

[63] E.S. Buzawa & C.G. Buzawa, *Domestic Violence: The Criminal Justice Response* (1990).

Perpetrators use a wide variety of manipulative tactics and techniques to exert and maintain control over victims. Some cease battering for varying periods of time,[64] while others self-regulate their behavior and only batter under certain conditions and circumstances.[65]

Following separation, batterers may threaten to report women to child welfare as unfit mothers; kidnap the children and take them out of state; threaten child abuse; or verbally, physically, or sexually abuse the children.[66] When women are on immigrant status, batterers may threaten them with deportation, or when child welfare is involved, women may not disclose child abuse because they fear the batterers will turn them in to the immigration authorities.[67]

Batterers may use visitation as a means to manipulate the children and/or undermine the mothers' parental authority.[68] Similarly, they may attempt to blame the mothers for alienating the children.[69] Some batterers exert their rights to visitation, yet spend little time with the children, often leaving them with other family members or new partners.[70] Some use problems between the mother and her children as evidence that the victim is neglectful, abusive, and incompetent.[71] When protection or no-contact orders exist, batterers may use visitation with children as a means to manipulate, verbally harass, or physically assault women.[72]

Women sometimes feel they are degraded, embarrassed, or treated in a condescending or patronizing manner.[73] Some women view this treatment as representing gender bias, the topic of the next section.

Gender Bias

When judges are required to determine whether DV is a factor in child custody decisions, judicial stereotyping sometimes results in women being determined unfit. This increases the likelihood that batterers will gain child custody.[74] Double standards may also operate whereby male parents are determined to be fit by virtue of attempts to gain custody, and female parents are determined unfit because they did not protect themselves or leave abusive relationships.[75] In other situations, mothers are judged on their past histories as parents, whereas fathers are judged on their future intentions.[76] When the same standard is applied to both males and females, it has positive outcomes for males and negative consequences for females. Similarly, gender bias is in operation

---

[64] Gelles, *supra* note 19.

[65] Dalton, Carbon & Oleson, *supra* note 59.

[66] Ptacek, *supra* note 43.

[67] L.A. Fontes, *Child Abuse and Culture: Working With Diverse Families* (2005).

[68] Bancroft, *supra* note 28; Bancroft, *supra* note 21; L. Bancroft & J.G. Silverman, "Assessing Abusers' Risks to Children," in P.G. Jaffe, L.L. Baker & A.J. Cunningham, eds., *Protecting Children From Domestic Violence: Strategies for Community Intervention* 101-20 (2004); Goelman, Lehrman & Valente, *supra* note 60.

[69] Jaffe, Crooks & Poisson, *supra* note 7.

[70] Bancroft, *supra* note 28.

[71] Dalton, Carbon & Olesen, *supra* note 59.

[72] McMahon, Neville-Sorvilles & Schubert, *supra* note 20.

[73] Ptacek, *supra* note 43.

[74] Schneider, *supra* note 41.

[75] Id.

[76] Bancroft & Silverman, *supra* note 19.

when consideration is given to reports suggesting children raised by single mothers are emotionally damaged due to lack of contact with fathers, whereas the same claim is not made against children raised by single fathers, particularly since overall reports of emotional damage are largely exaggerated.[77]

In addition to the problem areas just discussed, the emergence of the fathers' rights (FRs) movement has promoted use of Richard Gardner's Parental Alienation Syndrome concept and the friendly parent concept against DV victims seeking custody of children. These are the topics of the next three subsections.[78]

Fathers' Rights Movement

Feminist writer Louise Armstrong describes the development of the FRs movement as a response to pressures placed on fathers to provide child support.[79] She identifies the Men's Equality Now International Coalition as one of the first FRs groups to provide information on winning child custody and reducing child support through claims of alienation of affection and visitation rights being ignored.[80] Some lawyers associated with FRs groups maintain close relationships with judges. When women make accusations of child sexual abuse, court personnel may not respond promptly due to concerns that women's claims are largely fabricated.[81] Court personnel often find themselves in positions of conflict. On one side, FRs groups claim men are deprived of parental rights, and, on the other, DV advocates claim that the court fails to keep women and children safe. Afraid to act for fear of accusations of bias, the end result is an inept polarized system.[82]

Parental Alienation Syndrome

In 1985, psychiatrist Richard A. Gardner coined the term "Parental Alienation Syndrome" (PAS) to describe a disorder whereby children are programmed by one parent to alienate the other parent. According to Gardner, typically the parent doing the alienation is the mother, and the parent who is alienated is the father.[83] The American Psychological Association (APA) Presidential Task Force on Violence and the Family raised concerns about the scientific basis for PAS.[84] Their written report acknowledged that while many professionals routinely follow APA recommendations, claims of parental alienation are often mistakenly made in contested child custody cases. PAS is not recognized in the most current version of the *Diagnostic and Statistical Manual of Mental Disorders* (DSM-IV-TR) as a legitimate syndrome.[85]

---

[77] Bancroft, *supra* note 21.

[78] R.A. Gardner, *The Parental Alienation Syndrome and the Differentiation Between Fabricated and Genuine Child Sexual Abuse* (1987).

[79] L. Armstrong, *Rocking The Cradle of Sexual Politics: What Happened When Women Said Incest* (1994).

[80] Id.

[81] Neustein & Lesher, *supra* note 5.

[82] Jaffe, Lemon & Poisson, *supra* note 22.

[83] Gardner, *supra* note 78; R.A. Gardner, *True and False Accusations of Child Sex Abuse* (1992).

[84] American Psychological Association (APA), Presidential Task Force on Violence and the Family, *Violence and the Family* (1996).

[85] American Psychiatric Association, *Diagnostic and Statistical Manual of Mental Disorders-IV-TR* (4th ed. text revision 2000).

The National Council of Juvenile and Family Court Judges notes that PAS diagnoses and allegations of "parental alienation" are invalid. An argument is made that the diagnoses or allegations should not be admissible in court or should be stricken as not meeting the evidentiary standard for scientific evidence.[86]

According to Attorney Michelle Minor,[87] who has extensive experience working with victims of DV in contested custody cases, some judges are aware that PAS is not widely recognized as a psychological construct. They avoid using PAS, but use the words parental alienation interchangeably with the same intent and meaning associated with PAS. Hence, the shortened version, parental alienation, has the same detrimental effects on the victims as use of the PAS concept.

In situations whereby children either align themselves with victimized parents (most often women) or reject abusive perpetrators (generally men), the perpetrators often blame the women for alienating the children.[88] In situations where DV occurs and the perpetrator claims parental alienation, the perpetrator has typically caused the alienation through abuse of the children and/or his partner.[89] When expert witnesses who lack knowledge about the dynamics of DV make recommendations to the courts, perpetrators may be successful in gaining custody of children after making claims of PAS. This allows perpetrators to continue having power and control over victims and their children.[90]

Friendly Parent Concept

The friendly parent concept, like PAS, was created by Richard Gardner and may also be used in contested child custody cases.[91] Basically, this concept focuses on premises about the willingness of each parent to provide an opportunity for a frequent, open, and loving relationship between the opposite parent and the children. Friendly parent provisions promote and favor the parent who appears most willing to support and maintain a relationship between the other parent and the children. Women who have been battered may be advised to encourage a relationship between the perpetrators and children, even when this places them and their children in danger. If mothers do not comply, they risk losing custody.[92] These provisions work for perpetrators, as even false allegations of being denied access to children may increase the likelihood of gaining custody.[93] Women who attempt to limit children's contacts with perpetrators may be labeled as hostile and resistant to the efforts of perpetrators to maintain a

---

[86] C. Dalton, L.M. Drozd & F. Wong, *Navigating Custody and Visitation Evaluations in Cases With Domestic Violence: A Judge's Guide* (2006).

[87] M.V. Minor, personal communication, June 3, 2008 (on file with authors).

[88] J.W. Gould & D.A. Martindale, *The Art and Science of Child Custody Evaluations* (2007).

[89] Jaffe, Lemon & Poisson, *supra* note 22.

[90] E. Stark, "Preparing for Expert Testimony in Domestic Violence Cases," in A.R. Roberts ed., *Handbook of Domestic Violence Intervention Strategies*: *Policies, Programs, and Legal Remedies* 216–52 (2002).

[91] J. Zorza, "Child Custody Practices of The Family Courts in Cases Involving Domestic Violence," in Chapter 1 of this volume.

[92] Doyne et al., *supra* note 19.

[93] J. Zorza, "Protecting the Children in Custody Disputes When One Parent Abuses the Other," 29 *Clearinghouse Rev.* 1113 (1996); J. Zorza, "The 'Friendly Parent' Concept—Another Gender Biased Legacy From Richard Gardner," 12(5) *Domestic Violence Rep.* 74 (2007).

relationship with the children, and the court may correspondingly punish these women for their efforts to keep children safe.[94] In order to remedy this situation, some states have overcome these provisions by enacting legislation that recommends that frequent and continuing contact between an abusive parent and children places children at risk, and the safety and welfare of children should take precedence over other factors.[95]

The last two subsections of the literature review discuss how mediation, child custody evaluations, and psychological evaluations are used in contested custody cases. As will become evident, these frequently work against protective parents when DV is a factor in relationships.

Considerations of Mediation

The specialized needs of battered women and children in the court system placed emphasis on the need for services, and an early focus was placed on mediation, supervised visitation centers, and custody evaluations.[96] While the low costs associated with mediation are attractive to some women, they often end up coerced into agreements, accept limited child support, do not receive equitable decisions, and have no means to enforce agreements.[97] Furthermore, DV is often not reported to the courts, women remain at risk due to lack of supervised child exchanges, and children lack protection.[98] Battered women are also harmed because batterers seldom abide by mediated agreements. These cases often end up costing more and result in fewer protections for women and children.[99]

With growing knowledge of the damaging effects of DV on both women and children, court recommendations moved toward awareness that mediation and joint custody potentially place women and children at risk and might not be in the best interests of the children (BIC).[100] Mandated mediation and joint custody are considered ineffective due to a strong tendency to perpetuate situations of intimidation and unequal power distribution.[101] Although ethical considerations recommend that mediation be terminated when inequities in bargaining power exist, few mediators actually end sessions.[102] Since a primary focus on mediation is not to assign blame to either party, batterers are in a position where they do not have to accept responsibility for their behavior and frequently attribute their battering to provocation by the victims or relationship problems.[103] Finally,

---

[94] Bancroft, *supra* note 21; Jaffe, Crooks & Poisson, *supra* note 7.

[95] Jaffe, Lemon & Poisson, *supra* note 22.

[96] P.G. Jaffe, D.A. Wolfe & S.K. Wilson, *Children of Battered Women* (1990).

[97] A.R. Imbrogno & S. Imbrogno, "Mediation in Court Cases of Domestic Violence," 61(4) *Families in Soc'y* 392 (2000).

[98] N.E. Johnson, D.P. Saccuzzo & W.J. Koen, "Child Custody Mediation in Cases of Domestic Violence: Empirical Evidence of a Failure to Protect," 11(8) *Violence Against Women* 1022 (2005).

[99] Zorza, *supra* note 36.

[100] J.N. Bow & P. Boxer, "Assessing Allegations of Domestic Violence in Child Custody Evaluations," 18(12) *J. Interpersonal Violence* 1394 (2003); Johnson, Saccuzzo & Koen, *supra* note 98; A.D. Laviolette & O.W. Barnett, *It Could Happen to Anyone: Why Battered Women Stay* (2d ed. 2000).

[101] M.K. Pruett & C. Santangelo, "Joint Custody and Empirical Knowledge: The Estranged Bedfellows of Divorce, in R. M. Galatzer-Levy ed., *The Scientific Basis of Child Custody Decisions* 389–424 (1999).

[102] Zorza, 1995a, *supra* note 30; Zorza 1995b, *supra* note 30.

[103] Buzawa & Buzawa, *supra* note 63.

mediators, guardians ad litem (GALs), and custody evaluators often do not have the necessary skills and training to deal with custody situations when DV is an issue. This places battered women and children in harms way.[104]

Considerations of Child Custody and Psychological Evaluations

All states cite the BIC as the primary consideration when making child custody decisions. Due to some problems inherent in mediation, child custody evaluations are increasingly used by court personnel when making decisions.[105] This can be a problem because child custody evaluations do not necessarily equate to child safety, as DV and child abuse may not be documented in child custody evaluations.[106] Also, custody evaluators can be influenced by positive experiences with perpetrators or manipulated by them. In either case, feelings for perpetrators may override evidence of abuse.[107] Some custody evaluators accuse battered women of exaggerating violent episodes in order to manipulate the court and influence custody decisions.[108] Even when documentation exists, custody evaluators may not take DV into consideration when making recommendations.[109] Custody evaluators may choose not to investigate allegations of abuse, fail to contact third-party sources, dismiss allegations on the basis of favorable perceptions of perpetrators, or place too much reliance on the findings of psychological test results.[110] Other custody evaluators fail to use specialized assessment instruments, tests, and questionnaires specifically geared toward providing DV information[111] or use ones never designed for use with battered women or even in custody situations.[112] Many custody evaluators consider alienation to be a more important factor than DV in child custody decisions and, moreover, recommend against sole or joint custody to parents who alienate children.[113]

Custody evaluators may make recommendations consistent with previous rulings of judges.[114] At times, they may not follow the law, offer opinions where there is no scientific basis, and rely on test results that have no established basis for rendering child custody decisions.[115] Child custody evaluators often do not have the necessary skills and training to deal with custody situations when DV has been an issue. However, the second author of this chapter was excluded as a custody evaluator on the grounds that she had

---

[104] Roberts & Kurst-Swanger, *supra* note 35.

[105] Jaffe, Wolfe & Wilson, *supra* note 96.

[106] Bancroft & Silverman, *supra* note 19; L.S. Horvath, T.K. Logan & R. Walker, "Child Custody Cases: A Content Analysis of Evaluations in Practice," 33(6) *Prof. Psychol.: Res. & Prac.* 557 (2002).

[107] Bancroft & Silverman, *supra* note 19.

[108] Doyne et al., *supra* note 19; Jaffe & Geffner, *supra* note 34.

[109] Jaffe, Crooks & Poisson, *supra* note 7.

[110] Bancroft & Silverman, *supra* note 19.

[111] Bow & Boxer, *supra* note 100.

[112] Dalton, Drozd & Wong, *supra* note 86.

[113] M.J. Ackerman & M.C. Ackerman,"Child Custody Evaluation Practices: A 1996 Survey of Psychologists," 30 *Fam. L.Q.* 565 (1996).

[114] L.E. Stamps, S, Kunen & A. Rock-Faucheux, "Judges Beliefs Dealing With Child Custody Decisions," in C.A. Everett ed., *Child Custody: Legal Decisions and Family Outcomes* 3–16 (1997).

[115] R.E. Emery, R.K. Otto & W.T. O'Donohue, "Custody Evaluations: Limited Science and a Flawed System," 6(1) *Psychol. Sci. in Pub. Int.* 1 (2007).

too much training and knowledge about DV and contested child custody. On this basis, it was concluded that she would be unable to render impartial recommendations. Attorneys for batterers have a strong preference to use professionals for child custody evaluations who lack training and expertise. This increases the likelihood of them getting favorable outcomes for the batterers. Courts should be extremely cautious when using these professionals to make custody or visitation decisions,[116] and there should be a mechanism whereby custody evaluators are held to an established standard of practice.[117]

RECENT STUDIES: DATA AND METHODS

To this point, this chapter has presented a review of factors and practices that have detrimental effects on women and children when DV is involved in contested child custody cases. This section focuses on information from five recent studies that relate to this topic.

Alaska Study

The Alaska study[118] was prompted by exposure to two survey studies that had been conducted in Arizona[119] and Massachusetts[120] on the topic of DV and contested child custody. After the senior author reviewed the earlier studies, she decided to replicate them in Alaska, given Alaska's continuous high rates of DV and child abuse. Once funding for the project was secured, a survey instrument that was similar to those used in the Arizona and Massachusetts studies was completed and pretested. Before the data-gathering stage of the study, the project was approved by the University of Alaska Anchorage (UAA) Institutional Review Board.

Several methods of gathering data were used. First, study participants who were victims of DV in the past or who were presently involved in child custody disputes in the Alaska court system within the past ten years were identified and mailed a twenty-page survey. These respondents are referred to as protective parents, a term coined by H. Joan Pennington to describe parents, usually mothers, who enter the family court system as a means to protect their children from alleged sexual abuse by the fathers.[121] Second, one to two years later, the senior author contacted a sample of the protective parents who had previously completed the initial survey for an update of information. The data-gathering methods, sampling procedures, and statistical tools employed are described below.

Survey. The initial survey was patterned after studies of victims of DV who had been involved in child custody disputes in Arizona[122] and Massachusetts.[123] Using the same survey instrument in all three studies allows, after some editing, for more accurate comparisons than would be the case if the questions were different. Our study would then resemble a replication study.

---

[116] Bancroft & Silverman, *supra* note 19; Roberts & Kurst-Swanger, *supra* note 35.
[117] Emery, Otto & O'Donohue, *supra* note 115; Horvath, Logan & Walker, *supra* note 106.
[118] Araji, *supra* note 4.
[119] Arizona Coalition Against Domestic Violence, *supra* note 15.
[120] Cuthbert et al., *supra* note 16.
[121] H.J. Pennington, *The Hardest Case: Custody and Incest* (1993)
[122] Arizona Coalition Against Domestic Violence, *supra* note 15.
[123] Cuthbert et al., *supra* note 16.

The survey was twenty pages in length and included basic demographic questions about the victims (protective parents), their abusive partners, and their children. There were questions about types and duration of abusive acts by partners toward the victims and their children. Inquiries were also made about the relationship between alcohol and/or drug use and DV.

As the research is primarily on what happens to protective parents and their children once they get involved in child custody disputes in the courts, many questions were included about victims' experiences with judges, attorneys, custody evaluators, psychological evaluators, child protective services (CPS) workers, mediators, GALs, and the police. The survey contained both structured and open-ended questions, and went through various editing stages by the senior author and a colleague, André Rosay, as well as with others familiar with survey construction and/or the research topic.

Samples/Sampling Procedures. When funds had been secured through UAA faculty development awards, several women who had been involved in contested child custody cases in Alaska were contacted and asked to participate in the study. These women also agreed to help identify others (mostly women) whom they knew had been or were involved in similar cases in Alaska. Before the identified victims were contacted by the senior author, one person from the initial group of women contacted them and asked if they would be interested in taking part in a survey study. If they were, their names and contact information were given to the senior author. From that point on, a snowball approach was used to locate participants for the study. Some state and local advocacy groups and social service agencies also helped recruit study participants. The criteria imposed on participating in the study were that the contested child custody case had to have occurred within the last ten years (1996-2005) and been heard in an Alaskan court. Respondents were given an option of completing the survey by phone or having it mailed. Given the length and topic of the survey, all opted to have it mailed.

Over the course of two years, sixty-four individuals were sent surveys and, as a gesture of appreciation, offered $25 for participating in the study. We received thirty-four completed surveys, representing a 53 percent response rate.

To add a long-term dimension to the study, one to two years later, the senior author contacted a 20 percent convenience sample (N = 7) of protective parents who had completed the initial survey to determine what had happened to them and their children since that time. An open-ended question aimed at gathering this information was e-mailed to seven women whom we had maintained contact with over the two-year study period. All seven women (100 percent) responded to the request.

We included both structured and open-ended questions in our survey study and employed SPSS version 16.0 Family for Windows to analyze quantitative data. As the respondents in our study had written extensive answers to open-ended questions, we used HyperRESEARCH, version 2.6.1, for qualitative data analysis.

Arizona and Massachusetts Studies

The Arizona study[124] was most similar to the Alaska study, as it was based solely on survey data, so we patterned our survey after this. Fifty-seven women had participated in the study.

---

[124] Arizona Coalition Against Domestic Violence, *supra* note 15.

Questions asked in the Massachusetts[125] study were similar to the studies conducted in Arizona and Alaska,[126] but their methods of gathering data were much more extensive. This study consisted of interviews with forty victims of DV who were involved in contested child custody cases, a written survey completed by thrity-one advocates for DV victims, and focus groups that involved twenty-three women who were either survivors of DV and/or advocates for DV victims. In addition, interviews were conducted with sixteen state professionals familiar with DV and child custody issues.

Pennsylvania Study

Methods of gathering information in the Pennsylvania study[127] varied from those in Alaska, [128] Arizona, [129] and Massachusetts. [130] Data was gathered from seven different sources within the Domestic Relations Division of the Philadelphia Family Court. These sources included formal court observations, descriptions of experiences, telephone surveys, testimonies from court hearings, telephone calls, reviews of court information and notices, and information obtained from the final report of the Pennsylvania Supreme Court Committee. The unduplicated observations totaled information from 566 cases that involved protection orders from abuse and 218 cases that involved child custody.

California Study

The California study[131] was undertaken by the California National Organization for Women (NOW). Similar to the study done in Pennsylvania, [132] information was derived from a variety of sources. This included data from 212 usable questionnaires from around the United States, as well as information from eighty case studies, a review of court documents, and written case histories.

RECENT STUDIES: FINDINGS

Across the five studies, an effort was made to find themes—patterns of problems associated with contested child custody cases where protective parents had also experienced DV (see Table 6.1).

Problems With Joint Custody and Visitation

As can be seen, the responses of protective parents were categorized into seven themes. Theme I focused on problems with joint custody and visitation.[133] Factors

---

[125] Cuthbert et al., *supra* note 16.
[126] Araji, *supra* note 4.
[127] Women's Law Project, *supra* note 14.
[128] Araji, *supra* note 4.
[129] Arizona Coalition Against Domestic Violence, *supra* note 15.
[130] Cuthbert et al., *supra* note 16.
[131] Heim et al., *supra* note 17.
[132] Women's Law Project, *supra* note 14.
[133] After this chapter was completed in April 2008, we became aware of two other relevant studies. One was completed by the Voices of Women Organizing Project, *Executive Summary.*

related to this theme included (1) sole or joint custody being awarded to perpetrators of DV; (2) children being emotionally, physically, or sexually abused by perpetrators; (3) perpetrators abusing alcohol, drugs, and/or carrying weapons that endangered children's safety; (4) children witnessing DV between parents; (5) children and protective parents living in reduced financial circumstances; (6) other problems protective parents encountered related to child support; (7) greater finances of perpetrators favorably influencing child custody and court decisions; and (8) perpetrators creating multiple court hearings that caused protective parents to miss work, lose jobs, and incur financial problems.

With respect to the category of problems related to joint custody and visitation (see Table 6.1), all of these problems were found in the Alaska[134] and Arizona[135] studies. The Pennsylvania[136] study, at least in the report, did not address factor 1, that sole or joint custody was awarded to perpetrators. Of note, is the finding that reports from three out of the five states (Pennsylvania, Massachusetts, and California) did not address factor 4, the idea of children witnessing DV between parents, and none, to the best of our knowledge, discussed children witnessing the abuser abusing a new partner. The Massachusetts[137] study did not describe factor 7, regarding the issue of the greater finances of perpetrators favorably influencing child custody and court decisions.

Lack of Enforcement of Court Orders

Theme II involved issues related to lack of enforcement of court orders. Factors included (1) DV continues or starts after separation and (2) lack of enforcement of court orders. Four out of five studies (Alaska, Pennsylvania, Arizona, and Massachusetts[138]) reported that victims felt unsafe at court or that DV began, continued, or escalated after the victim and perpetrator had separated, whereas factor 1 was not reported in the California[139] study. All five studies noted that factor 2, lack of enforcement of court orders, was highly problematic.

Perceptions About Judges and Courtrooms

Theme III focused on perceptions about judges who were associated with contested custody cases, as well as the courtroom atmosphere. Factors included (1) judges making offensive or degrading comments about protective parents, along with perceptions that judges were disrespectful or uncaring; (2) rapid proceedings, insufficient

---

Justice Denied: How Family Courts in NYC Endanger Battered Women and Children (2008) for the Battered Women's Resource Center in New York, and the other was completed in Canada by M. Dragiewicz & W. DeKeseredy, *A Needs Gap Assessment Report on Battered Mothers Without Legal Representation in the Family Courts; Research Report* 2008) for Luke's Place and the Denise House. A scan of both studies revealed that the problems mentioned in this chapter are repeated in these studies.

[134] Araji, *supra* note 4.

[135] Arizona Coalition Against Domestic Violence, *supra* note 15.

[136] Women's Law Project, *supra* note 14.

[137] Cuthbert et al., *supra* note 16.

[138] Araji, *supra* note 4; Women's Law Project, *supra* note 14; Arizona Coalition Against Domestic Violence, *supra* note 15; Cuthbert et al., *supra* note 16.

[139] Heim et al., *supra* note 17.

Table 6.1
Themes and Concerns Associated With Domestic Violence
Victims Involved in Contested Child Custody Cases: Five Studies

	Alaska[1] (2006) N=34 Surveys and 20% Follow-up Surveys	Pennsylvania[2] (2003) N=784 Observations (Primary Sample); Supplemented by Narratives, Surveys, Reports, Hearings, Test Calls and Reviews	Arizona[3] (2003) N=57 Surveys	Massachusetts[4] (2002) N=40 Interviews (Primary Sample); Supplemented by Surveys, Focus Groups, Interviews	California[5] (2002) N=212 Surveys; 80 Case Studies
I. Problems With Joint Custody and Visitation					
1. Sole or joint custody awarded to perpetrators	X	O	X	X	X
2. Children emotionally, physically or sexually abused	X	X	X	X	X
3. Perpetrators abuse alcohol / drugs, carried weapons, result was unsafe visitation	X	X	X	X	X
4. Children witnessed domestic violence between parents	X	O	X	O	O
5. Children and mothers live in reduced financial circumstances	X	X	X	X	X
6. Problems with child support	X	X	X	X	X
7. Greater finances influence custody/court decision/ representation	X	X	X	O	X
8. Women must miss work to attend multiple court hearings, perpetrators drain resources	X	X	X	X	X
II. Lack of Enforcement of Court Orders					
1. DV continues or starts after separation	X	X	X	X	O
2. Lack of enforcement of court orders	X	X	X	X	X
III. Perceptions About Judges Decisions/ Courtroom Conduct/Courtroom Atmosphere					
1. Judges make offensive and degrading comments, disrespectful, uncaring	X	X	X	X	X
2. Rapid proceedings, not enough time, ongoing hearings	X	X	X	O	X

Table 6.1 (Continued)

	Alaska (2006)	Pennsylvania (2003)	Arizona (2003)	Massachusetts (2002)	California (2002)
3. Judges placed victims at risk, orders mediation, counseling, contact with abuser	X	X	X	0	X
4. Judges do not follow legal standards[2]	X	X	X	0	X
5. Judges do not explain court process, paperwork, legal rights	X	X	X	0	X
6. Judges fail to consider domestic violence as factor in child custody	X	X	X	X	X
7. Gender biases—women held to higher standards; women stereotyped as hysterical, unreasonable, pathological; biased toward perpetrators	X	X	X	X	X
8. Women not allowed to speak, heard in court, discuss DV or child abuse, physical barriers not available, court-room unsafe, no protection offered	X	X	X	X	X
9. Perceptions of conflict of interest, cronyism	X	X	X	X	X
10. Backlog of court cases	0	X	0	0	X
11. Support persons, witnesses, denied access to court	0	X	0	0	0
IV. Lack of Confidence in Court Appointed Psychologists, Review Bodies					
1. Custody evaluators untrained, biased toward perpetrators	X	0	X	X	X
2. Psychological testing used against victims, lose custody, discredit reports of abuse	X	0	X	X	X
3. Child protective services did not take concerns seriously, children at risk	X	0	X	X	X
4. Custody evaluators hold women equally responsible for abuse, blame for abuse	0	0	X	X	0

(Continued)

Table 6.1 (Continued)

	Alaska (2006)	Pennsylvania (2003)	Arizona (2003)	Massachusetts (2002)	California (2002)
6. Probation officers pressure women to participate in unsafe mediation	O	O	O	X	O
7. Court personnel not respected, disrespectful to women	X	X	X	X	X
V. Court Costs, Issues, Representation					
1. Lack of legal representation, lack of finances to pay lawyers	X	X	X	X	X
2. Lack of access to low cost or pro bono lawyers for poor	X	X	X	X	X
3. Lack of information and resources to handle cases	X	X	O	O	X
4. Litigants lack knowledge that DV is a factor in child custody	X	X	O	O	O
5. Litigants not informed of hearings or allowed access to records, reports	X	X	X	X	X
6. Perpetrators filed multiple harassing motions, retaliatory motions, many jurisdictions	X	O	X	X	O
7. System deprived women of due process, fair hearings	X	X	X	X	X
VI. Parental Alienation Syndrome					
1. PAS used against Victims	X	O	X	O	X
VII. After Custody Decisions					
1. DV continued	X	O	X	X	X
2. Victims stalked by perpetrator, repeated boundary violations	X	O	X	X	O
3. Children frightened by perpetrators, perpetrators create fear that visitation with protective parent will be refused	X	O	X	X	X
4. Children at risk of physical harm or physically abused by perpetrators	X	O	X	X	X
5. Children manipulated by perpetrator, made to feel sorry for perpetrators, or perpetrators blamed victims	X	O	X	X	X

Table 6.1 (Continued)

	Alaska (2006)	Pennsylvania (2003)	Arizona (2003)	Massachusetts (2002)	California (2002)
6. Perpetrators interrogated children, used visitation to get information about or to send violent messages to victims, alienated children	X	O	X	X	X
7. Perpetrators used courts to abuse victims, ongoing court hearings	X	X	X	X	X
8. Perpetrator threatened to steal, kidnap children, relocated to gain custody, refused to return children from visitations	X	O	X	O	X
9. Perpetrators abused alcohol and drugs, possessed firearms or other weapons during visitations/custody	X	X	X	X	X
10. Perpetrators engaged in illegal behavior, violation of court orders	X	X	X	X	X
11. Victims and children experienced continued financial harm, lack of child support, lack of access to resources and support.	X	O	X	X	X

X = Reported in study; O = Not reported in study

[1] = Araji, *supra* note 4 (Alaska)

[2] = Women's Law Project, *supra* note 14 (Pennsylvania)

[3] = Arizona Coalition Against Domestic Violence, *supra* note 15 (Arizona)

[4] = Cuthbert et al., *supra* note 16 (Massachusetts)

[5] = Heim et al., *supra* note 17 (California)

time, and multiple ongoing hearings; (3) placing victims at risk and ordering mediation, counseling, and contact with perpetrators; (4) failure of judges to follow legal standards; (5) judges' lack of explanation of the court process and rights; (6) failure of judges to consider DV as a factor when making child custody determinations; (7) gender bias; (8) protective parents not being allowed to discuss relevant issues in court and physical barriers that placed victims at risk; (9) perceptions of conflict of interest and cronyism; (10) a backlog of court cases; and (11) support and other persons denied access to courts.

Either all or a majority of these concerns were identifiable in the Alaska, Pennsylvania, Arizona, and California studies (see Table 6.1).[140] The Massachusetts study[141] did not specifically discuss factor 2, rapid proceedings, insufficient time, and multiple ongoing hearings; factor 3, placing victims at risk and ordering mediation, counseling, and contact with perpetrators; factor 4, failure of judges to follow legal standards; and factor 5, judges lack of explanation of the court process and rights. Three of the studies (Alaska, Arizona, and Massachusetts) did not report factor 10, a backlog of court cases, as well as factor 11, supportive and other persons denied access to court. Similarly, the California study did not discuss factor 11. None of the studies, to the best of our knowledge, discussed the issue of conflicting court orders.

Lack of Confidence in Court-Appointed Professionals

The problems protective parents experienced extended beyond judges and the courtroom. Theme IV that emerged from the five studies involved a lack of confidence in court-appointed professionals, with the view that personnel from these agencies acted in a manner or provided services that worked against protective parents. The six factors that relate to Theme IV included (1) custody evaluators being untrained and biased in favor of perpetrators; (2) psychological testing used against protective parents; (3) CPS not taking DV and child abuse concerns seriously, placing children at risk; (4) custody evaluators holding protective parents equally responsible for abuse and blaming them; (5) custody evaluators granted immunity; (6) probation officers pressuring women into unsafe mediation; and (7) court personnel not being respected and being disrespectful to protective parents.

The ways in which this theme was addressed showed some variability across studies. Studies from all five states were in concurrence with factor 6, court personnel not being respected and at the same time being disrespectful to women. Four states (Alaska, Arizona, Massachusetts, and California[142]) noted similar problems. These studies addressed factor 1, custody evaluators are untrained and biased toward perpetrators; factor 2, psychological testing is used against protective parents; and factor 3, CPS did not take concerns seriously, and children were at risk. Two states (Arizona and Massachusetts) emphasized factor 4, custody evaluators held protective parents equally responsible for abuse and blamed them; and, similarly, the reports of three states (Alaska, Arizona, and California) addressed factor 5, custody evaluators were granted immunity. Only the study conducted

---

[140] Araji, *supra* note 4; Woman's Law Project, *supra* note 14; Arizona Coalition Against Domestic Violence, *supra* note 15; Heim et al., *supra* note 17.

[141] Cuthbert et al., *supra* note 16.

[142] Araji, *supra* note 4; Arizona Coalition Against Domestic Violence, *supra* note 15; Cuthbert et al., *supra* note 16; Heim et al., *supra* note 17.

in Massachusetts, which uses probation officers in their family courts, but refers to them as family service officers,[143] described problems with factor 6, which referred to probation officers pressuring women to participate in unsafe mediation.

Legal Representation and Court System

Theme V addressed issues related to legal representation, court costs, fear of the courts, and court culture. This theme addressed seven different factors: (1) lack of legal representation and finances to pay lawyers, (2) lack of access to affordable lawyers for the poor, (3) lack of information and resources for protective parents to manage their cases, (4) protective parents' lack of knowledge that DV is a factor in child custody, (5) protective parents not provided with necessary court information or access to supportive documents, (6) perpetrators misuse of the court system through motions and jurisdictions, and (7) the court system depriving women of due process and fair hearings.

Studies conducted in all five states (Alaska, Pennsylvania, Arizona, Massachusetts, and California[144]) identified problems related to this theme with limited variability. All studies noted problems with factor 1, lack of legal representation and finances to pay lawyers; factor 2, lack of access to affordable lawyers for the poor; factor 5, protective parents not provided with necessary court information or access to supportive documents; and factor 7, the court system depriving women of due process and fair hearings (see Table 6.1). Two studies (Arizona and Massachusetts) did not address factor 3, lack of information and resources for protective parents to manage their cases, whereas three studies (Arizona, Massachusetts, and California) did not report on factor 4, protective parents lacked knowledge that DV is a factor in child custody. Finally, one study (Pennsylvania) did not discuss factor 6, perpetrators misuse of the court system.

Parental Alienation Syndrome

The sixth theme, PAS, is listed by itself, as it has received considerable attention in the literature. Three out of five studies (Alaska, Arizona, and California[145]) identified this as a problem facing protective parents in contested child custody decisions.

Problems Encountered by Protective Parents After Custody Decisions

Theme VII contained ten different factors related to problems that protective parents encountered or faced from their abusers after custody decisions. These included (1) the DV continued; (2) perpetrators stalked or violated the boundaries of protective parents; (3) perpetrators frightened children; (4) perpetrators put children at risk of physical harm or physically abused them; (5) perpetrators manipulated and controlled children; (6) perpetrators interrogated, used, or alienated children from their protective parents; (7) perpetrators used the courts as a form of continued abuse of their partners;

---

[143] J. Zorza, personal communication, May 26, 2008 (on file with authors).

[144] Araji, *supra* note 4; Women's Law Project, *supra* note 14; Arizona Coalition Against Domestic Violence, *supra* note 15;Cuthbert et al., *supra* note 16; Heim et al., *supra* note 17.

[145] Araji, *supra* note 4; Arizona Coalition Against Domestic Violence, *supra* note 15; Heim et al., *supra* note 17.

(8) perpetrators threatened to allow protective parents access to children or failed to return them from visitations; (9) perpetrators engaged in illegal behavior; and (10) protective parents and children experienced financial harm and devastation as a result of contested custody.

As can be seen in Theme VII (See Table 6.1), there were many similarities across the studies with respect to problems that occurred after custody decisions had been made. In all five studies (Alaska, Pennsylvania, Arizona, Massachusetts, and California[146]) problems associated with factor 7 were noted, perpetrators used the courts as a form of abusing their partners; and factor 9, perpetrators engaged in illegal behavior. Four studies conducted in Alaska, Arizona, Massachusetts, and California noted similarities across factor 1, DV continued during and/or after custody decisions; factor 3, children were frightened by the perpetrator and/or the outcomes of custody decisions; factor 4, perpetrators placed children at risk of physical harm or children suffered physical abuse; factor 5, perpetrators manipulated and controlled children; factor 6, perpetrators interrogated, used, or alienated children; and factor 10, protective parents and children experienced financial harm and devastation. Two studies (Pennsylvania and California) did not address problems related to factor 2, perpetrators stalked, or had others stalk, protective parents, or perpetrators violated protective parents' boundaries; and two studies (Pennsylvania and Massachusetts) did not report on factor 8, perpetrators threatened to let protective parents have access to children or failed to return them from visitations.

DISCUSSION OF STUDY FINDINGS

The purpose of the research discussed in this chapter was to apply a sociological approach to gathering data that would increase awareness of the problems victims of DV encounter when they become involved in contested child custody cases with their abusive partners. The review of relevant literature, data from primary research conducted in Alaska,[147] and a review of four other relevant studies[148] demonstrate that we are beginning to see, across the United States and Canada, a pattern of problems associated with these cases.

Custody Arrangements Used as Extension of Abuse and Control

As evidenced in the findings section (see "Recent Studies: Findings"), the pattern of problems protective parents encounter when sole or joint custody is awarded to abusive partners (Theme I; See Table 6.1) includes custody arrangements that are used as an extension of abuse and control by perpetrators to harm the protective parent and children emotionally, psychologically, physically, sexually, and financially. These findings are consistent with publications by researchers such as Lundy Bancroft,[149] an internationally

---

[146] Araji, *supra* note 4; Women's Law Project, *supra* note 14; Arizona Coalition Against Domestic Violence, *supra* note 15; Cuthbert et al., *supra* note 16; Heim et al., *supra* note 17.

[147] Araji, *supra* note 4.

[148] Women's Law Project, *supra* note 14; Arizona Coalition Against Domestic Violence, *supra* note 15; Cuthbert et al., *supra* note 16; Heim et al., *supra* note 17.

[149] Bancroft, *supra* note 28; Bancroft, *supra* note 21.

recognized expert in this area. His observations are especially relevant as he has worked with many batterers as both a probation officer and a clinician. In an interview he completed with the senior author for the purposes of developing an educational video program on the topic of DV and contested custody,[150] he noted that he was seeing batterers who used unsupervised visitations with their children as opportunities to destroy the children's relationship with their mothers. According to Bancroft, these were cases where children were clearly in danger of physical assaults, including sexual abuse, during visitation with the fathers. He indicated that even when therapists and police officers verified reports of harm, courts refused to restrict access of batterers to children. Bancroft believes that the problem of family courts granting too much unrestricted, unsupervised access to children with their battering fathers is a nationwide problem, whereby women experience ongoing difficulties with the courts taking their concerns seriously.

Penalties for Abuser Do Not Exist or Are Minimal

A second problem (Theme II; See Table 6.1) identified in the Alaska[151] study focused on the lack of enforcement of court orders surrounding DV[152] and how laws fail to protect women when they attempt to leave abusive relationships.[153] Across studies,[154] women frequently reported that even when court orders were issued, penalties for the abusive partners' noncompliance either did not exist or were minimal. This often resulted in women feeling profound anxiety, fear, and terror in anticipation of retaliation by their abusers. One woman in the Alaska study reported her fears eloquently when she described how the judge did not understand why she was afraid of her abuser when he sat twenty feet away from her in public events in violation of a no-contact order. A second woman summed up the experiences of women across studies when she stated that she did not feel that any mother could walk into the family court system today and have any confidence that she and her children would be protected from abuse.

Judges Make Offensive Comments and Show Disrespect

Another area of concern (Theme III; See Table 6.1) found in the five studies[155] revolved around what happens to protective parents, mostly women, when they enter the court arena. Some of the concerns voiced by the women or court observers were that judges made offensive and degrading comments, showed disrespect, and that there were gender biases that favored the abusive parents (Theme III). Across studies, judges told or even ordered women to cooperate with the perpetrators, accused them of being

---

[150] L. Bancroft, personal communication, Feb. 2005 (on file with authors).

[151] Araji, *supra* note 4.

[152] Bancroft & Silverman, *supra* note 68; S. Keilitz, "Improving Judicial System Responses to Domestic Violence: The Promises and Risks of Integrated Case Management and Technology Solutions," in A.R. Roberts ed., *Handbook of Domestic Violence Intervention Strategies: Policies, Programs, and Legal Remedies* 147–72 (2002); McMahon, Neville-Sorvilles & Schubert, *supra* note 20.

[153] Zorza, 1995a, *supra* note 30; Zorza 1995b, *supra* note 30.

[154] Women's Law Project, *supra* note 14; Arizona Coalition Against Domestic Violence, *supra* note 15; Cuthbert et al., *supra* note 16; Heim et al., *supra* note 17.

[155] Araji, *supra* note 4; Women's Law Project, *supra* note 14; Arizona Coalition Against Domestic Violence, *supra* note 15; Cuthbert et al., *supra* note 16; Heim et al., *supra* note 17.

"unfriendly parents," and accepted the allegations of perpetrators as truth, without documentation, while simultaneously requiring protective parents to submit extensive files that documented their allegations.

Two specific examples were found in our Alaska study.[156] One woman and her son experienced repeated DV and death threats by the perpetrator, and the judge in her case commented that their collective experience of DV was nothing more than a small "slap in the face." He went on to rule that their history of family violence was not DV and that there was no need for the perpetrator to be court ordered to attend a batterers' intervention program. A second woman described how she ended up being fearful of the court system in and of itself. It is her belief that her experiences are not unique, that courts nationwide are biased against believing women; it is the culture of the courts to not believe women, and it will take many years before this gender bias and disbelief of women are eradicated from the court system.

Another problem included protective parents being placed at risk when judges ordered mediation, counseling, and contact with abusers. As was noted in the literature review, such practices result in inequities whereby women reported being fearful of abusers and, correspondingly, being coerced and intimidated into accepting financial and other decisions that were not in the BIC and did little to alleviate their situation.[157] The present research corroborates previous literature that found women were placed in situations of continuing violence both during mediation and postcustody.[158] We also found that a few women in our study reported that their abusers used new partners, family members, and friends to perpetuate DV. Women described situations where new female partners of the abusers repeatedly harassed, threatened, and intimidated them in order to get demands met. During visitations with children, abusers and their family members frequently manipulated and lied to children. Finally, when women were unable to pay exorbitant sums required for professional visitations, they were forced to rely on the unsafe friends of abusers who were used to provide supervision.

The last group of concerns that was found in Theme III, across almost all five studies, related to the court proceedings themselves. The identified issues and problems relating to this theme focused on time and processes. Protective parents and court observers both expressed concerns that there was not enough time allotted to hearings, multiple hearings were held, and sometimes these multiple hearings occurred across many years. During a community forum conducted in Anchorage, Alaska, in 2005, one judge, who was serving as the moderator of a panel discussion following the viewing of a documentary about the problems associated with contested custody, commented that in some contested child custody cases he felt almost like a parent. He had become acquainted with the children when they were babies, and the hearings had continued until they were teens.

Accusations of Domestic Violence and Child Abuse Not Taken Seriously

A fourth problem revolved around lack of confidence in court-appointed professionals (Theme IV; See Table 6.1). Protective parents were often placed in situations whereby child custody evaluators failed to act in the BIC. They did not have their accusations of

---

[156] Araji, *supra* note 4.

[157] Imbrogno & Imbrogno, *supra* note 97; Pruett & Santangelo, *supra* note 101.

[158] Imbrogno & Imbrogno, *supra* note 97; Johnson, Saccuzzo & Koen, *supra* note 98; Zorza, 1995a, *supra* note 30; Zorza 1995b, *supra* note 30.

DV and child abuse taken seriously, were told to be fair, and were urged to keep abusers in the lives of children. Due to the many stresses related to their situations, protective parents often experienced mental health symptoms, and these symptoms resulted in labels related to mental illness or drug addiction. One woman, concerned with results, filed a malpractice lawsuit against the psychologist. She had her case dismissed on the grounds that the psychologist had immunity, even though subsequent psychologists reviewing the case cited malpractice.[159] Similarly, in our study, we found that even when an abuser is court ordered to have a psychological evaluation, repeated refusals resulted in lack of enforcement, with no legal consequences for his noncompliance.[160]

Attorneys' Expenses and Lack of Knowledge About Domestic Violence

Another area of concern (Theme V; See Table 6.1) in all five studies[161] centered around the costs of litigation, lack of access to affordable attorneys, litigants who lacked knowledge of DV, and other factors that prevented protective parents from receiving fair hearings or access to due process. There is abundant research that suggests that inadequate finances result in women not having access to consistent and ongoing legal representation or expert knowledge that affects child custody decisions.[162]

In our study,[163] respondents reported that the costs of litigation varied from $0, for women who lacked attorneys, to $125,000, with additional costs of up to $30,000 when court-appointed professionals were involved. A similarity we found across all five studies is that women did not believe that there was an equitable distribution of court costs in light of abusers having larger incomes, more discretionary income, and unfair control over mutual assets. In an interview with the senior author, Lundy Bancroft noted that batterers are tenacious fighters over custody and visitation, and it is not uncommon for women to have $100,000 or even $200,000 in legal fees over the course of litigation.[164] Allan Bailey, an attorney in Alaska, concurred, noting that any time there were allegations of physical or sexual abuse of children, costs of litigation escalate.[165] Also, when CPS and the court disagree with abuse allegations made by protective parents, those seeking to keep their children safe are expected to pay associated court costs while the state assumes the financial burden associated with abusers' claims of innocence.[166]

Court System's Reticence to Hear Women's Cases

The sixth problem (Theme VI; See Table 6.1) refers to allegations of PAS. Across all five studies,[167] the court system expressed reticence to hear women's claims about

---

[159] Araji, *supra* note 4.

[160] Id.

[161] Id.; Women's Law Project, *supra* note 14; Arizona Coalition Against Domestic Violence, *supra* note 15; Cuthbert et al., *supra* note 16; Heim et al., *supra* note 17.

[162] Hare, *supra* note 25; Jaffe, Crooks & Poisson, *supra* note 7; Kurz, *supra* note 26; Neustein & Lesher, *supra* note 5; Zorza, 1995a, *supra* note 30; Zorza 1995b, *supra* note 30.

[163] Araji, *supra* note 4.

[164] L. Bancroft, personal communication, Feb. 2005 (on file with authors).

[165] Bailey, *supra* note 10.

[166] *E.g.,* Neustein & Lesher, *supra* note 5.

[167] Araji, *supra* note 4; Women's Law Project, *supra* note 14; Arizona Coalition Against Domestic Violence, *supra* note 15; Cuthbert et al., *supra* note 16; Heim et al., *supra* note 17.

DV and child abuse, and when protective parents made allegations, their statements were often used against them. These women were labeled as being "unfriendly parents" or of PAS. Across the literature, there is abundant research suggesting that these labels are largely used against women in contested child custody cases, reflect gender bias, and result in harsh consequences for women and children.[168]

While the senior author was in Colorado, she met a woman who had been accused of PAS and court ordered into treatment for the disorder. The allegations of PAS arose when her daughter expressed reluctance to maintain a relationship with her stepfather because of his preferential treatment of another daughter who was the couple's biological child. The young girl also expressed fear, saying that the stepfather was threatening to harm her mother and others she loved. The child custody evaluator assigned to the case alleged that the daughter's reluctance to maintain a relationship with her stepfather was a direct result of her mother's attempts to prevent the child from visiting the stepfather. He diagnosed the mother with parental alienation/PAS, and, as an expert witness, noted this in court hearings. The mother was court ordered into treatment for PAS with a therapist approved by the GAL assigned to the case (in Colorado a GAL must be an attorney). After six months, the therapist reported that no further treatment was necessary. However, the GAL was not satisfied and ordered the mother back to therapy. This continued for about another six months. These treatment sessions represented a significant financial burden for this mother and her children. She had to pay for the therapy sessions, as no insurance covers the treatment because it is not recognized by the American Medical Association or the APA as a legitimate disorder. She also had to drive 170 miles to attend therapy sessions, and she estimates that she has spent thousands of dollars on just this aspect of her case, which has drawn on for years and continues.[169] This case study mirrors what was found in the literature we reviewed as well as from the findings from the five studies reported in this chapter. That is, it is the batterers themselves who cause children to be alienated through their own behavior, and they are typically quite good at shifting responsibility for their actions and convincing others of their good intentions,[170] but it is the protective parents who are diagnosed with PAS and suffer the consequences.

Violence Continues or Escalates

The final category (Theme VII; See Table 6.1) is extensive and focuses on what happens to protective parents, primarily women and children, once the judge has rendered visitation or custody decisions. Across the five studies,[171] there were consistent findings that violence often continued or even escalated. This violence took many forms including boundary violations, stalking, and physical assaults. Perpetrators who had committed acts of marital rape continued to do so. Sometimes marital rapes were committed in front of the children, and on other occasions protective parents were required to barter sex in order to obtain resources.[172]

---

[168] Doyne et al., *supra* note 19; Gould & Martindale, *supra* note 88; Stark, *supra* note 90.

[169] A. Warren, personal communication, June 13, 2008 (on file with authors).

[170] Jaffe, Lemon & Poisson, *supra* note 22; Dalton, Carbon & Olesen, *supra* note 59; Goelman, Lehrman & Valente, *supra* note 60.

[171] Araji, *supra* note 4; Women's Law Project, *supra* note 14; Arizona Coalition Against Domestic Violence, *supra* note 15; Cuthbert et al., *supra* note 16; Heim et al., *supra* note 17.

[172] Araji, *supra* note 4.

One example that clearly demonstrates boundary violations, stalking, attempted murder, and suicide is found in another project completed by the senior author.[173] During custody hearings, following a divorce and when restraining orders were in place, "A" would come home and find that her estranged husband had entered her home, which had an alarm system, and had left articles, such as guns, that would send a message that he could enter the home any time he wanted and harm her. One morning, disguised with a wig and long coat, he grabbed "A" as she was walking to work and forced her into the car. She struggled as he attempted to handcuff her to the steering wheel. Her cries for help attracted others in the parking lot, and the police were called. A gun battle occurred between her ex-husband and the police. "A" was seriously wounded as were several police officers, and her ex-husband committed suicide by shooting himself. Her case led to the implementation of a stalking law in Alaska. During the course of our research, we found examples of similar stories.[174]

Perpetrators often used children as a continuation of control and/or abuse of the protective parents, and this took many forms. They manipulated, harassed, and interrogated children in order to obtain information about the protective parent. Visitation was often used to send threats or violent messages. In our study, a perpetrator who was denied access to weapons by the court, returned the children from visitation with a full set of toy weapons in an effort to terrorize the protective parent. He accompanied his threat by making comments to the protective parent's family and friends that he could do whatever he wanted to her.[175] Some abusers threatened to or actually kidnapped children, while others failed to return children from visitations or relocated to other areas. When abusers had custody, it was not uncommon for them to refuse to allow the protective parents court-ordered visitation. Children often responded with extreme fear, anxiety, and distress. It was not uncommon for them to exhibit emotional, behavioral, and academic difficulties. Over half of the respondents with whom we conducted follow-up surveys or interviews over the two years after the initial survey, reported that the abusive partners continued to use the children against them, and their children were suffering.[176]

In addition to violation of court orders, DV, and child abuse, perpetrators often engaged in other illegal behaviors. Examples included drug trafficking, weapons possession, and fraud. In several cases in the Alaska study,[177] children became caught up in the dysfunctional and illegal lifestyles of the abusive partners. In one case, a teenage son had been suspended from school, and his abusive father began to enlist his participation in illegal activities. Both the father and son were apprehended by the authorities; the father was sent to prison, and the son was placed on probation. A second case involved a father who was a violent drug trafficker. His son witnessed extreme violence and often ended up in physical altercations with the father in an effort to protect the mother. The son expressed much anger and rage against the father, turning his anger and rage inward against himself by

---

[173] S.K. Araji (executive producer), Domestic Violence Case Study in UAA Distance Education Video Course, Violence In Intimate Relationships, Sociology 452, Anchorage, AK (University of Alaska Anchorage 2006).

[174] *E.g.,* Jaffe, Lemon & Poisson, *supra* note 22; Neustein & Lesher, *supra* note 5; Stark, *supra* note 90.

[175] Araji, *supra* note 4.

[176] Id.

[177] Id.

repeatedly skipping school and drinking alcohol. The son eventually began disappearing, and it was later found that he had joined a violent street gang.

Perpetrators also use the courts to continue their abuse of women. Consistent with our research, others have found that abusers repeatedly bring women to court by making ongoing claims for modifications in visitation and custody, and make many attempts to drain the financial resources of protective parents.[178] In our Alaska study,[179] several women reported having to pay larger than their fair share of court costs or those related to caring for children, due to the ability of the abusers to hide assets, divert money into businesses or property, refuse to work, or work only for cash that was not reported to the courts. Protective parents were often placed in positions of having to pay day-to-day living expenses, medical and counseling fees, and court costs, while abusers retained discretionary income that was sometimes used for alcohol and drugs, entertainment of friends, vacations, or luxury items.[180]

Overall, protective parents generally had fewer finances to use in seeking divorces and custody as compared to the abusive partners. This was partially a result of their lower earning power, the ability of abusers to hide and divert assets, as well as protective parents who had often assumed traditional gender roles associated with marriage and the family. It was not uncommon in the Alaska study to find that women, even with college educations and careers, were left homeless and forced to seek help from friends and relatives or end up in homeless shelters.[181] Together or separately, these factors led to protective parents who were also victims of DV losing custody of their children to abusive partners, along with them experiencing a substantial decline in their standard of living. This decrease in the quality of life also affected children if the protective parents received custody or visitation rights.

An overview of all the problems associated with DV and contested child custody (listed in Table 6.1) might lead to the conclusion that these problems are only associated with those who belong to minority groups, have little education, and/or have low incomes. This was not the case in our Alaska study.[182] Of the thirty-four respondents, the median age was forty-three, most were white (82 percent), had some college education (82 percent), and nearly a quarter had undergraduate or graduate degrees (25 percent). Their income ranged from $920-$104,000, with no clear median income. Their abusive partners' demographics were similar with respect to age and race. Over half (52 percent) of the abusive partners had only a high school degree or G.E.D., or less. The income of the perpetrators was much higher than that of the protective parents, with the range being from $6,000-$250,000, with the median being $50,000. These demographic findings led us to three conclusions:

1. As a group, the women's education was not translating into similar earning power as their abusive partners who had less education.

2. Higher educational levels as a group did not help protective parents to achieve desired divorce and custody decisions, in comparison to their less educated spouses.

---

[178] *E.g.,* Jaffe, Crooks & Poisson, *supra* note 7; Stark, *supra* note 90.
[179] Araji, *supra* note 4.
[180] Id.
[181] Id.
[182] Id.

3. Compared to their abusive partners, the women did not have the earnings to expend on legal services. This last finding is very congruent with what several attorneys told us during the course of our research, *namely, whoever has or controls the finances and other resources is the one most likely to win in divorce and custody cases.*[183]

CONCLUSION

DV victims who are usually women, experience many problems when they become entangled in contested child custody cases with an abusive partner. Part of the problem appears to stem from lack of, or access to, finances and other resources. Other problems are related directly to the legal system that includes judges, attorneys, custody evaluators, psychological evaluators, and CPS, among others. The present review of literature and findings from across five studies[184] in the United States indicate that this is not a localized problem that affects only a small number of DV victims and their children. It is a social condition that needs to be elevated to the status of a social problem, with the appropriate changes in social policies and legal training, with a focus on eradicating the biased attitudes and courtroom conduct that continues to place victims of DV and their children in harm's way. Some of the recommendations found in the five studies in the research project include the following:

1. Courts, court personnel, child custody evaluators, etc., need education on issues related to DV;

2. Courts must consider the effects of DV on women and children when awarding custody and visitation;

3. Courts need to place responsibility for DV on perpetrators and stop blaming victims;

4. Courts need to award custody, if at all possible, to the nonviolent parent when DV is an issue;

5. Courts really need to consider the BIC and not force children into unsafe and dangerous visitation; and

6. Judges need to follow existing laws.

These recommendations, however, address only one side of the problem. What we came to realize over the course of this research project is that victims of DV who find themselves in divorce and/or contested child custody cases need to educate themselves about the roles of attorneys and the court system. If they enter the court system without finances and resources and the belief that they, and in some cases their children, have been victimized and can get protection and justice in the court system, they will

---

[183] A. Bailey & H. Viergutz, Interview on Domestic Violence, Child Custody, and The Legal System, in Educational Videotape: S.K. Araji (executive producer), *Listen to Our Voices* (2007).

[184] Araji, *supra* note 4; Women's Law Project, *supra* note 14; Arizona Coalition Against Domestic Violence, *supra* note 15; Cuthbert et al., *supra* note 16; Heim et al., *supra* note 17.

be disappointed. As Lundy Bancroft has noted, the protective parent needs to educate herself on laws and procedures. She is going to have to work very hard to find some way to get represented. She needs to prepare for the long haul. There is not going to be a quick resolution to the case. It will not be easy.[185] But as one woman in our Alaska study[186] told us, even after educating herself, she found that the court system discriminated against her.[187]

Finally, the review of literature and information presented from the five studies has focused on the practices and services that victimize protective parents (mostly women) who are involved in contested custody cases where DV is a factor. In future studies, we also need to address the next step in the process wherein some victimized children, particularly males, become the future perpetrators of DV and sexual abuse.[188] The evidence of children modeling abusive language and behavior learned from the abusive parent and then using this against the protective parent was very evident in conversations between the senior author and several women in our Alaska study and also from women who were attending the Fifth Annual Battered Women's Conference in Albany, New York, January 2008. A familiar story was how their children, particularly males, were beginning to talk and act like the abusive parent and those in the environments to which the children were exposed. One woman commented that it was like witnessing a miniature of her abusive partner.

Given the issues discussed in this chapter, we conclude with a question. How can we ever reduce DV if those who are participants in court decisions continue to grant custody and unsupervised visitation to parents who have documented histories of DV and child abuse?

Authors' Note

The research reported on in this chapter was completed while Dr. Araji was Professor and Chair of Sociology at the University of Alaska Anchorage (UAA). Currently, she is Professor and Chair of Sociology at the University of Colorado Denver. Dr. Bosek is a Term Assistant Professor with UAA's Psychology Department. Thanks are extended to Gale Smoke, Adjunct Instructor in the Sociology Department at UAA, Dr. André Rosay, Director of UAA's Justice Center, and UAA students Carly Barron, Amanda Matthews, and Reem Sheikh for assistance with this project. Most of all we thank the protective parents who completed a lengthy twenty-page survey that served as findings for the Alaska study. The research was partially supported by several UAA Faculty Development awards to one or both authors. Findings from the study were presented at the Western Social Sciences Conference in Denver, CO, April 24, 2008.

---

[185] L. Bancroft, personal communication, Feb. 2005 (on file with authors).

[186] Araji, *supra* note 4.

[187] J. Doyle, Interview on Domestic Violence, Child Custody, and The Legal System, in Educational Videotape: S.K. Araji (executive producer), *Listen to Our Voices* (2007).

[188] There is an emerging social problem of children twelve years of age and younger, most of whom have been physically and/or sexually abused, now becoming the newest and youngest group of sexual abusers (S.K. Araji, *Sexually Aggressive Children: Coming to Understand Them* (1997)). The situation where custody and unsupervised visitations are being awarded to documented DV and child abusers can only exacerbate this problem—a problem most states are unwillingly to admit even exists.

Chapter 7

Do Judges Adequately Address the Causes and Impact of Violence in Children's Lives in Deciding Contested Child Custody Cases?

by Thomas E. Hornsby, J.D.

INTRODUCTION

Most victims of family violence will have some contact with the legal system that is not well designed to handle such cases. In addition, inequities in the application of the law, racial and class bias, and inadequate investigations have harmed rather than helped many families. The low priority given to funding for implementation of child protection laws results in a system that frequently fails to work. Many battered women find themselves in dangerous positions because the courts often do not give credence or sufficient weight to a history of partner abuse in making decisions about child custody and visitation. Racial bias often influences the court's decision about whether to order treatment or to imprison offenders.[1]

This chapter will explore the judicial decisions made by a sample of U.S. family court judges in contested child custody cases involving domestic violence (DV) and state court judicial disciplinary proceedings and outcomes. This chapter will also attempt to provide answers to the following questions:

1. Why are abusive fathers who batter mothers two times more likely to seek sole physical custody of their children than are nonviolent fathers?[2]

2. In Florida, where the Model Code on Domestic and Family Violence[3] has been partially enacted, why were violent fathers more likely to get sole custody of their children than the mothers who were the victims of DV?[4]

3. What can be done to assure that the best interests standard in child custody cases involving DV is applied rationally by the trial court?

The first section of the chapter will explain why trial judges often fail to recognize the effect of DV on the victim in deciding contested custody cases. It includes the chronology of a case, for which I served as a trial judge, that clearly illustrates the dynamics of DV and its effects on the victim. In the next section, statutes and case law are provided to explain the competing statutory factors, including the "friendly parent" provision that courts apply

---

[1] American Psychological Association, *Violence and the Family: Report of the American Psychological Presidential Task Force on Violence and the Family,* Executive Summary, at 4 (1996).

[2] Id. at 40.

[3] *See infra* note 57.

[4] Nancy K. Lemon, *Domestic Violence Law* 392 (2d ed. 2005), *discussed in* John Zorza & Leora Rosen, "Guest Editor's Introduction to Special Issue on Custody and Domestic Violence," 11 *Violence Against Women* 983 (Aug. 2005).

in determining the best interests of the children (BIC) in contested custody cases involving DV. The third section explores ethical issues in judicial decision making by analyzing the American Bar Association (ABA) Model Code of Judicial Conduct[5] and state court disciplinary proceedings that have applied their respective ethical codes to judicial misconduct. Finally, my recommendations for improving judicial decision making in contested custody cases involving DV are presented.

SOME JUDGES FAIL TO RECOGNIZE EFFECT OF DOMESTIC VIOLENCE ON THE VICTIM IN DECIDING CONTESTED CUSTODY CASES

A Classic Case

During the nineteenth year of my twenty-three-year tenure as a circuit court judge in the Fifteenth Judicial Circuit of the state of Illinois, my negative attitude toward female DV victims who sought orders of protection after I had granted them previous orders dramatically changed. Prior to this change in attitude, I did not understand the dynamics of DV, which often led to women staying in abusive relationships nor did I understand that women stay in these relationships because their abusive partners threaten to kill them, their children, and themselves if they leave. I was upset when the victims, often visibly injured, came into my court, and requested another order of protection. I was annoyed that the victims were wasting my time because I suspected that they would not require the abusers to obey the protective orders and would allow them back into their homes while the orders were in effect, often resulting in other incidents of domestic violence and necessary protective orders. The change in attitude came about after, as trial judge, I presided in the case of *People of the State of Illinois v. Machen*.[6] The Second District Appellate Court filed in the Appellate Clerk's Office Order No. 2-91-0479, in which it made factual findings, some of which are included herein. Mr. Machen was charged, indicted, and tried for several offenses and found guilty of attempt (first degree murder), six counts of aggravated battery, two counts of aggravated kidnapping, seven counts of kidnapping, and seven counts of unlawful restraint. All of the offenses were committed against his wife, Diane Machen. The defendant was indicted for attempted murder based on his intent to kill Diane Machen by starving her to death.

The case was a classic profile of a DV batterer and the effects of the battering on his wife. It illustrates a pattern of physical battering, isolation of the victim from her parents and friends, total control of her life in every aspect—financial, physical, emotional, and psychological—threats to kill her, and actual restraint of her liberty with a premeditated attempt to kill her.

History of the Case

When Diane married the defendant in August 1984, she was a healthy woman weighing 130 pounds. When she was taken to the emergency room by the police on July 22, 1990, the nurse found her to be unkempt, thin, pale, and expressionless. She

---

[5] *See infra* note 120.
[6] Order No. 2-01-0479 (2d Dist. Ill. App. Ct. Apr. 16, 1993) (decision without opinion at 656 N.E.2d 810).

weighed 101½ pounds. Her sister, Kathy Walters, testified that she saw her later in the day and that Diane was grayish in color and "didn't look like she was going to be around much longer."[7]

The battering began in July 1985 when Diane called her mother complaining that the defendant had been beating her. "Her mother took her to a domestic violence shelter where she stayed for a month before filing for a dissolution of marriage."[8] After testifying in the dissolution proceedings, she returned home in August 1985 before a judgment was entered.

"The defendant lost his job in 1985 and was thereafter with Diane almost constantly for the next five years."[9] He would drop her off at his mother's or sister's house while he was away from the home. "She complained of her treatment to the mother and sister"[10] but "stopped telling anyone of his actions, fearing that the defendant would fulfill his threat to beat her if she told anyone what he was doing to her."[11] The relatives denied ever observing any violence between the couple and denied that Diane had ever complained to them that the defendant had mistreated her.[12] The defendant continued to isolate her by "preventing Diane from contacting her family or making phone calls."[13]

> In January of 1988, the defendant told Diane that she was gaining too much weight, and he wanted her to start eating just once a day. She agreed because she was scared of the defendant. To enforce this rule, the defendant would stand behind Diane or sit in the kitchen when she cooked so she would not feed herself. He also accompanied her when she went shopping for groceries. Diane once told the defendant's mother, in the defendant's presence, that he was hitting her and not letting her eat right.[14]

Diane testified that she wrote a letter to the defendant on the occasion of their fourth anniversary in August 1988, expressing thanks for a "Happy Four Years" hoping "that her relationship with her husband would improve."[15]

> On September 13, 1988, the defendant and Diane were living in a trailer in Amboy, Illinois. On that day the defendant watched a television program about why women sometimes kill their husbands. That night, fearing that Diane would kill him, he beat her in the ribs and face until she agreed to let him tie her hands behind her back using a pair of toy handcuffs. She was handcuffed from 11:00 P.M. until late the next morning. On August 26, 1989, instead of toy handcuffs, the defendant started using chains . . . and a padlock to tie Diane's hands behind her back at night. On the morning of August 27, 1989, the children, Chad, born March 9, 1985, and Andrea, born in July of 1986, saw their mother tied up and attempted to free her.[16]

---

[7] Id. at 2.
[8] Id.
[9] Id.
[10] Id.
[11] Id.
[12] Id. at 9.
[13] Id. at 2.
[14] Id. at 3.
[15] Id.
[16] Id.

One evening, Diane attempted to run away from the defendant by sneaking out the back door of their trailer. The defendant awoke and caught her running on the road a half mile from their trailer, forcibly took her home, hit her head against an outside wall and then took her inside where he gagged, blindfolded and choked her.[17]

The defendant denied doing any of these acts. "He denied beating or tying Diane at anytime before August 26, 1989."[18] But instead, he "stated that around that date, he and Diane decided to try having sex with bondage. He stated that they experimented with bondage using chains and Diane's arms tied in front of her approximately 30 times between August 26, 1989 and February 1990, but stopped because they were not enjoying it."[19]

On November 1, 1989, the family moved to a house in rural Amboy, Illinois, to care for the defendant's grandfather. In January of 1990, the defendant told Diane that he was going to kill her because he was afraid that she would take the children away, because she was no good and because she did not deserve to live. He said he would tell everyone that she had died of anorexia. From January onward, he would not allow Diane to eat for three or four days in a row, and when he did allow her to eat, it would be a small portion of whatever food he had eaten for dinner. While around members of his family for birthdays and other gatherings, the defendant allowed Diane to eat because he did not want anyone else to know that he was restricting her food intake. "Four or five times in January 1990, the defendant stated to Diane that he was going to starve her to death. On February 12, Diane placed some food in a lower kitchen cabinet during the day so she could retrieve it later when her hands were bound. The defendant chained her hands at around 11:00 p.m. that evening. At approximately 2:00 a.m., Diane sneaked into the kitchen, retrieved the food, took it to the bedroom and began to eat it by kneeling on the floor on her hands and knees. The defendant woke up, saw her eating, threw her on the bed and choked her. He began punching her in the chest. She had trouble breathing for several days following the beating.[20]

[On April 12, 1990, at] 7:00 p.m., the defendant began to punch Diane in the ribs in the presence of the children. He threw her against a wall, and her neck and upper shoulders made a small dent in the wall. He kept hitting her and dragged her into a hallway where he hit her head against the wall, making a hole. At 11:00 p.m., he took Diane to the basement where his belt was nailed to a rafter. He had her stand on a chair, placed the belt around her neck and he removed the chair. She was hanging for a few minutes, forced her to use her hands to keep the belt off of her neck so she could breathe. The defendant again stated that he was going to kill her. Diane promised to be a better wife, and the defendant let her down. Her hands were chained that night.

---

[17] Id. at 3–4.
[18] Id. at 9.
[19] Id.
[20] Id. at 4.

Early in June of 1990, the defendant began to chain Diane's leg to a weight bench at night, to prevent her from going to the kitchen for food. ... The defendant told her that he would kill her if she told anyone what he was doing to her. That evening [June 1990], the defendant chained her arms and legs.

On July 9, 1990, the defendant accused Diane of being "mouthy" and hit her head against the bathroom wall, leaving a mark on the wall. Later that night, he chained her arms and leg. On the nights from July 9 to July 22, the defendant fell asleep watching television before chaining Diane. He then beat her every day during that period because she had not awakened him to tie her up the previous evening. "On July 18, the defendant caught Diane taking food from the kitchen. He took the food away, brought her to the bedroom, chained one of her hands to the weight bench and made her remove her shirt. He then held a lamp under his arm, doubled up the electrical cord and whipped her back, leaving severe welts that left scars.[21]

He later would deny doing any of these things.

On July 21, the defendant asked Diane to move their outside tower television antenna to improve the reception. When she tried to turn it, it fell on top of her, but she was not injured. When she told the defendant about the incident, he beat her head on the living room floor. At 4:00 a.m., he found Diane in the kitchen getting food. He grabbed her by the hair, threw her to the floor and beat her head against the floor until she began to bleed. He next had her take off her shirt. He beat her with the lamp cord numerous times and the plug on the cord broke off during the beating. Diane screamed for help, but he said that she deserved the beating for eating.[22]

The defendant admitted to drinking twenty beers and that the antenna had fallen on Diane.[23] He told the jury that "Diane had been threatening to kill him almost every day, in addition to threatening to take the children away."[24] And

on July 21st, 1991, he awoke at 4:00 a.m. to find that Diane had poured gasoline on him . . . and was standing close to him with some matches. He admitted to beating her with a lamp cord which had no socket attached to the end. He stated that he was drunk, and he could not recall how many blows he administered.[25]

At 9:00 a.m. on July 22, the police came to the Machen home to look in on Diane upon the request of Diane's sister. Diane told the officer that the defendant had been hitting her. The officer took Diane inside the trailer. The defendant asked her to remain, promising to let her eat and not to hurt her. She left with the officer.[26]

---

[21] Id. at 5-6.
[22] Id. at 7.
[23] Id. at 8.
[24] Id. at 10.
[25] Id. at 10.
[26] Id. at 7.

The officer then transported her to the law enforcement center and the hospital emergency room for an examination. She did not require intravenous feeding, and she was discharged two hours and forty-five minutes later.

The defendant was then arrested and taken into custody. While testifying at trial, he admitted striking Diane twice during the marriage but denied beating her or hanging her on April 12, 1990.[27] At the trial,

> Pathologist Larry Blum testified that he examined Diane on July 23, 1990. He found abrasions on the back of her scalp and scars on her scalp. On her back, he found long, strap-like horizontal bruises, "too numerous to count." There were deep abrasions on the back of each and a contusion to the right nipple. . . . The strap wounds were consistent with infliction by the lamp cord. . . . There were also scars and abrasions above the ankles, consistent with the use of chains. He further observed a recent bruise to the right eye, a faint bruise around the left eye, a scar on the chin, swelling in the left ear, scattered bruises on the thighs, bruising over the back hipbones, and bruises on the upper left abdomen. He also noted that she appeared malnourished and that she had lost normal body fat, especially in her face and neck.[28]

Before the trial, the prosecutor had informed me, the trial judge, of his intention to call six-year-old Chad Machen to the stand. I informed both the prosecutor and the defense attorneys that I wanted to make the courtroom "child friendly" and would do so by taking off my robe, placing Chad in a chair in front of the jury, and allowing him to have a stuffed animal and a soft drink. Neither side objected to this arrangement.

> Six-year-old Chad Machen testified for the state, after the trial court found him competent. He testified that he saw his father put chains on his mother at night, that his mother slept on the floor with chains on her arms under her back and that his father had a key which unlocked the padlock. He testified that he did not see the defendant ever hit his mother, but he also testified that his father would only allow his mother to eat breakfast consisting of cereal and milk, and not lunch or dinner.[29]

The defense called twenty witnesses who had contact with the couple. None of these witnesses noticed any marks on Diane.[30] The Lee County, Illinois, jury returned guilty verdicts on all counts, and as trial court judge I entered convictions on all counts. I sentenced the defendant on all counts and on the most serious count, attempt (first degree murder), Mr. Machen was sentenced to twenty-five years imprisonment.

On appeal, the Second District Appellate Court found that the prosecution had proven beyond a reasonable doubt the counts of attempted murder, five counts of kidnapping, two counts of aggravated kidnapping, and one count of aggravated battery, and reversed the convictions of unlawful restraint because it was a lesser included offense, and one conviction of aggravated battery because there was no differentiation between conduct supporting two separate aggravated battery charges arising from the same physical act (i.e., the striking of Diane with a lamp cord).

---

[27] Id.

[28] Id. at 8.

[29] Id.

[30] Id. 10.

Batterer Control Over Victim

The Machen case (see "A Classic Case" and "History of the Case") was a classic example of the control exerted by a batterer over the victim. Mr. Machen denigrated Diane's appearance and self-esteem; controlled the family finances; restrained her liberty; isolated her from her friends, family, and support systems; battered her physically at an escalating rate; threatened her with death if she left him; and escalated the threat into reality by attempting to starve her to death.

Why Women Stay

After the Machen trial concluded (see "A Classic Case" and "History of the Case") and the defendant was sentenced, I fully understood why women continue to stay in homes where DV exists. After having listened to the testimony and observed Diane's psychological state and physical condition, it became clear to me that victims of DV are often treated unfairly by judges who decide protection or custody cases within the family, dependency, and divorce court systems. It also struck me that the victims' wounded and fragile conditions were the result of the horrendous abuse and the unequal financial status they had to endure in their relationships with their batterers. This was a subject matter that had not been taught in any of my law school courses, judicial seminars, or other judicial trainings that were offered around the time I was first appointed to the bench by the Illinois Supreme Court in December 1972. I therefore became motivated to improve the ways in which our court processes and decides cases involving DV.

Becoming Part of the Solution

As a member of the National Council of Juvenile and Family Court Judges (NCJFCJ), I decided to become involved in the activities of the NCJFCJ Family Violence Department and subsequently became a member of the Family Violence Committee. Since that committee first began, the NCJFCJ has challenged judges to become a part of the solution to the problems associated with the judicial response to DV issues.

The efforts of the NCJFCJ began with a joint meeting of interested judges, advocates, prosecutors, public defenders, scholars, and other groups. That meeting led to plans to attack these problems. The first of many publications came out of the committee in 1990, entitled *Family Violence: Improving Court Practice*. As past president of the NCJFCJ, Judge Stephen B. Herrell of Portland, Oregon, stated in the preface to this pioneering work that "the whole area of family violence has been a troublesome one for the courts. Frankly, we have not handled these cases well."[31]

The activities of the NCJFCJ and the training programs will be discussed later as valuable resources to family court judges (see "Consideration of Domestic Violence Factor as a Presumption of Detriment to the Child"). But the question remains, What can the judiciary do to improve court practices in DV cases? The intent of this chapter is to identify the problem areas in child custody cases involving DV and to provide solutions to solve the problems.

The next section will explore the application by the trial judge of statutory factors in determining what is in the BIC in a contested custody case involving the presence of DV.

---

[31]National Council of Juvenile and Family Court Judges Family Violence Project, *Family Violence: Improving Court Practice* Preface (1990).

COMPETING STATUTORY FACTORS IN APPLYING THE BEST INTERESTS STANDARD IN CONTESTED CHILD CUSTODY CASES

Courts are required to apply the best interests standard in deciding custody issues. For example, Florida Statute Section 61.13(2)(a) provides that the court determines custody matters in accordance with the BIC and the Uniform Child Custody Jurisdiction and Enforcement Act (1997) (UCCJEA).[32] Under, the Florida statute, it is the public policy of the state, as mandated by the legislature, to assure that the minor child has frequent and continuing contact with both parents after dissolution and to encourage parents to share rights and responsibilities and joys of child rearing. In determining primary residence of the child, the statute also provides that the father of the child is to be given the same consideration as the mother irrespective of age or sex of the child—thus abolishing the "tender years doctrine" that required courts to favor the mother over the father in situations where the minor child was of a very young age.

When applying the best interests standard, what consideration should the court give to the effects of parental violence in contested custody and visitation cases? State statutes are divided in determining the weight to be given to the presence of DV as a factor in deciding a contested custody case. This division will be discussed in the following subsections by detailing cases that were decided in various jurisdictions.

Domestic Violence as an Equal Factor in Deciding the Best Interests of the Child

A majority of the states have statutes that require courts to consider DV as a factor on an equal basis with other factors enumerated in the statute in making custody determinations.[33] In making decisions of contested cases, often the DV factor and the friendly parent factor conflict with each other. Friendly parent statutory provisions encourage parents to cooperate with each other in visitation and custody situations in order to obtain maximum contact between the parents and the child after a divorce or dissolution. The problems arise when the trial judge tries to blend the friendly parent factor with the DV factor, which are often irreconcilable, especially where there is a no-contact provision in the valid order of protection.

The Florida statute contains friendly parent and domestic violence provisions. Florida Statute Section 61.13(3) provides that

> For purposes of establishing or modifying parental responsibility and creating, developing, approving or modifying a parenting plan, including a time-sharing schedule, which governs each parent's relationship with his or her minor child and the relationship between each parent with regard to his or her minor child, the best interests of the child shall be the primary consideration. . . . Determination of the best interests of the child shall be made by evaluating all of the factors affecting the welfare and interests of the child, including but not limited to:

---

[32] The UCCJEA was drafted by the National Conference of Commissioners on Uniform State Laws and by it approved and recommended for enactment in all of the states. Copies of the UCCJEA may be obtained from the National Conference of Commissioners on Uniform State Laws, 676 North St. Clair St., Suite 1700, Chicago, Illinois, 60611.

[33] Family Violence Department of the National Council of Juvenile and Family Court Judges, "Family Violence in Child Custody Statutes: An Analysis of State Codes and Legal Practice," 29 *Fam. L.Q.* 197, 199 (1995).

(a) The demonstrated capacity and disposition of each parent to facilitate and encourage a close and continuing parent-child relationship, to honor the time-sharing schedule, and to be reasonable when changes are required. . . .

(l) The demonstrated capacity of each parent to communicate with and keep the other parent informed of issues and activities regarding the minor child, and the willingness of each parent to adopt a unified front of all major issues when dealing with the child.

(m) Evidence of domestic violence, sexual violence, child abuse, child abandonment, or child neglect, regardless of whether a prior or pending action relating to those issues has been brought. . . .

(r) The capacity of each parent to protect the child from ongoing litigation with the child, not sharing documents or electronic media related to the litigation of the child, and refraining from disparaging comments about the other parent to the child.[34]

The Florida case of *Ford v. Ford*[35] is a classic example of a trial court ignoring DV in favor of the friendly parent provisions. The case illustrates the trial court's failure to take into consideration numerous instances of DV perpetrated by the husband against his spouse and an overreliance on the two friendly parent provisions found in the Florida statute. This failure resulted in a reversal by the appellate court on a finding of the trial court's abuse of discretion in awarding custody to the batterer. The Florida statute in effect at that time did not list the presence of DV as one of the factors to determine best interests, but the court relied on the then statute, which allowed the court to consider "(k) any other factor considered by the court to be relevant."[36]

The presence of DV was marked by at least two incidents that were the primary focus of the six-day hearing. The first incident occurring on Mother's Day, 1994, when "the husband ran out of the house screaming, and told his family they better get in the house before he tore off his wife's head. The husband took a walk with his sister-in-law and told her he hit his wife again."[37] The second incident of violence occurred on October 26, 1994, and

> involved the husband throwing the wife on the floor. The wife testified he began kicking her in the chest, ribs, and legs. The wife ran out of the house and called the police, eventually leaving the house because she feared for her safety, as well as that of her daughter. The husband stated he slapped the wife, but only after she kicked him.[38]

Following this incident, "the husband phoned Michelle Lampert [Michelle Lampert is not identified further in the opinion] and told her the wife left because he hit her."[39]

The testimony revealed a prior incident of violence occurring when the wife was four to five months pregnant.

---

[34] Fla. Stat. § 61.13(3) (2008).
[35] 700 So. 2d 191 (Fla. Dist. Ct. App. 1997).
[36] Fla. Stat. § 61.13(3)((k) (1995).
[37] Ford v. Ford, 700 So. 2d 191, 193 (Fla. Dist. Ct. App. 1997).
[38] Id.
[39] Id.

The former wife explained the husband was upset because she chose to attend her last day of work as an Emergency Technician. The husband threw her on the floor of her closet, shoving her in the stomach, and kicking her in the side. The husband recounted the incident as involving an argument, after which the wife threatened to abort the baby, and then began hitting herself in the stomach. The husband testified he restrained the former wife from this self-abuse by holding her wrists, and lowered her to the ground, holding her there for a period of time.[40]

The custody evaluator, Ms. Kay Jones, completed a court-ordered custody evaluation and "recommended [that] the former wife should have primary residential custody of Kylee because the former wife was more emotionally stable and would provide a better home setting for Kylee because the former wife lived with her father and grandmother in Miami."[41]

While the trial court found that Kylee was more closely bonded to the mother, the judge awarded primary physical residence to the former husband.[42] The court made its decision by finding that "the mother manipulated visitation during the litigation to the detriment of the father, using Kylee as leverage, concluding that the father would be most likely to allow frequent and continuing contact between Kylee and the nonresidential parent."[43] The court, in emphasizing the friendly parent factors of Florida Statute Section 61.13(3)(a) and (j),[44] "found the factor regarding willingness and ability to facilitate and encourage a close continuing relationship between the child and the other parent favored the father over the mother."[45]

The appellate court, in reversing the award to the husband of primary residence, found that the trial court's decision was an abuse of discretion as it was unsupported by substantial evidence. In support of its decision, the court found that the trial court's statement that it

has considered everything that each side has accused the other side of as well as all the good things that each side has presented about themselves, [is], under the compelling facts of this case, . . . standing alone as it does, . . . insufficient, and bolsters our finding an abuse of discretion. [The court was] troubled not only by the absence of any meaningful evidence of domestic violence, but also by the apparent misapplication of record evidence to the statutory factors contained in section 61.13, Florida Statutes (1995).[46]

The appellate court rejected "the trial court's expressed concern regarding difficulties encountered in visitation. [and stated the difficulties] reflect a problem commonly occurring in cases where evidence demonstrates a pattern of domestic violence. The trouble occurs when a court attempts to harmonize the

---

[40] Id. at 194–94.

[41] Id. at 194.

[42] Id.

[43] Id.

[44] Id. at 196 (quoting Fla. Stat. § 61.13(3)(a) (1995)). "The parent who is more likely to allow the child frequent and continuing contact with the nonresidential parent." Fla. Stat. § 61.13(3)(a) (1995)).

[45] Id. (quoting Fla. Stat. § 61.13(3)(j) (1995)). "The willingness and ability of each parent to facilitate and encourage a close and continuing parent-child relationship between the child and the other parent." Fla. Stat. § 61.13(3)(j) (1995)).

[46] Id. at 198.

non-abusive conduct with "friendly-parent" provisions. Here, the trial court failed to offset what it perceived to be the mother's violation of Florida's friendly-parent provisions, with what was recognized in the temporary order [of protection] as the mother's "justifiable reason to fear the Husband." This failure resulted in an unbalanced final judgment that found "the Mother has manipulated the visitation during this litigation to the detriment of the Father," and failed to recognize the probability that the mother's actions were justified.[47]

How Much Emphasis Should Courts Place on Presence of Domestic Violence?

Courts have discretion in any contested custody case to consider how much emphasis should be given to the presence of DV in the family. Often this factor is given little weight.

The Georgia Supreme Court in *Welch v. Welch*[48] found no abuse of discretion by the trial court in applying the Georgia statute[49] and granted custody to a father who had committed two acts of violence against his wife. Two days prior to filing the complaint for divorce, the wife lost her job and left the state of Georgia to reside in Greensboro, North Carolina, her hometown. The court concluded that it was in the children's best interests to remain in the Georgia county where the husband resides, because

Evidence of the children's close relationship with their father as well as extended family in the area, their ability to continue to attend the same Rabun County School where they have many friends, and their ability to continue as well-known members of their church congregation support the trial court's award of custody to the Husband.[50]

There was also evidence of the husband's acceptance of responsibility and remorse for those acts of DV, and there was a lack of evidence of ongoing acts. Even though the trial court was required by the statute to make a finding of the existence of family violence, the court did not do so, and its failure to do so, though noted by the Georgia Supreme Court, was still not considered to be an abuse of discretion by the trial court.

Was Mrs. Welch placed in an unfair position in this case because of her financial instability? If the court would have granted an adequate award of alimony and child support, Mrs. Welch may have been able to return to Georgia and provide an adequate home for herself and the children.

The Georgia Supreme Court in *Brock v. Brock*[51] found no abuse of discretion by the trial court in applying Georgia Statute Section19-9-3(a) and (b) and granted custody to a father who had "admitted hitting the Wife and crashing into her car after

---

[47] Id.

[48] 596 S.E.2d 134 (Ga. 2004).

[49] Id. (quoting Ga. Code Ann. § 19-9-3(a)(3)) ("which provides in part, wherein the trial court has made a finding of domestic violence, the trial court 'shall consider as primary the safety and well-being of the child and of the parent who is the victim of family violence [and] shall consider the perpetrator's history of causing physical harem, bodily injury, assault, or causing reasonable fear of physical harm, bodily injury, or assault to another person."

[50] Id. at 134.

[51] 610 S.E.2d 29 (Ga. 2005).

learning of her extramarital affairs"[52] and had previously pled guilty to specific acts of DV. The court found as a basis for its decision that "testimony from the final hearing demonstrates that both parents were fit and proper persons and each had a loving relationship with the children."[53]

The *Ford*,[54] *Welch*,[55] and *Brock*[56] cases illustrate decisions by trial courts that award custody to batterers when the presence of DV in the home is treated as an equal factor in applying the best interests standard in contested custody cases.

Consideration of Domestic Violence Factor as a Presumption of Detriment to the Child

Should DV be given greater consideration in custody disputes? Should it be elevated over all other factors in a BIC determination? The NCJFCJ,[57] a judicial membership organization, and the ABA[58] have recommended placing abuse of one parent against another over other best interests factors in contested custody cases by creating a legal presumption denying joint or sole custody to a person with a history of DV.

The Family Violence Department of the NCJFCJ advises that as of June 21, 2006, twenty-five states[59] have adopted versions of Section 401 of the Model Code by including

---

[52] Id. at 31.

[53] Id.

[54] *See* Ford v. Ford, 700 So. 2d 191, 193 (Fla. Dist. Ct. App. 1997).

[55] *See* Welch v. Welch, 596 S.E.2d 134 (Ga. 2004).

[56] *See* Brock v. Brock, 610 S.E.2d 29 (Ga. 2005).

[57] In 1994, the NCJFCJ adopted a Model Code on Domestic and Family Violence that stated

> In every proceeding where there is, at least, at issue a dispute as to custody of a child, a determination by the court that domestic or family violence has occurred, raises a rebuttable presumption that it is detrimental to the child and not in the best interest of the child to be placed in the sole custody, joint legal custody, or joint legal custody, or joint physical custody with a perpetrator of family violence.

Model Code on Domestic & Family Violence § 401, at 33 (Advisory Committee of the Conrad N. Hilton Foundation, Model Code Project of the Family Violence Department 1994) [hereinafter Model Code].

[58] The ABA recommended that "custody not be awarded in whole or in part, to a parent with a history of inflicting domestic violence, that visitation be awarded to such parent only if the safety and well-being of the abused parent and children can be protected, and that all awards of visitation incorporate explicit protections for the child and the abused parent." Howard Davidson (Reporter), American Bar Association, Center on Children & the Law, *The Impact of Domestic Violence on Children, A Report to the President of the American Bar Association* (1994).

[59] Ala. Code § 30-3-131; Alaska Stat. § 25.24.150; Ariz. Rev. Stat. Ann. §§ 9-15-215 and 9-13-101; Ark. Code. Ann. §§ 9-15-215 and 9-13-101; Cal. Fam. Code § 3044 (specifically sets forth that the friendly parent provision, under the BIC standard, cannot be used to rebut this presumption); Del. Code Ann. tit. 13 § 705A; Fla. Stat. § 61.13 (rebuttable presumption created when a parent has been convicted of a felony of the third degree or higher involving DV); Haw. Rev. Stat. § 571–46; Idaho Code Ann. § 32-717B; Iowa Code § 598.41; La. Rev. Stat. Ann. § 9:364; Mass. Gen. Laws. §§ 209C.10, 208.31A, and 209.38; Minn. Stat. § 518.17; Miss. Code. Ann. § 93-5-24; Mo. Rev. Stat. § 455.050; Nev. Rev. Stat. § 125C.230 (rebuttable presumption regarding custody), Nev. Rev. Stat. § 125C.220 (rebuttable presumption regarding custody and BIC when the parent of the child is convicted of first degree murder of the other parent), Nev. Rev. Stat. § 125C (rebuttable presumption

a rebuttable presumption against placing the child in the custody of a batterer when DV is prevalent in the family.[60] Following are various examples of statutes that have been adopted and cases that have been decided.

Denying Custody to Persons With History of Domestic Violence. The Louisiana statute is often cited as a model statute and contains a rebuttable presumption denying both the sole and joint custody to a person with a history of DV. To rebut the presumption, the batterer must document successful completion of a treatment program, demonstrate that he is not abusing alcohol and drugs, and show that it is in the BIC to give the abusive parent custody. If both parents have records of DV, sole custody should go to the less abusive parent. If the parent is a spouse abuser, that parent must be allowed only supervised visitation; he/she must complete a treatment program, not be abusing drugs or alcohol, and not be a danger to the child. In addition, the court must find that unsupervised visitation is in the BIC.[61]

Evidence of Pattern of Domestic Violence. The Wisconsin statute provides that in DV cases it is detrimental to a child to award joint or sole custody to a domestic batterer when there is evidence of a pattern or serious incident of DV. Custody may still be awarded if the abuser successfully completes a certified treatment program for batterers and is not abusing alcohol or drugs. The court may determine that it is in the BICs to be in that person's custody. Where both parents have engaged in incidents of DV, the court will identify the primary aggressor by taking into account prior acts of DV between the parties, the severity of the injuries, the likelihood of future injuries, and whether one of the parties was acting in self-defense.[62]

In requiring the completion of a batterer's intervention program (BIP) to rebut the presumption, both of the above statutes presume the effectiveness of BIPs as a factor in determining whether the presumption has been rebutted. However, research has questioned the effectiveness of these programs. A study of BIPs conducted by Richard M. Tolman and Jeffrey L. Edleson concluded that 53 to 85 percent of victims reported successful outcomes for their violent partners who had successfully completed batterer's programs.[63]

---

regarding child conceived by sexual assault), Nev. Stat. Ann. § 125.480 (rebuttable presumption regarding BIC) and Nev. Rev. Stat. § 432B.157 (rebuttable presumption regarding custody in protection of children from abuse and neglect chapter); N.D. Cent. Code. § 14-09-06.2; Okla. Stat. tit. 43 § 112.2; Or. Rev. Stat. § 107.137 (rebuttable presumption only when conviction of domestic abuse within the past five years or residing with a person who has been convicted of domestic abuse within the past five years); S.D. Codified Laws § 25-4-445.5 (rebuttable presumption only when conviction of DV); Tenn. Code. Ann. § 36-6-101; Tex. Fam. Code. Ann. § 153.004 and Tex. Fam. Code Ann. § 153.131 (joint custody is presumed but presumption is removed where there is a finding of family violence); Wis. Stat. § 767.24 (rebuttable presumption regarding legal custody only).

[60] Section 401 of the Model Code on Domestic and Family Violence provides that "In every proceeding where there is a dispute as to the custody of a child, a determination by the court that domestic or family violence has occurred raises a rebuttable presumption that it is detrimental to the child and not in the best interest of the child to be placed in sole custody, legal custody, or joint physical custody with the perpetrator of family violence."

[61] La.Rev. Stat. Ann. § 9.364.

[62] Wis. Stat. § 767.24.

[63] Richard M. Tolman & Jeffrey L. Edelson, "Intervention for Men Who Batter: A Review of Research," in *Understanding Partner Violence Prevalence, Causes, Consequences and Solutions* 262–73 (S.R. Smith & M.A. Straus eds., 1995), *available at* http://www.mincava. umn.edu/documents/toledl/toledl.html.

Anger Management Programs. Some courts require the batterer to attend an anger management program as a provision of the custody order. A New York court in *Millard v. Clapper*,[64] refused to modify an order granting custody to a batterer who had previously been incarcerated for DV. In this instance, the case worker testified that the children's welfare would be better served by custody remaining with the father who was currently enrolled in an anger management program.

However, in *Coulter v. Coulter*,[65] the Iowa Appellate Court found that the conditions imposed on the batterer requiring him to complete an anger management course, psychiatric evaluation, drug treatment, and drug testing prior to each visit with the children were an abuse of discretion by the trial court and would not be adequate to prevent a risk of harm to the mother or the children. The appellate court concluded, "at a minimum, Brendan should be required to complete a batterer's education course and provide satisfactory proof from his treating psychiatrist that he poses no risk to Lynn and the children."[66]

Custody in Cases of Serious Family Violence. Louisiana Revenue Statute Section 9.364 was applied in *Hicks v. Hicks*,[67] wherein the Louisiana Court of Appeal reversed the trial court without remand and decided the case *de novo* because the trial court did not apply the statutory rebuttable presumption in granting primary residence of the three minor children to the father. The court of appeal found that the father had a history of perpetrating family violence in that he had committed one incident of DV resulting in serious family violence and had committed more than one act of DV. In support of its finding, the court considered only the acts of DV that Mr. Hicks did not refute, even though there was corroborated evidence of other acts:

(1) More than once, he has hit her in the stomach while she was pregnant, causing her to have miscarriages.

(2) More than once, he has broken brooms over her.

(3) He has picked her up with a two by four under her neck and thrown her off the porch.

(4) He has forced her to have sex with him several times against her will.[68]

The court found that once the violent act has been triggered, it need not look at the other "factors relating to best interest until the perpetrator has satisfied all requirements delineated in the act."[69]

This case is a glaring example of the critical need for statutes that include rebuttable presumptions and requirements for rebutting those presumptions in child custody cases where DV is present. The trial court did not apply the Louisiana statute and went directly to the twelve factors in the statute, treating the extreme DV as an equal factor and stressing

---

[64] 679 N.Y.S.2d 434 (N.Y. App. Div. 1998).

[65] No. 02-0473, 2002 WL 31528589, at *1 (Iowa Ct. App. Nov. 15, 2002).

[66] Id. at *3.

[67] 733 So. 2d 1261 (La. Ct. App. 1999).

[68] Id. at 1263.

[69] Id. at 1265.

the importance of keeping the children together in a stable environment.[70] In deciding the case *de novo*, and reversing without remand, the court did not return the case to the trial court to take further evidence to rebut the presumption.

However, in *Jackson v. Jackson*,[71] where the trial court did not apply the statutory presumption after finding DV and granting custody to the batterer, the Civil Court of Appeal of Alabama reversed the trial court's decision awarding joint custody of the child to the perpetrator and remanded the case to the trial court to allow the perpetrator to present evidence to rebut the rebuttable presumption.

In a later Alabama case, *Lamb v. Lamb*, the civil court of appeal refused to reverse the trial court's decision granting custody to the husband, who was the alleged batterer. In *Lamb*, the wife presented several witnesses, each testifying as to the violent behaviors of the husband. A neighbor who lived across the street from the couple stated that he had to call the police on numerous occasions because of the violence he witnessed. He stated that he saw the husband slap one of the wife's children from a previous marriage to the ground. Another time the neighbor heard the couple yelling inside their home; then, when the couple went onto the porch, he saw the husband knock the wife down and almost off the porch. "On yet another occasion the neighbor called the 'animal control' when he saw the husband punch a puppy in the face."[72]

A former girlfriend of the husband also testified that while she was dating him, he was also violent towards her and their child. The wife's mother also testified that she saw the husband abuse her daughter and tie cats to a ceiling fan.[73]

The husband presented evidence to show that the wife was not a very involved parent. She did not involve herself in the education, hygiene, and general welfare of her children, four of whom were from a prior relationship. Additionally, the husband presented evidence to show that the couple's child was sent home by the school and missed many days of class because he was infested with lice.[74] By contrast, the husband presented himself as a stable person with a job who cared for his child's welfare and wanted the best education possible for him. Furthermore, the trial court did not find any evidence that the husband had been violent towards the child. It therefore granted custody to the husband.

The wife appealed the trial court's ruling, and the Alabama Civil Court of Appeal reviewed the trial court's findings *ore tenus*, meaning that the trial court's decision will be sustained unless it is plainly or palpably wrong.[75] The appellate court noted that the trial judge's characterization of the DV as a "skirmish" indicated that the judge did not fully believe that the incidents occurred.[76] Alabama Statutes Section 30-3-130 has a rebuttable presumption of not awarding custody to the perpetrator of violence. Additionally, it states that the court must also take into account what if any impact the DV has on the child. In *Lamb*, the trial judge made no express findings of any impact of the alleged violence on the child, nor did it make an express finding of DV.

The fact that the trial court did not make an express finding of DV prevented the appellate court from overturning the award of custody to the husband. Under established Alabama precedent, the appellate court cannot reweigh the trial court's findings

---

[70] Id. at 1264.
[71] 709 So. 2d 46 (Ala. Civ. App. 1997).
[72] Lamb v. Lamb, 939 So. 2d 918, 920 (Ala. Civ. App. 2006).
[73] Id.
[74] Id.
[75] Arzonico v. Wells, 589 So. 2d 152, 153 (Ala. 1991).
[76] Lamb v. Lamb, 939 So. 2d 918, 921 (Ala. Civ. App. 2006).

unless the judgment was plainly or palpably wrong, which the appellate court did not find here since there was compelling evidence on both sides. In a concurring opinion, Justices Thompson, Pittman, and Bryan wrote of the problem that presents when a trial court does not make express findings of domestic abuse. In the absence of express findings by the lower court concerning allegations of violence, an appellate court will be unable to ascertain whether the lower court applied Alabama Statutes Section 30-3-130 correctly, thus preventing meaningful review.[77]

The concurrence in *Lamb* invited the Alabama Supreme Court to reconsider its holdings in prior cases and required express findings by trial courts in cases involving allegations of DV. The latter would ensure that an appellate court could meaningfully review cases before it, that Alabama Statutes Section 30-3-130 is properly applied, and that the BIC are served.[78]

In *Heck v. Reed*,[79] a North Dakota case where both the father and the mother sought sole custody of the children, the North Dakota Supreme Court reversed the trial court's award of custody to the father based upon the trial court's finding that the evidence rebutted the presumption against awarding custody to the perpetrator of DV.

> At issue in the appeal [were] the 1993 Amendments to NDCC § 14-09-06.2(1) (j) in particular, the meaning and application of the language that there is a 'rebuttable presumption that a parent who has perpetrated domestic violence may not be awarded sole or joint custody of a child' and that "[t]his presumption may be overcome only by clear and convincing evidence that the best interests of the child require that parent's participation . . .
>
> The trial court, agreeing with the guardian *ad litem*, characterized both parents as having the ability to appropriately raise the children and as having great affection toward them. It then found that, although Shane had perpetrated domestic violence against Christie, by calling her bad names, pulling her hair and hitting her and punching her in her face, the presumption that a parent has perpetrated domestic violence may not be awarded sole or joint custody of the children was rebutted by other factors.[80]

The factors cited by the trial court were customary best interests factors: the mother's living arrangements, which the appellate court found to have been destabilized by the father's DV; the absence of DV against the children—the appellate court noting that that children suffer harm even when they do not witness the violence; little likelihood of continued violence—the appellate court finding that there was no evidence that the father considered or participated in any form of treatment program or counseling related to the DV; the mother's smoking in the presence of the children, even though one of the children is asthmatic, and the appellate court's noting that the latter can be solved by issuing an order prohibiting smoking in the presence of the children.[81]

In reversing the trial court's decision, the appellate court concluded that "[t]he legislature intended not only that domestic violence committed by a parent weigh heavily

---

[77] Id. at 924.

[78] Id.

[79] 529 N.W.2d 155 (N.D. 1995).

[80] Id. at 158 (citing N.D. Cent. Code § 14-09-06.2(1)(j)(6)).

[81] Id. at 165.

against that parent's claim for custody, but that it be overcome only by clear convincing evidence the best interests of the children demand the perpetrator of domestic violence serve as custodial parents."[82] In finding the trial court's opinion clearly erroneous because it found that ordinary custody factors could be used to rebut the DV presumption, the court looked to the intent of the legislature in subsection (j) of the statute and found that "[t]he statute is intended to counteract the myths that: domestic violence is not a serious crime; victims provoke or deserve the violence; victims habitually lie or exaggerate the extent of the violence; and domestic violence is a private family matter."[83]

What is necessary to trigger the rebuttable presumption? Following *Heck*,[84] in *Brown v. Brown*,[85] the court applied the amended North Dakota statute that triggers the rebuttable presumption when the trial court finds "credible evidence that domestic violence occurred, and there exists one incident of domestic violence which resulted in serious bodily injury or involved the use of a dangerous weapon or there exists a pattern of domestic violence within a reasonable time proximate to the proceeding."[86]

The trial court made findings on all thirteen of the BIC factors under the statute, and the supreme court affirmed the trial court's findings that the incidents of DV did not trigger the presumption. In support of the affirmance, the supreme court held that the trial court was correct in deciding that a pattern of behavior had not been established, and there was no evidence of any act that caused serious bodily injury. Letitia Brown alleged, in support of her claim of DV, that Michael Brown had thrown a can opener at her car while she was in the car and their child was nearby. The court rejected her allegation and found that "The can opener incident caused damage only to the front of the hood of Letitia Brown's car and did not hit or injure her."[87] In considering whether any serious bodily injury had occurred, the court found that in regard to the bruises allegedly inflicted on her, "[o]n the same day her bruises were allegedly inflicted, Michael Brown called the police and reported Letitia Brown had thrown things at him and had pushed to the ground. Neither party argues that either of these November 15, 1997, acts of domestic violence acts resulted in serious bodily injury."[88]

The court first found that both parties had committed DV, then considered whether the evidence was sufficient under the best interests standard, even though it did not trigger the presumption. The court affirmed the trial court's finding that the incidents did not "weigh more heavily in favor of custody placement with either party."[89] Letitia Brown claimed that the trial court erred because it did not consider Michael Brown's alienation of their child from her. The supreme court found that the evidence did not support her claim of alienation.[90] The court rejected Letitia Brown's claim that the trial "court erred in awarding custody of the parties' child to Michael Brown, due to his

---

[82] Id. at 161.

[83] Id. at 163.

[84] Id.

[85] 600 N.W.2d 869 (N.D. 1999).

[86] Id. at 873.

[87] Id.

[88] Id.

[89] Id. at 874.

[90] Id.

alienation of their child from her."[91] The court based the decision on its finding that there was no alienation of the child from Letitia Brown and that it has never reversed a custody award based solely on the threat of future alienation.[92]

In a custody modification case involving DV and the friendly parent provision, in *In re Marriage of Reidel*,[93] the California Court of Appeal affirmed the trial court's finding that the alleged batterer had rebutted the presumption against granting custody to the father who pled guilty to felony spousal abuse after he demonstrated to the trial court that he had successfully completed a batterer's treatment program. In supporting the trial court's decision, the court of appeal reasoned that because Sophia Reidel's conduct had made coparenting impossible, along with Donald Reidel's successful completion of the BIP, it was in the BIC to award custody to the father. The appeal court found that the trial court's findings and its decision to change custody from the mother to the father were supported by substantial evidence, which came not from Donald but from separate credible sources, including to wit

> the court-appointed mediator, ACCESS and Christian's attorney. . . . That evidence consisted of "(1) mother's continual referral to CPS (ACCESS) for issues which have been previously resolved (tickling scrotum), physical abuse of Christian (unsubstantiated and apparently unfounded); (2) her interference with visitation consisting of vacation scheduling, misinterpretation of visitation consisting of vacation orders of the court, and unwarranted termination of visits; (3) violation of the spirit, if not the letter of this court's previous order regarding the presence and assistance of law enforcement to enforce visitation orders; (4) continued demeaning comments regarding father in the presence of the child, despite protestations to the contrary; (5) clear evidence of attempting to manipulate the child to substantiate mother's fears and concerns over issues of physical and sexual abuse."[94]

The appeal court emphasized that "while many of these problems existed and were discussed in the court's initial decision, they persisted and increased in magnitude, leaving the trial court to conclude that a change of circumstances exists."[95]

The appeal court's conclusion that Donald had successfully completed the program was based on the testimony of his probation officer who testified that "Donald had successfully completed the court-ordered batterer's treatment program, voluntarily attending 80 sessions, 28 more than the court-ordered 52 session, and never provided a cause for concern about his attendance at the program."[96]

Sophia relied on the Florida case of *Ford v. Ford*,[97] in support of her argument that in a DV case where joint custody is detrimental to BIC, the friendly parent provision no longer serves the BIC.[98] In *Ford*, the appellate court found that the trial court's

---

[91] Id.

[92] Id.

[93] No. C036947, 2002 WL 2013461, at *1 (Cal. Ct. App. Sept. 4, 2002).

[94] Id. at *8.

[95] Id.

[96] Id. at *3.

[97] 700 So. 2d 191 (Fla. Dist. Ct. App. 1997).

[98] *In re* Marriage of Reidel, No. C036947, 2002 WL 2013461, at *12 (Cal. Ct. App. Sept. 4, 2002).

decision was against the manifest weight of the evidence and an abuse of discretion for failure to take into consideration the DV. The court distinguished the present case from *Ford* as follows:

> Here, the trial court made findings of fact regarding the parties' credibility, and specifically found Sophia's testimony lacked credibility. Moreover, the court considered the history of domestic violence, found that Donald had reformed and posed no physical threat to Christian, and further found that Sophia's efforts to distance Christian from his father were not justified and actually threatened to be harmful to his development.[99]

The court also found that the evidence did not support Sophia's argument that "the friendly-parent provision should not be applied in a rebuttable presumption case because it does not account for the fact that the parents cannot cooperate and that gender bias leads courts to blame battered mothers for the parents' failure to cooperate."[100]

In many child custody cases where DV is present, the victim is in an inferior economic position because of her victimization by the batterer. The court, while recognizing that reliance on the relative economic position is impermissible when determining the BIC, because the "purpose of child support awards is to ensure that the spouse otherwise best fit for custody receives adequate funds for the child,"[101] found in this case that "the trial court looked not to the relative economic position of the two parties, but to their relative stability and reliability in providing an appropriate home for Christian and meeting his needs."[102] The court rejected Sophia's argument that her instability was based upon her victimization.

Economic Factors. If the DV victim is not in a position to support herself and/or her children psychologically and financially because she is a battered spouse, is it then fair to apply a statutory factor inferring economic superiority on an equal basis to the presence of DV? Such a factor is found in Florida Statute Section 61.13(3)(c) as follows: "(c) The demonstrated capacity and disposition of each parent to determine, consider, and act upon the needs of the child as opposed to the needs of the parent."[103]

If the court applies such a provision, which implies that financial superiority is on an equal basis in the presence of DV, then how can a battered woman living with her children in a DV shelter, without a job and psychologically and emotionally impaired, possibly compete with a financially and stable batterer in a contested custody case? A possible solution is the use of a transitional housing facility. The Betty Griffin House in St. Johns County, Florida, provides a transitional housing facility for victims after they have left the shelter. The transitional housing facility of the Betty Griffin House provides housing, support services, and resources needed to make major life changes, in addition to a safe place to live after leaving the shelter. Emphasis is placed on the skills and education needed for income and permanent housing services.

---

[99] Id. at *12 n.12.
[100] Id. at *13.
[101] Id. at *14.
[102] Id.
[103] Fla. Stat. § 61.13(3)(c) (2008).

If a statutory amendment creates a rebuttable presumption of detriment to a child when DV is present in a custody case, does the amendment apply retroactively to create the presumption in a case tried prior to the effective date of the amendment but after the enactment of the amendment?

That question was answered in the negative in the Alaska Supreme Court case of *Van Sickle v. McGraw*,[104] wherein the court sustained the trial court's refusal to apply the rebuttable presumption when DV was present and awarded sole physical custody of the child to the father. The court found that under the friendly parent provision, the father was more capable than the mother of fostering an open relationship between the child and the other parent. The court also found that the trial court did not err in finding that the father's town was a better home, as the father's domicile was near his extended family and provided better cultural opportunities for the child of Tlingit heritage.[105]

Child's Preference. Where both parents are fit custodians but the child chooses the DV perpetrator over the victim, how much weight should be given to the child's preference as a factor to consider by the court? The New York Supreme Court considered this issue in *Wissink v. Wissink*.[106] The supreme court reversed the family court's award of custody to the batterer and remanded to the family court to order a comprehensive psychological evaluation; this assessment was to ensure that the award of custody to the father was in the child's best interest. The trial record contained seven incidents of DV and two orders of protection, the last being a permanent order. The incidents reported by the mother included hitting, kicking, pulling out chunks of her hair, leaving marks on her neck with a resulting sore throat, holding a ten-inch knife to her throat, punching her, squeezing her face leaving marks, and choking her.

> On June 24, 1999, a few days after the mother's return from the shelter, during a dispute over tax returns, the father tried to wrest papers the mother held in her teeth by squeezing her face in his hands, leaving marks and even enlisting the assistance of Andrea, their daughter; he allegedly directed the child to "hold [the mother's] nose so she can't breathe."[107]

The court found that

> Andrea's preference for her father and her closely bonded relationship to him were confirmed by her law guardian and the "mental health professional" social worker who interviewed her. Indeed, putting aside the established fact of his abusive conduct toward the mother, Andrea's father appears a truly model parent. He is significantly involved in her school work and her extracurricular activities. They enjoy many pleasurable activities, including movies, shopping, building a barn, and horseback riding. He provides her with material benefits such as a television set, clothing, a horse, a trip to Europe. He is loving and affectionate. She is his "princess," his "best girl." In contrast, Andrea's mother has not been significantly involved in her school work or her extracurricular activities, and Andrea does not enjoy her company.[108]

---

[104] 134 P.3d 338 (Alaska 2006).

[105] Id. at 342.

[106] 301 A.D.2d 36 (N.Y. App. Div. 2d Dep't 2002)

[107] Id. at 39.

[108] Id. at 37.

The supreme court stressed the importance of the availability to the trial court of a complete forensic report that examines the consequences of DV on a child and the likelihood that the evaluation would include clinical evaluation, psychological testing, and review of records and information from collateral sources.[109] After finding the mental health evaluation deficient based upon the social worker's two forty-five-minute interviews of Andrea and a one-hour interview of each parent, the supreme court ordered a new custody hearing to be conducted after a comprehensive psychological evaluation of both the parties.

While the *Wissink*[110] case viewed the child's preference as a factor to be considered but not determinative in deciding best interests, in Georgia, upon reaching the age of fourteen, the child's preference is binding on the court, unless the court finds the parent to be not a fit and proper person to have custody of the child.[111]

Mothers Who Work Long Hours. The case of *Kopec v. Severance*[112] illustrates a trial court's failure to address DV to a victim that had to work long hours to financially support herself and her children, and an award of primary residential custody of the child to the mother. While the Florida Appellate Court affirmed the trial court's opinion in granting custody to a husband who had committed DV, the strong dissenting opinion concluded that the trial judge's opinion was an abuse of discretion. The appellate court majority opinion found that while both parents love their son and are able to care for him, and the son is comfortable with both of them, because "this trial judge had in excess of a quarter-century of experience, had the witnesses in front of them, heard and saw the parties in person and considered a great amount of testimony, it is with the usual amount of deference we affirm the ruling."[113] The court compared the recommendations of the guardian ad litem (GAL) who had experience in one contested divorce and no previous guardianships, and the clinical psychologist who had much greater experience and training. The strong dissenting opinion found that the majority disregarded the numerous threats of DV directed primarily against Kopec and her other children, disregarding Florida Statute Section 61.13(2)(b)(2),[114] and Severance's dysfunctional background and alcohol abuse—drinking in excess on a daily basis throughout the marriage[115]—and that the trial court abused its discretion since

> it is arbitrary and capricious to fault Kopec because of her career and industriousness and success, period. This is particularly true in this case since there was no showing that her pursuit of her career in any way injured, endangered, or harmed her children. There was also evidence that Kopec had no choice but to work to support her children. No one else was doing it.[116]

The dissent also questioned the trial judge and the testimony of the psychologist in favoring the father, "Would, I wonder, the trial judge or the licensed clinical psychologist who testified as the court's witness, have so faulted a man for working at his job under these circumstances?"[117]

---

[109] Id. at 40.

[110] Wissink v. Wissink, 301 A.D.2d 36 (N.Y. App. Div. 2d Dep't 2002).

[111] Ga. Code Ann. § 19-9-3(a)(4).

[112] 658 So. 2d 1060 (Fla. Dist. Ct. App. 1995).

[113] Id. at 1060.

[114] Fla. Stat. § 61.13(2)(b)(2) (2007). Section 61.13(2)(b)(2) provides as follows: "The court shall consider evidence of spousal or child abuse as evidence of detriment."

[115] Kopec v. Severance, 658 So. 2d 1060, 1061 (Fla. Dist. Ct. App. 1995).

[116] Id.

[117] Id.

Mothers With Mental Disorders. Ironically, the friendly parent provision worked in favor of a DV victim whose abuser discredited her for having a mental condition caused by his DV. In the New York case of *Candy H. v. Justin G.*[118] the New York Family Court awarded custody to a DV victim whose bipolar disorder was properly treated with medication. In using the friendly parent factor against the batterer, the court found it in the BIC to award custody to the mother not only because she was clean from drug and alcohol abuse and her bipolar disorder was under control, and the father had engaged in DV, but also because of the father's great disdain and arrogance toward the mother because of her financial status. In the court's opinion, that would make the father unfit to be the custodial parent "since his attitude would substantially interfere with his own in fostering a continued relationship with the non-custodial parent unfit to be the custodial parent."[119]

ETHICAL ISSUES IN JUDICIAL DECISION MAKING

Justice does not depend upon legal dialectics so much as upon the atmosphere of the courtroom, and that in the end depends upon the judge.

—Judge Learned Hand

Does judicial bias, particularly gender bias, affect judges' decisions in contested custody cases involving DV? This section discusses the pertinent judicial ethical canons related to bias and improper demeanor in the courtroom and explains how these canons relate to judicial disciplinary proceedings.

General Ethical Standards for Judicial Conduct

All states have codes of judicial conduct setting forth standards governing ethical conduct for judges in both their official judicial duties and personal activities and, in general, have adopted some version of the ABA Model Code of Judicial Conduct.[120] On February 13, 2007, the ABA House of Delegates approved a Revised Model Code of Judicial Conduct that is now being considered for adoption by the states. However, the 2007 ABA Revised Code of Judicial Conduct will not be discussed for the purposes of this chapter, and all references will be to the prior ABA Model Code of Judicial Conduct.

The general standard for judicial conduct is set forth in Canon 2A of the ABA Model Code of Judicial Conduct, which provides that "a judge shall respect and comply with the law and shall act at all times in a manner that promotes public confidence in the integrity and impartiality of the judiciary."[121] Canon 2A also applies to both the

---

[118] No. V-3361-03, 2004 WL 690062, at *1 (N.Y. Fam. Ct. Mar. 29, 2004).

[119] Id. at *3.

[120] Model Code of Judicial Conduct (1990), *amended* Aug. 10, 1999, and Aug. 12, 2003. This can be ordered from the ABA Book Publishing: American Bar Association, 750 North Lake Shore Drive, Chicago, Illinois 60611 and at http://www.abanet.org [hereinafter Model Code of Judicial Conduct].

[121] Id.

professional and *personal* conduct of the judge and applies the reasonableness standard to the conduct according to the ABA Commentary to Canon 2A.[122]

The ABA Model Code of Judicial Conduct in Canon 3B(5) clearly requires judges to perform judicial duties without bias or prejudice based upon gender and also requires judges to not permit staff, court officials, and others subject to the judge's direction and control to do so.[123] Judges have been disciplined by various state disciplinary bodies for violating both Canon 2A and Canon 3B(5). In interpreting Canon 3B(5), the ABA Commentary to the canon sets forth courtroom standards for judges as follows:

> A judge must refrain from speech, gestures or other conduct that could reasonably be perceived as sexual harassment, and must require the same standard of conduct of others subject to the judge's direction. A judge must perform judicial duties impartially and fairly. A judge who manifests bias on any basis in a proceeding impairs the fairness of the proceeding and brings the judiciary into disrepute. Facial expressions and body language, in addition to oral communication, can give to parties and lawyers in the proceeding, jurors, the media and others an appearance of impropriety. The judge must be alert to avoid behavior that may be perceived as prejudicial.

Thus, judges must do more to assure fairness to DV victims than simply calling the balls and strikes. They must not only refrain from prejudicial and biased conduct,

---

[122] Id., Canon 2A cmt.

Public confidence in the judiciary is eroded by irresponsible or improper conduct by judges. A judge must avoid all impropriety and appearance of impropriety. A judge must expect to be the subject of constant scrutiny. A judge must therefore accept restrictions on the judge's conduct that might be viewed as burdensome by the ordinary citizen and should do so freely and willingly. Examples are the restrictions on judicial speech imposed by Sections 3(B)(9) and (10) that are indispensable to the maintenance of the integrity, impartiality, and independence of the judiciary.

See generally id., Canon 3.

The prohibition against behaving with impropriety or the appearance of impropriety applies to both the professional and personal conduct of a judge. Because it is not practicable to list all prohibited acts, the proscription is necessarily cast in general terms that extend to conduct by judges that is harmful although not specifically mentioned in the Code. Actual improprieties under this standard include violations of law, court rules or other specific provisions of this Code. The test for appearance of impropriety is whether the conduct would create in reasonable minds a perception that the judge/s ability to carry out judicial responsibilities with integrity, impartiality and competence is impaired.

See generally id. *See also* Cannon 2(C) cmt.

[123] Model Code of Judicial Conduct, *supra* note 120. Canon 3B(5) provides as follows: "A judge *shall* (emphasis added) perform judicial duties without bias or prejudice. A judge shall not, in the performance of judicial duties, by words or conduct, manifest bias or prejudice, including,, but not limited to, bias or prejudice based upon race, sex, religion, national origin, disability, age, sexual orientation of socioeconomic status."

but also protect the victim from being subjected to bias and prejudicial conduct from anyone else in the courtroom. This includes the attorneys as evidenced by ABA Canon 3(B)(6), which states,

> A judge shall require lawyers in proceeding before the court to refrain from manifestations, by words or conduct, bias or prejudice based upon race, sex, religion, national origin, disability, age, sexual orientation or sociological status, against parties, witnesses, counsel or others. This section 3(B)(6) does not preclude legitimate advocacy when race, religion, national origin, disability, age or economic status, or other factors are issues in the proceedings.

Not all states have adopted the ABA Model Code of Judicial Conduct in the same language. Therefore, to determine whether a given conduct violates their ethical responsibilities, judges must examine their own state respective codes of judicial conduct and any judicial advisory and/or disciplinary proceedings applying those codes.

The NCJFCJ recognized the need for removing bias in the courtroom and set forth suggestions for accomplishing this goal as early as 1989, as follows:

> Courts must be without bias as to race, gender, ethnicity, handicap, age, or religion, both in fact and in the perception of the community.
>
> A. Court personnel should be representatives of the composition of the community.
>
> B. Judges and court personnel should have continuous training to address and to be sensitized regarding bias by reason of gender, race, age and economics.
>
> C. Every state should create a state level task force on bias and the courts.
>
> D. Local bias review committees should be established to audit court practices and review systemic problems.
>
> E. Codes of judicial conduct should address judicial bias and treat it as severe transgression. The findings of any judicial disciplinary board, made after notice and an opportunity to be heard, should be made available to the public.[124]

Forty states, and the District of Columbia, have established gender bias task forces. Several federal task forces have also been established. Unfortunately, some of the task forces have been abolished.[125]

Many state courts systems have demonstrated leadership in identifying sources of bias and in eliminating bias in the courts through judicial training. Such leadership is exemplified by the endorsement by then Rhode Island Supreme Court Chief Justice Frank J. Williams of a pamphlet entitled *Equal Justice for All: Protocol to Ensure Fairness for All in the Rhode Island Courts*.[126]

---

[124] *Families in Court: Recommendations From a National Symposium* 12 (NCJFCJ May 1989).

[125] *Legal Momentum: Advancing Womens Rights, National Judicial Education Program (NJEP): Gender Bias Task Forces,* http://www.legalmomentum.org/site/PageServer?pagename=njep_17/.

[126] *See Equal Justice for All: Protocol to Ensure Fairness for All in the Rhode Island Courts* (Rhode Island Supreme Court Advisory Committee on Women and Minorities in the Courts 2001).

A one-day conference of all Rhode Island judges was held on September 20, 2002, in Newport, RI. I was a presenter at the conference on the topic of "Judicial Responsibility to Ensure Fairness in the Courts" and discussed the contents of the pamphlet and relevant ABA canons with case law and judicial advisory opinions as to particular judicial and extrajudicial conduct. The pamphlet discussed the "special role" of the judge as follows:

Because you are a viable leader in the courts, you have the added responsibility:

To establish and require a demeanor in your courtroom that is free of bias.

To intervene and take whatever steps are necessary to correct the biased attitudes or conduct of those around you.

To avoid any form of bias in your decision making and court interactions.

To demonstrate that all matters heard by the court are important, regardless of how busy the daily schedule may be.[127]

The pamphlet warned judges against stereotyping people as follows:

Reject stereotypes in the treatment of people in the treatment or the handling of cases in court.

Avoid making assumptions about individuals or their roles in the court based on stereotypes.

Guard against any tendency to label women or minority litigants as more troublesome or emotional or to regard cases typically brought by women or minorities as less important.

Avoid subjecting victims of crime to unnecessary scrutiny because of the nature of the alleged acts perpetrated against them or based on their gender, race, ethnicity, knowledge of English, or social status.

Do not expect women or minority attorneys to be more passive or aggressive in their advocacy or to be more tolerant of interruptions or reprimands than other attorneys.

Bias exists in our society, and it is very difficult to overcome preconceived notions in judging a case. Nevertheless, we must make every effort to prevent these assumptions form distorting our perceptions of individuals in the courtroom, our assessment of credibility, or our fact finding, decision making, and sentencing.[128]

Certainly, the advice to avoid bias is helpful to the judge when deciding contested custody cases where DV is involved. Do judges label women as more troublesome or

---

[127] Id. at 3.
[128] Id. at 5–6.

emotional? Are victims of domestic crimes subjected to unnecessary scrutiny because of the nature of the alleged acts perpetrated against them?

The following examples of judicial gender bias and improper demeanor in the courtroom and the judicial disciplinary proceedings that followed illustrate the persistence of gender bias among some members of the judiciary.

Disciplinary Proceedings for Violation of Judicial Codes of Conduct

In the case of *In re Greene,*[129] The North Carolina Supreme Court censured a judge for conduct prejudicial to the administration of justice and that brought the judicial office in disrepute in violation of Canons 2A, 3A(2), and 3A(3) of the North Carolina Code of Judicial Conduct. The conduct involved, in addition to the finding that the judge regularly drove in excess of the speed limit, statements made by the judge to a battered women's support group while presiding at a criminal case involving a charge of assault on a female. In support of the censure, the court accepted the findings of the Judicial Standards Commission as follows:

> The respondent demeaned the dignity and integrity of the proceeding and his judicial office when during proceedings in State v. Sheffield, . . . he embarrassed [sic] and humiliated the seven-months pregnant victim of the assault by telling her she would ruin her children's lives if she did not reconcile with her estranged husband, . . . he referred in a derogatory manner to the representative of the support group who was with the victim and the support group itself, which he later came to know as Interact, as a one-sided, man-hating bunch of she-dogs; and he polled the courtroom spectators as to how many of them had little spats during their marriages.[130]

Judge Marko was reprimanded by the Florida Supreme Court in a disciplinary proceeding[131] for rude, improper, and inappropriate remarks to a wife in a dissolution proceeding. The court approved the stipulation, which contained the findings of the commission, in pertinent part, as follows:

1. You have conducted yourself in a manner designed to lessen public confidence in the dignity, integrity and impartiality of the judiciary in violation of Canons 1, 2, 3A(2) and 4A(3) of the Code of Judicial Conduct.

2. You have exhibited rude, improper and inappropriate behavior at a dissolution of marriage hearing in Price v. Price, in that you used inappropriate language when you remarked to the wife to ". . . go out and get another guy . . . the single bars are all full of them . . . there are all kinds of bimbos in those places, and there are all kinds of guys running around in open shirts with eagles on their chests. There are great guys out there . . . go find a brain surgeon."[132]

---

[129] *In re* Greene, 403 S.E.2d 257 (N.C. 1991).
[130] Id. at 261.
[131] *In re* Marko, 595 So. 2d 46 (Fla. 1992).
[132] Id. at 46.

In another case involving allegations of displaying bias and improper demeanor in a number of cases, the New York Court of Appeals, *In the Matter of Roberts,*[133] accepted the recommendation of the New York State Commission on Judicial Conduct and removed an elected village court judge from office. The commission found that one of the charges "demonstrates a gross insensitivity and an applied dereliction of duty in regard to judicial responsibilities in the area of domestic abuse crimes and related matters."[134] This is exemplified by a statement the judge made to his clerk ("Every woman needs a good pounding now and then."[135]) and that his comments as to protective orders "reflect an attitude or predisposition that orders of protection are worthless and foolish, and to fail to issue an appropriate protective order in the particular circumstances and matter, are appropriately weighed together and in context for the sanction review in this case."[136]

In the case of *In re Romano,*[137] the New York of Court of Appeals removed a part-time judge who, in a series of incidents, exhibited intemperate behavior against victims of DV, disregard for the law, and an egregious assertion for private gain. The most recent incident occurred at an arraignment where a defendant was charged with violating an order of protections and assaulting his wife. At the arraignment, the judge stated from the bench, "What's wrong with that? You've got to keep them in line once in a while."[138] The judge was found to be in violation of many of the New York Rules Governing Judicial Conduct, among them Rule 100.2(A) (requiring a judge to "avoid impropriety and the appearance of impropriety in all of the judge's activities") and Rule 100.3(B)(4) (prohibiting a judge from manifesting bias or prejudice by words or conduct).

In the case of *In re O'Dea,*[139] the supreme court of Vermont publicly reprimanded Judge Arthur J. O'Dea for violations of Code of Judicial Conduct Canon 3A(3) and prohibited him from sitting in the family court for a period of two years. The charges involved misconduct in two cases, *Green* and *Georges*, both family court proceedings. The court found that

> In Georges, which concerned a visitation dispute, respondent exhibited similar impatience and discourtesy. He refused to grant a continuance so that the litigant mother could obtain counsel, even though she had appeared at the court expecting the matter to be mediated or continued. He cut off the mother's attempt to briefly cross-examine the father, gave her no opportunity to present testimony or evidence of her own, and questioned in a harsh and intimidating fashion the parties' daughter, who was not a party or sworn as a witness. When the mother began to comfort her daughter, who had begun to cry, he directed the mother to "just leave her alone and let her listen." He also threatened to transfer custody of the daughter to the parties if the parties did not adhere to the visitation schedule, although the father neither requested nor wanted such a transfer. Respondent directed the parties to agree to a visitation schedule during a recess, which the mother, feeling powerless to object, signed with the notation, that she was agreeing "under duress of the court's order."[140]

---

[133] 91 N.Y.2d 93 (1997).

[134] Id. at 94.

[135] Id.

[136] Id.

[137] 712 N.E.2d 1216 (N.Y. 1999).

[138] Id.

[139] 622 A.2d 507 (Vt. 1993).

[140] Id. at 509.

Has there been any progress in eliminating judicial bias in custody cases? Unfortunately, judicial bias and misconduct continues as evidenced by the removal of a Virginia juvenile and family court judge as recently as November 2, 2007, in *Judicial Inquiry and Review Commission of Virginia v. Shull*.[141] This case exemplifies a judge continuing to demean litigants appearing before him, even after being warned by the Virginia Judicial Inquiry and Review Commission in an appearance before the commission in May 2004. "At the time the Commission dismissed these allegations, the Commissioner's chairman stated, 'You haven't been a full-time judge for very long, and the Commission is hopeful that this is the initial learning process that is going to help you sort everything out.'"[142] The court in *Shull* concluded "by its action, the Commission plainly gave Judge Shull the opportunity to change his future conduct and to treat litigants with due respect."[143] Judge Shull was removed from office for grave and substantial violations of several canons. The court found that

> Judge Shull violated the Canons by his conduct because his actions failed to uphold the integrity and independence of the judiciary, and tended to impair public confidence in the integrity and impartiality of the judiciary. See Canons of Judicial Conduct 1 & 2. Judge Shull also violated the Canons by failing to maintain and exhibit professional competence in the law, by failing to require decorum and civility in the courtroom, and by failing to be patient, dignified and courteous to a litigant. See Canons of Judicial Conduct 3(B)(2), (3) & (4). Finally, Judge Shull's action initiating an improper ex parte telephone call also violated the Canons because that action precluded the parties from participating in a disputed matter material to their proceeding. See Canons of Judicial Conduct 3(B)(7).[144]

The court concluded that "the essence of Judge Shull's judicial misconduct has been his disregard for the dignity of litigant's appearing before him and for the dignity of the judicial process."[145]

The underlying factual findings that constituted the violations were supported by the testimony of several witnesses whom the court found to be credible. The court found as a matter of fact that, in a custody and visitation hearing over which he presided, during which Tammy Giza claimed that Keith had inflicted a wound on her thigh,

> Giza lowered her pants in the courtroom because Judge Shull directed her to display her wound after she was unable to expose it by lifting her pants leg. We also find as a matter of fact that Giza lowered her pants to her knees on both occasions after being directed to display her wound, and that, as a result, her buttocks were exposed.[146]

The court determined that the judge's conduct "ignored the dignity of a litigant who was not represented by counsel and who had a clear history of mental instability."[147] The court also found that in twice tossing a coin in the courtroom to

---

[141] 651 S.E.2d 648 (Va. 2007).
[142] Id. at 659.
[143] Id.
[144] Id. at 658.
[145] Id. at 659.
[146] Id. at 657.
[147] Id. at 659.

resolve a visitation dispute, Judge Shull "denigrated both the litigants and our justice system."[148] In addition, the court stated also that Judge Shull's improper *ex parte* telephone call during the Giza custody hearing to obtain information on a disputed factual matter "serves to illustrate again Judge Shull's lack of concern for litigants appearing before him."[149]

Could Judge Shull's removal from the bench have been prevented if remedial action had been taken when he received his initial warning from the 2004 Judicial Inquiry and Review Commission Hearing? If so, what remedial action would have been effective? Gender bias sensitivity training? Education about the dynamics of DV and its effect on its victims? The next section explores these questions and offers suggestions for improving the judicial system in its treatment of DV victims in child custody cases.

RECOMMENDATIONS FOR IMPROVING JUDICIAL DECISION MAKING IN CONTESTED CUSTODY CASES INVOLVING DOMESTIC VIOLENCE

No problem can be solved by the same consciousness that created it.

—Albert Einstein

A 1996 report of the APA Presidential Task Force on Violence and the Family—Executive Summary[150] concludes that training is needed for all actors in the cases involving DV:

Child Custody and visitation decisions must be made with full knowledge of the previous knowledge of the previous family violence and potential for continued danger, whether or not the child has been physically harmed. Most lawyers, judges, and others in the justice system are not trained in the psychology of the family violence and abuse.[151]

Education on the causes and effects of DV should begin at the earliest possible stage of a legal career in the law school curriculum. In fact, progress toward this goal has already been made in law schools throughout the country. The ABA Commission on Domestic Violence conducted a survey of law school programs in 2002 and found that at least ninety-five schools incorporated DV issues into their curricula.[152] Some of those schools, such as the Florida Coastal School of Law (FCSL) in Jacksonville, Florida, teach a DV course and integrate DV issues into the family law and criminal law courses. Other law schools include DV clinics in their clinical programs. Continuing legal education (CLE) programs for practicing attorneys should include DV topics to ensure that attorneys have the requisite knowledge to effectively represent litigants in cases involving DV.

---

[148] Id.

[149] Id.

[150] American Psychological Association, *supra* note 1.

[151] Id. at 3.

[152] American Bar Association Commission on Domestic Violence, *Teach Your Students Well: Incorporating Domestic Violence Issues Into Law School* (U.S. Department of Justice 2003).

Has any progress been made in helping judges and lawyers understand not only the psychology of the family violence and abuse, but also how to determine what is in the BIC in contested child custody cases involving DV? Progress has been made, but as demonstrated by the cases in this chapter, ongoing legal and judicial training is still very much needed.

The Family Violence Department of the NCJFC has been conducting trainings as well as producing and distributing tool kits to assist family court judges with these cases. Ongoing and mandated judicial training in handling DV cases has occurred in some states. I have conducted judicial trainings on bias and related issues throughout the country for the NCJFCJ, the National Judicial College, and various state judicial systems. Trainings by the National Judicial Institute of the NCJFCJ to approximately 3,900 judiciary and multidisciplinary individuals were completed between 1999 and the end of 2007.[153] The trainings consisted of "Enhancing Judicial Skills in Domestic Violence Cases" (EJS), "Continuing Judicial Skills in Domestic Violence Cases" (CJS), and roundtable and steering committee meetings.

Several recent publications are excellent roadmaps for judges to follow in handling DV cases. One recent publication includes a valuable checklist for judges hearing DV cases involving children.[154] In a contested custody case, it is not unusual for the trial judge to order a child custody evaluation as authorized by statute.[155] Judges therefore need to avoid some of the pitfalls in choosing the evaluator and relying on his/her recommendation. The NCJFCJ publication, *Navigating Custody & Visitation Evaluations in Cases With Domestic Violence: A Judge's Guide*,[156] offers an excellent resource for judges in reviewing an evaluator's testimony. The publication contains bench card checklists and supplementary materials to "help judges critically review expert testimony of child custody evaluators, determine whether the evaluator's testing methods were accurate and reliable, or tease out the biases of individual clinicians, particularly when domestic violence is involved."[157] In addition, "it is designed to be a practical tool for judges on how to order, interpret, and act upon child custody evaluations."[158] This tool is designed to help judges

---

[153] E-mail from Tracy Keever, Resource Specialist, NCJFCJ, Family Violence Dept. (Nov. 8, 2007, 17:31:29 EST) (on file with author).

[154] *A Judicial Checklist for Children and Youth Exposed to Violence* (National Council of Juvenile & Family Court Judges, Reno, Nevada, 2006).

> The Checklist was developed with the input of juvenile and family court judges as well as professionals who have worked closely with children and youth exposed to violence. The Checklist was then piloted by a select group of judges form the Model Courts who have extensive experience adjudicating judicial benchcards and checklist tools. The five participating judges had an average of 12.5 years on the bench and preside over an average of 370 juvenile-related cases each year.

Id. at 11.

[155] Fla. Stat. § 61.20(1) (2007).

[156] *Navigating Custody & Visitation Evaluations in Cases With Domestic Violence: A Judge's Guide,* (National Council of Juvenile & Family Court Judges 2006). This document was developed under grant number SJI-03-N-103 from the State Justice Institute.

[157] Id. at 3.

[158] Id.

- determine whether the case is one that requires an evaluation;

- determine what the content of the evaluation should be;

- select the right person to conduct the evaluation;

- tailor the evaluation to your needs;

- critique it carefully; and

- know, at the end, whether or to what extent you can rely on the evaluator's report.[159]

DV victims frequently appear pro se in contested custody cases and are unable to properly represent themselves, as evidenced by the previously discussed difficulties Mrs. Giza encountered in the *Shull* case (see "Disciplinary Proceedings for Violation of Judicial Codes of Conduct").[160] The NCJFCJ has published a manual to assist such litigants in divorce cases in contested cases.[161] One of the articles, "How to Gather Evidence to Present at Trial at Trial" by Ruth Jones, J.D.,[162] may be useful in preventing objections to a pro se litigant's lack of knowledge regarding the rules of evidence. Another article, "Do's and Don'ts for Pro Se Litigants in Divorce and Child Custody Cases: A Judges's Perspective," by Hon. Michael Town, Hon. Linda Dakis, Hon. Stephen Herrell, and Hon. Scott Jordan,[163] provides guidance to the pro se litigant in presenting one's case to the court and in knowing what to expect from the judge in the courtroom.

This publication should be distributed without charge to pro se litigants who are battered women upon the filing of a divorce or dissolution complaint and, if possible, even before the case is filed.

Each day, across America, family court judges make difficult and critical contested custody decisions determining what is in the BIC in cases involving DV. In order to safeguard the well-being of both children and their parents, judges must base their decisions on a thorough understanding of the dynamics of DV and of the relevant statutory and case law. Throughout the decision-making process, judges also must be aware of their own potential biases as well as those of family law attorneys, GALs, and custody evaluators working on the case. This could ensure that members of the judiciary and of the bar would be better educated and, therefore, better equipped to make decisions that are in the BIC and the family unit as a whole.

Author's Note

I am grateful for the research assistance of Ms. Rosa Celeste and Ms. Jessica Smagacz my student research assistants at Florida Coastal School of Law and the advice and assistance of Library Assistant Director Colleen Manning of the Florida Coastal School of Law.

---

[159] Id. at 7.

[160] Judicial Inquiry and Review. Comm'n of Virginia v. Shull, 651 S.E.2d 648 (Va. 2007).

[161] *Managing Your Divorce: a Guide for Battered Women, Family Violence* (Department of the National Council of Juvenile & Family Court Judges, Resource Center on Domestic Violence: Child Protection 1998).

[162] Id. at 17–23.

[163] Id. at 31–33.

Chapter 8

Truth Commission: Findings and Recommendations

by Mo Therese Hannah, Ph.D.

INTRODUCTION

The Battered Mothers Custody Conference (BMCC)—one of the few forums that focuses exclusively on family/divorce court processes that punish battered women for trying to limit their children's contact with abusive biological fathers—emerged out of a sense of growing outrage over the dysfunction that permeates the nation's family court system. Each year, the BMCC has gathered an unusually heterogeneous audience, the majority made up of mothers who have been victimized by these practices, along with their personal and professional supporters; practitioners who work within the confines of the court system, such as family law attorneys, social workers, domestic violence (DV) advocates, and victims' rights advocates; investigative journalists and other media professionals; scholars from fields like women's studies, law, criminal justice, and psychology; and the occasional policy maker, politician, or government agency leader. Similarly, those who have presented at the BMCC come from every region of the country and comprise an equally diverse group that include grassroots activists who were formerly battered mothers, attorneys working for mothers' custody rights, and retired judges who are outraged over the flawed practices of fellow members of their profession.

It ought to be noted here that the BMCC is but one of several vehicles that have been devised by mothers' custody advocates as a means of speaking truth to power. Nonetheless, as recently as a decade ago, unless you happened to work inside the family court system or had gone through a custody battle yourself, the increasingly widespread phenomenon of fit mothers losing custody of their children probably had not appeared on your radar screen. Even if you had in fact heard about it, it is likely you were unaware of the actual severity and prevalence of these problems. There have been, in fact, earlier outcries over this issue; one notable example from the print media is Phyllis Chesler's prescient book, *Mothers on Trial*.[1] Additional books, like Myers'

---

[1] Phyllis Chesler, *Mothers on Trial* (1986).

A Mother's Nightmare,[2] comment on the risk of custody loss by separating or divorcing mothers who report child sexual abuse by their children's father. Only much later, in 2005, did we see a definitive treatise devoted exclusively to this issue: Neustein and Lesher's *From Madness to Mutiny: Why Mothers Are Running From the Family Courts—And What Can Be Done About It.*[3]

So, although the court system's track record at protecting abuse victims went from bad to worse over the last two decades, public awakening began only recently, and it has progressed quite slowly. We saw similar prolonged periods of public ignorance in relation to what are now well-recognized and notorious patterns of abuse—the sexual abuse of children by members of the Catholic clergy being a notable example. It seems that whatever societal system you choose to examine—our legal, financial, religious, educational, or political system—wherever there is a juxtaposition of vulnerability, power, money, and secrecy, you are likely to discover abuse.

But discovering a pattern of human rights abuse, like the one we have found in the family courts, and convincing the powerful to do something about it, are very different ventures, with the latter more difficult than the first. Further, even public exposure of an abuse does not necessarily lead to restoration for the victims, nor does it always guarantee against further commissions of the abuse. Complicating matters is the fact that, like other victims of human rights atrocities, mothers who have been cut out of their children's lives by the order of a family court judge are usually too traumatized, too damaged, and therefore too paralyzed to advocate effectively on their own behalf.

BATTERED MOTHERS CUSTODY CONFERENCE

Mission

As documented in its original mission statement, the BMCC's objectives are as follows:

1. To draw public and media attention to the bias and injustices faced by battered women and their children in their interactions with the family court system in the United States;

2. To enlighten court personnel, legislators, government agencies, and policy makers about these realities, and to press for change;

3. To educate professionals, including attorneys, DV counselors, social workers, legal advocates, and others who work with battered women about the ways in which abusive dynamics manifest within the context of family court legal processes;

4. To discuss and disseminate strategies for improving the outcomes of child custody cases of battered mothers; and

---

[2] J. Myers, *A Mother's Nightmare—Incest: A Practical Legal Guide for Parents and Professionals* (1997).

[3] A. Neustein & M. Lesher, *From Madness to Mutiny: Why Mothers Are Running From the Family Courts—And What Can Be Done About It* (2005).

5. To facilitate communication and collaboration among experts, scholars, professionals, advocates, and lay persons who work on behalf of battered mothers and their children.[4]

Contributors and Outcomes of Battered Women's Family Court Experiences

During the seven years the conference has been held (each January of 2004 through 2010), conference faculty collaborated with audience members to define and trace the contributors and outcomes of battered women's family court experiences. Among the causes identified, there was consensus regarding those with the greatest negative impact, which include the following:

1. The prevalence of gender bias, which has been documented by studies of trial courts in over forty states;

2. An absence of meaningful oversight and regulation of family court professionals, including law guardians (guardians ad litem (GALs)), attorneys, and judges;

3. The routine denial of due process to protective mothers; and

4. The routine use of flawed testimony based on pseudoscientific theories and biased practices of forensic or custody evaluators.

One could safely say that so far, over the course of its relatively short lifespan, the BMCC made significant strides towards accomplishing at least some of its objectives. At minimum, it has become an accepted forum for public truth-telling about these matters. It also, quite clearly, has helped generate national discussion about a human rights violation that had previously been shrouded in far greater secrecy. Even further, the conference facilitated what has become a clearer understanding of a complex problem that requires complex solutions.

But by no means has this conference succeeded in halting family court injustice. As noted in the chapter this author wrote for an e-book published by the California chapter of the National Organization for Women (CA NOW), "Naming an injustice brings validation to those who have been victimized: I am confident that now, in comparison with several years ago, fewer battered mothers feel all alone; fewer believe the lies that they are unfit and that they deserve what happened to them."[5]

Perhaps most notable is the fact that the BMCC has helped solidify a sense of shared mission and solidarity between the decades-old battered women's movement and the nascent protective mothers' movement. Again, as this author noted in the CA NOW e-book:

In obvious and important ways, the protective mothers' movement resembles many other movements that have rallied for social change. The move to organize unions, the movements against war, apartheid, and nuclear proliferation,

---

[4] Taken from the Mission Statement of the first Battered Mothers Custody Conference, held January 6-9, 2004, at Siena College, Loudonville, New York.

[5] M.T. Hannah, "The Protective Mothers' Movement: An Activists' Notes," in *Disorder in the Courts: Mothers and Their Allies Take on the Family Law System* 91 (H. Grieco, R. Allen & J. Friedlin eds., 2006), http://www.canow.org.

the women's suffrage, civil rights, anti-rape, feminist, and gay/lesbian rights movements, among others, share features in common with our own. And in fact, movements build upon one another: a protective mothers movement would be impossible—there would be no basis for a mother's right to keep her children away from an abusive father—if the domestic violence movement had not [first] done the work of establishing that domestic violence is harmful.[6]

FROM THE MOUTHS OF MOTHERS: THE TRUTH COMMISSION

When it comes to reforming a corrupted system, no conference, regardless of the prestige of its presenters or the credibility of its content, can have quite the same impact as hearing the voices of those victimized by that system. Activists may not always agree on tactics, but they generally agree that unless and until a critical mass is reached, change will not occur. In turn, what helps bring a human rights movement to the brink of that critical threshold are the following:

1. Powerful allies familiar with the workings of the system;

2. Public outrage;

3. Investigative authorities who have integrity; and

4. Courageous exposure by media who refuse to bend under pressure.

Since the battered mothers' movement has been handicapped by the lack of virtually all of the above, it needs to avail itself of any and all means—preferably proven ones—to promote allies and outrage, investigation, and exposure. Rather than invent the wheel, this author decided to use a truth commission,[7] at the Fourth Battered Mothers Custody Conference (held in January 2007), a methodology that has been used before, which gives victims a stage and an audience for providing testimony regarding the injustices they suffered.

According to the charge given to those sitting on the BMCC IV Truth Commission:

The BMCC IV will devote a portion of its sessions to taking testimony from approximately 16 battered mothers . . . Each [mother] will have approximately 20 minutes to give testimony, which will be heard by both the Commission members and the audience attending the conference. In addition, battered mothers and professionals will have the opportunity to submit written statements [if they so choose]. . . . The hearing of testimony will be followed by a "think tank" period, during which Commission members will sequester themselves to discuss the testimony and to formulate a response—e.g., a

---

[6] Id. at 92.

[7] Truth commissions (also called truth and reconciliation commissions) have been held throughout the world in response to gross and systematic human rights abuses. Among the many were those held in various South American nations subsequent to the fall of governments run by dictators or brutal military juntas. A good deal of information about the history, purpose, and structure of truth commissions is available online; *see, e.g.,* http://www.truthcommission.org.

summary of the problems and proposed solutions. The commission members will then have a two-and-a-half hour period to present their findings to the general audience and to respond to questions from the entire audience. . . . The findings will later be written up in the form of a "white paper," which will be disseminated in venues agreed upon by the Commission.

During the year or two since the BMCC IV Truth Commission issued its final report, the document (reproduced in Exhibit 8.1) has served as a comprehensive summary of what we know about the revictimization of battered women by the custody courts of our nation. The report is available at a variety of online sites.[8]

TRUTH COMMISSION FINDINGS AND PROPOSED SOLUTIONS

Members of the BMCC IV Truth Commission consisted of eight members, including four attorneys specializing in mothers' custody issues, a victims' rights professional, two leaders within the DV movement, and a grassroots organization president.[9] The commission reported as follows:

Sixteen women [who collectively had gone through custody battles within the family court systems of eleven different states] testified about their family law cases before the Truth Commission at the Fourth Battered Mothers Custody Conference. The common theme that emerged from the testimony is that there is a widespread problem of abusive parents being granted custody of children and protective parents having their custody limited or denied, and/or being otherwise punished.

There is a crisis in the custody court system, which has resulted in thousands of children being sent to live with abusers while safe, protective parents, primarily mothers, are denied any meaningful relationship with their children. The court system has failed to respond appropriately to domestic violence and child abuse cases involving custody. The Commission found many common errors made by the courts and the professionals they rely upon that contribute to these tragedies. These same mistakes have negatively impacted battered women and children in other cases, with less extreme results.

From these and other case histories and issues raised by concerned professionals throughout the country, the Commission made the following findings and proposals recommended for further study. Not all members of the Truth Commission agree with every proposed solution, but all members are in agreement that solutions need to be developed to address these findings.[10]

---

[8] *See* http://www.battered motherscustodyconference.org; http://www.stopfamilyviolence. org; http://www.nownys.org.

[9] These individuals were Richard Ducote, Esq, Chair; Nancy Erickson, Esq; Barry Goldstein, Esq.; Eileen King; Patti Jo Newell; Connie Valentine, M.S.; Gwen Wright; and Joan Zorza, Esq.

[10] Truth commission member Connie Valentine, in collaboration with other commission members, wrote the official and final report of the BMCC IV Truth Commission, entitled *The Truth Commission: Findings and Solutions*. All members of the truth commission are considered coauthors of the report, which is reprinted in Exhibit 8.1 with permission.

Exhibit 8.1

Truth Commission Findings and Proposed Solutions

Findings	Proposed Solutions for Further Study
Court appointees, state actors, and other professionals are frequently biased, particularly gender-biased, misogynistic, incompetent, and inadequately trained in DV and child abuse. Many exhibit a shocking lack of knowledge about incest and child sexual abuse, and how DV affects parenting, and may lie with impunity. They appear to have scant understanding of, or interest in, the negative effects of substance abuse as it pertains to parenting. There is a lack of training and availability of qualified, ethical professionals, particularly attorneys to represent nonabusive protective parents. This problem is mostly hidden from the general public.	*Public Education:* The situation of family courts endangering children and punishing women must be exposed in the media. State and national policy makers in all three branches of government and other allies must be advised of the problem of family courts placing children in the unsupervised custody of abusive parents and be told that this is happening with alarming frequency. *Research:* More and better research on family court cases with allegations of DV and child abuse is needed to determine how many children are sent to live with abusers and how often custody scandal cases occur. Research should be done about how jury trials might work in custody cases to determine if this method of family court adjudication improves children's safety. Any changes to the law must be examined to rule out unintended consequences of the abusers using the law to assist their cause. *Training:* Effective, quality, in-depth training on DV, child sexual abuse, child physical abuse, substance abuse, and the negative effects of abuse and violence on parenting and healthy child development must be developed and provided to all court professionals. A standard national training curriculum must be developed by a consortium of nationally recognized experts in DV, child physical and sexual abuse, substance abuse, parenting, and child development. The approved curriculum must be taught by certified, qualified experts who must pass rigorous examinations in the subject matter. This training must be based on publications such as the 2006 *Navigating Custody and Visitation Evaluations in Cases with Domestic Violence: A Judge's Guide* and *1996 American Psychological Association Presidential Task Force.* It must be required for and provided to *all* court personnel and associated professionals, *including judges.*

(Continued)

Exhibit 8.1 *(Continued)*

Findings	Proposed Solutions for Further Study
Judges: Judges who preside over custody cases exhibit clear bias against women. They are sometimes closed to new information and research. Many judges improperly delegate judicial authority. They frequently rely on court appointees and abrogate their judicial authority by uncritically following recommendations of appointees. The judges may select appointees in a biased manner from a small pool, using problematic lines of friendship and trust. This leads to appointees pleasing the judge in order to be reappointed.	*Judges:* Judges who demonstrate gender bias, fail to protect children and vulnerable adults, and show favoritism in court appointments must be identified and successfully trained to conduct themselves appropriately or be removed from the bench. Judges must be prohibited from improperly delegation of judicial authority in custody and visitation cases. Judges must not be allowed to abrogate their decision-making duties to court appointees.
Court Professionals: Court professionals often do not rely on facts and make recommendations based on bias, frequently endangering children and vulnerable adults by so doing.	*Court Professionals:* Court personnel and court-related and court-connected professionals must only gather facts to provide to judges, not make recommendations.

The level of integrity for all court personnel and court-related professionals must be dramatically raised to ensure that children and vulnerable adults are not placed at risk. |
| *Child Advocates:* Guardians ad litem, law guardians, and attorneys for the minor often assume inappropriate roles, do inaccurate fact-finding, and present incompetent, biased recommendations that place children at substantial risk of continued abuse. They often fail to gather or report information from their child clients. They may distort the child's wishes and advocate for positions that harm rather than help and protect the child client. They are often appointed when there is no defined need, and it is difficult to remove them once they are on the case. In some states, they may stay on the case until the child reaches the age of majority. The child is unable to fire the attorney. The attorneys often do not argue the law or call witnesses. Often their fees are paid by parents who have no say in their appointment. | *Child Advocates:* The role of the guardian ad litem, law guardian, or attorney for the minor must be limited to the American Bar Association standard of practice (37 *Family Law Quarterly* (2003)) or eliminated entirely. Children must be able to dismiss any advocate or attorney who does not ensure their physical and sexual safety and does not represent their wishes. If appointed by the court, the advocate or attorney shall be paid by the court or volunteer his or her services. |
| *Evaluators and Investigators:* Evaluators often perform inadequate, incompetent, and biased investigations and assessments. Many are selected for reasons other than competency in evaluating DV, child sexual abuse, or child physical abuse. They may utilize junk science such as so-called parental alienation syndrome (PAS) to make recommendations that place children at risk of continued abuse. They are often appointed when there is no defined need. Their fees, often prohibitively expensive, are usually paid by parents who generally have no say in their appointment. Some do not make written reports, and when they | *Evaluators and Investigators:* Evaluators are to be used only to gather specific factual information that could be helpful for the court to make custody and visitation decisions as directed and defined by the court. Evaluators must be prohibited from usurping judicial authority by making recommendations in custody cases as to which parent should receive custody and what type or schedule of visitation should be granted. |

(Continued)

Exhibit 8.1 *(Continued)*

Findings	Proposed Solutions for Further Study
do write a report, parents are often not allowed to see the report or they may be treated with systems therapy in which the problem is considered a family problem and not the criminal behavior of the abuser.	Any appointment of an evaluator should be limited to only specific issues that require scientific expertise in his or her area of expertise, such as a mental health professional expert might be appointed when there is credible evidence that a party and/or child may suffer from a mental health problem that would significantly affect parenting. After-effects of violence and abuse, such as posttraumatic stress disorder, depression, or anxiety, must not be used against victims by any mental health professional. Junk science such as PAS and alienation are inadmissible and must be disallowed. Behavior may be defined but must be proven, not just alleged.
	When a custody or visitation case involves allegations of domestic violence, child physical or sexual abuse, or substance abuse, the court must appoint a trained investigator who is a documented qualified expert in the discipline area being investigated (i.e., DV, child physical or sexual abuse, or substance abuse). The investigator must have a qualified expert investigator conduct or approve any discipline area in which he or she is not a qualified expert.
	A standardized template report format must be required for all investigators to complete, to ensure statewide uniformity and compliance with laws and rules of court. A format example can be found at http://www.childabusesolutions.com. Such reports must be based only on accurate, scientific evidence.
Mediators: Mediators are used inappropriately in DV and child abuse cases, and, in some states, mediators make recommendations to the court based on brief meetings with the parties. They seldom take abuse allegations seriously and generally push protective mothers to accept inappropriate shared custody and unrestricted access by abusers to the children. Often they credit junk science PAS accusations made by abusive parents, but do not realize that abusers who raise PAS allegations are doing so for their own tactical gain. Most are trained in systems therapy in which the problem is considered a family problem and not the criminal behavior of the abuser.	*Mediators:* Mediators must never make recommendations to the court. Mediation must be entirely confidential. Mediation must be specifically prohibited in any case where there are allegations of DV, child physical or sexual abuse, or substance abuse, in which cases, the court would order an investigation.

(Continued)

Exhibit 8.1 *(Continued)*

Findings	Proposed Solutions for Further Study
Other Court Connected and Court-Appointed Personnel: Special masters, parenting coordinators, and other court personnel are often biased and incompetent and are used inappropriately. Most side with the fathers and take a punitive role against mothers. They illegally intrude themselves into the lives of families.	*Other Court Connected and Court-Appointed Personnel:* Such personnel must be specifically prohibited in child custody and visitation cases. Parents and their children must be free of illegal state intrusion except when a child is at risk in a home where there is DV, physical or sexual abuse, or substance abuse.
Supervised Visitation Monitors: Monitors lack training and are often biased. They scrutinize the protective parents, but they do not report children's disclosures of abuse. They may fail to protect the children appropriately. Most do not take long-term cases because their caseloads are high. The monitors often misuse and misinterpret data from the supervised visits. Most are more supportive of giving fathers access to children than in protecting the children and their mothers.	*Supervised Visitation Monitors:* Supervised visitation must be standardized. Supervision by relatives or friends of the abuser must be prohibited. Supervised visitation is to be used only to protect children from violence and abuse, not to punish a parent for reporting abuse or for attempting to protect the child.
Judges may fail to send appropriate cases to supervised visitation, and inappropriately place nonabusive parents on supervised visitation.	Supervisors should make a record of statements by a child that indicate a danger to the child's health or safety. Supervised visitation reports should not be used to determine if a parent is safe enough for unsupervised visitation, but rather an investigation by a qualified expert investigator should be ordered.
Attorneys are sometimes biased against women, unethical, and incompetent. Abusers' attorneys are often overaggressive and may suborn or encourage perjury. Attorneys for protective parents may abandon their clients before a court date and may fail to work on behalf of their protective parent clients, setting them up for countless delays and often the loss of custody.	*Attorneys, Therapists, and Physicians* involved in custody and visitation, DV, child physical and sexual abuse, and substance abuse matters must be closely regulated by an independent citizen oversight committee to ensure that child and victim protection is their primary concern and to prevent abuse of power.
Therapists for the child are sometimes biased, fail to make mandated reports of suspected child abuse or neglect, and may be trained in systems therapy, in which the problem is considered a family problem, not the problem of the abuser.	
Physicians may be friendly toward the abusers and fail to make mandated reports of suspected child abuse. Few truly understand the dynamics of DV, and few take the victim's fears seriously. Some violate the victim's confidentiality and tell their abusers what was said.	

(Continued)

Exhibit 8.1 *(Continued)*

Findings	Proposed Solutions for Further Study
Child Protective Services (CPS) frequently does poor investigations, fails to gather information from the children, and does not protect children, particularly when there is a custody case involved. CPS may not do a new investigation when there are sequential reports of abuse. When abuse is not founded by CPS, children are usually reunited with the identified abusers and silenced. Cases that cover multiple counties or states and involve multiple agencies and jurisdictions allow children to fall through the cracks. There is little or no coordination. *Law Enforcement:* Law enforcement officers frequently do not investigate abuse allegations thoroughly.	*Child Protective Services/Law Enforcement:* Specialized integrated DV courts with multidisciplinary panels and specialists in child abuse and substance abuse must be developed. Clear lines of communication, process, and jurisdiction, particularly when multiple counties or states are involved, must be established for all agencies and professionals, including CPS and law enforcement officials, in custody and visitation cases when there are allegations of DV, child physical and sexual abuse, and substance abuse.
District Attorneys: District attorneys sometimes do not prosecute the criminal actions of the abusers, and when they do prosecute, they often continue cases without findings or accept plea bargains down to meaningless levels that result in no clear record of child physical or sexual abuse. In some cases, they inappropriately prosecute protective parents.	*District Attorneys:* District attorneys must cease filing bogus charges against protective mothers and begin consistently and vigorously filing charges against abusive, violent fathers. Laws and practices must be changed so that the pattern of a defendant's DV tactics are shown in context.
DV, child abuse, and substance abuse are ignored, minimized, and trivialized. This results in a failure to protect children and vulnerable adults.	Courts must be mandated to err on the side of physical and sexual safety for children and vulnerable adults.
Professionals fail to give credence to abuse and disregard the safety of the children and their mothers. If violence occurred in the past, it is considered no longer a relevant issue even thought the victim and children are still afraid.	Clear guidelines and protocols must be established to identify DV, child physical and sexual abuse, and substance abuse.
There is a reliance on myths, not research. Parental alienation and other junk theories are used against mothers, completely defeating and trumping any abuse allegations. Mothers are pathologized, misdiagnosed and demonized with mental health labels. Good faith efforts by mothers to protect themselves and their children are frequently misunderstood to be an attempt to interfere with the father's relationship with the children.	All family court cases must be screened at the outset for DV, child physical or sexual abuse, and substance abuse through the use of a nationally recognized valid DV screening instrument, a valid child trauma screening instrument such as the Trauma Symptom Checklist (John Briere, Ph.D.) and a valid substance abuse screening instrument such as the Addiction Severity Index (ASI) in conjunction with alcohol/drug urine or hair tests.

(Continued)

Exhibit 8.1 *(Continued)*

Findings	Proposed Solutions for Further Study
The "friendly parent" standard is used inappropriately, to say that abusers are more likely to share parenting. Ironically, once abusers gain custody, they then isolate and estrange the children from the protective parents. Courts seldom punish the abusers or switch custody back to the protective parents.	Pending an investigation when there is any evidence of DV, child abuse, or substance abuse, or during an appeal, the child must be protected by remaining in the custody of the safe, protective parent. DV must be taken seriously and a DV advocate provided for both adults and children in family court. DV advocates are an important resource in the community and should not be treated as partisans, since the state and the courts claim their policy is to end DV. Accordingly, the courts should seek appropriate input from the DV community in determining the qualifications of professionals with respect to DV. Lack of police reports should not be used to discount DV. DV must be defined appropriately. One recommendation would be "coercive control by an intimate partner involving physical, sexual, psychological/ emotional and/or economic/ financial abuse." The court should be aware of and strongly skeptical about men who feign that they are physically victimized by women, particularly when the males are larger or stronger. The term primary aggressor needs to be clearly defined. It is recommended that the definition include the following factors: • A bigger, stronger (usually male) aggressor hits harder and causes more damage; • The reason for hitting: males hit for control/ get their way versus females hit in self-defense; • Women "give in" due to fear of bodily harm; men virtually never give in due to such fear. There must be a presumption that DV primary aggressors, child abusers, and habitual substance abusers are prohibited from gaining joint or sole custody of children. Primary aggressors and child abusers identified in family courts through initial screening and careful investigation must be limited to supervised visitation until they complete an extensive batterers program, anger management program, and/or child abuse prevention program, and the program center certifies them safe to be in unsupervised contact with children.

(Continued)

Exhibit 8.1 *(Continued)*

Findings	Proposed Solutions for Further Study
	If a primary aggressor fails to complete a program for batterers or anger management, supervised visitation must continue. The court would need to hold a new hearing to determine what visitation would be safe and beneficial for the child.
	If the child abuse was sexual in nature, or an abuser physically attacks the child after being declared safe by the treatment center, the abuser shall be limited to only supervised visitation during remainder of the child's minority.
	Mediation and couples counseling are inappropriate and not to be used in DV cases due to power and control exercised by the primary aggressor.
	Programs where child protective agencies work together with DV agencies and consult DV advocates about cases that may involve DV must be developed and expanded.
Joint custody is presumed to be in the best interests of the child even when the parents are unable to communicate, and violence is occurring.	The "approximation standard" (i.e., the approximate parenting timeshare prior to separation) must become the standard for sharing parenting after separation. The court must ensure that supervised contact only is allowed for perpetrators when there is DV, child physical or sexual abuse, or substance abuse, unless and until the behavior is remediated to ensure safety of the children and vulnerable adults.

Note: Permission is hereby granted for use and dissemination of this material by those working to strengthen the movement and promote the cause of bringing justice to battered women and their children.

Part 2

Survivors' Stories

Chapter 9

Courageous Kids: Abused Children Sharing Their Experiences

by Karen Anderson

INTRODUCTION

In recent years, the public has heard more and more horrifying and heartbreaking stories about kids killing kids. Childhoods have been wiped out in a split second by criminally negligent or pathologically disturbed peers. The media presents these stories as tragic aberrations demonstrating the dangers faced by today's youths. The reality of children committing murder is enough to cause widespread despair over the current state of our society.

As a grassroots activist and a protective mother, I hope readers will receive encouragement and inspiration by reading the story of the Courageous Kids (CKs)—a group of young people working to save other kids from the parental and governmental abuses that they themselves experienced. The CKs present a different face of today's youths, one that reflects the commonality of their stories of stolen childhoods caused by the negligence and maliciousness of the family courts. In many cases, the courts not only failed to protect these young people from abusive parents, but actually participated, directly or indirectly, in the abuse these children suffered. The CKs are kids who are helping other kids survive the destructive effects of their experiences with the family court system. Their stories, which have gone largely unreported by the mainstream media, are finally being told.

SYSTEM FAILURE SPARKS A MOVEMENT

Protection Denied

No one was prepared for the scene that follows: A little eight-year-old boy sat quietly in the front row of the giant cathedral. With his curly, tousled hair and freckled face, he looked like the perfect model of an all-American boy from a Norman Rockwell painting. In stark contrast, he had lived a life far from the ideal portrait of a carefree childhood in the "land of the free." Oblivious to the hundreds of people looking on, the boy quietly got out of his seat and approached the closed casket that was about to be taken to the long, shiny black vehicle waiting outside. The little boy laid his head gently down and stretched his arms out, embracing his mother for the last time through the thick, polished wood that surrounded her. He remained motionless, refusing to let go, his somber expression revealing a profound sense of loss, hopelessness, and utter despair. He would never again curl up in her lap, feel the softness of her skin, hear the comfort of her voice, smell her motherly fragrance, and enjoy the security of her protective arms wrapped around him.

His mother had finally won a war waged against the judicial and child protective systems so that her son could live safe from the man he identified as his sexual predator—his father. Nevertheless, the years of stress had taken a toll on his mother's body, and she lost her battle with cancer. Now the little boy was left with no one who had legal standing to carry on his mother's fight to protect him. Intellectually mature far beyond his years, he intuitively knew what was coming. Shortly thereafter, at the instruction of a social worker, he was removed from his maternal grandmother, his most precious remaining connection to his mother. It was a grisly scene, as two armed policemen, grasping the boy by his ankles and wrists, carried him air borne, kicking, screaming, and writhing to free himself from the impending isolation of life with his father. By living with his father, the boy would be separated from everyone and everything familiar and beloved. All of the years during which this child could have enjoyed being with his mother were consumed, instead, by the trauma of paternal abuse and the endless court proceedings that protected his father instead of him. Finally, the little boy's outcries were silenced forever; the evidence of his need for safety got buried with his mother.

Friends, family members, advocates, a deputy district attorney, a state legislator, and even the governor had tried to intervene on the boy's behalf to insure that he would be protected. His own paternal grandmother had fought to protect the boy from his father—her son. However, all of these voices went unheeded by the court, which, following the mother's death, granted custody to the abusive father.

One Case Like Many Others

The case described above is sadly representative of many others, where the voices of protective advocates have been drowned out by the family court's battle cry of judicial revenge against protective parents, whose complaints about domestic violence (DV) or child abuse are routinely dismissed as "alienation" or some other psycho-babble term, instead of being understood as crimes perpetrated by an abusive parent.

As the phenomenon of protective parents losing custody to abusers in family courts became widely recognized as an escalating national problem, adult victims, family violence prevention advocates, and professionals dedicated to the protection of children began to speak out against the courts' barbaric, victim-blaming practices. However, their cries were met by a deafening silence on the part of the public and the political system. Those most capable of correcting the problem seemed to be ignorant of, desensitized to, or detached from the tremendous suffering of the afflicted.

California Protective Parents Association Advocates for Children

Out of the death of this boy's mother was born an organization dedicated to continuing the fight to protect the safety of abused children and the custodial rights of their nonoffending parents in family court litigation. Over the five years that followed, the California Protective Parents Association (CPPA), a nonprofit child advocacy organization based in Sacramento, California, worked to educate judicial officials, lawmakers, and public agencies about the crisis in domestic courts, which was leaving a trail of human suffering in its wake like none ever before. With the assistance of a few insightful and heroic legislators, progress was made. New laws were passed, giving rise to better legal protections, at least on paper, for abused children and their nonoffending parents. But it was a slow, arduous process that met strong resistance from the status quo, whose members were offended by the implication that they, as public servants, were failing to protect the most vulnerable citizens in our society: our children.

Those who were most offended tried to "shoot the messenger," thereby positioning themselves as being part of the problem rather than part of the solution. But then, as the child victims started to speak out, the tide began to turn.

CASES FROM CHILDREN'S LIVES

The seriousness of the problem cannot be overstated, as illustrated in the following actual case examples from the CKs of the CPPA.[1] These are not fictional vignettes; they are very real tragic situations. The case examples presented below occurred between 1998 and the present. In one case, a CPPA member's appearance on the *Leeza* show attracted 200 calls to CPPA.

Case #1: The Million Dollar Question

Her long brown hair frames her tan face. Her expression is apprehensive as she surveys the crowd of people waiting expectantly for her to speak. Barely sixteen, she has the look and aura of innocence. No one would guess that she had lived two years as a fugitive, running away, hiding, fending for herself, and couch-hopping to escape an abusive father whose rage at her mother and, by extension, at her, was terrifying. When her parents divorced, her father used his superior financial power—which translated into legal power—to wrestle custody of her away from her mother. The young girl describes how scared and alone she felt and how she begged and pleaded to see her mother but was denied. Years went by without contact. The young woman talks about how her father and court officials tried to make her believe that her mother was mentally ill while her father seemed to transfer his hostility toward her mother to her.

The girl goes on to tell of running away from her father's abuse. She wanted to return to her mother but knew that if she sought her mother's safety and comfort, her father would surely make good on his threats to have her mother arrested and jailed for violating a family court order. The order prohibited contact between the girl and her mother except under rigidly controlled, expensive, supervised conditions that her mother could not afford. Unable to go back to her mother, the girl sought refuge with friends. Throughout her ordeal, the family court and "child protective" systems were deaf to her disclosures of paternal abuse and neglect, and ignored her pleas for safety. When she checked herself into a youth shelter for asylum after her father physically assaulted her, the court promptly ordered her back to her abuser. Now, her dark eyes staring into a television camera, she asks the world a provocative question: "How can you say you're a good father when you hurt someone so bad." She pauses, fighting back tears. Biting her lip, she continues, "that it makes you feel like you want to die?"

Case #2: Hiding the Bruises

Another child recounts her father's brutal assault on a sister, only eight years old at the time, for refusing to pick up shoes. She remembers the blood pouring from her sister's mouth, the black and blue bruising that followed, and how she and the rest of her siblings were sequestered from public view until the physical signs of child abuse had faded. In a matter-of-fact tone, she talks about her father shooting the family dog. She discloses how, several years later, he threw her and one of her sisters against a wall and then called the police, reporting that his children were assaulting him. She describes the degradation she would feel when her father would unapologetically walk into her bedroom while she was dressing or into the bathroom

---

[1] The names of the children have been omitted for safety and legal reasons.

while she was showering. As she tried to hide from his staring eyes, he seemed to feel entitled to these invasions of her personal privacy. The fact that the girl's paternal aunt had been molested as a child by the girl's father, who was the aunt's older brother, only added to the girl's sense of vulnerability.

After the girl and her siblings were placed in the custody of their father, she packed the younger kids into her car one night and fled with them to the mountains, where they stayed until they were forced to go back to their father. Shortly thereafter, the girl's younger sister called law enforcement for protection from their father. Her sister was not protected; instead, she was placed in a psychiatric hospital for a week by their father. When the girl's father threatened to place another sibling in the psychiatric hospital and the girl in juvenile hall, she fled with her siblings once again, this time to the safety of their mother, who was residing in another state. While attempting to modify custody through legal proceedings, her mother was arrested and jailed for kidnapping, and the girl and her siblings were immediately returned to their father. However, her father would not allow the girl to return to his home. So at the age of seventeen, she was living in her car in freezing weather, banished by her father and unable to access her mother.

Case #3: Violence Begets Violence

Hesitantly, a fifteen-year-old boy approaches the podium. He begins to read his story of abuse, written in smudged pencil on paper stained from sweaty hands and crumpled from taking it in and out of his pocket repeatedly while preparing for his presentation. Part way through his talk, losing his place on his paper, he rubs his hand back and forth over his buzz haircut and blurts out, "Gosh, I'm so nervous!" His spontaneity reveals an endearingly childish candor. The group of kids sitting at the long table to the left of him instinctively responds with words of encouragement. The boy continues, eventually abandoning the recitation of the words written on the tattered paper and lifting his head to speak directly to the audience. He tells how he was removed from the custody of his safe, nurturing mother and placed in the custody of his abusive father. He describes living in terror of the beatings that became a daily routine in his life, inflicted on him by a man calloused to his son's pain by years of association with gang violence. Driven by the uncertainty of what the next beating would bring, and fearing for his life, the boy ran away. However, like so many others in similar situations, he could not run to the safety of his mother, for fear of the punishment that might be meted out to her by a family court system that was as calloused and brutal as his father.

Case #4: Not Saved by the Bell

The two siblings stand side by side, a tall, lanky, fourteen-year-old boy and his short, going-on-twelve sister. The younger child is not scheduled to speak but wants to be near her big brother to emotionally support him. These two kids have been through more courtroom drama in the short span of their years than most adults go through in a lifetime. Between family and juvenile dependency proceedings, for years their lives have been full of chaos. When the boy speaks, he describes being safe and well cared for in his mother's custody and the contrast of what his life was like when he was forced into his father's custody: living in filth, not having a bed to sleep on, not being fed, and trying to survive the constant terror of physical and sexual abuse.

The boy recalls the occasion when he locked himself in his bedroom, then crawled out of a window and ran to the neighbors' house, banging frantically on their front door, heart pounding, and begging them to call the police because his father had threatened to kill him. There is despondency in his voice as he wonders why the police would not help him, but instead sent him back to the danger of his father's murderous anger. He does not trust police anymore, he says. He talks about contemplating suicide in the months prior to being allowed to move out of state with his mother, not because he really wanted to die, but because he could not think of any other way to escape his nightmarish life of abuse. He had lost all faith in the systems designed to protect him, and he no longer believed, or even dared to hope, that anyone, with the power to rescue him, would.

The boy moves to return to his seat, but his younger sister takes the microphone before he can replace it in its holder. Empowered by the courage of her big brother, she spontaneously decides to make her voice heard as well. She is amazingly articulate for an eleven year old, expressing her feelings of humiliation and hopelessness after being interviewed by a series of social workers who asked her embarrassing questions about being sexually abused. She describes how betrayed she felt by those who did not believe her, and her great sense of relief and gratitude for the ones who did, resulting in the out-of-state move and followed by a short-lived time of assured protection.

She then recounts the day when, after a phone rang in her school classroom, she was sent to the principal's office. There, she was told that her father had arrived from out of state with a court order giving custody back to him. She describes a feeling of disbelief that was quickly replaced by panic as the words sunk in. What she describes next sounds like a mass confusion of phone calls and adults arguing around her while she sat terrified, with her future hanging in the balance. Though an emergency appeal prevented her father's order from being enforced, the trauma of that day made a lasting impact on her. She relates that, ever since that experience, she has had a hard time concentrating in school because of tormenting thoughts that she will be called to the principal's office for a replay of the same traumatic event. Now, whenever she hears a phone ring at school, the same fear grips her, her stomach knots up, and her heart races. She says, "It makes me feel like I am having a heart attack."

Case #5: For His Sisters' Sake

A handsome youth, quiet and expressive, talks candidly about the fear, loneliness, and grief that prevented him from sleeping for the seven years he was forced to live in the custody of his abusive father. The boy lived separated from his mother and older brothers, after his younger sisters disclosed that their father was sexually abusing them. He tells about how he was taken away from his protective mother when he was ten years old, how he was suddenly snatched away from his happy and familiar life, allowed to take nothing with him but the clothes on his back and a few schoolbooks. There were no good-byes and no explanation.

With heaviness of heart, he describes his life as being "shattered apart" on that day, as though he had been kidnapped. He tells of the deep despair and emptiness he felt as he and his little sisters sat unattended on a curb in a strange city, while his father worked at the construction site behind him. He recalls that he "wondered where his life had disappeared to." He talks about how living a life of isolation, oppression, and emotional abuse, in terror of his father's outbursts of rage, caused him to slip further and further into depression. His depression was exacerbated by his feelings of helplessness and powerlessness to prevent his father's continual nighttime visits to his younger sisters' bedrooms, where the seclusion of darkness hid what he could not bear to think of. He describes how, feeling that he could no longer go on living in that situation, he escaped from his father and returned to his mother, where he could finally "find a reason to live."

He has been free of his abuser for two years, but he still hurts. He struggles to maintain his composure as he reflects back on a childhood ravaged by emotional pain, beginning the day he was taken from his mother. When he speaks of his torment over having to leave his sisters behind and the enduring trauma of trying, but being unable, to rescue them from their secret hell, he breaks down and cries. Moved, the audience cries with him. "Sorry," he says, apologizing for the emotion that interrupts the flow of his presentation. His head drops, and he closes his eyes as he takes heavy, deep breaths to control the pain. He wills himself to finish. As he returns to his seat, he softly cries again, the camera capturing his barely audible words, "I hurt so bad for my sisters."

VICARIOUS PUNISHMENT

When we, as Americans, read about children in third world countries being sent into battle, sacrificed for political gain in wars they have no capacity to even understand, we shudder at the thought. We proclaim that America would never send its children into battle. But the children whose stories are told in the previous section are American children who were held hostage, abused, and deprived of their human rights on orders issued by their own government. They, too, were sent into battle in a war promoted by greed, power, and politics. For them, America has not been the internationally touted "land of the free." It has been a land of state-sponsored psychological torture, oppression, violence, and injustice.

The CKs speak out publicly at conferences, judicial trainings, state legislatures, and to the media against the court-ordered abuse of their fellow American children. They have chosen to come forward, pure in their altruistic motive, to educate the public about the dire need to reform the family courts. They hope to prevent other children from having to suffer the lives of abuse that they were forced to endure. While their individual experiences, circumstances, and after-effects may vary somewhat, the sentiments unanimously expressed by these kids are haunting memories of trauma and a profound sense of how irretrievably their childhoods were lost.

The governmental systems meant to protect children did not merely fail them miserably, they also vindictively punished the mothers who dared to seek protection for their children. In doing so, those systems also punished the children.

CHILDREN OF PROTECTIVE FATHERS

Lest the fathers' rights proponents begin screaming about "male bashing," let me state right now that these are *not* the only children in the country who have suffered at the hands of ignorant, biased, dysfunctional, lazy, and/or corrupt family courts, law enforcement, and social service officials and systems. These children are only a few of a multitude of similarly situated children. These are some of the few who were able to unite and who had the emotional strength and the opportunity to share their stories. There are thousands more like them throughout America, some of whom have been abused by mothers while their fathers have tried in vain to protect them.

Case #6: Maternal Sexual Abuse Ignored

Years before the CKs Network was formed, a protective father sought resource assistance from the CPPA. His ten-year-old son had disclosed that his mother had continually sexually abused him by shoving things up his penis. Medical reports of a sexual assault examination confirmed the boy's statements, as physicians on the child protection team of a highly regarded university medical center found physical evidence of bleeding and internal tearing in the urethra. Yet, the criminal justice and child protection systems seemed to turn a blind eye to the evidence of abuse. The boy's father and grandparents spent thousands upon thousands of dollars trying to protect him through family court litigation—all to no avail.

While this father was not demeaned or treated with hostility by the family court, child protective services (CPS), or law enforcement, as mothers routinely are, he was not given the relief he sought. No protection order was ever granted to him on behalf of his son. The mother retained primary custody of the child, despite the boy's repeated disclosures of sexual abuse supported by medical evidence and the fact that there were no allegations of misconduct on the part of the father. Eventually, the father gave up trying to get help from the "system," fearing that the boy's mother would successfully induce the family court to curtail his visitation for continuing to pursue safety for his son, leaving the child with no time of reprieve from the abuse. The boy's stress from continued visits with his sexually abusive mother caused recurrent illnesses and failing grades.

Case #7: Supervised Visitation as Lifestyle

Another father supported by the CPPA who tried to protect his two daughters from abuse fared much worse. Each of his two daughters was from two different previous relationships. One daughter was being physically abused by her mother, who was a counselor in the school system. The father had videotape and photos of the four-year-old child depicting bruises on her left temple in the shape of a handprint. Both the mother and the child admitted that the mother struck the child. The father and the child's pediatrician reported this and other incidents of physical abuse, including a dislocated elbow, to CPS. The father was granted an order to prohibit the mother from using corporal punishment on the child, but, astoundingly, on the same day the father was stripped of joint custody of this child, and supervised visitation was imposed on him. There were no findings that the father was detrimental to the child.

This father's younger daughter (by a different mother) disclosed being sexually abused by one or more maternal uncles who provided day care while her mother worked. The family court refused to believe the allegations of sexual abuse and denied the father's request requiring the mother to provide alternative day care. The child was subsequently seen by her pediatrician for vaginal discharge and irritation and an unexplained bruise on her lower back. The child disclosed to the pediatrician that one or more of her uncles were molesting her, which the pediatrician reported to law enforcement and CPS. The positive findings of a sexual assault team's examination of the child, which indicated a damaged hymen consistent with penetration, were suppressed. The father subsequently discovered that one of the reported uncles had previously been arrested and charged with battery and molestation of an (unrelated) child younger than fourteen years of age, thereby corroborating the father's assertion that his daughter needed to be protected from the uncles. The court, however, would not acknowledge its error and modify its punitive rulings against the father; instead, it further violated his rights by prohibiting him from filing any further motions without prior approval from the court.

When the father wrote a letter to the editor of the local newspaper about the court's failure to protect his children, the case took a turn for the worse. The family court summarily dismissed his concerns for the safety of his children while viewing with contempt his dissent from its opinions. The harder the father fought to protect his daughters by publicizing the court's indifference toward their safety, the more he was judicially punished. Eventually, he was restricted to supervised visitation for *twelve years,* while his children's mothers were allowed to remain uncooperative in restoring him to unsupervised visitation.

Case #8: Sex Offender Approved as a Stepfather

One of the first and clearly most tragic protective parent cases that the CPPA was asked to support was that of a protective father whose former wife retained custody of their two children after she had gotten remarried to a convicted child molester. The father's ability to represent himself in court was severely diminished by his broken English and highly emotional reaction to his children's predicament. This high-profile case, in which the family court was obviously biased against the father and violated every conceivable due process right to which he was entitled, gained the attention of high-level government agencies that attempted to intervene on his and his children's behalf, without success. Astoundingly, the court opined that despite the stepfather's identification as a child molester, the children "seemed to be doing fine" in the custody of their mother and sex offender stepfather.

As the protective father continued to fight to rescue his children, he was increasingly viewed by the court, as routinely happens to similarly situated mothers, as "the problem parent" for refusing to accept the unacceptable by trying to overturn the court's mystifying rulings. His visitation was incrementally restricted.

CREATING A CHILDREN'S FORUM

When Telling Is Healing

In 2003, as executive director of the CPPA, I had been working for five years seeking to rescue family violence victims from dangerous custody placements. In addition, for the previous two years I had been employed full-time as a DV and sexual assault counselor at a violence prevention agency, where I counseled both male and female adult and child abuse victims. From my experience working with domestic abuse victims, I was aware that many adults who had long kept their abuse a secret were eventually able to obtain safety and find their own voice. I also knew that many felt an urgent need to tell their stories, as one of their first steps towards healing. The telling of their stories seems to help them validate the reality of what they lived through and to purge themselves, to the greatest extent possible, of the toxic emotions produced by the trauma. There seemed to be a sufficient number of venues where adults could tell their stories: abuse-survivors' support groups, candlelight vigils, church groups focused on spiritual healing, or, for those who numbed their pain with substances, Alcoholics Anonymous or Narcotics Anonymous meetings. Some, with or without prior professional literary skills, wrote books or magazine articles based on their experiences.

While serving as an advisory board member for the Little Hoover Commission,[2] I had heard young adults testify before the commission about their experiences of abuse, neglect, and systemic negligence in the foster care system. As I sat facing the commission members listening to the horror stories of these young people, I was aware of how attentive the commission members were. From their verbal responses to the youths, it seemed that the reams of paper in the reports they laboriously read took on new meaning as the real human beings, negatively affected by the failures in the system, spoke. Though I had not forgotten the impression the foster youths made on everyone in the room that day, nor their selfless reasons of social change for appearing to testify, the memory was not at the forefront of my mind. So, creating a venue for the abused children served by the CPPA to tell their stories had not yet occurred to me.

Then one day, while reading a declaration to the family court written by a seventeen-year-old boy, where his silence was broken in an explosion of feelings poured out on paper in story form, I was stunned by these words: "This is what I've been dying to say for seven years."

I wanted to talk to this victim about his obvious sense of relief in being able to unload his burdens in a public way, on a permanent court record. I had no problem finding him. He lived with me. These were the words of my own son, the boy who cried for his sisters. I was away at a conference in San Diego when he wrote his declaration, which he presented to me when I returned. When he left for the evening to hang out with his friends, I sat down to read what he had written. By the end of the first page, I was sobbing. The vicarious trauma I suffered from reading about the extent and depth of the emotional pain my son had lived with for so many years in the custody of his abusive father, yet invisible to the outside world, shocked and devastated me to the point that it literally took my breath away. I felt as though something was crushing my chest, and I had to struggle to breathe. Though my vision was blurred and my eyes stinging from tears mixed with leaking mascara, I forced myself to keep reading the minidiary of my son's seven-year "sentence" to custodial abuse. There, on the last page, was the expression of liberation that came from the telling of his story and the releasing of so much buried hurt.

In the next days, I thought about the other "escapees" of custodial abusers who had openly discussed their situations with the CPPA while seeking advocacy. I contemplated the experience of one girl, a thirteen-year-old from Santa Clara County, who had already testified on May 6, 2003, before the Senate Judiciary Committee for a family law bill the CPPA was supporting. Though somewhat intimidated by the formality of the hearing, where the committee members sat in large chairs behind an elevated circular platform of rich wood, the youngster forged through her testimony with grace. She was a slight girl who looked much younger than her age and, from the vantage point of the committee members, must have looked even smaller than she was. The response by the committee members was unanimously favorable and protective. She felt exhilarated by the experience because people in an obvious position of power really listened to her for once and said they were sorry for what she had gone through.

Creation of a Support Network for Abused Children

All of the kids served by CPPA advocacy had conveyed a feeling of aloneness throughout the years they were trapped in the custody of their abusers, believing at the

---

[2] The Little Hoover Commission is appointed by the governor of California and is designed to investigate various problems in the state. *See* http://www.lhc.ca.gov/.

time that their court cases were anomalies and that they were the only ones who had gone through such a perverse ordeal. Thinking about this young girl's testimony, my son's words in his declaration, and the healing power of speaking out in a supportive forum, something occurred to me (see "When Telling Is Healing"): the kids for whom we had advocated might benefit from meeting and getting support from other kids in similar situations, along with having a safe and supportive forum in which to tell their stories. So Connie Valentine (my colleague and president of the CPPA) and I contacted the kids who had received services from the CPPA. When asked if they were interested, their response was a resounding, "Yes!"

First Meeting. One of the girls suggested that everyone could meet at her house. After checking out the game system and arming themselves with an arsenal of soda and snacks, the kids all sat down at the dining room table for formal introductions. One of the boys broke the ice by asking if any of the others had been "stuck with" the same court-appointed attorney he had. He then went on to describe what happened in his family court case and how he was betrayed by the people appointed to represent his interests. As each child related a saga of being uprooted from a contented life to one of abuse and misery, the others listened intently, hanging onto each word and soaking up the validation of their own experiences. Each expressed utter amazement at the stories of the others, not because the stories were unbelievable, but because they were so much like their own.

They eagerly agreed to tell their stories at an upcoming child abuse conference cosponsored by the CPPA. With much humor, they bantered around possible names for their group. The boys, employing typical comic antics of high school male competition, tried to outdo each other in amusing the girls with the implausible names they suggested. Having instantly bonded through the sharing of their experiences, their mood had become relaxed and jovial. In just a few short hours, these total strangers had become comrades with a common goal: to change the systems that refused to protect them and turned a blind eye to their agony. They settled on the name, "Courageous Kids."

It is hard to describe the atmosphere permeating the room that evening, but, to me, it was as though a cathartic cleansing had taken place right before my eyes, a cleansing of long-imprisoned souls who had suddenly burst free. The transformation was incredible. As they would later reveal, this was a life-changing experience for each of the kids. They came feeling isolated and alone, having suffered from a governmental abuse so invisible to the rest of the world that they did not know a name for it. They left energized, and they felt *connected.* Their feelings of aloneness dissipated with the knowledge that there were others in the world like them, others who could truly understand the bizarre, life-altering traumas they had endured at the hands those charged to protect them. They left with a name for this abuse: legalized kidnapping.

Forward Movement. The newly formed CKs Network presented for the first time at the Tenth Annual Child Sexual Abuse Awareness Conference in Davis, California, on April 4, 2004, which was cosponsored by the Incest Survivors Speakers Bureau and the CPPA. These children had been disbelieved and betrayed in the past by professionals—the attorneys, social workers, mental health evaluators, and other court-related personnel who were supposed to be child centered and knowledgeable about abuse. Because of this, they approached the conference with some trepidation, aware that the audience was predominantly made up of legal and mental health professionals, just like the people who betrayed them.

Putting aside their fears, the CKs made their way to the microphone, one at a time, and presented their stories. The audience was more than attentive and polite. In comments made after the kids' presentations, audience members showed outrage at the needless trauma that had been inflicted on these young people. They expressed compassion for the years of deep emotional pain that the kids had endured as well as respect and gratitude for the courageous leap of faith the CKs had taken in sharing their stories.

The audience response was precisely what the kids had been longing for but had been denied for so many years: they were *believed*. Being heard, validated, and encouraged provided them with a degree of healing that often takes years of psychotherapy to accomplish. They hoped that speaking out would teach lawyers, social workers, and judges how much ruin results from bad decisions. They hoped to make a positive difference for other kids in custody battles with abusive parents. Yet, none of them had the slightest idea as to the importance of what they had done or where it might take them in the future. They were pioneers, treading through the undiscovered territory of victim advocacy initiated by children.

The conference was videotaped by a volunteer. The recording was far from professional-level quality, but, nonetheless, it was sufficient to allow a viewer to feel the impact of the kids' presentations. After the conference, with the help of CPPA volunteers, the kids opened a Web site and posted their stories on it. News of the CKs Network spread quickly through the DV and child abuse prevention communities, culminating in an invitation from Dr. Robert Geffner for the CKs to present at the main plenary session of the Ninth International Conference on Family Violence in San Diego in September 2004. The invitation was accepted by the kids with great enthusiasm.

Arranging the trip for this group of teens and their protective mothers, all financially destitute as a result of their court battles, proved to be quite a challenge. Thanks to financial assistance, the details came together, and the group made it to the San Diego conference.

At the appropriate time, they climbed the stairs and took the stage in front of approximately 1,200 people. With great poise, one by one, they gave powerful victim impact statements, bringing the audience to tears and, finally, to their feet with a standing ovation that seemed to go on forever. Before leaving the stage, each kid, on behalf of the CPPA, was presented with a heavy gold medal inscribed with his or her name and the words "For Courage" by a representative of the California Attorney General's Office, Victim Services Division. Everyone present seemed to be bursting with pride over these young people who had so bravely come forward to speak about their painful experiences, not for personal gain, but for the sake of making a positive difference in the world. Even Dr. Geffner, a veteran witness to traumatic stories, was moved to tears. Later on that same day, the kids conducted a workshop in which they put on a humorous satirical skit involving a specially made board game called "Family Courtopoly." They told their stories in greater detail, with the audience having the opportunity to ask questions.

In the fall of 2004, when the Second Battered Mothers Custody Conference (BMCC), held annually in Albany, New York, was in its planning stages, the CKs were invited to present at the conference. Around the same time, the videotaped footage of the CKs' presentations at the San Diego conference found its way to French television producers Dominique Lasseur and his wife, Catherine Tatge, who were based in New York City. After researching the protective parent issue, Dominique and Catherine decided to make a PBS documentary about the failure of American family courts to protect abused children. Plans were made for the taping to be done at the Second BMCC.

Once again, the CKs and their protective mothers boarded planes for a history-making excursion. With confidence, the kids told their poignant stories, while tears streamed down the cheeks of the protective parents and seasoned professionals attending the BMCC. All were captivated, and some were vicariously traumatized by what they were hearing. Each presentation they made was an opportunity for the kids to receive validation, both from their audience and from one another. This cemented a stronger bond among the CKs, which helped bring about further healing. There was an unspoken comfort and a deep loyalty that existed among them, similar to what happens with frontline combat veterans whose horrendous experiences cannot really be understood by anyone except other soldiers who have faced the same enemy.

In October 2005, PBS released the Tatge/Lasseur production of *Breaking the Silence: Children's Stories.* Prior to the documentary's national release, the PBS affiliate in Sacramento, California, held a special premier attended by the producers, Dominique and Catherine Lasseur, and by the kids and parents who appear in the film.

During the following two years, the CKs received numerous invitations from victim advocacy groups to speak at conferences, court trainings, and California legislators. The group started to expand, as other young people from throughout the country joined the ranks of child victims of custody wars. The older teens in the CKs Network were finally free to live normal lives, to the extent that was possible, considering the emotional fallout of their traumatic childhoods, the financial deprivation of their mothers due to litigation, and the fact that some of the kids were still trying to rescue their younger siblings. Despite all that they had been through, the CKs gradually began to concentrate on their educations and their futures. They continued to mentor younger kids who were seeking their help in breaking free from their abusers or who had already done so and now wanted to join the CKs in speaking out.

Clearly, one of the most profound moments I witnessed as an advisor to the CKs was in watching some of the older CKs give medals to the younger ones after they made their first presentation at the annual Child Sexual Abuse Awareness Conference. With words of pride and encouragement, the veteran CKs draped medals around the necks of the neophytes, promising their continued moral support and solidarity.

HOW PARENTAL ALIENATION SYNDROME ADVERSELY AFFECTS THE LIVES OF CHILDREN

Legalized White Slavery

In a personal meeting I had with (former) California Assist Attorney General Jack Stevens, he described the phenomenon of children being "sentenced" by court order to live in the custody of their abuser as "white slavery." Indeed, in protective parent cases throughout the county, especially those involving children's disclosures of incest, the "legalized" abuses visited upon these parents and their children were eerily similar to the violations of human rights once perpetrated by masters upon their slaves. From the ripping of a wailing infant from the breast of its enslaved mother, to putting that infant up for sale to the highest bidder, to the condoning of rape as an entitlement of slave ownership, to the modern-day taking of children to punish their fit mothers for engaging in protective behaviors that are contrary to judicial determination, the end result is the same: legalized enslavement and bondage to abusive, ultracontrolling, patriarchal power.

While perfectly fit fathers also may become enslaved by tyrannical family court orders that infringe on their liberty interests, the oppression of protective parents is overwhelmingly inflicted upon women.

There are remarkable similarities in the legal histories of the CKs' cases. With callous disregard, each child was abruptly removed, literally snatched away like a slave baby, from the custody of a fit mother with whom the child was closely bonded. This experience, likened to the sudden death of a loved one, was perpetrated on these children because of the family court's *presumption* that a mother's disclosure of paternal abuse is prima facie evidence of Parental Alienation Syndrome (PAS), which alleges that the accusing mother is trying to interfere with the father-child relationship by "alienating" the children from their father. Whether the word syndrome is included in the accusation of parental alienation, the result was the transfer of child custody from the alleged alienator (the safe parent, according to the children) to the alleged abuser (whom the children considered unsafe). After or in conjunction with the custody transfer, court orders consistent with alienation theory effectively kept the mother and her children in bondage to the abuser and court officials, allowing them control over virtually every aspect of their lives, even their thoughts and beliefs (e.g., their conviction that the abuse occurred).

Courts' Encouragement of Children's Loss of Contact With Mothers

Ironically, *in each case without exception*, once the children's fathers obtained custody of the children via accusations of PAS, the fathers then engaged in the very same behaviors of which they had (falsely) accused the mothers—and to an exponential degree. That is, these fathers did, in fact, interfere with the children's relationships with their mothers by petitioning the court to severely restrict or eliminate mother-child contact. However, when it came to the fathers' interference in parent-child relationships, the courts *encouraged* that behavior via court orders. In other words, the courts opined by their orders that *attempting* to interfere in a parent-child relationship is harmful behavior if *allegedly* perpetrated by a mother, but such interference is in the child's best interests when *provably* perpetrated by a father. This diabolically opposed "reasoning" clearly evidences gender bias in these PAS cases.

There is a distinction being made here between *alleged* behavior and *proved* behavior. It is critically important to note that in the described cases, the children had regular contact with their fathers while they were in their mothers' custody; however, once they were transferred to their fathers' custody, their contact with their mothers was severely restricted or even eliminated. Yet, the courts accepted as true the fathers' accusations of interference. Such outcomes, which are repeated every day in courtrooms across the country, result from the branding of fit mothers with labels based upon hearsay and the subjective opinions of mental health professionals who work for the courts. Instead of relying on actual *behavior* that can be proved using statutory standards of evidence, the courts rely upon unproven pseudoscience when making custody decisions.

Even after talking with many kids and hundreds of protective parents about their cases as well as experiencing it first hand, I still find it difficult to understand how people who are intelligent enough to pass bar exams (lawyers and judges) or mental health licensing exams (mediators, custody evaluators, social workers) could be so inept at applying reasoned logic to a set of circumstances that it results in the creation of a slave/master-like relationship between the abuser and his victims. This is particularly ironic because, even with their youthfulness, the CKs clearly understood the lack of common sense and logic, the perversity and backwards thinking that drive accusations of PAS.

In the cases presented earlier, the children's fathers were extremely controlling and aggressively tried to destroy the children's bonds and relationships with their mothers. In addition to fighting for custody orders that severely restricted or completely terminated contact between the children and their mothers, they also fought for orders that controlled all other aspects of the mothers' and children's lives. The children's mothers were excluded from any decision making in their lives, restrained from going to their schools or participating in any of their extracurricular activities, prevented from providing medical care for them, prevented from sending them gifts on special occasions, etc. For those children who had supervised visitation with their mothers, their fathers refused to pay or help pay for monitors, refused to agree to unpaid monitors, and/or threatened and harassed monitors until they withdrew their services, in order to prevent the mothers from exercising the visitation. Some children were direct witnesses to their father's harassment and abuse of monitors.

With mothers entitled to unsupervised visitation, the fathers either refused to produce the children for visitation or coerced the children into refusing visits. They were allowed by the courts to do so with impunity. After their fathers obtained custody, many of the CKs literally spent years without any contact whatsoever with their mothers. They were not allowed to send or receive cards from their mothers on birthdays, Mother's Day, or Christmas, much less have contact with them. Based on these and other facts, it seems patently obvious that by spuriously making allegations of alienation against the mothers, the fathers were projecting onto the mothers their own destructive intentions, attitudes, and behaviors.

Children Put in Untenable Situations

According to all of the CKs, their fathers used isolation and brainwashing in an attempt to convince the children that their mothers were mentally unstable and therefore deserved to lose custody and be exiled from their children's lives. The fathers enmeshed their children in the litigation by framing the mothers' efforts to regain custody or even a semblance of normal contact as an attack on both the fathers and the children. The fathers denied their histories of abuse to their children and demanded, through overt or covert pressure, that the children form an alliance with them against their mothers. In fact, the vast majority of CKs have reported that their fathers either told them or led them to believe that their mothers were unfit, did not love them, did not want them, or had abandoned them for selfish reasons.

Because the children clearly understood that their fathers were backed up by the courts and therefore had the power to do to the children whatever they wished, the kids had no choice but to go along with the program. They allied with their fathers against their mothers, even when they knew that what their father told them was untrue. They did what they had to do in order to survive. However, the forced betrayal of their own convictions, and their submission to their fathers' demands to bad-mouth or reject their mothers, created feelings of weakness and shame, especially for the boys. However, all the CKs expressed feelings of guilt over being unable to help themselves or defend their mothers against their fathers' attacks.

The sense that these children had of no longer having a "real" mother (though some lived with stepmothers) caused them a great deal of shame, which in turn affected their social and peer relationships. It was particularly painful on those occasions when other children's mothers came to attend school parties, sports events, plays, award assemblies, graduations, and so forth. Children generally understand early on that mothers are supposed to be fixtures at school events. When members of the CKs were asked by their peers why their mothers did not come to a school event, they would be at a loss for an explanation. Most of the CKs did not understand why their mothers were not in attendance much less have the ability to explain it to others. Some did not even know where their mothers were living, since their fathers refused to provide them with any information about their mothers, except for the fatal flaws the fathers claimed these mothers to have. As an additional assault on the children's self-esteem, the absence of their mothers made the kids feel unworthy, unloved, and inferior to peers whose mothers loved them enough to attend their school functions. Every school event was another painful reminder to these children of the absence of their own mothers, which further exacerbated their feelings of grief and loss.

While the children lived with their abusers, fear was their constant companion: fear of further abuse, abandonment, failure, and rejection; fear of disclosing information they were demanded to keep secret; fear of telling the truth, disappointing their abusers, forgetting their mothers, or having their mothers forget them; fear of holding out false hopes that they would ever again have a normal life, of being caught as a runaway, of being placed in foster care, of their fathers' retaliation towards their mothers, of feeling and of not feeling anything at all. Some of these children even feared success, because their self-worth had been so damaged that they did not believe they deserved success.

DIRECT ABUSE BY COURT-APPOINTED PROFESSIONALS

As cruel as the behaviors of CKs' abusive fathers were, it is possible to grasp how an abuser obsessed with power and control, combined with a vested interest in "winning," could behave so egregiously at the expense of his own child. After all, batterers feel entitled to use and abuse other people as a means to an end. But the cold hearted, even malicious conduct often exhibited by court officials toward the children whose best interests they are assigned to protect simply defies comprehension. Some of the examples presented in this section are so shocking to the conscience, and so completely in contrast with the image the public holds of our court system, that they may be difficult to even conceive, much less believe.

The opening pages of this chapter presented the story of an eight-year-old boy whose mother died. What was not revealed was what was done by the child protective social worker who had been assigned to his case for a long period of time and who was, therefore, very familiar with his situation. She sought out this child immediately after his mother died, before the funeral and before she was buried, to tell him that he would be taken away from his grandmother and returned to the custody of his father. The social worker did not even allow the child to grieve his mother's death in peace, not even for the few days before she was buried. Instead, she further traumatized him with the news that he would also be losing his grandmother and everything that went along with living with her: his sense of safety, security, and consistency; his relatives, pets, neighborhood, school, and friends—in sum, his entire life as he knew it.

At the time of his mother's death, the boy had been living with her and his grand-mother. His grandmother was perfectly fit to take care of him, so there was no need to rush to remove him from her care. What would motivate this social worker to further tear at this child's fresh wound by exacerbating his grief with the devastating news that more loss was to come?

One of the CKs (whose story has not yet been mentioned) described how a moni-tor of supervised visitation, in league with his father, used him as a pawn to hurt his mother by coercing him to refuse to visit her. The boy described how his mother would fly from California to Arizona and then rent a car to meet him for a few hours of super-vised visitation once a month. When his mother arrived, the monitor would present the boy to his mother from a distance, where he would wait in silence, instructed not to speak. The monitor would then walk up to his mother and say, in the boy's presence, "He doesn't want to visit you today." The monitor would then demand from his mother a fee for having shown up to supervise the now-cancelled visit. After collecting her fee, the monitor would turn her back on the boy's mother, leaving her engulfed in an inferno of pain while she joined the boy and his father, with the three of them leaving the exchange location together.

This scenario was repeated until the boy's mother gave up trying to visit. But each time he had to participate in this perverse game with his father and the monitor, knowing how much it hurt his mother and feeling responsible for her pain, the boy became more racked with guilt. He began to hate himself. This boy, an only child, had disclosed from a very young age that his father was sexually abusing him. He was left with severe psychological problems from his years of custodial abuse, as his mother's fight to protect him had resulted in him being removed from her custody and placed with his father. He eventually ran away from his father as a teen and returned to his mother. His trauma left him with large gaps of memory loss, which has taken years of intensive therapy to resolve.

Another CK, who was forced to move from the West Coast to the East Coast when the court placed him in the custody of his abusive father, repeatedly begged his court-appointed attorney to allow him to remain in the custody of his mother, and he stated all the reasons for his request. The boy's court-appointed attorney ridiculed him, called him a liar, made the accusation that his mother instructed him to call, and told the boy to call back "when he had something truthful to say." This boy was very active in a 4-H program where he was learning responsibility and confidence-building skills through individual and community service projects. He had won many impressive awards for raising and showing his animals, hard-earned successes that made him feel good about himself. And, moreover, his animals were not just "projects." They were pets. They were a source of comfort to him while his family was disintegrating.

The boy's court-appointed attorney, however, showed no compassion for the heart-break his young client would suffer in having to leave not only his mother, but also his pets behind to move across the country and be thrust into an entirely different lifestyle. Nor did this attorney show any compassion for the boy's sense of loss, loneliness, and desire to maintain a relationship with his mother after being placed in his father's custody. Instead, he assisted the father in keeping the boy completely isolated from his mother. After years of being denied even phone conversations with his mother, the boy ran away from his father. He stayed underground for two years, moving from place to place and going outside only at night to avoid getting caught as a runaway.

In another case, a CK recalled the day a court-appointed "investigator" (lawyer) came to her home to speak with her. The investigator, a man, entered the girl's bedroom to talk with her. He sat on her bed next to her, and, before long, he was urging the girl to hug him, which frightened her immensely. She described feeling "frozen," not knowing what to say or do, wanting to bolt out of the room, but fearing the consequences if she did.

Many of the CKs were court ordered to PAS "therapy"[3] (also known as threat therapy) after being removed from their mothers and were severely emotionally abused by the PAS therapists. The therapists told the kids that their mothers were mentally ill, emotionally unbalanced, liars, evil, unable to care for them, unwilling to care for them, etc. One CK was forced by her therapist to call her mother on the telephone and tell her she did not want to see her. This young girl spoke about how guilty and ashamed she felt at having done this to her mother, albeit unwillingly. She described each therapy session as "an hour of listening to my therapist bad-mouth my mother, making me feel wrong and guilty for loving her. I left each session wanting to die." Several of the kids who were subjected to PAS therapy were told by the therapists at the onset of their "treatment" that they would never live with their mothers again. One can only imagine the impact of sadness, a sense of loss, and hopelessness those words had on the children who were already grieving so many losses, and longing for their mothers. They were not allowed to have photos of their mothers or of anything related to their lives with their mothers before the change of custody, as if to completely erase their memories of happier times.

My own son has frequently described, in presentations, the severe emotional abuse inflicted on him by the court-appointed PAS therapist assigned to our case, chosen and paid for by his father. He described how the therapist used fear tactics, making veiled threats that he and his sisters would never see me again if they "broke any of her rules." These rules included not showing or expressing affection for me, not sharing their feelings with me, not discussing with me a list of subjects that covered basically every aspect of their lives, including their school activities, and never asking when they would see me again. These are his words, recalling the pain of his experience at ten years old:

> Every week after the hour with my mom was over, I would go home wondering if I'd see my mom again. I wished with all my heart I would, because the agency workers discouraged us to hug our mom and I figured that if I could keep seeing her every week that one week I'd sneak a hug in. Until then I had to just look at her and wave . . . I felt like crying every time I walked away from my mom but I hid it so my dad and [PAS therapist] wouldn't get upset with me.

Some of my son's traumatic memories and my own are inextricably intertwined, such as when my son came to a supervised visit appearing upset and withdrawn. I asked him if something was bothering him, and he began telling me how much he hated being taken out of school early to see the therapist every week. He said it drew attention to him, and the other kids at school made fun of him for being "the kid with the problems" (which caused him to isolate himself from the other children in shame).

---

[3] I have placed quotation marks around the term "therapist" in this section because the role of such therapists in connection with PAS work is the opposite of what real therapists do. Therapy helps patients heal, cope with problems, and improve health. When children are forced into PAS therapy, the purpose is to benefit the abuser (and to some extent the court) and unqualified professionals that promoted the bogus and unscientific theory. Such "treatment" is harmful to children, interferes with their ability to heal, and will have long-term harmful effects on them. To call this treatment is to bastardize the term.

When I empathized with my son, telling him that I was sorry for his discomfort, and that maybe the therapy times could be changed to after school, the monitor became vicious and announced that the visit was over because I was perpetrating "parental alienation syndrome." My son, who was about ten years old at the time, and his younger sisters began to cry hysterically when the monitor ordered them to leave, and they desperately clung to me. The monitor called others from the agency into the room. Together they physically pulled on my children while they held on to me, sobbing, until they were physically overpowered. Their PAS therapist subsequently wrote a letter to the court stating that she spoke with the children immediately after this incident and explained to them how their mother was bad for "breaking the rules," alleged that they were "not upset" over termination of the visit, and had not asked about me since. This terrorism and manhandling of my children was done to instill such fear in them that they would cease making complaints about their miserable circumstances that demonstrated how severely the court's orders were harming them.

On another occasion, my son described how he and his sisters tried to tell the PAS therapist about their father's abuse and their misery in his custody. This only resulted in the therapist bringing their father and court-appointed attorney into the therapy session, where all three authority figures sat side by side on a couch across from the children and made veiled threats to stop making complaints about their father's treatment of them or their living situation. My son described the utter hopelessness he felt, which manifested in depression, from being mentally brutalized *en banc* by "his therapist," "his attorney," and his father, referring to them as "the big three." My son also described that he personally witnessed this PAS therapist force his sister to write letters to her little school friends recanting disclosures of molestation by her father. This was after his sister disclosed to her friends that her father was molesting her and complained to the therapist of her father's abuse. My son watched while the PAS therapist placed paper and writing instruments in front of his sister and dictated to her letters of recantation. These letters were then addressed and sent by the PAS therapist, in her business envelopes, to the homes of the children to whom my daughter had disclosed molestation by her father.

One of the first kids to speak out about her experience in the family court, long before the CKs Network was formed, described in a letter, which was published in a San Francisco newspaper, how she was abused by court officials who deliberately protected her offending father and acted hateful and vicious toward her protective mother. She revealed how her PAS therapist (who she declared was sleeping with her father) assisted her father in having her institutionalized out of state at the age of eleven, alleging that she was mentally ill, after a teacher witnessed and reported a physical assault on her by her father. The girl described how she was abused at the lock-down facility by older youths and was mentally tortured and browbeaten by therapists who repeatedly told her that until she accepted the opinion that her father was a good parent and her mother was a bad, "alienating" parent, she would not be considered "well." She figured out that if she just parroted whatever the PAS gurus wanted her to say, she would be released. After using this tactic for several months, she was returned to her father, who then sent her away to boarding school. When she had to return to her father from boarding school, this young girl ran away. She vividly described literally running, even crawling under barbed wire fences, to evade capture by police. Eventually she was protected by the Los Angeles juvenile court and allowed to return to her mother, after her father pleaded no contest to abusing her. Upon reaching the age of majority, she successfully sued her father for abusing her.

One has to wonder what demons of their own must live in the minds of these court "professionals" who would inflict such heinous psychological cruelty on children.

JUDGES AS SECONDARY ABUSERS

The court officials, who directly abused the children as described in the preceding section, were obviously not ordered by judges to do, specifically, the grossly unethical and damaging things to these children that they did. But by virtue of their attitudes and rulings, such as refusing to believe children's accounts of abuse, violating their due process rights to full presentation of their cases of abuse in the court proceedings, failing to provide qualified and *effective* counsel for the children, relying on testimony to a legally invalid theory that does not pass *Kelly-Frye* and *Daubert* standards of admissibility, appointing PAS therapists to promulgate the invalid hypothesis, failing to provide the children with any protective mechanism to report abuses perpetrated on them by court appointees, and improperly delegating authority to family court service providers, the judges in these cases acted as secondary abusers of the children.[4]

Judges who, whether *sua sponte,* on the recommendation of court appointees, or at the request of the abuser, ordered micromanagement and control over the lives of the children's mothers equally abused the rights of the children. By orders from unconstitutional prior restraint on speech to making the mothers responsible for the actions and speech of the general public who questioned or criticized the court's handling of the cases, the children were collaterally deprived of redress for the wrongs done to them, as the effects of the oppressive orders spilled over onto the kids.

As they have described, the prior restraint on speech prevented spontaneous conversation between the kids and their mothers, as they were forced to observe their "master's" rules of discourse in order to protect their ability to maintain contact with their mothers. Freedom of association with extended relatives and peers was also curtailed for many of the kids, who were not allowed by their abusers to have contact with anyone who might be supportive of their mothers or who was not outwardly hostile toward the mothers on behalf of the abusers. This meant, for some of the CKs, loss of relationships with long-time family friends, schoolmates, and even with siblings; these losses were piled on top of the losses of their mothers to create deep chasms of loneliness and grief—all because of orders made by judges in their cases.

---

[4] People v. Kelly, 17Cal. 3d 24, 549P.2d 1240 (Sup. Ct. 1976), Frye v. United States, 293 F. 1013 (DC Cir. 1923), Daubert v. Merrill Dow Pharms., 509 U.S. 579 (1993). *Frye* was the key federal case regarding the standards for admissibility of expert medical testimony. In order to permit such testimony, it must refer to a well-recognized scientific principle or discovery that has gained general acceptance in the particular field it belongs. As discussed in other chapters, PAS does not meet these standards because it is not recognized by any reputable professional organization and has not been included in the American Psychological Association, *Diagnostic and Statistical Manual of Mental Disorders* (4th ed. 2000). The *Kelly* case is California's adaptation of the *Frye* standard. *Daubert* adds additional requirements to *Frye* in order to qualify for admission into evidence. The judge makes an initial determination and, among other standards, would not admit evidence unless it is relevant and reliable and scientifically valid. These standards would further disqualify the use of PAS. California never adopted *Daubert*, so it continues with a lower standard from *Frye*. Many attorneys and others who oppose PAS believe custody courts repeatedly allow PAS testimony in violation of the evidence standards established by *Frye* and *Daubert*.

Some orders were so tyrannical for the punitive agenda of the court that they can only be said to border on pure lunacy, such as forbidding mothers from even waving to their children in the event that they passed by each other in vehicles on the road or spontaneously ran into one another at a store. What might a child who recently experienced the loss of his mother by custody orders feel if he saw her pass by in the car and excitedly waved to her, only to receive no response? It would be quite natural for the child to internalize his mother's lack of response to his wave as a sign of abandonment or something negative about himself that caused her to reject him. This type of self-blaming behavior was best described by a CK (whose case is not described in this chapter) when she spoke of the years she was isolated from her mother, with no comprehension of why the relationship dissolved. She said, "I wondered what I had done to make my mother not love me anymore." She then described years of feeling worthless over the shame of believing that she had done something so wrong that her own mother had rejected her.

The long and short of it is, judges who are abusing the children's mothers are also abusing the children, just as batterers who abuse their children's mothers are also abusing their children. Judges just happen to be more powerful abusers.

LONG-TERM REPERCUSSIONS FOR CHILDREN

While there is no accurate way to predict how any individual child will respond to being separated from a nurturing parent while forced into the custody of an abusive parent, it is understood that the child will suffer immeasurably. Overwhelmingly, the CKs who were physically abused reported less trauma from the physical abuse than from the verbal and emotional abuse, and the worst trauma reported was from sexual abuse. Based on the accounts of the CKs, the most common self-identified emotional/psychological problems they suffered as a result of their traumas were feelings of anxiety, insecurity, sadness, depression, guilt, shame, confusion, loneliness, grief from loss, hypervigilance, helplessness, inability to trust, insomnia, loss of faith in governmental systems, low self-esteem, fear of abandonment, and fear of failure. Significantly, these were long-standing maladies, as all of these children spent at least several years away from their protective parents and with their abusive parents.

Hypervigilance in assessing their abusers' unpredictable moods and/or violent outbursts emerged as a common theme in the disclosures of the CKs. Even in times of relative calm, the children lived in perpetual fear of "the other shoe dropping," most often described by victims of DV as "walking on eggshells." They watched carefully nuances in their abusers' facial expressions and behavior that might signal danger, and they adapted their own behavior to ameliorate their abusers and/or protect against becoming their targets. Some CKs reported not asking for even basic necessities like food, fearing that making any request would upset their abusers. Some felt forced to take sides with their abusers in thrashing their mothers, to ensure their safety.

Perhaps surprisingly, the CKs that expressed feeling the greatest fear of their abusers were those who had *not* been physically abused, but rather those who described behavior by their abusers that is commonly referred to as repressed rage. These kids explained that their fear was of the unknown: the consequences of their abusers' uncontrolled rage. The kids' gut instincts told them that if their abusers ever let go of all their pent up rage, they might kill them. Yet, no one in the "system" listened to their fears, believing them to be unreasonable or fabricated.

On the other hand, the CKs who were physically abused had a good sense of how far their abusers would go because their abusers' rage was expressed outwardly and so was known to them and, therefore, more predictable. As is often the case, the unknown can be more frightening than the known. Moreover, in some cases, *repressed* rage may be more lethal than *expressed* rage. The best example of this type of situation was that of fourteen-year-old Evan Nash, the San Diego boy killed by his father while running with his high school track team.[5] The father (a teacher), who publicly presented himself as a wonderful, doting father, had never physically abused the boy. Nevertheless, the boy knew the repressed rage that boiled in his father and instinctively knew his capabilities. After his mother obtained a restraining order on Evan's behalf, his father shot and killed him at point blank range in front of his schoolmates. Evan's gut instinct was proved correct, and his fear reasonable.

What could have possibly saved Evan? If his mother had run with him and hidden him to protect him, Evan's picture would have probably ended up circulated all over the country by Missing and Exploited Children; his mother would have likely been hunted down by the FBI, caught, prosecuted, and sent to jail. Undoubtedly, Evan's gut instinct would have proved to be of little value in her defense on abduction charges or in a motion for his custodial placement with someone other than his father. Kids with gut instinct fears like Evan's who are not listened to, or whose fears are ridiculed, learn to mistrust or deny their instincts.

Most importantly, all of the CKs reported that some or many of their emotional problems continued even after they were free of their abusers and were in safe and stable environments. Though not labeling it as such, many described symptoms of posttraumatic distress lasting for several years after being freed from their abusers (both parental abusers and "system" abusers). One boy described feeling anxiety whenever he saw a mailbox, because court papers bringing bad news regularly arrived in his mailbox.

As described previously in Case #4, one child suffers a startle response to the sound of a phone ringing. My son has described such an extreme and continuing aversion to being anywhere near his father's county of residence, marked by physical symptoms of emotional distress (a sickening feeling of dread accompanied by tension, anxiety, and stomach upset), that he avoids traveling in the proximity of the county. Sadly, several of the youths who were either delivered to their abusers by law enforcement officers, or returned to their abusers by law enforcement officers after running away, described having an upsetting physical reaction to the sight of a squad car or police officer.

Not surprisingly, negative triggers to reminders of their traumatic experiences are common problems for children in protective parent cases who were revictimized by the "system." Because the older kids in the CKs Network have just recently passed the teen years, it is impossible to know how the fallout from their traumatic exposure to the legal system will affect their futures, and particularly their adult intimate partner relationships, and relationships with their own future children should they become parents. Considering that *all* of the CKs have stated that their negative experiences with the court system have caused them to have difficulty trusting other people, as well as their government, it stands to reason that this will negatively influence many aspects of their adult lives. While the ability to trust is a key element in forming healthy close interpersonal relationships, a propensity to mistrust is likely to have a negative effect on both close interpersonal relationships as well as extended social relationships.

---

[5] Joe Hughes, "Grieving Mom Battles to Save Others' Children," *San Diego Union Tribune,* May 16, 2004, *available at* http://www.signonsandiego.com/uniontrib/20040516/news_1m16mom.html.

OVERCOMING TRAUMA

It is amazing, given the extent of trauma they suffered, that each of the CKs overcame all of their fears and the obstacles placed in their paths, escaped the custody of their abusers, and returned home to their mothers. What is most perplexing is that some of them had siblings, in precisely the same circumstances, who succumbed to the manipulations and brainwashing of the abusers and turned against their mothers. Some siblings were older, and some were younger, so it is unclear what impact, if any, age or birth order in the family may have on a child's ability to persist in efforts at self-protection despite adversities.

There are so many variables to consider. How old were they when they were removed from the protective parents? What was the relationship with each of the parents at the time they were removed? Do they have siblings? What support or close relationships did they have outside of their families? How did that change after the custody switch? What form of abuse did they suffer and to what extent? What type of personalities do they have: strong willed, passive, somewhere in between? What changes took place in their lives after being placed with the abusers; did they move away from their protective parents? Was there introduction of a stepparent and/or new siblings? What type, if any, therapy did they have after being removed from their protective parents?

With the limited comparative information available, at this point, it is anyone's guess why some children isolated with abusers do not give up the fight to free themselves and others do. Anecdotally, it appears that the CKs are the exception not the rule. From all accounts, it appears that most children in circumstances of isolation with custodial abusers become traumatically bonded to the abusers, causing them to accommodate to the abuse itself, as well as to the abusers' oppressive control over them. They do not attempt to escape because of fear of the abusers and a sense of powerlessness inherent with the realization that the authorities (courts, law enforcement, CPS, etc.) are supporting the abusers. Moreover, they study the world around them and learn to blend in so others cannot see the pain they live with day and night, their lives morphing into a self-created *Truman Show*,[6] directed and produced by their abusers with the assistance of enabling family courts.

This presents a tremendous problem for the protective parent who is trying to rescue the child who, from superficial outward appearances, looks and acts "normal." With only one exception, all of the CKs I have spoken with admit that, at times, they became so confused by the constant barrage of criticism of their mothers, coupled with the continual support of the abusers by authority figures, that they began to believe their abusers' defamatory statements about their mothers. This was a result of having no ability to receive opposing information. Yet, their souls could not rest. Something kept them from giving up, no matter how hopeless their circumstances seemed. Some of them prayed, even when they thought God had forgotten them.

Wherever the strength of the CKs comes from, it is remarkable. *They* are remarkable. Their determination is contagious. They inspire others to act. They provide a light in the darkness, a ray of hope, and encourage the rest of us, no matter how weary, to keep fighting the good fight for the sake of safety and justice for all children who will have to walk through the mine fields of family court. My deepest respect and unending thanks goes to each one of them with whom I have been privileged to work. Thanks CKs, for the tremendous difference you have made in the protective parent movement.

---

[6] *The Truman Show* (Paramount Pictures 1998) is a movie about a child raised on a movie set, which the child did not know to be a false representation of reality.

EPILOGUE—CASE UPDATES

Readers of this chapter will want to know what happened to the CKs whose cases were described earlier. Here is a brief follow-up report (as of October 2009):

- *The Motherless Boy.* The little boy whose mother died turned eighteen in April 2008. In 2007, a teen foster child living with the boy's grandmother and paternal aunt asked the grandmother why she was so despondent. The grandmother told this girl about her grandson, who she had not seen for many years and missed so badly. Without telling the grandmother, the girl found the boy on MySpace and sent him an e-mail. Making small talk, she asked the boy what he would want more than anything in the world if he could have a wish granted, thinking his answer would be something like having a Mazaratti sports car. Instead, he responded, "I would just like to talk to my mother one more time." Since then, the grandmother has been communicating with her grandson by e-mail, hoping to see him in person after he turns eighteen and is legally unbound from his father.[7]

- *Case #1: The Million Dollar Question.* The girl turned eighteen, graduated from high school, and is working. An arrest warrant issued against her mother several years ago for failure to appear in court for what the mother termed another "legal torture session," was recently vacated, enabling the mother to finally live free from the fear of incarceration and to renew her driver's license. While the girl was a runaway and did not reside with her father for two years, he continued to collect child support from her mother's meager income, thus impoverishing her. Though the girl and her mother were finally freed from the control of the court and able to live together in peace, they were made homeless because of poverty. The years of trauma and stress have had a devastating effect on the health of both the mother and the girl, who, at her young age, was just diagnosed with Graves disease, echoing the results of Dr. Vincent Felitti's Adverse Childhood Experience Study.[8]

- *Case #2: Hiding the Bruises.* This girl has also turned eighteen. She left California and moved in with an older sister in close proximity to her mother and another older sister. When her mother was released from jail, she was able to reunite with her. A new judge took over the family law case—one who regularly presides over criminal cases. He heard testimony from the girl and her siblings and on March 15, 2008, the mother was able to take her minor children

---

[7] The boy is now a college student. He has visited his grandmother and reconnected with many relatives from his mother's side of the family. After one visit, he said he feels so loved. While visiting his grandmother, his grandfather who was separated from his grandmother died. He went to the funeral where he met two women who knew him when he was a young child. They had also been molested by their fathers. He plans to stay with one of the women rather than return to his father's home during college breaks.

[8] The Adverse Childhood Experiences (ACE) Study is a major research study that compares current adult health status to childhood experiences decades earlier. With the cooperation of 17,421 adult health plan members and with the ongoing collaboration of Dr. Robert Anda at the Centers for Disease Control and Prevention (CDC), the study is being carried out in the Department of Preventive Medicine at Kaiser Permanente (KP), San Diego—where for many years, detailed biomedical, psychological, and social (biopsychosocial) evaluations of more than 50,000 adult Kaiser Permanente Foundation Health Plan members per year have been conducted. Vincent Ferlitti, M.D., 6(1) *The Relationship Between Adverse Childhood Experiences and Adult Health: Turning Gold Into Lead* (Winter 2002), *available at* http://xnet.kp.org/permanentejournal/winter02/goldtolead.html.

home after the judge returned custody to her. Finally, the girl, her mother, and siblings were able to be a family again.

- *Case #3: Violence Begets Violence.* This boy continued to run away and, at the same time, he wrote letters to the state bar and other public officials complaining that his court-appointed attorney was not protecting him. He finally convinced his attorney to take legal action that would allow him to live with his mother, where he is happy and doing well.

- *Case #4: Not Saved by the Bell.* The California appellate court relinquished jurisdiction to the state where the children's father lives, and so the children were ordered back to live in his custody. They ran away, and warrants were put out for their arrest. Three years later, in May 2009, they were found. Reportedly, six U.S. marshals broke down their door, pointed automatic rifles at them, and took them into custody. Each child is now residing in separate out-of-home youth placement facilities. The boy will turn eighteen years old within weeks and be free from the jurisdiction of the court. When released, he plans to return home to his extended maternal family. For her attempts to protect her children, the mother is being held in jail on child abduction charges *without bond*, though suspects charged with violent crimes, even murder and child rape, are often allowed to post bond.

- *Case #5: For His Sisters' Sake.* This young man is now working as a firefighter. After he left his father's custody, his father disowned him, sought retribution against him, and succeeded in turning his sisters against him, severing their sibling relationship. In December 2007, his mother won an appeal. However, the family court judge refused to comply with the appellate decision and would not reverse custody of the boy's sisters to his mother, despite the fact that a new court evaluator substantiated sexual and psychological abuse of the children by their father, and despite the fact that the father was criminally prosecuted by the district attorney, as well as being found guilty of contempt in family court for violating custody orders, and was sentenced to jail for his offenses. Both sisters are now aged out of the jurisdiction of the court, and each immediately left her father's home when she graduated from high school; they are living away from his county of residence. As a result of their father's coercive control, they are estranged from their maternal family. This young man continues to grieve for the loss of a relationship with his sisters and clings to the hope that someday they will be reunited.

- *Case #6: Maternal Sexual Abuse Ignored.* No one has heard from the father since he gave up trying to protect his son.

- *Case #7: Supervised Visitation Imposed as a Lifestyle.* In their teen years, both of this father's daughters began to complain about the stifling and artificial environment of the supervised visits. The visitation monitor declared to the court that there was no evidence that supervision was necessary and recommended traditional unsupervised visitation. The court's reaction to the girls' objections and the monitor's opinion, though, was not to dispense with supervision of visits, but rather to continue the order for supervised visits and allow the girls to refuse the visits. The father then lost all contact with his daughters. He has not seen them in years. Tragically, their younger half-siblings, the two children from the father's subsequent marriage, have not seen their sisters either.

- *Case #8: Sex Offender Approved as Stepfather:* This father's children began refusing visits in their teen years, which the court allowed them to do. After having no contact with his children for several years, the father had a heart attack and died. While his unhealthy weight undoubtedly had a negative impact on his health, those who knew him believe he died of a broken heart.

Chapter 10

From the Mouths of Mothers

by Wendy Titelman, Annette Zender, Paige Hodson, B.A., and Larissa Pollica, R.N., B.S.

EDITORS' INTRODUCTION

This chapter presents the stories of four protective mothers. It is intended to help the reader understand what it is like to experience the crisis in the custody court system.

We have included Ms. Titelman's account because it is a fair representation of what happens when mothers raise allegations of sexual abuse of children in custody cases. We are familiar with the specifics of this case and believe the presentation accurately reflects the circumstances. For a variety of reasons discussed elsewhere in this volume, custody courts have an especially poor record of responding to sexual abuse allegations. Ms. Titelman's experience illustrates the personal consequences caused by these courts' mistakes.

Ms. Zender's story (presented here as told to Carroll White) is a good example of the kinds of retaliatory actions courts often take against protective mothers who challenge a court's mistakes. We are familiar with this case and believe it illustrates the problems faced by protective mothers. Here the court ignored overwhelming evidence of the father's abuse and permitted him to take a safe and loving mother out of the child's life. When the mother attempted to expose the court's mistakes, the court responded with retaliatory threats and attacks that harmed the child the court was supposed to protect.

In an otherwise grim landscape, one of the few good things to come from the custody crisis is that protective mothers have been working to help other victims of the custody court system. Paige Hodson serves as an inspirational example of someone who learned about the problems affecting domestic violence (DV) and child abuse custody cases and used this knowledge to help others in similar situations. She is active in the community working on behalf of battered mothers and has made an important difference in the lives of many other women.

After providing testimony about her custody case to the Truth Commission at the Fourth Battered Mothers Custody Conference, and with the help of other advocates, Ms. Pollica became an activist for court reform in her jurisdiction. We are aware of the details of Ms. Pollica's case and believe it accurately reflects what other mothers are going through. The judge refused to hear the testimony of an expert (Barry Goldstein, coeditor of this volume) because he had been a family court judge for seventeen years and believed his knowledge of DV was sufficient. The law guardian also refused to speak to the mother's expert and had limited discussions with others familiar with the children, while uncritically accepting the statements of the abusers' witnesses. The evaluator had no training in DV. These mistakes led the court to send Ms. Pollica's children to two different abusive fathers. After obtaining custody by promising to promote the children's relationships with their mother, the fathers did everything they could to limit contact.

SEXUAL ABUSE IN CUSTODY COURTS—WENDY TITELMAN'S STORY

Another season has come with the changing color of the leaves and the drop in temperature, and school is back in session. Children can be heard laughing while waiting for the bus at our local stop. My daughters, ages fifteen and thirteen, are not among them; they live with their father several hundred miles away, and I do not know which school they attend. I do not know anything about them anymore. It has been seven years since I last saw them.

Boxes of legal files fill my bedroom. My desk is covered with legal papers along with another motion for criminal and civil contempt that was delivered to me by the sheriff this past week. Responses are due within a few days in four different legal actions. I am not an attorney, but I must do the work of one. Seeking protection for my children through the courts has left me indigent. Anxiety continuously clutches at my chest and my throat. The grief that only a childless mother could know tears at my heart and fills my very soul. Once again, I try to empty myself of the negative emotions that rob me of life. Again, I turn to my faith for justice, peace, reunification, accountability, and forgiveness. These are the only things that give me the strength to carry on.

Seven years ago, the Cobb County, Georgia, Superior Court, at a hearing where neither I nor my attorney was present, issued an order forbidding me and my family to come within 3,000 yards of my two children. This order was a permanent one, issued outside of due process and without any finding that I am an unfit parent. My children and I had a very close and loving bond before our relationship was totally severed by the court. During our marriage, my husband wanted nothing to do with the care of our children or with making decisions about their lives; I was their sole nurturer. Our marriage was tumultuous due to my husband's abuse. During divorce proceedings, my husband told me that he was going to make things as difficult as possible for me. He announced that he wanted full custody of our children and asked the court to appoint a guardian ad litem (GAL).

When we separated, a temporary custody order was issued whereby the girls were to rotate between their father and me each week, in a 50/50 time division. Almost immediately, the girls began to disclose that their father was sexually abusing them and that they did not want to return to his home. Psychologists and forensic specialists substantiated their allegations. The GAL, Diane Woods, was supposed to protect my children but instead chose to advocate for my husband. She said that I was attempting to "alienate" the children from him; therefore, I should be allowed only supervised visitation with my girls. She appointed her good friend, Dr. Elizabeth King, as a court-appointed psychologist, and she told her friend that there was no abuse. My daughters continued to cry out for help to Dr. King, to medical doctors, psychologists, supervisors, and friends, all of whom—with the exception of Dr. King—reported child abuse to the agencies that are in place to protect children.

Dr. King testified that I was mentally ill because I believed my daughters' disclosures. In her custody evaluation report, she stated, "The issue of parental alienation must be a concern. Alex meets six of the eight criteria, and Jenny meets seven of the eight for Gardner's parental alienation syndrome [PAS]."[1] Dr. King also found that I was suffering from a disorder she characterized as "Snow White Syndrome." Further, Dr. King opined that I was "implanting or reinforcing false memories" that created problems "with regard to parental alienation." She presented us with a videotape made by my ex-husband over the course of two days, stating it was proof that he had not molested the girls. This videotape has been examined by numerous experts, who all agreed that it shows my ex-husband "browbeating" the girls to recant their allegations of abuse. He is seen standing over them in an overbearing and threatening manner, angrily making demands for them to say exactly what he wants them to say. The court never bothered to view the tape. King recommended that the court award my ex-husband full custody of our children.

When the girls continued to disclose abuse by their father and the number of reports substantiating the abuse increased, the court held an unlawful *ex parte* hearing and issued an *ex parte* order preventing my family and me from having any contact or communication with my children. My ex-husband and his attorneys, along with Ms. Woods and Dr. King, had me arrested and thrown in jail. I was prosecuted on a felony charge of custodial interference, which carries up to a five-year jail sentence. I was acquitted after a very short jury deliberation. The outraged jurors took the unusual and extraordinary step of writing a letter to the prosecuting district attorney, Patrick Head, and to Judge James Bodiford, the judge presiding over the custody case, calling the prosecution an inexcusable "cover-up" of the state of Georgia's malfeasance and failure to protect the children. The letter was presented by jury foreperson Bryan Wilson and states, in part,

> We were perplexed as to why our state would pursue such a case so diligently when there were obvious errors in the indictment and credible reports indicating sexual and emotional abuse to two small children and the prosecution of the mother who sought to protect them from harm's way.

Diane Woods, the GAL who met with my children only once, charged over $22,000 for handling the case. Dr. King who, acting in dual roles, used junk science to bolster her opinion and ignored my children's pleas for help, charged over $55,000. It cost me $2,000 a month to see my children for twelve hours a week under supervised visitation.

The court gave my ex-husband all of my property, all of my savings, and other financial awards that were supposed to have been assigned to me. It ordered me to pay five and a half years of mortgage payments to him for a home that was supposed to be signed

---

[1] "Richard Gardner's theory positing the existence of 'parental alienation syndrome' or 'PAS' has been discredited by the scientific community. Testimony that a party to a custody case suffers from the syndrome should therefore be ruled inadmissible both under the standards established in *Daubert* and the stricter *Frye* standard." National Council of Juvenile and Family Court Judges and the State Court Institute, *Navigating Custody and Visitation Evaluations in Cases With Domestic Violence: A Judge's Guide,* 19 (2004, rev. 2006) developed under grant number SJI-03-N-103 from the State Justice Institute.

over to me per a property settlement agreement. I was ordered to pay him $158,000 within thirty days. As a result, I filed for bankruptcy. A second contempt motion under a new case number has been filed, with an additional $20,000 claim. My constitutional due process rights, my right of notice and the opportunity to be heard, my right to discovery, and my right to protection against double jeopardy were all violated.

Appeals were made to the Georgia Supreme Court, but the court dismissed them. On May 18, 2007, I was one of ten petitioners who filed a complaint against the United States with the Inter-American Commission on Human Rights. On September 6, 2007, I filed a petition for a writ of *certiorari* in the U.S. Supreme Court. The Supreme Court failed to grant the writ.

I have been jailed, prosecuted, and found not guilty. I have published a book, *A Mother's Journal: Let My Children Go*, and sent approximately 1,000 copies to legislators and the government of Georgia, where my children reside. I walked 518 miles across the historic "Trail of Tears" to bring attention to a legal system that desperately needs reform. I receive numerous phone calls from other parents who, like me, have lost their abused children because they turned to the courts for help. I continue to endure attacks by a court that seeks revenge because I spoke out on this issue and continued my attempts to protect my daughters. The court has threatened the attorneys who represented me with the loss of their licenses. The judge has called my friends, supporters, and expert witnesses "kamikazes," and threatened the jurors with the loss of their homes, cars, and livelihoods for writing their letter.

One day, my daughters will know that I love them more than life and that I did everything I could to protect them. I am still their mother, and a mother protects her young.

IN HER BEST INTERESTS—ANNETTE ZENDER'S STORY

My daughter was only five years old when I had to leave an abusive and violent man who is her biological father but was never my husband. When she was between six and nine years of age, she told some of her teachers, the school principal, other adults, and two counselors, that her father was scary and violent, he was touching her, sleeping with her on a regular basis, and taking nude photos of her. They thought it was in her best interests to contact the local authorities.

In 1997, a Minnesota judge, having presided at trial, issued a court order awarding me sole custody and awarding her father restricted visitation. Unhappy over being held accountable for his behavior, he sought a friendlier jurisdiction[2] (Illinois) in which to challenge the custody order, contending that it was not in *his* best interests to live under court orders issued by the state of Minnesota.

When I sent my daughter to school on the morning of September 11, 2001, it seemed like any other day. But on that especially fateful day, parents across America and throughout the globe would be moved to hug their children especially hard, promising to keep them safe in the face of the 9/11 terrorist attacks. That was also the day my daughter was taken from her school, and from me, and placed in the arms of her violent father. There had been no due process of law, no notice, no time to respond, no hearing, and no presentation of evidence from both sides. I did not even know that a ruling had been made until after my child was virtually, and legally, kidnapped from me.

---

[2] This is known as "forum shopping."

Despite the Illinois court's assumption that the father would act in our daughter's best interests, he did not enroll her in school. He exposed her to pornography, entered her room late at night wearing nothing but his underwear, kept loaded weapons in his home, including an Uzi assault rifle (according to his own admission in a police report), and continued to expose her to his fits of rage. This is according to eyewitnesses who had the courage to come forward in the face of threats to their safety.

What statutory foundation of law was the basis for this unconstitutional court order? None! There is no statutory basis in Illinois law for allegations of "alienation," a watered-down version of the PAS fabrication of Richard Gardner and the "fathers' rights" (FRs) movement, which was never proven by research or peer-reviewed studies and has been thoroughly de-bunked. However, in a "child custody evaluation" report rendered by Daniel DeWitt, of Barrington, Illinois, I was accused of coaching my child to tell stories of abuse by her father. I allegedly traumatized my child during supervised visitation. Why was I accused of such noncrimes? My daughter cried and begged me to take her home (to my home). She begged a judge, in an *in camera* proceeding, to be allowed to see me unsupervised.

I have never been accused of abuse, maltreatment, or neglect of my children or the foster children that have been placed in my care since I became a licensed Illinois foster parent in 1998.

From June 2006 to October 2006, three witnesses came forward to protect my child whom they witnessed being abused, isolated, and not sent to school by her father. Two of these witnesses served as caregivers and employees of the father in his home. They gave sworn eyewitness testimony of the father's violence in the home toward themselves, our child, and animals. They testified to the father's excessive use of alcohol, his threats involving guns, his use of pornography and coercion of our daughter to view pornography with him, his invasion of her room late at night while he wore nothing but underwear, and to the fact she never attended school.

Counsel for the father, Norman Kurtz, and GAL Gary Schlesinger, when questioning the eyewitnesses, focused singularly on discrediting the witnesses on character first and foremost and then on point of fact as an afterthought. There was no significant contrary point-of-fact testimony with which to discredit the witnesses.

Gary Schlesinger, whose job was supposed to be protecting my child, argued that there was no material change in circumstances because the father was violent before the change in custody, and he is still violent. Despite the evidence from neutral witnesses, Judge Joseph Waldeck, ruled there had been "no material change of circumstance" in the best interests of the child, as is the statutory basis for overturning child custody decisions under Illinois law.

In other words, according to the court, my child's best interests are being served in the household of a violent man who, according to neutral eyewitness testimony, engaged in inappropriate sexual activity, lack of schooling, violence to animals, weapons in the home, violent tirades, and excessive use of alcohol.

While the court has been unwilling to protect my daughter, it has had no such compunction about protecting itself and retaliating against me, the protective parent. The court imposed $50,000 in sanctions to punish me for presenting the evidence by the two neutral witnesses to my daughter's abuse. Unable to pay the retaliatory sanctions, I face jail and financial ruin for trying to protect my daughter.

In 2006, the court sought to silence me by imposing a gag order designed to prevent the parties or their attorneys from discussing the case with third parties. This was retaliation for the negative publicity the court received for failing to protect an innocent child. The court's violation of my First Amendment rights backfired when I walked into the office of the local newspaper. In compliance with the court's illegal order, I said nothing and instead wore a purple scarf over my mouth. This picture appeared on the front page of the newspaper with an article exposing the improper actions of the court. Nevertheless, my daughter remains with her abuser, unable to see me, her mother.

HELPING MYSELF AND HELPING OTHERS—PAIGE HODSON'S STORY

In 1998, I made one of the toughest decisions of my life. I finally got the courage to leave my eleven-year marriage to a man who had physically, emotionally, and mentally abused me. I had tried to leave once before but had been charmed back by his promises to change and by my own guilt over depriving my child of an intact family. But this time, I was resolute: he had begun to abuse my daughter in similar ways. Hurt me? Maybe. But hurt my children, and you get no more chances.

At the time, I had a newborn baby boy and a six-year-old daughter to consider. When I filed for divorce, I assumed that the legal process would be 100 percent child centered and that it would make custody and visitation decisions based on what would be safe and developmentally appropriate for small children. I was not surprised when my ex-husband contested custody, as he had been threatening to do so. My attorney agreed to use the services of a custody evaluator. I assumed, once again, that the evaluation process would be fair and impartial and that there was no predetermined outcome.

Instead, what I encountered from the legal system was the imposition, at all costs, of a joint physical custody agenda, along with improper *ex parte* communications between the evaluator and my husband's attorney, and little if any concern for the children's developmental needs, my husband's DV, or the children's own statements and preferences.

After I reported the DV perpetrated by my ex-husband, and once the custody investigation process had begun, the mud-slinging by the other side came fast and furiously.

The wild and unfounded accusations made by my ex and his attorney were given more credence than my own and my children's accounts, which were documented by history, by collateral witnesses, and by voluminous documentation. The court professionals working on my case diagnosed me with bizarre, misogynistic syndromes, claiming that I suffered from psychological dysfunctions I had never heard of: enmeshment, PAS, and Munchausen Syndrome by Proxy (MSBP). Astonishingly, the judge accepted their gender-biased theories and junk science diagnostic labels.

At the end of the first custody trial, I was warned that if I did not accept a 50/50 custody arrangement, after our case was reviewed a year later, the father just might receive full custody of our two children. Upon hearing the judge's decision, I went into a state of dazed bewilderment, feeling like Alice falling down the rabbit hole in Wonderland. The judge had stripped me and my child of confidentiality as far as what we said in therapy. He punished me for reporting abuse, and he warned me to stop talking about it under threat of losing my children. None of this made a shred of sense. I had to find a solution, and quickly.[3]

---

[3] Ultimately I received sole custody and my ex-husband received visitation every other weekend and half of the summer. His actions have caused problems in his relationships with the children.

As an alternative to psychotherapy, I sought out services from my local DV agency. The staff there was supportive and guaranteed confidentiality, but they had no real experience dealing with abusers' legal strategies in custody cases. Knowing next to nothing at that time about the Internet, I spent night after night searching for answers. Whenever I conducted a search using keywords such as child custody, mothers and custody, parental alienation, and similar terms, I was directed to Web pages touting "fathers' rights." It seemed as though, while I had been asleep, my value to our society as a mother had fallen to zero. The more I researched, the more I found disturbing ties between those who developed the bogus syndromes used by court professionals and leanings toward perversions like pedophilia and incest. The FRs Web sites dismissed all claims of abuse as false. I discovered the growing use of Machiavellian and draconian measures to punish women who complained about abuse that had been perpetrated by their ex-partners on themselves or their children.

Finally, I found an online noncustodial mothers' support group. I eventually learned that roughly 90 percent of the 100 or so women on this news list had experienced some form of DV; in some cases, they had been in relationships with men who were substance abusers and/or neglectful or uninvolved fathers of their children. In our exchanges, we joked that we had all married the same man, since our partners' abuse, manipulation, control, and perversion of the system sounded eerily similar.

I began asking around for referrals to experts of national caliber who were trained in DV, child abuse, and trauma. Names slowly emerged, although most mothers could ill afford to pay the fees charged by these experts. Still, as the women in our group began to realize that they were not alone, the seeds of activism began to sprout. Many of our members were motivated to agitate for change on a broader level, while an even larger number wanted to form local support groups.

In working with others who walked in my shoes, and by sharing support and information with each other, I found that we all desperately needed many of the same things—first and foremost, education about the legal system. I began to work on creating an educational Web site to fill the gap. Thus, "Custody Preparation for Moms" (http://www.custodyprepformoms.org) was born. Today, almost ten years later, the Web site is getting thousands of hits per day.

To this day, there are many battered mothers struggling to navigate a legal system that has been turned upside down. The good news is that the movement toward women helping women with family court issues has grown exponentially. This is a trend that I hope and believe will continue.

BECOMING AN ACTIVIST—LARISSA POLLICA'S STORY

My first sense that my family court case was only one of thousands that had gone horribly awry came while I was attending the Fourth Battered Mothers Custody Conference in January 2006. Looking across the room at all the faces of mothers who had been treated unjustly, I realized that I was one of many; therefore, something was very wrong—not with me, but with the family court system itself. Armed with the knowledge I gained at the conference, I began looking around my area for other mothers like me. I felt driven to do whatever I could to help my own children as well as

---

My daughter is now eighteen, but when she was younger, she often refused to go for visitation after unpleasant incidents with her father. My son, now eleven, dislikes visitation but goes grudgingly. My children are doing well academically and socially, and I am so proud of them.

others who would go through the meat grinder of the family court machine. Through word of mouth, I located approximately fifteen mothers who had been mistreated by the system and whose children were suffering. We were a diverse group, consisting of stay-at-home moms and career women—teachers, nurses, lawyers, and others.

When we met, we discussed our individual cases and identified the amazing similarities we shared. The common thread weaving us together was that all of us had petitioned the court for protection from an abusive husband/partner or a sexually abusive parent. Instead of being allowed to keep ourselves and our children safe, we were blamed for "provoking" our partners' abuse, or we were accused of being "irrationally concerned" about child sexual abuse. Despite providing all manner of reliable documentation, we were simply not believed.

We learned that the law guardians and the court-appointed psychologists were the biggest players and the worst offenders here, as judges were known to frequently rubber stamp whatever these professionals recommended. We found out that those responsible for rendering these life-changing decisions were not educated or otherwise knowledgeable about DV and its effects on children. For example, a mother might speak to her child's court-appointed law guardian for only a few moments before the guardian would make a written recommendation regarding her child's future. Despite seeing our tears and our anxiety, these court agents viewed our desperate attempts to protect our children from their fathers' violence as "not promoting a positive relationship with the father." All of us were accused in some way of being "crazy." (I found it peculiar that most of us were given the same vague diagnosis: "possibly a personality disorder of some type.")

We all live in Ithaca, New York, a small community where relationships between court personnel—law guardians, court psychologists, and judges—inevitably become intertwined and symbiotic. We came to realize that divorce has generated a huge industry and that the money made by those who run the industry, the lawyers and other family court professionals, is exorbitant.

Our first idea for changing the divorce industry was to remove the secrecy by which the court works. Our goal was to publicly expose what the court was doing to children by shining a spotlight on it in hopes of holding the court players accountable for their actions and decisions. We wrote articles for the local newspaper on what we had experienced, especially with the law guardians and psychologists who worked in the area. We wrote lengthy complaints about the law guardians to our local Tompkins County Bar Association, to the director of the law guardians' program in Albany, and to the New York State Committee on Professional Standards. We wrote equally detailed complaints about the court-appointed psychologists to the American Psychological Association and to the psychologists' Office of Professional Discipline. We wrote to the governor. We invited DV experts, lawyers, the police chief, members of a family court advisory committee, and a member of our state assembly to come to our group to brainstorm solutions to the problems we were encountering. We held a demonstration in front of the local courthouse, which was covered by our local news station. Our regional paper, the *Ithaca Times,* featured a photo of our demonstration on the front page, accompanied by an article about how the family court system is failing children and families. In the photo, we were shown carrying big signs with statements like, "Law Guardian Aligns With Abuser," "Judge Separates Siblings," and "Court-Appointed Psychologist Has No Domestic Violence Training."

It felt tremendously empowering to announce to the public that the people working inside the courthouse were damaging so many lives. But our hope of exposing the corruption and incompetence that we had witnessed in the court system and for bringing about immediate change was beginning to fade. In response to our written complaints, we were receiving short, sterile letters from the responsible agencies who made claims such as, "The serious concerns of the complainant do not meet cause for action," or "The alleged violations have already been adequately addressed in another forum," or "This matter will now be considered by our staff, although the Committee is prohibited by law from revealing the nature of the action taken." Elliot Spitzer, New York's governor at that time, never even bothered to write back. In other words, we found that the psychologists, law guardians, and other court agents were being allowed to run amok. There seemed to be no governing body to monitor, evaluate, or control what was taking place in the court, no responsible authority willing and able to reprimand them for a job poorly done.

There was, in addition, a backlash against some of the mothers who were active in our group. The two judges in our town clamped down hard on them for their perceived transgressions, and they were punished more harshly than ever for objecting to the cruel and inept treatment being dished out to them and their children by the family court. One of the lawyers I consulted with practically begged me to "stay under the radar."

Our consensus was that our cases were not about our competence and strength as mothers, but rather about the embarrassment we were causing the court by our complaints, objections, and noncompliance with the judges' authority. The court was certainly not used to having a group of infuriated mothers demonstrating at its doorstep, and so it went to great lengths to discredit us and separate us even further from our children.

The best thing that has come out of our activism is the network of friendship and support that we created. We call each other on the phone when our children are acting out their grief and confusion, when we receive dreaded court papers in the mail, when we go to court, and when one of us has to go pick up our children from a dangerous ex-partner. Our old friends, our acquaintances, and even our family members have become overwhelmed by the battles generated by the family court system. We have, at least, each other to provide us with a measure of comfort and hope.

Authors' Note

Annette Zender's story is presented as told to Carroll White. Carroll White is a cofounder of the Illinois Coalition for Family Court Reform, a freelance writer, and a protective parent. For more information, see http://www.icfcr.org.

Part 3
Causes of and Contributors to the Problem

Chapter 11

Reframing Child Custody Decisions in the Context of Coercive Control

by Evan Stark, Ph.D., M.S.W.

INTRODUCTION AND BACKGROUND

The prevailing conceit in family court is that children are best served when their access to both parents is preserved to the maximum extent feasible after divorce. Indeed, seventeen states plus the District of Columbia have statutory presumptions favoring joint custody.[1] Nowhere are the prospects for future contact by both parents more in doubt than where one or both of the parties allege violence or other forms of abuse. Nor are other problems encountered by family judges or evaluators comparable to battering in prevalence, duration, scope, dynamics, effect on personhood, and their significance for children's well-being. Domestic violence (DV) may affect one adult woman in five and a considerably higher proportion of those engaged in custody disputes. As the chapter by Crooks, Jaffe, and Bala (Chapter 22) in this volume makes abundantly clear, it is a major context for a range of medical, behavioral, and mental health problems that can affect parenting and is the context for almost half of all child abuse,[2] much of it occurring after couples separate or divorce. Indeed, both women and men who are separated have a higher risk of being killed or severely assaulted by a partner than if they are married, though the absolute numbers for men at risk are small. Some researchers believe that mere exposure to parental violence can have traumatic and long-term effects on children that resemble child abuse. Moreover, as this chapter will make clear, the spectrum of harms in partner abuse cases extends far beyond the violence that has been widely studied. These less tangible harms affect basic dimensions of personhood such as autonomy and decision making and may threaten children's well-being even more fundamentally than threats to their or their parent's physical safety.

Despite the significance of DV in disputed custody cases, judges, lawyers, evaluators, and advocates who work with families remain sharply divided about the appropriate response. So do litigants. Horrific stories of women who have lost custody to abusive partners or been punished, even jailed, for disobeying court orders to provide unsupervised visitation to these men are commonplace. On the basis of interviews with female custodial litigants in Massachusetts, the "Battered Women's Testimony Project" at the Wellesley Center for Women documented a pattern of discrimination, mistreatment, and arbitrary or biased rulings they framed as human rights violations.[3] Using the same approach, the Arizona Coalition Against Domestic Violence uncovered identical grievances.[4]

Fathers also tell dramatic stories about being unjustly accused of physical or child sexual abuse by their wives and exiled by the family court to a lifetime of alienation from their children. Building on these stories, "father's rights" (FRs) groups and their supporters use their Web sites to insist that husbands, not wives, are the real victims of bias, to discount documented injustice to mothers, and to attack "feminists," "protective mothers," and their supporters. When PBS aired *Breaking the Silence* in 2005,[5] a documentary that featured critics who dubbed the use of Parental Alienation Syndrome

---

[1] K.T. Bartlett, "Improving the Law Relating to Postdivorce Arrangements for Children," in *The Post-Divorce Family: Children, Parenting and Society* 71 (R. Thompson & P.R. Amato eds., 2000).

[2] E. Stark & A. Flitcraft, *Women at Risk: Domestic Violence and Women's Health* (1996); E. Stark, "The Battered Mother in the Child Protective Service Caseload: Developing an Appropriate Response," 23(2) *Women's Rts. L. Rep.* 107 (Spring 2002) [hereinafter Stark (2002)].

[3] K.Y. Slote et al., "Battered Mothers Speak Out: Participatory Human Rights Documentation as a Model for Research and Activism in the United States," 11(11) *Violence Against Women*, 1367 (2005).

[4] D. Post & Arizona Coalition Against Domestic Violence, *Battered Mother's Testimony Project: A Human Rights Approach to Domestic Violence and Child Custody* (2003).

[5] *Breaking the Silence: Children's Stories*, a documentary produced by Dominique and Catherine Lasseur (http://www.tatgelasseur.com) was broadcast on most PBS stations in October 2005.

(PAS) to counter abuse allegations as junk science, a letter-writing campaign spearheaded by FRs publicist Glen Sacks won support from the station's "advocate," a watchdog appointed by President Bush, and PBS hastily produced a more "balanced" film. From California to Maine and Alaska, coalitions of protective mothers and court reformers have challenged legislation making joint custody the default disposition in family disputes, advocated for the presumption of sole custody in abuse cases, and demanded greater transparency and accountability for the range of professionals involved in family court, including judges. In response, researchers from Canada, the United States, and Great Britain recently convened a national conference to challenge what they believe is a "feminist" stranglehold on research and policy in the DV field, asking, "Does Gender Matter?" and answering in the negative. FRs groups have initiated lawsuits in Minnesota, California, and elsewhere demanding that public funds be equally spent to support shelters for "battered men."

Amidst the practical realities that constrain their work, judges and evaluators are expected to set these political conflicts aside, envision a unique family whose willingness or capacity to resolve critical disputes has broken down, perhaps irretrievably, and to dispassionately apply the law as well as their training, experience, and the limited assessment tools at their disposal to map a workable postseparation arrangement least likely to harm children. Given the complexity of this process, the huge variation in the qualifications of those involved, and the often contradictory legislative contexts in which family court decisions are made, it is inevitable that some proportion of outcomes will appear unfair and leave abuse victims and their children at risk. Biased treatment of even a small proportion of litigants is a concern. But is the number of persons put at risk by court bias and the resulting harm significant enough to merit a public response? Even if bias is commonplace in family court, does it constitute a discriminatory pattern? In other words, is the proportion of abuse victims who receive differential treatment sufficient to suggest that bias is systemic, that it advantages a class of persons because of their sex, race, or social class, or is it the byproduct of individual prejudice, ignorance, or malfeasance? If the latter is true, training and monitoring should provide sufficient correctives. More fundamental reforms are needed to correct systemic bias.

THE LONG MARCH

Confrontation with the family court is only the latest step in a "long march" through which advocates for DV victims have tried to rid public institutions of practices they insist are discriminatory against women. Previous efforts have largely succeeded, in part because the arguments defending the status quo are so transparent, and the political forces advancing these arguments are relatively weak. When the first battered women's shelters opened in the early 1970s, it was still widely believed that DV was a male prerogative. It had no standing in the social sciences. Psychiatry and psychology assumed it was rare and attributed it to maladaptive family dynamics or to personality problems (such as masochism or "dependent personality disorder"). Today, largely as a result of federal and state legislation promoted by advocates and their supporters, laws and policies throughout the United States and in hundreds of other countries reflect the prevailing understanding that DV is a widespread and criminal act primarily committed by men to gain "power and control" over female partners or former partners. Equally widespread is the belief that states are obligated to extend protections afforded to women through arrest, court orders, and counseling to their children.

One basis for the societal revolution in how we approach DV is lawsuits arguing that failing to protect persons from partner abuse violated their Fourteenth Amendment right to equal protection. In finding for the plaintiffs in these suits, courts made it clear that neither the site of an assault nor the fact that the parties are married or intimate compromised their right to legal protections, the same view that had extended the protections of rape laws to partners starting in the 1970s. While the sex discrimination protections afforded in Title VII of the 1964 Civil Rights Act[6] have yet to be formally extended to personal life, the Violence Against Women Act passed in 1994[7] in the United States defined abuse as a crime motivated by "an animus based on the victim's gender" and allowed DV victims to seek civil rights relief based on the view of abuse as a group-based harm rooted in inequality, giving victims a common point of reference to counter the claim that it is a private concern or the result of their complicity. Although this provision was found unconstitutional in *United States v. Morrison*,[8] it received bipartisan endorsement in the Congress.

SEPARATE PLANETS?

If the link between sexual inequality and partner abuse is not universally recognized, the belief that DV is a gendered crime from which women and children particularly require institutional protection is widely accepted in policy circles, the criminal justice system, medicine, and the social services. But it remains controversial in the civil arena and particularly in family court, where the tenet remains strong that the private sphere of family life should be immune from the principles of formal justice that govern criminal law and that "discrimination" (assumed to be a problem best left to federal courts) and the relationship problems seen in state family courts are mutually exclusive phenomena. Resistance to a gendered analysis of abuse in family court and the tenacity with which key players in this arena hold arguments discredited in criminal court also reflect the financial stakes at risk in family proceedings and the relative privilege and political power of the men who would be disadvantaged by acceptance of this view compared to those who typically bear the brunt of criminal sanctions.

British scholar Marianne Hester[9] has dramatized the different and often contradictory assumptions that criminal and family courts bring to bear in DV cases by referring to them as "separate planets." In criminal court, a woman who presents evidence of abuse is considered a strong and cooperative witness. But if she presses these same claims in family court, she risks being identified as vindictive or uncooperative with "friendly parent" assumptions. The criminal court addresses equity concerns by using its authority to redress the imbalance of power exploited through abuse; in family court, abusive fathers are assumed to have an equity interest in custody. The "perpetrator" of DV may now be reframed by an evaluating psychologist as "the good enough father." No-contact orders are commonplace in DV proceedings. But they are extremely rare in custody cases, even in the face of identical evidence. To the contrary, even victims who hold a no-contact order may be held in contempt if they fail to provide access to an abusive father. At best, family courts can help couples set

---

[6] Pub. L. No. 88-352, 78 Stat. 241 (July 2, 1964).

[7] Pub. L. No. 103-322, 108 Stat. 1796 (Sept. 13, 1994).

[8] 529 U.S. 598 (2000).

[9] M. Hester, "Future Trends and Developments—Violence Against Women in Europe and East Asia," 10(2) *Violence Against Women* 1451 (2004).

aside long-standing grievances for the sake of the children. At worst, the normative emphasis on cooperation leads court professionals to misread partner abuse as a form of "high conflict," rationalize unworkable proposals for contact, and then turn on victims when these plans fail.

In 1997, in part to overcome inconsistencies between family and criminal court practice, Congress passed the "Morella resolution," so-named after its sponsor, Congresswoman Connie Morella (R-Maryland), recommending that state courts give presumptive custody to victims of DV. Some variation of this recommendation has been adopted by most states. While the language of these statutes is gender neutral, it was widely understood that their primary beneficiaries would be battered women. FRs groups claim these statutes have exacerbated the prevailing antimale bias in the family court.

A less extreme position, the so-called gender neutral approach, acknowledges that men commit the more serious forms of DV.[10] Even so, insist proponents of this argument, the DV seen in family court is less serious than the types seen by police or criminal courts, which typically consist of isolated episodes provoked by the stress of separation rather than chronic abuse and is rooted in the dysfunctional interpersonal dynamics specific to a given relationship, in personality deficits, or in the sorts of childhood experiences key to other psychiatric or behavioral problems. Research psychologists in Canada and England have extended this claim to abuse generally.[11] Although this argument echoes the victim-blaming psychiatric explanations of abuse that prevailed when the DV revolution began, this does not mean it is wrong. Moreover, framing DV as one among the many personality or behavioral problems seen in family court gives the argument an intuitive appeal to judges and custody evaluators. If a pattern of maladaptive or dysfunctional behavior is the core obstacle, then shared custody can be facilitated by some combination of adjustment counseling, family systems work, or psychotherapy, short-term interventions that are commonly recommended to ease the difficult transition faced by divorcing couples. In contrast to the mainstream view of DV as volitional, instrumental behavior rooted in sexual inequality and sexist cultural norms, the "gender neutral" approach holds that the sheer existence of DV is insufficient to justify restricting parental access, particularly when the only evidence is of minor or isolated assaults.

The remaining sections of this chapter set the questions being debated in the context of a new body of knowledge about the scope and dynamics of abuse, distinguishing DV from the pattern of "coercive control" I and others have identified with "battering" and explaining why the current focus on violent episodes can mask the most devastating facets of abuse. In making the argument that DV is a sentinel event in custody cases, advocates and researchers have focused on how children are harmed by exposure to parental assaults. Much less is known about the dynamics and consequences of coercive control, a situation in which children commonly become both direct objects of an abuser's control and instruments of his attempts to control their mother. Coercive control may involve relatively minor levels of physical violence, leading judges and evaluators to conclude that abuse is not serious. In fact, because

---

[10] J.W. Gould, D. Martindale & M. Eidman, "Assessing Allegations of Domestic Violence," 4(1/2) *J. Child Custody* 1 (2007).

[11] D.G. Dutton, "Domestic Abuse Assessment in Child Custody Disputes: Beware the Domestic Violence Research Paradigm," 2(4) *J. Child Custody* 23 (2005) [hereinafter Dutton (2005)]; D.G. Dutton, "On Comparing Apples With Apples Deemed Nonexistent: A Reply to Johnson," 2(4) *J. Child Custody* 53 (2005).

the tactics used to isolate, intimidate, and control partners in coercive control directly target a mother's autonomy, they often compromise parental decision making even more profoundly than physical assault. If the risks associated with coercive control are typically more far reaching than when DV alone is involved, they are also more difficult to identify, particularly when attempts are made to interpret the significance of abuse through the prism of discrete acts of violence. Because victims of coercive control are subjected to multiple tactics often over many years, its cumulative effects are likely to include high levels of fear, anger, dependence, or confusion. These effects are likely to seem grossly disproportionate when weighed against documented or alleged incidents of physical assault, most of which are likely to be relatively minor. As a result, the consequences of coercive control are often attributed to exaggeration, duplicity, malevolence, or foundational deficits in parenting that justify limiting or denying access to a protective mother.

Clarifying the extent and dynamics of abuse and the risks it poses gives us a basis against which to measure evaluation and decision making in disputed custody cases. If the FRs groups and their supporters are correct about the antimale bias in family court, we would expect to find that restrictions are being placed on men's access in cases where partner abuse is merely alleged (falsely in the view of FRs groups) as well as where hard evidence of prior abusive behavior is presented. If the protective mothers are correct, we would find that courts, evaluators, and other related professionals are minimizing or denying the significance of abuse or even responding punitively to women who raise abuse as an issue in custody disputes, possibly by giving custody to abusive fathers. If the family courts are behaving equitably, as defenders of the status quo claim, we would expect to find a greater sensitivity to abuse in family court decisions but not bias. This would be reflected, for example, if protective measures were being routinely implemented when abuse is proved, an outcome FRs groups would be hard pressed to oppose, but not where it is merely alleged. In this case, the major challenge would be to find better ways to collect, communicate, and present evidence of abuse in family court.

The final question addressed is whether the pattern of response to abuse by family courts can be usefully framed as the sort of "discrimination" that formerly characterized the response to abuse by other institutions, "reverse discrimination" as the FRs groups contend, or as too idiosyncratic to be considered systemic. The outcomes of custodial disputes involving abuse bear on the long-term health and safety of several million children annually as well as on the happiness, health, and safety of their parents. If a condition of systemic discrimination in abuse cases exists and is allowed to persist, the overall legitimacy of the family court as an institutional arbiter of marital dissolution may be jeopardized.

THE NATURE OF ABUSE SEEN IN THE CUSTODIAL CONTEXT

In the majority of divorces that involve children, including those precipitated by abuse, couples arrive at custodial arrangements either by agreement or default. Partner violence is a factor in anywhere from one-third to one-half of the minority where custody is disputed.[12] In about half of these cases, somewhere between 15 and 25 percent of all disputed cases, there is substantiating evidence of physical abuse such as

---

[12] M.P. Johnson, "Apples and Oranges in Child Custody Disputes: Intimate Terrorism vs. Situational Couple Violence, 2(4) *J. Child Custody* 43 (2005).

a prior arrest for DV, a criminal court finding, or court order.[13] Given its prevalence and potential significance, it would seem clear that routine assessment for abuse in disputed custody cases is a prerequisite for any reasonable determination of equity and a child's best interest.

From Domestic Violence to Coercive Control

Between the early 1960s, when we learned that a higher proportion of police calls involved "domestics" than all other violent acts combined, and the adaptation of mandatory arrest statutes in the 1980s, society's response to abuse was revolutionized. These changes were elicited by the legal challenges already mentioned, a grassroots movement that opened shelters in hundreds of communities to which women who identified themselves as "battered" flocked in droves, and a burgeoning research literature on the extent and seriousness of abuse and the relative effectiveness of sanctions.

Hallmarks of Physical Abuse

Since the mid-1970s, more than 12,000 research monographs have been published documenting the prevalence of partner violence in the general population as well as among various subgroups, including medical and mental health patients, mothers of abused children, and petitioners for divorce.[14] This research documented the three most salient dimensions of abuse: its significance as a source of injury and a range of other physical and psychological problems, its frequency, and its duration. In the early 1980s, on the basis of a randomized review of the medical records of more than 3,500 women who came to Yale's emergency room, Dr. Anne Flitcraft and I reported that DV accounted for about four times as many injuries presented to the hospital as auto accidents (40 percent versus 11 percent), considered the most common source of adult injury at the time, and affected almost twice as many patients (18 percent versus 11 percent).[15] Physical abuse was also shown to be frequent, with rates varying from 3.7 to 8 assaults annually in community samples,[16] and as many as 35 percent of female victims reported being abused daily in cases where police arrest the offender.[17] Our hospital data and longitudinal studies of battered women show that abuse continues for between five and seven years on average, a fact that has elicited a broad ranging debate about "why women stay" with abusive men.[18] In a comparison of battered and

---

[13] M.A. Kernic et al., "Children in the Crossfire: Child Custody Determinations Among Couples With a History of Intimate Partner Violence," 11 *Violence Against Women* 991 (2005).

[14] H.L. MacMillan & N. Wathen, "Family Violence Research: Lessons Learned and Where From Here?" 294 *J. Am. Med. Ass'n* 618 (2005).

[15] Stark & Flitcraft, *supra* note 2.

[16] R.H.C. Teske & M.L. Parker, *Spouse Abuse in Texas: A Study of Women's Attitudes and Experiences* (Criminal Justice Center, Sam Houston State University, 1983); P. Klaus & M. Rand,. *Family Violence: Special Report* (Bureau of Justice Statistics, 1984).

[17] D. Brookoff et al., "Characteristics of Participants in Domestic Violence: Assessment at the Scene of Domestic Assault," 277(17) *J. Am. Med. Ass'n* 1369 (1997).

[18] Stark & Flitcraft, *supra* note 2; J. Campbell et al., "Voices of Strength and Resistance: A Cntextual and Longitudinal Analysis of Women's Responses to Battering, 14 *J. Interpersonal Violence* 743 (1998).

nonbattered women in the hospital population, Dr. Flitcraft and I discovered that, after the onset of abuse, battered women's risk of attempting suicide, becoming homeless, and developing secondary medical, behavioral, and mental health problems such as alcoholism increased dramatically, and that abuse was a major context in which these problems emerged for women generally. No similar risk profile characterizes other populations of assault victims, including persons assaulted by strangers, men abused by female partners, or men or women abused by same sex partners. An outstanding challenge, therefore, was to identify the distinguishing features of woman battering by male partners that elicited this profile. Another important finding was that the vast majority of abuse seen in the helping system is long standing rather than "new." This fact has two implications, that effective intervention can substantially impact the burden abuse places on women, children, and the community and that current interventions are largely ineffective in protecting women and their children from further abuse.

Translating these findings for custodial decision making is complicated by three flaws in how abuse is understood: its equation with discrete episodes of physical violence, applying a calculus of physical harms to assess seriousness, and the identification of DV with marriage or intact relationships. Absent evidence that an injurious assault has occurred, it is hard to justify protective intervention. Moreover, protection orders and many other interventions are predicated on the mistaken notion that separation effectively curtails DV, even if it does not end completely.

Most states do not require evidence of injury to arrest a perpetrator for DV. As a practical matter, however, arrests and other interventions are set in motion by demonstrable harm. This is problematic for victims, however, because, despite their significance for injury, the vast majority of abusive episodes are relatively minor, involving pushing, grabbing, holding, slapping, hair pulling, and the like. This is true even at those sites, like the military or the emergency room, where we would expect to find the most injurious violence. Of 11,000 substantiated abuse cases reported to the military in 2001, for example, 57 percent involved no injury at all, another 36 percent prompted one visit to outpatient care, and only 7 percent could be classified as "severe."[19] In our study of the emergency medical population, fewer than one in fifty women required hospitalization.

Since the vast majority of incidents of partner violence are minor, and few of the protections or sanctions won by advocates are set in motion by minor incidents, we need look no further than the incident-specific focus in DV law to understand why, in most states, DV crimes are treated as second-class misdemeanors for which almost no one goes to jail. The belief that abuse is minor if there have only been minor acts of violence misses the hallmarks of a victim's experience documented above, the devastating fear and dependence elicited by frequent abuse over an extended period. But the present approach does more than trivialize women's experience. When the incident-specific approach is used to frame allegations of abuse in family court, the cumulative fear victims experience can appear grossly disproportionate to "the evidence," lending credibility to a perpetrator's insistence that they are exaggerating, lying, crazy, or trying to "alienate" their children. A related problem arises when the duration of abuse claimed or the absence of documentation by police, criminal

---

[19] Caliber Associates, *Symposium on DV Prevention Research* (Department of Defense, 2002).

courts, shelters, or other service sites are taken to mean that the partner's abuse cannot have been frequent or serious.

Issue of Sex Parity in Abuse

Another result of the flawed thinking is the deduction that fathers are as likely to be battered as mothers.[20] This belief is based on evidence from community surveys that female partners are as likely as male partners, or almost as likely, to use violent tactics in conflicts. The most comprehensive review of these surveys finds that women are somewhat more likely than men to use tactics considered minor (such as throwing an object); that "mutual" violence is more common than violence used by one partner alone; and that men are significantly more likely to engage in behaviors (such as "beat up," "choke or strangle") considered "severe" and many times more likely, by a ratio of 4:1, to use forms of coercion identified with control, such as pinning or holding a partner down.[21] The National Violence Against Women Survey (NVAWS), the largest and most reliable national population survey to date, also reports that women are three times more likely than men to have suffered DV over their lifetime and seventeen times more likely to have been "badly beaten."[22] Still, the annual female to male victimization ratio of DV reported by the NVAWS is only 1.4:1, a significant difference and certainly equivalent to ratios that have led public health and medicine to identify sex as a major risk factor, but not nearly so dramatic as one might intuitively expect.

The community surveys have been faulted for neglecting motive, meaning, and consequence. Apart from determining whether a partner's violence is defensive or retaliatory, this omission is probably not significant for the severest forms of violence, since these are serious regardless of their context. However, context is critical in distinguishing the types of minor violence men and women may use in "fights" from the routine use of minor violence as part of an ongoing pattern of battering. One factor that distinguishes "fights," in which both parties are assumed to have an equally instrumental stake in aggression, from "abuse," in which one partner uses coercion to subjugate another, is the perceived need by a victim for outside assistance. It is instructive, therefore, that, apart from the growing proportion of women arrested for DV, most in the context of "dual" arrests, not one of the thousands of point-of-service studies have identified a significant proportion of male victims who seek help.

---

[20] Dutton (2005), *supra* note 11; Gould, Martindale & Eidman, *supra* note 10.

[21] J. Archer, "Sex Differences in Aggression Between Heterosexual Partners: A Meta-Analytic Review," 126 *Psychol. Bull.* 651 (2000). While methodologically sophisticated, Archer's work relies heavily on studies of dating violence, omits the results of the National Violence Against Women Survey (NVAWS; *see infra* note 22), the largest and most comprehensive assessment of domestic violence nationwide, and minimizes the significance of the very large differences between female and male partner victimization over the life course.

[22] M.A. Straus & R. Gelles, *Physical Violence in American Families: Risk Factors and Adaptations to Violence in 1,145 Families* (1990); R. Gelles, *Domestic Violence Not an Even Playing Field* (1998), *available at* http://thesafetyzone.org/everyone/gelles.html (no longer available); P. Tjaden & N. Thoennes, "Prevalence and Consequences of Male to Female and Female to Male Intimate Partner Violence as Measured by the National Violence Against Women Survey," 6(2) *Violence Against Women* 142 (2000).

FRs groups and their supporters explain the absence of "battered men" from the rolls of help-seekers by pointing out that the "feminist"-driven legal and policy framework that shapes intervention targets men as perpetrators and women as victims almost exclusively. In this reasoning, "woman" battering was only widely recognized after shelters for women opened. The "hidden" population of battered men to which the surveys point would surface if only funds were properly redirected in a "gender neutral" way.

Such arguments are historically deaf. "Wife-beating" was first outlawed in the United States in seventeenth-century Massachusetts, hardly a hotbed of feminism, and has periodically surfaced as a social problem, almost always because religious and "law and order" constituencies have joined advocates for women's rights. In much of the world even today, as in the United States until relatively recently, it is a husband's "right to chastisement" that makes women vulnerable to abuse, a right for which there is no female counterpart, and is inextricably tied to their second-class status. It is true that the worldwide proliferation of shelters called attention to battering as a social problem that governments should address. But the success of this movement was itself a byproduct of the fact that millions of women self-identified as victims of their partners' abuse and courageously left their homes or other property, jobs, communities, and often their families to come to shelters or other services because they felt this was their only way to remain safe. Moreover, as the research from police and hospitals showed clearly, DV victims had been calling or coming for help in huge numbers for years before the social problem of woman abuse was publicly acknowledged. There is no comparable evidence to support the belief that a population of abused men in need of help remains hidden.

In fact, the "problem" of "battered husbands" to which FRs groups point became a focal point for attacks on the "gender" model of abuse only in the face of two developments: the state's willingness to support sanctions of perpetrators and an array of protections for battered women and their children, and the growing concern that assaulting a wife might have financial consequences in civil proceedings or result in a loss of custody. Claims that police respond differently to males and females who request assistance with an abusive partner have not been supported.[23] Thus, gender bias cannot explain why so few of the men who are hit or assaulted by women seek outside help.

Large numbers of women assault male or female partners and for many of the same reasons men assault same sex and female partners. But this in no way mitigates the rationales for special protections for female victims of male violence, the special vulnerability of women as a class due to persistent sexual inequalities, the fact that the vast majority of those seeking help for abuse are women, and the historical failure of the courts and police to protect women from male partner violence. The distinctive health profile identified with woman battering is merely an extension of the unique nature of the abuse women suffer. The coauthors of the NFVS,[24] the most frequently cited source of support for a "gender neutral" approach, are clear that the violent conflict tactics they document must be distinguished from the

---

[23] E. Buzawa & G. Hotaling, "The Impact of Relationship Status, Gender, and Minor Status in the Police Response to Domestic Assaults," 1 *Victims & Offender* 1 (2006); D. Hirschel et al., *Final Report. Explaining the Prevalence, Context, and Consequences of Dual Arrest in Intimate Partner Cases* (National Institute of Justice, 2007).

[24] *See* Gelles, *supra* note 22.

"abuse" or "battering" that is beyond the scope of their surveys. Richard Gelles[25] expressly classifies as a myth the belief "that Men and Women are equal perpetrators of 'domestic violence," calling this "a significant distortion of well-grounded research data." He concludes, "it is misogynistic to make it appear as though men are victimized by their partners as much as women." Similarly, Murray Straus defends the legitimacy of studying the use of physical force in families, as would I. But he too distinguishes the incidence of physical violence from the pattern of coercive and controlling behaviors that comprise battering. He writes, "it would be ridiculous and unethical" to ignore "the psychological assaults, sexual coercion, subjugation, and economic situation of battered women, or the behavior of men who engage in other forms of degradation."[26]

A large, heretofore "hidden" population of abused husbands may yet surface in family court. But this seems highly unlikely since they have not surfaced to any extent in other settings.

Coercive Control

Even more far reaching than the problems that result from the incident-specific approach are the dilemmas created for abuse victims in family cases by the equation of battering with physical violence. In somewhere between 20 and 40 percent of cases, DV is the principal source of abuse, usually accompanied by forms of psychological abuse such as chronic name calling or put downs. For the rest, however, in as many as four out of five cases in which victims seek outside assistance, the history of physical and/or sexual assaults is accompanied by a combination of tactics to intimidate, humiliate, exploit, isolate, and control a partner. In these instances, the nonviolent forms of coercion and control are at least as harmful as violence and almost always more consequential for the range of concerns about parenting and child well-being that underlie custodial decision making. Variously referred to as intimate terrorism,[27] psychological maltreatment,[28] and coercive control,[29] the term I prefer, this abusive pattern remains largely outside the scope of evaluation and decision making in family court.

In a typical case of coercive control, violence involves frequent, even routine, minor assaults, often accompanied by coerced sex. Interestingly, however, several well-designed studies have found all of the characteristic effects of battering may be produced even when no violence has occurred or when violence has not occurred for some time.[30] In a national survey, for instance, Finnish researchers reported that the

---

[25] Id.

[26] *Quoted in* D. Ellis & N. Stuckless, *Mediating and Negotiating Marital Conflict* 13 (1996).

[27] M.P. Johnson, "Patriarchal Terrorism and Common Couple Volence: Two Forms of Violence Against Women," 57 *J. Marriage & Fam.* 283 (1995); Johnson, *supra* note 12.

[28] R.M. Tolman, "The Development of a Measure of Psychological Maltreatment of Women by Their Male Partners," 4(3) *Violence & Victims* 159 (1989).

[29] L. Okun, *Woman Abuse: Facts Replacing Myths* (1986); J. Jones & S. Schechte, *When Love Goes Wrong* (1992); E. Stark, "A Failure to Protect: Unraveling the Battered Mother's Dilemma," 27 *W. St. U. L. Rev.* 101 (2000) [hereinafter Stark (2000)]; E. Stark, *Coercive Control: How Men Entrap Women in Personal Life* (2007) [hereinafter Stark (2007)].

[30] C. Lischick, Coping and Related Characteristics Delineating Battered Women's Experiences in Self-Defined, Difficult/Hurful Dating Relationship: A Multicultural Study (1999) (unpublished (Ph.D. dissertation, Rutgers University) (on file with author).

older women who had not been abused for at least ten years evidenced the highest levels of fear and abuse-related mental symptoms.[31]

Intimidation Tactics. The complementary intimidation tactics that characterize coercive control extend from open threats, stalking, and harassment via phone or computer to more subtle warnings whose meaning is only grasped by the victim. An example of the latter is a husband who would show up at his wife's softball games and offer her a sweatshirt when she struck out several batters in a row, a gesture others interpreted as loving. Only his wife understood that this sweatshirt offer was an ominous warning that the attention had made him jealous, and she would have to "cover up" her arms that night due to a beating. The purpose of intimidation is to instill fear, enforce obedience, and raise the cost of disobedience. Apart from literal threats to hurt or kill a wife or someone she cares for, husbands in my caseload have engaged in the following:

- Embarrassed their wives on social occasions to get them to do as instructed;
- Forced their wives stand and listen to "lectures" at all hours ("Its done, when I say its done");
- Openly followed their wives;
- Accidentally left "porno" sites or a love letter open on the computer;
- Given their wives the "silent treatment" for days after the wives refused a sexual demand or otherwise displeased them;
- Engaged in frequent sexual inspections;
- Described in detail how they could have them killed without detection;
- Told the children in their wives' presence that if the wives were not home when the children returned from school, they could find their mothers in the ground next to the dogs;
- Had their wives followed at the mall;
- Called their wives repeatedly at work or showed up there unexpectedly;
- Sent anonymous "reports" about their wives' moral indiscretions to clients, business associates, or co-workers;
- Revealed personal secrets to family members or friends;
- Engaged in periodic house "cleanings" by burning toys, pieces of furniture, or the wives' clothing;
- Secretly monitored their wives' cell phones;
- Driven recklessly with the children in the car;
- Gone through their wives' diaries;
- Called back anyone whose voice they did not recognize; and
- Allowed children to have "accidents" while they were baby sitting.

---

[31] M. Piispa, "Complexity of Patterns of Violence Against Women in Heterosexual Partnerships," 8(7) *Violence Against Women* 873 (2002).

Acts that victims find intimidating, such as "surprising" them by jumping out of a closet or playing too roughly with a young child, are often excused as "games." Gas-light games are also used to make a wife feel she is crazy by sabotaging a common activity like turning off the stove after she has turned it on and then asking innocently about dinner or moving her car without her knowledge or putting her car keys in a strange place. Seemingly anonymous acts whose authorship is transparent are particularly shaming in the context of physical threats and coercion because a partner cannot "know what she knows" without putting herself at risk, a condition termed "perspecticide" in the hostage literature.

Isolation Tactics. Isolation involves a set of tactics designed to enforce dependence on victims, secure exclusive possession, monopolize their time, skills and resources, and "keep the secret" of abuse by cutting them off from core sources of support and reality testing, such as family, friends, co-workers or helping professionals. Examples from my practice include the following:

- Forbidding wives from calling family or friends;
- Timing or limiting the wives' conversations;
- Destroying mementoes or photographs of family members;
- Stopping the wives from going to the gym;
- Calling back numbers the abusive husbands do not recognize;
- Calling all the wives' friends "whores";
- Forcing the wives to sit in one place ("and don't move") when they are at a bar;
- Refusing to provide money for plane trips home;
- Where the husband is a doctor, having a partner write prescriptions for psychiatric medicines (without meeting the women) so they do not "need" to see someone else;
- Pulling the phone out of the wall; and
- Forbidding the wives from leaving the house, going to church, or forcing them to quit the home-schooling network, which were the wives' only source of contact besides their children.

In one case where the husband continually belittled his wife's failure to attend college, he constructed elaborate lies about the education and careers of his father and his colleagues' wives. When she relied on this information in social gatherings with his family or friends, she was humiliated. Isolation evolves a cat and mouse game in which victims attempt to establish, and their partners to locate and destroy, "safety zones" where the victims can ponder their options and preserve autonomy. Studies in the United States and England reveal that 40 to 89 percent of women who are physically assaulted by their partners are also kept from socializing, seeing their families, or leaving the house.[32] In attempts to placate husbands who interpret even accidental social

---

[32] Tolman, *supra* note 28; A. Rees, R. Agnew-Davies & M. Barkham, Outcomes for Women Escaping Domestic Violence at Refuge (paper presented at Society for Psychotherapy Research Annual Conference, Edinburgh, 2006).

contacts by exhibiting a jealous rage, many women will voluntarily cut themselves off from friends or family members. In extreme cases of isolation, battered women can experience a "Stockholm Syndrome," where they cling to the husband who is abusing them because he is their only source of reality and self-esteem.

Control Tactics. Control tactics that install a husband's dominance directly are at the heart of most battering relationships. This is accomplished primarily by three means: exploiting a partner's capacities and resources for personal gain and gratification, depriving her of the means needed for autonomy and/or separation, and regulating her behavior with formal or implicit "rules" to conform with stereotyped gender roles. These tactics begin with a partner's control over the necessities of daily living, including money and other assets, food, sex, sleep, medication, housing, transportation, and communication with the outside world. But control tactics can extend to taken-for-granted arenas of autonomy such as toileting, eating, or which chair a wife can use. Husbands in my practice have removed the doors from bathrooms, timed how long their wives and children could use the toilet, and denied them toilet paper when they were "bad." If the exploitation or regulation of access to material necessities is the material foundation for coercive control, its infrastructure involves the micromanagement of minute facets of everyday life, particularly in areas like cooking, cleaning, and child care associated with women's default roles as homemakers or mothers. In two studies of service populations, more than half of the abusive men monitored women's time as well as took their money.[33] I have had several cases in which women were given written "rules" for daily behavior covering everything from how high the bedspread was to be from the carpet to descriptions of which clothes they were to wear. More often, rules are implicit, often too general to be obeyed literally (e.g., "you will be a 'good girl' at all times" or "you will never make me jealous") or contradictory, making it virtually impossible to obey them. One wife was punished "for thinking for yourself" as well as for waiting for her husband's permission to purchase a new appliance; another was told she had to answer the phone by "the third ring or else" but was then given a long list of daily chores each morning. Rules are often arbitrary, with no obvious connection to a husband's needs. For example, one husband measured the space available in the refrigerator and demanded his wife make a dish that would fit exactly. The more arbitrary or petty the rule, the more women experience compliance as demeaning.[34]

Studies on Coercive Control. Several large-scale, well-designed studies have shown that control factors predict fatality and the psychological, physical, and psychosocial outcomes heretofore attributed to DV far better than do levels or frequency of physical assault and may elicit these outcomes even in the absence of physical assault or long after physical assault has ended.[35] With stalking, telephonic harassment, and control over money as the most obvious examples, many of the tactics used in coercive control also cross social space as well as extend over time, making them particularly effective as a way to continue abuse after couples are physically separated. These behaviors are part of a comprehensive strategy built around a husband's privileged access to his

---

[33] Id.

[34] Stark (2007), *supra* note 29.

[35] N. Glass, J. Manganello & J.C. Campbell, "Risk for Intimate Partner Femicide in Violent Relationships," 9(2) *DV Rep.* 1 (2004); Lischick, *supra* note 30; Rees, Agnew-Davies & Barkham, *supra* note 32.

wife and the personal knowledge of her whereabouts, habits, and fears rather than a response to "conflict" in any obvious sense. In fact, 60 percent of British victims who use shelters report having been beaten in their sleep.[36]

Coercive control is far more difficult to decipher than physical violence, is unlikely to be documented by court or police records, and can easily be concealed from evaluators or made to appear odd, eccentric, even "crazy" rather than malevolent. Like the offer of the sweatshirt (above), numerous gestures that elicit high levels of psychological distress in an abused wife and children may seem meaningless or loving unless put in the context of the larger pattern of coercive control. Here again, a victim's expressed fears can appear exaggerated, her claims histrionic or paranoid, and her personality "borderline"—observations that may be supported by a husband's history of his wife's "acting out" or reports from friends that the wife "acted crazy."

Case Example. In a recent case, violence was minimal. The wife testified that her husband had pointed a gun at her on two occasions, slapped her, thrown her off the bed, locked her out of the house in the snow, and choked her once. The largest number of incidents involved shoving, which he claimed had been mutual. On the basis of having attended a DV seminar, the judge insisted that there was no "real" DV in this case and disallowed my testimony. The gun had not been loaded, for example. What never got into evidence was that isolation and intimidation tactics had been continual in this home. Several times a week the husband made his wife stand next to the bed while he lectured her about her faults, often for hours. After 9/11, he claimed to have received special information that their suburban Connecticut town was a target of Al Qaeda and stopped letting her leave the house without him, only allowing the cleaning woman (with rubber gloves) to go to the mailbox. Under the interim agreement, the couple was to communicate via e-mails—his consisted of numerous, lengthy, and abusive lectures on the areas of her life that needed correction—and to have no personal contact without mutual consent. Although the evaluator made no effort to verify the wife's claims of abuse, she advised the wife to set clear boundaries with her husband and joined the law guardian in recommending that the wife get primary custody, largely because the husband had serious mental health problems. Shortly before the final disposition, the daughter had a karate tournament during her mother's time. The husband told his wife he was coming to observe the tournament. But when he arrived, he insisted on sitting with them, became verbally abusive when she said no, followed them when they attempted to leave, blocked their exit, and then shoved his wife down when she tried to get around him, all in front of witnesses. The wife called the police, and the husband was arrested. Instead of supporting the wife, however, the professionals agreed that her "overreaction" constituted a "selfish, self-centered attitude," which showed "she could not distinguish the child's interest in being with her father from her own." The evaluator and the child's lawyer changed their recommendation, and the husband got primary custody and the wife very limited visitation.

The original recommendation was that the wife get primary custody and the husband generous visitation with his daughter. But the husband became increasingly agitated as the settlement date approached, and he faced the prospects of losing not only a substantial portion of the assets he had controlled but the hold he had over his wife. His increasingly accusatory and threatening e-mails (which the child's lawyer and therapist saw) caused his wife to fear that her husband would do something to

---

[36] Rees, Agnew-Davies & Barkham, *supra* note 32.

hurt her or their daughter, as he had in the past. Her reaction at the karate tournament was only intelligible in this context. To the guardian and evaluator, and ultimately to the judge, the karate incident could either mean that the husband was more dangerous than they had suspected—a conclusion that was incompatible with their assessments and recommendations for liberal visitation, or that the wife was "crazy" or malicious, hence unable or unworthy to have primary custody. Victims of coercive control suffer many of the same physical or psychological effects as victims of DV. But its major effects involve harms to autonomy, personhood, and decision making that bear directly on parenting but are less tangible than physical injuries. In this case, when the effects of the coercive control to which the wife was subjected were de-contextualized, the guardian, evaluator, and judge attributed the behavioral consequences of literal regulation, intimidation, deprivation, and control to the wife's psychological dysfunction, compounding the effects of her husband's abuse.

Coercive Control Mostly Committed by Men. While DV is committed by women as well as men and is often mutual, coercive control is almost wholly committed by men. There is a growing sentiment among FRs activists and their supporters that abusive men represent a deviant subtype who suffer from some combination of borderline, paranoid, or impulse control disorders that are often manifest in childhood. Well-designed studies of batterers in treatment, however, show that only one in four have serious psychological problems, although the proportion rises to 40 percent among those who commit chronic physical abuse.[37] Nor has any convincing data emerged that links these problems to abusive behavior. By contrast with psychological models, which researchers claim can predict up to 20 percent of future violence, 50 percent of the variance in future violence can be predicted by simply knowing whether there has been a previous assault.[38]

There is no research that directly bears on whether perpetrators of coercive control are more or less likely to evidence psychiatric disease than men who limit their abuse to violence. Of the several dozen DV assessment tools available that have been tested for construct validity, only a handful consider aspects of abuse other than violence, and all are scaled to reflect the array of violent tactics, and/or the frequency of their use and physical or psychological effects. Moreover, the long-term strategic planning and instrumental calculations involved in coercive control are generally incompatible with the personality types most commonly identified with violence.

DOMESTIC VIOLENCE, COERCIVE CONTROL, AND CHILDREN

Research on the overlap of woman abuse and harms to children differs greatly in quality, uses varying definitions of harm to children, and often disregards the incredible resilience shown by women who mother through DV and their children or the mediating role of coping skills, parental support, and developmental age[39]—issues

---

[37] E.W. Gondolf, *Final Report: An Extended Follow-Up of Batterers and Their Partners* (Centers for Disease Control and Prevention, Grant No. R49/CCR3l0525-04-06-1, 1997–2001, 2002).

[38] K.D. O'Leary, "Through a Psychological Lens: Personality Traits, Personality Disorders, and Levels of Violence," in R.J. Gelles & D.K. Loseke eds., *Current Controversies on Family Violence* 7–31 (1993).

[39] Stark (2002), *supra* note 2; L. Radford & M. Hester, *Mothering Through Domestic Violence* (2006).

emphasized in the chapter by Crooks, Jaffe, and Bala (Chapter 22 in this volume). Whatever the limits of this work, however, there is no question that abuse of a female primary caretaker is far and away the most common context in which evaluators are likely to confront behavior that jeopardizes a child's best interest.

Where DV is identified, child abuse is a common consequence. Over thirty well-designed studies using a conservative definition of child abuse show a robust link between physical and sexual child abuse and DV, with a median co-occurrence of 41 percent and a range of 30 to 60 percent.[40] One large, multicity study found that children were directly involved in adult DV incidents from 9 to 27 percent of the time (depending on the city) and that younger children were disproportionately represented in households where domestic assaults occurred[41] as they are in family court cases. Although an abused woman is more likely than a nonabused woman to abuse her children, the father who is abusing the mother is more than three times more likely to be abusing the children than is the battered mother.[42]

Witnessing and Exposure to Violence

Much of the research on children's responses to DV focuses on the psychological, behavioral, and cognitive harms caused by "witnessing" one of the more tangible facets of what is referred to as "exposure" rather than to literal physical or sexual abuse. It must be assumed that any child in a home where abuse occurs has witnessed violence, particularly when we consider the repeated nature of violence in these relationships. Around 70 percent of abused women report their children have witnessed their father's violent behavior. But adults dramatically underreport children's exposure. As Jaffe, Wolfe, and Wilson[43] found, children often provide detailed recollections of the very events they were not supposed to have witnessed.

On average, children exposed to adult DV exhibit more difficulties than those not so exposed. Witnessing violence has been linked to a range of psychological, emotional, and behavioral problems, including many of the same problems classically identified with physical and sexual abuse, with exposure to other behavioral problems such as parental alcoholism, or with traumatic events such as divorce or the death of a parent. Children exposed to DV exhibit more aggressive and anti-social behaviors (externalized behaviors) as well as fearful and inhibited behaviors (internalized behaviors) when compared to nonexposed children.[44] Exposed children also show lower social competence than other children,[45] lower cognitive

---

[40] A.E. Appel & G.W. Holden, "The Co-Occurrence of Spouse and Physical Child Abuse: A Review and Appraisal, 12 *J. Fam. Psychol.* 578 (1998); J.W. Fantuzzo & W.K. Mohr, "Prevalence and Effects of Child Exposure to Domestic Violence," 9 *Future of Child.* 21 (1999); L.A. McCloskey, A.J. Figueredo & M.P. Koss, "The Effects of Systematic Family Violence on Children's Mental Health," 66 *Child Dev.* 1239 (1995); Stark (2002), *supra* note 2.

[41] J.W. Fantuzzo et al., "Effects of Interparental Violence on the Psychological Adjustment and Competencies of Young Children," 59 *J. Consulting & Clinical Psychol.* 258 (1991).

[42] Stark (2002), *supra* note 2.

[43] P. Jaffe, D.A. Wolfe & S.K. Wilson, *Children of Battered Women* (1990).

[44] H.M. Hughes, D. Parkinson & M. Vargo, "Witnessing Spouse Abuse and Experiencing Pphysical Abuse: A 'Double Whammy'?" 4 *J. Fam. Violence* 197 (1989); Fantuzzo et al., *supra* note 41.

[45] J.L. Adamson & R.A. Thompson, "Coping With Interparental Verbal Conflict to Spouse Abuse and Children From Nonviolent Homes," 13(3) *J. Fam. Violence* 213 (1998).

functioning,[46] and higher-than-average anxiety, depression, trauma symptoms, and temperament problems than children who are not exposed to violence at home.[47]

The relationship of the child to the violent adult appears to influence how a child is affected. A recent study of eighty shelter-resident mothers and eighty of their children revealed that an abusive male's relationship to a child directly affects the child's well-being without being mediated by the mother's level of mental health.[48] Violence perpetrated by a biological father or stepfather was found to have a greater impact on a child than the violence of nonfather figures (e.g., partners or ex-partners who played a minimal role in the child's life). Children whose fathers or stepfathers were the abusers showed lower scores on self-competency measures when compared to the other children. The researchers concluded that, "there may be something especially painful in the experience of witnessing one's own father abuse one's mother."[49]

Despite the importance of DV to children's well-being, it cannot be assumed that all children exposed to any type of abuse in the home suffer long-term or severe consequences or that any manifestation of psychological or behavioral problems in exposed children results from abuse. As Crooks, Jaffe, and Bala emphasize (Chapter 22 in this volume), whether serious problems will develop depends on the resilience of a particular child, the available support system, the child's developmental age, and the nature and extent of abuse to which the child is exposed, with the probability of harm increasing sharply if abuse is chronic. Although infants and small children are too young to appreciate what other people are feeling, they respond to cues like crying, shouting, or bleeding in the same ways as older children.

At the same time, even if they do not suffer behavioral or cognitive difficulties because of exposure, children living with abuse are more actively engaged than the relative passive term "witnessing" suggests. They interpret, predict, assess their roles in causing "fights," worry about the consequences, engage in problem solving, and/or take measures to protect themselves, their siblings, and their primary parent physically and emotionally. Intervening to protect an abused mother is a common source of physical harm to children as well as the guilt when their intervention "fails." Psychological defenses may be at work even when they appear unresponsive. Peled offers this chilling account, for instance: "I wouldn't say anything. I would just sit there. Watch it . . . I was just, felt like I was just sitting there, listening to a TV show or something. . . . It's like you just sit there to watch it, like a tapestry, you sit there."[50]

---

[46] B.B.R. Rossman, "Descartes's Error and Posttraumatic Stress Disorder: Cognition and Emotion in Children Who Are Exposed to Parental Violence," in *Children Exposed to Marital Violence* 223-56 (G.W. Holden, R. Geffner & E.N. Jouriles eds., 1998).

[47] A.H. Maker, M. Kemmelmeier & C. Peterson, "Long-Term Psychological Consequences in Women of Witnessing Parental Physical Conflict and Experiencing Abuse in Childhood," 13 *J. Interpersonal Violence* 574 (1998).

[48] C.M. Sullivan et al., "How Children's Adjustment Is Affected by Their Relationships to Their Mothers' Abusers," 15(6) *J. Interpersonal Violence* 587 (2000).

[49] Id. at 598.

[50] E. Peled, The Experience of Living With Violence for Preadolescent Witnesses of Woman Abuse (1993) (unpublished Ph.D. dissertation, University of Minnesota), *cited in* J.L. Edleson, "Children's Witnessing of Adult Domestic Violence" 14(8) *J. Interpersonal Violence* 839 (1999).

Coercive Control and Children's Welfare

While the unique effects of coercive control on children have not been studied, given the prevalence of coercive control in partner abuse cases, it is clear that many of the harms attributed to physical violence alone are actually elicited by exposure to a combination of abusive tactics among which assault (because it is often low level) may not be the most important.

The limits that shape the general misunderstanding of DV in family court extend to how the potential harms to children are assessed. Either explicitly or by implication, research on children's witnessing adapts an incident-specific definition of violence that highlights the potentially traumatic effects of exposure, particularly for very young children, showing that even infants exposed to severe violence may experience symptoms similar to adult posttraumatic stress disorder. While children can be traumatized by witnessing a severe assault, their more typical experience is prolonged exposure to repeated but minor assaults and to the combination of violence, intimidation, isolation, and control in coercive control. Because children's experiences of parental abuse are typically ongoing and multifaceted, the psychological, behavioral, and cognitive harms they suffer are not adequately encompassed by traditional trauma models and cannot be accurately measured using these models. To the contrary, in clinical evaluations using the standard battery of psychological tests, the cumulative effects of prolonged exposure to abuse cannot be distinguished etiologically from the effects of convergent developmental, personality, and behavioral influences in the environment, including other situational stressors. With respect to the more diffuse pattern of coercive control, what the child "witnesses" is one parent being humiliated and systematically deprived of liberty and autonomy in everyday affairs, an "exposure" that elicits far less tangible signals of distress than are associated with violence and may be difficult to discern than those induced by seeing a primary parent physically injured. Still, the long-term effects of such exposure may be quite dramatic and affect a child's gender identity, sense of autonomy, as well as their behavior as a "citizen." Few of these effects are picked up by the standard psychological tests used in custody evaluation, and none are linked to abuse.

Battered Mother's Dilemma

In addition to the direct physical risks children face in any cases involving DV, in coercive control, they are also endangered by two common patterns: "the battered mother's dilemma" and when child abuse occurs as "tangential spouse abuse."

The battered mother's dilemma refers to the choices an abusive partner forces a mother to make between her own interests, including her physical safety, and the safety or interests of their children. A particular incident may bring this dilemma into sharp focus, as when a woman realizes that she may be hurt or killed if she attempts to protect her child from her partner's abuse. In custody disputes, common examples involve abusive husbands who threaten extended custody battles unless the wives abandon all claims for financial support, or the husbands threaten the wives with physical harm if they pursue custody. Typically, however, the battered mother's dilemma describes an ongoing facet of abusive relationships where the victimized caretaker is repeatedly forced to choose between taking some action she believes is wrong (such as using inappropriate forms of corporal punishment with her child), being hurt herself, or standing by while the abusive partner hurts the child.

Ignorance of the external constraints to which a caretaker is responding often leads courts or service professionals to aggravate the battered mother's dilemma. This happens, for instance, when, instead of providing appropriate protections for an abused mother, a court threatens to shift primary custody to an abusive partner if she fails to facilitate his access to their child, as in the case example (above). Another common example involves charging a mother who reports DV with "neglect," a practice found unconstitutional by a federal court in New York.[51]

A related dynamic involves child abuse as tangential spouse abuse, when the abusive partner uses the child as a tool to solidify control over a mother's behavior. While this pattern often begins when the couple is living together, it typically escalates when they separate, and the perpetrator has less access to his victim. While they are together, the perpetrator may suggest the children's misbehavior is the reason the primary parent must be beaten or encourage children to abuse their mother, frighten children by threatening to harm them or their pets, or use them to spy on the victimized parent. Children may also be held hostage or abducted as a way to hurt or control their mother. This dynamic often underlies a woman's hesitation about separating or securing a protection order. Examples of this dynamic in an intact couple include threats to report the mother to child protective services, moving for custody despite no real interest in care taking, punishing a mother by denying her access to the children, hurting the children whenever the mother does something that makes the abuser jealous, being passive-aggressive by consenting to care for the children so the mother can work and then neglecting them, and telling the children that the abuser will hurt himself or the mother if he does not "win" custody. In two large studies, 44 percent of battered women in the United States reported their partners had threatened to take or report them to child welfare "at least once," and 44 percent of the women in England reported their partners had done so "often" or "all the time."[52] Mothers caught in this dynamic are particularly susceptible to guilt, whether induced by the abusers' accusations or by institutional victim blaming.

Children may also be harmed indirectly because of the secondary consequences of coercive control (such as depression, substance abuse, or attempted suicide) or because nonviolent abusive tactics may extend to the children through neglect, manipulation, or undermining a victim's ability to parent. Child outcomes in these instances include depression, suicidality, aggression, delinquency, anxiety, developmental delay, substance use, and inappropriate behavior at school.[53] Because a victim's access to money is a major target of coercive control, it can have a major impact on her income, earning capacity, and employability, all factors that are critical to children's support. In a randomized sample of low-income women, Susan Lloyd from the Joint Center for Poverty Research in Chicago found that those women who had been physically abused, threatened, or harassed by male partners in the twelve months prior to the study had lower employment rates, lower income, and were more likely than nonabused women in the sample to exhibit depression, anxiety, anger, and other problems that affect their labor market experience over time.[54] All of these outcomes bear on custodial and support decisions in family court.

---

[51] Nicholson v. Williams, 203 F. Supp. 2d 153 (E.D.N.Y. 2002); Stark (2002), *supra* note 2.

[52] Tolman, *supra* note 28; A. Rees, R. Agnew-Davies & M. Barkham, *supra* note 32.

[53] Stark (2002), *supra* note 2.

[54] S. Lloyd, *The Effects of Violence on Women's Employment* (Joint Center for Poverty Research, MacArthur Foundation 1997), http://www.spc.uchicago.edu/PovertyCenter/violence.htm.

Coercive control may also affect children indirectly because it induces less tangible changes in a nonoffending mother. A victimized woman may believe she is an inadequate parent because her partner has consistently portrayed her as unfit or as the cause of their children's deficits, a view that he has reinforced by isolation and threats. Additionally, a victimized woman may lose the respect of her children. This may happen because children grow to devalue or feel shame about their mother or learn to disregard her authority or her rules. A victimized woman may also believe a man's excuses for abuse and reinforce them with her children. Further, a victimized woman may change her parenting style in response to the abuser's parenting style. A woman may become too permissive in response to the authoritarian parenting of an abuser or too punitive because she is trying to keep children from annoying the abuser. If the abuser simultaneously undermines his wife's disciplinary authority and insists she punish children or he will do "worse," an example of the battered mother's dilemma, she may escalate the use of corporal punishment. I frequently see this pattern in cases where mothers are charged with risk of injury or failure to protect their children.[55] In the context of coercive control, some children come to see their mother as a legitimate target of abuse. She may make age-inappropriate or unreasonable demands on children to placate the abuser or because she is constrained from meeting her needs for affection in more appropriate ways. Finally, coercive control may compromise a victimized mother's bond to her children. As a result of coercive control, children may be angry at a mother for failing to protect them or to evict the abuser or to comfort them when they are distressed. In some of these cases, children become "parentified," assuming caretaking roles for their mothers or other siblings that are inappropriate for their ages. Some abused children "identify with the aggressor" and become alienated from their mothers either to protect themselves by an alliance with the stronger parents or as a magical way to protect their mothers. Some children become coabusers of their mothers.

Men's Interference in Women's Parenting During Custodial Disputes

All forms of abuse extend into the postseparation period, a major reason why "separated" women actually face a higher risk of abuse than married or cohabiting women.

Child visitation and shared custody are common contexts for reassault during the postseparation period.[56] Leighton reported that one-quarter of the 235 Canadian women he interviewed had been threatened or assaulted during child visitations.[57] As many as one-third of violations of court orders occur during child visitation exchanges.[58] Studies of so-called high conflict marriages and divorce indicate that

---

[55] Stark (2000), *supra* note 29.

[56] C. Shalansky, J. Ericksen & A. Henderson, "Abused Women and Child Custody: The Ongoing Exposure to Abusive Ex-Partners," 29(2) *J. Advanced Nursing* 416 (1999); Kernic et al., *supra* note 13.

[57] B. Leighton, *Spousal Abuse in Metropolitan Toronto: Research Report on the Response of the Criminal Justice System* (Report No. 1989-02) (Solicitor General of Canada, 1989).

[58] M. McMahon & E. Pence, "Doing More Harm Than Good: Some Cautions on Visitation Centers," in *Ending The Cycle of Violence: Community Responses to Children of Battered Women* 186–206 (E. Peled, P. Jaffe & J. Edleson eds.,1995).

children continually exposed to abusive encounters between parents in shared custody arrangements or in noncustodial visits have more behavioral problems in childhood and early adulthood than children in sole custodial arrangements.[59]

Typical of control tactics during postseparation is interference with a woman's parenting. In a study that is quickly becoming seminal to our understanding of abuse, Bancroft and Silverman argue that men who batter systematically undermine and interfere with their partner's parenting and that this interference often extends into the postseparation period when perpetrators may use children to sabotage parenting and to spy on or otherwise intimidate their mothers.[60] This pattern is often signaled by efforts to win custody by a father who has had little previous involvement in parenting. The collusion of the legal system in a batterer's use of repeated legal motions in an attempt to bankrupt a former partner, protect his assets, and intimidate her into "compromising" her interests in the protection of the children is another common tactic used to disrupt parenting.

Coercive control poses a particular challenge in cases where the child's expressed preference is to live with the abusive father, or the child denies witnessing abuse despite compelling testimony to the contrary. Explanations for a child's apparent closeness to an abusive parent range from identification with the aggressor and frank Stockholm Syndrome to the child's belief that he/she can magically protect the victimized parent by placating an abusive father, perhaps in response to his threats to hurt himself if he loses custody or his complaints about abandonment. As an extension of this self-presentation, children often imagine their abusive fathers as the weaker of two parents and as requiring their support. Children may also deny abuse or express a preference for abusive fathers simply because they share their mothers' fears, which they often observe directly, a reaction that can lead mothers to be charged with "alienation." In one of my cases, two teen boys denied seeing their father use violence though the mother provided convincing descriptions of how they had responded, and neighbors reported the boys had shared their fears of "daddy's big hands." Too great a focus on the children's wishes in these cases can keep judges, evaluators, and children's attorneys from following the implications of parental abuse wherever they may lead. The quality of a child's relationship to the abusing parent is important but less because it points to whether limits should be placed on access and protections implemented than to how separation from an abusive parent should be facilitated. Protective custody arrangements may certainly involve providing an opportunity for a child to say goodbye to an abusive father or for the abusive parent to relieve the child's burden of guilt by accepting responsibility for creating chaos in the home, particularly if a supervised visitation center is available in the area where this meeting can take place safely.

RESPONSE TO ABUSE BY THE FAMILY COURTS

How have family courts and evaluators responded to the realities of abuse and its effects on children?

Following passage of the Morella resolution in 1997 (see "Separate Planets?"), all but two states changed their custody laws to favor abuse victims either by giving them

---

[59] E.M. Hetherington & M. Stanley-Hagan, "The Adjustment of Children With Divorced Parents: A Risk and Resiliency Perspective," 40 *J. Child Psychol. & Psychiatry & Allied Disciplines* 129 (1999).

[60] L. Bancroft & J. Silverman, *The Batterer as Parent: Addressing the Impact of Domestic Violence on Family Dynamics* (2002).

the presumption of custody, instituting a rebuttable presumption against joint custody, banning sole custody or unsupervised visitation for perpetrators, or identifying abuse as an important factor that judges have to consider. The National Council of Juvenile and Family Court Judges (NCJFCJ) has promoted its support for rebuttable presumption legislation through its "Green Book" initiative. Available data do not provide a sufficient longitudinal picture of whether judicial decision making in abuse cases has changed significantly as a result of these laws. But there is growing concern that it has not, particularly relative to changes in how police, child welfare, or the criminal courts respond in abuse cases. For example, sole physical custody was given more often to fathers than to mothers in states where statutes favoring joint custody or friendly parent statutes competed with statutes denying custody to perpetrators of abuse.[61] In New York, fathers were more likely to receive visitation when the mother had a protection order than when she did not.[62] At best, family courts remain deeply ambivalent about the changing normative response to abuse.

In addition to statutes favoring joint custody or friendly parents, the family courts' responses to abuse are constrained by their reliance on the best interests of the child as a guide to custodial decisions. Since children's actual wishes are rarely polled directly, in practice, this has meant relying on "therapeutic jurisprudence," an approach in which psychological interpretations of what children need, however weak their empirical foundation, trump the sort of justice concerns put in play by abuse allegations. By placing a significant proportion of custody cases outside the realm of psychological evaluation, presumptive custody rules threaten the professional infrastructure of therapeutic jurisprudence. By contrast, absent evidence of direct harm to a child, the best interests standard allows family judges to exclude DV as tangential to a child's psychological well-being. Because the psychological and behavioral harms to children caused by the most common forms of abuse are rarely detected using conventional models of assessment, forcing victims of DV or coercive control to adopt a psychological argument to convince courts to provide needed protections disadvantages victimized mothers.

Available evidence suggests that, with marked exceptions, most family courts continue to interpret partner violence as an instance of "high conflict" rather than as abuse and to view the illegitimate exercise of power and control to hurt and subjugate loved ones as different only in degree, but not in kind, from other types of animosities and family problems that bring disputants in custody litigation to court.

There are mixed findings about how framing abuse as "conflict" has affected the actual outcomes in contested custody cases, and much of the research that highlights its negative effects is based on self-reports from selected or volunteer samples. But the most relevant fact for our current purpose is that, in a disturbing proportion of cases, abusive partners continue to be given primary or shared custody and to be allowed unrestricted access to protective mothers and children. Even where abuse is well documented, it rarely surfaces as a major determinant of case outcomes.

When evaluators are asked about their practices, a substantial proportion report that they not only consider DV allegations, but also use DV assessment tools and make specialized referrals or protective recommendations when appropriate.[63] But

---

[61] J. Morrill et al., "Child Custody and Visitation Decisions When the Father Has Perpetrated Violence Against the Mother," 11(8) *Violence Against Women* 1076 (2005).

[62] L. Rosen & C. O'Sullivan, "Outcomes of Custody and Visitation Petitions When Fathers Are Restrained by Protection Orders," 11(8) *Violence Against Women* 1045 (2005).

[63] J.N. Bow & P. Boxer, "Assessing Allegations of Domestic Violence in Custody Evaluations," 18 *J. Interpersonal Violence* 1394 (2003).

these self-reports do not appear to reflect the reality. Research in Kentucky found DV was not only overlooked by evaluators as a general rule, but that it played no role in recommendations even when it was mentioned in the report.[64] Moreover, studies in both Kentucky and California found that DV couples were as likely as those without such allegations to be steered into mediation and that mediators held joint sessions in nearly half of the cases where DV was substantiated in an independent interview, even though this was against the regulations.[65] In San Diego, mediators failed to recognize DV in 57 percent of abuse cases. Perhaps more importantly, revealing DV was found to actually be detrimental to outcomes for victimized mothers. In fact, mediators who said they were aware of abuse were less likely to recommend supervised exchanges than those who were not so aware.[66] This finding helps explain anecdotal information that family lawyers are now advising clients not to discuss DV with evaluators.

An important limit of research on DV in custody cases is failure to distinguish outcomes involving partner abuse from cases where child abuse or other forms of parental unfitness are alleged. In a well-designed study that was able to isolate the response to partner abuse, Kernic et al. studied all Seattle couples with minor children petitioning for dissolution of marriage in the target year, merged the marital dissolution files with police and criminal court files, and compared the outcomes for mothers with a documented history of abuse (as well as those with allegations of abuse in the dissolution file) with those without this history.[67] Importantly, of the cases with a documented preexisting history of abuse (n = 257), almost three-quarters had either no mention of DV in the marital dissolution file (47.6 percent) or only unsubstantiated allegations (28.9 percent). In other words, the court was made aware of documented abuse in less than one case in four. After adjusting for a range of potential confounders (such as allegations that the mother had used violence), mothers with a history of abuse were no more likely than the nonabused mothers to be granted child custody. Moreover, while fathers whose abuse was substantiated in both criminal and family court files were significantly more likely to be denied child visitation and assigned to relevant services than comparison fathers, the vast majority (83 percent) of abusive fathers had no such restrictions. The outcomes in cases that involved fathers with documented histories of abuse, but whose abusive histories were not included in the dissolution file, and those with documented histories, whose abuse was included only as an allegation by their wives, were no different than the outcomes for nonabusive fathers. This last finding is particularly disturbing because the low level of violence typical of DV and coercive control rarely prompts an arrest or protection order. Contrary to the claims of FRs groups and their supporters, there is no empirical evidence that fathers are disproportionately denied visitation where their wives merely allege abuse. Indeed, no special restrictions are being placed on their visitation even in the vast majority of cases where there is documented evidence of abuse.

---

[64] L.S. Horvath, T.K. Logan & R. Walker, "Child Custody Cases: A Content Analysis of Evaluations in Practice," 33 *Prof. Psychol: Res. & Prac.* 557 (2002).

[65] A.M. Hirst, *Domestic Violence in Court-Based Child Custody Mediation Cases in California.* (Research Update, Judicial Council of California, Administrative Office of the Courts, Nov. 1–12, 2002).

[66] Johnson, *supra* note 12.

[67] Kernic et al., *supra* note 13.

Kernic and her colleagues did not specifically assess the role of evaluators.[68] But, like the findings from Kentucky and San Diego,[69] their research indicates that evaluators fail to assist the courts in reaching an appropriate disposition in these cases. They typically fail to recognize DV even when documentation is readily available, as it was in Seattle, or easily identified, as it was in San Diego, almost never report a finding of DV in response to allegations by mothers where there is no documentation, and fail to include DV in their recommendations.[70] Indeed, when Meier[71] reviewed a sample of custody cases, she concluded that recommendations by evaluators and law guardians were a principal reason abusive men won custody. These findings indicate that therapeutic jurisprudence is completely failing battered women and their children, even on its own terms, since children's welfare is clearly being put at risk in these cases.

The most positive finding from these studies is that judges who possessed information about abuse were more likely to take protective action that favored mothers and children. Undoubtedly, the proportion of judges who responded protectively in abuse cases would increase if they were heard in "integrated" courts, if communication between courts was improved, or if allegations were properly investigated by evaluators. But the fact that family judges failed to provide appropriate protections in the vast majority of documented abuse cases points towards a systemic constraint on appropriate decision making that is not likely to be remedied by training alone.

NATURE OF ABUSE IN CUSTODY CASES

Defenders of therapeutic jurisprudence have recently taken a new tact in response to the consensus among researchers that DV harms children, arguing that the type of violence that surfaces in custody disputes is substantively different and less serious than abuse seen in other service settings such as shelters or criminal courts. In a recent review purportedly summarizing knowledge of DV for custody evaluators, Gould, Martindale, and Eidman write,

> It is our belief that the nature of allegations of DV that most often are brought to the attention of child custody evaluators reflect "separation engendered violence" or "post-divorce trauma" described by Johnston and Campbell (1993). . . . males and females identified (with-E.S.) this category . . . display acts of violence that were uncharacteristic of their everyday lives. Increased aggressiveness was associated with increased tension around the separation and divorce. Physical violence was absent during their marriage and abuses of power and control were also absent.[72]

To Gould and his coauthors, violence in custodial settings is rooted in dysfunctional marital dynamics rather than in individual behavior and poses little long-term risk to children, largely because it is episodic, unlikely to continue once the finality of

---

[68] Id.

[69] See Horvath, Logan & Walker, supra note 64; Hirst, supra note 65.

[70] Kernic et al., supra note 13.

[71] J. Meier, "Domestic Violence, Child Custody and Child Protection: Understanding Judicial Resistance and Imagining the Solutions," 11(2) J. Gender, Soc. Pol'y & L. 656, 709 n.186 (2003).

[72] Gould, Martindale & Eidman, supra note 10, at 10.

separation is accepted, and is not linked to other forms of violence or control. Rather than rush to judgment in abuse cases and so "cast a dark shadow" over the perpetrator's life by labeling him abusive, they argue that courts should treat the episodic violence they see as transitory, search for its cause in "family factors," and recommend therapeutic interventions that can manage trigger events or otherwise facilitate the ongoing cooperation and access of both parents.

Gould and his co authors rely on a single empirical source to support their argument, a study in which Johnston and Campbell test a typology of violence in a convenience sample of divorcing couples.[73] Employing the calculus of physical harms I have shown to be suspect (see "Hallmarks of Physical Abuse"), Johnston and Campbell limit their identification of abuse to cases where unilateral violence "rises to dangerous, life threatening levels," a definition that excludes most cases of coercive control or DV. The researchers also exclude from their abuse category what they term "male-controlled interactive violence" where a controlling male who is willing to use force to win compliance escalates his assaults if his partner physically or otherwise resists his efforts at control. This situation is termed "interactive" because there would be no severe violence, hence presumably no threat to children, if the wife complied with her husband's demands. This interpretation raises significant ethical issues. By putting a woman's resistance to control on a par with a husband's abuse, the researchers lend normative weight to coercive control, the most devastating form of interpersonal oppression seen in family court. As Dalton argues, insisting that abuse is only real when violence is unidirectional has helped to rationalize moving the vast majority of abuse cases into the "conflict" or "high conflict" categories.[74] By contrast, sociologist Michael Johnson[75] describes the identical phenomenon as "violent resistance" and tracks the wife's violence to the husband's illegitimate use of control, which he labels abusive. By reframing this dynamic as a form of dysfunctional interaction, Johnston and Campbell obliterate the lines of power to which a court must respond if it hopes to protect the child.

But even on its own terms, Johnston and Campbell's research lends no support to the belief that custody cases involve a unique type of violence.[76] The typology assessed by Johnston and Campbell is derived theoretically rather than empirically and is impervious to modification based on actual reports, let alone on conflicting reports from members of a couple. The researchers were not interested in how common each type was, report no tests of statistical significance, and have no way to know what proportion of actual divorce cases involve what they term "separation and post-divorce" violence. So, they make no claim, one way or the other, about whether separation violence is common, let alone typical of the abuse seen in custody disputes. They attribute "separation engendered violence" to the "intolerable sense of abandonment and loss" that prompts some partners to engage in "one, two or several incidents" of violence, including "sometimes very serious ones." In marked contrast to the normal sense of loss common in divorces, I have found that the sense of "intolerable . . . abandonment" that leads to violence is elicited by a felt loss of control over a spouse, rather than by separation per se, and can excite a murderous rage, sometimes

---

[73] J. Johnston & L. Campbell, "A Clinical Typology of Interparental Violence in Disputed Custody Divorces," 63(2) *Am. J. Orthopsychiatry* 190 (1993).

[74] C. Dalton, "When Paradigms Collide: Protecting Battered Parents and Their Children in the Family Court System," 37 *Fam. & Concilation Courts Rev.* 273 (1999).

[75] Johnson, *supra* note 27; Johnson, *supra* note 12.

[76] Johnston & Campbell, *supra* note 73.

followed by the perpetrator's suicide.[77] According to the recently released report of the Violence Policy Center, a nonprofit agency that tracks violence in America, there were some 554 murder-suicides in the first half of 2007, including 320 homicides. Not only were the vast majority of the homicide victims female (227) or children (45) and the killers male (95 percent), but these proportions hold up on the solely intimate-partner murder-suicides, which account for nearly three in four of all murder-suicides.[78] The controlling husband obsesses over his loss, deprives himself of food or other basic necessities, "slips" in his personal hygiene, and experiences many of the same health and behavioral symptoms due to the loss of control over his partner that we observe in women who are being abused. Far from being relatively benign, this type of violence can almost always be identified with a prior history of violence and control. When the couple separates, the husband blames his wife for disloyalty, uses the court system to the fullest extent his assets allow, and takes every opportunity, including visits with his children, to denigrate his wife for abandoning him, an example of "child abuse as tangential spouse abuse." The narrow definition employed by Johnston and Campbell would hide this pattern. Of course, violent outbursts can be stress-related and respond well to short-term counseling and arrangements for "parallel parenting." But they are more likely to be prompted by distress induced by a loss of control and to present a high risk to mother and children. Neither an evaluator nor the family court can take this risk. Where any violence surfaces during separation, the most conservative approach requires that a pattern of abuse or coercive control be ruled out before assuming the assault is an isolated incident.

A rich literature is emerging that attempts to type the varied contexts in which abusive partner violence occurs. While none of these typologies has a sufficient empirical foundation to be considered definitive, they can be used to target clinical resources and determine which protections are likely to be effective. For the purposes of the family court, the most relevant of these typologies divides abuse into "situational" violence, where force is used to resolve conflicts; "intimate terrorism," a complex much like coercive control where control tactics accompany violence; and "violent resistance," where an abused partner responds violently to intimate terrorism.[79] According to Johnson, situational violence is often mutual and/or initiated by female as well as male partners; "intimate terrorism" is primarily initiated by men, though not exclusively, largely because control strategies are facilitated by sexual inequality; and "violent resistance" is primarily used by women in response to a male partner's abuse, the type Johnston and Campbell term "interactive."[80] In my work, situational violence is further subdivided into "fights," where violence is typically mutual and neither party feels "abused," and frank partner assaults, where the primary intent of violence is to hurt or dominate a partner rather than to resolve differences.[81] Although exposure to violence of any kind can disturb children, fights are probably the least harmful, and intimate terrorism is the most threatening. The effects of violent resistance are complicated by the frequency with which it is protective and is perceived as such by children.

Gould, Martindale, and Eidman argue that the separation violence they describe more closely resembles the situational violence reported to community surveys than

---

[77] Stark (2007), *supra* note 29.

[78] Violence Policy Center, *American Roulette: Murder Suicide in the United States* (3d ed. 2008).

[79] Johnson, *supra* note 27; Johnson, *supra* note 12.

[80] Johnston & Campbell, *supra* note 73.

[81] Stark (2007), *supra* note 29.

the intimate terrorism more typical of service recipients.[82] Johnson shares this view.[83] However, where Johnson clearly classifies situational violence as abuse and insists we should assume all cases involve intimate terrorism until proved otherwise, Gould, Martindale, and Eidman conclude that the violence is typically not serious enough to require protective intervention and that it is motivated by something other than a desire to control or exploit. At least one study finds that close to 70 percent of the incidents classified as "situational" involve severe violent acts, and approximately 50 percent cause minor or serious injury.[84] This is a slightly lower level of injury than elicited by "intimate terrorism," but it is clearly a significant concern. Equally important, the same proportions (30 percent) of situational violence cases and cases of intimate terrorism are motivated by money or children, issues that are central to custody disputes.[85] Thus, these phenomena are distinguished by the tactics deployed, but neither are distinguished by their motive nor the degree to which the encounters are abusive.

As we have seen, FRs supporters turn to population surveys to counter evidence from service sites. The violence reported to these surveys is more likely to be mutual than at service sites, and the women identified as abused report lower frequency rates of victimization than are reported in "clinical" samples from shelters or in criminal justice proceedings. Even so, virtually every one of these surveys shows that abused persons are assaulted on average three to four times annually and that 25 to 30 percent report being beaten once a week or more—so-called serial abuse. There is no way to know how much of this low-level violence occurs in the context of coercive control. Nor is there evidence that these frequency rates are altered by separation or divorce.

In sum, the claim that the violence seen in disputed custody cases is any different than the partner violence seen elsewhere cannot be supported. Even where victims first acknowledge their abusive history in the context of a divorce action, it is usually because they feel it is safer to do so at that point rather than because abuse is new.

When Glass, Manganello, and Campbell, conducted a multicity study to determine which factors were associated with lethal outcomes in abuse cases, they identified three that increased a woman's risk nine-fold: separation, the presence of a weapon, and the existence of control.[86] By contrast, factors commonly thought to signal dangerousness, such as the frequency or the severity of previous violence or the role of substance abuse, did not do so. Since separation is a constant in divorce cases, and control is also likely to be present in a majority of abuse cases, there is good reason to suspect that, if anything, the types of abuse in the custodial setting are more dangerous than abuse seen in other service settings, not less so.

WHAT SHOULD BE DONE?

For the family court, the critical questions are how the power dynamics at work in an abusive relationship jeopardize the physical and psychosocial integrity of the

---

[82] Gould, Martindale & Eidman, *supra* note 10.

[83] Johnson, *supra* note 12.

[84] K. Guzik, Governing Domestic Violence: The Power, Practice, and Efficacy of Presumptive Arrest and Prosecution Against the Violent Subjectivities of Intimate Abusers (Ph.D. dissertation, University of Illinois at Urbana-Champaign, 2006).

[85] Id.

[86] Glass, Manganello & Campbell, *supra* note 35.

mother and the children and how to protect them during separation and after divorce. As has already been suggested, therapeutic jurisprudence is little help in answering these questions.

So critical is the presence of coercive control to the future prospects of a mother's relationship to her child, so elusive and eclectic are the signs and symptoms of intimidation, isolation and control, so easily are the behavioral dynamics of coercive control hidden from view, and so commonly are the reactions to control mistaken for psychological dysfunction that, much like a cardiologist confronted by complaints of chest pain, any professional called to advise the court in these cases should conduct a full workup to rule out this worst-case scenario at any hint of its presence.

CONCLUSION

In the late 1970s, it was still widely believed that women's failure to seek help explained why DV was so rarely a focus of medical concern. By the early 1980s, researchers had documented what the shelter experience confirmed—battered women were seeking help in huge numbers. If official numbers were low and the response inappropriate, this was because a range of blinders kept service providers from recognizing the significance of abuse. In hospital research, we found that clinicians were correctly identifying only one case of battering in twenty.[87] The medical paradigm led physicians to abstract injuries and other symptoms from their social and historical context, treat each symptom as a discrete incident, and, then, when this approach failed to keep women from returning to the hospital or from developing secondary problems, such as depression or alcoholism, from the stress of ongoing abuse, to use pseudopsychiatric labels that identified these women as the problem to be managed rather than their abusive partners. Interventions actually reinforced their entrapment.

Three decades of advocacy, professional education, and legal reform have greatly enhanced the response of hospitals, police, child welfare, the criminal courts, and other services to battered women and their children. But the family court remains largely outside this process. Here, the same pattern of denial, minimization, and victim blaming that heretofore characterized other institutions, continues to dominate practice, particularly in disputed custody cases. As the studies from Kentucky, New York, Washington, and California suggest, even when a history of abuse is well documented in a man's criminal records, DV is rarely identified or validated by custody evaluators and is even less often included in custodial recommendations to the court. One consequence is that, in a disturbing proportion of cases, abusive husbands are given sole custody, joint custody, or unsupervised access to children to whom they continue to pose a significant risk. While judges do respond more appropriately when a criminal case of DV is documented in the family file than when it is merely alleged, even in this instance, only one case in four results in a no-contact order. Moreover, this response does not distinguish family courts in the United States from similar proceedings abroad. In 2003, fewer than 1 percent of the applications for child contact in Family Courts in England and Wales (601 of more than 67,000) were refused,[88] a stunning outcome given what we know about the prevalence of DV.

---

[87] Stark & Flitcraft, *supra* note 2.

[88] Department for Constitutional Affairs CMND 6251, Judicial Statistics England and Wales for the year 2003 (May 2004). Department for Constitutional Affairs, *available at* http://www.official-documents.gov.uk/documentcm51/6251/6251.pdf (no longer available).

Well-designed research in New York and California suggests something more—victims and their children may actually fare worse in the family court when abuse is identified than if mothers remain silent about DV, a dramatic example of the battered mothers' dilemma. Stories abound of abused mothers who have been forced to provide access to perpetrators, been given pseudopsychiatric labels because of their aggressive attempts to protect their children, had severe constraints placed on their own access, been ordered to supervised visitation, been denied access altogether, or even been jailed for their reluctance to "cooperate."

In sum, although DV is far and away the most prevalent threat to children in disputed cases, the family courts not only deny its significance, but appear to discriminate against battered women and their children as a class, even when state policies explicitly direct judges to give presumptive custody to battered women. The question is, "why?"

One explanation is structural. The family court occupies a unique place in the legal system because of its substantive concerns with personal life and character, its informal evidentiary procedures, and a decision-making process that lacks the sort of accountability to formal law, public scrutiny, and empirical validation that characterizes other legal, medical, or criminal justice institutions. To some extent, this reflects its function, to reconcile the conflicting needs and wishes of particular individuals rather than to administer equity and justice, for example. But its combination of a personalistic focus and relative insularity also allows social prejudice with respect to gender, sexual identity, race, or social class to play an inordinate role in its decision making. At best, therapeutic jurisprudence lends a certain objectivity to the process of assessing needs and reconciling interests. At worst, as in the case of DV, it gives stereotypes the imprimatur of science.

Another explanation for the inappropriate response by the family court is paradigmatic, as it was in the medical system. The prevailing conceit favoring coparenting implies that fathers have an inalienable "right to contact" if they choose to exercise it. Therapeutic jurisprudence recasts the same man who appears as a perpetrator in criminal court as a "good enough father" in family court, rationalizes this interpretation as in the child's best interest, and reframes women who persist in seeking protective interventions as "uncooperative" or worse, punishing them for vindictively alienating their children from their fathers and giving these fathers primary custody. At the same time, when courts equate abuse with violence, take an incident-specific approach, and apply a calculus of injury to assess severity, the result is to trivialize partner assault—which typically involves frequent, but minor violence—and to render coercive control, the context of violence that is most devastating to victims and their children, virtually invisible. This approach makes the cumulative fear expressed by victims of battering or coercive control appear exaggerated or, in the case of children, to be a byproduct of deliberate alienation, two of the more common rationales for dismissing allegations of DV.

A third explanation reflects the socioeconomic and political context in which custodial decisions are made. Without a principled theory of primary parenting or equity to constrain the exercise of prejudice in disputed family proceedings, decisions follow the dollar, in this instance, the advantaged status of husbands both relative to their wives and to the offenders seen in criminal court. Therapeutic jurisprudence rationalizes this dynamic. By applying psychological theories discredited in other settings, evaluators reframe legitimate allegations of abuse as transparently self-interested efforts to sabotage the benefits of coparenting and fathers' access to children.

A final explanation involves the nature of abuse itself. Battering and coercive control are behavioral strategies intended to exact privileges by oppressing and exploiting an adult partner. Although these strategies have psychological dimensions and effects, they are not psychological conditions, nor are they typically rooted in psychological problems. Perpetrators of abuse have a self-interest in concealment, minimization, and blaming others for their strategies that far exceeds the detection capacities of evaluators, family judges, and most other professionals who work in and around the family court. Appropriate assessment in abuse cases requires a new type of forensics, including new types of evidence, assessment conducted by persons with extensive experience working with abuse perpetrators and their victims, and expert testimony from persons whose investigative skills more closely resemble those of police detectives than psychologists. Given the prevalence of DV in disputed custody cases, adapting this approach means sharply reducing the role of therapeutic jurisprudence in custody cases. Most family lawyers are not prepared to appropriately present a case for abuse, let alone to decipher its more subtle dimensions. Scatter-shot training for judges or evaluators, the current approach, is as likely to reinforce as to curtail the prevailing bias evident in family court decisions in abuse cases. In the end, mounting an effective response to abuse in disputed custody cases requires major changes in family court procedure as we know it.

Given convincing evidence of abuse, the primary concern of the family court should be to limit access by the perpetrator to his former wife and children, provide appropriate protections against future assault, and offer support services to all parties. Adhering to this program would help a significant proportion of abusive husbands (and some wives) reframe their behavioral choices, as many now do in the context of criminal proceedings and some do in batterer programs. But there should be no illusions. Appropriately retooling family courts to respond to abuse would dramatically up the ante in custodial disputes, lengthen the time and cost of these proceedings, add a level of conflict to already acrimonious proceedings, and make evaluators and judges targets of criticism by FRs groups and their supporters. Frank assessments of abuse would also challenge the prevailing ideology of family courts by pitting justice concerns, the importance of safety, and moral judgments about right and wrong against deeply held beliefs in equity, fairness, privacy, and cooperation. But it is also likely that strengthening the family court commitment to just outcomes in abuse cases may actually move us towards rather than away from an ideal of joint parenting after divorce. As Justice Wall, the Lord Justice of Appeal in England put it, "it is . . . high time that the Family Justice System abandoned any reliance on the proposition that a man can have a history of violence to the mother of his children but, nonetheless, be a good father."[89]

Incorporating this insight into family court practice may be a first step towards responsible fathering and allowing victimized women to properly protect and mother their children.

---

[89] N. Wall, *Report to the President of the Family Division on the Publication by the Women's Aid Federation of England Entitled Twenty-Nine Child Homicides: Lessons Still to Be Learnt on Domestic Violence and Child Protection With Particular Reference to the Five Cases in Which There Was Judicial Involvement* 8.22 (2006).

Chapter 12

Parental Alienation Syndrome

by Paul Jay Fink, M.D.

INTRODUCTION

As originally defined, Parental Alienation Syndrome (PAS) proposes that when a parent (most often the mother) in a custody battle accuses the other parent (typically the father) of child abuse, especially sexual abuse, she is most likely doing so fraudulently, and with deliberate malice, in order to cause estrangement ("alienation") between the child and the other parent. The mother is therefore "diagnosed" as causing the "disorder" of PAS in her child. Or, instead, she may be accused of engaging in "parental alienation" or "alienating behaviors" by teaching or "coaching" the child to believe and make false allegations against the father. In either case, the "expert" who "diagnosed" these problems in the mother will often recommend full custody to the "targeted," that is, alienated, parent (usually the biological father). The court might also order that the "alienating" mother not be allowed, at least temporarily, any contact with her children outside of a supervised setting. There are numerous cases, both anecdotal and documented, in which such mothers never see their children, either supervised or unsupervised, again.[1]

Is there such a thing as parental alienation? Negative attitudes, conflict, even occasional hostility are extremely common among separating partners. Children often feel resentment toward one or both parents. Within some, there may be a deep-seated desire to hurt the other party. In such cases, one parent often says nasty things about the other parent, sometimes in front of the children. One parent may inform the children

---

[1] Reports abound with testimony and other findings of how frequently fit mothers lose custody of their children to abusive ex-partners. For details, see the list of recommended reading and resources in Appendixes A and B of this book.

about the other parent's infidelity or other egregious behavior; one parent may try to assassinate the other parent's character. Such messages are absorbed by the children, who often repeat them to the accused parent, thus setting off another round of accusations and counteraccusations. As a result, alienation may occur at some point between parents and children, but it is neither a syndrome nor a disorder, as PAS proponents contend.

PAS has not been recognized by the American Psychiatric Association, the American Medical Association, or the American Psychological Association as a legitimately researched, evidence-based condition. Since it seems to bear the imprimatur of both psychological science and the judicial system, however, PAS appears cloaked in a mantle of credibility.

ROLE OF PARENTAL ALIENATION SYNDROME IN CHILD CUSTODY CASES

PAS is partly if not wholly responsible for the many family court decisions in which battered mothers lose custody to abusive men. Some of these mothers have been deprived of access to their children for months and years. How could this possibly happen, unless these mothers were unfit—which they overwhelmingly are not?

First, courts often accept at face value the recommendations listed in a forensic (or custody) evaluation report. These recommendations are formulated by a so-called forensic expert, often but not always a psychologist or psychiatrist, on the basis of any number of junk science theories, on test scores that are invalid for the purpose of determining custody, on sexist assumptions, or on personal biases.

PAS epitomizes the reasoning, or lack of reasoning, behind these egregious court decisions. Since the expert testifying to the alienation or other offenses is usually a respected member of the psychiatric or psychological profession and is therefore viewed as credible by the court, this amounts to an extraordinary misuse of the legal system. The ultimate outcome—custody awarded to an abusive parent—is likely to inflict extreme psychological damage to the children and to the mother who is denied free access to them.

For court agents who lean toward awarding joint custody as a way of solving complex and difficult custody cases, PAS offers a useful sound bite. Many judges, law guardians, and other court agents cite PAS, or its variations, in deciding such cases.

ORIGINS OF PARENTAL ALIENATION SYNDROME

PAS was invented by a psychiatrist who often testified in child custody cases, Dr. Richard Gardner. Gardner claimed to be a professor of child psychiatry at Columbia University School of Medicine. However, he was a *volunteer* clinical professor; he was not on the teaching staff of the university. He based PAS on his own observations and conclusions about what motivates accusations of child abuse (especially child sexual abuse) in these cases. Gardner devotees who performed custody evaluations promoted his theories both here and abroad, citing, in their court testimony, the many "scientific" articles and books Gardner published. Yes, there are quite a few. But almost all of his books were self-published through Creative Therapeutics, which Gardner ran from his home in New Jersey. Gardner also published in several journals—almost always in legal journals or journals edited by his friends. He never published his articles in any medical journal. Thus, his theories were never subjected to the scientific scrutiny of his peers.

Although Gardner claimed that PAS was not exclusively directed against women, the vast majority of cases in which it has been used involve a father who accuses the mother of being an alienator. His published ideas about sex between adults and children are directly opposed to societal norms. Gardner's writings, in fact, are resoundingly sexist.

Some quotes from Gardner's writings will give the reader a clearer sense of the pathology from which PAS sprung forth:

- "Pertinent to my theory here is that pedophilia also serves procreative purposes. . . . [T]he child who is drawn into sexual encounters at an early age is likely to become highly sexualized. . . . Such a 'charged-up child' is more likely to become sexual active . . . and more likely, therefore, to transmit his (her) genes to his (her) progeny at an early age."[2]

- Pedophilia "is a widespread and accepted practice among literally billions of people."[3]

- Similarly, "intrafamilial pedophilia (that is, incest) is widespread and . . . is probably an ancient tradition."[4]

- "Sexual activities between adults and children are a universal phenomenon. . . . Such encounters are *not* [italics in original] necessarily traumatic. The determinant as to whether the experience will be traumatic is the social attitude toward these encounters."[5]

- "The [sexually abused] child might be told about other societies in which such behavior was and is considered normal. . . . In such discussions the child has to be helped to appreciate that we have in our society an exaggeratedly punitive and moralistic attitude about adult-child sexual encounters"[6]

- "It is because our society overreacts to it [sexual abuse] that children suffer."[7]

- Some children experience "high sexual urges in early infancy" and "the *normal* child exhibits a wide variety of sexual fantasies and behaviors, many of which would be labeled as 'sick' or 'perverted' if exhibited by adults."[8]

- "Females . . . who, by merely a small extension of permissible attitudes, may become masochistic—thereby gaining sexual pleasure from being beaten, bound, and otherwise made to suffer. It may very well be that for some masochistic women, allowing themselves to be beaten into submission is the price they are willing to pay for gaining the gratification of receiving the sperm."[9]

---

[2] R.A. Gardner, *True and False Accusations of Child Sex Abuse* 24 (1992).

[3] R.A. Gardner, *Child Custody Litigation: A Guide for Parents and Mental Health Professional* 93 (1986).

[4] R.A. Gardner, *Sex Abuse Hysteria: Salem Witch Trials Revisited* 119 (1991).

[5] Gardner, *supra* note 2, at 670.

[6] Id. at 572.

[7] Id. at 595.

[8] Gardner, *supra* note 4, at 12 (emphasis in original).

[9] Gardner, *supra* note 2, at 26. For a more thorough discussion of Gardner's theories on child sexual abuse, see S.J. Dallam," Dr. Richard Gardner: A Review of His Theories and Opinions on Atypical Sexuality, Pedophilia, and Treatment Issues," 8(1) *Treating Abuse Today* 15 (1998).

Although I was never in a courtroom when Gardner was testifying, he was, reportedly, a masterful witness for whose testimony litigants paid royally. Gardner thus exemplifies the dangers of allowing pseudoscience to enter the courtroom. In reality, even pseudoscience will find adherents to buy into its notions and become excellent sales persons on its behalf.

GENDER BIAS AND CHILD ABUSE

Just as racism and ageism are alive and well in America, sexism pervades many areas of our society. Bias against women and the abuse of children take on numerous forms and show up in a wide range of venues. PAS is one of the ways gender bias manifests in our legal system.

Although I have not personally witnessed a father being labeled an alienator, Gardner and his allies claim that there have been such cases. Yet by far, the majority of PAS allegations are launched against mothers. Even when sexual abuse has been proven, the mother may still be accused of PAS, thus enabling a child abuser to hurt and violate a woman just as he has already hurt and violated his own child.

Another often overlooked aspect of this bias is seen when judges find the woman's hysterical behavior in court reprehensible and often punish the woman for her performance rather than based on the facts of the case. Can I prove this? No.[10] But I know how I myself often feel when the woman presents in a very dramatic fashion, with lots of tears and accusations. After I run out of empathy, I get annoyed. I have no standard of decorum in my office that is in any way analogous to what is expected in the courtroom.

As suggested by the title of Goldstein, Freud, Solnit, and Burlingham's book, *Beyond the Best Interests of the Child*,[11] custody courts should focus on the interests of the children who are at the center of the battle. By using PAS against mothers who are trying to protect their children from abusive fathers, custody courts, in effect, overlook, excuse, and even enable the abuse and reabuse of children.

LEGAL SYSTEM

The U.S. court system is highly fragmented. County courts and state courts have many levels of jurisdiction; laws vary from state to state. Therefore, any campaign to educate all of the family court judges in the country about the illegitimacy of PAS would be hindered by the complexity of our system (which some refer to as a "nonsystem").

In almost every court that has held a *Frye*[12] or *Daubert*[13] hearing to address the admissibility of PAS, the theory has failed as a science, and the expert—including Gardner himself—has been disqualified. However, once a PAS allegation is raised, unless a

---

[10] The common phenomenon in which judges and other court agents base their impressions of a battered women's credibility on her *in-courtroom demeanor or litigating behavior*, as opposed to the legal merits of her case, is thoroughly examined in A. Neustein & M. Lesher, *From Madness to Mutiny: Why Mothers Are Running From the Family Courts—And What Can Be Done About It* (2005)..

[11] J. Goldstein et al., *Beyond the Best Interests of the Child* (1984).

[12] Frye v. United States, 293 F. 1013 (1923).

[13] Daubert v. Merrell Dow Pharm., 509 U.S. 579 (1993).

hearing is requested, the case proceeds as though the theory were legitimate. Consequently, PAS-tainted testimony and recommendations make it into the court record and are allowed to guide the judge's decision. This might shock those who are not familiar with the inner workings of the family court system, especially the extraordinary power held by judges. In fact, in the courtroom, the judge is king, and the king's decisions are final.

In one notorious Marin County, California, case, the children and youth agency in the county had already substantiated the sexual abuse of the two daughters by their biological father. However, the judge in that same county would not allow the evidence to be presented. Ultimately, custody of the children was given to the known predator. The judge might call this justice. Almost anyone else would call it a miscarriage of justice.

Mental health and legal professionals who work in the system get used to the autocracy of the court and the strange methods it uses in the quest for justice. For example, time and human relationships mean little to the court. A mother who has been ordered to cease contact with her children will likely become more and more anxiety ridden, with her rage, frustration, and worry continuing to build as time passes. Unless her relationship with the children is restored, she is likely to develop a deep sense of hopelessness. Since the court system has little empathy for her predicament, it may delay scheduling the next hearing until weeks or months into the future, thus further amplifying the mother's anguish. This is just one of many ways in which the judicial system's operation—business as usual—inflicts harm on families.

Related to this is that, often, a father has enough money to delay, appeal, and hire the best lawyers and expert witnesses. Mothers generally have less money, if any, by comparison, so their options are much more limited. Rarely is there an even playing field between the two parents. Even women who can afford a good lawyer have complained of hiring several different attorneys in a row because, one after another, each failed to competently or vigorously defend the woman against PAS allegations.

IN DEFENSE OF THE CHILDREN

Thousands of cases of child abuse—physical, sexual, or emotional–as well as childhood trauma and child neglect are verified annually. These experiences may be life altering, as they have been shown to have deleterious effects, both medically and psychologically, on short- and long-term adjustment. One line of research on this relationship uses the Adverse Childhood Experiences (ACEs) instrument, developed by Dr. Vincent Felitti of the Kaiser Permanente Program in San Diego, California, and Dr. Robert Anda, a senior researcher at the Centers for Disease Control (CDC).[14] These two have discovered that a child who experiences four or more of the list of ACEs has a greater chance of being involved with negative lifestyle behaviors—smoking, drinking, drug abuse, obesity—which may lead to serious medical diseases such as heart disease, diabetes, and liver disease as well as serious mental illnesses and early death. The ACEs include recurrent physical abuse, recurrent emotional abuse, sexual abuse, an alcohol or drug abuser, an incarcerated household member, someone who is chronically depressed, suicidal, institutionalized, or mentally ill, mother being treated

---

[14] V.J. Felitti, *The Origins of Addiction: Evidence From the Adverse Childhood Experiences Study, available at* http://www.partnershipforsuccess.org/uploads/200701_AddictionfinalASF2. pdf. Published in Germany as V.J. Felitti, "Ursprünge des Suchtverhaltens—Evidenzen aus einer Studie zu belastenden Kindheitserfahrungen," 52 *Praxis der Kinderpsychologie und Kinderpsychiatrie* 547 (2003).

violently, one or no parents, and emotional or physical neglect. The relationship of trauma and abuse to psychophysiological disorders came through very clearly in findings on a sample of over 17,000 patients.

This study and others tell us how badly we treat children, who are weaker and more vulnerable than adults and therefore subject to greater damage. Early in the history of psychoanalysis, Freud believed that serious neurosis was the result of childhood trauma related to sexual abuse. He changed this theory after being consulted by the daughter of a good friend. He could not believe that this man had sexually abused his daughter.

Almost 100 years later, a major biological researcher repeated the same sentence: "I can't believe a nice man like that would have sex with his daughter." But now we also have documented knowledge that lots of nice guys "screw" their children. Sexual abuse, as we know it, is not limited to any specific socioeconomic or ethnic group. The use of PAS at every level of society is therefore not only possible but plausible, due to the huge number of children and adolescents who are raped, fondled, or otherwise misused by pedophiles throughout the country.

THE ABUSED AND TRAUMATIZED DO NOT TELL

Children as well as adults who suffer from being sexually abused are very reluctant to reveal their stories. This is similar to what is commonly known about Holocaust victims, who often refuse to reveal the horrors they experienced, even to their spouses or children. Likewise, many abuse victims repress their experiences. To some, the perpetrator has issued dire threats if the child tells anyone about what has been done to him/her—threats to either kill the child or hurt the other parent or siblings. These threats complicate cases of PAS, because someone is always claiming that the child cannot be believed or has been coached to lie by the "alienator."

To determine whether sexual abuse has occurred, a thorough evaluation should be carried out by an expert psychiatrist or psychologist who has been trained to interview children about these matters. All too often, clumsy investigators with no credentials make such an investigation impossible. Police, lawyers, or social workers may pressure the child with inappropriate direct questions, which may frighten the child and render information useless forensically. The most important antidote to this is careful investigation that includes an examination of the child, the parents, and the siblings.

In some cases, a frightened, silent child is told he/she is lying, while the mother is accused of planting the lie in the child's mind. However, it is well known that child abuse memories may be repressed; the abuse experience may cause dissociation as a way for the child to escape from the horror of recalling the repeated events. Those who claim that there is no such thing as repression and/or dissociation or that abuse symptoms are induced by the therapist are denying the prevalence of sexual abuse, the damage it causes to children, and the ways in which it manifests.

WORK OF LEADERSHIP COUNCIL TO COUNTER MISINFORMATION

Creation of Leadership Council

Almost a decade ago, a number of psychiatrists, psychologists, lawyers, and other mental health professionals formed the Leadership Council on Child Abuse and

Interpersonal Violence (http://www.leadershipcouncil.org). In the 1990s, after hard-fought advances in the awareness and treatment of child abuse, we witnessed a vitriolic backlash against child victims, adult survivors, and anyone who spoke out on their behalf. The backlash was orchestrated by accused child molesters, pedophile advocacy groups, defense attorneys, insurance companies, and professional expert witnesses. As a result of a successful media, legal, and academic campaign, the extreme views promoted by the backlash began to be expressed in mainstream journals and newspapers. As a result, fewer instances of child abuse are being substantiated by child protective agencies, and fewer sex offenders are investigated or charged by the legal system.

As things went from bad to worse, a group of concerned professionals gathered to discuss how best to address the situation. At a meeting in 1998, we searched our hearts for ways to use our unique position to educate the public on what we know about trauma and to counter the increasing stream of misinformation attacking the credibility of abuse victims. As a result of this meeting, the Leadership Council was formed. The Leadership Council is a nonprofit scientific organization, and our advisory board contains over forty internationally known and respected researchers, clinicians, legal scholars, public policy analysts, and leaders in the fields of child abuse and severe trauma. Members of the Leadership Council are working professionals dedicated to the health, safety, and well-being of abused children and other victims of trauma or interpersonal violence.

Mission

The Leadership Council is the only professional group in the United States whose foremost mission is to expose and counter the attitudes and misinformation that allow the widespread abuse of children in our society to persist. Through scientific means, we actively counter the pseudoscience employed by those who seek to misrepresent science in order to discredit child abuse victims, protect child abusers, or challenge laws that criminalize sex with children. We fight misinformation wherever it takes root, whether in the media, the court system, or the scientific community.

The number of *amicus* briefs the Leadership Council has produced is extensive, and samples appear on our Web site. We receive a significant number of calls and e-mails from mothers, whom we try to refer to excellent, knowledgeable lawyers, psychiatrists, and psychologists (expert witnesses) who might help create an even playing field in court. Too often, these women are totally without funds and are desperate as a result of the lengthy litigation they have already been through. Except for money spent on research, Leadership Council members work pro bono to educate not only victims, but the general public about the many problems related to custody battles and family distress related to the abuse of children in our society, especially sexual abuse.

To give an example of the typical calls for help that we receive, while I was writing this, the Leadership Council received a call from a woman living in a mid-sized city in Texas. She reported that a number of women had been "abused" by a social worker/counselor who was pro-PAS. Reportedly, this counselor had repeatedly lied to her clients and betrayed the women by calling the opposing spouse in the case and then essentially testifying against them in court. We agreed to read the material she would send and try to help if we could.

In the last five years, we have been contacted by hundreds of mothers claiming to have lost custody or who are in danger of losing custody of their children because they are accused of PAS. In almost every case, the crime committed by the mothers was seeking to protect their child from abuse. In some of these cases, the abuse was substantiated by pediatricians and child protective service workers. Yet even hard evidence of abuse is often not enough to counter the alleged abuser's claim that the child suffers from PAS. This is because PAS is based on the belief system of the evaluator rather than any real diagnostic criteria. The syndrome has no scientific basis, and thus there is *no* valid or reliable means of making a diagnosis. This, of course, means there is also no way to disprove a diagnosis once it has been made.

BOTTOM LINE: STEPS TO TAKE

There are several things that need to be done to stop the use of PAS in custody cases. First, we need to find a way to educate legal professionals—judges, lawyers, guardians ad litem, evaluators, and so forth—about the facts of PAS. It is vital that they disallow the use of PAS in court. Jennifer Hoult studied the use of PAS in court extensively and has found that PAS has failed *Daubert* and *Frye* and has been known to lack validity.[15]

The following list of facts provides proof that PAS fails to satisfy *Daubert*:

1. Differential diagnostic criteria (DDC) cannot diagnose PAS according to Gardner's definition.

2. DDC cannot logically diagnose any identifiable entity.

3. There is no evidence that PAS is a medical syndrome; its cause and remedies are legal, not medical.

4. Gardner's expert certification was questionable.

5. PAS is a mere *ipse dixit*—"subjective (belief) and unsupported speculation."[16]

Second, we need to raise consciousness among members of the general public regarding the sexual abuse of children and the terrible, lifelong effects it has on those who are abused.

Third, we must better train those who conduct interviews of sexually abused children. We need well-trained professionals to do exquisite multilevel evaluations in which the child and both parents are evaluated. Judges, too, need training in these matters.

Fourth, the evidence concerning PAS's failure to meet *Daubert* and *Frye* standards must be widely promulgated. It is essential that we finally put this pseudoscience to rest, no matter how committed Gardner devotees are in pushing the PAS agenda.

Fifth, prosecutors should diligently question any case law or article that is cited as supporting PAS theory. Some Web sites refer to case law as supporting the reliability of PAS theory, but the opinions in these cited cases are often not adequately explained, or they prove to be less supportive of PAS theory than argued. Prosecutors reviewing literature that is cited as being favorable toward PAS should scrutinize it carefully.[17]

---

[15] J. Hoult, "The Evidentiary Admissibility of Parental Alienation Syndrome: Science, Law, and Policy," 26(1) *Child. Legal Rts. J.* 1 (Spring 2006), *available at* http://stopfamilyviolence.org/media/Hoult_PAS_admissibility.pdf, also presented at International Conference on Violence, Abuse, and Trauma, San Diego, California, Sept. 17, 2006.

[16] Id.

[17] Articles on PAS that have been published in peer-reviewed journals are listed on the Web site of Creative Therapies (http://www.rgardner.com), the publisher of many texts on PAS by Dr. Gardner.

Chapter 13

Why Do Judges Do That?

by Mike Brigner, J.D.

INTRODUCTION

The American public does not understand what motivates men to beat up women they supposedly love. This results mainly from the misperception of domestic violence (DV) as solely physical assaults rather than its more common pattern of malicious coercive control of female intimate partners, with physical violence as only one of its weapons. To remedy this public confusion, an insightful veteran who works with abusive men published a revealing volume that systematically explains why men beat and manipulate their intimate partners. In *Why Does He Do That? Inside the Minds of Angry and Controlling Men,*[1] author Lundy Bancroft dissects the motivations of the millions of men who assault their partners every year.

The general public badly needs such education. Not so most battered women, who already understand abusive men. They observe firsthand the male rewards of coercive control that female partners pay for with their bodies and souls: financial supremacy,

---

[1] Lundy Bancroft, *Why Does He Do That?: Inside the Minds of Angry and Controlling Men* (2002).

absolute discretion over family activities, sex on demand, servitude of spouse and children, and the psychic rewards of cruel power.

Women trapped in relationships with abusers come to expect horrendous misbehavior from their partners. What they cannot fathom is the maddening reinforcement commonly provided to abusive men by the justice system and the public at large. Almost all of the weapons at the command of an abuser, including fear, despair, isolation, impoverishment, and manipulation of children, can be fortified by police officers, prosecutors, judges, child protective services, faith leaders, employers, and even the battered woman's own family.

This chapter focuses on only one of those abuse collaborators—what this author considers the key one. Of all the individuals and agencies who touch the lives of DV victims, this is the one with the power to nullify every attempt by a battered woman to escape her partner's abuse and protect her children, to nullify every service provided to her by every community agency and the entire justice system, and to nullify even the DV law itself.

That key abuse collaborator is the custody judge. Of all of the actors in a battered woman's life, none wield more power over her children and financial future than the custody judge. It is beyond infuriating when women discover that their custody judges lack understanding of DV and are colluding with abusers to take away women's financial resources and, even worse, their children.

When the public asks, "Why does he do that?" it is the violent abuser they are trying to understand. When battered women cry, "Why does he do that?" they are more likely to be in despair over the abusive nature of their judges than the abusive nature of their partners. Cruel behavior from their partners they have come to expect. When abuse comes from the same judges these women turned to for help, they are blindsided. So, with thanks to Lundy Bancroft, we will ask the question, why do judges do that? To find the answers, we will go inside the minds of uneducated and biased judges.

CHILDREN LIMIT SAFETY OPTIONS IN DOMESTIC VIOLENCE CASES

The first question an experienced attorney asks the new DV client is, "Do you have minor children with the abuser?" The course of the entire case hinges on the answer. A battered woman without children can usually focus exclusively on her own personal safety, cooperate with prosecution, seek protective orders freely, change her name and social security number, or even flee the jurisdiction and go into hiding. But her safety options change or disappear when children are involved. She cannot hide from his abuse, upon pain of federal kidnapping charges. Custody litigation will bind her to her current jurisdiction. Changing her name or social security number is fruitless; not only can the children be tracked regardless of these protective measures, but custody courts will usually order her to disclose her whereabouts as long as the children are minors. To the cruel but frequently asked question, "Why don't you just leave?" an abused mother can honestly answer, "Because the courts won't let me."

Utterly disastrous to an abused mother's future well-being is the willingness of many abusers to manipulate the children as part of their endless campaign of coercive control. Even more disastrous is the court's willingness to allow abusers to do just that.

Motherhood appears to make a woman a target for intimate partner abuse. The rate of abuse for women with children under twelve years is twice that of women without young children.[2] Further, studies show that at least 20 percent of disputed custody

---

[2] Amy Farmer & Jill Tiefenthaler, "Explaining the Recent Decline in Domestic Violence," 21(2) *Contemp. Econ. Pol'y* 158, 160 (2003), citing 2000 U.S. Department of Justice Study.

cases involve DV.[3] This means that (1) mothers with small children are more likely to be abused and (2) mothers who appear in divorce court are at very high risk for abuse. The public rightly assumes that custody courts—courts with broad equitable jurisdiction plus a statutory mandate to protect battered women and children—will zealously protect victims from abusers. But all too often, the public is wrong.

HOW ABUSIVE MEN MANIPULATE THE CUSTODY SYSTEM

Children living in homes with abusers face a greater danger than the public or even the custody courts seem to realize. At least one-third of children living in a home where a man is abusing their mother are themselves abused physically and/or sexually by the same man. Some research places this figure as high as 70 percent.[4] The research also indicates that the longer the duration or the higher the severity of the violence, the more likely it is that the children are victimized as well. "The probability of child abuse by a violent husband increases from 5% with one act of marital violence to nearly 100% with 50 or more acts of marital violence."[5] Such stunning revelations ought to invite severe scrutiny of the custody and visitation demands of fathers accused of battering the children's mother but, as discussed below, such scrutiny is far from universally practiced. It would be logical for the public to assume that state laws and judicial discretion would combine to discourage violent men from laying claim to child custody—logical, but once again, wrong. A widely quoted statistic notes that fathers who batter the mothers are more likely to seek sole custody of their children than are nonviolent fathers.[6]

Even if abusive fathers' prospects for success in custody courts were not so promising, powerful motivations encourage them to pursue child custody despite an apparently disqualifying history of violence against their partners or the children. Simply stated, these men have nothing to lose because *they do not really want the children anyway*.

This author, in a quarter century of practice as an attorney and as a judge in child custody litigation, found that fathers who had been accused or convicted of family violence frequently parlayed a meritless custody claim into unjust financial concessions and unsafe visitation agreements from the mothers they were abusing. Even if these fathers had no real interest in the daily care of children, aggressively pursuing expensive custody litigation is, for them, a winning strategy. The children make handy weapons to force mothers to give up property and support rights or to agree to unsafe child access demands. The prospect of child support avoidance if custody or shared parenting is won provides additional incentive for meritless child custody battles.

The monetary incentive for abusive fathers in custody litigation is hard to miss. Protests of love for their children are not matched by financial support for the children's

---

[3] Susan L. Keililz, *Domestic Violence and Child Custody Disputes: A Resource Handbook for Judges and Court Managers* 8 (1997).

[4] Naomi R. Cahn, "Civil Images of Battered Women: The Impact of Domestic Violence on Child Custody Decisions," 44 *Vand. L. Rev.* 1041, 1058-59 (1991); Anne E. Appel & George W. Holden, "The Co-Occurrence of Spouse and Physical Child Abuse: A Review and Appraisal," 12(4) *J. Fam. Psychol.* 578 (1998).

[5] S.J. Dallam & J.L. Silberg, "Myths That Place Children at Risk During Custody Disputes," 9(3) *Sexual Assault Rep.* 43 (Jan/Feb. 2006), *available at* http://www.leadership-council.org/docs/Dallam&Silberg.pdf.

[6] American Psychological Association Presidential Task Force on Violence and the Family, *Violence and the Family* (1996).

needs. It has been calculated that fathers who batter the mothers are three times as likely to be in arrears in child support as are nonviolent fathers.[7] It is safe to say that abusive fathers also tend to be "deadbeat dads."

PROTECTING ABUSED CHILDREN

Of all the utensils in the judicial toolbox for protecting children from an abusive father, the one with the greatest potential for creating safety is the one that judges seem reluctant to use. Some safety shield is provided by stay-away orders, suspension of visitation, supervised visitation, weapons surrender, and similar protective orders. But what courts are loathe to admit is that the justice system cannot adequately protect children from violent fathers. Police cannot provide round-the-clock surveillance. Judges are not going to follow the children home. No armed guard is going to be assigned to watch over the children.

Typically, there is only one person who has a chance of protecting a child from abuse, and that is the nonoffending mother. It is likely that she served that policing role prior to separating from the children's father. "While couples are still living together, a batterer's danger to children can be mediated to some extent by their mother's ability to protect them."[8] In fact, abused mothers often report that they stay in relationships with abusers to serve as a shield between the abuser and the children.

After separation, there is only one way for the justice system to put a nonoffending mother in a position to protect her children from abuse, and that is to restore her to economic self-sufficiency. It has long been recognized that lack of financial resources is another one of the primary reasons women stay in relationships with abusers.[9] Therefore, granting protective mothers the economic relief to which they are entitled by law is the single most important tool judges have to provide for their safety and for the safety of their children. There is no way for battered women to escape abuse, no matter how many times they are admonished to "just leave," without the financial wherewithal to create new and safe places to live.

Judges should recognize that when they issue court orders that create economic justice, orders that are essential for battered women to rebuild their lives, the court imposes no injustice on the batterers. Abusers cannot claim it is unfair to place upon them the financial costs of restoring their victims to economic stability. Many abusers qualify as the financially advantaged partners and thus are already bound by state law to support their families, under pain of criminal penalties.

In a recent study, an extraordinary 99 percent of the battered women participants reported that they had experienced economic abuse at some time in their relationships with their batterers.[10] Therefore, in DV cases, monetary payments beyond mere sustenance support can be viewed as a form of restitution for the financial damage inflicted on the victim and the children by the abuser:

> Though greatly underutilized, civil protection order codes include provisions
> that enable survivors to pursue economic relief, including access to material

---

[7] Id. at 40.

[8] Lundy Bancroft & Jay G. Silverman, *Assessing Risk to Children From Batterers* (2002), *available at* http://www.lundybancroft.com/pages/articles_sub/JAFFE.htm.

[9] Ann Jones, "Why Doesn't She Leave?" 73 *Mich Bar J.* 896 (1994).

[10] C. Sullivan, "Development of the Scale of Economic Abuse," 14(5) *J. Violence Against Women* 563 (2001).

resources. . . . Safety for survivors of domestic violence requires economic security. Domestic violence impoverishes battered women and exposes them to increased risks of violence. . . . Indeed, access to economic resources is the most likely predictor of whether a survivor will be able to permanently separate from her abuser.[11]

Unfortunately, judges often leave the device of economic relief in their judicial toolbox, untouched and unused. This is most often, and most unjustifiably, the case when they are considering protection orders under statutes designed specifically to provide for victim safety. Some "forty-three percent of domestic violence service providers report that judges are unwilling to consider awarding remedies (in civil protection order cases) that are clearly authorized by statute, especially custody, child support, and other forms of financial relief."[12] When so many courts do not appear to care whether they support their children or not, it is little wonder that abusive fathers feel free to become "deadbeat dads."

To the extent that a court accepts any responsibility for the safety of children, failure to provide economic justice to their protective parent constitutes dereliction of duty. But reluctance to grant battered women economic justice is only one of the failures of the judiciary, especially custody judges.

SOME CUSTODY JUDGES THINK LIKE ABUSERS

Among the tools men find effective for controlling their victims are intimidation, emotional abuse, isolation, financial restrictions, and manipulation of children. Sociology professor James Ptacek was one of the first to recognize that each of the dozen or so most common abuse weapons are often wielded against women *by judges* as well as by their abusers.[13] Five examples follow:

- The abuser can threaten dire consequences if the victim does not obey; the judge can do the same.

- The abuser can berate the victim as unstable, stupid, and not credible; the judge can confirm her inconsequence by paternalistic demeanor, denial of protection, and by treating her claims as lies.

- The abuser can cut the victim off from her job, friends, family; the judge can keep her from moving away from the abuser and from family and resources by threatening loss of custody if she relocates.

- The abuser can make sure the victim does not have the financial resources to escape; the judge, by refusing to issue or enforce adequate support orders, can reinforce this control.

- The abuser can threaten to take the victim's children away from her through a custody battle; the judge can make this nightmare come true.

---

[11] Erika A. Sussman, "The Civil Protection Order as a Tool for Economic Justice," 2006(3) *Advocate's Q.* 1–2 (Office of Violence Against Women Center for Survivor Agency and Justice).

[12] Deborah Epstein, "Redefining the State's Response to Domestic Violence: Past Victories and Future Challenges," 1 *Geo J. Gender & L.* 127, 143 (1999).

[13] James Ptacek, *Battered Women in the Courtroom* (1999).

One comprehensive, ongoing study documents the scandalous ways battered women and their children suffer from a broken justice system:

> To better understand the problems that protective parents face in the legal system, researchers at California State University, San Bernardino, are performing an on-going national survey. To date, over 100 self-identified protective parents have completed the 101-item questionnaire. The results are quite shocking. Prior to divorce, 94% of the protective mothers surveyed say that they were the primary caretaker of their child, and 87% had custody at the time of separation. However, as a result of reporting child abuse, only 27% were left with custody after court proceedings. Most protective parents lost custody in emergency ex parte proceedings (where they were neither notified nor present) and where no court reporter was present.

> The vast majority of these mothers (97%) reported that court personnel ignored or minimized reports of abuse. They reported feeling that they were punished for trying to protect their children, and 65% said they were threatened with sanctions if they 'talked publicly' about the case. In all, 45% of the mothers say they were labeled as having Parental Alienation Syndrome (PAS).

> The protective parents reported that the average cost of the court proceedings was over $80,000. Over a quarter of the protective parents say they were forced to file bankruptcy as a result of filing for custody of their children. Eighty-five percent of the protective parents surveyed believe that their children are still being abused; however, 63% say they stopped reporting the abuse for fear that contact with their children will be terminated. Eleven percent of the children were reported to have attempted suicide.[14]

The public might expect that the legal and economic coercion motivating such abusive custody litigation would be throttled by strong judicial policies that discourage abusive men from proposing that children be entrusted to their proven-unsafe care. But unfortunately, the opposite is true. The American Judges Foundation reports that judges grant custody to abusers 70 percent of the time they ask for it.[15] Allegations of DV raised by protective mothers have no demonstrated effect on the rate at which fathers are awarded custody of their children, nor do such allegations affect the rate at which fathers are ordered into supervised visitation.[16]

Two poignant examples from this author's own files illustrate the dilemma faced by nonoffending mothers when custody judges use their legal muscle to reinforce abusers' behaviors. A mother we will call Sarah had three DV felony convictions against her husband. The third time he cracked her skull with a bowling ball, and she had the X-rays to prove it. When this evidence did not seem to be of any interest to the divorce court judge, and it became evident that the court would allow the father unsupervised contact with the children, Sarah took the children and fled to another

---

[14] Dallam &. Silberg, *supra* note 5, at 43 (citations omitted).

[15] American Judges Foundation, *Domestic Violence and the Court House: Understanding the Problem . . . Knowing the Victim*, http://aja.ncsc.dni.us/domviol/page5.html.

[16] Mary A. Kernic et al., "Children in the Crossfire: Child Custody Determinations Among Couples With a History of Intimate Partner Violence," 11(8) *Violence Against Women* 991 (2005).

state. The judge ordered the FBI to track her down, ordered Sarah arrested and jailed, and then awarded custody of the children to the violent ex-husband.

Amanda (another fictitious name) fled her state when she discovered her husband was secretly poisoning her with something that could harm or terminate her pregnancy. She gave birth to a healthy son while she was in hiding. But, despite the fact that her ex-husband arguably had tried to harm or kill the infant boy before he was even born, the custody judge in the father's home county refused to restrict the father's contact or to even consider supervised visitation. The judge threatened Amanda for moving out of state and standing in the way of the father's visitation rights. Finally, Amanda moved back to the state and county where the father lived. She explained, "I'm now more afraid of the judge than I am of my ex-husband."

Attorney Richard Ducote, one of the nation's leading experts on the legal representation of battered mothers in custody cases, described in a published law review article the maddening dilemma custody courts impose on battered mothers. Ducote blames, in part, judicial thumbs that tilt the scales away from statutory abuse factors toward statutory "friendly parent" factors.

> One of the most perplexing failures in family court custody litigation is the lack of protection and support for women and children fleeing homes with violent partners, despite the abundant legal and societal demand for abused women to leave their abusers and protect their children. This "damned if you do, damned if you don't" dilemma causes battered women to risk losing custody in juvenile court for neglect if they stay, and to also risk losing custody in family court if they leave and insist on the child's protection. The primary reason for this calamity is the clash between the pervasive statutory emphasis on the parent who will encourage the child's relationship with the other parent, and the domestic violence law and policy that supports parents who insist on proper protection and the separation of the abusive parent and the child.[17]

The very legitimacy of the family court system itself might be called into question, should the public closely examine the abuse battered women receive from the judiciary. But it also may be that the concept of judges intentionally placing so many children at risk is so irrational as to defy public belief. Regrettably, we continue to hear reports to the contrary.

> Concerns about how family courts are handling cases involving abuse were also raised by the findings of [a study published by two researchers in 1999]. They examined judicial responses to protective parents' complaints of child sexual abuse in 300 custody cases with extensive family court records. The investigators found that in only 10% of cases where allegations of child abuse were raised was primary custody given to the protective parent with supervised contact with alleged abuser. Conversely, 20% of these cases resulted in a predominantly negative outcome where the child was placed in the primary legal and physical custody of the allegedly sexually abusive parent. In the rest of the cases, the judges awarded joint custody with no provisions for supervised visitation with the alleged abuser.[18]

---

[17] Richard Ducote, "Guardians Ad Litem in Private Custody Litigation: The Case for Abolition," 3 *Loy. J. Pub. Int. L.* 106, 136 (Spring 2002) (citations omitted).
[18] Dallam & Silberg, *supra* note 5, at 43 (citations omitted).

Battered women with children, especially protective mothers trying to shield their children from physical and sexual abuse, are stunned to discover that the justice system is not willing to dispense justice. It seems inconceivable that rational decision makers, especially judges, would intentionally grant unsupervised contact, joint decision making, and even full custody to men who have harmed their children and have threatened to do so again. In reality, however, battered women and their children suffer unconscionable disregard for their safety from the legal system. This occurs so often[19] that the family court system has been excoriated in investigative reports,[20] in damning documentary films,[21] and in searing commentary.[22] Egregious custody outcomes, when publicized, have spurred the creation of national organizations that advocate for battered mothers who have lost custody of their children or face that imminent prospect.[23] Scattered jurisdictions have seen courthouse protests by mothers who say they lost custody when they raised abuse charges,[24] while demonstrations in other locales spurred legal actions against offending judges.[25]

By mandating judicial education before judges have had the opportunity to make mistaken rulings that endanger women and children, states could succeed in saving not only innocent lives, but also the public's trust in family court judges and in the courts.

---

[19] The extent of the problem of parents losing custody to abusers is documented by The Leadership Council on Child Abuse & Interpersonal Violence, Bala Cynwyd, PA, a nonprofit independent scientific organization composed of respected scientists, clinicians, educators, legal scholars, and public policy analysts. The collected evidence includes media reports, http://www.leadershipcouncil.org/1/pas/media.html, scholarly articles, http://www.leadershipcouncil.org/1/pas/2.html, and research studies, http://www.leadershipcouncil.org/1/pas/dv.html.

[20] Amy Neustein & Michael Lesher, *From Madness to Mutiny; Why Mothers Are Running From the Family Courts—And What Can Be Done About It* (1995); Ptacek, *supra* note 13.

[21] Mary M. Rall, "Woman Points Camera at Domestic Violence; Documentary to Show How DV, Courts Impact Children," *Alaska Star*, Aug. 10, 2006, http://www.alaskastar.com/stories/081006/new_20060810001.shtml; Catherine Tatge & Dominique Lasseur (producers), *Breaking the Silence: Children's Stories* (2005), video documentary that chronicles the recurring failings of family courts across the country to protect children from their abusers.

[22] Jana Bommersbach, "Parental Alienation—'Jana's View,'" *Phoenix Magazine*, May 2006, *available at* http://harfordmedlegal.typepad.com/forensics_talk/2007/07/phoenix magazin.html#more.

[23] Battered Women, Abused Children, and Child Custody: A National Crisis, a grassroots organization formed in 2003, "to host a national public forum to address the many complex issues facing battered women and their advocates as they strive to protect themselves and their children in and out of family court," http://www.batteredmotherscustodyconference.org/index.htm. Other organizations with similar missions are documented by The Leadership Council at http://www.leadershipcouncil.org/1/pas/1.html.

[24] *See, e.g.,* WUSA9.COM, TV 9, *Losing Custody to Abuse Accusations,*, http://www.wusatv9.com/news/news_article.aspx?storyid=51107; Emily Previti, "Custody Case Raises Energy, Awareness," *Antioch J.*, Sept. 29, 2006, http://www.weeklyjournals.com/articles/2006/09/29/antioch/local_and_region/county02.txt; Glynis Hart, "Group Pushes for Family Court Reform," *Tompkins Weekly*, Apr. 9, 2007, http://www.tompkinsweekly.com/index.html.

[25] Mike Wiser, "County Judge, State's Attorney Sued for $300M; A Suit Claims That the Officials and a Local Attorney Conspired to Deny Custody Rights," *Rockford Register Star*, http://www.rrstar.com/apps/pbcs.dll/article?AID=/20070517/NEWS0107/105170074; Assoc. Press, "Wilson County Judge Reprimanded in Child Custody Case," Sept. 8, 2007, http://www.tennessean.com/apps/pbcs.dll/article?AID=/20070908/COUNTY10/70908004/1/RSS05.

WHY DO JUDGES DO THAT?

Universally, battered women who experience the anguish of watching the children they are trying to protect from abuse yanked away into the care of their abusers, cry, "Why?" What possibly could motivate judges to intentionally put children in harm's way? The judicial response of "It's the law" fails logic. The laws of forty states require judicial consideration of DV in custody cases. What is more, the discretion of judges in custody matters is so unfettered that no child should ever be subjected to living in a dangerous environment by judicial decree.

Having worked for three decades as a family law litigator, domestic relations court judge, and judicial educator, I would like to offer my perspective on why so many judges, particularly custody judges, make themselves coconspirators with batterers.

Judges Are Overworked

Cases rush at courts in a torrent. Domestic relations judges, especially in urban counties, may be faced with divorcing ten couples a day just to stay even with filings. Criminal dockets, especially in misdemeanor courts, are equally crushing. As a result, DV cases often are deprived of the attention warranted by their deadly potential.

What judges, especially those with little or no education on DV, fail to realize is that across their entire judicial career, there is no other type of case that carries a greater risk of a fatal outcome than a case involving intimate partner violence. Men kill their female partners at the rate of about 1,400 a year in this country, and, in addition, women kill several hundred men.[26] Remarkably, those deaths often occur while a case is actively pending in the justice system—in other words, while some judge has some degree of control over the parties and thus the opportunity to deter violent behavior. It is rare for courts to encounter criminals who kill crime victims and witnesses while their cases are still pending. Assault or murder of witnesses is rarely seen in cases with highly dangerous defendants, such as organized crime or drug gangs. In DV cases, however, physical violence against complainants is a daily event.

These cases deserve the highest degree of judicial scrutiny, regardless of docket pressures. The use of danger assessment instruments to triage the high-risk defendants from the rest of the docket list is an essential step in the competent judicial management of DV cases.

Judges Are Uneducated

DV is damnably counterintuitive, which is one reason why it mystifies casual observers. The enigma of DV, combined with the prodigious breadth of judicial intuition

---

[26] Callie Marie Rennison, *Intimate Partner Violence, Bureau of Justice Statistics Special Report* (NCJ 178247, May 2000). Bureau of Justice statistics show that during the 1976–1998 period in the United States, intimate partner murder fell by 36 percent, from 3,000 (1976) to 1,800 (1998). The number of U.S. women murdered by intimates fell from 1,600 in 1976 to 1,317 in 1998. The number of men murdered by intimates during the same period decreased from 1,357 (1976) to 512 (1998); reported in Reuters, "Protecting Battered Women Saves Lives of Men," Jan. 4, 2001. *See also* Neil Websdale, Maureen Sheeran &Byron Johnson, *Reviewing Domestic Violence Fatalities: Summarizing National Developments* (July 7, 2000), *available at* http://www.vaw.umn.edu/documents/fatality/fatality.html.

(under the guise of "judicial discretion") that judges bring to bear in DV cases, makes uneducated judges a menace to battered women and their children. A judicial officer whose discretion is guided by (1) a lack of understanding of abuse and of abusers, (2) the belief that violent husbands can be good fathers, (3) feelings of antagonism toward women who do not cooperate in litigation processes, and/or (4) hostility toward women who claim that men have been violent toward them and their children—to mention a few common biases cited publicly to justify destructive judicial decisions—paints that judge as a poster child for mandatory judicial education on DV.

Unfortunately, that education—often amounting to, quite literally, a matter of life and death—is rarely mandatory. Few law schools provide DV courses, and few states mandate any judicial education in DV. Despite the hazardous nature of DV cases, judges are allowed to pick up a gavel and make perilous decisions with little or no specialized training. By contrast, most states require well over a thousand hours of education for a citizen to pick up a pair of scissors and start work as a beautician.

Judges Erroneously Believe That Violence Ends Upon Separation

Judges sincerely but wrongly believe that DV will end when a couple becomes legally divorced or separated. This misconception is as dangerous as it is widespread. "We commonly encounter the mistaken assumption among professionals, including judges and custody evaluators, that children are in less danger from a batterer once a couple is no longer living together, when the reality is often the opposite."[27] This error leads some judges to adopt a dismissive attitude toward men's violence; they see it as irrelevant to the divorce case and believe that dealing with it will only slow down the proceedings and delay the "solution" of a permanent judicial dissolution of the relationship. Worse, this misconception justifies the gross mishandling of cases by judges who labor under the myth that a violent husband and father becomes magically anointed with new nonviolent behaviors once a divorce decree is issued.

In fact, the very act of seeking a divorce may be the most dangerous decision a battered woman will ever make. This is because her action confirms to a possessive husband or boyfriend that he is in danger of losing his female property. Studies now confirm what police and shelter workers have known for decades: some proprietary men pursue and kill the women who leave them.

> The results of our analyses indicate that wives are much more likely to be slain by their husbands when separated from them than when co-residing . . . One implication is that threats which begin "if you ever leave me . . ." must be taken seriously. Women who stay with abusive husbands because they are afraid to leave may correctly apprehend that departure would elevate or spread the risk of lethal assault. As one Chicago wife, a victim of numerous beatings by her husband, explained to a friend who asked why she didn't leave her husband, "I can't, because he'll kill us all, and he's going to kill me." He did. Fear must be added to the economic and other reasons why battered wives sometimes do not leave.[28]

---

[27] Bancroft & Silverman, *supra* note 8.

[28] Margo Wilson & Martin Daly, "Spousal Homicide Risk and Estrangement," 8(1) *Violence & Victims* 8–10 (1993) (citations omitted), *available at* http://psych.mcmaster.ca/dalywilson/SpousalHomicide.pdf.

Risk of death and sublethal assaults does not decrease when abused women attempt to escape, as many judges mistakenly believe; in fact, they increase. Data indicate that women are especially at risk for the first two months after leaving.[29] Despite the advice most women get to "just leave him," separation is a hazardous thing to do. Advocates who assist battered women have long observed that a woman is most likely to be killed when a man realizes "She's really going to leave me this time." A woman, on the other hand, kills a man when she believes, "He's really going to kill me this time."

In assessing the threat an abuser poses, it is important in this context to recognize that "separation" does not necessarily mean packing up and moving away. Women often separate temporarily without being assaulted by their partners. The increased risk to a woman of lethal-level violence appears to hinge not just on physical separation, but also upon a proprietary abuser's perception that the woman intends a final departure from the relationship. Thus, the signal event could be the filing of a divorce or protection order, the woman's visit to a lawyer, discovery of hidden safety funds, or a variety of similar events that awaken the abuser to the likelihood of her leaving for good. It is dangerous for judges to be uneducated about the realities of separation violence. It is equally dangerous for judges to assume that physical separation is the sole trigger for separation violence.

It is not just battered mothers who face increased danger after separation: children are at higher risk as well during this period. Experts observe that batterers' attempts to intimidate and control their victims by abusing, threatening, and manipulating the children increase after separation, due to the loss of other means of maintaining control.[30] Erroneous judicial assumptions that women and children will suffer less violence after separation lead to erroneous divorce, custody, and visitation orders that disregard the risk of further violence. Widespread recognition that the courts frequently fail to ensure postseparation safety, economic justice, and protection for the children convinces many battered mothers to stay in an unsafe relationship. In other words, mothers have learned to be more afraid of judges than they are of their abusers.

Judges Wrongly Believe Violent Husbands Can Be Good Fathers

Judicial ignorance of the high correlation between partner abuse and child abuse, combined with judicial misconception of the increased danger women and children face after separation, leads judges to treat batterers the same as nonviolent fathers, when making custody decisions. Despite laws in over forty states requiring judges to consider DV as a custody factor, judges often foreclose even the discussion of abuse with a desk-pounding declaration that "every father has a god-given right to see his children!" Both legally and morally, they could not be more wrong.

Dr. Peter Jaffe, a widely recognized expert on parenting in DV cases, put it succinctly:

> Somebody who is abusive to their spouse can't be a good parent. I think judges used to feel that somebody could be a violent husband but still be a kind and loving father. And those things just don't go together. Once you're a violent

---

[29] Id. at 10.

[30] Lundy Bancroft & Jay G. Silverman, *The Batterer as Parent: Addressing the Impact of Domestic Violence on Family Dynamics* (2002).

husband, in fact, you're offering a terrible role model for children. You're exposing children to fear and terror. You're traumatizing children in a variety of ways. You're undermining often their primary caretaker.[31]

Children deserve to benefit from the long arm of the law by receiving legal protections. Instead, what they often get is the opposite: "A high rate of serious assaults by batterers occur post-separation, and children are likely to witness these incidents. The risk that the batterer will assault the mother sexually also increases during and after separation. When a batterer kills his former partner, children commonly witness the homicide or its aftermath, or are murdered themselves."[32] A batterer's manipulation of the justice system combined with judicial incompetence creates a perfect storm for child endangerment to occur *by court order*.

Judges Fail to Recognize Litigation Abuse

Litigation is frequently used as a powerful instrument of abuse by those who can afford it against those who cannot. It should not be surprising that economically advantaged spousal abusers would use the courts to continue their campaign of coercive control. In fact, fathers who batter the mothers are twice as likely to seek sole custody of their children as nonviolent fathers, according to the American Psychological Association, and with predictably dangerous consequences:

[Child] custody and visitation disputes appear to occur more frequently when there is a history of domestic violence. Family courts often do not consider the history of violence between the parents in making custody and visitation decisions. In this context, the non-violent parent may be at a disadvantage, and behavior that would seem reasonable as a protection from abuse may be misinterpreted as a sign of instability.[33]

Judges Think Women Are Lying

In providing judicial education across the country, I have heard, without fail, each judicial audience ask the same shocking question: "What can I do about all these women lying to me?" Challenged to provide evidence, judges cite these examples: women claim abuse for the first time when they are seeking a divorce; women call for police or court help and then reconcile with their abuser; women file for *ex parte* protection orders and then fail to return for a contested second hearing; and women use protection orders to get a "leg up" in custody litigation. None of these reported behaviors justifies the widespread judicial misapprehension that women who report DV are liars.

Nonreporting Victims. Battered women do not often report abusive behavior when it first occurs. Studies show that they typically suffer multiple assaults before they

---

[31] Peter Jaffe, Ph.D., C. Psych., National Judicial Institute presentation, San Francisco, CA, Feb 19, 1999.

[32] *See supra* note 20.

[33] American Psychological Association Presidential Task Force on Violence and the Family, *supra* note 6, at 100.

contact authorities or apply for protective orders.[34] For a host of reasons, including denial, fear of the abuser, poverty, acceptance of the abuser's apologies, reluctance to involve police in family matters, and a conviction (apparently well-placed) that judges will not believe them, women generally wait until physical abuse and other coercive tactics escalate before turning to the justice system for help. Why judges tend to view this pattern of behavior as an indication of bad faith on the part of complainants, instead of recognizing that first-time defendants are very rarely first-time offenders, is puzzling.

Victims Who Reconcile. Judges seem to expect that battered women will attempt reconciliation, even after they have initiated court action. For a variety of very rational reasons, including threats, coercion, family pressures, children, financial dependence, promises of reform, lack of family or community support, and religious beliefs, battered women usually make repeated attempts to reconcile before making a final decision to leave an abuser. At least half of all DV victims attempt reconciliation at least once.[35]

This reconciliation pattern may frustrate those who work in the justice system, but judges should remember that DV laws give them responsibility for punishing and preventing family violence, not for regulating personal relationships. Judges would make their communities safer if they encouraged victims to return to the justice system for help if reconciliation fails rather than threaten or punish them for not leaving an abuser as quickly as judges think they should.

Victims Who Withdraw From Litigation. The National Center for State Courts investigated the issue of victims who obtain *ex parte* protection orders and then later decide to pursue no further legal remedies. The study found that when victims did not return for hearings on permanent orders, in 45 percent of the cases, the abuser had either stopped bothering them or had left the area. In another 25 percent of the cases, the victims had found help devising safety plans and felt safe without further court intervention. Yet another 17 percent had reconciled with their abuser.[36] Thus, fully 87 percent of petitioners saw the *ex parte* proceeding as sufficient for their safety and self-determination. Unfortunately, as judicial grumbling verifies, court systems unanimously see such decisions as failures that interfere with established court procedures. Worse, many judges view nonreturning victims as liars and manipulators who misuse the court system to achieve their own ends.

Myth of False Allegations. The incredulity with which courts greet reports of abuse from battered women is well known. Author Lundy Bancroft discusses this phenomenon:

---

[34] R. Felson, J. Ackerman & C. Gallagher, *Police Intervention and the Repeat of Domestic Assault* (U.S. Department of Justice, 2002-WG-BX-2002, National Institute of Justice, NCJ 210301, 2005).

[35] Jacquelyn C. Campbell, "Safety Planning Based on Lethality Assessment for Partners of Batterers in Intervention Programs," in Robert Geffner & Alan Rosenbaum eds., *Domestic Violence Offenders: Current Interventions, Research, and Implications for Policies and Standards* 129–43 (2001).

[36] Joan Zorza & Nancy K.D. Lemon, "Two-Thirds of Civil Protection Orders Are Successful; Better Court and Community Services Increase Their Success Rates," 2(4) *Domestic Violence Rep.* 51 (April/May 1997).

Court personnel and other service providers look skeptically at allegations of abuse that arise during custody and visitation battles. Batterers try to feed these doubts by saying, "She never said I was abusive before; she's just using this accusation to get the upper hand." In fact, there is no evidence that false allegations rise substantially at this time, and there are many reasons why an abused woman may not have made prior reports.[37]

Bancroft also assesses the reasons why abuse allegations may arise for the first time in the context of a divorce case:

It is not at all uncommon for a battered woman to tell no one about his abuse prior to separation because of her shame, fear, and desire to help the abuser change. Many victims quietly hope that ending the relationship will solve the problem, a myth that most professionals share; when she discovers that his abuse is continuing or even escalating after separation, she finds herself forced to discuss the history of abuse in hopes of protecting herself and her children. It is not uncommon for an abuser to be more frightening after separation than he was before, and to increase his manipulation and psychological abuse of the children.[38]

What judges ought to be concerned about is the opposite problem: Why do women have such little faith in the court system that they are reluctant to ask it for help? As Bancroft further notes:

In reality the overwhelming majority of women who report abuse are telling the truth, and an even greater number do not report the abuse. . . . Most abused women do not disclose victimization, even when reporting such information may be of vital importance to them . . . [O]f course, it is important to sort through varying accounts to ensure that no one is falsely accused of violent behavior. Nevertheless, studies continue to confirm that underreporting of violence is a much more significant problem than false accusations.[39]

Judges' obsession with the mythological problem of women making false allegations in protection order and custody cases reflects, at minimum, their failure to understand the dynamics of DV, which ultimately prevents them from grasping the specific facts in front of them. At worst, given the gender-targeted nature of DV, such judicial focus on "lying women" raises ethical concerns, especially given the judiciary's deafening silence regarding the corresponding issue—men whose denials of abuse are proven false by the evidence.

---

[37] R. Lundy Bancroft, *Understanding the Batterer in Custody and Visitation Disputes* (1998), *available at* http://www.lundybancroft.com/pages/articles_sub/CUSTODY.htm. This article is the precursor to Chapter 5 of Bancroft & Silverman, *supra* note 30.

[38] Id.

[39] Nancy K.D. Lemon, Jack Sandler, David A. Wolfe & Peter G. Jaffe, *Working Together to End Domestic Violence* (1996).

Judges Believe Competence in Domestic Violence Undercuts Judicial Neutrality

Fanned by the hot wind of vocal men's rights advocates, some judges complain that focusing judicial education and resources on battered women and their children taints the judiciary as being unfair to men. If American courts are biased toward men, this will come as a surprise to the hundreds of judges, lawyers, and other citizens who comprised the gender-bias task force studies in forty states and six federal appellate districts.[40] After extensive fact-finding and research, those independent studies found unanimously that court systems all across the nation practice degrees of gender bias *against women.* Faced with such overwhelming evidence, declarations from men's rights groups and some judges advocating the unsupportable theory that courts are gender biased against men can unfortunately be seen as further evidence of societal and judicial gender bias against women.

Based on the measure that is the most reliable, which is fatalities, it is impossible to claim that the legislative and judicial initiatives of the past thirty years have harmed the interests of men. A Department of Justice study that began in the late 1970s—an era when all states and the federal government adopted new DV laws—shows indisputably that it is *men* who have benefited most from societal action against DV. The Department of Justice statistics show that murders of women by intimate partners have declined slightly, from about 1,600 a year to about 1,400. But it is men who gained the most dramatic benefits: deaths of men at the hands of intimate partners in the studied time frame dropped by an incredible two-thirds. Whatever DV laws in this country have accomplished, by the most important measure—physical survival—it is men, not women, who have gained the most.[41]

Expressions of judicial grievance toward calls for DV competence under the banner of judicial neutrality are also misguided. It is anything but neutral for judicial officers to ignore the extremely gender-targeted nature of DV. Intimate partner violence is overwhelmingly a crime of men against women. The most recent reliable and comprehensive studies of DV[42] show the following:

1. Women are more likely than men to be victimized by intimate partners. In fact, about 85 percent of intimate partner violence is committed against women.

2. Women are harmed more severely in those assaults.

3. Males who are victims of assault are generally assaulted by other males.

4. In the most serious of DV assaults, those resulting in homicide, federal statistics show that males make up 83 percent of spouse murderers, and males account for eight out of every ten homicides of a family member.[43]

---

[40] As documented by the National Organization of Women (NOW) Legal Defense Fund, http://www.nowldef.org/html/njep/tfstate.shtml.

[41] *See supra* note 26.

[42] Julie Kunce Field, *Screening for Domestic Violence: Meeting the Challenge of Identifying Domestic Relations Cases Involving Domestic Violence and Developing Strategies for Those Cases*, 39 *Court Rev.* 4 (Summer 2002) (citations omitted).

[43] U.S. Department of Justice, Bureau of Justice Statistics, *Family Violence Statistics, Including Statistics on Strangers and Acquaintances* (June 2005), *available at* http://www.ojp.usdoj.gov/bjs.

Consequently, the great majority of cases where there is DV will have female victims and male perpetrators.

Judicial attempts to impose gender-neutral outcomes in such circumstances constitute not neutrality, but yet another vivid demonstration of gender bias against female victims. If judicial neutrality was a bona fide objection to achieving judicial competence in DV cases, it would be unlikely that a unanimous supreme court of one of the country's largest states would declare, "Courts have an obligation to carry out the legislative goals to protect the victims of domestic violence."[44]

CONCLUSION

Abused mothers may find cold comfort in understanding "why judges do that." A custody court system that undermines their ability to support and protect their children, even if the system is more understandable, will remain indefensible to these women. They also will find little comfort in the small likelihood that they can correct the injustices of the custody system. The typical options for individual or systemic change are limited: public advocacy or political action against a judge is unrealistic, given that the same judge is likely to retain, for many years, continuing jurisdiction over a woman's custody and support rights. Even a cursory reading of case files suggests that disciplinary complaints could sometimes be justified, but the continuing jurisdiction problem, coupled with the infrequency of serious sanctions in such cases, discourages that avenue of pursuit.

Another tool for systemic change of the justice system can be quite powerful, as an advocacy group, "Mothers Against Drunk Driving," has proven in the past several decades. Intense court watch programs to document judicial abuses, coupled with legislative and community advocacy, wrought dynamic changes in how recalcitrant courts handled cases of drunk drivers. (Unfortunately, this was achieved through the loss of critical judicial discretion, but judges have no one but themselves to blame for that outcome.) That same kind of community action could help to remedy the abuses committed by custody courts.

However, at this juncture we lack the necessary core group of committed citizens who are strongly motivated to accomplish change. While drunk drivers often leave behind highly motivated survivors with resources, DV survivors are usually too busy surviving and raising children to devote the energy it takes to achieve major structural changes in societal systems.

The greatest promise for improving justice for abused mothers and their children lies in the public's insistence that judges gain competence in understanding and managing DV cases. However, this would require overcoming the extreme reluctance of many judges. Judicial hostility toward DV education and proficiency must be countered by the explanation that judges are not being asked for favoritism, but for *competence*. Judges are not being requested to act unethically; to the contrary, improving the administration of justice is a key component of the judicial code of ethics.

Judges should understand that rather than being asked to favor battered women, they are being asked to stop favoring abusers. When faced with battered women's requests for economic relief and safety for children, judges should recognize they are not being asked to unfairly assist women in their attempts to achieve justice. Rather,

---

[44] Felton v. Felton, 79 Ohio St. 3d 34 (1997).

judges are being asked to prohibit men from blocking women's attainment of justice. Judges are being asked not to bend the rules, but rather to remove the barriers to justice that litigants face in their court systems. If judges simply provided justice, DV victims and their children would at least have a fair chance.

The public should be outraged over the persistent rate of homicide of battered women, which has hovered near 1,400 a year every year for the past three decades.[45] Whatever legislators and judges have done for over a quarter century, it is obvious that their actions have accomplished nothing toward saving the lives of battered women. Long overdue is a self-examination by all judges, but especially custody judges, as to whether they are part of the solution or part of the problem. Until courts engage in that reform, battered women and the public will continue to demand, "Why do judges do that?"

---

[45] *See supra* note 26.

Chapter 14

Batterer Manipulation and Retaliation Compounded by Denial and Complicity in the Family Courts

by Joan Zorza, J.D.

INTRODUCTION

The most common form of violence that the nation's police officers see is domestic violence (DV) in which one spouse or lover beats up the other one. Police learn about close to eight million of these incidents each year in the United States, making DV "more common than all other forms of violence combined."[1] Each officer in this country responds on average to 170 DV calls per year or almost one such call for every day that every officer works.[2] Most of the parties the police see end up in the courts whether because criminal charges are brought against the abuser; one or both parties go to family or divorce courts (hereafter "family courts") to obtain an order of protection, a divorce, custody or visitation, child support, an order for return of a child, permission to move with the child out-of-state, or other relief; because the state moves to take custody away from the parents, often based on the DV; or only very occasionally, because the victim sues the offender to obtain restitution for the damages that result from his abuse. If there are minor children or the parties are married, sooner or later these cases almost always end up in the family courts. While there is a belief that mothers almost always win custody cases, this chapter will show that this is simply not a given and that men who abuse their female intimate partners, largely through false accusations, harassment, manipulation, and intimidation, have been surprisingly successful in wining custody and often driving their victims into poverty. Abusive men not only harass their victims, many harass their partners' lawyers and manipulate those in and connected with the court system who are supposed to insure that children are placed with their better parent in a safe, nurturing environment, making it all the stranger that about half of the time batterers win custody in family courts and are actually more likely to win custody than men who do not abuse their partners.[3] The intimidation, harassment, and manipulation by abusers of their victims and everyone else in the family court or criminal justice systems has been little recognized, and sometimes courts knowingly or inadvertently collude with the abusers. This chapter concludes with some suggestions about how courts can proactively help to stop this abuse of victims as well as the courts.

LEGAL SYSTEM HAS A PRO-MALE BIAS

The legal system in America evolved from the British common law and for many years afterwards, was developed almost entirely by men with little input from women who did not even have the vote in the United States until the Nineteenth Amendment was enacted in 1920.[4] Even when the first DV laws were proposed in the 1970s, largely by women and feminists,[5] they had to be enacted by largely male legislative bodies and signed into law by overwhelmingly male governors. So it is not surprising that U.S. DV laws are somewhat gender biased in favor of men

---

[1] Lawrence W. Sherman, *Policing Domestic Violence: Experiments and Dilemmas* 1 (1992).

[2] Id. at 5-6.

[3] Joan Zorza & Leora Rosen, "Guest Editors Introduction," 11(8) *Violence Against Women: Special Issue on Child Custody and Domestic Violence* 983 (2005).

[4] Catharine A. MacKinnon, "Women and Law: The Power to Change," in *Sisterhood Is Forever: The Women's Anthology for a New Millennium* 447 (Robin Morgan ed., 2003).

[5] Evan Stark, *Coercive Control: How Men Entrap Women in Personal Life* 26–38 (2007).

and against women, although their enactment represented a huge improvement for battered women.[6] Furthermore, there was so little awareness of DV, despite how common it has always been, that battered women's advocates had to focus initially on just increasing public awareness of the issue and how it harmed battered women. Accordingly, they focused primarily on men's physical abuse of women, not the subtler aspects, such as the isolation, monitoring, stalking, coercive control, and course of conduct, or even the emotional abuse, all of which have since been shown to cause far greater harm.[7] While many abuser accusations lack such specifics, courts often fail to hold them to the same pleading requirements. Indeed, it is not uncommon for courts to never actually have an evidentiary hearing on whether a mother alienated the children, and it is almost unheard of for a court to allow testimony on whether the abuser's allegations of parental alienation are motivated by tactical or personal gain.[8]

When mental health professionals (MHPs) or judges hear men's alienation allegations, they may readily believe them, often because of the gender bias of individual practitioners or judges. But often their beliefs are exacerbated because the legislature enacted laws that favor men. While most states—Washington State is an exception—encourage courts to consider, in granting custody, which parent will encourage a better relationship and more frequent contact between the children and the other parent, courts consider only behaviors that mothers are more likely to do under this criteria, leaving out behaviors that men primarily do. Thus, failing to pay spousal or child support, or failing to legitimate the other parent's immigration status when a spouse can do so are not seen as hurtful, "unfriendly" behaviors. Yet what could be more harmful to a relationship with the children than depriving the other parent of adequate support or even the right to remain in the United States? Indeed, changing custody because a parent has not paid child support is illegal in most states; yet custody is changed all the time when mothers do not give fathers access to their children, or bad-mouth the father in the children's presence, or when abusers allege that they did one of these things, as it is nearly impossible to disprove that something did not happen. But while fathers often speak badly in front of their children about their mothers, few mothers speak badly about their former husbands,[9] although courts are notorious in assuming that they do, often to the point that they credit a father's allegations without ever giving the mother a chance to rebut them.

MALE MISBEHAVIOR IS LARGELY DISCOUNTED BY COURTS

Most family court judges believe that people going through custody and divorce cases are good people, but these people often behave very badly because they are so stressed out by the pressures of the separation and court dispute.[10] The judges primarily say this regarding men who batter their female partners, assuming that none of the abuse from these men predated the separations and custody fights and that, once the stress is over, these men will resume being what they assumed was their former

---

[6] *See, e.g.,* Chapters 1 and 5 in this volume.

[7] *See, e.g.,* Stark, *supra* note 5, at 104; Susan Schechter, *Women and Male Violence: The Visions and Struggles of the Battered Women's Movement* 161–69 (1982).

[8] Id.

[9] Demie Kurz, *For Richer: For Poorer: Mothers Confront Divorce* 181 (1996).

[10] ABA Center on Children and the Law & State Justice Institute, *A Judge's Guide: Making Child-Centered Decisions in Custody Cases* 4 (2001).

good selves.[11] As will be discussed later in this chapter, this view is reinforced if not actually taught to them by most of the MHPs (who may act as mediators, custody evaluators, parent educators, or guardians ad litem (GALs)) appointed to represent the children's best interests, as well as many of the MHPs brought into judicial trainings to educate them (see "Mental Health Professionals Seldom Know Much About Domestic Violence"). It is also reinforced by many lawyers representing the children (the law guardians or children's attorneys) and especially by the lawyers representing men who misbehave, at least those who are even willing to admit their clients sometimes misbehave. Simultaneously, or alternately, many of these MHPs and lawyers seek to shift responsibility onto the women who, they claim, provoke the men, whether by having new partners, alienating the children, or any one of the alleged myths noted by the gender-bias studies of courts starting almost thirty years ago. This chapter will discuss many of the misdeeds of abusive men against their partners and the courts, and the chapter will further discuss how courts and MHPs excuse the men's abuse, blame the victims for it, or otherwise collude with the abusive men, all to the detriment of battered women and their children.

MALE ABUSERS ARE DIFFERENT FROM OTHER MEN

Massachusetts, which has a very comprehensive records system involving intimate partner violence, has found that relatively few of the men who abuse their female intimate partners and children (called either "abusers" or "batterers" in this chapter) do so for the first time after the case is filed, and the stress theory is simply another excuse to discount, trivialize, or rationalize male violence against women. Since 1978, Massachusetts, has allowed its criminal court judges to issue civil restraining orders (as civil orders of protection are known in that state) against abusers, and it now urges all judges—even the family court judges, who also have the authority to issue such protective orders—to consult the probation records of both the alleged perpetrator and the victim whenever a petition for protection in any abuse prevention case is filed. Furthermore, the state periodically analyzes its carefully kept records. It has found that almost 80 percent of the male abusers against whom protective orders are sought have criminal records,[12] 46 percent for violent offenses. In addition, 39 percent have prior restraining orders entered against them, and the criminal justice system data shows that 15 percent of the male abusers violated those orders within the first six months (undoubtedly the number is much higher, as there is no information about cases when the police were not called or no charges brought). The men with prior orders are almost equally divided between those who have repeatedly abused one victim and those who have abused multiple victims.[13] In addition, many of the supposedly stressed-out good men seen in divorce and custody cases abusing their intimate partners were previously very well known to the criminal courts for other types of not-so-honorable problems, like writing bad checks. While many of these are the same criminal defendants previously

---

[11] Contradicting the view that it is only temporary behavior caused by stress is another commonly expressed view; their behavior should be excused because "boys will be boys," implying that this is a permanent behavior and that men never grow up into responsible individuals.

[12] James Ptacek, *Battered Women in the Courtroom: The Power of Judicial Responses* 89 (1999).

[13] Donald Cochran, Sandra Adams & Patrice O'Brien, "From Chaps to Clarity in Understanding Domestic Violence," 3 *Domestic Violence Rep.* 65, 77–78 (1998).

mentioned with a record of violent crimes on their probation records, some only show up in evictions, bad check cases, failure to pay child support cases, or other nonviolent crimes.

Massachusetts also was the first state in the country to create a statewide registry for its restraining orders, and these protective orders are also entered onto the defendants' probation records, so that judges considering issuing a restraining order can automatically become aware of both parties' prior abuse histories. Unlike in most states (which remove data once the case is over), Massachusetts' probation records retain information entered on them forever, even in juvenile delinquency cases that occurred when the individual was a minor. They also retain criminal case information filed against an individual, even if that case was later dismissed or continued without any finding or resulted in an acquittal. A person's probation record will show the disposition in each case involving that person (e.g., whether the defendant served out the entire sentence or even received a pardon). All of the events will be listed on that person's probation record, and this includes any cases filed against that person involving DV, even civil protection orders, as well as whether a temporary abuse prevention order became a final order or was later extended, violated, or dismissed. Unlike in most states, nothing put on a person's probation record is ever taken off, although, as already noted, all further major actions in the same case are also added to the probation record. This is not to say that all abusive men have records or abnormal personalities[14] or that no female partners of abusers ever have records. However, abusive men, although they tend to be considerably older, better educated, and are more likely to be white than other criminals, and hence to have been given far more breaks in the criminal justice system, usually have probation records, often showing multiple prior crimes.

The Massachusetts probation record system thus demonstrates that these men are simply not the stressed-out good guys as assumed by the family courts and are the sole abusers (i.e., this is not a mutual abuse problem). The probation records also show that MHPs are also wrong in assuming the divorce or separation is temporarily causing the problem, and this includes the MHPs who are creating new typologies that downgrade most of the dangerousness or those MHPs who assume the abuse will end once the stress is over.[15] Rather, the Massachusetts data system supports those battered women's advocates and batterer intervention providers who claim that the men who abuse their intimate partners and children do so intentionally and deliberately and not because the men are stressed out or provoked by the women; only very rarely is the abuse mutual. Instead these men abuse as a matter of choice, as a way to assert power and control over their female partners and children, to punish them, or (much less often) because

---

[14] American Psychological Association, *Violence and the Family: Report of the American Psychological Association Presidential Task Force on Violence and the Family* 37 (1996) [hereinafter APA.]

[15] See, for example, Michael P. Johnson, *A Typology of Domestic Violence: Intimate Terrorism, Violent Resistance, and Situational Couple Violence* (2008) for one of the more interesting analyses of these typologies. However, one reason to be suspicious of such categories as situational couple violence is that these new relationship categories have never been studied prospectively so that some of the supposedly less dangerous patterns may be describing abuse that recently started, which might later escalate into typical intimate terrorism. Likewise, some apparent mutual abuse happens only after the police and courts have failed to protect the victim, leaving her to conclude she has no option except to resort to her own self-protection. Yet, what Johnson says about intimate terrorism rings absolutely true, and there probably are some individuals who properly belong in his other categories as well.

they enjoy inflicting pain.[16] The reality is that few if any of these men are merely react-ing to the stress of divorce (and it is not even clear if divorce is that stressful or if stress actually can create such abuse), but rather the men are instead using the divorce and other excuses to rationalize their bad behaviors, rationalizations in which the courts and MHPs, upon whom judges rely, are complicit in encouraging or accepting and therefore in reinforcing.

BATTERED WOMEN DO NOT DIFFER FROM OTHER WOMEN

In contrast to male abusers, female victims seldom have prior records. Although many MHPs and family courts assign comparable blame to the men's victims, Massachusetts' records show that the female victims are extremely different from their male abusers. In fact, battered women are generally no different from other women, except for having been abused and suffering the effects of that abuse. Research has shown that, prior to being abused, battered women are no different from other women,[17] meaning that it is only by knowing who their partners are that one can predict whether these women will be battered. It is the effects of male abuse that later makes battered women frightened and creates other manifestations, which often make the women seem unstable and appear less credible as witnesses.[18] Courts, police, and prosecutors often refuse to help battered women and discourage them from pursuing cases, but then they blame the victims for dropping their cases. However, battered women are no more likely to drop cases than are other victims of violent crimes, including male ones, who have been rethreatened by a stranger who previously assaulted them. What is different is that most violent criminals who assault acquaintances or strangers never reassault or even contact their victims again, but the average battered woman is beaten up three times by her batterer dur-ing the pendency of a criminal DV case,[19] and virtually all are recontacted directly by the abuser or indirectly by the abuser's friends and family, sometimes as often as every day. These contacts often begin with pleas to reconcile or drop the charges, but they usually escalate to include implicit or explicit threats if the case continues or the woman does not reconcile with her abuser. Also, in contrast to victims of stranger crimes, many battered women are forced by fear or circumstances, and even by insensitive courts, to continue living with their abusers, or at least to continue having frequent contact through visitation or court-ordered or coerced mediation, couples counseling, or dubious custody evaluations that make light of battered women's fears of continued contact with their abusers, all of which reinforce their abusers' violent behaviors and denials of responsibility for the abuse.[20]

All victims (both male and female), and in all types of cases, who are threatened with further assault want to drop their criminal cases. Battered women are actually

---

[16] Evan Stark & Anne H. Flitcraft, *Spouse Abuse. In Violence in America: A Public Health Approach* 123, 132–33 (Mark L. Rosenberg & Mary Ann Fenley eds., 1991); Ola W. Barnett & Alyce D. LaViolette, *It Could Happen to Anyone* 63 (1993).

[17] Stark & Flitcraft, *supra* note 16, at 140–44.

[18] Id. at 134.

[19] Joan Zorza, "Battered Women Behave Like Other Threatened Victims," 1(6) *Domestic Violence Rep.* 5 (Aug./Sept. 1996).

[20] Lenore E.A. Walker, *The Battered Woman Syndrome* 194 (2d ed. 2000).

more willing than other threatened victims to pursue their cases,[21] a display of bravery that gets entirely missed by the courts and those in the mental health system, which forgets how common DV is and is far more forgiving of other victims' fears. Many people in the court system, frustrated that they are not stopping the violence, blame the victims for the abuse or for not having left their abusers much sooner, blame that only colludes with the women's abusers and exacerbates the victims' problems, actually increasing the likelihood that the abuse will continue.

BATTERERS MINIMIZE, DENY, BLAME, LIE, OR MAKE EXCUSES

Battering is a very rewarding behavior in that it gets abusive men much of what they want. Yet the men who batter have been so successful at distracting attention from all the rewards battering gives them—their main losses are their capacity for empathy and compassion, and the potential for real intimacy in their relationships—that almost all of the attention is focused on the women and not the abusers' behaviors.[22] Men who batter are not only adept at minimizing and denying their own abusive behaviors and their responsibility for it, they are also adept at blaming circumstances or their victims, thereby shifting responsibility and projecting their own behaviors onto their victims.[23] Yet while their excuses, such as alcohol,[24] poverty, and other circumstances may aggravate a situation, they do not cause violence, as most people (even other men) in such circumstances do not abuse. Even having grown up in an abusive environment, although it increases the risk that a man will be abusive when he grows up, does not cause men to abuse their female partners; 90 percent of boys who grow up in abusive homes, and even 80 percent who grow up in the most abusive homes where they were abused, do not end up abusing their wives.[25] The reality is that most men who beat their female intimate partners grew up in nonviolent homes. Similarly, victims are not to blame for the violence. These same men seldom attack their secretaries, waitresses, or others—even female others—who do the very same misdeeds or possess the identical ostensibly aggravating behaviors, showing that abusive men use a cost-benefit analysis to do what they can get away with without serious repercussions.[26] Unfortunately (and also showing court collusion with abusers), abusive men have been very successful in convincing courts and juries that their own behaviors are their female victims' fault, or that their partners provoked them, or that their partners wanted the abuse, or that bad circumstances caused the abuse. Yet, in reality, most of their partners' alleged misdeeds are projections of the men's own behaviors onto their victims, which also enables the abusers to see themselves as blameless and project themselves as the real victims.[27] Contrary to the beliefs of most MHPs, batterers do not have a problem with their own anger, but rather with their partners' anger, twisting it—as so often they do—so that

---

[21] Zorza, *supra* note 19; APA, *supra* note 14, at 36-37.

[22] Lundy Bancroft, *Why Does He Do That? Inside the Minds of Angry and Controlling Men* 151–57 (2002).

[23] APA, *supra* note 14, at 81–82.

[24] Barnett & LaViolette, *supra* note 16, at 77.

[25] Evan Stark & Anne Flitcraft, *Women at Risk: Domestic Violence and Women's Health* 79 (1996).

[26] Lenore E.A. Walker, *The Battered Woman Syndrome* 101 (3d ed. 2009).

[27] Bancroft, *supra* note 22, at 28.

abusers use it against their victims.[28] Because their battering and coercive control is so effective at getting them what they want, and they are seldom held accountable by society, including the courts, battering and manipulation are highly rewarding behaviors,[29] which is probably why it is virtually unheard of for abusive men to make substantial and lasting changes in eliminating their abusiveness, even when they are in therapy.[30]

Although women's allegations of DV are being more and more ignored within the courts, increasingly there is more of an assumption that women are responsible for much of the abuse, or at least they are being faulted for supposedly fighting back, only some of which is probably actually happening, given abusers' tendencies to make false accusations, project their own behaviors onto their victims, and to lie "persuasively, with soulful facial expressions, good eye contact, and colorful details" that generally convince others, including most MHPs and judges that they are being truthful and their victims are not.[31] Some researchers who are sympathetic to the plight of battered women are noting that most of women's actual fighting against their intimate terrorist abusers is a violent resistance, which, even if it may not always meet the technical standards for self-defense, is done to protect themselves or their children from injury from their male abusers.[32] Yet, most of those who discuss women's violence against their partners seldom stop to analyze what is likely going on. In my own practice, in which I represented more than 2,000 battered women starting thirty years ago, I saw that most women only began using violence after their attempts at seeking help proved futile, particularly after police or courts failed to protect them from their abusers, or actually made their situations worse, for example, by denying them protective orders, issuing mutual orders of protection (which are more dangerous than no orders at all), giving their abusers an order of protection, forcing them to coparent or go to mediation or couples counseling, or turning the case into a parental alienation one. These women effectively learned that they had nobody else to rely on except their own resources to keep themselves and their children safe, not the lesson that the criminal justice and family court systems should be teaching. When it was the courts that failed women, it was often as a result of the MHPs whom the courts rely on to advise them.

MENTAL HEALTH PROFESSIONALS SELDOM KNOW MUCH ABOUT DOMESTIC VIOLENCE

The family courts increasingly rely on mental health experts to assist them in a large variety of ways, particularly when the parties have children in common. Most courts use MHPs as mediators, evaluators of the parties when custody is contested, parent coordinators, or supervisors of visitation, and they may refer one or more members of the family to counseling. Batterers not only manipulate their partners, as will be discussed later in this chapter (see "Batterers Manipulate and Retaliate Against Their Victims"), they are adept at and very likely to manipulate MHPs to their advantage, something that few MHPs seem to realize,[33] including (and perhaps particularly) the ones they encounter in custody disputes.

---

[28] Id. at 59.

[29] Id. at 151–58, 170, 197.

[30] Id. at 25.

[31] Id. at 195, 264.

[32] *See, e.g.,* Johnson, *supra* note 15, at 51–52.

[33] APA, *supra* note 14, at 102.

Lack of Training in Domestic Violence

There is an assumption in the courts, and among most MHPs, that MHPs are knowledgeable about DV. Unfortunately, the vast majority of the experts upon whom courts rely have never received adequate training in intimate violence or child sexual abuse; indeed, their professional schools seldom teach the subjects, and 40 percent of those working in mental health fields in the United States admit they have never received *any* training about intimate partner violence *ever* in their careers, and, with the possible exception of being told they need to report child sexual abuse, even fewer MHPs have ever received training about child sexual abuse.[34] The content of what little training exists in schools and in continuing education programs is often questionable or outright misleading, or so short (one hour is not that uncommon over the course of a career)[35] that it is clearly inadequate, and it is highly unlikely that on-the-job training is likely to produce genuine knowledge. Furthermore, even when they get good training in these areas, most MHPs are already so indoctrinated in crediting what men say, or blaming women, or disbelieving women's allegations about DV and incest, that few are able to absorb what they are being taught. One of the country's best experts in child sexual abuse maintains that only 10 percent of custody evaluators know enough about incest to not be dangerous to women and children in cases in which such allegations are raised.[36]

In addition to the custody evaluators and mediators, the GALs, who are supposed to represent the children's best interests to the court, generally lack training or knowledge in any aspect of family violence, and many even lack knowledge about child development.[37] Without the training and sensitivity to abuse issues, which few get when there is so much tendency to blame abused mothers, particularly for not protecting their children,[38] few MHPs even screen for DV or follow up when told about it.[39] When MHPs do follow up, batterers are adept at manipulating them, appearing very together and, in the relatively rare instances when a batterer does admit his abuse, appearing contrite and regretful, justifying his abuse or making it appear that it happened as part of a substance abuse or depression problem, or that it was instigated or caused by his partner.[40] All this usually convinces the MHP that the abuse was at most an aberration that will be controlled in the future, although this is most unlikely.[41] Mental health evaluators and GALs, having been trained in a system that blames mothers for most problems that people have,[42] are particularly vulnerable to being

---

[34] Felicia Cohn, Marla E. Salmon & John D. Stobo, *Confronting Chronic Neglect: The Education and Training of Health Professionals on Family Violence* 3–5 to 3–8 and 4–5 (2001).

[35] Id. entire book; APA, *supra* note 14, at 13.

[36] John E.B. Myers, *A Mother's Nightmare—Incest: A Practical Guide for Parents and Professional* 104 (1997).

[37] APA, *supra* note 14, at 102.

[38] Lorraine Radford & Marianne Hester, "Overcoming Mother Blaming? Future Directions for Research on Mothering and Domestic Violence," in *Domestic Violence in the Lives of Children: The Future of Research, Intervention, and Social Policy* 135, at 149 (Sandra A. Graham-Berman & Jeffrey L. Edleson eds., 2001).

[39] Edward W. Gondolf & Ellen W. Fisher, *Battered Women as Survivors* 133–34 (1998).

[40] Id. at 132.

[41] Id. at 81.

[42] Barnett & LaViolette, *supra* note 16, at 9–10.

persuaded by fathers who deny their abuse and blame their partners, and, hence, most MHPs discredit the mother's accusations and fears, and recommend that custody be given to fathers, even when the men are abusive. The result is that DV is seldom considered in the vast majority of child custody determinations,[43] particularly when there are allegations of physical or sexual abuse against a child.[44] This is an amazing omission, given that all fifty states and the District of Columbia require courts to consider DV when making child custody determinations,[45] knowing that the effects of custody disputes are devastating to battered women and children, and how adversely affected they are, particularly when these cases become protracted,[46] as tends to happen when MHPs become involved.

Ignorance About the Research on Intimate Partner Abuse

Compounding this lack of effective training (see "Lack of Training in Domestic Violence"), most good research on intimate partner abuse is published in journals specializing in interpersonal violence, which are simply not read by people who do not make that field their specialty. This research conclusively shows how detrimental it is for children to be exposed to abusive fathers and how much better both children and mothers do when they have no contact with abusive fathers.[47] Since most research that is published in the journals read by the MHPs affiliated with the family courts deals with the positive effects of fathering and the negative effects of having an absent father, they are further reinforced in favoring fathers and disfavoring mothers. Indeed, the benefits of fathering is much more lucratively funded and emphasized in the social science research, to the degree that there is virtually no research on the effects of mothering on children or how children are hurt by mother absence,[48] so that any assumption that fathers are more valuable than mothers would be like assuming that smoking cigarettes is much better than not smoking after having read only the literature put out by the tobacco companies (which was all that was available for many years in this country). Also generally ignored is the increasing evidence of the direct and intentional link between abusive men battering their intimate partners and sexually abusing children in their homes.[49] Seldom are MHPs taught that studies show that a cessation in contact between the children and an abusive father improves both the welfare of the children and the mother's ability to parent.[50]

---

[43] Joan Zorza, "Domestic Violence Seldom Considered in Psychologists' Custody Recommendations," 2 *Domestic Violence Rep.* 65, 68 (1997).

[44] Myers, *supra* note 36. Mothers of abused children are themselves blamed for the abuse and traumatized by it and other's reactions. *See, e.g.,* Betty Joyce Carter, *Who's to Blame? Child Sexual Abuse and Non-Offending Mothers* 188 (1999).

[45] Linda D. Elrod & Robert G. Spector, "A Review of the Year in Family Law: Redefining Families, Reforming Custody Jurisdiction, and Refining Support Issues," 34 *Fam. L.Q.* 607, 652 Chart 2 (2001); Zorza & Rosen, *supra* note 3.

[46] Lundy Bancroft & Jay G. Silverman, *The Batterer as Parent: Addressing the Impact of Domestic Violence on Family Dynamics* 126 (2002).

[47] Radford & Hester, *supra* note 38, at 150.

[48] Id. at 141.

[49] Id. at 142.

[50] Id. at 150.

Gender-Biased and Inaccurate Assumptions

Judges, like MHPs (and often because of what they have learned from these supposed experts on these issues), make the gender-biased and inaccurate assumptions that most DV and child abuse accusations made by mothers in custody cases are falsely made for tactical gain, with the result that they take these cases far less seriously than they should, or they completely discount them.[51] As Professor Joan Meier notes, Dr. Evan Stark, a widely read, published, and highly respected researcher and scholar of DV has testified under oath that there is no documented case of a woman fabricating a history of DV but that he (and many others) observe that women vastly understate or even deny the amount of their abuse.[52] In fact, incest allegations are only made in 2 to 3 percent of custody cases, and mothers make few false accusations either of DV[53] or of child sexual abuse.[54] Although no psychological test can definitively prove that someone has battered or sexually abused someone,[55] many family courts require women to conclusively prove the abuse—a virtually impossible burden—or they refuse to believe that any abuse happened. This unfair burden is also legally incorrect, since civil courts generally require only a preponderance of the evidence standard, or at most a compelling evidence standard, both easier standards than the criminal standard of beyond a reasonable doubt. However, and completely illogically (although this is another indication of gender bias against mothers in family courts), it is the experience of many DV attorneys and advocates that it is often easier to obtain a criminal conviction against an incest-perpetrating father than to get a family court to find that the father committed the abuse. Furthermore, some family courts even refuse to make such findings knowing that the father had previously been convicted in criminal court of incest, so the family court should have made the finding automatically, pursuant to the legal principles of *res judicata* or issue preclusion. Professor Margaret Drew notes "that it is very difficult, even rare, to get a finding in a family court that a father committed incest" as "family courts seem more engaged in denial that incest happens."[56] This is not to say that criminal guilt findings are easy to obtain; fewer than 10 percent of child sexual abuse cases that the criminal justice system knows about ever go to criminal prosecution,[57] and fewer yet of these result in convictions; the corresponding rates for incest cases are probably even lower. The overwhelming discounting of DV and incest evidence happens in both trial and appellate courts, even in states that have a presumption against batterers being awarded custody. Professor Joan Meier's research in examining thirty-eight appellate custody decisions in the United States showed this

---

[51] "A Typical Week of Restraining Orders in Massachusetts," 1(4) *Domestic Violence Rep.* 3, 4 (Apr./May 1996).

[52] Joan S. Meier, "Domestic Violence, Child Custody, and Child Protection: Understanding Judicial Resistance and Imagining the Solutions," 11 J. *Gender, Soc. Pol'y & L.* 657, 684 (2003).

[53] APA, *supra* note 14, at 12.

[54] Id.

[55] Myers, *supra* note 36, at 46–48.

[56] E-mail message from Margaret Drew, associate professor of clinical law, University of Cincinnati College of Law and former chair of the American Bar Association's Commission on Domestic Violence.

[57] Gregory F. Long, "Legal Issues in Child Sexual Abuse: Criminal Cases and Neglect and Dependency Cases" in *Handbook on Sexual Abuse of Children: Assessment and Treatment Issues* 137, 139 (Lenore E. Auerbach Walker ed., 1988).

gender bias against mothers. She found that only two trial courts credited the mother, and that while appellate courts upheld only thirteen of these decisions (an amazingly high reversal rate given that appellate courts must find that trial courts abused their discretion in order to overturn a trial judge's decision in family cases, a very difficult standard to meet), one of the two cases granting custody to the mother was also reversed on appeal.[58] While it is of considerable encouragement that appellate courts did reverse many of the awards of sole or joint custody to abusers, the reality is that the cost of appealing cases is so large that few mothers can afford to appeal adverse decisions.

Misleading Assessment Tools

In addition, because most assessment tools used in custody evaluations were never developed to take into account the effects of DV on victims, the tools distort the results to incorrectly show that most frightened victims are paranoid or have other psychiatric disorders, such as major depression, paranoid schizophrenia, dependent personality disorder, or borderline personality disorder,[59] diagnoses that will hurt battered women in any custody fight.[60] Without experts able to refute the faulty diagnoses (and few battered women have the money to pay for such experts, even if any are available who are both knowledgeable about these issues and willing to criticize their colleagues), battered women and mothers of children who have been abused risk being assessed as incompetent mothers, with the result that they so often lose custody to their batterers and reinforce the already gender-biased and erroneous beliefs of the judges and MHPs involved in making custody determinations.

Biased Evaluations

The biased evaluations that result from these unknowledgeable and often biased custody evaluators amount to collusion with abusive fathers. This becomes apparent when one realizes how often MHPs connected with courts, particularly those supervising visitation or acting as parent coordinators, end up policing or punishing mothers, while repeatedly ignoring or excusing the misdeeds of fathers. Their inquiry, even when they are appointed to monitor a child's safety, typically changes to focusing on the mother's hostility to the father, her badmouthing him, or her slighting of his visitation rights, particularly if she brings the child late or otherwise unprepared for visitation or to an appointment with a MHP. The National Council of Juvenile and Family Court Judges (NCJFCJ) notes that Parental Alienation Syndrome or parental alienation allegations are junk science that should not be admissible in evidence, although it also says that abusers "commonly sabotage their respective partner's parental authority over and relationship with the children." Instead it urges custody evaluators and judges to first look to see if there is DV, which would explain a child's hostility to the abuser.[61]

---

[58] Meier, *supra* note 52, at 657, 662 n.19, app. 726–31.

[59] Edward W. Gondolf, *Addressing Woman Battering in Mental Health Services* 81 (1989).

[60] Barnett & LaViolette, *supra* note 16, at 74; Gondolf, *supra* note 59, at 81.

[61] Clare Dalton, Leslie M. Drozd & Frances Q.F. Wong, *Navigating Custody and Visitation Evaluations in Cases With Domestic Violence: A Judge's Guide* 24–25 (2006), *available at* http://www.ncjfcj.org/images/stories/dept/fvd/pdf/navigating_cust.pdf.

BATTERERS MANIPULATE AND RETALIATE AGAINST THEIR VICTIMS

Despite myths put out by fathers' rights advocates that mothers always win custody cases, the findings of the most credible studies to date of trial court decisions range from showing that fathers actually win sole or joint custody in 70 percent of contested custody disputes,[62] to those showing that fathers win residential custody half of the time,[63] which is fairly consistent with the findings of Professor Meier based on appellate cases. This is true even though the men who abuse women and children are far more likely than other fathers to fight for custody and engage in prolonged litigation.[64] Even though every state's custody statute requires judges to take DV into account and protect children when there is violence in the family, men who abuse their wives and children are actually more likely to win custody and not be given supervised visitation than nonabusive fathers.[65] One of the main reasons that this happens is because batterers are so adept at manipulating everyone in the system and, should that fail, intimidating them as a way to enhance their manipulation and get their way.

How It Starts

Batterers start by manipulating their would-be partners into believing they are perfect partners. At this stage the women often describe the men as being "Prince Charming," a "knight in shining armor," or "too good to be true," and others who see them at this stage often agree. That the men can do this shows that they know how to behave when it is to their advantage, particularly if they want to attract a partner. Batterers wait to show their abusive side only when they are sure of the relationship, after they and their partners are living together or married, and in any case after it would be too difficult or embarrassing for their victims to leave.[66] Most batterers slowly escalate their abuse, checking if they can get away with what they are doing, backing off for a while if they fear that their victims will leave them or if they will suffer significant consequences. Rather than going through a buildup or attacking during a dispute, many abusers attack with no prior warning, leaving their female victims fearing another attack and feeling as if they are walking on eggshells.[67] A small majority of batterers in this country apologize for their first abusive episodes, something that varies depending on the abusers' cultures[68] and what they think is necessary to keep their victims from leaving them. In fact, abusers' apologies are few,[69] as even the ones who start out apologizing for their abusiveness, over time start blaming their

---

[62] Ruth I. Abrams & John M. Greaney, *Report of the Gender Bias Study of the Supreme Judicial Court [of Massachusetts]* 62–63 (1989), also citing similar findings from California and the entire nation.

[63] Zorza & Rosen, *supra* note 3.

[64] APA, *supra* note 14, at 40.

[65] Zorza & Rosen, *supra* note 3.

[66] *See, e.g.,* Leslie Morgan Steiner, *Crazy Love* 240 (2009).

[67] Stark, *supra* note 5, at 246.

[68] *See, e.g.,* Sakhi, *A Life Without Fear* (Intermedia, 1994). This video documentary about family violence in the South Asian community describes how it is virtually unheard of for men to apologize even to their brides after physically abusing them.

[69] Stark, *supra* note 5, at 246.

victims for "making me have to do this to you." To maintain control, abusers also isolate their victims from anyone who could support them, again something they only do gradually. All of the men's tactics, particularly as they are reinforced by isolating their victims from any of existing or potential support networks, serve to greatly confuse and disempower their victims, making it increasingly difficult for them to leave their abusers or even to try to seek help.[70] As part of these tactics, the abuser also isolates the victim from the economic means to be able to survive on her own and become self-sufficient.[71]

Retaliation Studies

Batterer retaliation has been recognized, though usually not under that name in much of the DV research that has been done, particularly the studies on the effectiveness of different police responses to DV. In those federally funded studies, the concept examined was recidivism, repeat violence, or even an escalation or increase in the batterer's violence in response to how police responded to a DV incident, for example, whether there was any appreciable difference in recidivism or repeat violence depending on whether the responding officer arrested the parties, separated the parties, mediated the dispute, ordered the abuser to show up in court, or gave an oral warning that the next time the police have to come to the home that somebody would be arrested, although not every study used all of these responses.[72] Although the first experiment clearly indicated that recidivism was lowest when abusers were arrested, only half of the later experiments were claimed to validate that first result, although all experiments when reanalyzed for the National Institute of Justice and the Centers for Disease Control showed that in the first six weeks after a police response, the arresting of male abusers made female victims less likely to be reabused.[73] The initial claim that arrest deterred white abusers but not African American ones was later shown to be false, as it was found that while the effect was stronger with white abusers, even unemployed African American abusers were less likely to reoffend if police arrested them than if law officers responded in some other way. In addition, the research did not find that "arresting an offender . . . increased the risk of subsequent aggression against women."[74] While these experiments certainly showed that some batterers did reoffend against their victims, the study found no evidence that they were retaliating as other facts explained their recidivism rates, like their prior records. It found that over time recidivism rates went up considerably for most abusers, but there were some abusers who reoffended almost immediately and continued to do so, regardless of how the police responded. In any case, it is not likely that what happened six months or even longer after the police response was dependent on that initial response, especially since abusers are highly impulsive, so that any retaliation would happen very quickly.

---

[70] These patterns have been described repeatedly in women's personal accounts, including Steiner, *supra* note 66, and in the academic DV literature.

[71] Johnson, *supra* note 15, at 38–39.

[72] Sherman, *supra* note 1; Lawrence W. Sherman, "Symposium Issue on Domestic Violence," 83(1) *J. Crim. L. & Criminology* 1 (1992).

[73] Sherman, *supra* note 1, at 16–18.

[74] Christopher D. Maxwell, Joel H. Garner & Jeffrey A. Fagan, *The Effects of Arrest on Intimate Partner Violence: New Evidence From the Spouse Assault Replication Program* (July 2001), http://www.ncjrs.gov/textfiles1/nij/1888199.txt.

Another study, which was based on the National Crime Victimization Survey and looked at both male and female offenders, also found that police involvement had a strong deterrent effect. It additionally found no evidence that offenders retaliate more when their victims (as opposed to somebody else) called the police or if the victims signed complaints. That study suggests that victims and third parties should be encouraged to report DV incidents to the police.[75]

Retaliatory and Manipulatory Tactics

When male batterers feel that their authority is being threatened, they begin or escalate their violent and terroristic tactics, often threatening to kill or seriously injure their victims,[76] their families, children, or loved ones,[77] and even themselves.[78] After separation, they often carry out these threats, hurting their partners fourteen times as often after separation as when they were together.[79] Studies show that most of these men also rape their female partners. Male batterer rapes of their female partners are more brutal and more likely to cause serious injuries than stranger rapes, and they are often done to terrorize and disempower the children as well, particularly the 10 percent of marital rapes that are perpetrated in front of the children.[80] Batterers are notorious for destroying the things most valued or needed by their victims, something deliberately done to intimidate, demoralize or punish them (often economically), or prevent them from obtaining help. They do this by disabling or taking telephones, cars (or the keys), or money from their partners (e.g., by stealing or forcing them to hand over their pay checks or welfare benefits), destroying their photographs, destroying or selling their clothing (which sometimes renders the victims unable to go outside with any dignity or protection from the elements and therefore less able to flee or seek help), or destroying household goods. It is not uncommon for an abuser to shut off or cause his victim's utilities to be shut off or cause her to be evicted or her house to be put in foreclosure. Male batterers also hurt or kill the pets cherished by their female partners or children, often in brutal and sadistic ways, knowing that this will devastate their family members and also send them the message that their abusers have no qualms about inflicting enormous pain and that the victims or the children may be next. Their farm animals are also vulnerable, because these too are often loved, and may be a, or even the, only source of economic support for battered women and their children, particularly in rural areas. Furthermore, society seldom treats animal abuse very seriously, regarding the animals as merely personal property. Not surprisingly, many battered women are afraid to leave their abusers for fear of what their abusers will do to their pets and farm animals.[81]

---

[75] Richard B. Felson, Jeffrey M. Ackerman & Catherine Gallagher, *Police Intervention and the Repeat of Domestic Assault* (June, 2005), http://www.ncjrs.gov/pdffiles1/nij/grants/210301.pdf.

[76] David Adams, Identifying, "Assaultive Husbands in Court: You Be the Judge," 33 *Boston B.J.* 23–24 (July/Aug. 1989).

[77] Id.; Barnett & LaViolette, *supra* note 16, at 50.

[78] Donald Dutton & Susan K. Golant, *The Batterers: A Psychological Profile* 49 (1995).

[79] Caroline Wolf Harlow, *Female Victims of Violent Crime* 5 (Dept. of Justice, Bureau of Statistics, NCJ-126826 Jan. 1991).

[80] Ptacek, supra note 12, at 74; Walker, *supra* note 20, at 486; Jacquelyn Campbell, *Nursing Assessment for Risk of Homicide With Battered Women* (1986); National Council of Juvenile and Family Court Judges, "Batterer Manipulation of the Courts to Further Their Abuse, and Remedies for Judges," 12(1) *Synergy* 12 (Winter 2008) [hereinafter National Council].

[81] Judee E. Onyskiw, "The Link Between Family Violence and Cruelty to Family Pets," 7(3)

When I practiced law, my clients told me of many instances of each of the foregoing behaviors, as well as many that they feared would never be believed or were too embarrassing or far fetched for them to be willing to relate to the courts. These included abusers threatening their lives with motor vehicles (a practice that Lenore Walker found in almost 10 percent of her clients[82]), usually by deliberately trying to run them over and, in a few instances, actually doing so; repeatedly banging their cars into their victims' vehicles or chasing them off of the road; shoving their victims out of rapidly moving vehicles, often into oncoming traffic or at the edge of steep cliffs; or putting them in other highly dangerous situations. Many abusers sabotaged their victim's medical situations, for example, by hiding, destroying, or substituting needed medications; preventing them from seeing doctors, particularly after they themselves had seriously injured their partners; ripping open stitches after major surgery; or raping them the day they returned from the hospital after childbirth. It was also common for the abusers of victims with disabilities to destroy or withhold needed equipment (e.g., hearing aids or wheelchairs) or to drug or intoxicate them, greatly endangering them and rendering them unable to obtain help. In addition, many of these acts almost guaranteed that their victims would not appear credible if they somehow managed to seek help. Although many of these health-related abusive practices are well noted in the elder and sometimes child abuse literature, they are seldom discussed in the DV literature, except that a few states criminalize or give special recognition in their protective order statutes to destroying or disabling telephones to prevent victims from calling the police.

Batterers commonly demean, shame, or humiliate their victims as a way to deprive them of self-respect, control them, demonstrate their subservience, or show others that they are owned. These behaviors may lead the victim to loathe herself or even attempt suicide. There are many ways that an abuser can force his victim into "subservience through the making and enforcement of a behavior or ritual that is either intrinsically humiliating or is contrary to her nature, morality, or best judgment."[83] For example, several Jewish clients told me how their Jewish husband abusers forced them to have sex (i.e., raped them) when they were menstruating, knowing that their religion forbade them from having sex at that time of the month. Similarly, a Roman Catholic client told me how her abuser forced her to spit in the holy water at church, threatening that if she refused, he would later beat up one of her children (something that she had every reason to believe he would do). It was so offensive to her religious beliefs and humiliating to be forced to do this in front of her priest and congregation, as her husband knew it would be, that she stopped going to church, which further isolated her. She was only welcomed back to her church two years later when I went with her to talk to her priest, so that he would understand the circumstances. She also learned that her husband had set her up to be discredited by talking to the priest and others in the congregation about her supposed strange behavior a few days before he made her spit in the holy water, revealing that what he did (as most batterers do) was premeditated and not impulsive.

As part of their manipulation and control, many abusers enlist members of their families to monitor and even abuse their victims. One apparent exception is the role that many abusers' mothers play, at least as long as the marriage lasts. Many battered women report their mothers-in-law have been their best and most supportive friends, making sure they went to the hospital after their husbands seriously injured them.

J. Emotional Abuse 7 (2007).
[82] Walker, *supra* note 20, at 194.
[83] Stark, *supra* note 5, at 259–61.

(Often these abusers isolated their female partners from anyone else who could play that role, and not uncommonly in these cases the abusers' fathers battered their own wives, so that the women's mothers-in-law had a fairly good understanding of what their sons were putting their wives through.) Yet the women also almost always report that the roles of their mothers-in-law dramatically change once the women leave their abusers, often shocking the women at how suddenly hostile their mothers-in-law become (see "Fighting for Custody").[84]

Abusers also manipulate their victims by frequently calling them demeaning names or swearing at them, or telling them how stupid or selfish they are, often in public and more often in front of the children. Many force their victims to bear marks of ownership, such as tattoos, bite marks, or burns, which convey both that they own the victims and that the women are vulnerable to further abuse by others.[85] Abusers also spit on their partners surprisingly often, which is something that many police DV officers report having witnessed.[86] Particularly in poor communities, some batterers force their victims into highly illegal and compromising situations as a way to prove their loyalty or as the only way the women can protect or feed themselves or their children, such as by forcing them to prostitute themselves; use, deliver, or sell illegal drugs; or commit burglaries or robberies, making them too afraid or ashamed to seek services and fearful that their abusers will retaliate against anyone who helps them, particularly family members. These women often rightly fear that the police will arrest them or put their children in foster care, or that shelters will refuse to take them knowing or suspecting they have a substance abuse problem.[87] However, in more middle- and upper-class communities, it is not that uncommon for batterers to force their victims to flee or lock them outside, particularly when they are scantily clad or naked, or inadequately protected from the elements, often after having forced them to become intoxicated (whether with drugs or alcohol). These abusers often combine these indignities with others, such as claiming the women were having affairs or insulted their (the men's) sexual prowess, all behaviors that leave their victims vulnerable to neighbors or responding police thinking the worse of the women, assuming that they are crazy or substance abusers or deserved what they got, and ultimately causing the police and neighbors to distance themselves from such women and their children as well.[88] For abusive men, this is part of their manipulative strategy to isolate their victims from anyone who might help them[89] as well as to discredit the women, knowing that

---

[84] Walker, *supra* note 26, at 101.

[85] Stark, *supra* note 5, at 260.

[86] Anne O'Dell, now retired from the San Diego Police Department, often talked of how common it was for abusers to swear at, use demeaning names, or spit on their partners, even in front of police. In many states, these behaviors would probably not rise to being arrestable offenses unless there were protective orders in effect.

[87] Beth E. Richie, *Compelled to Crime: The Gender Entrapment of Battered Black Women* (1996); Jody Raphael also writes of these issues in her trilogy of books, *Saving Bernice: Battered Women, Welfare, and Poverty* (2000), *Listening to Olivia: Violence, Poverty, and Prostitution* (2004), and *Freeing Tammy: Women, Drugs, and Incarceration* (2007).

[88] See, for example, *Custody of Vaughn*, 664 N.E.2d 434 (Mass. 1996), in which the state's highest court adopted the finding of the trial judge "that [the mother], 'when rejected after demanding sexual favors from [the father] followed him from the house to the public road. She was naked and directed foul language at him. This . . . was done in the presence of [Vaughn—the child].'"

[89] Johnson, *supra* note 15, at 9.

nobody would likely believe or be sympathetic to them, or to such a tale, even if they are brave enough to relate it (and few women want such stories known). All of these tactics set up battered women to look bad and be discredited in the courts, should they end up there.

BATTERERS MANIPULATE THE COURTS

Batterers not only manipulate their partners within the relationship, but they retaliate against their partners in many other ways as well, often being extremely imaginative and unpredictable (see "Batterers Manipulate and Retaliate Against Their Victims"). In their desire to punish their victims for leaving, they are often quite willing to drive them into economic ruin, even if in many cases it causes financial hardship to themselves as well. It is very common for batterers to threaten to drive their victims into bankruptcy, put them on welfare, make them homeless, or otherwise prevent them from ever achieving financial stability,[90] and, in using their cost-benefit analysis, they are far more likely to do this after separation when they themselves may escape some of the resultant hardship they cause. A few do this by seriously injuring their victims, preventing them from working or attracting a mate; many abusive men telling their partners, "If I can't have you, no one will," and taking concrete steps to make this a self-fulfilling prophesy, often killing them.[91] When batterers feel their power over their victims is slipping, they frequently enlist the courts in various ways to act as one of their agents.

In the past, many abusers often had their wives committed to mental hospitals for the rest of their lives. While changes in health law and health economics have made permanent commitments much harder to do in recent years, it is still quite common for abusers to hospitalize their victims for shorter periods, sometimes with court complicity, and even have Electroshock or Electro Convulsive Therapy (ECT) used on them, although medical studies show that ECT causes significant to severe brain damage causing permanent memory loss and impaired functioning, and other studies have found ECT produces no psychological benefit to those to whom it is administered. Furthermore, ECT is overwhelmingly used against female patients and overwhelmingly by male doctors, often as a way to punish or control women for not being submissive wives or because they are lesbians or hold other nonconforming views or positions.[92]

But perhaps the most common way that batterers retaliate against women for leaving is through the family courts. Many court practices, such as mediation, mutual orders of protection, gag orders, and the abusers' allegations that the mothers are alienating the children from them, are techniques that abusers promote and encourage courts to promote, which ultimately give the abusers more court orders and court players that they can use against their victims, thereby increasing their power and control over them (see Chapter 1 in this volume). With these types of gender-biased court orders, they have more tools to have their victims arrested or punished by the courts.

---

[90] Id. at 38–39.

[91] Walter S. DeKeseredy & Martin D. Schwartz, *Dangerous Exits: Escaping Abusive Relationships in Rural American* 15 (2009).

[92] Bonnie Burstow, "Electroshock: The Gentleman's Way to Batter Women," 14 *Domestic Violence Rep.* 17–18, 25–32 (2009).

Fighting for Custody

Abusers are notorious in fighting for custody,[93] even though most of them never paid much attention to the children while they were together with the children's mothers.[94] Just as many abusers deliberately hurt, kidnap, or kill pets, most batterers seek custody of the children, or threaten to or actually abduct the children, knowing that depriving the mothers of custody is by far the best way to punish and hurt them.[95] Many abusers admit they do so to punish, control, or harass their victims, and some even admit it is to financially drain them. Compared to other fathers, batterers are notoriously poor at paying child support,[96] but most men know that winning custody not only absolves them from having to pay child support, it may obligate the mothers to pay child support to the fathers, which abusive men see as another way to punish their female partners for leaving them. Although most men do very little parenting after divorce (it is not uncommon for them to use their own mothers, sisters, new girlfriends or wives, or even have the children's own mothers do the parenting—but with the threat that the last type of arrangement will cease immediately if the mothers move to switch custody back or even reveal to the court that they are in fact still the children's caretakers), most MHPs seem oblivious to the fact that three-quarters of fathers threaten custody fights after divorce and that men use custody fights to blackmail their partners, typically to get the women to agree to receiving lower child support or even to force the women into paying the men child support.[97] Women commonly give up many property rights in their effort to keep custody or not to further inflame their already hostile former partners.

Not only will the abuser likely fight his wife in any way that he can in the courts, but, after the breakup, it is common for his mother to come to court to do everything she can to bolster her abusive son's custody or visitation claims, to discredit all of the woman's claims, or even to seek custody for herself, particularly if her son is unable to do so, such as when he is in jail or on active military duty. The woman's mother-in-law is there to vindicate the family honor of the abuser's family, and she and her son now are there to demoralize and destroy the woman whom they both "clearly" see as their enemy. Often the woman's father-in-law or others (e.g., his siblings, grandparents) in the abuser's family join in as well. Indeed, the ones from whom the abuser learned to be abusive in the first place often do this spontaneously. Fortunately, such third-party attempts to wrest custody from the battered woman were made considerably harder by *Troxel v. Granville*,[98] the U.S. Supreme Court decision that struck down Washington State's grandparent visitation statute, which permitted visitation against the wishes of the parents. Just as the batterer may do, many paternal grandparents also often file false or trumped-up charges against their daughters-in-law or their sons' girlfriends to get them in trouble and discredit them, most often with child protection agencies,

---

[93] Barnett & LaViolette, *supra* note 16, at 50; APA, *supra* note 14, at 100; Marsha B. Liss & Geraldine Butts Stahly, *Domestic Violence and Child Custody, in Battering and Family Therapy: A Feminist Perspective* 175, 181 (Marsali Hansen & Michèle Harway eds., 1993); Walker, *supra* note 26, at 35; Barcroft & Silverman, *supra* note 46, at 113.

[94] Catherine Kirkwood, *Leaving Abusive Partners* 54–55 (1993); Einat Peled & Duane Davis, *Groupwork With Children of Battered Women: A Practitioners' Manual* 8 (1995).

[95] Liss & Stahly, *supra* note 93, at 181-83.

[96] Id. at 181; Mildred Daley Pagelow, *Family Violence* 311 (1984).

[97] Kurz, *supra* note 9, at 151, 161, 168.

[98] 530 U.S. 57 (2000).

but also alleging that the women perpetrated welfare or immigration fraud or other criminal activity, allegations they often make to family courts.[99]

In contrast, the battered woman, whose abuser has usually alienated her from her own family (to the point that some of her family may even come into court supporting her abuser or give him, but not her, money or housing or other assistance[100]), usually has nobody coming to court with her, particularly if she is one of the vast majority of battered women who cannot afford a lawyer. Even if she has a lawyer, the abuser may charm the lawyer into not believing the battered woman, or may so frighten the lawyer that the lawyer withdraws or does an inadequate job representing the woman. As noted previously, the abuser often manipulates any court-related mental health witnesses so that they too become his advocates.

Controlling the Victim's Experts and Her Lawyer With Litigation Tactics

In court, abusers often use endless litigation tactics, filing huge numbers of motions, asking for court delays once the victims show up in court, as a strategy to exhaust and continue controlling the victims, as well as depleting them financially and emotionally, and maybe getting them fired from their jobs, if they are employed. Some abusers list the victim's lawyer as a witness they plan to call, or they file grievances against her lawyer or any experts who will bolster her position to force them off the case.[101] If the victims have lawyers, this perpetual litigation may exhaust the lawyers as well, although more likely the lawyers stops representing the women because the women can no longer afford the exorbitant costs that their abusers have set them up to owe.

Threatening or Abusing the Victim and Children

Batterers also retaliate by threatening their former partners and their children during visitation, or by shifting their abuse onto the children. It is quite common for batterers to begin abusing the children physically or sexually after the separation and for such abuse to escalate, just as their violence tends to escalate after separation against their former partners.[102] Many abusive fathers threaten to and actually abduct the children,[103] and these abductions are as harmful to the children as when strangers kidnap them.[104] When batterers do have custody, they often refuse to let the mothers see their children. Yet the same courts that are outraged and vindictive upon hearing that a mother failed to make the children available to the father seldom punish a father who denied visitation to the mother, even when he has been doing so repeatedly over a long time. Many abusive men get their partners to drop legitimate demands or force them to do something the women did not want (e.g., submit to abhorrent sexual practices or

---

[99] Zorza, *supra* note 43, at 68, 75.

[100] See, for example, Steiner, *supra* note 66, a true story, where the victim's father assisted her abusive husband after he tried to kill her and she fled, but he did nothing to help her from the personal and economic devastation that her abuser caused her.

[101] Peter G. Jaffe & Claire V. Crooks, "Assessing the Best Interests of the Child Visitation and Custody in Cases of Domestic Violence," in *Parenting by Men Who Batter: New Directions for Assessment and Intervention* 45, 48 (Jeffrey L. Edleson & Oliver J. Williams eds., 2007); Walker, *supra* note 26, at 36.

[102] Harlow, *supra* note 79.

[103] Geoffrey L. Grief & Rebecca L. Hager, *When Parents Kidnap* 4 (1992).

[104] Id. at 205–06.

to abort a child) by threatening to or actually beating one or more of the children until the women agree to whatever the abusers demand.[105]

Claiming to Be the Victim

Batterers have also become more sophisticated in claiming to be the victims, rushing into civil or criminal courts to beat out their victims in filing criminal complaints or obtaining orders of protection, often getting custody and an order forcing the women to leave the homes as well. Lundy Bancroft, who long ran programs for abusive men, says of such families, "It would be difficult to find anyone more self-satisfied than the man who repeatedly assaults his partner verbally or physically and then has the pleasure of handing her a court order that bars *her* from the residence," causing her shock and yet more resignation and bitterness.[106] Most batterers know that when women file complaints after they have already done so, both complaints usually cancel each other out, or even work in turning the courts against the women, and, in any case, seldom result in the batterers being given any jail time. Often the courts may well grant the batterers protection orders or issue mutual protection orders in such situations,[107] providing the batterers with another tool to use against their victims, as they can then claim the victims violated the orders.

Abusers also increase the harm by making outrageous accusations as to what their victims supposedly did to them (whether false accusations of infidelity, or claiming that the women attacked them in particularly improbable ways).[108]

Contacting Child Protection Agencies

Not uncommonly, abusers set up their partners to look vulnerable and then report them to child protection agencies, an emotionally terrifying and often financially devastating intrusion to the women, who risk losing custody to the state. Since in many states child protection agencies will take the children if they realize the mother is being battered (New York is an exception, see *Nicholson v. Scoppetta*[109]), the mother is in a terrible bind, because even if she can convince them that there is no merit to his allegations, child protection may still remove the children upon realizing that the abuser's false allegations are part of his pattern of physically and emotionally abusing her.

Discrediting the Victim

Since batterers cannot punish their victims without knowing their transgressions, they use another common ploy to turn their friends, relatives, neighbors, and even the

---

[105] See, for example, the discussion of a Roman Catholic victim who was forced to spit in the holy water in "Batterers Retaliatory Tactics Against Their Victims."

[106] Bancroft, *supra* note 22, at 310.

[107] Id. at 204.

[108] For example, it is not uncommon for an abuser to claim the woman attacked his genitals, something for which it is most unlikely that he would not have had to obtain medical treatment but for which he has no medical documentation. The case of John and Lorena Bobbitt (in which she cut off his penis after he raped her) was so unusual that it received enormous media and public attention (including "a flurry of jokes") around the world for many years. *See, e.g.,* John and Lorena Bobbitt, http://en.wikipedia.org/wiki/John_and_Lorena_Bobbitt.

[109] 820 N.E.2d 840 (N.Y. 2004).

MHPs involved into agents for them to monitor their partners' behaviors, especially after they separate when it becomes harder for them to know what the women are doing every moment.[110] The abusers alert people who know their partners, feigning genuine concern about them, asking each of them to watch their partners because they are drinking, abusing the children, or otherwise acting strange or dangerous. At the same time, the batterer has made his agents become more suspicious and probably less supportive of his victim and also much less likely to believe or want to assist her. Some of these agents may start monitoring her and reporting on her whereabouts and any transgressions to him. These abusers are generally believed in their accusations, in part because the men seem so sincere and concerned in their use of manipulation, and their victims, often sensing an increase in the monitoring, may start to act more suspicious and fearful, which makes them seem paranoid and even a bit crazy, which tends to support what their abusers said about them. Some abusers even succeed in turning some of these agents into witnesses to bolster their cases, either directly in court or with the MHPs. Those who are more experienced with the court system, such as police officers or probation officers, are particularly likely to use and be successful in using all of these types of tactics.

The female victims, who seldom know of the actual attempts to discredit and harm them, are usually unable to defend against any rumors and accusations that their abusers have made against them. Even in the courts, when some of the abuser's accusations may finally surface, the victim often learns of them with no time to prepare a rebuttal. Furthermore, the system fails to blame the men who set the women up, particularly when this occurs in the child custody context, since the court itself and the MHPs it uses are supposed to be impartial and check into anything that might endanger the children or affect a parent's ability to parent well. Because of gender bias, MHPs are primed to look into accusations of poor mothering but overlook men's transgressions.[111] Batterers also can take advantage of the fact that most of them have worked hard to have good public images within their communities, which makes the batterers seem more credible at the expense of their victims,, while simultaneously diminishing the victims' self-confidence and increasing their reluctance to believe that anybody would believe them if they sought help.[112] It is also nearly impossible to prove that something never happened, particularly when men make vague accusations such as that the victims alienated the children from them.[113]

Terrorizing the Victim

Many batterers so harm and terrorize their victims that they are forced to flee with the children. Instead of exploring why the woman left, courts typically give the batterer immediate, and often permanent, custody of the children, and upon her return or being found, the victim is often jailed as punishment, which punishes the children as well as her. Federal law gives victims of DV a complete defense for fleeing to another country with the children from an incidence or pattern of DV,[114] but state courts still punish mothers under state laws for doing so, and few mothers flee beyond the country's borders.

---

[110] Johnson, *supra* note 15, at 27.

[111] *See, e.g.,* Meier, *supra* note 52, at 685.

[112] Bancroft, *supra* note 22, at 68.

[113] *See* "Parental Alienation Syndrome and Its Progeny" and "Friendly Parent Concept" in Chapter 1 in this volume.

[114] 12 U.S.C. § 1804(c)(2).

Many battered women are usually precluded from obtaining recognition for much of their abusers' wrongdoing (or restitution for it) because they seldom can provide the courts with the specific dates on which each wrongdoing occurred[115] and, even if they can, seldom will have evidence to prove the abuse. Furthermore, the victim is usually precluded from alleging the course of conduct that an abuser used against her over a period of time, although virtually all DV involves a course of conduct, something implicit in the stalking laws but not generally in DV laws. This omission largely contributes to preventing most battered women from ever obtaining justice in the form of guilty verdicts in criminal trials, court findings as to the wrongdoings in civil cases, and restitution in any court proceedings regarding their abusers' wrongdoings. Recently the omission of the course of conduct component is being recognized by some feminists as a serious and perhaps even the worst flaw in our legal understanding of what DV is and how it harms victims of intimate partner violence, causing a few of them to propose revising the definition of DV to focus on the coercive control and course of conduct.[116]

Speaking Positively About Current Partners

Another reason that courts have not been quicker to catch on about men's projecting their own behaviors onto their victims[117] and being highly vindictive against their former female partners is that while they speak very negatively about their former partners, they generally speak very positively about their current ones.[118] This is typical of men, but few courts or MHPs are aware of it, and they are fooled into thinking the men must be objective, so what they say about their former partners must be accurate. Yet once the men break up with their current partners, they start publicly devaluing them as well.

Abusing the Courts

Some courts are wising up to men's retaliatory tactics, because many involve abusing the courts. Many abusers learn that cross- or counterclaims often cancel out the claims of their victims and that filing contempt charges shifts the focus to their victims.[119] Most batterers know they can bring criminal and contempt charges at virtually no expense to themselves but that any litigation takes an enormous financial and emotional cost on their victims. The result is that many abusive men prolong the litigation and file spurious claims, some openly acknowledging they are trying to drive their victims onto welfare or into homelessness or bankruptcy. They are successful in impoverishing their

---

[115] This seems to be more of a problem for women, and particularly battered women, many of whom experience posttraumatic stress disorder or have been brain damaged as a result of the abuse or less commonly from having received electroshock treatment.

[116] *See, e.g.,* Deborah Tuerkheimer, "A New Approach to Criminalizing Domestic Violence," 14(6) *Domestic Violence Rep.* 81 (2009); Stark, *supra* note 5, at 5, 282.

[117] Dutton & Golant, *supra* note 78, at 105.

[118] David Schuldenberg & Shan Guisinger, "Divorced Fathers Describe Their Former Wives: Devaluation and Contrast," in Sandra Volgy Everett, *Women and Divorce/Men and Divorce: Gender Differences in Separation, Divorce, and Remarriage* 61–87 (1991).

[119] Jeffrey L. Edleson & Richard M. Tolman, *Intervention for Men Who Batter: An Ecological Approach* 31, 34 (1992).

victims, as litigation is very expensive, with the result that filing for bankruptcy is very common among divorcing and particularly battered women.[120] Some studies have found that half of all homeless women and children in the United States are homeless because of DV.[121] A study of battered women in contested custody cases in America found that their average court-related expenses exceeded $90,000,[122] hardly an amount that most women can sustain and particularly not battered women whose abusers deprive them of money and their ability to earn it. While couples and men used to be the main ones filing for bankruptcy, new data from the bankruptcy courts shows that women filing as individuals now do so in much greater numbers than either couples or men[123] and that it is primarily divorcing women who are responsible for this increase.

Occasionally, it is only when abusers accuse judges or other court players of impropriety or attack them or those helping their partners, such as shelter workers,[124] that the courts catch on to their tactics. Unfortunately, some judges (and other court players, including most mental health experts) become too frightened[125] or vicariously traumatized[126] to act sufficiently to believe or act to protect battered women. However, most abusers are far too savvy to make such accusations, attacking only their former partners.

Some court actors are openly hostile to battered women, denying them protection or issuing restraining orders to their abusers to use against the battered women. Lundy Bancroft notes that many courts are extremely skeptical of women who complain about abuse from their partners, in large part "because of prejudices against the complainants as well as misconceptions about what 'type' of man would commit such a crime."[127] Bancroft notes that there are many excellent players in the court system but also that some are highly collusive with the abusers, for example, "probation officers . . . who buddy up to the abuser with a wink and a nod, who bond with him in the belief that there exists an anti-male bias in the court system and who signal him that he needn't take the abuser [treatment or intervention] program seriously."[128]

Threatening Victims, Even Prosecutors and Judges

Prosecutors know that when they are threatened by criminals, it makes their jobs much more dangerous and much harder for them to continue prosecuting these criminals. This is true even when federal marshals protect them and any of their threatened

---

[120] Margaret Dore, The "Friendly Parent" Concept: A Flawed Factor for Child Custody, 6 *Loy. J. Pub. Int. L.* 41, 53–54 (2004); NOW Legal Defense and Education Fund, *Legal Resource Kit: Divorce Planning* 18 (2008), http://www.legalmomentum.org/assets/pdfs/divorce_final_2008.pdf.

[121] Joan Zorza, Woman Battering: A Major Source of Homelessness, 25 *Clearinghouse Rev.* 421 (1991).

[122] Geraldine Butts Stahly, *Protective Mothers in Child Custody Disputes: A Study of Judicial Abuse,* Presentation at Battered Mothers' Custody Conference, Albany, NY, Jan. 14, 2007.

[123] Marcy Gordon, "Women Filing for Bankruptcy More Than Men," *Buffalo News,* June 22, 1999, at 6D.

[124] Ptacek, *supra* note 12, at 63.

[125] Id.

[126] Joan Zorza, "Why Courts Are Reluctant to Believe and Respond to Allegations of Incest," in 3 *The Sex Offender: Theoretical Advances, Treating Special Populations and Legal Developments* 33–8 (Barbara K. Schwartz ed., 1999).

[127] Bancroft, *supra* note 22, at 294.

[128] Id. at 295.

family members.[129] Such threats are increasing against judges as well, despite much greater security and protection for both judges and prosecutors.[130]

Victims tell DV advocates that their male abusers are also making more threats against them, particularly when there are criminal charges pending. A Vera Institute of Justice study found that the average battered woman pursuing misdemeanor criminal charges against her abuser was injured as severely as 90 percent of stranger felony victims and got beaten up three times while awaiting trial. The battered women who had been subjected to further physical violence from their abusers were considerably more likely to continue cooperating with prosecutors compared to those felony victims who were later revictimized or even though their offenders had made some effort to recontact them—often after receiving one hang up call, which, of course, might or might not have been from their offenders. This was true even comparing the battered women with male felony victims.[131] Although battered women are much braver than other victims, including male victims, they have the reputation for always recanting and dropping charges, even though many of them continue living with their abusers or have to see them repeatedly because of their court cases or, when they have minor children in common, for court-ordered visitations. When there are criminal cases pending, many batterers make repeated serious threats against them or convince their friends or family members to make such threats. Even when abusers are ordered out of the home, many of them move close enough in proximity to their victims' homes as to insure running into them repeatedly. Stark describes how common it is for obsessive abusive men to stalk and monitor their victims, both before and after they separate, how they

> harass them at work; park outside their job; hold children hostage when a partner goes to the hospital; repeatedly call them at work or at home; leave threatening messages on their cell phones; show up at their new residence at odd hours; perform periodic "house checks" or "inspections"; break in and leave anonymous "calling cards"; demean them to business clients, co-workers, and family members; cancel or run up debt on their credit cards, forge their names on personal checks, and raid their bank accounts; show up unexpectedly at social or family gatherings; move in next door; take a job in the same workplace; appear spontaneously at the children's school or soccer game without notice; check their mail; hide outside their apartments; and hire or solicit friends to watch or follow them.[132]

But unlike prosecutors and judges, there are no federal marshals protecting battered women, and the recent U.S. Supreme Court's case of *Castle Rock v. Gonzales*[133] exonerated police from any liability for not having protected the children of a battered woman from her abuser, even though the woman had an order of protection against her batterer, and her state law mandates that police arrest anyone violating an order of protection.

---

[129] Keith L. Alexander, "Killers Fear This Woman: With Cuts and Grit Prosecutor Takes on Infamous Defendants," *Wash. Post,* June 7, 2009, at C1 and C4.

[130] Jerry Markon, "Threats to Judges, Prosecutors Soaring: Worried Court Personnel Resort to Guards, Identity Shields, Weapons," *Wash. Post,* May 25, 2009, *available at* http://www.washingtonpost.com/wp-dyn/content/article/2009/05/24/AR2009052402931.html.

[131] Vera Institute of Justice, *Felony Arrests: Their Prosecution and Disposition in New York City's Courts*(1981); Zorza, *supra* note 19.

[132] Stark, *supra* note 5, at 130–31.

[133] 545 U.S. 748 (2005).

COURTS CAN CURB BATTERER MANIPULATION OF THE COURTS

There are some good models for courts to proactively deal with batterers who abuse the courts, making the courts victims as well their past or current partners. However, courts must first be aware that actions that appear to be the same on the surface can be very different in reality, based upon the context of the action. In many cases, at different stages of the proceedings, the mother and father each attempts to limit the contact between the children and the other parent. Courts often treat these actions as if they were the same (although they tolerate a father's interference probably believing that the mother's relationship with the children is stronger and thus would not be harmed as much by such interference), but parents' actions are usually done for very different purposes. The mother seeks to limit the interaction in order to protect the children from a father that has abused the mother and often the children. The father seeks the limitation to punish or control the mother, but of course that is not what he tells the court.

Similarly, both parties in contested custody cases may file complaints against professionals working in the court system. The parents complain the professionals acted improperly and seek various relief and sanctions. On the surface, the complaints seem similar, but the mother is seeking to redress mistreatment by these professionals, and the father is trying to prevent anyone from helping his victim.

Before considering whether to sanction a parent, courts must scrupulously look for patterns in these actions in order to understand them in context. If there is evidence that during the relationship the father sought to interfere with the mother's relationships and support network, or her ability to be gainfully employed, this would be important information to understand that his complaints against professionals attempting to help her is a continuation of his tactic of isolating his victim. If the mother has provided evidence of the father's abuse of her and the children, this supports the belief that she is seeking to limit contact with the father in order to protect the children. Professionals who look at each issue or incident separately fail to understand the pattern of behavior.

As noted by the NCJFCJ, courts often make these mistakes by appointing or listening to MHPs who do not have the training to recognize DV or the patterns of abuse, or know of its dangers associated with separation.[134] Until judges and other professionals receive the specific training they need to recognize these patterns (and as noted previously, many have such strong preconceived notions that they will not learn anything from even the best training), they must consult with genuine DV experts, particularly DV advocates. Otherwise, as shown in many parts of this book, courts often make mistakes that place the lives and safety of protective mothers and their children in jeopardy. In this context, it is important for courts that rule against alleged victims of DV to be open to the possibility that they made a mistake. Courts should be reluctant to take punitive or retaliatory actions against mothers who continue to believe their partners abused them. Similarly, it is important for courts to encourage attorneys and other professionals to speak up and challenge judges they believe have mistreated their clients. Gender bias and other common mistakes are often made unconsciously. Courts are less likely to learn of their mistakes if they seek to silence or retaliate against those who are willing to challenge mistakes courts make against victims of DV.

Keeping all of this in mind, courts, particularly if asked, although courts can do this on their own, can sanction abusers for having filed frivolous suits or motions,

---

[134] Dalton, Drozd & Wong, *supra* note 61, at 17–18.

or causing repeated delays. One of the most helpful responses is for the court to make findings of fact about what the abuser did. Indeed, such findings are probably necessary to provide the foundation for any further sanctions that a court makes against an abuser. Courts could consider the appropriateness of doing some or all of the following:

- Order the abuser to pay his victim's attorneys' fees and her costs (e.g., her lost wages, baby sitter expenses, and transportation expenses, which could include staying in a hotel if the courthouse is far from her home), and any costs to pay for her witnesses who may have had to come to court multiple times before they could testify.

- Order the abuser to pay all of the costs resulting from his abuse, including, but not limited to, her or the children's expenses for housing, health care, travel, and repair, or replacement costs.

- Forbid the abuser from filing any further action or motions involving the victim without prior permission of the court.

- Fine the abuser.

- Order the abuser to post bond to cover the cost of future wrongdoings.

- Fine the abuser with civil or criminal contempt of court.

- Refuse to let some or all of the abuser's witnesses testify or to use some of his exhibits or custody evaluations.

- Refer the abuser's attorney, or other professional who participates in the misconduct, to bar disciplinary or other professional licensing organizations.

Of course, courts can and should be creative and are not limited to only one of these possibilities. Courts should not only fashion orders to protect the court, but they should more importantly insure the safety of the abuser's victims as well as others the abuser is threatening or harming. Often this includes other agencies, so that protective orders forbidding the abuser from reporting his victim to the police, with or without court permission, might be both an appropriate and effective way of curbing an abuser's fraudulent accusations against his victim as well as any others he may be retaliating against for supporting her.

An article in the NCJFCJ publication, *Synergy,*[135] noting how batterers use custody proceedings to harass and control their former partners, discusses the federal district court case of *Davey v. Dolan*[136] as an excellent model that courts can use or lawyers can ask courts to use against abusers. After losing in the divorce court, Davey (the former husband and an attorney) sued his ex-wife and two of her children who had been granted an order of protection, his own son, two of her family members, his wife's lawyer, and their respective law firms. He also sued the judge who granted the divorce and the state of New York. He sought several million dollars in damages from all of these parties. He had already filed claims in state court and only filed in federal court after he lost in the state court. The federal court held that he had already litigated or could have litigated any of his claims in the state court, and that the claims he filed

---

[135] National Council, *supra* note 80, at 12–13.
[136] 496 F. Supp. 2d 387 (S.D.N.Y. 2007).

in the federal court failed to state any cognizable claim against any of the defendants he sued, and that the claims he filed were frivolous. Accordingly, the court ordered that no future claims should be filed relating to the divorce. Not one to be discouraged or hear a "no," Davey filed a motion asking the court to reconsider its 2006 decision. The court not only reaffirmed its prior decision[137] but it ruled that it was proper for the court to have issued an injunction against him from pursing any related litigation, saying his litigation had an "utter lack of merit," was vexatious and continuing, and that as a lawyer he should have known as much. It also found that given what he had done, the attorneys' fees and expense sanctions that it ordered him to pay were "quite reasonable, given the utter lack of merit of [Davey's] claims and his evident intent to harass [his ex-wife and her sister]."[138]

The article concludes with some ideas that are similar to the ones previously suggested in this section, although the last one goes further, "for bolstering the safety of domestic violence victims and avoiding waste of judicial resources includ[ing]" the following:

- "Not letting first or subsequent violations of any order go by without consequences."

- "Ordering the abusers to pay all reasonable costs, expenses and attorney's fees incurred by the defendants in responding to the violation of any order or filing of frivolous lawsuits, including lost wages of the victim."

- "Even if not required to do in your jurisdiction, making findings in your order that will be helpful to [the court] and the parties should additional actions follow, such as requiring prior authorization from the court before filing further litigation or requiring the abuser to attach the court's opinion and order of injunction to all subsequent filings."[139]

CONCLUSION

When courts blame victims and fail to hold abusers accountable, they reinforce abusers' behaviors, subvert justice, disempower the victims, teach children that abusive behavior is permissible, and may even be rewarded, and reinforce the cycle of violence. While some courts have colluded with abusers, courts can and should stop doing so and instead be more proactive in holding abusers accountable, thereby sending them a message that DV and abuse of the courts will not be tolerated. Courts should also be mindful of fully protecting the partners and children who are at risk of abuse from abusers.

---

[137] Id.

[138] Id. at 390.

[139] National Council, *supra* note 80, at 13.

Chapter 15

The Yuck Factor, the Oprah Factor, and the "Stickiness" Factor: Why the Mainstream Media Has Failed to Expose the Custody Court Scandal

by Garland Waller, M.S.

INTRODUCTION

When it comes to protecting and doing justice for abused children and their mothers, the family courts have failed miserably. But the mainstream media (MSM) has played its own role in this failure: The rare news coverage of the family court arena, with its ugly and acrimonious custody battles, is typically sensationalized and usually victim-blaming. The stories seldom dig below the surface explanations given routinely by attorneys or other legal actors who are contacted about the rare family court horror story—the favored one being that the complainants are "disgruntled litigants" whose reports, therefore, warrant little or no credibility.

How, and why, did journalism in such a compelling area—the nexus between the fates of parents and children and the role of the legal system—end up so blacked-out and so whitewashed? I believe that, when it comes to exposing the ugly collision between child custody and abuse and the lack of responsible media coverage, the "Yuck Factor," the "Oprah Factor," and the "Stickiness Factor" all play a part.

There was a time in this country, before the Reagan era's deregulation of media corporations, when TV news operations were sometimes willing to take the heat and the risks that arise when exposing social injustices, government corruption, or a volatile combination of the two. Think, for example, of Edward R. Murrow calling out Senator McCarthy or of the great documentary *Harvest of Shame,*[1] which exposed the cruel living and working conditions of migrant workers. You might recall the conscience-afflicting black and white footage of dogs and fire hoses being used against civil rights marchers. These media images, and their messages, were enough to swing the pendulum of public opinion. That is the power of media.

But over the course of a few decades, the media landscape changed—and not in a good direction. Now, the near-deafness, dumbness, and blindness of the media regarding the hopelessly flawed condition of the nation's family court system have risen to the level of complicity. In a nation that prides itself on respect for family values, human rights, and justice for all, how can this possibly be? How could a national scandal of such destructive and monumental proportions go unnoticed and unaddressed?

SOME STORIES ARE JUST TOO DARK TO TELL

In the introduction to my documentary, *Small Justice: Little Justice in America's Family Courts,*[2] I cite a statistic taken from the American Judges Foundation Web site: "Studies show that batterers have been able to convince authorities that the victim is unfit or undeserving of sole custody in approximately 70% of challenged cases."[3] Also included

---

[1] Edward R. Murrow, *Harvest of Shame* (CBS 1960).

[2] Garland Waller, *Small Justice: Little Justice in America's Family Courts* (Intermedia, Inc., 2001).

[3] American Judges Association, *Domestic Violence & the Courtroom Understanding the Problem . . . Knowing The Victim,* http://aja.ncsc.dni.us/domviol/page5.html.

is the statement, "Fathers who battered the mother are twice as likely to seek sole physical custody of their children as non-violent fathers."[4] These quotations have a well-deserved ring of authenticity and generally grab peoples' attention from the get-go.

There are plenty of other statistics I could cite. But the bottom line is that the MSM not only refuses to cover this issue, to look deeply into it and expose the horrific abuses many of us see every day in the family courts, they make it worse, simply by their silence. In a nation that prides itself on respect for family values, human rights, and justice for all, how can this possibly be? How can what is truly a national scandal go uncovered?

This chapter draws from personal experience to explain why the media's coverage of custody battles tends to be so myopic. I once was speaking to a reporter from a network magazine about the family court problems. As our conversation progressed, I realized that he did not get it. He did not understand what was really going on behind the scenes in many child custody cases involving abuse. At every turn, this reporter challenged everything I was saying—about the cases I had studied, the horror stories I had heard from mothers, and the statistics I had collected on this issue. His behavior struck me as odd. Usually, when I am talking "producer to producer" to a fellow journalist, there is an implicit exchange of professional courtesy as well as a cutting to the chase shorthand. Forget the niceties. Skip all emotion. Tell me whether there is really a story I can use.

Later, when my colleague, Eileen King, a child advocacy professional at Justice for Children in Washington, DC, started dissecting this particular case, she commented, "I still can't get the image out of my mind. He sat there in court, and when the children were testifying about their abuse by their father, he rolled his eyes. In the end, in order to be able to see her children at all, the mother of the children in question agreed to give up sole custody of her kids."[5] Those kids have lived with their abuser ever since the trial.

Many reporters do their homework, but some do not, and any of them can be taken in by an abuser's charm just as easily as a family court judge. After all, when a normal looking man gets accused of raping a child, the specter is so repulsive, so unbelievable at such a deep level that, just like reporters, the family courts cannot believe it either. It is just yucky. Remember that word.

Another example comes from a February 9, 2008, headline in the *New York Times*: "Slain Dentist's Wife Is Charged with Murder and Conspiracy."[6] It was the story of a woman charged with conspiracy in her ex-husband's murder. The husband was shot and killed at a playground in New York City during a visitation hand-off of their daughter. The article mentioned a custody dispute, but there was no mention of child abuse allegations against the husband.

Smelling a rat, I decided to act on my suspicions regarding the truth behind this story. I e-mailed the reporter to ask if any allegations of child sexual abuse had been raised in the case and, if so, whether the allegations had been founded or not. A day later, in his reply, the reporter stated that it was another *New York Times* reporter who had told him that a child abuse allegation had been made about the father, "but it didn't seem to be warranted— which would fit into the pattern of the mother's apparently extreme behavior."[7]

---

[4] American Psychological Association, *Violence and the Family: Report of the American Psychological Association Presidential Task Force on Violence and the Family* 40 (1996).

[5] Eileen King, Justice for Children, Boston, telephone conference, Feb. 21, 2008.

[6] Bruce Lambert, "Slain Dentist's Wife Is Charged With Murder and Conspiracy," *N.Y. Times,* Feb. 8, 2008, *available at* http://www.nytimes.com/2008/02/08/nyregion/08dentist. html?_r=1&scp=1&sq=%22Slain%20Dentist%E2%80%99s%20Wife%20Is%20Charged%20 with%20Murder%20and%20Conspiracy%22&st=cse. She has since been convicted.

[7] Bruce Lambert, e-mail to author, Feb. 10, 2008.

At this point, there was no evidence of anything; there were only charges filed against the wife and allegations launched against the husband. Nevertheless, the *New York Times* was willing to publish the unproven allegations of murder and conspiracy against the mother, while at the same time refusing to dig deeper into the allegations raised in the courtroom against the father. My point here is not whether the mother was guilty or innocent or whether sexual abuse had occurred. The point is that both the courts and the press refused to consider sexual abuse allegations.

This brings up a haunting reminder of Elsa Newman's case. I have been communicating with Elsa since before she was sent to jail, in Jessup, Maryland, in 2003.

Her case is extremely complicated because it also involves conspiracy to commit murder. The case reveals all too well the failures of both the mainstream press and the courts. In Elsa's case, someone else shot her ex-husband. When I first spoke with her, she was a loving mother working as a labor lawyer. She was concerned about her children being abused, and she wanted *Small Justice* to be shown at her temple. Elsa was nowhere nearby when her ex-husband was shot, but she was sentenced to prison for conspiracy. She will serve more time in prison than will the person who pulled the trigger. Elsa is now incarcerated with criminals, including women who have killed their own children. The *Washington Post* reporters wrote that at the time he was shot, Elsa's ex-husband was in bed with his child.[8] What they left out was that the ex-husband had been naked from the waist down while in bed with his son.

As a TV producer for over twenty years, someone with contacts in the business and the ability to talk in a way that most TV, newspaper, and magazine reporters can hear, I have come to realize that it is not that the story of family court injustice is not a good one (i.e. one that will work for or sell the TV or newspapers). It is that the MSM today lacks resources, time, patience, and, above all, guts.

There are patterns to reporting on TV and in newspapers, not just in the family courts themselves, but also in how the media covers domestic violence (DV) and child sexual abuse in general. Sometimes, there is little to no coverage. Sometimes the coverage is short-lived and flimsy. Sometimes it is hot, hot, hot—a camera flash and then gone. Sometimes the story is promoted and aired but under pressure is later denied. These patterns reflect the larger state of news and media coverage in the United States today. The media, which could serve as a vehicle for social change, often ignores significant human rights issues in its quest for "eyeballs" and "advertising." And let there be no mistake here, what is happening in American family courts is a human rights issue.

SMALL JUSTICE: WHAT I LEARNED

I learned just that, in no uncertain terms, when in 2001, I produced *Small Justice: Little Justice in America's Family Courts.*[9] The program follows a paralegal and her attorney husband as they try to prevent three loving mothers from losing their children to the very people the children said abused them. In my documentary on family court injustice, I sought balance. I was interviewing women who were seeking custody of their children, who were victims of DV, and whose children had also reported sexual abuse at the hands of their fathers. I tried to speak to the men

---

[8] Michael Ruane & Phuong Ly, "Wife Is Charged In Md. Shooting; Her Whereabouts Unknown; Couple Feuded Over Custody." *Wash. Post,* Jan. 10, 2002, at B01.

[9] *See supra* note 1.

as well as the women. The men refused to speak to me. In my opening stand-up, I addressed the issue head on. I tried to speak to both sides, but only the women wanted to speak. What you will see in *Small Justice* is the women's side of the story. Rather than ignore the issue, rather than give up on getting the story out, I presented one side. I did not let silence by one side prevent coverage of the issue. I thought this would take care of the MSM's primary concerns, and that, when presented with a powerful story, it would be a scandal they would want to expose, much like the Catholic priest scandal from years before.

As a professor and as a producer, there are rules of the documentary TV and film business that had to be respected. I teach them. I know them. I used those rules to create a respectable production that would make a difference. I felt that I would be able to sell it. I was not a kid.

I assumed that my contacts in the business would help. This is how I started. I pitched *Small Justice* to numerous production companies, TV shows, and networks. I expected openness and excitement about an uncovered scandal. I sent letters and made calls to many networks—Oxygen, HBO, The Independent Film Channel, CNN. I called several TV shows directly—*20/20, Prime Time, 48 Hours*. Would they want to air the documentary? Would they air part of the documentary or use a clip? I just wanted the media to do something—to do anything.

As time passed, *Small Justice* won awards at independent film festivals like the New York International Independent Film and TV Festival and The Key West Indie Festival. It was screened at the Museum of Fine Arts in Boston and was being distributed by Intermedia Inc. But no one from the MSM picked up the piece. There was, however, a pattern that I was beginning to discern: interest, excitement, then silence. Reporters would take the call, be interested, call back enthusiastically for more details, and then boom—nothing. One day, I received two negative responses. One was from the TV show *60 Minutes* who said it looked too much like The Independent Film Channel, and the other was from the Independent Film Channel who said it looked too much like *60 Minutes*. For me, this is when the light dawned. *Small Justice* was never going to see the light of day on TV. Something about it was too scary, too difficult—too something. I could not put my finger on it.

Since that time, I have been following media coverage of DV and family court issues, and I have put some of the pieces of the puzzle together.

Let us break down the media silence and, ultimately, complicity and then see what we can do about it.

WHAT THE MEDIA REALLY WANTS: RATINGS

To fully understand how things got this bad, and why the MSM refuses to expose a national scandal that affects thousands of women and children, one must look first at how all stories are chosen and covered today. To begin with, ratings are at the heart of *all* TV decisions. Ratings mean money. Local and national newspapers and television news and magazines are heavily dependent on advertising dollars. In order to attract advertisers, the media has to guarantee a certain numbers of viewers or, as we call it in the industry, "eyeballs." The more eyeballs a show or article attracts, the higher the ratings. The higher the ratings, the more secure the show will be in attracting advertisers. The more advertisers, the more likely the show will continue to air. It is a circle that provides millions of dollars to stockholders and CEOs.

It is important for people to understand that this is how the system works. Once you understand ratings, a lot of things fall into place.

Thomas Berman, a producer at ABC, told me,

> In a place like ours, you have so many producers and bookers pitching stories. The people who decide what stories go on the air are the ones who are looking at what people who watch our show want to watch. I wish I could do more, but it's a ratings game . . . we're a weekly news magazine and there is really no market for the court system.[10]

There is also a myth that news broadcasters report the news and only the news—a sort of "Just the facts, m'am" mentality." But that is not true. The news reports information that is accessible, easy to understand, and can be reported in two to four minutes (less is preferred). Solid government sources and/or authorities are even better because without digging, without spending any real time or resources on the issue, the information appears to be credible. If a star can be quoted, then putting the celebrity on the air is a no-brainer. It may or may not be true, but it *looks* true, or as Steven Colbert would say, it has "truthiness."

There is something else to consider. Frequently, news sources will not report news if it is not already being covered by another news media outlet. It is copycat news. That is why you see so many cameras covering one story like OJ Simpson or Britney Spears. It validates the importance of the topic. Take a look at the lead stories on network and cable news. Have you ever wondered why everyone seems to be covering the same story, sometimes even at the same time? Flip from channel to channel some night and just see how often this happens. And just for a hoot, take a look at *The Daily Show* with Jon Stewart. This is the meat and potatoes of his program—or at least the starch. He runs clip after clip of reporter after reporter saying almost the identical thing. "Repeat something often enough and people will believe it," goes the old adage. This is nowhere truer than in American political journalism.

Eric Alterman's book, *What Liberal Media? The Truth About Bias in the News*[11] addresses these issues in the context of politics, but the message is the same for social issues. His chapter, "You're Only as Liberal as the Man Who Owns You," is clearly inspired by the famous journalist, A.J. Liebling, who wrote in the *New Yorker*, "Freedom of the press is guaranteed only to those who own one."[12] Stockholders and corporate titans own the media outlets. *Mother Jones* magazine reported that by the end of 2006, there were only eight giant media companies dominating the U.S. media from which most people got their news and information:

- Disney (market value: $72.8 billion);

- AOL-Time Warner (market value: $90.7 billion);

- Viacom (market value: $53.9 billion);

- General Electric (owner of NBC, market value: $390.6 billion);

- News Corporation (market value: $56.7 billion);

---

[10] Thomas Berman, telephone conversation, ABC *Prime Time,* Mar. 6, 2008.

[11] Eric Alterman. *What Liberal Media? The Truth About Bias in the News* 14 (2003).

[12] A.J. Liebling, *New Yorker,*1960, *cited in* Ralph Keyes, *The Quote Verifier* 172 (2006).

- Yahoo! (market value: $40.1 billion);

- Microsoft (market value: $306.8 billion);

- Google (market value: $154.6 billion).[13]

Ted Turner, in his 2004 *Washington Monthly* article, noted,

> Consolidation has given big media companies new power over what is said not just on the air, but off it as well . . . Disney recently provoked an uproar when it prevented its subsidiary Miramax from distributing Michael Moore's film *Fahrenheit 9/11*. As a senior Disney executive told *The New York Times*: "It's not in the interest of any major corporation to be dragged into a highly charged partisan political battle." Follow that logic, and you'll clearly see what lies ahead. If every media outlet in operation is run by a major corporation, then controversial or dissenting views may never get aired at all.
>
> Naturally, corporations would claim that they never suppress free speech. But it is not their intention that matters; it is their capability. Consolidation gives them more power to tilt the news and to cut important ideas out of the public debate.[14]

As a country, we need to look closely at which policies and issues actually get covered in the MSM and which ones do not. The media, because of its corporate structure, does not have society's best interests at heart. That is not their job. Their job is to return a profit to the shareholders. High ratings return a profit. Whether it is political journalism or social justice journalism, the point is this: TV is not brave. It does not take risks. If a reporter spends too much time on a story, that is expensive. If the story is too controversial or does not suit the corporation's own financial interests, then it is not good for the bottom line. Stories that require digging and time, like complicated legal issues, are going to die on the vine.

One of the best examples of ratings as the driving force for what is covered in the "news" is "To Catch a Predator" (TCAP). John Hockenberry, a former producer for *Dateline* and one-time MIT Media Lab fellow, describes the TCAP experience in an article he wrote for *Technology Review*. His primary goal in the article was writing about the convergence of new technology with television, but what he says now that he is no longer working at the network is very, very powerful.

> The culmination of *Dateline*'s Internet journalism strategy was the highly rated pile of programming debris called *To Catch a Predator*. The *TCAP* formula is to post offers of sex with minors on the Internet and see whether anybody responds. *Dateline*'s notion of New Media was the technological equivalent of etching "For a good time call Sally" on a men's room stall and waiting with cameras to see if anybody copied down the number.[15]

---

[13] Eric Klinenberg, "Breaking the News," http://www.motherjones.com/politics/2007/03/breaking-news; Dmitry Krasny, "Informational Graphic," *Mother Jones,* Mar./Apr. 2007, http://www.motherjones.com/files/legacy/news/feature/2007/03/and_then_there_were_eight.pdf.

[14] Ted Turner, "My Beef With Big Media," *Washington Monthly,* July/Aug. 2004, *available at* http://www.washingtonmonthly.com/features/2004/0407.turner.html.

[15] John Hockenberry, "You Don't Understand Our Audience," *Tech. Rev.*, Jan./Feb. 2008, http://www.technologyreview.com/infotech/198451 (registration required).

TCAP is a perfect example of ratings-driven journalism. It brought in tons of viewers. Advertising revenue was a nice bedtime story for the network. One of my graduate students told a story to me that her friends, all of whom are in their late-twenties and early thirties, and none of whom have children, loved this show. They gleefully got together to watch whenever it aired and fondly called it "The Pervert Show."[16] It was their Superbowl. So yes, people talked about this show and watched the show. There was an "OMG (Oh My God) Factor," but somehow not a "Yuck Factor." It was so bizarre, so tawdry, yet somehow so removed from people, that they could watch it over beer and a pizza.

In the *Columbia Journalism Review,* Douglas McCollam said of TCAP in his article, "The Shame Game,"

> since its debut in the fall of 2004, "To Catch a Predator" has been the rarest of rare birds in the television news world: a clear ratings winner. The show regularly outdraws NBC's other primetime fare. It succeeds by tapping into something that has been part of American culture since the Puritans stuck offenders in the stockade: public humiliation.[17]

McCollam goes on to point out that, although TCAP was continuously bringing the issue of Internet predators to the attention of the American public, a

> more recent study by the Crimes Against Children Research Center at the University of New Hampshire found that the number of kids getting unwanted sexual advances on the Internet was in fact declining. In general, according to data compiled by the National Center for Missing and Exploited Children, more than 70 percent of sexual abuse of children is perpetrated by family members or family friends.[18]

Is there any other issue that has received that much airtime? The question is whether the level of coverage is proportional to the actual problem.

This was about ratings though. It was not about doing the right thing or even the relevant thing. Personally, I have always wondered why TCAP did not follow up with lots of those married men who showed up. Did any of them have full custody of their own kids? One man even brought his child with him. What happened to that kid? Where was that story?

Ratings and the bottom line do not apply just to TV. Consider the 2006 firings of several *Los Angeles Times* big shots—one quickly replaced after the other for not cutting back on reporters.

"Dean Baquet, the editor of The Los Angeles Times, who defied orders from his corporate bosses to cut jobs, was forced out of his own job yesterday, shocking the newsroom just as it was gearing up to cover election returns."[19] The article goes on to say, "Mr. Baquet's departure follows that of the paper's publisher, Jeffrey M. Johnson, who openly objected to cuts ordered by the Tribune Company in September and was fired last month."[20]

---

[16] Eleanor Greene, interview, Boston, Feb. 12, 2008.

[17] Douglas McCollam, "The Shame Game," *Colum. Journalism Rev.,* Jan./Feb. 2007, http://cjr.org/feature/the_shame_game.php.

[18] Id.

[19] Katherine Q. Seelye, "Los Angeles Paper Ousts Top Editor," *N.Y. Times,* Nov. 8, 2006, *available at* http://www.freepress.net/news/18961.

[20] Id.

The word bloodbath comes to mind. Even when there are good media folks out there who know you cannot get something for nothing, they are not the owners. And at the end of the day, the owners (stockholders) call the shots.

Dr. Mo Hannah (coeditor of this volume), Professor of Psychology at Siena College in New York and the chair of the Battered Mothers Custody Conference (BMCC) takes it a step further. "Corporate media is often affiliated with right-wing causes. It also has a desire to maintain the status quo, and even patriarchy to some extent. It actually affects not just this issue, but other social issues as well."[21]

WHY FAMILY COURT STORIES WORK AT FIRST

With the understanding that media is a ratings-driven business and that journalism thrives on stories like TCAP, it is easy to assume that TV and newspapers would want to cover a story like custody and abuse in the family court. After all, there are seriously high levels of conflict and drama. In fact, early on, a lot of producers and reporters feel that they have hit the mother lode when they hear about these contested custody cases. After all, they involve sex, violence, and child abuse. This could be a front page or lead story. Sex and violence do sell. And when it is layered with a sense of outrage and need for social justice, well, call Clark Kent.

But if we break down the elements of popular story reporting into what works for media coverage and what does not, we see how coverage of DV, child sexual abuse, custody laws, and the family courts is sort of in the scary movie department to the MSM. Somewhere along the road to publication and eyeballs, family court stories almost always get axed or they simply pass into the media graveyard.

WHAT KINDS OF STORIES WORK FOR THE MEDIA?

The media is a beast that must constantly be fed. It needs stories. Stories are their meat. But the stories have to get good ratings and sell papers and generate advertising dollars.

What they want are stories that have the following elements:

- Are easy to understand;

- Have clear pros and cons;

- Are simple to write;

- Contain drama and excitement;

- Have lots of visuals;

- Are celebrity-packed;

- Have the blessing of the legal department; and

- *Appear* balanced and unbiased.

---

[21] Dr. Mo Hannah, telephone conversation, Boston, Feb. 22, 2008.

FAMILY COURT STORIES: WHY THEY DO NOT GET COVERED

To explore why the MSM has shied away from covering the family courts, let us look at how the characteristics of family court issues conform to the features listed above.

Family Court Stories Are Not Easy to Understand

Easy to understand involves having a beginning, a middle, and an end to the story. The chronology is simple, clear, and unambiguous. Easy also means that the issues at hand are relatively familiar to the reader or viewer; that way, a long learning curve is not needed, and explanations do not have to be too lengthy. An easy story comes tied up in a neat little package that fits snugly into a couple of newspaper columns or a few minutes on the air.

Since time is money, there is rarely enough of either for any news story that needs to give detailed explanations. The news, in fact, does not typically give a lot of actual airtime to any one topic. When I was a special projects producer, for example, I had to *beg* for thirteen extra seconds on a TV story. This was typical.

Newspapers, too, aim for concise stories that are fast reads and can be easily understood by an audience with a broad range of education and reading levels. If stories do not meet these standards, they are unlikely to see the light of day.

Complicating matters further is the fact that family court processes are not easily understandable to lay persons. The criminal courts, with their glamorization through TV shows like *Law and Order*, are far more familiar to the general audience. Think of it this way: As *Law and Order* presents it, crime is black and white. Somebody committed a crime, so they have to pay. In *Judging Amy*, a show focusing on the family courts, matters were much more complicated. Most of the time, there was no black and white—just a lot of gray.

Reporters looking for a simple story that builds to a strong close will be hard pressed to find one in the family court system. Family courts do not operate like the more familiar criminal courts, so cases are hard to follow and even harder to summarize into a concise story. If the case has dragged through the courts for months, years, even decades, the time span alone makes the story nearly impossible to cover.

Thomas Berman, a producer at ABC's *Prime Time*, agrees. "These stories are so complicated. When we try to tell a story, if anything is confusing, if there is anything that is apt to have them tune out, the story is less appealing to us."[22]

Family Court Issues Do Not Have Clear Pros and Cons

Stories promoting pro-Parental Alienation Syndrome (PAS) and pro-fathers' rights (FRs) propaganda are being hawked to the same media organizations that battered mothers' advocates are trying to reach. At present, PAS and its derivatives have become so entrenched in the mentality of the courts that the same drivel is routinely passed along to reporters, who often buy into it.

Complicating matters is the inclination of reporters to take experts' opinions at face value. When reporters are seeking an expert for a story on PAS (whether pro or

---

[22] Thomas Berman, telephone conversation, ABC *Prime Time,* Mar. 6, 2008.

con), they often locate the pro-PAS lobby first, since PAS proponents are well organized through the Internet. The pro-PAS group is made up of FRs advocates along with
their enablers, few of whom are too battered and bankrupt, like noncustodial mothers,
to organize. If reporters are not strongly committed to getting the whole story, they
might be duped by the pro-PAS regiment. So it does not take much for reporters to
miss half the story, or get it wrong entirely, all the while thinking they have done their
due diligence by getting quotes from "experts." (Notice how quoting only pro-PAS
experts violates MSM's usual policy of getting both sides of the story.)

Attorney Richard Ducote says,

> If they say they are going to do a story on the courts and how the courts don't
> protect children, and that they have to give both sides, well, what *is* both sides?
> False allegations are not the "other side."[23]

What I, personally, have heard over and over again from reporters is that family
court stories are of the "He Said-She Said" variety. The family court judge can prevent certain evidence from going on the record. When a reporter learns that a medical
report stating clearly that the child was anally raped, or any other evidence against
the father, is not on the record, that is the same thing as there being no evidence. Any
"proof" that is not on the court record is no proof at all.

"Every media outlet is pitched so many stories, but without a finding from the
court, there's just not much they can do about it," says attorney Richard Ducote.
"Criminal courts—with the heavy burden on proof beyond a reasonable doubt–will
convict people for crimes of abuse on the same evidence that family court judges deem
to be no evidence at all."[24]

A network reporter said to me, off the record,

> There's always a shadow of doubt. The testimony of a child could have been
> manipulated by an adult. There are huge gray areas. I know abusers count on
> this. That is the biggest problem. We can't go on the air. We could get sued.[25]

Brandon Bodow, a producer at *Good Morning America*, told me,

> These cases are so difficult to cover when we, as editorial producers, struggle
> between the outcome of the cases and what we feel might be the real truth. But
> how can we report injustice when the evidence is often so unclear?[26]

Family Court Stories Are Not Easy to Write

Not long ago, I was speaking to a reporter at a national newspaper who was interested
in exploring family court injustices. He was trying to wrap his mind around some of the

---

[23] Richard Ducote, Esq., telephone interview, Boston, Feb. 22, 2008.

[24] Richard Ducote, "What I Learned in the Courthouse," in *Exposé: The Failure of Family
Courts to Protect Children From Abusers* (Elize T. St. Charles & Lynn Crook eds., 2002), *available at* http://www.taliacarner.com/backgroundarticles/ducote.html.

[25] Telephone interview with anonymous major network producer, Boston, Feb. 22, 2008.

[26] Brandon Bodow, Producer, *Good Morning America,* telephone interview, Boston, Feb.
21, 2008.

issues. He was confused as to why PAS was illegitimate; to him, it made a certain amount of sense. "Listen," I advised him, "Parents say bad things about each other all the time. Divorce can be messy. But there is a big difference between a mother who doesn't get along with her ex and a mother who reports that her child told her, 'My dad put his pee-pee in my mouth.'"

Joan Zorza, founding editor of *Domestic Violence Report* and *Sexual Abuse Report*, told me, "The courts have bought into the idea that the woman is making false allegations."[27] Statistically, false reports of sexual abuse are rare, but reporters usually overlook that point. The real irony is that fathers are sixteen times more likely than mothers to make false allegations during custody battles.[28]

When a reporter contacts a woman going through a custody battle, the mother is usually so frantic over the possibility of losing her children that when talking about her case, she obsesses over each and every detail. This strategy almost always backfires on her. Reporters are in a hurry; they want to get the key elements of the story quickly, so that they can do a quick turn around and sell the story to an executive producer/boss.

Family Court Stories Lack Drama and Excitement

Television is always looking for great drama. Newspapers and magazines need it for their life blood. But they are not looking for the kind of drama that is seen in family court litigation. Since these cases seem to go on forever, there is no closure, no grand conclusion to bring it all to fruition. Leaving a story in midair makes a story deeply unsatisfying.

Another point is that *real* sexual abuse and *real* DV makes people sick. When it is unfiltered and presented to you over dinner, it is not entertaining; it is just plain uncomfortable. Of course, *The Burning Bed* is about DV, but it stars Farrah Fawcett. *Erin Brockovitch* is about cancer and corporations poisoning water supplies, but it also has Julia Roberts. *Michael Clayton* has George Clooney. All of that is entertainment. But long trials, with sad, worn out people and children talking about being raped are not drama. That is disgusting. This may be why it is easier to expose important social issues in TV dramas rather than on the news. There is emotional distance in dramas, because discomfort comes under the guise of fiction, therefore requiring no action on the part of the viewer.

John Hockenberry, in *Technology Review,* claims that it is, in fact, the nightly fictional dramas that have the network's blessing to explore real-life issues.

> Entertainment programs often took on issues that would never fly on *Dateline.* On a Thursday night, *ER* could do a story line on the medically uninsured, but a night later, such a "downer policy story" was a much harder sell. In the time I was at NBC, you were more likely to hear federal agriculture policy discussed on *The West Wing*, or even on Jon Stewart, than you were to see it reported in any depth on *Dateline*.[29]

---

[27] Joan Zorza, telephone interview, Boston, Feb. 21, 2008.

[28] Nicolas M.C. Bala et al., Allegations of Child Abuse in the Context of Parental Separation: A Discussion Paper (Canada Department of Justice 2001), http://www.justice. gc.ca/en/ps/pad/reports/2001-FCY-4.html.

[29] Hockenberry, *supra* note 15.

It is also not easy to get producers to talk on the record the way Hockenberry does. He is very candid about the content decisions that news and networks make. The reason Hockenberry could talk so openly was because he did not have the network legal eagles breathing down his neck. His paycheck came from MIT, not the network. He is a free man, which makes a big difference as far as what he can say or not say.

Crimes Make Better Headlines

Reporters find it easier to report on a crime that was committed and that led to someone's arrest. Most of us grew up in a society that teaches that crime is bad and that criminals are bad people who should be punished. If a crime has been committed, there will probably be a trial (if not a plea bargain), a verdict, and possibly a sentence. That is an easy and intuitively appealing story.

In fact, some family court cases have attracted media coverage once the case found its way to criminal court. Other cases got attention from the press when one of the parties went to jail or died.

Let us look at a case in which someone went to jail. Genia Shockome's case received coverage and a headline from the *New York Post*: "Pregnant Ma Lands in Jail."[30] The article stated, "The ruling on May 5th by Poughkeepsie Family Court judge Damian Amodeo sent Russian-born Shockome, a 33 year old IBM software engineer, to prison for Mother's Day."

In a press release, Attorney Barry Goldstein (coeditor of this volume) commented,

> Genia's husband abused her throughout the marriage. He had little to do with the children before the separation, but did engage in physical and sexual abuse of the children. When the mother decided to separate from her abuser, he threatened that he would take the children and destroy her life. It would be one of the few times that he told the truth.[31]

Virtually everything that happened in this case was outrageous, but there were no headlines until the mother, who was seven months' pregnant, was gagged, then jailed for three weeks, causing her and her children to be separated on Mother's Day. The stories in the press expressed considerable outrage. People were shocked that a pregnant woman who was once named a "Mother of the Year" could land in jail for purportedly speaking too vigorously and persistently to a judge while defending her maternal rights.

In *Small Justice*, we see Kathy Smigelski, the protective mother who took her abused daughter underground, go to jail. TV and newspapers heavily covered her criminal trial. Here was this sweet, blonde mother going off to jail in shackles for try- ing to protect her child. It was TV manna from heaven. "I was put in jail with women who had killed their children. I went to jail for trying to protect mine," she says in *Small Justice*.[32] Although Kathy was exonerated in criminal court, the family court gave custody of her daughter to her ex-husband.

---

[30] Brad Hamilton, "Pregnant Ma Lands in Jail," *New York Post,* May 15, 2005.

[31] Barry Goldstein, Esq., Background Press Release, http://www.thelizlibrary.org/outrage/ shockome.html.

[32] *See supra* note 1.

If Someone Dies, the Media Will Cover It

Unfortunately, a bullet is sometimes what it takes to get a story about DV on the front page. (Occasionally, a woman can be hospitalized, instead of dead, for the news to pick up her story.) Think about Charles Stewart, the furrier who made up the lie that a black mugger murdered his pregnant wife for some jewelry. That story got national attention. According to *Time Magazine*, "Instead of suspicion, Stuart was showered with sympathy. The media apotheosized the couple as starry-eyed lovers out of Camelot cut down by an urban savage."[33]

Darren Mack, who murdered his wife and shot the judge in his divorce case, got coverage from Fox News. "Reno businessman Darren Mack is suspected of shooting the judge whom he blames for the 'unjust' conditions of his divorce. He is also charged with slashing his estranged wife Charla to death."[34] More recently, we saw wall-to-wall coverage of a murdered pregnant Marine. "Pregnant Marine Cpl. Maria Lauterbach was believed to have been killed by a crowbar blow to the head, a federal law enforcement official involved in the case tells the Blotter on ABCNews.com."[35]

Attorney Joan Zorza knows all about the proclivities of the media. She described a case of a husband who threw gasoline on his wife and tried to burn her alive. "This woman had been trying to get the courts to protect her from him for months. Once she was in the hospital, she got some media coverage." Zorza went on to say, "A kid has got to be dead. At that point, everyone rushes to cover it, but months before, the mother was screaming to the courts for protection. To the media, though, it's not a story unless it's totally dramatic."[36]

So the media accepts death, injury, or jail as ways to wrap up a story.

Family Court Stories Lack Visuals

In many criminal and civil courtrooms, cameras are allowed. You can take pictures of people in handcuffs. You can see who is accused of setting the fire or raiding the corporation's 401(k) plan. You can see the pain and horror on the faces of the witnesses. This creates powerful images.

A real obstacle to getting coverage of DV and custody cases is that viewers cannot see for themselves what is going on inside the family courtroom. No cameras are allowed. This is supposedly for the protection of the children, who might have to testify about being sexually abused. But another reason for this, I believe, is because whether an alleged abuser is guilty or innocent, once the victim's testimony is broadcast, the accused will no longer be able to hold his head up in public. Alleged abusers can be very litigious, and that scares the daylights out of the media. "I can't have faceless people in my story. I can't have everyone in silhouette. It's not like the old days," an off-the-record reporter told me.[37]

---

[33] Margaret Carlson, "Presumed Innocent," *Time Magazine,* Jan. 22, 1990, *available at* http://www.time.com/time/magazine/article/0,9171,152635,00.html.

[34] Wendy McElroy, "Fathers Rights Movement Must Condemn Darren Mack," Foxnews.com, June 27, 2006, Views, http://www.foxnews.com/story/0,2933,201251,00.html.

[35] Brian Ross, "Official: Marine Killed by Crowbar, Baby Was a Girl," ABCNews.go.com, Jan. 18, 2008, http://abcnews.go.com/Blotter/story?id=4155874&page=1.

[36] Ruben Castaneda, "After Burning of Woman, Judge's Cases Are Limited," *Wash. Post,* Oct. 14, 2005, at B05.

[37] Interview with anonymous network reporter, Feb. 28, 2008.

ABC's Tom Berman admitted that any story related to the family courts raises a red flag. "But mostly, it means that there can be no camera in the courtroom. For what it's worth, we shy away from federal court stories, too. It would have to be a pretty big story for us to do it."[38]

Sound has similar issues. Sound bites are short, clear statements (sometimes incomplete sentences) that capture the essence of a thought, idea, or issue. It is like a campaign slogan or a rallying point; it is what people remember. Who does not recall the name of the person who said, "I did not have sexual relations with that woman"?[39]

In DV and custody cases, sound bites are hard to get. Often, that is because the entire story is too complicated to boil down to a sound bite. In addition, the protective mother, unfortunately, is sometimes her own worst enemy. She has a hard time telling her story chronologically, or in brief. She wants to explain each and every detail. This turns reporters off. They have nothing to work with: there are no sound bites; the issues are not clear-cut, what the courts are doing is incomprehensible, and so the story goes nowhere.

Celebrity Custody Battles Are Newsworthy

If a celebrity is attached to a story, news organizations react like they have hit the bonanza. The drive for high ratings partly explains the attractiveness of celebrity-based news, but also relevant here is the fact that we live in a celebrity-obsessed culture. Reporters cover Brad Pitt going to build houses in New Orleans. They salivate over Angelina Jolie as a UN Ambassador. They will embrace George Clooney or Mia Farrow in Darfur. But when serious questions are raised about the actions of the power elite in our court system, reporters and editors want to run for cover.

A friend of mine was talking to a network magazine reporter about using the Darren Mack case as the thread for story on the family courts. (This is the case where a man shot a judge and killed his wife.) The expert in the case, Dean Tong, would later be arrested himself on DV charges. The Darren Mack story was interesting, this reporter told my friend, but he knew his network would not cover it. "Give me a star. Have the star go to court. Then I can do something."[40]

The Alec Baldwin voice mail incident is a good example of how a celebrity can attract media attention to a custody battle. Baldwin got angry when his daughter (the child of Baldwin's marriage to actress Kim Bassinger) did not respond to a phone call from him. "You are a rude, thoughtless little pig," he screamed as he left a voice mail message for his daughter. "You don't have the brains or the decency as a human being."[41] The taped message was leaked, then played incessantly on the radio and TV and over the World Wide Web. *Newsweek* and other national publications carried this story.

What people may not remember about this incident is that Kim Bassinger (Baldwin's ex-wife) took a lot of media heat for allegedly releasing the audio tape (although there is

---

[38] Thomas Berman, telephone conversation, ABC *Prime Time,* Mar. 6, 2008.

[39] President William Jefferson Clinton, White House Press Conference, Jan. 26, 1998, http://www.washingtonpost.com/wp-srv/politics/special/clinton/stories/clinton081898.htm.

[40] Telephone interview with anonymous network reporter, Feb. 28, 2008.

[41] Alec Baldwin, as heard on "Alec Baldwin's Threatening Message to Daughter," *TMZ Staff,* Apr. 19, 2007.

no proof that she did so). In contrast, Baldwin—a very famous celebrity caught angrily castigating his child—was viewed with considerable sympathy. He also received, along the way, free advanced publicity for the pro-PAS book he was writing.

From radio shock jocks to *The View*, from the *New York Times* to small town papers, everyone was talking about this "rude, thoughtless, little pig" tape. But the really important information lying in the background—such as how custody was decided in the Baldwin-Bassinger case, or whether Baldwin's taped message constitutes verbal abuse—was lost on the media. They had their stars—Baldwin and Bassinger—and they were going for broke.

The same thing happened with coverage of the gory custody battle between Britney Spears and Kevin Federline. The questions that might have been raised about how the family court handled this case were never raised. Instead, Britney Spears herself was the real story here.

Attractive People Attract Coverage

"'Beauty is Natures coin,' [seventeenth century poet] John Milton wrote in 1634. It is currency in today[']s labor market, as well. Since 1994, numerous studies have found that workers of above-average beauty earn 5 to 15 percent more than those with below-average looks. [']Those differences are of a similar order of magnitude as the premiums we associate with race and gender,['] says associate professor of economics at Wesleyan University, Markus Mobius."[42] Mobius coauthored "Why Beauty Matters," which was published in the *American Economic Review*.[43] The article adds, "We attribute all kinds of positive things to people who look good."[44]

This is especially true for the family courts and for the media. Both are quite taken in by appearance. While I was shooting *Small Justice*, when I saw the men accused of abuse go to court, even I had a few moments of doubt. These men looked really normal. They went to church. They had decent jobs. They looked like your neighbor next door.

This is what the courts and the media do not seem to understand: People who abuse and batter others are often incredibly charming. That is why they are so successful at attracting romantic partners. Charm is an essential tool enabling them to do what they do—which is abuse and control others—while convincing people that their victim is to blame.

Sandra Horley describes this further in *The Charm Syndrome*.

> The "syndrome" is described as one whereby men use attentiveness and romance as controlling mechanisms. The charm visible to the outside world, and to the woman herself at the outset of the relationship, makes it difficult for others to believe that this man can really be capable of any abuses which are alleged by his victim.[45]

---

[42] *Quoted in* Harbour Fraser Hodder, "The Beauty Bounty," *Harv. Mag.,* Nov./Dec. 2006, *available at* http://harvardmagazine.com/2006/11/The-Beauty-Bounty.html.

[43] Markus M. Mobius & Tanya S. Rosenblat, "Why Beauty Matters," 96(1) *Am. Econ. Rev.* 222–35 (2006).

[44] Hodder, *supra* note 42.

[45] Sandra Horley, *The Charm Syndrome: Why Charming Men Can Make Dangerous Lovers (*1991), *cited in* Linda Walton-Brown, "Charmers Who Use Romance and Attention to Hide Their Violence," *The Scotsman,* June 27, 2000, *available at* http://www.highbeam.com/doc/1P2-18737459.html.

In *Small Justice*, Diane Hofheimer commented on this phenomenon: "Some of the judges are very good people. But the courts just don't believe that these men could do the horrible things they are accused of. They look so normal, but you know, they have spent their lives fooling people. The judges just don't get it."[46]

These con men seem so cool, calm, and reasonable. That is how they get what they want: first, the woman; then, the children. Family courts and the media share an inability to see through their manipulative behavior. "Experts, judges, friends will say of a man accused of abuse, 'He's such a nice man.' They don't realize that these things are irrelevant. These are men who are interested in controlling their image," says Joan Zorza.[47]

How a woman looks also makes an impression. Like so many other women, Bridget Marks had a horrific custody battle. But unlike most other women, her case got a lot of TV coverage. She appeared on *Dr. Phil, The O'Reilly Factor*, and *Prime Time Live*, among other shows. She got stories in the papers as well. After sexual abuse allegations were raised during the custody hearing, the wealthy, married man who fathered Bridget's two girls was given sole custody of the children. There is widely viewed footage of the two girls screaming not to be taken away from their mother, who is seen kneeling at their level as they cling to her. However, there was an additional visual component to this story: Ms. Marks was once a *Playboy* model, and she looks it. This is not to detract from the seriousness of her story. But she got media coverage in large part because of her beauty—not her story.[48]

In a *New York Times* op-ed piece, Nicholas D. Kristof commented on another issue, when he wrote about "The Elizabeth Smarts and Natalie Holloways . . . who fill the cable niche for a "missing blonde" story,"[49] I was reminded of this issue. Once again, it is about images that are attractive, that sell, that tap more into pop culture than to important news and information. The essence of the story gets lost in the blizzard of sellable paparazzi shots.

Bernard Goldberg, a producer for *48 Hours*, admitted, "All we do is murder, murder, murder, sex. And only about white people."[50] To which I would add, "And attractive people."

Returning to Genia Shockome's case, at the time she got coverage, she was seven months' pregnant and had been sentenced by a family court judge to a month in jail for contempt. That is what got her in the news—not the unending abuse her ex-husband had inflicted on her or the fact that she had lost all meaningful contact with her two young children. When a very pregnant battered mother goes to jail, that works. That is newsworthy.

Appearance also plays a role in how the courts view battered mothers. Lundy Bancroft and Dr. Jay Silverman, in their remarkable book, *The Batterer as Parent*, commented,

---

[46] *See supra* note 1.

[47] Joan Zorza, telephone interview, Boston, Feb. 21, 2008.

[48] For detailed records of press coverage of the Bridget Marks case, see http:judicialaccountability.org/articles/expertsinchildcustody.htm.

[49] Nicholas D. Kristof, "The Pimp's Slave," *N.Y. Times,* Mar. 16, 2008, *available at* http://www.nytimes.com/2008/03/16/opinion/16kristof.html.

[50] Bernard Goldberg, Producer *48 Hours,* telephone interview, Feb. 21, 2008.

One reason is that these mothers have been so abused and terrorized by their husbands is that they don't look good in court. They seem frazzled and out of control when they go before a judge. They might have been living in a shelter or on the run, so they look disheveled. The batterers, on the other hand, understand how the system works. They also have been living at home, have the money and resources to pay an attorney. They are dressed properly, and they appear calm and in control.[51]

In *Small Justice*, Dr. Carolyn Newberger, who is affiliated with Harvard University and Boston Children's Hospital, commented,

What I'd like people now to know is that when women are abused, they do not come out looking like paragons. They come out looking tired, angry, sleep-deprived, with symptoms and difficulties that need to be understood for what they are. Women are often blamed for what they look like instead of being understood and helped.[52]

The things that make a woman look bad in court are the same things that make her not a great "sell" for TV. Beauty, motherhood, and apple pie work better than battered, victimized, and angry.

Legal Department Has to Bless It

When the legal department of a TV station, network, or newspaper reads the notes or a story written by a reporter, no matter how true, well written, or substantiated the story may be, it can get axed on the spot. Legal is paid to be alarmist. It is the legal department's job to protect the company from lawsuits, because if you have to go to court, it costs money; if you lose, it costs even more money.

Many advocates and protective parents have told me that when they first spoke to a reporter about their story, he/she listened, took notes, seemed genuinely interested, and promised to follow up. I also can say, from my own experience, that when I contact producers of TV shows like *20/20, 60 Minutes, Prime Time,* and *48 Hours*, they show initial interest. But in every instance, once the story reaches the eyes and ears of the news organization's legal department, the piece ends up getting killed. Legal counsel wants incontrovertible proof that the allegations are true before the story goes to print; otherwise, it is too risky.

My ex-husband, a civil rights attorney, used to say that all cases that go to court are complicated. If they were easy, they would settle. Anyone who has worked on these family court cases knows that the reason they are in court is because spousal or child abuse is hard to prove in family court, where the criminal rules of evidence do not apply.

A sympathetic network reporter who requested anonymity told me,

I know with [an unnamed protective mother] that she had documented everything. She was giving me this story on a silver platter. But the child,

---

[51] Lundy Bancroft & Jay G. Silverman, *The Batterer as Parent: Addressing the Impact of Domestic Violence on Family Dynamics* (2002).

[52] *See supra* note 1.

who was living with the father, was unwilling to testify, and the father denied any and all abuse. You know, even if the child spoke on the record, it was her word against her father's. [Our] legal [department] would just never let this pass.[53]

Legal concerns are one of the main reasons why the national media retreats from these stories at the last moment. The legal department is usually the last hurdle for the producer or writer. The legal department is what causes immense frustration to a lot of battered women's advocates. The advocates spend hours with a reporter. They send the reporter enough material to sink the Queen Elizabeth II. But the story's plug is likely to get pulled once the legal department discovers that the story includes allegations of sexual abuse or DV—unless the battered mother is already dead or the perpetrating father has been found 100 percent guilty by the court.

A producer friend said to me, "You know I can't talk to you. I am owned by the network."[54] This is a reporter who would like to blow this scandal wide open. But my friend has remained silent, like almost everyone else in the media. The media knows that the legal department would nix the story, anyway. They know who the boss is and what the rules are; so rather than waste everyone's time, they simply decide that they cannot do the story. That way, the story dies by way of self-censorship.

Eric Alterman points out,

Focusing on examples of direct censorship in the U.S. media misses the point. Rarely does some story that is likely to arouse concern ever go far enough to actually need to be censored at the corporate level. The reporter, the editor, the producer, and the executive producer all understand implicitly that their jobs depend in part on keeping their corporate parents happy.[55]

Fair and Balanced

In my opinion, the notion that news must be "fair and balanced" may be the biggest obstacle to getting coverage of family court corruption. News organizations are committed to getting both sides of the story, which requires interviewing the accuser and the accused. If a man accused of abuse will not talk, or if a woman alleging abuse is under a gag order and therefore cannot talk, there is no way for the reporter to get both sides of the story. Under the fair-and-balanced mandate, then, there can be no story.

Gag orders are especially problematic. Many protective parents are so traumatized by what has happened to them that they try to tell their stories to anyone who will listen. They believe that since they live in America, if it becomes known that children are being hurt, people will want to know and do something about it. But when a judge in a family court issues a gag order, these parents cannot talk for fear of the consequences. As Joan Zorza commented to me, "The gag orders that are imposed are the most powerful tool the courts use under the guise of protecting children. They are weapons used to control and silence what is really going on in the family courts."[56]

---

[53] Interview with anonymous, major network producer, Boston, Feb. 21, 2008.
[54] Interview with anonymous major network producer, Boston, Feb. 22, 2008.
[55] Alterman, *supra* note 11, at 14, 23.
[56] Joan Zorza, telephone interview, Boston, Feb. 21, 2008.

Annette Zender, a protective mother from Illinois, was not about to be intimidated by a gag order (see Chapter 10 in this volume). Along with organizing a group called the Illinois Coalition for Family Court Reform (ICFCR),[57] she got hundreds of protective mothers to write down what happened to them during their custody battle. Annette understood that battered mothers tend to give too many details or have problems presenting the facts of their case. This is why Ms. Zender posted a form on the ICFCR Web site for mothers to use to summarize their stories for the media.[58] That made the Illinois courts nervous. In fact, it made Ms. Zender's family court judge mad enough to place a gag order on her. In protest, Annette defied the judge's order, contacted the press, and wore a purple scarf over her mouth—a visually impressive action that made the front cover of the *Lake County News Sun*. The headline was "SHUT UP!—She Can't Discuss Custody Case With Any Third Person, Including This Newspaper."[59] Barry Goldstein, Genia Shockome's former attorney, noted how the case drew press attention after Ms. Shockome was gagged and sent to jail:

> A local radio program, "Scams and Scandals," and two local cable shows covered it. Interestingly, when we received the publicity, other victims of [the biased judge in the case] came forward, which is exactly what the gag order was intended to prevent.[60]

The waves of publicity that follow the imposition of gag orders on Annette Zender and Genia Shockome had nothing to do with the fact that a loving mother had lost custody of her children. It had everything to do with the First Amendment—a gag order that effectively bans the publication of a newsworthy story? To reporters, *that* is scary. Freedom of speech amounts to their bread and butter. When people cannot talk to the press, a reporter's job becomes difficult if not impossible. Reporters recognize that a gag order placed on a witness is not a big leap away from a gag order placed on a member of the press. Many reporters would be willing to go to jail rather than give up their First Amendment right to do a story. Therefore, if packaged properly, a case in which a protective parent is gagged could attract press coverage. Usually, though, the fear factor silences those who have been gagged, and since a reporter needs both sides of a story, without one side or the other, there can be no story.

On a related note, I believe that the refusal of alleged abusers to talk to the press is a strategy used by FRs groups to keep the media from covering these stories. If, as it claims, the media is required give both sides of the story, if one side will not talk, that guarantees the media's silence. The MSM may use "fair and balanced" as an excuse for a number of their failings, but I maintain that it is fear that is preventing the media from exposing the family court problems.

In fact, both sides are *not* required for all stories. We do not feel the need to cover both sides of hate crimes. We do not require reporters to talk to people arrested for pushing drugs in order to get both sides of the story. Certainly, for most topics, the goal is to get and present both sides. But why must every news story have two sides? Should

---

[57] Illinois Coalition for Family Court Reform, http://icfcr.org/index.html.

[58] Id.

[59] Art Peterson, "'SHUT UP!' She Can't Discuss Custody Case With Any Third Person, Including This Newspaper," *Lake County News Sun,* Aug. 31, 2006, *available at* http://www.stopfamilyviolence.org/ocean/host.php?page=340.

[60] Barry Goldstein, e-mail to author, Jan. 26, 2008.

a story be killed if the reporter *cannot* get both sides? Should the Nazi war criminals have been granted coverage equal to that given to their prosecutors to ensure that the reporting was fair and balanced?

FALLOUT

The fairness-and-balance issue brings up to two different documentaries. The first is *Small Justice*,[61] where, as stated earlier, I explicitly informed the audience that they would be hearing only one side of the story. This admission, stated at the outset, might be the primary reason why *Small Justice* never aired on network TV. "We could never air this on our news magazine," an executive producer told me. "We always show both of sides of the issue."[62] *Small Justice* has been shown at many conferences to great acclaim. It has won Indie awards. But it has never been aired on network TV.

The second documentary did get network time, but it also got a volley of retribution hurled at it by FRs proponents, who lambasted the documentary for what they called one-sided storytelling. *Breaking the Silence: Children's Stories*[63] aired on the Public Broadcasting Service (PBS) in the fall of 2005. A year or so earlier, the documentary's co-producer, Dominique Lasseur, had shot footage at the BMCC. He listened to the experts and spoke to many women who had lost or were losing custody to abusers. The Mary Kay Cosmetics Foundation funded the documentary to the tune of $500,000. The show was produced in accordance with the PBS underwriting guidelines. Advocates hoped this would be the breakthrough show and that it would, indeed, break the silence.

But even before it had aired, FRs groups launched an attack on the documentary claiming it was not fair and balanced. According to PBS ombudsman Michael Getler, 4,000 letters were written to PBS about *Breaking the Silence*.[64] Of those, 3,500 were against the show. More than 90 out of 105 calls were also negative.

Although in their formal press release[65] PBS stood behind the integrity of *Breaking the Silence*, they eventually buckled under. As attorney Barry Goldstein put it, "There was an important campaign around that film in which the male supremacy movement attacked the film before even seeing it. We sought to support it [*Breaking the Silence*], but PBS caved in to the pressure."[66]

Dr. Mo Hannah, chair of the BMCC, commented,

I got to witness this up close. PBS leaned in the direction of the bully. They were listening to the loudest voices. It felt abusive—that is the word for it. In the end, it was another experience of being subjected to an abusive system.[67]

---

[61] *See supra* note 1.

[62] Interview with anonymous major network producer, Boston, Feb. 22, 2008.

[63] Catherine Tatge & Dominique Lasseur (producers), *Breaking the Silence: Children's Stories,* aired on PBS in October 2005.

[64] Michael Getler, "A Little About Me, A Lot About "Breaking the Silence," *The Ombudsman Column,* Dec. 2, 2005, http://www.pbs.org/ombudsman/2005/12/introudction_ and_breaking_the_silence_print.html.

[65] PBS Statement on *Breaking The Silence: Children's Stories,* Dec. 21, 2005, http://www. pbs.org/aboutpbs/news/20051221_breakingthesilence.html.

[66] Barry Goldstein, Esq., telephone conversation, Feb. 21, 2008.

[67] Dr. Mo Hannah, telephone conversation, Feb. 21, 2008.

As a way to respond to the complaints of the FRs groups, PBS commissioned a second documentary. (This kind of response to pressure is extremely unusual in the TV industry.) That subsequent production, *Kids & Divorce: For Better or Worse*[68] never received the kind of buzz that *Breaking the Silence* got, but it did pacify FRs proponents. In a review of *Kids and Divorce* for the publication *Domestic Violence Review,* Dr. Hannah summed it up this way:

> What I anticipated, then, from *Kids and Divorce* was a cohesive, statistically rich counter-punch to *Breaking the Silence*. I expected a point-by-point rebuttal of what was stated in the earlier documentary–for example, the statistic that 50%–70% of abusers who seek joint or sole custody are successful in doing so, or the claim that battered mothers and their children often are re-victimized by what goes on in the family courts. What I did not expect was a piece that deflected attention away from the heart of the matter, namely the family courts' handling of custody cases when there is domestic or family violence. Instead, *Kids and Divorce* completely failed to dispute, challenge, or even respond to the bleak picture portrayed in *Breaking the Silence.*[69]

It is not just the networks that have to deal with complaints from angry fathers, though. Sometimes the writer/producer is the one under attack. I personally have received hate mail in response to my own documentary, *Small Justice,* so I take my hat off to those who have had to deal with the backlash on a regular basis.

Reporter Kristen Lombardi last worked for the *Village Voice*. Before that, she wrote for the *Boston Phoenix*. I spoke to her while she was working on the *Boston Phoenix* piece, "Custodians of Abuse." It was a powerhouse of an article, similar to what she wrote when she broke the Catholic priest sexual abuse scandal years earlier.

She began "Custodians of Abuse" with no holds barred.

> If you're a parent, it's your worst nightmare: finding out that your child is being molested–by your spouse. If you seek a divorce as a result, or are already going through one when you make the discovery, you hope that family court will do the right thing: grant you sole legal and physical custody of your child. In fact, you can't even imagine that there could be any other outcome in the custody judgment. But for many parents—in nearly every instance, mothers—just the opposite occurs: the alleged abusers don't just get unsupervised visitation rights, they get full custody. How can this happen?[70]

The answer to that question made a lot of people scared and a few people very angry. One man who was named in the article sued the *Boston Phoenix*. For a journalist, a lawsuit can be a very big problem. Lombardi's livelihood and reputation were on the line. The *Boston Phoenix* stood behind her. Still there was a lawsuit. That lawsuit was settled, but her career trajectory was affected.

---

[68] David Iverson (Producer), *Kids & Divorce: For Better or Worse* (2006).

[69] Dr. Mo Hannah, telephone conversation, Feb. 21, 2008.

[70] Kristen Lombardi, "Custodians of Abuse," *Boston Phoenix,* Jan. 09, 2003**,** *available at* http://www.stopfamilyviolence.org/get-informed/custody-abuse/news-on-custody-abuse/custodians-of-abuse.

Richard Ducote commented to me about the article, "Before, during the 1980s and even the 1990s, there was local and national coverage, and much of it was good. After Kristen Lombardi's article in the *Boston Phoenix,* there has been a chill."[71] Indeed!

OPRAH FACTOR

You cannot discuss the media's handling of these horror stories without looking at the *Oprah* phenomenon. What if Oprah were to do a show on this issue? She is, after all, the leading lady as far as making people stand up and shout for change. Attorney Barry Goldstein told me that numerous women have proposed to him the idea of contacting Oprah about their cases.

> Every protective mother victimized by the court system has the same idea: She should appear on *Oprah.* Protective parents often believe that their story is so awful, so horrific, that of course the press will want to cover it, especially Oprah. Once Oprah hears the truth, she will put this story on the air, and women and children across the country will be saved. This is not just because of Oprah's great influence and the exposure an appearance on her show would provide, but because she is perceived as caring about human issues.[72]

I put in a call to the senior supervising promotions producer at Harpo Productions, which produces *Oprah.* I wanted to know how many stories Oprah gets pitched a year, what they look for in stories, and how they weed through all of them. Her assistant was courteous; she asked me to provide questions and some background information about myself. To be honest, I did not really expect a call back. I did not get one either.

At the beginning of this chapter, we discussed ratings and the central role they play in media decisions. If you look at the *Oprah* Web site, you can see that there has been a seismic shift in the topics she is covering currently in comparison with those from when she first started on TV. This may explain why heavy topics like custody, DV, and child abuse are not being addressed on her show. Yes, she is looking for people to be on her show, but take a look at the prevailing topics: "How do you feel about your body?" "Does your family need a makeover?" Oprah Radio focuses on things like the law of attraction and how to clear up all that clutter in your house. On Oprah.com's Web page, notice that Nabisco and 100 Calorie Packs and Three Musketeers are sponsors.[73] Oprah at Home is sponsored by Target. It is all about ratings and advertising.

It is important to give credit where credit is due, however. The magazine *Oprah* did a magnificent story "Please Daddy, No."[74] I think this article by Jan Goodwin is one of the best ever written on child sexual abuse and the crisis in the family courts— certainly the best since Lombardi's "Custodians of Abuse."[75]

---

[71] Richard Ducote, Esq., telephone interview, Boston, Feb. 22, 2008.

[72] Barry Goldstein, e-mail to author, Feb. 21, 2008.

[73] *See* Oprah.com, http://www.oprah.com.

[74] Jan Goodwin, "Please Daddy, No," *Oprah Magazine,* Nov. 2006.

[75] Lombardi, *supra* note 70.

Goodwin drives the point home with, "A child molested by a stranger can run home for help and comfort. A child sexually abused by a parent cannot. And that tragedy will repeat itself again and again until we stop looking the other way." She continues, "Whoever it is—the GAL [guardian ad litem], the judge, the lawmaker, mother, 'the people responsible for placing children back with their sex offenders are, at the very least, criminally negligent in any subsequent sexual abuse,' says Randy Burton of Justice for Children."[76] There is nothing soft about this story in *Oprah*. This is bold. Thank you, Oprah.

And Oprah has done numerous shows on abuse. She even had Yvette Cade, the woman, whose husband burned her with gasoline, on her show.[77] Oprah also has spoken publicly about her own abuse. But to date, she has not looked at how loving mothers, once they go to family court, can lose custody of their children to men who batter and abuse.

Richard Ducote makes a good point.

> There is a paradox in getting all these stories covered, whether it's for Oprah or any other show. Everyone runs to the media with an individual story. In the end, it makes it more difficult. A better strategy is to present a bunch of cases at the same time. It's much better than inundating them.[78]

Well, yes and no.

Ducote makes a valid point. Yes, it is better when women and advocates and lawyers work together to compile names, stories, lawyers, and judges in the cases. The no comes from seeing that the media, even if they could determine a pattern of abuse, would probably not cover it because it is too expensive, too time consuming, too complicated, and it probably will not do well in the ratings.

But there is one more thing that must be asked. When there have been stories in the media, and there have been some, they often do not stick. They do not generate a buzz, they do not make people outraged, and they rarely lead to any form of corrective action. Why is that?

STICKINESS FACTOR

I first met Kathy Lee Scholpp at the BMCC. I later helped get her story on TV. My husband, Barry Nolan, the former host of the Comcast Channel's *Nitebeat*, agreed to interview Kathy Lee and Boston attorney Barry Polack on custody issues. Barry also invited Dr. Ned Holstein, chair of the board and founder of "Fathers and Families First," to present the "other side." Kathy Lee had just lost custody of her young son in a Massachusetts family court. She commented, "I thought that once I went on the show that the media exposure would shine a light on the court and I would get my son back."[79] Needless to say, that did not happen.

---

[76] Goodwin, *supra* note 74, at 351.

[77] Allison Kline, "On 'Oprah,' a Wife's Tale of Terror," *Wash. Post,* May 4, 2006.

[78] Richard Ducote, Esq., telephone interview, Boston, Feb. 22, 2008.

[79] Kathy Lee Schopp, conversation with author at the BMCC, Jan. 13, 2008.

In September 2006, *Newsweek* published an article written by Sarah Childress.[80] The article profiled Genia Shockome's case, but the real target was PAS. Childress notes, "Parental Alienation is now the leading defense for parents accused of abuse in custody cases, according to DV advocates." She writes that the National Council of Juvenile and Family Court Judges "denounced the theory [of PAS] as 'junk science.'" She quotes Richard Ducote, an attorney with expertise in custody matters, as saying that PAS has "been a cancer in the family courts." So here is a major publication exposing a serious problem in the family courts, and yet it dies on the vine. There is no public outrage.

There is a common misconception that once the media disseminates information about an egregious injustice, the public will rise up and demand change. But when it comes to reports about family court injustice, the public does not do this. There is something about these stories that makes people so uncomfortable that, rather than getting enraged and engaged, they run and hide.

PUBLIC RESPONSIBILITY

I am reminded of one of the most important speeches in TV history, "The Vast Wasteland."[81] It is a speech that I teach every year to my students at the College of Communication at Boston University. The speech focuses on the power of television to do great things along with its abysmal failure to do those very things.

In 1961, Newton Minow, who was then the chair of the Federal Communications Commission, gave a speech to the National Association of Broadcasters. It was one of the most courageous talks ever given to the very group that controls the airwaves. They did not like the speech then, and they hate being reminded of it now. Minow states,

> I invite you to sit down in front of your television set when your station goes on the air and stay there without a book, magazine, newspaper, profit and-loss sheet or rating book to distract you—and keep your eyes glued to that set until the station signs off. I can assure you that you will observe a vast wasteland.

I, too, can assure you that things have not changed much since Minow spoke those words almost a half-century ago. When describing the principles that guided his work, Minow emphasized Principle #1:

> The people own the air[waves]. They own it as much in prime evening time as they do at 6 o'clock Sunday morning. For every hour that the people give you, you owe them something. I intend to see that your debt is paid with service.[82]

This is something few Americans know: These media corporations are making billions of dollars using *your* airwaves. News divisions were once viewed as beholden to the public. Holders of broadcast licenses had obligations to the public, who are the *real* owners of the airwaves. In the past, news divisions were more or less exempt from ratings pressures. Now, many news programs are profit centers, the economic engines

---

[80] Sarah Childress, "Fighting Over the Kids," *Newsweek*, Sept. 25, 2006.

[81] Newton R. Minow, "Vast Wasteland," Address to the National Association of Broadcasters, *available at* http://www.americanrhetoric.com/speeches/newtonminow.htm.

[82] Id.

of broadcast operations. If the news flops, the news director gets chopped, and so, too, does the attractive anchor reading the teleprompter.

Minow aimed his message right between the eyes of broadcasters.

> Television and all who participate in it are jointly accountable to the American public for respect for the special needs of children, for community responsibility, for the advancement of education and culture, for the acceptability of the program materials chosen, for decency and decorum in production, and for propriety in advertising. This responsibility cannot be discharged by any given group of programs, but can be discharged only through the highest standards of respect for the American home, applied to every moment of every program presented by television. Program materials should enlarge the horizons of the viewer, provide him with wholesome entertainment, afford helpful stimulation, and remind him of the responsibilities which the citizen has toward his society. . . . I urge you to put the people's airwaves to the service of the people and the cause of freedom.[83]

This is the point. Whether it is TV, radio, newspapers, or magazines, it is time for those of us who recognize the misuse of the MSM for profit to demand they get back to the "service of the people and the cause of freedom."

TIPPING POINT

"Much of what we are told or read or watch, we simply don't remember. The information age has created a stickiness problem" says Malcolm Gladwell.[84] Gladwell's book, *The Tipping Point: How Little Things Can Make a Big Difference,* discusses why serious concerns like the family court crisis are not sticking to the public psyche. Using terms like "sticky" to describe topics that attract media interest, Gladwell provides some insights that are useful for gaining exposure for family court-related issues.

Change in Presentation

Gladwell notes that stickiness may be enhanced by "a subtle but significant change in presentation."[85] This point is particularly relevant to battered mothers' stories. Mothers and their advocates typically try to give the press too many details too soon, and at warp speed. Their presentation, instead, should be more like an outline than a full-fledged story: spare, clean, clear, and concise, just the necessary details, just the facts. They need to know how to create and use sound bites, which are pithy summations that are easy for a reporter to understand and run with. Their stories need to start with the most important part first, instead of at the end. They need to speak in a way that makes the media listen. They need to get to the heart of the matter right away (e.g.,"My daughter told me her father makes her play the 'marriage game'").

---

[83] Id.

[84] Malcolm Gladwell, *The Tipping Point: How Little Things Can Make a Big Difference* 98-99 (2000).

[85] Id. at 257.

But even more important, we need to stop presenting a given case as though it were isolated and happenstance. We need articulate, powerful, and persuasive individuals, advocacy groups, and experts to constantly reiterate that these problems are systemic and endemic.

For example, custody expert Richard Ducote shows the masterful use of a soundbite when he made this comment: "the family court is a cabal and a cartel."[86] Another excellent sound bite, by author, advocate, and attorney, Andrew Vachss, goes, **"If enough citizens step up this time, we can finally eliminate the law that gives a special bonus to those who grow their own victims."**[87] The sound bite consists of the final phrase about "grow[ing] your own victim." It is haunting and disturbing, and it sounds true.

In *The Tipping Point*, Gladwell points out that to make a message stick, you have to consider "The Law of the Few":

> There are exceptional people out there who are capable of starting epidemics. All you have to do is find them. The lesson of stickiness is the same. There is a simple way to package information that, under the right circumstances, can make it irresistible. All you have to do is find it."[88]

That, in a nutshell, is the job of those who want to protect battered women and abused children. The information must be packaged in a way that a lot of people can quickly and easily understand. "We throw up our hands at a problem phrased in an abstract way, but have no difficulty at all solving the same problem rephrased as a social dilemma," writes Gladwell.[89]

Leveraging Entertainment

If a major TV or movie actress could star in a *Burning Bed* or *Erin Brockovitch* type of movie about family court corruption, this could generate enough public interest to break the real story behind the film. The issue needs big name celebrities—Reese Witherspoon, Julia Roberts, Jodi Foster, and Geena Davis, to name a few—with money, power, and their own production companies. A good number of actresses are highly committed to social justice causes, including women's issues. They could use their resources, power, and media access to shift the message.

National Spokesperson

The battered mothers' movement needs a single and visible national spokesperson who can speak calmly but forcefully to the press. This must be a person who, at the first sign of a media frenzy, like the Alec Bladwin tape, can jump in with a press release to *all* news organizations that day, not two days later. It is not just someone who cares. It is someone who has the skill-set to talk to the press in strong, clear sound bites.

The spokesperson would also be able to coordinate with the myriad of groups who are working on mothers' custody problems. All are well intentioned, but, at this

---

[86] Richard Ducote, Esq., telephone interview, Boston, Feb. 22, 2008.

[87] Andrew Vachss, "The 2004/2005 California Circle of Trust Campaign Senate Bill 1803," *The Zero,* http://www.vachss.com/updates/ca_incest.html.

[88] Gladwell, *supra* note 34.

[89] Id.

juncture, these groups are too numerous and scattered throughout the country. They need to be organized, centralized, and united.

Legislation

Legislation needs to be drafted in ways that elicit bipartisan support as well as wide support from the public. In framing and presenting this legislation, we need to take back the "family values" line from FRs groups and other male supremacists. The battered mothers' issue is all about the protection of the family, whose core purpose is the propagation and protection of vulnerable children (the FRs movement, with its sole focus on the rights of males, espouses precisely the opposite value).

CONCLUSION

At the very least, we know that the media's failure to cover stories about the serious and pervasive pattern of family court injustice to battered mothers and their children is a danger to society and a disservice to the public, not to mention the field of journalism. I, personally, believe in advocacy journalism, and so I consider it incumbent upon the media to do the right thing simply because it is the right thing to do. But I also believe that, without pressure being brought to bear by an outraged public, the networks and other media outlets will continue their strategy of minimizing risk and maximizing profits, meanwhile sacrificing social justice altogether.

I would like to close with the promised postscript to the story I related earlier, which I heard from Eileen King of Justice for Children. This was about the reporter who wrote a sympathetic story about an abusive father who got custody of his kids. "The kids weren't able to talk about the abuse because they have had to live with him," Eileen said. "But when one son got to college, he was given an assignment to write about his hero. He wrote about his mother, because she 'believed him and tried to keep him from being abused.'"[90]

The flaws in the family court system should have been exposed long ago, but they have not. I lay that omission at the feet of the MSM. When children are mandated by the family courts to live with abusers, it amounts to a crime against humanity. When battered women can lose custody of their children simply for making a good-faith claim of abuse, it amounts to a national scandal. When the MSM turns its back on everything except simple, noncontroverial stories and the almighty dollar, it is time for the media to turn in its licenses.

In fact, this is where the public has some power. I advise people to pay attention to what is going on at the national level, as far as Federal Communications Commission rulings and federal legislation addressing corporate media ownership. Keep in mind that on a local level, TV stations are required to do certain public service programming in order to maintain their licenses.

There is one more important consideration, as far as this issue reaching the "tipping point." That is, the fact that the many children who have been forced by the courts to live with their abusers are now grown up, with many more close to having "aged out" of the courts. A number of these now-adults are beginning to talk. When they do, a good number will be naming names. With a little help, they will sue the

---

[90] Eileen King, Justice for Children, telephone conference, Feb. 21, 2008.

people who facilitated that abuse by their courtroom procedures and behaviors. We, the public, need to be there for them. Maybe one of them will have the story that sticks, and the "Yuck Factor" will ultimately lead to what Gladwell calls an "epidemic" of understanding. Maybe the story will become pretty simple to tell after all. Oprah, and Dr. Phil, and Maury, and *60 Minutes*—all of them—will want those kids on their shows. The legal department will just have to deal with it because it is the truth.

Author's Note

The author wishes to thank Eleanor Greene for her research assistance.

Part 4
Solutions and Strategies

Chapter 16

Leveling the Landscape: Family Court Auxiliaries and How to Counter Them

by Michael Lesher, M.A., J.D.

FAMILY COURT'S DANGEROUS REALITIES

Family court is treacherous terrain for mothers, doubly so because few mothers know what to expect when they enter it. The reality of family court, with its seemingly omnipotent decision makers and its casual approach to evidence, often confounds a woman's naïve expectations of the justice system. A mother of a child who may have been abused by the child's father understandably looks to various institutions connected with the courts—child protective services (CPS) agencies, law guardians, court-appointed mental health "experts"—for guidance and support in the unfamiliar setting of courtroom litigation. But far too many find themselves the victims of exactly the professionals they hoped would be their allies.

In *From Madness to Mutiny,*[1] Dr. Amy Neustein and I analyze in detail how the institutional "auxiliaries" that cling like barnacles to the family court system can all too easily stand in the way of justice. As a lawyer who often works with protective parents—that is, mothers who suspect that their children are victims of abuse perpetrated by their children's fathers—I have found myself having to repeat to client after client the warnings Dr. Neustein and I articulate in our book in order to help these women avert the most nightmarish of outcomes: losing custody of a child to a man precisely because of the actions that the mother tries to take to keep him from abusing the child.

---

[1] Amy Neustein & Michael Lesher, *From Madness to Mutiny: Why Mothers Are Running From the Family Courts—And What Can Be Done About It* (2005).

That nightmare is, alas, much more common than anyone but a veteran of the system would likely believe. But the news is not all bad. I have found that certain litigation strategies can maximize the protective parent's chances of success in the treacherous landscape of the family court system.

What follows is a summary of the worst dangers posed to protective parents by the court-related institutions that, in theory, exist to help them. Most importantly, I provide a description of the legal approaches I have used in such cases to help my clients avoid these pitfalls.

CHILD PROTECTIVE SERVICES

Today, child abuse allegations are generally referred to child welfare agencies, known in some states as "presentment agencies," which function much as prosecutors do in criminal cases. On the surface, this appears logical; funneling child abuse allegations to special agencies was clearly intended to aid in the investigation and presentation of those charges, which by their nature tend to require the intervention of experts.

But as Dr. Neustein and I reported in *From Madness to Mutiny*,[2] CPS agencies are just as likely to hinder as to help a protective mother worried about the possible abuse of her child. First, if an agency is not convinced abuse occurred (and sexual abuse of children, especially, is notoriously difficult to prove) and, as a result, declines to press the charge, the mother's chances of having her concerns taken seriously by the family court judge are sharply reduced. Second, agencies do not stop at not pursuing a sex abuse charge against a father; all too often, they move on to the ultimate betrayal of a protective parent: actually pressing "child neglect" charges *against the accusing mother*. In other words, for suspecting her ex-husband of having sexually abused her children, a mother finds herself accused of harming her own children by virtue of that suspicion. Worst of all, with CPS against her, such a mother will generally end up losing custody to the alleged abuser.

A mother in that sort of imbroglio is certainly not to be envied. Still, aggressive and carefully chosen tactics can bring good results.

Case Examples

In two of my own recent cases, CPS accused protective mothers of having "neglected" their children because each one believed her child's report of having been sexually abused by the child's father. In one instance, the mother took the small child for medical examinations each time the child reported having been fondled or penetrated in her vaginal or anal areas (twice on medical advice, once on instructions from CPS itself). The early examinations revealed no physical evidence of abuse, but that was hardly surprising; physical signs of abuse detectable by doctors are rare in cases of child sexual abuse.[3] In fact, in this case, the child's most recent examination

---

[2] Id.

[3] According to Kathryn Bowen & Michael B. Aldous, "Medical Evaluation of Sexual Abuse in Children Without Disclosed or Witnessed Abuse," 153(11) *Pediatrics & Adolescent Med.* 1160 (Nov. 1999), 83.5 to 94.4 percent of children whose genitals were examined were "normal or nonspecific," even where their histories indicated sexual abuse.

by a pediatrician did reveal an abnormality in the vagina that, according to the doctor, could have been evidence of penetration.

CPS had rejected the abuse allegations because its caseworkers (none of whom appears to have had any particular expertise in interviewing children about sexual abuse) did not elicit additional disclosures from the child. Nevertheless, the agency had continued to monitor the case and recommended therapy for the young girl. Its attitude only hardened further when the child's pediatrician recommended that she be examined with a colposcope[4] to determine whether, in fact, her recently observed vaginal abnormality constituted physical evidence of abuse. CPS caseworkers were unmoved even when the child's psychotherapist concluded, at almost the same time, that the child had been sexually abused (presumably by her father) on the basis of her behavior and precocious sexual knowledge.

What did CPS do? The agency accused, not the father, but the *mother* of "neglect-ing" the child. Its caseworkers claimed the medical examinations had been "intru-sive" and that, by taking the child to the doctor when she described being abused, the child's mother had caused the girl emotional harm. To this breathtaking logic, CPS added the claim that the mother must have "coached" the child to say that her father was "mean," even though the child had spontaneously described abusive acts by the father to at least two people when her mother was elsewhere—not to mention that the girl's therapist had explicitly rejected the possibility that the girl had been "coached." As for the therapist's diagnosis of sexual abuse and the newly discovered physical evidence requiring a colposcope to examine possible signs of penetration, CPS had a jadedly simple answer: the agency recommended that the girl be barred from having an internal examination of her vagina and demanded that she no longer be allowed to see her therapist.

The second case involved very similar features. The divorced mother's five-year-old son made a report to a school psychologist that he was being sexually abused by his father. The father had a documented history of domestic violence against his ex-wife and had even been found guilty of neglecting the child, due to an incident in which he had attacked the mother in the boy's presence. Nonetheless, CPS refused to be per-suaded. And after the psychologist's report was presented to the family court, the CPS agency in the county in which the father lived (since separation, the parents resided in different counties within the same state) became his active ally. Their advocacy on his behalf extended to the point where they filed a petition in court accusing the mother of "child neglect" based on allegations virtually dictated by the father. The mother was said to have made false reports of abuse by the father, when in fact all of the reports in question had come from the psychologist and other sources. CPS also accused the mother, vaguely, of planning to run away with the child out of state, a claim for which there was no evidence of any kind.

Legal Approaches

My approach to both cases was essentially the same. I have noted already that CPS agencies play a role in domestic litigation akin to that of prosecutors in criminal courts. When prosecutors file charges that are clearly impossible to sustain—either because the charges rest on false claims of fact or because the specifics they allege

---

[4] A coloscope is "a lighted instrument used by a gynecologist to examine the tissues of the vagina and the cervix"; *see* http://www.medicinenet.com.

are not crimes at all—defense attorneys fight back by asking the judge to dismiss the charges outright. I take the same approach to bogus "neglect" charges against protective mothers. In both of the cases just described, I drafted motions seeking dismissal of the charges against my clients before even preparing for trial.

Taking the legal fight directly to CPS is not the strategy endorsed by most matrimonial attorneys. Most prefer to negotiate with CPS; in fact, they will press their clients to sign almost any agreement the agencies offer that contain a withdrawal of the neglect charges—even when the mother clearly did nothing wrong. This approach implicitly acknowledges CPS agencies as all powerful in matters of child abuse, literally above the law.

I am skeptical of such a strategy. True, CPS goes into battle armed with many advantages: credibility with the judge, social workers wielding impressive-sounding "diagnoses," a state-financed prosecutorial role. But when CPS officials can be shown to have ignored the law and to have made demonstrably false statements, I believe they must be challenged. It is better to put the agency on the defensive and demand that it prove its case than to allow CPS's shadowy and often illegal claims to gain substance by tacitly endorsing them.

In both of the cases just described, CPS's petitions were built—to put it bluntly—on lies. The mother accused of making false reports had not, in fact, made the reports; the child whom CPS claimed was subjected to repeated "invasive" examinations had only one internal vaginal exam, which was hardly invasive (since no instrument was used) and actually revealed possible evidence of penetration. These lies threatened my clients with the loss of custody of their children. Even worse, these false charges arose transparently from the agencies' desire to protect *themselves*: Instead of admitting that they might have made a mistake by overlooking credible evidence of real abuse, in both cases the agencies chose to throw themselves into the service of a possible child abuser to protect their own image. In doing so, they were not only maligning an innocent parent, but betraying children they were sworn to protect.

Rather than let my clients suffer such conduct silently, I insisted that CPS provide documentation for its claims. My motion papers took CPS's claims apart point by point, exposing each and every claim that contradicted the record. I was equally adamant that CPS explain why the course of conduct taken by both of these mothers qualified as illegal "child neglect." On the contrary, I argued, these mothers could have been neglectful had they *not* acted as they did. Any mother who disregarded medical advice and failed to have her child professionally examined after the girl had reported being sexually violated, or who did nothing after a psychologist reported the suspicion that the mother's young son had been abused, might actually face legal action for her negligence. If CPS could accuse these mothers of "neglect" when they *do* take appropriate action, then these mothers literally could not win: they were guilty no matter what they did!

My approach paid off for these clients. In one case, the agency actually withdrew its petition accusing the mother, rather than attempting to justify its provably false claims. In the other, although the case was not dismissed outright, CPS did admit that some of its key accusations against the mother were false: It acknowledged that the child, whose mother was formerly accused of subjecting her to repeated "invasive" examinations, had never yet had an internal examination. That concession significantly narrowed the evidence CPS would be able to present against this mother at trial.

From my reading of the relevant cases, and from discussions with other lawyers, I believe that this approach, of filing motions to dismiss false CPS charges as soon as they are made, is a novel tactic. This is all the more reason for using it. CPS agencies are not accustomed to strong challenges, and I find that an aggressive and well-written motion can put the agency, as in the cases I just described, on the defensive.

I know that challenging the status quo is dangerous, and that as a lawyer I have no right to gamble with a client's life, no matter how compelling my larger agenda. But I also feel that there are great risks, less often acknowledged, in acquiescing to business-as-usual from an agency that is violating the law. If a falsely accused mother allows the charge against her to stand, it soon acquires its own perverse reality in the world of the courts, where "facts" are the outcome of formally orchestrated procedures. This "fact" will then dog her for as long as she remains in family court. Even if further evidence of abuse by her ex-husband surfaces, she will not be able to present it; even if she does, such evidence will be disregarded, and she will be accused of "alienating" behavior or of somehow emotionally damaging the child. A genuinely abusive father is likely to take advantage of this fact and abandon restraint, so that the mother is driven ever closer to a Hobson's choice: do nothing and allow the child to be abused, or try to protect the child and be cut off from the child altogether. Meanwhile, the CPS agency, knowing it is safe from any challenge, may be even less scrupulous in its next set of attacks on the mother. (I know of protective mothers who "compromised" with a hostile CPS agency only to lose custody later on, precisely because evidence of abuse intensified.)

Given the risks attendant on both courses of conduct, I often advise the more aggressive approach. The civil rights protections that are part of every legal system, even family courts, do not always work for protective parents. But they will never work if we do not try to use them.

LAW GUARDIANS

No one familiar with the family court system will question the power of law guardians or guardians ad litem, who are responsible for representing children in cases involving allegations of abuse. As Dr. Neustein and I observed in *From Madness to Mutiny*,[5] law guardians can use their positions to fight for a child's protection—or, in less fortunate cases, to ensure that the child's needs are ignored or violated.

For instance, after one child disclosed to his mother that his father had molested him—and confirmed this to a pediatrician—the boy's law guardian, without even meeting with the boy, convinced a family court judge to remove two small children from the mother's home without even considering the boy's charges against his father.

I have watched this same ugly pattern unfold in my clients' cases over the years. Again and again, I encounter lawyers charged with protecting a child's interests who instead seem to operate as though their real client was the father accused of abusing the child. They ignore or misrepresent the child's reports of being hurt by the accused parent; they reject the child's expressed wishes regarding custody and visitation; they may even expose the child to danger.

Law guardians, like CPS, have developed a special and powerful relationship with family court judges. Consequently, their recommendations can be decisive, even when these same recommendations are contradicted by substantial evidence. It is not surprising that many matrimonial attorneys advise their clients not to fight the law guardian's recommendations, no matter how unfair. Family court judges are quick to defend law

---

[5] *See supra* note 1.

guardians and even quicker to condemn litigants—read "protective mothers"—who accuse the law guardian of injustice or unethical conduct.

Legal Approach

Although I am well aware of these facts and of the dangers they pose for my clients, I often take a different approach. I believe law guardians can and should be challenged when their actions violate legal guidelines, trample the laws of evidence, or subvert my client's civil rights. Law guardians, after all, are lawyers; fundamentally, they are just like any other lawyer, with the same legal and ethical obligations to their clients and to the courts. They have no right to be treated as if they were above the law. What is more, law guardians have reputations and images to protect; like other professionals, they are sensitive to criticism that attacks their professional integrity. This does not mean all such criticism will have the desired effect. But when the criticism is carefully documented and powerfully argued, it can provide a strong disincentive for improper behavior by the law guardian and, in the meantime, give the child a critical opportunity to be heard, sometimes for the first time, by the figure most deeply responsible for safeguarding his/her interests.

I have used this approach to counter renegade law guardians in several of my cases.

Case Examples

I became involved in one postdivorce battle in which the mother had suddenly lost custody of her two daughters after initially sharing joint custody with the girls' father. The girls had repeatedly accused their father of striking and confining them, imposing excessive and cruel discipline, and subjecting them to furious, frightening tirades. After the involvement of a biased "expert" (a common danger I will address below), the court concluded that the children's complaints were somehow driven by their mother's attitude toward her ex-husband (who had treated her to similar behavior over the years). As a result, the children were transferred to their father's custody, and the mother was permitted to see her daughters only under supervision. Even then, many of the visits were thwarted by the father, who, in one instance, took the children unexpectedly on a long trip overseas. He also brought along his live-in female companion to school functions and counseling sessions for the children. It was as though *she* were their mother when, in fact, the real mother was barred even from entering the school grounds.

The girls' law guardian attacked the mother repeatedly in court hearings, usually citing hearsay "evidence" that often, in fact, did not exist. He claimed—without evidence—that she had violated court orders; he accepted all the father's accusations as facts, and he castigated the mother to the judge as a woman with a "disorder" whose "delusions" were causing all the trouble in the case. (The mother was never found to be delusional or to suffer from a mental illness or disorder.)

After close to a year of this, I felt she had had enough. It was clear that if a much-needed reunification between mother and daughters was to begin, the mother was going to have to make clear the difference between the reality of her case and the unflattering *manqué* shaped by the law guardian and fed to the court, over a ten-month period, as though it were fact.

In the motion I drafted on the mother's behalf, I made sure to specify how the law guardian had improperly filtered the evidence received by the court. For example, the law guardian had repeatedly told the court that the girls' passionate complaints against their father were the result of their mother's hostility toward her ex-spouse. The judge had accepted this view without question. But my motion cited documentary evidence that it was the *father*, not the mother, who had repeatedly tried to stifle contact between the girls and their other parent (no telephone, no e-mail, all letters to be intercepted, a reduced number of strictly supervised visits), and had written threatening letters to a visitation supervisor whose reports of the mother were favorable. The father's actions—which were precisely the mirror image of what the law guardian (inaccurately) had accused the mother of doing when he urged the court to switch custody— were well known to the law guardian. But he had never raised the matter in a court hearing. What is more, after getting custody of the two girls, the father had excoriated the mother in an e-mail to the remaining child (then thirteen years old), in which the father insisted that my client was dangerous and harmful and would "run your life into the ground and control you forever."[6] The law guardian never even bothered to mention this to the court while simultaneously, at the father's request, recommending that the *mother* be penalized, even though *no* evidence supported his accusations against *her*.

The judge was favorably impressed with the motion I drafted and restored my client's unsupervised visits with her daughters. The long process of reunification was finally allowed to begin. I am convinced that this would not have happened had I allowed the law guardian to continue to slander the children's mother, without evidence, every time the children complained about their father.

In another case, a mother came to me immediately after losing custody to a father whom her child had accused of abusing him. In writing the appellate brief on her behalf, I made sure to describe in detail several astonishing lapses on the part of the law guardian. Among the most important were the following:

1. The law guardian had used inaccurate statements to have the child summarily taken out of the mother's custody. This law guardian claimed to have reviewed a videotape that proved the mother had threatened to punish the boy for showing affection to his father. When the videotape was finally played in court, none of the statements claimed by the law guardian could be made out on the tape.

2. The law guardian never asked the child how he had received bruises on his arm while he was with his father. She ignored an expert (a police detective) who explained that the bruises were caused by the strong pressure of a man's fingers, even after it was clear that the father had lied about the cause of the injury.

3. The law guardian failed to ensure that the child, her client, got proper medical treatment for motor tics triggered by the father's fierce reprimands, even though these were clearly visible on the videotape she herself presented to the court.

Repelled by this conduct, the attorney who handled the trial for the mother had devoted part of his summation after trial to a request for the law guardian's disqualification. Knowing how family court judges protect law guardians (particularly those

---

[6] In order to protect the mothers and child(ren) involved in the following cases, identifying information for specific cases is not provided. Relevant case material is on file with the author.

who cater to the judges' prejudices, as the law guardian in this case had clearly done), I was not surprised that the trial judge had ignored the request. Nor was I confident the law guardian would be removed by the appellate court. However, I felt it was essential to show the appellate court how the trial court's reliance on the law guardian's unsupported opinions had seriously undermined its objectivity. I knew that if I did not, the appellate court would be reluctant to reexamine the findings of fact announced in the trial court's decision, many of which were clearly wrong and all of which echoed the claims made in court by the law guardian.

I knew I had reasoned correctly when the law guardian's appellate brief hardly even attempted to deny the facts underlying my criticisms of her. She did not deny causing the mother to lose custody by claiming she could discern statements on a videotape that no one else was able to hear. She did not deny that she had failed to investigate how the child had been bruised while in the father's keeping. She did not deny that the father had lied about the injury, and she did not deny that the sole expert opinion was that somebody had crushed the child's arm in his fingers. Amazingly, the law guardian merely pointed out that no eyewitness had actually seen the father grab the child's arm, as if that excused her from investigating the matter. (Of course, no eyewitness had ever seen or heard the mother disparage the father either, but that had not prevented the law guardian from accusing the *mother* of that charge.) As for the child's motor tics and the medical condition they implied, the law guardian limited herself to complaining that the mother's trial lawyer had only produced an affidavit from a health care professional describing the seriousness of the tics *after trial*; as a result, she had lacked time to "rebut Mother's Exhibit, arguments, and claims."[7] (Yes, "rebut": the law guardian openly implied that it was her job to defend the accused father rather than represent the interests of the child.) When I saw her response, I knew that I would have been wrong to let this law guardian's conduct pass without comment.

I wish I could report that the appellate court angrily condemned the law guardian's breach of duty and immediately ordered the child back into his mother's custody. Unfortunately, that is not what happened. Nevertheless, the unflattering truths I had pushed forward in the appellate briefs had their effect. The appellate court nervously evaded the issue of the law guardian's misconduct on technical grounds, arguing that it should have been raised during trial. (The court ignored the fact that this very issue had been raised in closing arguments.) But it did not reject a single factual allegation I had made against the law guardian on the mother's behalf.

Meanwhile, and (I suspect) not coincidentally, the law guardian approached my client, told her she was unhappy with the way the case was going, and said that she wanted to turn over a new leaf. It was the friendliest meeting the child's mother had ever had with the child's law guardian, and it seemed to signal new hope for her after months of gloom and despair. Could this have happened if I had allowed the law guardian's conduct to go unchallenged?

MENTAL HEALTH EXPERTS

Psychologists and other "experts" hold a very special place in the new legal landscape of child abuse/custody litigation. As Dr. Neustein and I wrote in *From Madness to Mutiny*, "The influence they can wield is often out of all proportion to the weight their methods and theories hold among their professional peers."[8] Many a protective

---

[7] Id.

[8] *See supra* note 1, at 26.

parent has learned, to her dismay, that once a prominent family court psychologist accuses her of some sort of "alienating" disorder—Parental Alienation Syndrome (PAS), Munchausen Syndrome by Proxy (MSBP), enmeshment, etc.—she not only cannot prove an abuse case against the other parent, but also stands a good chance of losing custody altogether.

PAS and similar theories have been debunked time and again: they are unscientific; they beg the question they set out to resolve; they are virtually impossible to rebut with objective evidence; and for all these reasons, they are very poorly suited to the needs of courtroom litigation. Unfortunately, however, they are still very much in use.

How does one defend the interests of a protective mother whose efforts to probe credible evidence that her child has been abused are used against her, by an "expert," as evidence that *she* is a threat to the child's well-being? As with CPS agencies and law guardians, most such "experts" have been given far too much leeway in family courts, in part because family court attorneys are reluctant to challenge them. There are valid reasons for this hesitation. An attorney who attacks an expert may soon need that same expert for a different case. Courtroom controversies over questions of science are complicated and expensive. Most important of all, such attacks are not often successful. Family court judges who decide these questions (there are no jury trials in family court) have gained their experience of the mother-blaming theories within the insular family court institutions in which such nostrums are the norm, and they view challenges to those theories with suspicion.

Still, I have had some success challenging tendentious experts in my defense of protective mothers. In most cases, I do this by attacking the experts in the two areas that are the least subjective, and therefore the most productive, in an unwelcoming judicial environment: (1) the expert's grasp of the facts of the case and (2) his/her use of objectively correct methods.

Expert's Grasp of the Facts

However credulous a judge may be about PAS, he/she will begin to have doubts about anyone who expresses opinions about a case while misrepresenting what actually happened in it. An expert who is shown during cross-examination, or in motion practice, to have made provably false statements about the case will not be able to counter with abstractions about alienation theory. This means that an attorney who thoroughly masters the facts of his client's case can make headway against the most determined of hired-gun witnesses.

For example, one of my clients was a mother who was accused by her ex-husband's hired expert of suffering from MSBP. The expert had produced a "report" that purported to show that the children were in such danger from their mother—not the father, who was accused by the two girls of abusing them—that the court, accepting the report at face value, immediately stripped the mother of custody. When I entered the case, I made sure to document every statement the expert had made that was belied by provable facts.

The expert denied that there was any evidence that "the father is the cause of physical or emotional problems with regard to any of his children."[9] I showed that this claim was false: I presented proof that both CPS caseworkers and a competent psychologist had substantiated allegations of emotional abuse of the girls by their father. The expert insisted that the daughters had never made any complaints against their father before

---

[9] Expert's report, August 2004. *See supra* note 6.

the parents separated. (Here, the expert attempted to blame the children's disclosures on "coaching" by their mother.)

I produced letters, journals, and handwritten notes from the girls that showed significantly earlier dates, proving the mendacity of the expert's statement. The expert accused the girls of being "exceedingly discourteous and rude in the most basic ways . . . manipulative, and . . . very untruthful."[10] I documented that those who knew the girls found them to be almost the exact opposite of the expert's description. The expert's criticism, therefore, was intended to discredit the girls, thereby justifying making light of their serious accusations against their father.

This same expert also accused the mother of "subjecting" two of her daughters to "gynecological examinations" in order "to attain her own emotional/internal needs."[11] I presented the medical records, which revealed that there had never been a "gynecological examination" of either child. After I made this showing, the judge gave CPS officials supervisory authority over the case. CPS then wrote to the "expert," stating in no uncertain terms that her evaluations would no longer be heeded. In the end, custody of all of the children was restored to the mother.

The same approach can be used to counter an "expert" who flagrantly ignores appropriate methodology.

Expert's Use of Objectively Correct Methods

The second of the two areas I focus on when challenging "experts" is different from the first mainly in the form of proof. To make *this* showing, it is nearly always necessary to produce an expert of one's own, whose job is to evaluate the first expert's handling of the evidence, the test results, and whatever procedures are appropriate to the kind of conclusions the expert has claimed to reach.

For instance, one of my clients was a divorcing mother who had moved with her young daughter, with her husband's consent, to another state. According to his version of events, the father had agreed to this move only for a period of six months, but when the six months were up, the mother had refused to return. She pointed out that she had parents and other family members near her in her new location. In addition, she had started graduate school there to enable her to pursue a teaching career that would allow her to devote more time to her daughter as a single mother. Her husband's state did not offer her similar opportunities; what is more, he objected to paying her any alimony.

Despite having excellent reasons to remain where she was—for the child's welfare as well as her own—the mother's right to keep her six-year-old daughter with her was attacked by the court-appointed "expert" who evaluated both parents. He claimed that she was "narcissistic" and "histrionic" and that her "excessive hostility" would prevent her from allowing an appropriate relationship between the young child and her father. According to the expert's conclusions, this single mother had to travel back to her ex-husband's state, where she could not afford to live, would not receive alimony, had no family, and could not prepare herself for a career that would allow her to raise her child properly; otherwise, she would lose custody of the child.

To challenge the expert, I brought to court an expert of our own, one with particular expertise in the scoring of psychological tests. I forced the court's expert to provide copies of the raw scores and test data to our expert (which the court's expert did most

---

[10] Id.
[11] Id.

reluctantly). The results were quite remarkable: it turned out that the court's "expert" had flagrantly ignored the most reliable of the psychological tests he had given the mother, basing his conclusions entirely on another, less reliable test, which he did not even score correctly! Not only was I able to bring this out through our expert's testimony, but under cross-examination, I was even able to make the court's expert admit most of the crucial points himself. This made him highly vulnerable to our expert's final attack on his methodology in a written report:

> His failure to resolve, nor even acknowledge, the discrepancy between the two psychological tests administered is troubling, particularly given the fact that the more widely accepted and well-validated of the two tests revealed essentially no problematic behaviors or personality characteristics. . . . [H]is apparently exclusive reliance on the MCMI-III test results . . . is both troubling and simply inaccurate.[12]

As a result, the family court judge largely disregarded the court-appointed expert's testimony. Of course, this being family court, my client was still subjected to attacks because, it was claimed, she did not sufficiently "respect the importance of the child's relationship with the father."[13] Still, things could have been much worse if she had been stigmatized as mentally ill or as suffering from a personality disorder that rendered her a bad parent. That is precisely what would have happened, if I had not taken forceful action at trial.

CONCLUSION

Nothing I write here is meant to minimize the dangers and obstacles protective mothers face in family courts. In far too many cases, their motives are questioned; their reasonable acts are treated as crimes, and their every effort to protect their children is held against them. There is never any guarantee that a cogent case on behalf of a protective parent will be met with sympathy by the family court.

Still, as I have tried to show, lawyers can take steps to reduce the oppressive power of CPS agencies, law guardians, and mental health experts when these family court auxiliaries abuse their functions. Wherever this is possible, I believe it is obligatory. We lawyers need to insist, as often and as vigorously as necessary, that mothers be allowed to litigate on level ground with their ex-spouses and with the professionals involved in every case. We should insist that attorneys not be silent when their clients' right to a fair trial, based on accurate evidence and constitutional procedures, is denied simply because "family court is family court." Fighting to extend the rule of law into family court procedures is essential not only for the protection of individual clients but for the improvement of the system as a whole. One of the first steps toward curing any system's ill health is refusing to accept the status quo.

---

[12] Expert's report, April 2003. *See supra* note 6.
[13] Court decision, July 2003, at 13.

Chapter 17

Organizing in Defense of Protective Mothers: The Custody Rights Movement

by Lundy Bancroft

INTRODUCTION

Can we change the way family law courts treat protective mothers? The annual Battered Mothers Custody Conference (BMCC) in Albany, New York—viewed by many as an accurate barometer of national sentiment among protective mothers and their allies—would answer this question with a powerful, "Yes we can. And we must."

At the same time, the prevailing sentiment at the January 2009 BMCC was that we have not begun to win significant improvements in the family law system—not just yet. Responses by judges, custody evaluators (including guardians ad litem, psychological evaluators, and court-appointed advocates), parenting coordinators, mediators, and other court-involved personnel appear to be remaining the same or even getting worse. Although we have no good way to count how many of these cases are occurring throughout the country, those of us who actively advocate for protective mothers are hearing about more cases of severe human rights abuses than we ever have before.

In order to turn this tide, we need to understand more about why the trend currently is moving in the wrong direction. From analyzing these dynamics, we can form a strategic approach to establishing recognized and enforced rights for protective parents. Therefore, I will begin by exploring the particular challenges and difficulties we face in the custody rights movement at this juncture. I will then go on to lay out a proposal for how we can most successfully and rapidly move forward toward deep systemic change and, ultimately, the reestablishment of justice.

WHY THE MOVEMENT IS LOSING GROUND

In order to keep this analysis succinct and useful, I am going to explore only the problems that appear to be the most critical, along with the ones we have the greatest chance of affecting positively through our own activist efforts. Please note that, in this chapter, I refer to the organized opposition to the rights of protective mothers as the "father-supremacy movement."[1]

Abusive and Male-Supremacist Fathers Organized Effectively

Over the past fifteen years, abusers and father-supremacists have been remarkably successful at grassroots organizing through the creation of the euphemistically named

---

[1] I have chosen to use the term "father supremacists" to refer to the individuals and groups who are collectively working to undermine protective mothers, spread the belief that abuse allegations in divorce are usually false, and promote joint custody and father involvement at all costs. I have chosen to use this term after years of reading "fathers' rights" (FRs) materials in newsletters, Web sites, and books. These writings have little to do with promoting the legitimate rights, needs, and interests of fathers; their focus is primarily on fighting against abuse allegations; spreading vituperative statements about feminists, mothers, domestic violence activists, and sexual assault activists; decrying homosexuality; and giving false information about various kinds of social trends, including claiming that fathers are at a huge disadvantage when custody is contested. Some of these groups were visible in fighting the renewal of the Violence Against Women Act (passed as Title IV, Sections 40001-40703 of the Violent Crime Control and Law Enforcement Act of 1994, H.R. 3355 and signed as Public Law 103-322 by President Bill Clinton on September 13, 1994), a telling stand. Visible FRs Web sites excused and justified the shooting of a family court judge by a father in Nevada in June of 2006 (the father allegedly murdered his estranged wife the same day). Although the adherents of this movement state that "The Best Parent Is Both Parents," in practice they work aggressively and hypocritically to drive mothers away from their children through such accusations as parental alienation. The overall flavor of their writings, policy stands, and actions on cases is indicative of men who are abusive and intimidating in their actions and beliefs, and who believe that fathers are more important and more positive in children's lives than mothers. I therefore believe that we should refer to their efforts with a term that accurately reflects what they are promoting.

"fathers' rights" (FRs) movement. This organizing has often occurred court-by-court and community-by-community, accompanied by lots of meetings, street actions, letter writing, community outreach, and image building. In the early 1990s, this movement was very small, but its activists have been tireless (one might say obsessive) and willing to do the work of gradually building a movement from scratch.

One of the keys—and there are several—to the success of the father-supremacist movement is that court-involved fathers themselves have been at the forefront. Their presence at pickets and at conferences, their interviews with journalists, and their personal stories on their Web sites have empowered them to get the public to believe the facts as the abusers present them. This has enabled the FRs movement to be effective in winning sympathy from those who hear what these men claim to have suffered. Putting fathers at the forefront also has benefited their movement by harnessing the energy of those who have a profound personal investment in the issue around which the FRs movement is organized. This permits FRs proponents to work with a kind of commitment and intensity that is difficult for mothers' allies to match.

Another key to the power of the FRs movement has been local, court-by-court organizing. By organizing locally, father-supremacy activists have been able to put tremendous direct pressure on judges, other court personnel, and community members to side with fathers who are accused of abuse and to punish mothers who attempt to protect their children and themselves. Face-to-face contact, the building of personal relationships, and relentless hammering through phone calls, letters, and pickets have served to wear down resistance to the FRs stand and to persuade the public that these men must be suffering genuine injustices. Court personnel can sometimes be heard expressing concern about how their local FRs group will react if the court makes a certain ruling or promulgates a particular policy. Such apprehension suggests that the organized response of allegedly abusive fathers is far more effective than the corresponding response of protective mothers. It is no wonder, therefore, that the courts find it easier to bend in the wrong direction.

I do not mean to suggest that good organizing is the whole reason for the success of the father-supremacy movement. That movement has had numerous advantages, including far greater financial resources than protective mothers have, support from a conservative (and financially motivated) forensic psychology industry, direct support from the last federal administration, and a willingness to use spin, distortion, and outright fabrication to promote both their alleged victimization and their collective cause. For these reasons, the FRs movement has been able to present itself as representing the voice of "fathers," rather than the voice of "fathers who are alleged perpetrators of abuse." However, it has been the FRs efforts and success at organizing that has generated their success on all other fronts.

Protective Mothers Have Been Less Well Organized

Numerous individuals and organizations across the continent are involved in promoting the custody rights of protective mothers and are working for family court reform. There is no dearth of passion or understanding regarding the extent of the human rights nightmare that is taking place within the family court system. Yet, despite all of our energy and commitment, we are feeling frustrated over the ineffectiveness of our actions. No groups or individuals have emerged as strong national leaders, with the charisma, resources, and singleness of purpose needed to effectively inspire and coordinate the efforts that are currently ongoing. As a result, activists across the country end up working largely in isolation. Groups in one state unwittingly duplicate the efforts of groups in other states, expending tremendous energy in the process. Individuals approach the media with what appears to be a very small number of voices, and so they are unable to demonstrate convincingly how large our constituency actually is. We do not do well at large-scale fundraising, because we have trouble showing persuasively that thousands of women and their children are being harmed by the actions of our family courts.

The motivations that drive activists to work on this issue are myriad and diffuse, as well. Here are just a few of the ways in which people involved in this work currently characterize their core view of the issue:

1. Working against child abuse and children's exposure to witnessing domestic violence (DV);

2. Working for the rights of mothers;

3. Working for equality between the sexes;

4. Working against corruption and ignorance;

5. Working against junk science and unqualified experts, with a particular emphasis on fighting Parental Alienation Syndrome (PAS);

6. Working toward accountability for state actors who currently behave with impunity;

7. Working equally for the rights of all protective parents, whether female or male; and

8. Working to fix a broken family court system that gives custody to abusers.

All of these goals need to be part of our work. But the difficulty lies in having too many different ways of defining the most *central* principle of our movement. The result is not only a lack of organizational unity, but also a lack of focus in our arguments, which causes us to lose persuasive power with the media and the public. We are all over the place with our statements, making perhaps thirty different points, all of them valid and important but all of them, also, likely to get lost in the background in today's age of sound bites.

This cacophony should be contrasted with this simple formulation chanted by FR activists: "Fathers should be considered just as important as mothers in the lives of children." This statement is a profoundly misleading one, both because it suggests that courts currently favor mothers when, in fact, the opposite is true, and because it hides the antimother nature of their movement's agenda. This observation, however, is quite beside the point. In practical terms, of greatest significance is the fact that abusers and their allies have succeeded at positioning themselves as the people who are seeking equality and fairness. They have hammered away at this theme repeatedly and mantra-like, presenting a succinct, limited number of demands and claims (including the steady stream of references to "false allegations," which they use to make a statistically rare problem sound like a common one).

Battered Women's and Child Sexual Abuse Movements Lost Their Activist Force

What was once a cage-rattling, defiant movement against the domestic abuse of women has become almost entirely a large-scale service delivery system. Similarly, the outrage about child sexual abuse that was given voice by the feminist conflu-ence of the 1970s has faded into a situation in which child sexual abuse is treated as an individual experience of victimization, with the perpetrator either excused and defended (if he is the child's father) or pathologized as "sick" and "deviant" if he is not the father. The social and political dimensions that create and protect perpetra-tors are rarely publicly challenged. DV and child sexual abuse have joined the ranks of other "social problems" that require social workers to provide treatment to victims and perpetrators rather than work toward changing the way society treats women and children and empowers abusers.

The battered women's movement gradually has become professionalized. More and more programs require advocates to have master's degrees, though it is difficult to identify any way in which a degree helps an advocate be more effective. Executive directors of programs may now be people with little or no history of working in the movement and whose skills are in management and fundraising, not community orga-nizing and social change. Those who work in DV programs are increasingly feeling pressured to use gender-neutral language, to depoliticize this profoundly political kind of violence, and to avoid taking stands that might alienate funders, judges, government officials, and other powerful players.

One problem arising from both the diminishment of feminist activism and the cooptation of feminist movements is that DV and child sexual abuse advocates are no longer in a strong position to take on an issue as contentious as child custody. This is especially true given that the antimother side has a huge and strong network of professionals and attorneys collectively making untold millions of dollars per year, and journalists are reluctant to cover mothers' custody cases "because it's just he-said she-said." The damage being done to battered women and children, especially sexu-ally abused children, through custody litigation is one of the greatest human rights crises facing the United States and Canada today. Yet, the very organizations created to address domestic abuse tend to be afraid to touch this issue out of fear of losing funding. While protective mothers often tell us of quiet assistance and support they have received from battered women's programs, which at times can certainly make a significant difference in the woman's life, it is much less common to hear of programs that have been willing to confront judicial behavior publicly. And in the absence of this kind of overt resistance, courts are free to continue abusing human rights with impunity.

Recent Difficulties for Progressive Movements in General

Organizing for any form of progressive social change has been unusually diffi-cult in recent years, largely due to the policies and covert actions of the former Bush administration, coming specifically and heavily from the manipulation of the 9/11 tragedy to quell domestic dissent. This trend, combined with twenty years of antifemi-nist backlash in the United States, has contributed to a climate in which organizing for the rights of women as mothers faces steep challenges. Activists within numerous progressive causes often feel isolated from each other, despite the tremendous number of citizens who share their concerns and opinions. Conservative trends among elites and politicians can create the impression of a conservative trend within the population in general, when actually there is no evidence that public opinion is any less progres-sive than it used to be.

The father-supremacy movement has developed links of various kinds with the right wing of the United States. These collaborations have included the Bush administration's placing of father-supremacist sympathizers in top leadership positions (most notably, Wade Horn, who formerly occupied a high position in the federal Department of Health and Human Services); the organized opposition to child protective services; right-wing Christians; opponents of the Violence Against Women Act;[2] and antigay fanatics.[3]

By coupling itself to growing right-wing efforts, the movement against protective mothers has been able to strengthen its position and tap into greater resources. That movement also appears to have succeeded in building some significant academic links, judging by the numbers of Ph.D.s and professors that appear on FRs Web sites and discussion groups.

HOW TO SUCCEED IN TURNING THE TIDE

Despite the many challenges and discouraging trends I have pointed out, there is good reason to believe that we are nonetheless approaching the most favorable moment so far for building a successful movement for the custody rights of protective mothers. I travel to about twenty different states each year, and the level of concern and outrage that I have been hearing about the systemic abuse of protective mothers has reached the highest pitch I have ever seen.

The PBS documentary *Breaking the Silence: Children's Stories,* which aired in October 2005,[4] put the family court issue before the public on a large scale, reaching perhaps the largest audience that has ever heard about what is occurring. The *Newsweek* article "Why Parents Who Batter Win Custody"[5] offers another indication of the emergence of this scandal into the public eye.[6]

A growing number of groups across the country are devoting themselves to taking on the family court challenge, with notable efforts occurring in New York, California, Florida, Arizona, Minnesota, and other states. Even more encouraging are signs that activism in general is on the rise again in the United States. This is increasingly the case as time continues to pass since the 9/11 attacks, which generated an intimidating and dissent-suppressing atmosphere that was exacerbated by the extremist policies of the Bush administration.

Over the next few years, there is a good possibility that these forces may coalesce into a powerful nationwide initiative, one with a reasonable likelihood of culminating in tangible gains. I believe the experiences we have accumulated to date point our movement in the direction of the following salient steps toward success:

---

[2] Id.

[3] These points of contact can be verified by going to various FRs Web sites and by reading exposes of that movement, such as those available online; *see, e.g.,* R.Tarpaeian, "Why Gay Marriage Matters for Fathers Rights," http://www.fatherhoodcoalition.org/cpf/newreadings/2007/gay_marriage_RT.htm; "Homosexual Activism," http://www.equalparenting-bc.ca/issues/homosexual_activism.htm; cyncooper, "Hand That Feeds," http://www.talk2action.org/story/2007/3/3/184933/3474; *see also* Appendix A of this book for Web-based resources.

[4] *Breaking the Silence: Children's Stories*, a documentary produced by Catherine Tatge and Dominique Lasseur (http://www.tatgelasseur.com).

[5] Sarah Childress, "Why Parents Who Batter Win Custody," *Newsweek* Sept. 26, 2006.

[6] *See also* Appendix B of this book.

1. Putting protective mothers at the forefront of our movement, with the rest of us acting as allies and support people;

2. Working to develop a unified philosophy and to foster a degree of centralized, accountable leadership to provide coordination and inspiration;

3. Using our influence to reawaken the activist tendencies of the battered women's movement and the movement against child sexual assault, thus locating ourselves within the overall goals of women's liberation; and

4. Linking our movement to other efforts for justice and social change nationally and internationally, so that we come to be understood as part of the global effort for progressive action and human rights.

Putting Protective Mothers at the Forefront of the Movement

Protective mothers have already started many different grassroots organizations and nonprofit groups dedicated to family court reform. The movement could rapidly increase in strength and influence if we were to focus our efforts over the next few years on supporting and encouraging mothers to serve as leaders.

Many of us struggle with misconceptions and overgeneralizations about mothers who are going through custody litigation. These images tend to portray mothers as incapable of dynamic leadership because they are too traumatized by personal and systemic abuse, too economically strapped, too busy trying to take care of their own children and fight their own cases, and too afraid of retaliation by the court to dare show resistance. These images certainly capture certain aspects of life for mothers who are battling abusers for custody, but they do not accurately capture the totality of this group of women. Mothers to whom I speak are, more often than not, eager to take public action, find collective empowerment, and make an impact. They repeatedly make statements to me like, "I want to get involved in this issue, but I don't know where to plug in. I would love to know what I could do." A fair number describe efforts in which they are already engaged, such as organizing letter-writing campaigns, getting people to come to meetings, or planning marches or other public actions. Those of us who are not protective mothers need to move beyond our stereotypes about those who are.

As a mother strives to pursue her own litigation while simultaneously caring for her children—to the extent that the court permits her to do so—she is developing and honing a set of skills that have precise relevance to community organizing. These skills include the following:

1. Making good decisions under extreme pressure;

2. Operating well while being very emotionally upset;

3. Knowing how to identify and use community resources;

4. Expressing herself clearly, both orally and in writing, when explaining the details of her case;

5. Persuading people to value her perspective and to help her protect her children;

6. Functioning while sleep deprived;

7. Managing money well, especially when in short supply;

8. Persuading others (such as friends and relatives) to contribute money for her case;

9. Finding allies; and

10. Getting along with people, like lawyers and therapists, even when that is very hard to do.

This list could go on, but I believe the point has been adequately made; in fact, the skills I have listed above could virtually serve as an outline for a training program in community organizing and political activism.

Unity and Solidarity. Those of us who are already involved in the custody rights movement, whether as protective mothers or as allies, should adopt as one of our top goals the simple but crucial work of assisting mothers to find other women with cases in the same courts. Every time a protective mother tells her story to a friend, a staff person at an abused women's program, an attorney, a therapist, or anyone else, we should ask her, "Do I have your permission to give your name and phone number out to other protective mothers in your geographical area, so that you can locate each other?" Overwhelmingly and enthusiastically (over 80 percent, in my experience), protective mothers answer "yes" to this question. If we can put mothers in contact with each other on a community-by-community or court-by-court basis, we will take a giant leap toward building a successful movement.

We should also offer each woman ideas about steps she can take to find other local protective mothers, through such efforts as the following:

1. Volunteering to be a contact hub for her local abused women's program, who could then refer other litigating mothers to her;

2. Placing notices at the court house, on community bulletin boards, in newspapers, on local radio stations, and other public locations advertising a support group for mothers in custody litigation, along with her name and contact information. (If she cannot safely use her own name, she could consider finding an ally who would be willing to take phone calls.);

3. Sitting in at court hearings and then approaching protective mothers in the courthouse;

4. Creating a brochure for her local mothers' custody group; or

5. Asking local therapists and social workers to refer protective mothers to her.

Materials. There is also a need for good materials for protective mothers on how to organize an effective group, how to facilitate a meeting, strategies for taking effective public action (including suggestions for specific actions), and approaches to dealing with the difficult dynamics that can arise when groups are largely made up of abuse survivors. Protective mothers could also benefit from a guide to handling phone calls from other mothers, including strategies for protecting one's own privacy from the occasional caller who may be invasive or dishonest (as has arisen in some cases I have been involved in). Mothers and allies who might be interested in developing such materials should be encouraged to do so.

Developing a Unified Philosophy, Centralized Leadership, and Nationwide Coordination

The philosophy and political program of a movement must of course develop over time, through discussion and debate among activists. A philosophy that is too rigid can become an obstacle, but one that is overly amorphous and undefined may become an equal hindrance to building a movement. In order to sharpen the effectiveness of our arguments and our organizing, I believe we have to struggle together to formulate definitive answers to the central questions:

- Why are these abuses of protective mothers and their children occurring?

- What causes have we identified, and of those causes which do we believe have the most destructive impact?

- Given our analysis of these causes, how do we best proceed?

Proposed Framework. I am going to offer a proposal here for helping us to frame our movement's outlook. I hope this "first draft" can serve to stimulate debate and help to move forward the analysis of our movement:

We exist in a society that remains, in the year 2009, profoundly discriminatory toward women and that subjects women systematically to violence, intimidation, child sexual abuse, and sexual assault. The fact that all of these things also happen to men does not in any way change the fact that they are carried out in huge systematic ways that are targeted *specifically at women, because they are women.* One part of this societal oppression of women involves the widespread, endemic devaluation of motherhood as an occupation and the denigration of women as mothers.

When a woman finds herself in custody litigation with a man who has been violent or threatening to her, or who has been sexually abusive or violent to her children, she enters the court system *as a woman* in a system that has deep historical roots as an institution serving the interests of men. She faces attorneys and judges (both male and female) who are conditioned to dismiss a woman's concerns about her children postseparation. She faces custody evaluators and clinical evaluators who have been trained in a long history of psychological theories and approaches that demonize women and mothers, and that define "normality" as meaning "operating emotionally and behaviorally the way men do." She confronts a culture that still views children to a great extent as the personal possessions of the father, despite decades of struggle— with some progress, certainly—to overcome this view. And she faces a society that is still remarkably reluctant to take seriously the level of damage being done by perpetrators of DV and child sexual abuse.

In addition, she faces a civil court system that is not guided by any strong set of rules of evidence or rules of procedure, over which appeals courts have kept very little watch and in which there is no right to publicly-paid counsel.

The result is that the prejudices and deep forms of disrespect described in the above paragraph are free to run roughshod over the lives of women and children, with litigants typically having little or no recourse.

Our issue is thus, above all, one of *the human rights of women and their children* and an issue of *the liberation of women as an oppressed group,* including *the liberation of mothers.* Although there are protective fathers who are badly mistreated by family courts, their experience is different in many important ways and needs to be thought about separately. (At the same time, the success of our movement will greatly improve conditions for genuine protective fathers.)

Symptoms and Causes. As part of the above framework, we would be wise to use the language and concepts of international human rights activism, including specific references to the treaties that protect the rights of women and the rights of children.[7]

Many of the problems we observe in family court are, I believe, symptoms rather than causes. These include the irrationality and capriciousness of judges, attorneys, and custody evaluators; the failure of states to mandate that these players receive in-depth training on DV and incest perpetration; and the additional failure of states to provide any meaningful oversight of the conduct of these players. We will not succeed in bringing about the necessary sweeping changes if we attempt to address these problems singly, in isolation from their wider context.

At the same time, I do not wish to promote "either/or" kinds of thinking. We need to move forward on all fronts, attacking both the symptoms and their underlying causes in any way that we can. But we will become more effective in drawing allies into the movement, building successful collaborations with other groups, and presenting the material to the public in a way that will "click" and make sense for our audiences if we ground our points in the realities of sexism, mother-blaming, and human rights, along with striving to simplify and unify our arguments.

Another crucial advantage of the above framework is that it creates the potential to strongly link our movement to other efforts for gender justice, as well as to the even wider efforts for human rights and progressive social change, and thus to be able to draw on the resources of those movements. This collaboration is essential in order to combat the success of the father-supremacy movement in drawing upon the resources of the right wing in general.

Increased Effectiveness. In addition to creating a more focused and succinct analysis, we could increase our effectiveness by placing, at the forefront of our efforts, a set of primary goals. The reforms we are demanding—and there are of course dozens of them—could be productively distilled and prioritized as follows:

1. Equality of mothers and fathers before the court in disputed custody *based on the parent's actual involvement in child rearing, including pregnancy, childbirth, nursing, and all of the aspects of raising children that follow.* In other words, mothers should be winning the great majority of contested custody cases simply because they still do the lion's share of caring for the children.

---

[7] For an analysis of these laws and how to use them, see Carrie Cuthbert, Kim Slote, Monica Ghosh Driggers, J.D., Cynthia J. Mesh, Lundy Bancroft, Jay Silverman, *Battered Mothers Speak Out: A Human Rights Report on Domestic Violence and Child Custody in the Massachusetts Family Courts* (2002), available at http://www.wcwonline.org/component/page,shop.product_details/flypage,shop.flypage/product_id,679/option,com_virtuemart/Itemid,175/vmcchk,1/.

2. Creation of meaningful rules of procedure and rules of evidence for family court processes, to eliminate capriciousness and failures of due process.

3. Creation of the right of low-income parents to have public representation in custody disputes and creation of a clear system for the parent of greater resources to pay the other parent's appropriate legal fees.

4. Creation and mandated use of appropriate protocols for investigating and responding to allegations of intimate partner abuse and child abuse, including child sexual abuse.

5. Creation of meaningful oversight of all players in the system, including private attorneys.

Organizational Unity. In addition to pursuing unity in our underlying philosophy and major goals, our movement needs to pursue a significant degree of organizational unity in the years ahead. We might, for example, consider creating a seven or eight-member national coordinating council, made up of at least 50 percent protective mothers, to facilitate cooperation and growth of the many disparate groups and individuals currently active in our nationwide movement. In addition to or instead of the coordinating council, another approach would be to pool our resources to create a national resource center staffed with people trained to handle calls from protective mothers, help mothers find attorneys and experts, help activists find groups to join, and keep everyone informed of protest strategies and other national efforts.

A related, more complicated, but potentially more far-reaching effort would be the creation of an umbrella organization to coordinate and drive a nationwide initiative on behalf of protective mothers. Such an organization would increase our ability to approach possible funders, enabling the creation of more paid staff positions, which in turn would be a huge leap forward. A national conference or a national coordinating council, or both, could take on the work of forming and launching such an umbrella organization (of which the above-mentioned resource center might then become a part). A number of individuals in the custody rights movement have already proposed this goal. The national organizations that have already begun to take leadership on this issue, such as the National Coalition Against Domestic Violence and the National Organization of Women, might be well positioned to assist in the creation of a custody rights umbrella group. Many other organizations with national visibility and resources have contributed to the building of the movement into its current form; these could play a role in creating a unified national effort. Groups that come to mind include the BMCC, Protective Mothers Alliance, Justice for Children, the Battered Women's Justice Project, Legal Momentum, and the Wellesley Centers for Women, to name just a few. We might also be able to interest influential groups that have not been part of the effort to date, such as the Center for Constitutional Rights and the National Lawyers Guild.

At the same time, experience teaches us that when activists start to focus on large-scale coordinated national efforts, they often lose sight of fostering leadership among the constituencies whose interests they are fighting for. The battered women's movement, for example, has repeatedly forgotten to focus on putting battered women and formerly battered women at the forefront. It is thus my fervent hope that we will not make this elitist mistake and instead be mindful of supporting protective mothers in taking on the primary positions of leadership as we build a larger movement and a more centralized structure.

Reawakening Activism in the Domestic Violence and Sexual Assault Movements

The custody rights movement does not have to start from the ground up in building a supportive audience and finding potential activists; we already have a huge potential structure in place in the form of the existing networks addressing DV and sexual assault. As I discussed earlier, these networks have largely lost their cage-rattling tendencies, and as a result their funding has been cut every year, followed by the inevitable reductions in services. (Historically, movements that win government funding gradually see that funding slip away once the activist force of the movement fades.) Thus, at this point in history, they need us, and we need them. By this I mean that we need the numbers, resources, and political connections that these networks have, and they need our activist energy, our fury, our urgency, our "fire-in-the-belly" to take uncomfortable stands, and our commitment to renewing the demand for the liberation of women.

In order to succeed in this effort, we need to declare loudly and without reservation that our issue is a gender-justice cause, driven by a feminist understanding of fairness and decency. In recent years, I increasingly find myself in situations where individuals who are involved in one of these three interwoven causes (DV, sexual assault, and custody rights) are bending over backward to use gender-neutral language, to say that victims can just as well be male as female, or even to deny that the oppression of women is at the root of the problem. I not only find this trend unfortunate but also maintain that we should be moving precisely in the opposite direction, being more direct and overt about our gender analysis. By doing so, we would make much stronger arguments and move our audiences more effectively to action. Perhaps even more importantly, we would connect ourselves to an entire world of feminist thinkers and activists. It is they who are our natural allies and who can help us build a movement that can win.

Linking the Movement to Other Efforts for Progressive Social Change

I discussed earlier how the right wing of the United States has come to recognize the FRs movement as its own and the way in which this alliance has strengthened the influence of father-supremacists (see "Recent Difficulties for Progressive Movements in General"). No such connection has happened yet between the custody rights movement and the broader agenda of progressives and populists working for equality and social justice. When a community forms a coalition of progressive groups, as sometimes happens, it never occurs to the coalition builders that we are natural allies of theirs and should of course be at the table. So, just as we need to forge our links to feminists, we need to build even wider than that, positioning ourselves as part of the overall progressive tendency in this country, including antiracist, labor rights, and other justice groups.

In order to succeed in this effort, we need to develop written materials that better explain the connection between the abuse of the human rights of mothers and their children by family courts, on the one hand, and the global exploitation of women and children, on the other. We also could spread a better understanding of perpetrators and their ways of operating in communities and in organizations (such as churches, workplaces, and community groups). In doing so, we could help the greater community of activists better understand how batterers and incest perpetrators are having negative impacts on their own progressive efforts. (We might begin, for example, by generating a short piece to be called, "Why Progressives Should Care About the Custody Rights Movement.")

One valuable first step in this regard is for everyone to approach the local progressive and charitable groups in their community and ask permission to make a short presentation on the battered mothers' issue at one of their meetings. Those who live near a college or university might begin with the women's studies, peace studies, labor studies, or other progressive academic departments of those institutions, asking to discuss with them how you might forge links with them.

CONCLUSION

I have written this chapter from the perspective of a person who is a trainer in his professional life and an activist in his off hours. I believe in the value of the training work I do, but I am also repeatedly reminded of its limitations. Similarly, I believe in the value of any work our movement does to train professionals, create oversight commissions, generate better materials, pass improved statutes, and our many other efforts to address symptoms. At the same time, these efforts will make only small gains unless they are accompanied by a massive upsurge of grassroots, court-by-court organizing across the continent to empower protective mothers as leaders and to demand full human rights for mothers. This wave will, in turn, succeed only if it builds strong links to wider efforts to end violence against women, end sexual assault against women and children, and defend the economic and welfare rights of all poor and low-income people, who are disproportionately women and children. I look forward to seeing you all on the front lines.

Chapter 18

Recognizing and Overcoming Abusers' Legal Tactics

by Barry Goldstein, J.D.

INTRODUCTION

Domestic violence (DV) concerns tactics men use to maintain control over their intimate partners and to exercise what they believe is their right to make the major decisions in the relationship. Although courts and the professionals who work within the court system focus primarily on physical abuse, most of the DV that is committed is neither physical nor illegal. Understanding and uncovering a pattern of abusive and controlling behaviors is the key to detecting DV.

Significant progress toward ending DV has been made since the start of the modern movement in the mid-to-late 1970s. Women partnered with abusive men can now more easily obtain orders of protection, criminal prosecution, divorce, financial support, shelter, and community support. Communities in fields including education, medicine, mental health, business, media, and religion have adopted practices to help women seeking to leave their abusers. The DV homicide rate has come down, as society has moved to hold abusers accountable for their crimes.[1]

Abusers, upset with what they believe is their right to control their partners, have responded with new tactics designed to maintain their control. Male supremacist groups[2] have worked to create a backlash to the progress made by the movement to end DV. A wide range of tactics have been designed to punish women for leaving or to force them to return. Courts and the professionals they rely on have been slow to recognize these tactics (for more information about the male supremacists, see Chapter 4 in this volume).

The real agenda of these male supremacist groups is to reduce or eliminate child support, minimize the enforcement of DV laws, and in some cases justify or encourage incest. If members of these groups were honest about their objectives, courts would have an easy time determining what would be in the best interests of the children (BIC). Instead, these men manipulate the courts through the use of concepts like "friendly parent," Parental Alienation Syndrome (PAS), shared parenting, cooperation, and other out-of-context manipulations.

RECOGNIZING DOMESTIC VIOLENCE

Many of the tragic outcomes in custody cases are due to the courts' failure to recognize DV. Even the term "domestic violence" is problematic, since it focuses on

---

[1] S. Huntley, "Covering Domestic Violence," in *Covering Crime and Justice* ch. 12 (Criminal Justice Journalists eds., 2003), http://www.justicejournalism.org/crimeguide/chapter12/chapter12.html.

[2] These groups like to call themselves "fathers' rights" groups, but since their real agenda is to maintain men's control over women, I use what I view as a more accurate label.

physical violence, which accounts for only a small percentage of DV tactics. DV has been an important public issue for approximately thirty years. Nevertheless, the courts and the professionals on whom they rely are often unfamiliar with the substantial research on this topic (see Chapters, 6, 11, and 14 in this volume). Many people have some personal experience as either victims or offenders, or they know someone who has been involved in a DV situation. Many draw general conclusions from the one or two cases they know about. They may not understand the way abuse is sometimes disguised in these cases or the context in which men abuse women.

Men in the New York Model Batterer classes that I teach often make good faith suggestions about how to respond to DV, only to learn that their ideas have been tried before, without success. DV stems from sexism, and gender bias often permeates discussions of this issue. DV advocates engage in this work full time but are rarely treated as the experts they are. I have witnessed many judges refusing to listen to a DV expert, asserting that they have been judges for many years and therefore know everything they need to know about DV. They often proceed to send the children to live with an abuser because they failed to recognize his abuse *as* abuse.[3]

In one case, the court permitted a psychologist with one hour of training in DV to testify as if he were an expert and then refused to hear the testimony of a genuine expert with thousands of hours of DV training. The mother taped a phone conversation with her abuser. The abuser's statements were filled with the most degrading and sexist language. Although that was the focus of the debate about the tape, even more revealing was the subject matter of the abuser's tirade. His entire conversation was about how he would hurt and punish the mother if she did not give him custody of their baby. There was not one word of why he thought the baby would be better off living with him (e.g., he had more time available, his home was nicer, the schools were better). The conversation epitomized DV. He sought to use tactics to pressure, threaten, and intimidate his victim; yet the judge, the law guardian, and an evaluator with little or no experience did not know what to look for. They blamed the mother for provoking the father, and made the baby live with an abuser.[4]

Why Courts May Fail to Recognize Abusers' Tactics

There are many reasons why good judges have been slow to recognize abuser tactics. The reasons include inadequate training, gender bias, reliance on professionals with

---

[3] It is instructive to contrast a statement by Judge Thomas Hornsby in Chapter 7 in this volume that in his nineteenth year on the bench, he finally learned how to properly respond to requests from women for orders of protection. In the Tompkins County, New York, case described *infra* note 4, the judge refused to permit me to testify as an expert stating he was a family court judge for fifteen years and therefore did not need a DV expert. In Broome County, New York, in a case (*BJ v. MJ*) involving a protective mother, the judge refused to hear my testimony, essentially making the same argument that he was a judge for seventeen years and did not need a DV expert. In a Yonkers, New York, family court case (*RA v. MLA*) involving a protective mother, a new judge with less than six months' experience also claimed she did not need the testimony of an expert witness I sought to call to testify. In all three cases, the judges sent the children to live with abusers. I have not provided more identifying evidence because the cases are ongoing and for safety concerns.

[4] This case (*EC v. LPC*) is from Tompkins County, New York. I am familiar with the circumstances because I was to be one of the expert witnesses, but the court refused to hear any genuine experts. In consideration for the mother's safety, and because the case is still ongoing, I am not providing the exact title of the case.

little or no experience in DV, use of myths and stereotypes, and the ability of abusers to manipulate the courts (see "Factors Characterizing Contested Custody Cases"). Another factor that is often overlooked is the need to judge each case on its own merits.

Judges need to recognize DV as a pattern of behavior. I have seen many judges acknowledge that research demonstrates that abusers are extremely manipulative (see Chapter 14 in this volume); yet they believe that they cannot apply this information to a given case, stating, in effect, for example, "Just because most abusers act one way does not mean this father does." Often, the judge's findings in a case defy reality (e.g., determining that the father abused the mother only once or twice and then, for some unknown reason, stopped on his own).

Under the law, a trier of fact is supposed to use common sense and consider whether alternative scenarios are realistic. This is what we all do in everyday life; when a child, for example, tells a teacher the dog ate his/her homework, the teacher is fully aware that this commonly used excuse is rarely true. Accordingly, the teacher would be skeptical but might also be open to the possibility that some unusual circumstance had occurred (for example, by being informed through a note from the child's parent). Most of the time, however, a teacher using his/her common sense would disbelieve such an excuse.

Training

Training for judges and other court professionals should include what to look for in order to recognize DV. Courts should look for patterns of controlling behavior. Most abusers seek custody to punish their partners for leaving or to pressure them to return. They often admit this openly, but courts ignore this crucial evidence. In the *Shockome*[5] case, for instance, the father acknowledged telling his wife that he brought her here from Russia and that she had no right to leave. He further said she would never get away from him. The judge ignored this evidence, in which the abusive father unwittingly gave an honest explanation of his tainted motivations for demanding custody of the children.

Recognizing Which Men Are Most Dangerous

One of the problems courts face in DV cases is understanding which abusive men are most dangerous. Most men who use abusive tactics against their partners never kill or seriously injure their partners. Although researchers have made lethality studies, I believe we need research about abusers who believe their partners have no right to leave. Most men who kill their partners do so after they have left.[6] The motivation

---

[5] Shockome v. Shockome, 30 A.D.3d 528 (2d Dep't 2006). The citation is from the custody appeal in which the appellate division failed to deal with this or any of the other issues raised on appeal. I was the attorney for the mother for most of the case (I appeared after the children were taken from the mother but before the trial). I will refer to this case throughout this chapter because it provides a good example for many of the common mistakes courts make in these cases. Readers should know, however, that the judge in this case filed a complaint against me that resulted in my license to practice law being suspended. The circumstances of this controversy are discussed later in the chapter (see "Author's Note"). The case was also featured in Sarah Childress, "Fighting Over the Kids: Battered Spouses Take Aim at a Controversial Custody Strategy," *Newsweek,* Sept. 25, 2006, *available at* http://www.newsweek.com/id/45654.

[6] B. Hart, "National Estimates and Facts About Domestic Violence," 1989 *NCADV Voice*: *J. Battered Women's Movement* 12 (Winter).

appears to be the belief that she had no right to leave. Similarly, the extremely contested DV custody cases disproportionately involve abusive fathers seeking to pressure their partners to return or punish them for leaving.

The father's admission in the *Shockome*[7] case was unusual only because he acknowledged *to the court* stating to his wife that she had no right to leave him. Battered women often complain that their partners frequently threatened to kill them or go after the children if they dare to leave.[8] While it is possible for a man to have a belief system that a woman has no right to leave and not act on his belief, I believe responsible professionals should be concerned when a man's behavior seems to be based on this belief system.

I would encourage researchers to look at the connection between this belief system and the most extreme abuser tactics of murder and seeking custody for reasons of control. Obviously, just because a father seeks custody does not mean he is motivated by his desire to pressure his partner to return or punish her for leaving. In addition to threats an alleged abuser may have made, professionals should look for supporting evidence such as attempts to go out with his ex or get back together, use of phone calls to speak with the children for getting information about the mother or demanding to speak with her, interest in her private life, demands to have control of the children when he is not available to be with them, and other similar controlling behavior. When the mother has been the primary parent before separation, professionals should closely scrutinize the motivations of fathers seeking custody.

I am making an assumption throughout this chapter that safety issues ought to be paramount. The connection between a belief that a woman has no right to leave and murder or bad faith custody claims should raise serious safety concerns. We have seen abusive custody tactics lead to murder in all too many cases.[9] Courts and the professionals they rely on should pay careful attention to evidence that an abuser is seeking custody in order to control or punish the mother. In such cases, the safety of children and mothers should be the highest priority.

Improving the Justice System's Response

Attempts to improve the justice system's response to DV are often thwarted by unintended consequences. For example, activists in the movement to end DV lobbied for a pro-arrest policy, only to see victims of DV arrested for actions they had taken in self-defense. As will be discussed later (see "Complaints to Child Protective Agencies" and "Other Common Abuser Strategies"), male supremacists have developed a strategy of filing false criminal reports in order to gain an advantage and avoid the legal consequences of their own abuse.

Some professionals have heard about the concept of looking for a pattern of abusive behavior but then fail to apply this information. The idea is to look for a wide range of controlling behaviors that include many tactics that are perfectly legal. Instead, these professionals might see proof of one or two physical assaults but fail to

---

[7] Id.

[8] I base this on hundreds of statements from my clients and similar statements by DV advocates.

[9] The so-called Beltway Sniper, John Mohammed, received support from male supremacist groups when he sought custody of his children. Although his motive for the murders of strangers was a desire to kill his wife who was hiding in Maryland, the media downplayed the significance of the custody issue.

consider other tactics that an abuser is using against a mother. The professionals then conclude that this is not a DV case, because they do not see the pattern of abuse.

Professionals with little or no experience in DV often overlook the differences between the actions taken by an abuser and those taken by his abused partner. For example, typically, researchers will seek to understand DV by counting the hits. A man hits a woman, a woman hits a man, and both appear to be engaging in the same act. But there are three important differences: men, in general, are bigger and stronger than women, hit harder, and cause more serious injuries. There are exceptions, but this is generally true. Further, men hit women for different reasons than women hit men. A man hits a woman to maintain control of her and get his way; a woman hits a man in self-defense and to stop his abuse. We know this in part because 75 percent of men who murder their female intimate partners do so after she leaves,[10] which is not true of women who murder their partners. It is common for a woman to be afraid her partner will kill her, so afraid that she will give in, do whatever she thinks he wants, and let him make all the decisions so that he will not hurt her. It practically never happens that a man is so afraid that his partner will kill him that he will give in, do whatever he thinks she wants, and let her make all the decisions so that she will not hurt him.

Importance of Context

Professor Deborah Tuerkheimer wrote an important article[11] about the importance of context in DV criminal cases. The problem is that most DV crimes involve allegations of physical abuse. Usually there are one or two such acts that constitute the crime. The prosecution is often prevented from presenting evidence of other DV tactics that do not constitute crimes. All the jury knows is that one or two incidents of abuse are alleged to have taken place within the context of what appears otherwise appropriate behavior. This can by itself create a reasonable doubt, since it is hard to believe that someone who usually treated his partner well suddenly assaulted her. Context is similarly important in DV custody cases. Even when contextual evidence is admitted, courts rarely recognize its significance.

An abuser usually wants to speak of only a single incident (usually the one that resulted in his arrest or a restraining order) and to explain how there was nothing wrong with his actions. We refer to this as the "snapshot." More useful in understanding the abuser's behavior would be a video, showing the entire course of the relationship, which demonstrates his last act in the context of his pattern of abusive behavior towards his victim.

Why would a father suddenly seek custody after a separation when he had minimal involvement with the children during the relationship? Too often, professionals with little or no experience do not even consider this basic question, or, if they do, they assume the father's motive is his devotion to his children.[12]

In most cases, when the parents separate, the children live with their mother. Typically, this is by agreement between both parents, since over 95 percent[13] of custody

---

[10] Hart, *supra* note 6.

[11] D. Tuerkheimer, "Recognizing and Remedying the Harm of Battering: A Call to Criminalizing Domestic Violence," 94(4) *J. Crim. L. & Criminology* 959 (Summer 2004).

[12] For an example of this tactic, see B. Goldstein, *Scared to Leave, Afraid to Stay: Paths From Family Violence to Safety* 149-60 (2002).

[13] The exact percentage varies with methodology and the definition of contested custody. Many of the cases that start out contested in court are resolved without a trial. Only

determinations are made more or less by agreement. Mothers most often receive custody based upon such voluntary agreements. Male supremacists like to cite this to support their claim that the courts favor mothers. The reality is very different. We continue to live in a sexist society where mothers provide most of the child care.[14] When a couple separates, a nonabusive father might prefer to have more time with the children, but he recognizes that the mother has provided most of the child care, has better parenting skills, has more time available, and the children are more attached to her. Although there are exceptions, a father who really loves his children will sacrifice his needs in the BIC, and a custody-visitation agreement will be worked out without court intervention.

It is the approximately 5 percent of custody cases that are contested that cause most of the problems. In these cases, 90 percent of the fathers are abusers, but the courts do not detect abuse as the motivation for a previously uninvolved father's application for custody. As a result, between 70 and 83 percent of these fathers receive either full or joint custody.[15] It is within this context that DV custody cases are presently handled.

FACTORS CHARACTERIZING CONTESTED CUSTODY CASES

The most common question asked about DV cases is, "Why does she stay?" DV advocates say that, increasingly, more and more women are staying because their abusers threatened to take the children away from them or to seek custody of the children.[16] This is a most cruel and effective tactic, since it attacks a woman in her most vulnerable spot: her love for her children and her desire to protect them. In reality, the family court system often sends children to live with abusers; therefore, protective mothers need to take this threat very seriously.[17]

What some people refer to as "custody-visitation scandal cases" are those extreme but common cases in which an abusive father is granted physical custody of the children while a safe, primary caretaking mother is ordered to have only supervised visitation with her children and, in some cases, no contact with them at all.

3.8 percent of all custody and access cases are finalized through contested hearings; BC Network of Second Stage Programs, with funding from Status of Women Canada, *Raising the Profile of Second Stage Programs in British Columbia* (Sept. 2001), *available at* http://www.atira.bc.ca/files/RaisingtheProfile.pdf. *See also* J.P. Jafee, C.V. Crooks & S.E. Poisson, "Common Misconceptions in Addressing Domestic Violence in Child Custody Disputes," 54(4) *J. & Fam. Ct. J.* 57 (Fall 2003).

[14] S. Coltrane, "Research on Household Labor: Modeling and Measuring the Social Embeddedness of Routine Family Work," 62(4) *J. Marriage & Fam.* 1208 (2000).

[15] Jafee, Crooks & Poisson, *supra* note 13; *Breaking the Silence: Children's Stories*, a documentary produced by Catherine Tatge and Dominique Lasseur (http://www.tatgelasseur.com) was broadcast on most PBS stations in October 2005; *see also Are Good Enough Parents Losing Custody to Abusive Ex-Partners?* *available at* http://www.theleadershipcouncil.org./1/pas/dv.html.

[16] Voices of Woman Organizing Project (VOW), *Justice Denied: How Family Courts in NYC Endanger Battered Women and Children, Executive Summary* (2008), http://www.leadershipcouncil.org/docs/VOW_JusticeDenied_sum.pdf; R.L. Bancroft, *Understanding the Batterer in Custody and Visitation Disputes* (1998), http://www.thelizlibrary.org/liz/understanding-the-batterer-in-visitation-and-custody-disputes.pdf.

[17] For a detailed description of the basis for this conclusion, see *Crisis in the Custody Court System*, http://barrygoldstein.net.

Custody-visitation scandal cases unreasonably deny children a meaningful relationship with the parent with whom they have their primary attachment. What is going on in any one case might be hard to understand for anyone who has not studied the pattern of these cases. One is tempted to believe that there must have been something wrong with the mother, given the extreme remedies used by the court. This belief also is likely to sound feasible given that abusers commonly demonize their victims. When we look at hundreds or thousands of these cases, however, it is easy to recognize the pattern of mistakes that are made, resulting in decisions that jeopardize children.

On the basis of my years of practice, study, consultation, and experience with victims, DV experts, other attorneys, and activists, I have identified fourteen factors that characterize common mistakes in typical contested custody cases involving DV and/or child abuse, which lead to results that are harmful to children. They are as follows:

1. An allegation of domestic violence and/or child abuse made by the mother and/or child(ren);

2. A failure or refusal by court agents (attorneys, law guardians, forensic evaluator, therapists, and/or judges) to take such allegations seriously;

3. An outcome that places the children at serious risk;

4. An outcome that appears to be 180 degrees from what it should be;

5. An outcome that gives custody to the alleged abusers and restricted visitation to the protective mother;

6. Use by an abusive father and his attorney of "standard abuser tactics" (e.g., seeking custody to punish the mother or maintain control, using visitation or custody to harass the mother, claiming that unfounded child protective claims were made falsely and maliciously by the mother; and attempting to manipulate the children);

7. Propagation of myths and stereotypes about domestic violence (i.e., mothers and children frequently make false allegations of abuse to gain an advantage in litigation) by the court and its agents;

8. Failure to consider and use up-to-date DV research;

9. Gender bias and double standards (i.e., mothers being held to a higher standard than fathers);

10. Use of experts with little or no training and understanding of DV;

11. Use of approaches that blame the victim;

12. Use of biased or unsupported theories (e.g., PAS, "angry women," "vindictive women," alienation, or masochism);

13. Use of extreme penalties against protective mothers; and

14. An outcome that makes it appear like the judge was bribed even though that is usually not the cause of the judicial abuse.

A number of these factors are discussed in the following sections.[18]

Failure to Take Domestic Violence and Child Abuse Seriously

The failure to take DV and child abuse seriously includes failing to seek evidence that could determine the abuse occurred as well as the consequent failure to provide adequate protection for the victim. Judges and the professionals they rely on need to remember that an important part of the male supremacist agenda is to minimize the significance of their abuse. PAS (see "Parental Alienation Syndrome" below and Chapter 12 in this volume) is designed to accomplish this by assuming that all allegations of abuse are symptoms of alienation. This assumption has been highly successful in preventing adequate investigation of DV or child abuse allegations in custody cases.

Courts minimize the importance of DV and child abuse in the following ways:

1. Appointing evaluators lacking in DV expertise;

2. Refusing to permit genuine DV experts to testify or minimizing the significance of testimony by genuine experts;

3. Treating contextual or nonphysical abuse evidence as unimportant;

4. Interpreting a protective mother's desire to minimize contact with her abuser as an attempt to interfere with the father's relationship with the children; and

5. Basing decisions on myths, stereotypes, or gender bias rather than on up-to-date research.

When a father has committed what has been referred to as "low-level" DV while the mother is a safe, protective parent, research demonstrates that children benefit from the mother having custody of the children and the abusive father having only supervised visitation.[19] Low-level DV refers to verbal and emotional abuse. An unsafe mother would be one with a serious substance abuse problem or a mental illness, which prevents her from taking proper care of the children, or one who has a demonstrated pattern of abusive or neglectful behavior toward the children. Many of the mistaken decisions made by the courts are based on negative statements that the mother has made about the father or on her attempts to protect them. Even if such behavior could be construed as harmful to children (and such behavior usually is not harmful), it still would not rise to the level of being unsafe for the children. To whatever extent a court deviates from these best practices, it fails to take DV seriously.

Use of Myths and Stereotypes

One common stereotype about victims of DV is that they are always cowering in a corner afraid to speak. Protective mothers are, in fact, often afraid, but they find the

---

[18] B. Goldstein, "Custody-Visitation Scandal Cases," 2006 *NCADV Voice: J. Battered Women's Movement* 7 (Fall).
[19] L. Bancroft & J.G. Silverman, *The Batterer as Parent: Addressing the Impact of Domestic Violence on Family Dynamics* (2002).

courage to speak up because they are trying to protect their children. When a judge sees a woman challenging her abuser and, sometimes, also challenging the judge, he/she concludes that the woman cannot possibly be battered, since she is not afraid to challenge her abuser. In the *Shockome*[20] case, a custody evaluator wrote that the mother was a strong and articulate woman, and so she could not possibly need a DV advocate. The genuine experts who testified in this case were outraged at the evaluator's statement, while the professionals on whom the court relied did not understand what they were seeing.

If I walk into a police station and complain that, a year ago, someone assaulted me, it is unlikely the case would even be investigated. Because I had waited so long to make the report, the police would question my credibility. The same thing happens when, in the middle of litigation, a woman complains that her partner abused her years ago. She will be asked if she has police or medical records. If her answer is no, court agents tend to assume that she is fabricating the report of abuse in order to gain an advantage in the custody litigation. In reality, it is common for a woman to refrain from filing a police report or seeking medical assistance, particularly while she is living with her abuser. She may not feel safe in seeking assistance, or she may be afraid to get the abuser in trouble. This is why DV so frequently goes unreported. Nevertheless, courts continue to cite the lack of police reports as proof that the woman was not abused.

Failure to Use Up-to-Date Research

Custody-visitation scandal cases result in decisions that are the exact opposite of what up-to-date research tells us is in the BIC. Courts often rely on outdated research because much of the research regarding DV is relatively recent. The Battered Mothers Custody Conference (BMCC) Truth Commission (see Chapter 8 in this volume) recommended that judges and other professionals receive training on specific issues such as recognizing DV, the effects of DV on children, and gender bias in the courts, instead of more general information on DV. An important decision in New York responded to this problem of failing to take DV seriously in custody cases by requiring courts to consider up-to-date research.[21]

In the 1970s and 1980s, if a mother sought to limit visitation because of the father's DV, the judge would ask one question: is the father also assaulting the children? If the answer is no, the court would treat the father as though he were just as fit to have custody and visitation as was the mother he had abused.

Thereafter, more and more research became available demonstrating the harm caused to children who witness DV. Witnessing was defined broadly to include seeing or hearing the violence, seeing her bruises, or feeling her fear. The research found that children were harmed as much by witnessing abuse as by being directly abused. Witnessing DV was found to cause dysfunctional behavior, including substance abuse, suicide, self-mutilation, prostitution, teen pregnancy, school dropout, crime, and depression. Boys were found to be at risk of abusing their partners in adulthood, and girls were at risk of getting into relationships with abusive partners.[22] As a result of this research, states passed laws to protect children. Some states required courts to consider DV in custody and visitation decisions; other states went further by creating a rebuttable presumption that abusers should not have custody (although such laws are often not enforced).[23]

---

[20] *See supra* note 5, in second evaluation report.

[21] Wissink v. Wissink, 301 A.D.2d 36 (2d Dep't 2002).

[22] *See McKinney's Session Laws of New York* ch. 85, Memorandum of Support and studies cited therein (1996).

[23] A. Levin & L.G. Mills, "Fighting for Child Custody When Domestic Violence Is at

More recent research has demonstrated that all batterers, even low-level batterers, engage in harmful parenting practices, including undermining the children's relationship with their mother, teaching bad values (such as sexism), and being a bad role model for the children.[24] Application of this research would mean that batterers would receive custody only in extremely rare circumstances such as when the mother is unsafe and there is no alternative placement for the children.

Gender Bias

It is easy for well-meaning people to engage in gender bias without realizing they are doing so. This was illustrated in an article by Lynn Hecht Shafran,[25] which describes the evaluation of a young couple by an inexperienced psychologist. The evaluator went to the father's home and found a complete mess and no food in the refrigerator. In her report, she noted that the father lives in a typical bachelor's apartment. In the mother's apartment, she found some food in the refrigerator but not an ideal amount, and the home was messy but not as bad as the father's. The evaluator wrote that the mother lived in a messy apartment with inadequate food. This psychologist worked with a supervisor who asked if she saw what she had just done. The evaluator suddenly realized that she had engaged in gender-biased reasoning and quickly corrected her report. Despite the fact that she was a woman and was acting in good faith, she still failed to avoid this error.

Many states have developed commissions to study gender bias in their court systems. In all parts of the country, widespread gender bias has been found, indicating that women are often disadvantaged in trial court proceedings. In custody cases, gender bias results in giving abusers more credibility than their victims, forcing protective mothers to meet a higher standard of proof than their abusers, and blaming mothers for their abusers' actions (see Chapter 5 in this volume).

The *Shockome*[26] case presents an unusually clear example of gender bias. The evaluator used a certainty standard to judge the mother's allegations of domestic violence and the usual probability standard regarding the father's allegations of negative statements by the mother.[27] What parents would have any chance to maintain custody when they have to satisfy a certainty standard?

Issue: Survey of State Laws," 48 *Social Work* 463 (2003). P.G. Jaffe, C.V. Crooks & D.W. Wolfe, "Legal and Policy Responses to Children Exposed to Domestic Violence: The Need to Evaluate Intended and Unintended Consequences," 6 *Clinical Child & Fam. Psychol. Rev.* 205 (2003); A. Bailey, "Comments About Domestic Violence and Child Custody," in S.K. Araji (producer), *Listen to Our Voices* (educational video 2003).

[24] Bancroft & Silverman, *supra* note 19.

[25] L.H. Schafran, "Evaluating the Evaluators: Problems With "Outside Neutrals," 20(6) *GPSOLO Mag.* (2003), *available at* http://www.abanet.org/genpractice/magazine/2003/sep/evaluating.html.

[26] *See supra* note 5.

[27] These disparate standards were contained in the third evaluation and in the transcripts of the cross-examination of Dr. Meg Sussman. I raised this issue in my closing arguments, appellate brief, and later in the retaliatory disciplinary proceeding against me to confirm the truth of my statement that the judge was biased. None of the other attorneys challenged the fact that different standards were used, and all of the judges involved in the cases failed to respond to the issue of a violation of the due process and equal protection rights of Ms. Shockome and later myself by virtue of the different standards of proof.

Use of Experts With Little or No Training

Another important feature of custody-visitation scandal cases is the use of experts with little or no training. Traditionally, courts have relied on mental health professionals to evaluate DV cases. While there are many wonderful mental health professionals with expertise in DV (including experts writing chapters in this book), most mental health professionals have little or no real understanding of DV. Until five or ten years ago, most mental health professionals could complete all of their formal coursework without encountering any information about DV. Even now, their training in this topic is generally insufficient. As a result, the experts relied on by courts often do not recognize the signs of DV in custody cases. Instead their evaluations are based on their own personal values, stereotypes, and biases.

Courts often do not know how to evaluate the relevant expertise of their "experts," and they often have a limited number to choose from within their geographic area. Most custody experts use tests that reveal little if anything about parenting ability or DV. This practice is especially harmful when the test-scoring system has a built-in gender bias, so that, were both a mother and a father to give the same answer to the same test item, only the mother's answer would be interpreted negatively, that is, as a sign of pathology.[28]

These tests give a false sense of scientific credibility when used as a basis for making custody and visitation recommendations. This misuse of tests by mental health professionals compounds the problems created by the biases of the attorneys, law guardians, and guardians ad litem (GALs) who work on these cases, and by the judges who appoint evaluators with sexist or male supremacist orientations.

There is only one profession devoted exclusively to the work of combating DV. DV advocates have far more expertise in DV than do the vast majority of mental health professionals. Courts fail to recognize these advocates as a vital source of expertise in DV custody cases. Too often, advocates are viewed as partisan, even though their ultimate goal—to end DV—is supposedly the same goal as the courts'. The courts' use of these authentic experts in DV cases would help to reduce the prevalence of custody-visitation scandal cases and thereby greatly improve how the courts handle DV custody cases.

Blaming the Victim

"Get over it" is a phrase often used by abusers after they commit DV. Court agents all too often echo it. Recently, courts and legislatures have developed alternative approaches designed to limit conflict between divorcing or separating couples. Therapeutic jurisprudence approaches, such as mediation, use of the "friendly parent" standard, parenting coordinators, parenting training, and demanding cooperation between the biological parents, might be useful in some instances, but these strategies are always ill advised in DV cases.

Protective mothers who have experienced their partners' abuses of themselves and, often, their children have valid concerns about the children's safety. The protective stance these mothers take is reasonable, given their experiences with the children's fathers. Nevertheless, mothers who seek to restrict their children's contacts with the fathers or who want their children to have some time and space to heal from the fathers' abuses are often accused of interfering with the fathers' relationships with the children. This blame-the-victim attitude on the part of the courts often leads to children being ordered to live with abusive fathers.

---

[28] See Chapter 21 in this volume for a detailed explanation of this practice.

Of particular concern are courts that refuse to believe a protective mother's allegations of abuse. Often, these courts impose on a mother, as a condition for maintaining a meaningful relationship with her children, the necessity of giving up her belief, or at least expressing the belief, that the father is abusive. Deliberate, false allegations of abuse occur far less frequently than is reflected by the courts' decisions in these cases. Accordingly, judges should be extremely circumspect in limiting a mother's normal contact with her children merely because she expresses the belief that her partner is abusive. This harmful practice is one of the key components of custody-visitation scandal cases.

Extreme Penalties Against Protective Mothers

Even if a father is proven to have sexually abused his children, he is likely to receive at least supervised visitation (and all too often more than that). There is no other legal situation in which victims are forced to have regular contact with the persons who abused them. In fact, up-to-date research recommends that, if a father has abused his children's mother, he should be limited to supervised visitation with the children. In practice, courts routinely award fathers unsupervised visitations if not joint or sole custody.[29]

In custody-visitation scandal cases, if a mother is alleged to merely have made negative comments about the father, or if she is accused of otherwise discouraging his relationship with the children, she often is punished by being given no contact, or at best supervised visitation, with her children. This happens despite the absence of any research proving that her behavior toward the father causes greater harm than does removing her from the children's lives.

In the *Shockome*[30] case, the mother received the Dutchess County (New York) Mother of the Year Award. Many other mothers claimed that they learned to be better parents by watching Ms. Shockome interact with her children. There was no dispute she and the children had a close and loving relationship. Nevertheless, she currently is allowed less contact with her children than would a rapist. This type of extremely harmful outcome— one far from being in the BIC—is at the heart of custody-visitation scandal cases.

Judicial Abuse?

At times, the outcomes of cases make it appear as though judges were bribed, but this is not usually the cause of the judicial abuses.

Genia Shockome grew up in the Soviet Union, where it was not surprising to see totally unjustified decisions by the courts. She had heard that American justice would always be fair, and, so, as she prepared to divorce her abusive husband, she expected no real difficulties.

The evidence at the trial was overwhelmingly in favor of Ms. Shockome. Mr. Shockome had only minimal involvement with the children while the family lived together. At trial, the father was his only witness. He admitted to calling Ms. Shockome ten to twenty times a day, often late at night, when he knew the family was sleeping. Ms. Shockome, on the other hand, presented eleven witnesses, including five experts and

---

[29] J. Zorza, "Why Courts Are Reluctant to Believe and Respond to Allegations of Incest," in 3 B.K. Schwartz, *The Sex Offender* ch. 33 (1999); J. Zorza, "Child Custody Cases, Incest Allegations and Domestic Violence," 4 *ABA Comm'n on Domestic Violence, Quarterly E-Newsletter* 1 (July 2006), *available at* http://www.abanet.org/domviol/enewsletter/vol4/custodyandincest.pdf.

[30] *See supra* note 5.

neutral professionals such as the school nurse, the son's therapist, and a couple's counselor. The court's appointed evaluator admitted that Ms. Shockome was a safe parent who did not engage in parental alienation. The evaluator testified that the father probably abused the mother physically, verbally, and emotionally throughout the marriage, that the children had witnessed his abuse, and that the father's abuse was so severe that it induced posttraumatic stress disorder in the mother.[31]

What happened in this case, where the overwhelming evidence was entirely one-sided—on the side of the battered mother—was precisely the opposite of what should have happened. The abusive father received custody while the protective mother ended up having no contact with her children. Custody-visitation scandal cases typically involve decisions that appear to go against most if not all of the evidence, and that, further, are blatantly harmful to the children. As a result, people observing the case often come to believe that some type of corruption must have been involved.

How can the courts get these cases so wrong? In my opinion, most custody-visitation scandal cases are not due to bribery or corruption. Rather, these cases are the result of gender bias, ignorance about DV and child abuse, and a lack of openness to obtain research and information. Despite this being perhaps the most benign possible explanation of what causes these court-imposed tragedies, the courts nonetheless often retaliate against those who dare criticize their decisions in these cases.

COMMON LEGAL TACTICS AND STRATEGIES USED BY ABUSIVE FATHERS

This section provides a sampling of the tactics and strategies used by abusers in child custody litigations. Male supremacist groups continue to invent tactics in service of their goal of perpetuating men's rights to control their partners and their children.

Seeking Custody

I frequently met with clients at the courthouse, often with their DV advocates, before conferencing custody cases. We strongly believed that the abuser sought custody as a tactic to maintain control and to avoid paying child support. However, when I conferred with the other attorney and the judge or law secretary, it became clear that they thought it was wonderful that the father wanted to maintain a relationship with his children. This is true even when the father had minimal involvement with the children prior to separation or when his work schedule made it impractical to place the children in his custody.

Male supremacist groups advise their members to seek custody in order to prevent their victims from leaving or to punish the victims if they do choose to leave. Many attorneys advise abusers to seek custody as a bargaining tool. In one case, a father with minimal involvement in the upbringing of his daughter and very limited parenting skills followed his attorney's advice to file for custody. This advice turned what should have been an amicable separation into a bitter divorce. The parties wasted tens of thousands of dollars in legal fees, but the father received a favorable financial arrangement. When the little girl became ill, the mother did not have the money for needed medical care. Ultimately this strategy led to the tragic suicide of the mother.[32]

---

[31] *See supra* note 5.
[32] Goldstein, *supra* note 12, at 91–115.

Although 90 percent of contested custody cases involve abusive fathers,[33] with most of these fathers seeking custody for inappropriate purposes, courts continue to give these litigants the benefit of the doubt. Doing so amounts to the courts' failure to hold abusers accountable for their abusive behaviors. It is, therefore, the court system that makes this common abuser strategy—seeking custody to punish a woman for leaving—so successful.

Essential to this tactic is the abuser's willingness to hurt the children in order to maintain power and control over the mother. Abusers know that the most effective and devastating way to hurt a mother is to harm her children. Further, the children can be used as an excuse for the abuser to continue interacting with the mother, thereby giving him ample opportunity to harass and further abuse her.

In the *Shockome*[34] case, the court repeatedly pressured and threatened the mother to make sure the children spoke on the phone with their father. The audio recordings that the father made of these calls demonstrated how he used phone calls with his children as a guise for asking about the mother or demanding that she speak to him. This is one of many examples showing that, when an abuser seeks custody or visitation, it usually has little to do with his desire for a relationship with his children. Abusive fathers have very different motives than other divorcing or separating fathers.

Male supremacists engage in many other tactics designed to help fathers win custody battles, regardless of the merits of their case.

The pursuant custody battles are then riddled with the mistakes common to custody-visitation scandal cases:

1. Using "junk science" or misapplied theories such as PAS and Munchausen Syndrome by Proxy;

2. Believing in myths and stereotypes about women, especially battered women;

3. Using hired guns as experts; and

4. Blaming or demonizing the victim.

Other tactics, which will discussed below, include the following:

1. Using the abuser's greater financial resources;

2. Misusing orders of protection, especially "mutual" orders of protection;

3. Making false allegations of criminal or child protective violations against the mother; and

4. Attacking the credibility, status, or safety of witnesses who try to help the victim.

In many cases, a man's physical abuse of his partner ends with the separation, since he no longer has unfettered access to her. Court professionals all too often view this cessation of physical abuse as evidence that the abuser is no longer dangerous or has stopped trying to control the victim. But abusers' custody litigation tactics are just another means towards the same end: maintaining power and control by continuing to abuse the victims.

---

[33] *See* Jafee, Crooks & Poisson, *supra* note 13.

[34] *See supra* note 5.

Overcoming Abusers' Strategies in Custody Cases

Unless a protective mother is able to prove otherwise, courts tend to assume that a father seeking custody is motivated by love for his child. The mother's attorney, therefore, should respond by referring to the father's application for custody as "playing the custody card." The attorney should, in fact, raise this issue at the very start of the custody proceeding. He/she may also provide research articles and/or solicit expert testimony stating that most of the fathers who seek custody of their children are abusers. This is particularly true when the mother has always been the primary caretaker of the children and is a safe, fit, and loving parent.

Attorneys for protective mothers should educate judges and other court professionals about how harmful DV is to children. They should point out research on the long-term harmful effects of children's witnessing DV as well as more recent research about the harmful parenting practices of so-called low-level batterers (see Chapter 22 in this volume).[35]

No matter how judges or lawyers try to frame it, the court's decision to give custody or unsupervised visitation to an abusive parent sends a destructive message to children. Courts should assume that children are more cognizant of the father's abuse than anyone suspects. Many boys learn that society permits men to abuse their partners when they witness their father abusing their mother without experiencing any negative repercussions.

Some states have responded to the harms that DV poses to children by creating a presumption against awarding custody to abusers (although far too often, abusers win custody despite these laws). The BIC standard should result in custody for safe, protective mothers because the harm of witnessing DV and the poor parenting practices of batterers makes custody to an abuser against the BIC.

When courts fail to take DV seriously, a protective mother can prevail by documenting the importance and stability of her primary caretaking of the children, including, especially, evidence of her children's having a primary attachment[36] to her. Removing children from the parent with whom they have their primary attachment can cause serious harm such as depression, low self-esteem, and suicide.[37] To avoid these worst-case outcomes, attorneys for protective mothers must present ample credible evidence of the mother's reliable and high-quality care for her children as well as their strong attachment bond with her.

DV stems from the belief that men are entitled to maintain control over their intimate partner or children. Abuse is caused neither by a characteristic or behavior of the nonabusive partner nor by aspects of their relationship. Therefore, merely separating or ending a relationship does not make a dangerous abuser any less dangerous. Further, abusive males have a relatively high risk of reperpetrating abuse with future

---

[35] Bancroft & Silverman, *supra* note 19.

[36] Primary attachment (or "attachment bond") as proposed by developmental theorists, particularly those operating within the school of thought known as Attachment Theory, is the mutually interdependent bond that forms between a mother and her infant during the earliest months of life. Some attachment theorists propose that the mother-child attachment bond comprises a critical component of the growing child's psychosocial development. 1 J. Bowlby, *Attachment and Loss* (2d ed. 1999).

[37] S. Goldberg, *Attachment Part Three: Attachment Across the Life Span* (Nov. 2004), http://www.aboutkidshealth.ca/news/Attachment-Part-Three-Attachment-across-the-life-span. aspx?articleID=7966&categoryID=news-type.

intimate partners (and with those partners' children). If an abuser is given custody or unsupervised visits with his own children, they, too, may be further harmed by watching their father abuse yet another female partner.

Protective mothers are often pressured or even threatened into agreeing to a shared parenting arrangement with their abusers. When protective mothers complain about uninvolved fathers who are suddenly seeking custody, they are informed that both parents have an equal right to a hearing on custody or other claims. Even if the courts will not fully correct for this double standard, they should at least take action to discourage the use of "scorched earth" tactics against mothers in custody battles. Judges should, in fact, interpret any barrage of spurious, harmful litigation as evidence of that litigants' abusiveness. Judges could warn these litigants (and their attorneys) that if evidence demonstrates that the father pursued custody in order to punish or control his ex-partner, the court will impose sanctions such as charging the abusive litigator for his partner's attorney's fees.

Bancroft and Silverman[38] recommend that batterers be held responsible for any costs incurred due to inappropriate legal actions taken by the batterers. If batterers knew using the "custody card" came with high costs to them, they might very well stop using the legal system to continue abusing the mothers of their children. This, in turn, would result in positive benefits to the mothers and children as well as to the court system, which would then have fewer custody cases to adjudicate.

Seeking Joint Custody

An especially common tactic is for an abusive father to seek joint custody or a "shared parenting" plan, even when his previous involvement with the child was minimal.

Courts usually accept wholesale fathers' claims that they just want to stay involved in their children's lives. In reality, when given to a batterer, joint custody forces the abuser's victim to have regular contact with him. The abusive father then is free to use discussions about the children as a guise for harassing and controlling his former partner. Courts are often slow to recognize how an abuser uses his parental rights as a weapon and instead blame mothers who object to joint custody for this very reason. Courts like the solution of granting joint custody or shared parenting because it is viewed as a compromise in difficult "high-conflict" situations, which, in actuality, are usually DV cases. This is especially tempting to courts trying to meet standards for clearing up their caseloads. Consequently, there is widespread bias in favor of granting joint custody, even in cases for which joint custody is totally inappropriate or even dangerous to women and children.[39]

Overcoming Tactics for Obtaining Joint Custody

I was recently involved in a custody case in which I was hired to cross-examine an evaluator who held a male supremacist point of view.[40] The evaluator is an experienced psychologist who has testified extensively as an expert witness. During the course of his

---

[38] Bancroft & Silverman, *supra* note 19.

[39] J. Zorza, "What Is Wrong With Mediation?" 6(9) *Domestic Violence Rep.* 81, 91–94 (Aug./Sept. 2004) P.G. Jaffe, N.K.D. Lemon & S.E. Poisson, *Child Custody and Domestic Violence: A Call for Safety and Accountability* 59 (2003).

[40] This is a custody case in the family court of Queens County, New York. The title of the case is *SS v. TY*, I am not including the full name because the case is ongoing and for the safety of the DV victim.

involvement in the case, in an interview for a *New York Times* article, he was quoted as a being a supporter of shared parenting.[41] Throughout the cross-examination, he minimized the father's DV, blamed the mother for the father's abuse, and tried to justify a shared parenting arrangement, despite the father's history of DV (which the evaluator failed to recognize). Whenever I asked about the research on which he based his opinions, he tap danced around the question without citing any research. He accused the mother of being an extreme fundamentalist, because she proposed giving the father (who often worked 80 to 100 hours a week) visitation every other weekend, plus one weekday evening, instead of a 50/50 division of the children's time. I asked the evaluator if there were any research supporting his belief that a 50/50 time division worked better for children than, say, a 70/30 split. For the first time, he attempted to cite some research from Judith Wallerstein but could not cite a specific book or article. A colleague put me in touch with Ms. Wallerstein, who sent me an e-mail with information to use during the cross-examination. She stated that earlier research had supported the idea that a shared parenting approach benefited children, but, as she conducted more research, she found that shared parenting was not beneficial to most children, even when the parents are on good terms.[42]

If shared parenting does not work for parents who are reasonably cooperative with one another, it has to be a nightmare in cases involving abuse. Joint custody should never be considered where there are allegations of DV. When the allegations are true, forcing a victim to interact with her abuser is equivalent to court-ordered abuse. Even when such allegations are false, the level of contentiousness between the parents would make it impossible for them to effectively coparent. A relationship in which one parent abuses the other creates a fundamentally unequal relationship, so that the victim may feel too afraid of the perpetrator to challenge his position. Courts need to stop blaming the victim in these situations; the problem is not the mother's failure to cooperate, but rather the fact that the father's continued abuse makes it unsafe for her to do so.

Although the laws of each state vary, joint custody usually means shared decision-making power between parents, as opposed to dividing up the children's time between the parents' two residences. Under joint custody, the parties are supposed to come to an agreement on major decisions affecting the children's lives such as school placement, choice of medical doctors and therapists, and so forth. Agreement is required even when a given decision places greater responsibility or more inconvenience on one parent versus the other. For example, if the mother is the one who takes the children to day care or to doctors' appointments, it is she who must transport the children and interact with the medical or other providers. Yet under joint custody, the nonresidential parent has the ability to force his/her own will in making decisions. In one of my cases, the father used his status as joint custodian to insist, over the mother's objections, that their child go to kindergarten at the school the father preferred, which was several miles away from where the mother and child lived, because he thought the school was a more orthodox institution than the one the mother preferred, which was a block away from the home she shared with their child. Both parties had agreed that the child would attend a private kindergarten at a religious school. Obviously there were no academics involved at that

---

[41] M.S. Fischler, "Divorced Fathers Push for Greater Role," *N.Y. Times,* June 19, 2005, *available at* http://query.nytimes.com/gst/fullpage.html?res=9B02E5DC133EF93AA25755C0 A9639C8B63&sec=&spon=&emc=eta1.

[42] *See* J.S. Wallerstein & S. Blakeslee, *What About the Kids? Raising Your Children Before, During and After Divorce* (2003); J.S. Wallerstein, J.M. Lewis & S. Blakeslee, *The Unexpected Legacy of Divorce* (2000); J.S. Wallerstein, & S. Blakeslee, *Second Chances: Men, Women and Children a Decade After Divorce* (1989).

age, and this was only for kindergarten. The mother did not have a car. Thus, the father was able to use his power of joint custody to force the mother to spend the time and money for unnecessary travel. She found it particularly burdensome on the child when the weather was bad. This is not like a suburban mother just driving the child to school. Why should an abusive father be given the power to impose a waste of the mother's time and money and the child's time and risk of illness without any benefit?

Batterers often use their decision-making authority to maintain power and control over the mothers. Therefore, mothers whose primary motivation is the well-being of the child, as opposed to power and control, may be at a severe disadvantage when battering fathers use joint custody for their own purposes. The abuser often does not care if he and the mother cannot reach an agreement; the protective mother, on the other hand, very much cares about making decisions that will be of benefit to the child. Some courts have used mediators and parenting coordinators to help parents resolve conflicts, but this works poorly in DV cases and may even add to the abuser's arsenal.[43] Unfortunately, many mediators and parenting coordinators hold male supremacist ideas, and few have been adequately trained or have experience in recognizing DV.

When there is a history of DV, there should be, at the very least, limited contact between the parties. The legitimate rights of the nonresidential parent could be accommodated while minimizing many of the problems that arise in a joint custody arrangement. Visitation orders can state specifically whether the nonresidential parent should receive reports and notifications such as report cards, medical visits, extracurricular activities, and so forth. The mother can be ordered to authorize school personnel and providers to provide the father with the necessary information, so that he has the burden to contact the providers. Only if the nonresidential parent has demonstrated respectful communication should the order require consultation between the parents before making major decisions. This would allow the residential parent to act in the BIC while preventing obstructionist tactics by an abusive nonresidential parent.

Visitation Exchanges

In DV cases, an abuser often uses visitation exchanges as an opportunity to harass, threaten, or seek to resume his relationship with the mother. If the mother complains to the court about this, the father may claim that he was merely trying to communicate with her regarding the children.

Abusers often use incidents that they provoke during visitation exchanges to prolong the litigations. Each incident can result in new motions or petitions, thus requiring additional hearings and perhaps extensive testimony. In cases where the court schedules trial dates only a day or two at a time, with dates being as long as a month or more apart, the future days of trial may end up being consumed by the incidents that occurred between court dates. Since abusive fathers typically have greater financial resources than mothers, the extended litigations place severe financial stressors on mothers. Further, at the same time the mother and her children are struggling to heal from years of abuse, having to report and review the unpleasant visitation exchanges in court over and over again is retraumatizing and therefore impedes the healing process.

---

[43] J. Zorza, "How Abused Women Can Use the Law to Help Protect Their Children," in E. Peled, P.G. Jaffe & J.L. Edleson eds., *Ending the Cycle of Violence: Community Responses to Children of Battered Women* 147–69 (1995). J. Zorza, "Recognizing and Protecting the Privacy and Confidentiality Needs of Battered Women, 29 *Fam. L.Q.* 273 (1995).

Overcoming Visitation Exchange Tactics

The mother's attorney must take the lead in raising exchange issues, with the safety of the mother and children being considered the highest priority. Exchanges should be made in a public place, with parties kept as far away from each other as possible. Even when the mother is not concerned about her physical safety, exchanges should be structured in ways that minimize contact between the parents. Exchanges also are not a good time for the parents to discuss issues related to the children. Communication by e-mail is preferable, because it makes a record of the exchanges and is not generally as threatening to battered mothers as are in-person discussions and phone calls.

In DV cases, it is imperative that visitation orders include details about the visitation exchange, including the time of the exchanges, the location, how the parties are to behave, what to do when a parent is late, the amount of notice to be given should a visitation be cancelled, and other methods for ensuring safety.

Many supervised visitation programs also provide supervised exchanges. These programs increase safety and prevent unpleasant communication between the parties during the exchanges. Protective mothers should have someone with them as a witness during exchanges, if supervised exchanges are not possible. Courts should hold abusers strictly accountable if they attempt to use exchanges to harass or threaten the mothers.

"Sex Abuse Card"

Male supremacists groups refer to allegations of child sexual abuse as the "atomic bomb of custody." They want people to believe that whenever a mother accuses the father of sexual abuse, she will be awarded custody, with the father being denied normal visitation. These groups deliberately propagate the myth that women and children frequently make false allegations of abuse. In reality, attorneys often discourage protective mothers from bringing up valid allegations of sexual abuse. Tragically, in too many cases, even when allegations are supported by credible evidence, custody is often awarded to the abuser, while the mother, who usually is accused of coaching the child or of trying to alienate the child from the father, is placed on supervised visitation.[44] This occurs for many reasons, including the fact that sexual abuse is hard to prove. Courts and their professionals are reluctant to believe that a father, particularly one who "cares enough to file for custody," could do something so horrible. In fact, sexual abuse is common: by the time they reach the age of eighteen, one-third of girls and one-seventh of boys have been sexually abused.[45] Cases in which strangers abuse children receive substantial publicity; however, most sexual abuse is committed by someone known to the child such as fathers, step-fathers, and other relatives.[46]

Although sexual abuse is discussed more openly now than in previous generations, there continues to be a strong taboo against believing it has occurred. In sexual abuse cases, children are asked to describe extremely painful and embarrassing incidents.

---

[44] A. Neustein & M. Lesher, "From Madness to Mutiny: Why Mothers Are Running From the Family Courts—And What Can Be Done About It," 35 *Contemp. Soc.* 478 (2006).

[45] C. Bagley, "Development of a Measure of Unwanted Sexual Contact in Childhood, for Use in Community Mental Health Surveys," 66 *Psychol. Rep.* 401 (1990).

[46] R. Lieb, V. Quinsey & L. Berliner, "Sexual Predators and Social Policy," in M. Tonry ed., *Crime and Justice* 43–114 (1998); D. Finkelhor, G. Hotaling & A. Sedlak, *Missing, Abducted, Runaway and Throwaway Children in America* (U.S. Department of Justice, May 1990).

They are aware that their statements could get someone they love in serious trouble. They may have been threatened into silence or believe they will be punished if they reveal what happened. No one should be surprised if a child does not reveal incidents of sexual abuse, especially the first time he/she meets a child protection worker, law guardian, GAL, or evaluator. Further, very young children may not have the verbal ability to describe what was done to them, while older children may be reluctant to testify or may even recant out of fear, shame, or loyalty toward their abusers.

Proving a child abuse case is fraught with many of the same difficulties involved in proving that DV has occurred. Both of these offenses are rarely committed in front of witnesses. Both often lack physical evidence. Therefore, court professionals tend to view with great suspicion all allegations of child abuse, especially sexual abuse that a mother raises during custody litigation. Many judges, evaluators, and other professionals believe that such complaints are usually false or at least exaggerated. Despite research demonstrating that sexual abuse complaints are infrequently made during custody battles and that it is rare for mothers or children to deliberately fabricate these complaints, court agents generally assume that abuse allegations arise from a woman's desire to retaliate against the father of her children.[47]

In one case, a mother learned that the father's girlfriend had a nervous breakdown during a birthday party attended by her son. The court had appointed an experienced evaluator to help resolve conflicts over the child. The mother called the evaluator and explained what had happened. He responded appropriately to the issue. He then added that, when she first called him, he was afraid that she was going to raise an allegation of child sexual abuse that, he informed her, he was fully prepared not to believe.[48]

Overcoming the "Sex Abuse Card" Strategy

Attorneys for protective mothers should debunk the myth that women frequently make deliberately false allegations of abuse to gain an advantage in custody litigation. They should use expert testimony and cite research as evidence that deliberately false allegations of sexual abuse are rare.[49]

Attorneys for protective mothers need to request sufficient time for the child protective investigator or other evaluator to work with the child, so that he/she feels safe and comfortable enough to disclose what happened. Even more important, courts must keep in mind that "unfounded" does not mean that the abuse did not occur; rather, it means that there is not sufficient evidence to support the allegation. In other words, an "unfounded" allegation is not the same as a "false" allegation. Likewise, even when it is concluded that no abuse occurred, that does not mean that the mother or other reporter made a deliberately false report.

---

[47] Studies of the low frequency and high validity of child sexual abuse allegations in custody cases include the much-cited article by Nancy Thoennes & Patricia G. Tjaden, who estimate that less than 2 percent of custody and visitation disputes contain an allegation of sexual abuse. N. Thoennes & P.G. Tjaden, "The Extent, Nature, and Validity of Sexual Abuse Allegations in Custody/Visitation Disputes," 14 *Child Abuse & Neglect: The Int'l J.* 151 (1990).

[48] This information was related to me by a client discussing an evaluator who was frequently used by the courts in Westchester County, New York.

[49] *See* Jafee, Crooks & Poisson, *supra* note 13; S.J. Dallams & J.L. Silberg, "Myths that Place Children at Risk During Custody Litigation," 9(3) *Sexual Assault Rep.* 33 (Jan./Feb. 2006).

I had a case in which the children told the judge, law guardian, child protective worker, and evaluator that their father was physically and sexually abusing them. All of these professionals concluded that the mother was brainwashing the children, and they threatened to take custody from her if she did not stop. Later on, before the children's first unsupervised visit with the father, the babysitter confronted the father with information that forced him to admit kissing his daughters on their private areas. The law guardian joined me in a motion to stop the visitation. The judge, however, consulted the evaluator[50] and then decided to permit unsupervised visitation. During the visitation that followed, the father penetrated the four-year-old for the first time. I called child protective services (CPS), and they responded by conducting a new investigation. This one revealed that the father's abuse was far worse than we had suspected. The mother received full custody, and the father was never allowed anything but supervised visitation thereafter. After the mother won custody, at a celebratory dinner the children announced that they had a name for me and the new child protective worker: they called us "believers." We had believed them when they told us about the father's abuse, while all of the other professionals who were supposed to protect them did not.[51]

It takes a lot of courage for children to reveal sexual abuse. If authorities do not respond by protecting them, it is less likely they will disclose incidents of abuse in the future. Accordingly, it is important that professionals working with such children are willing to be believers.[52]

Qualified professionals are critical to an investigation of sexual abuse allegations. The professional should have experience specifically working with children and sexual abuse issues. Training in play therapy is particularly helpful in cases involving young children. Expertise in DV is also important, because it helps the professional to understand the context within which much sexual abuse takes place. Many professionals with little or no experience claim expertise in DV. A good question to ask them is, how often do mothers and children make deliberately false allegations of abuse? The answer should be in the 1 to 7 percent range.[53] If they are not sure of the answer or give a higher percentage, they are likely to believe the common myths and stereotypes about sexual abuse claims in custody cases.

When a court is considering criminal penalties, a high standard of proof is required, and only specific acts constitute a crime. However, there are many potential behaviors that, although not constituting a crime, are harmful to children. Some experts in the *Shockome*[54] case determined that the father's actions violated the children's boundaries. Such boundary violations tend to lead children to believe that such behavior is normal, thus making them more susceptible to being abused in the future. Instead of dismissing the sexual abuse allegations altogether, the court could have responded more effectively by discouraging the father's behavior without treating him as a sexual predator. Instead, the court punished the mother for expressing her genuine concerns, which were supported by the neutral experts she consulted. In this case, the tactic worked: the mother's sexual abuse complaint was transformed into a counteraccusation that she was trying to interfere with the father's relationship with the children.

---

[50] The same evaluator referred to *supra* note 48.

[51] Goldstein, *supra* note 12, at 23–48.

[52] Abusers have developed a tactic of pressuring children to make child abuse complaints against protective mothers as part of her punishment for leaving. Professionals need to be aware of this tactic.

[53] *See* Jafee, Crooks & Poisson, *supra* note 13; Dallams & Silberg, *supra* note 49.

[54] *See supra* note 5.

The abuser's tactic worked even though the mother was careful to avoid exaggerating the father's actions.

A scenario like the one above happens all too frequently to mothers.[55] Fathers, on the other hand, are rarely blamed when their reports of child abuse against the mother are unfounded. But in fact, it is abusive fathers—not mothers—who are far more likely to make deliberately false reports.[56]

Complaints to Child Protective Agencies

The work of child protective agencies is, at best, uneven. The work is difficult and taxing; training, especially in DV-related issues, has been far from sufficient. Many custody-visitation scandal cases have been facilitated by the mishandling of cases by child protective agencies. Their mistakes are especially common in responding to allegations of child sexual abuse.[57]

In one case where I represented the mother in Yonkers, New York, the father falsely reported to CPS that his wife had abused one of their daughters.[58] He had the daughter speak to professionals whom he knew were ethically required to report child abuse claims to CPS. He manipulated his child into affirming these false reports; he then repeatedly pressured the CPS workers to rule against his wife. His campaign eventuated in four "indicated" cases of child abuse against the mother. Around the same time, he cut himself, claimed his wife had assaulted him, and filed criminal charges against her. She was arrested. The judge at the integrated domestic violence court,[59] after considering the indicated child abuse charges and the pending criminal charges against the mother, awarded the father temporary custody of both children. In turn, the custody evaluator recommended that the father receive custody. Thereafter, in a separate hearing on the CPS charges, the mother was able to prove that the father had pressured the child who was the focus of the complaint to lie. As a result, all of the charges against the mother were dismissed while two indicated cases against the father were left standing. At a separate hearing on the divorce, the court found that the father had made false charges against the mother to CPS and to the police. The court also found that the father had engaged in a pattern of abusing the mother. Given these favorable rulings, in the midst of trial, I made a motion to immediately return custody of the children to the mother. The judge responded by stating that it would be fairer to wait until the trial was completed.

This mother came close to being pressured to give up custody before she had a chance to disprove the false charges against her. She has also become bankrupted by

---

[55] Neustein & Lesher, *supra* note 44.

[56] N.M.C. Bala et al., *Allegations of Child Abuse in the Context of Parental Separation: A Discussion Paper* (2001), *available at* http://www.justice.gc.ca/en/ps/pad/reports/2001-FCY-4.html.

[57] Neustein & Lesher, *supra* note 44.

[58] The case is *DM v. CA* in the Yonkers Integrated Domestic Violence Court (*see infra* note 59 for an explanation of integrated domestic violence courts). I have not provided more identifying evidence because the case is ongoing and for safety concerns.

[59] Integrated domestic violence courts are specialized courts designed to handle only DV cases. The idea is for the judge and support personnel to become more familiar with these issues and for all issues from criminal prosecution to custody and child support to be handled in one court. This is designed to prevent common abuser practices like forum shopping or delaying the criminal case until custody is decided.

the case while excessive child support was ordered. So, even under the best of circumstances, this tactic can be devastating to protective mothers.

The findings against the abuser by CPS and the supreme court judge made it likely the mother would win custody once the trial could be finished. The father's attorney was frequently unavailable for potential trial dates. This further delayed the conclusion of the case. The father filed additional false complaints with the child protective office in the Bronx, New York (the father lived in the Bronx, but the previous cases were from Westchester, New York). Although the mother advised the caseworker of the father's history of false allegations, the caseworker chose to indicate the cases against the mother before seeing the prior file. Eventually they reviewed the complete file and dismissed the charges, but in the interim the abuser used the findings against his victim.

The abuser then created an incident during a visitation exchange and claimed the mother grabbed the child's wrist and squeezed so hard as to cause a black and blue mark. The district attorney (DA) brought criminal charges against the mother and sought, as the father wanted, to interfere with the mother's visitation. I advised the DA of the father's history of false complaints including pressuring the daughter to make false complaints. Having made the mistake of filing charges without a full investigation, the DA was unwilling to dismiss the bogus charges and insisted on a trial. At the trial, a police officer testified that she did not see any evidence of marks or bruises on the child's wrist, and a witness the DA failed to interview testified that the alleged incident never occurred. The case was dismissed after trial, but the father used the charges to prevent several visitations. The court imposed no consequences, not even make-up visitation for the father's violation of the visitation order. As we have seen throughout this book, if a mother did this, custody would have been switched, and the mother would be looking at a contempt of court charge. This is the kind of double standard caused by gender bias that the courts regularly fail to see.

After the criminal case had imploded, but before the trial could be completed, the abuser went to see his daughters during the mother's visitation. This occurred while the children were in church. The father demanded to see the children and scared the nun at the school. The mother did not know about the incident. When the children returned to school on Monday, the daughter who was the focus of the previous complaints made a new complaint to the school nurse. This time she had bitten her arm to create "proof" of the mother's abuse. Despite the long history of the father pressuring the child to make false complaints and a lack of any corroborating evidence, CPS brought new charges against the mother and filed a neglect complaint. The caseworker made her determinations without knowing the history of the case, and once she was informed of the history became defensive in attempting to justify her mistake. As I write this, the mother cannot get a trial on the false charges for several months, and, in the interim, she is limited to supervised visitation, while the father has used the time to further alienate the children.

This and other cases (see Chapters 9 and 10 in this volume) demonstrate the destructive repercussions of the courts giving full reign to the legal tactics of abusers. Our broken system has placed mothers in an impossible position. If they fail to report suspected child abuse, they can lose custody due to failure to protect their children. However, if they do make such reports, abusive fathers can use these reports as proof of the women's determination to alienate the children from the fathers. In these and other instances, protective mothers are placed in a lose-lose situation. The higher standards faced by women is caused by gender bias, but the court system has failed to create remedies for problems caused by the use of gender bias by judges and other court professionals.

Overcoming the Strategy of Making False Child Abuse Reports

Attorneys for protective mothers need to educate judges about this tactic by, for example, using expert witnesses and citing research explaining the technical difficulties of proving child abuse, especially when it involves young children. Attorneys should also speak frankly about the well-documented flaws in the child protective system. Also relevant here are findings suggesting that abusive fathers make sixteen times more false reports of abuse than protective mothers do.[60]

If the court is using an evaluator or other expert, it must be someone with the requisite experience and training in child abuse—how it manifests and how to accurately assess it. Attorneys need to raise the selection of an appropriate expert early on, before any experts are suggested. If possible, the attorney should collect names of local qualified experts before appearing in court.

Parental Alienation Syndrome

As discussed elsewhere in this book (see Chapter 12 in this volume), PAS is an unscientific, gender-biased theory originally proposed in the 1980s by psychiatrist Richard Gardner. Since then, proponents of PAS and other "alienation" theories have modified or elaborated upon Gardner's theory—without, however, dismissing his central propositions. Since fuller explanations of these theories are provided in other chapters in this volume, I will focus here primarily on how PAS is wielded as a legal weapon against mothers.

PAS is a tactic that is frequently used by fathers who have abused their partner and/or their children. PAS and related theories turn the principles of child protection on their head: they assume, for example, that contact with the father is always beneficial to children, no matter how demonstrably abusive the father may be. Following this logic, mothers who object to their children's contact with the father are viewed as pathological and vindictive, and they are often punished by custody loss. In this manner, children receive the exact opposite of what they most require: they not only fail to receive protection from further abuse but are essentially forced to endure it when they are ordered to visit or live with their abuser while, in the meantime, their protective mother is forbidden and prevented by the court from protecting them.

One of the strategies of male supremacist groups is to minimize or eliminate the possibility that an abuser will be held accountable for his abuse. That is why these groups are so supportive of PAS: under PAS theory, allegations of DV or child abuse are viewed as symptoms of PAS; therefore, no investigation of his abuse is needed. PAS is used almost exclusively by abusers against protective mothers. Accordingly, court agents should consider the raising of an allegation of PAS against a mother by the man she accused of abusing her as a strong indicator that the man is, indeed, abusive.

Overcoming the Strategy of Claiming Parental Alienation Against Protective Mothers

From the first moment allegations are raised that a mother is alienating the children against their father, the protective mother's attorney must strenuously object. PAS is not

---

[60] Bala et al., *supra* note 56.

among the disorders recognized by the American Psychiatric Association, the American Psychological Association, or any other mainstream mental health organization. It is not listed in *The Diagnostic and Statistical Manual of Mental Disorders*,[61] the compendium of all mental health illnesses. Therefore, anyone who labels a protective mother as having PAS is, in effect, diagnosing a nonexistent disorder, a point that should be raised, strongly and repeatedly, by the mother's attorney.

The gender bias inherent in the use of PAS is clearly demonstrated by the fact that it is rarely diagnosed in fathers. Ironically, abusive fathers frequently engage in the tactic of undermining the mother's character and parenting, both in the eyes of her children and of outsiders. In the *Shockome*[62] case, for example, after several years of living with their father while being denied any contact with their mother, the children began to say that they did not want to see their mother. Further, they eventually claimed they could not remember ever having any good times with her. This, in short, is what true alienation looks like. Yet the same court that claimed its decisions were aimed toward ensuring that the children would have both parents in their lives refused to take any action against the father.

Accordingly, to overcome allegations of PAS or similar alienation theories, attorneys need to seek the testimony of genuine experts. Publications that provide research and other supporting evidence for debunking PAS are available in print and online (see Appendixes A and B in this volume).

Mutual Orders of Protection

Courts would be better situated to deliver justice to battered mothers if they clearly understood the motives underlying abusers' uses of custody battles to take mothers' children away from them. These motives are a form of backlash or retaliation against the progress made by the battered women's movement in holding abusers accountable for their behavior.

Mutual orders of protection nicely fit this agenda. Abusers want mutual orders of protection because this serves to nullify the protection their victims would otherwise receive. When a mutual order of protection is in place, should a woman call the police because her male partner physically assaulted her, all the man has to do to claim innocence is to deny her report and claim, instead, that she assaulted *him*. Typically, in such instances, the police will offer to arrest both parties or neither. Given the authorities' failure to hold him accountable, the abuser can rest assured that, in the future, the system will once again fail to protect her. As a result, he may use a mutual order of protection as a means of pressuring her to come back to him or to otherwise compromise her own position.

Courts that grant mutual orders of protection display a gross misunderstanding of the myriad ways in which DV manifests. For their part, women—who have no intention of violating a no-contact order—often unwittingly agree to the orders out of a misplaced desire to appear cooperative. Only later, after their ex-partners have falsely accused the women of violating the orders, do they realize that mutual orders of protection can do them more harm than good.

---

[61] American Psychological Association, *The Diagnostic and Statistical Manual of Mental Disorders* (4th ed. 1994).

[62] *See supra* note 5.

Overcoming the Strategy of Seeking Mutual Orders of Protection

Courts focus on whether the actions claimed on a request for a protective order satisfy the statutory requirements. Courts give less attention to the real purpose of the order, which is to provide safety to victims. In one case, my client obtained an order of protection against her husband, an attorney, after he assaulted her. A few weeks later, the abuser sought his own protective order in order to neutralize the wife's order. He fabricated an allegation that his wife had pushed him. The judge kept asking him questions about why he needed an order of protection. In responding, the man kept bringing up only the single incident. Physically, this man was bigger, stronger, and more powerful than his wife (as are the majority of men). When he could not justify needing the protective order, the judge denied his application.[63]

Probably the most important issue for the court to consider is which partner is afraid of the other. States should consider outlawing mutual orders of protection, which should be used rarely if at all. Attorneys for protective mothers must strongly object to these orders, explaining to the court their built-in harm and danger. They should never agree to a mutual order as a compromise, even if the terms are otherwise favorable. As far as protecting victims of DV, a mutual order is about as effective as no order at all.

Hiding Income and Assets

Money is an important means by which abusive men control their partners. Battered mothers commonly report that their abusers controlled most if not all of the parties' money during their relationships. Then, after they separated, the abuser used their combined assets to pay for an attorney to legally abuse her and to finance other methods of abuse. In the meantime, the typical battered mother can barely pay her own (and the children's, if they are in her custody) living expenses, not to mention high attorney's fees. Many women run out of money, and therefore are deprived of competent representation, well before the litigation is over. In this kind of case, the court should level the playing field by requiring the party with superior resources to pay the legal and other fees of the poorer party.

Abusers also use their superior resources to bribe and manipulate the children. I have rarely seen the court take this tactic seriously, even in cases where the mother complains about it. There is, of course, nothing illegal about giving children money and gifts. Nevertheless, abusers use it for their own purposes in order to sway the children away from their mothers.

Men are more likely than women to own cash-based businesses, which makes obtaining proof of their income more difficult. Further, the burden of proof is placed on the party who does not have possession of the financial records, thus placing women at a significant disadvantage.

This problem is compounded by bias revolving around child support. There is substantial anecdotal evidence of a double standard in child support enforcement. Some courts appear to be more willing to put mothers than fathers in jail for lack of child support payments. Determining whether this discrepancy is, indeed, factual would require additional research.

---

[63] This was a case in White Plains, New York, family court in front of a judge who had previously been criticized for not appropriately issuing orders of protection. Thankfully, this case had a better outcome. I have not provided identifying information due to safety concerns.

Overcoming the Strategy of Hiding Income and Assets

Attorneys for protective mothers should point out when abusers are using superior financial resources to gain unfair advantages in custody litigation. At the same time, mothers need to pay close attention to finances, especially by keeping records. An abusive father may lie about his income and respond accordingly; sometimes it can be demonstrated that the father's lifestyle is not commensurate with his reported income. Financial experts can be helpful in such matters. It also is considered good practice to use discovery, regardless of the expense. When DV victims have limited assets, the attorney must plan to do discovery in ways that are efficient and affordable.

Laws and practices should be changed so that the burden of proof in financial matters is on the party in possession of the information. If one attorney is collecting all the legal fees billed while the other has to wait for the end of the case to collect his/her fees, the first party has an important advantage. Protective mothers are often ridiculed for repeatedly changing attorneys, but finding, maintaining, and paying for an attorney who understands and knows how to manage DV cases is very difficult. For this and other reasons, judges should be more aggressive in rendering decisions that level the playing field.

Other Common Abuser Strategies

Blaming the victim is another common abuser tactic. When a court blames the woman for her reactions to a man's abuse, rather than understanding those reactions as caused by his abuse, this constitutes blaming the victim. This is why context is so important in understanding DV: the victim's reaction, which may appear as an over-reaction to casual observers, springs from an ongoing pattern of abuse and control that the abuser has been inflicting on the woman, usually in private and often for a long time.

Abusers are filing more criminal complaints as a legal tactic against ex-partners. This not only places a woman at a distinct disadvantage, both legally and custodially, but also discourages her from filing her own complaints against her abuser. Police, prosecutors, and judges need to view allegations of criminal conduct within the context of the entire relationship of the parties. They should remain skeptical of an alleged abuser's complaint against a woman until the matter is fully investigated.

Isolating the victim is another frequent tactic. Many abusers try to discourage anyone, especially professionals, from helping the victims. In one case, an abuser made hundreds of hang-up calls to me over a weekend after he heard I would be representing his wife. He did the same thing with potential witnesses. He did not stop until I taped one of his calls, and the DA brought criminal charges against him. This same abuser filed a grievance against me with the attorneys' discipline board, claiming he did not like the advice I was giving his wife. The grievance committee, intimidated by his repeated phone calls and threats, granted him a hearing.[64]

In the *Shockome*[65] case, the opposing side complained to the mother's insurance company about the mother's therapist, causing the therapist to lose substantial business. They also filed a complaint with the Board of Education against a courageous nurse who testified for the children.

---

[64] Goldstein, *supra* note 12, at 49–59.

[65] *See supra* note 5.

In another case, originating in Ohio, the abuser's side filed a complaint against me and against the psychologist who testified for the mother. They also threatened a rabbi who was trying to help the daughter.[66]

Courts should remain cognizant that abusers are highly manipulative and persuasive. Abusers do not "look like" abusers; they appear to be normal, friendly, and cooperative individuals. They may make limited or partial admissions of what they have done wrong in order to impress others with their feigned honesty and remorse. Likewise, abusers may sometimes enroll in therapy or an anger management course to convince the court (and sometimes his victim) that he is sincerely trying to change. Although therapy is often helpful to people, abusers are unlikely to benefit. This is partly because abusive behaviors are not caused by mental illnesses or emotional distress. Men abuse women because of society's message that men are more powerful and deserving than females; therefore, they have the right to control their partners and to make the major decisions in a relationship or family. Most abusers do not assault or intimidate anyone except their partners, which is why we so frequently hear that family members, friends, and others who know the partners believe the women must be fabricating the abuse. The man could not be an abuser, they reason; he is such a "wonderful guy."[67]

Abusers are particularly adept at minimizing the severity of their abuse and shifting the responsibility onto others, especially their victims. Ironically, battered women, too, are known to minimize the seriousness of abuse and to take on a measure of responsibility for it. Part of a woman's recovery from abuse is recognizing her distorted perceptions of the abuser's behavior and of her own responses to it.

CONCLUSION

An article published in the September 25, 2006, edition of *Newsweek* used the *Shockome* case to illustrate the typical pattern of mistakes made by our family court system. The reporter, Sarah Childress, interviewed both Genia Shockome and her ex-husband, Tim, along with their attorneys and several leading experts from across the country. She also interviewed representatives of male supremacist groups and reviewed extensive documentation from the case. This enabled her to grasp and write about the pattern of mistakes that have sent so many children to live with abusers.[68]

Courts often fail to recognize the signs of DV, especially as they appear in custody battles, or courts assume that abuse ends when the relationship is over. Recognizing abusers' legal tactics can help courts understand that the abusers have not changed—only the tactics. The abuser's attitudes and beliefs remain the same.

Retaliation more commonly attacks DV victims directly. Courts often determine that the protective mother's allegations of abuse against her ex-partner are false and then demand that she stop believing or at least referring to his abuse. Often when a mother complains of new incidents of the father's abuse, the court takes this as interference with the father's relationship with the children and as an affront to the court's determination that the father did not commit prior incidents of abuse. Most of this information is anecdotal, however, and I believe this would be a useful focus for future research.

---

[66] This case, *SS v. JS,* was tried in Ohio and New York. I have not provided more identifying evidence because the case is ongoing and for safety concerns.

[67] P.B. Frank & G.K. Golden, *Mental Health Treatment With Men Who Batter* (2000), http://nymbp.org/reference/MentalHealthTreatmentMB.pdf.

[68] *See supra* note 5.

Most often protective mothers are penalized by supervised visitation or a denial of all contact with their children. Some mothers have been subjected to contempt findings, criminal prosecution, financial sanctions designed to destroy them, unfair financial decisions favoring the fathers, gag orders,[69] and, in some cases, jail sentences. As discussed earlier, women rarely make deliberately false allegations of abuse, but the courts frequently find against mothers' allegations of abuse. This does not prove the courts wrong in any individual case, but it demonstrates that they are using flawed procedures and biased belief systems, which result in many mistakes against mothers. Courts should be more circumspect about penalizing protective mothers based on their findings in such cases.

In fairness to the courts, some of the cases in which the courts fail to find DV are caused because the woman is afraid to present evidence of her abuser's behavior, or her attorney fails to present the evidence effectively. The failure of the courts to recognize DV cases is particularly harmful because it replicates the pretend world she was living in with her abuser. Men often abuse their partners and then boldly deny what they just did or blame the victim for his abuse. The abuser maintains this pretend world because it is unsafe for the woman to challenge his interpretation of events. Up-to-date research has found that the best thing we can do for the children in these cases is to help the mother heal.[70] Accordingly, when courts make findings denying the father's abuse and then compound the error by pressuring the woman to reaccept this pretend world, the court is causing severe harm to the mother and children. I believe courts need to have the humility to avoid placing such harmful pressure on women making DV allegations.

In my opinion, a double standard, which favors the fathers, exists in the way courts treat the parties. While mothers are regularly penalized for complaining about their partners' abuses or continuing to believe they are dangerous, courts rarely penalize fathers, found to have abused their intimate partners or children, from continuing to deny their abuses after the finding. In some cases, where a father is found to have sexually abused his child, he is not pressured to admit his abuse, which would facilitate the therapy he may be required to undergo. Significantly, while there is substantial research about the harm of a father's abuse to the long-term well-being of the children, there is no credible research that a mother's false or inaccurate belief that the father is an abuser is harmful to the children. This common double standard is another example of the gender bias that pervades today's custody court system.

One of the Courageous Kids (see Chapter 9 in this volume) was forced to live with an abusive father as a result of the family court's failures. He described being a ten-year-old boy lying in bed and hearing his father go into his sisters' room to molest them. To this day, he struggles with blaming himself for not protecting his sisters, who continued to live with their abuser until they reached eighteen. Courts and the public assume that once a court makes a decision, the facts are as determined by the court. The reality for this boy and many other children discussed throughout this book is very different. Some judges have refused to correct their errors based on new and compelling evidence for fear that admitting their prior errors would undermine public acceptance of court decisions. Ironically the opposite is true. The research and information establishes that a high percentage of DV custody cases are wrongly decided as a result of widespread outdated and misguided practices (see Chapters 1, 6, and 14

---

[69] The courts usually claim the gag orders are designed to protect the privacy of the children, but, in reality, they are used to prevent criticism of the court. The orders tend to be enforced only against the mother.

[70] Bancroft & Silverman, *supra* note 19.

in this volume). Many women are choosing to stay with their abusers rather than risk being separated from their children.

Courts cannot keep abusers from using the tactics discussed in this chapter. The tactics, while abusive, are legal. However, recognizing the tactics for what they are could greatly help courts make better decisions in these important cases. The well-being of the next generation, and of generations to come, hinges on whether courts and the professionals working in the court system are able to come to this recognition.

Author's Note

After this chapter was submitted to the publisher, the New York court system retaliated against me for pointing out a judge's problematic responses to my zealous advocacy for a protective mother by suspending my license to practice law for five years. Accordingly, the publisher asked that I explore how this decision affects the suggestions in this chapter.[71]

Ordinarily the public's response to a lawyer's disciplinary decision is one of disappointment in the lawyer for violating ethical rules or perhaps a belief that the attorney's many good deeds should have been considered in moderating the penalties. The public's response to this case was most unusual. The male supremacist groups gleefully cheered the court's attack and punishment of me because they disliked having a prominent male attorney speak out about the mistreatment of women in the court system.[72] The leaders in the movement to end DV condemned the unprincipled decision of the court and strongly supported me. The BMCC passed a resolution that was later endorsed by the National Coalition Against Domestic Violence (NCADV), New York National Organization for Women (NOW), National Organization of Men Against Sexism (NOMAS), and Stop Family Violence. The resolution was sent to Governor Patterson, Attorney General Cuomo, and the Appellate Division of New York saying as follows:

> The attendees at the Sixth Annual Battered Mothers Custody Conference, held in Albany, New York in January, 2009, voted to strongly protest the Appellate Court's recent decision to suspend, for five years, the license of attorney Barry Goldstein. We view Mr. Goldstein as one of the most dedicated and hard work-ing advocates for battered mothers and their children, not only in New York state but in this nation. As called for by the ethical canons of his profession, Mr. Goldstein has vigorously defended battered mothers who, in trying to protect their children from abusive ex-partners, have been re-victimized by unjust and harmful decisions by family court judges. This egregious action on the part of the appellate court can only serve to discourage and suppress the efforts of attorneys to vigorously defend battered mothers for fear that they, too, will face retaliation by the court system. As fellow advocates for battered mothers, we pledge to widely publicize and condemn this decision.[73]

---

[71] It is not my intent here to discuss the merits of my case except to the limited extent it impacts on the issues discussed in this section. For more information, *see* http://www.barry-goldstein.net/legalethics.pdf.

[72] *See* http://glennsacks.com/blog/index.php?tag=barry-goldstein; http://deanesmay.com/2009/01/07/court-delivers-devastating-blow-to-leading-feminist-attorney-barry-goldstein/.

[73] *See* http://www.nownys.org/pr_2009/pr_021309.html.

The role of the NCADV is particularly important in understanding my case and other cases of retaliation. They are the leading organization in this country working to end DV. In other words, the NCADV represents the most important resource and expertise regarding DV issues. For the NCADV to repudiate a court's decision involving DV issues makes it virtually certain that the court has caused tremendous harm to battered mothers and their children. The NCADV is concerned about the failure of the custody court system to take DV seriously and, particularly, the increasingly common practice of retaliating against protective mothers and their supporters.

The widely differing views between those who seek to end DV and those who wish to go back to a time when society tolerated men's abuse and control over women demonstrates the impropriety of using the attorney disciplinary system to promote a particular political or social view. This is why courts usually place a high value on our rights under the First Amendment, particularly when discussing public policy issues.

Gender bias against women is widespread. It is easy for well-meaning professionals to unconsciously engage in gender bias. What is an ethical attorney supposed to do when he/she recognizes the double standard that has been found by gender bias committees in over forty states? The decision in my case would seem to say the attorney should stay quiet, refrain from challenging a judge's mistakes, and watch silently as his/her client and her children's lives are destroyed. In my case, even the judge admitted that I never cursed him or said anything similar. All of my statements, which the grievance committee took out of context, could be printed in a family newspaper or heard on radio or television. Most of the statements were my opinions or my interpretations of particular events. My long years of training and expertise about DV, which made my opinions informed, did not matter to the court. Neither did a finding by the referee that I sincerely believed what I said.

The canons of legal ethics require attorneys to zealously represent their clients. These rules are at the heart of an attorney's ethical responsibility toward his/her client. In my legal arguments, I informed the court that even a one-day suspension would force me to stop practicing law because it would be unethical to represent a client if I had to be afraid to challenge a judge when the judge makes a mistake harmful to my client. The decision in my case appears to encourage attorneys to violate fundamental legal ethics.

The decision in my case creates an unfortunate conflict for attorneys. They are forced into a choice between what is ethical and what is safe. There is no question that it would be safer for attorneys to avoid challenging judges or providing information that contradicts a judge's beliefs or positions. Although many protective mothers have complained about the failure of their attorneys to zealously represent them, I am not aware of any consequences any attorney has suffered for this ethical violation. In the present court system, courts and grievance committees can be relied on to protect attorneys from complaints about their failure to zealously represent protective mothers. Ethically, it is clear that attorneys are required to zealously represent their clients and that includes respectfully challenging judges who they believe have mistreated their clients.

The strategies discussed in this chapter have been used by many attorneys without causing them to be retaliated against. Accordingly, I would continue to recommend the strategies discussed in this chapter. Lawyers should be aware of the risk of retaliation. They should consider the best ways to present the information to help a judge hear the research and other facts. This is beneficial not only to protect the attorney, but also to give the clients the best chance of success.

Chapter 19

DV Case Preparation and Trial Examination: A Heavy Burden

by Marjory D. Fields. J.D.

INTRODUCTION

Essential Role of Lawyers

Legal representation for women victims of domestic violence (DV) is indispensable to obtain the statutory protection, child custody, and financial remedies they require. Early studies showed that women rate lawyers as their most important resource.[1] Only diligent legal advocacy utilizing documentary and real evidence, fact and expert witnesses can convince judges to grant women relief. The security provided by protection orders and child support enable women to make new lives for themselves and their children and resolve the depression that results from emotional or physical abuse.[2]

Another reason lawyers are essential for battered women is to protect their rights in different parts of the legal system. Marianne Hester, the British sociologist, described the contradictory responses to a battered woman in the multiple court systems where she may find herself. Dr. Hester made a "three planet" model[3] to illustrate this. The DV victim is:

- The victim of a crime, who is protected by the state in a criminal court prosecution of her violent partner;

- The respondent mother, who is prosecuted by the state in a family court child protection proceeding, in which she is accused of failing to protect her child from the father or stepfather who beat the mother; and

- The "uncooperative" mother who is sued by the father in a private law custody and visitation proceeding in a family or divorce court, and accused of parental alienation for opposing unsupervised access by the child's father, who is the man who beat her.[4]

---

[1] Lee H. Bowker, "Battered Women as Consumers of Legal Services: Reports From a National Survey," 10 *Response* 10-17 (1987).

[2] J. Zorza & N. Lemon, "Two-Thirds of Civil Protection Orders Are Never Violated; Better Court and Community Services Increase Success Rates," 2 *Domestic Violence Rep.* 51 (Apr./May 1997); M.A. Kernic, V.L. Holt, J.A. Stoner, M.E. Wolf & F.P. Rivara, "Resolution of Depression Among Victims of Intimate Partner Violence: Is Cessation of Violence Enough?" 18 *Violence & Victims* 115 (2003).

[3] M. Hester, "Future Trends and Developments: Violence Against Women in Europe and Asia," 10 *Violence Against Women* 1431 (2004). Cathy Humphreys & Rachel Carter et al., *The Justice System as an Arena for the Protection of Human Rights for Women and Children Experiencing Violence and Abuse, Final Report,* at 7 (Co-ordination Action on Human Rights Violations, European Commission Project, 2005), available from Rachel.carter@gldvp.org.uk.

[4] Parental alienation is a charge made against mothers exclusively. *See* Chapters 12 and 20 in this volume.

On a fourth planet, the DV victim is an undocumented alien resisting deportation by the federal government after her violent husband withdrew his immigration spouse petition sponsoring her permanent residence visa.

Protection of women and their children requires integrated legal strategies and consistent presentation of evidence on all four planets. Violent men should be portrayed as violent fathers and DV offenders who pose continued risk of harm to children and their mothers,[5] as shown in many studies of the emotional, psychological, cognitive, and physical harm suffered by children who had lived with DV.[6]

The second and third planets appear to apply family systems theory in child protection and custody cases. Family systems theory is based on the view that "problems" in families result from the interactions among family members. It requires focusing on the behavior of both DV offenders and victims. Equal responsibility for violent acts is placed on the victims.

Thus, a family systems analysis ignores prior court decisions and orders and criminal convictions to look at the underlying "causes" of DV. It is contrary to the provisions and legislative intent of the criminal laws, civil protection order laws, and child custody and child protection laws, which are intended to hold abusive and violent partners responsible for their acts and to protect the other members of their families.[7]

A third reason that abused women need legal representation is that judicial education programs provided by court systems, judges' associations, and private organizations[8] do not affect the fact-finding processes and outcomes in individual cases.[9] Judges decide cases based on the evidence presented: the record made in individual cases. Thus, a safe outcome is accomplished by diligent lawyers, one case at a time.

In addition, lawyers persuade judges to grant life-saving protection. Some judges in family law matters deny each party part of the relief to which he and she are entitled. These judges appear to believe that if both parties are dissatisfied with the decisions, the parties will be less hostile toward each other and not return to court. In reality, denying both parties part of their relief can have the opposite effect. It can enable the violent partner's hostile acts by failing to protect the victim. Victims with strong advocates are more likely to obtain the protection provided in the statutes. Good legal representation also makes a trial record to support an appeal.

Another rationale that sometimes leads judges to deny DV victims all of the protection to which they are entitled is the mistaken belief that setting limits will inflame DV offenders and lead them to retaliate against the victims. Lawyers, therefore, must show judges that weak responses that do not restrict offender behavior are likely to lead to retaliation against the victims. The value of having

---

[5] Hester, *supra* note 3, at 1445; A.C. Morrill, J. Dai, S. Dunn, I. Sung & S. Smith, "Child Custody and Visitation Decisions When the Father Has Perpetrated Violence Against the Mother," 11(8) *Violence Against Women* 1076 (2005).

[6] Governor's signing message 1994 NY DV law, Sessions Laws of New York, 1994.

[7] American Bar Association Commission on Domestic Violence (2007). Charts of all state domestic violence laws are available at http://www.abanet.org/domviol/statutorysummary-charts.html.

[8] For example, the National Council of Juvenile and Family Court Judges, the Association of Family and Conciliation Courts, and the National Judicial College.

[9] Institutional judicial education may be useful to judges who are motivated to learn new dispositional alternatives.

courts take control from DV offenders and set limits on their bad behavior is effective. Studies protection orders show that stop violence in most cases.[10]

Research shows that weak criminal justice responses to DV—police refusal to arrest, prosecutor refusal to prosecute, and judicial dismissals or lenient sentencing—produce a retaliation effect.[11] The same need for robust judicial response is present in civil cases with DV issues. Full orders of protection, barring contact and communication and limiting or denying visits with the children, are needed to keep victims and their children safe from retaliation or continued abuse.

Lawyers are important also because they cite the laws that give judges the authority to grant DV victims protection and restrain DV offenders and the legislative intent that is the basis for these laws. They also present expert witnesses who describe the scholarly literature. At the conclusion of the testimony, lawyers submit proposed orders containing provisions tailored to the facts of their cases.

Court systems, however, encourage judges to settle cases for reasons of judicial economy. Referrals to mediation, pretrial conferences with the lawyers and parties, and trial adjournments are used to encourage the parties to settle (or succumb to litigation fatigue, run out of funds to pay lawyers, or have no more leave time from work). Settlements that sacrifice the safety of DV victims and their children should be avoided. The alternative is to insist on a trial, which is feasible only when one has marshaled the evidence to prove the case.

When the evidence is weak or a trial is impossible because the client is unwilling to testify, cannot pay the costs of trial, or is unable to take leave from employment, then settlement is the only choice. Lawyers develop settlement offers and negotiate for their clients, thereby protecting DV victims from direct exposure to their violent partners. Sometimes settlements work well because the parties control the outcome and decide how much they can give up safely. Settlements also remove the risk of bad judicial decisions and, therefore, may be appropriate when the judge is known to disbelieve women and blame DV victims.

Gender Stereotypes and Double Standards Persist

"Just because he beats his wife does not mean he is a bad father."[12] The woman judge who made this "ruling" in a divorce case in which I represented the physically abused wife in 1978 was assigned to preside in all the divorce cases in Brooklyn, New York, for many years. Today, judges would not make this statement, but this attitude persists. It is the only explanation for many rulings in which judges grant extensive, unsupervised visits or custody to fathers who have been held to have beaten the mothers of their children.

Another woman judge who made findings of fact that the father had been violent toward his wife (who had been granted a protection order) and that the father had

---

[10] Joe Surkiewicz, "Of Service—House of Ruth Study Shows Protective Orders Protect Battered Women," *Daily Record,* Apr. 29, 2005 (Baltimore, MD); Zorza & Lemon, *supra* note 2.

[11] Laura Dugan, Daniel S. Nagin & Richard Rosenfeld, "Exposure Reduction or Retaliation? The Effects of Domestic Violence Resources on Intimate-Partner Homicide," 37 *Law & Soc'y Rev.* 169 (Mar 2003).

[12] Statement to me by a woman judge presiding in divorce cases in Brooklyn, New York, in 1978. Humphreys & Carter et al., *supra* note 3.

driven recklessly causing an accident with the children in his car, was abusing cocaine (including testing positive during the course of the trial and failing to take court-ordered drug tests), failed to engage in drug treatment and psychotherapy, failed to comply with discovery, misrepresented his income at trial, and failed to pay court-ordered child support, also found in the same decision that the mother was undermining the children's relationships with their father and failing to encourage the children to have a good relationship with their father.[13]

Blame Shifting

While the public perception may be that women have achieved equality in the courts and are protected from DV, the reality is different. Women are perceived as less truthful than men in court proceedings.[14] Unfortunately, the defensive, apologetic testimonial style of some women reinforces this bias. Women are blamed for provoking the violence of their partners and being equally responsible for DV,[15] although provocation is not a defense to the crime of assault. Women are denied protection after the first incident of DV because there is "no pattern of abuse" (yet), but also when they have been subjected to years of abuse because they "tolerated" the abuse and are using DV to gain a litigation advantage in the financial aspect of a divorce or in a custody case.

Family Systems Theory Is Inappropriate for Domestic Violence Cases

Reinforcing negative stereotypes of victims of DV, family systems theory has reemerged and is a source of analysis of DV cases used by judges, sometimes regarded as a "common sense" view. Family systems theory, however, is inappropriate for assessing or responding to DV.[16] Mental health professionals and judges who adopt the family systems perspective in DV cases blame victims for provoking violence and abuse. They perceive DV as the result of "reciprocal interactions" within the family system.[17] This approach contradicts the provisions and intent of both criminal and family law by failing to hold the DV perpetrator responsible for his actions.

---

[13] Beth M. v. Joseph M., (Supreme Court Nassau County, July 25, 2006) unpublished, slip opinion NYS Courts Web site, http://www.courts.state.ny.us.

[14] E. Sheehy, "Evidence Law and 'Credibility Testing' of Women," 2 *Queensland U. Tech., L. & Just. J.* 8, 11 (2002).

[15] *See* Chapter 5 in this volume.

[16] M. Hansen. & M. Harway, "Feminism and Family Therapy: A Review of Feminist Critiques of Approaches to Family Violence," in M. Hansen & M. Harway eds., *Battering and Family Therapy* 69-80 (1993); M. Harway & M. Hansen, "Therapist Perceptions of Family Violence," id. at 42-53; M. Hansen & M. Harway, "Intervening With Violent Families: Directions for Future Generations of Therapists," id. at 232-37.

[17] Marsali Hansen, "Feminism and Family Therapy," id. at 76-77; but see a contrasting view, Christine Murray, "Controversy, Constraints, and Context: Understanding Family Violence Through Family Systems Theory," 14(3) *Fam. J.* 234 (2006); *see generally* P.H. Neidig & D.H. Friedman, *Spouse Abuse: A Treatment Program for Couples* (1984); L Bancroft & J.G. Silverman, *The Batterer as Parent: Addressing the Impact of Domestic Violence on Family Dynamics* 140-49 (2002).

These perceptions result from the flawed structure of family systems theory when applied to DV. It ignores all aspects of the family system other than communication and dyad interaction. It does not include the legal, social, and political "systems" or contexts within which families exist. Differences in size and strength, social status, and economic and political power between men and women are omitted from the family systems analysis of DV.[18] Family systems theory "directs the focus away from the violence and fails to address" the safety needs of weaker family members.[19]

MENTAL HEALTH EVALUATIONS MAY BE UNRELIABLE

Mental health evaluations are ordered too often. They are unnecessary in most custody and visitation cases because these are disputes based on facts, not mental illnesses or disorders. Mental health evaluations are not useful to the court in DV cases because there is no diagnosis of DV offender or DV victim.

Mental health reports are based on the parties' statements to the interviewer, statements that are better made under oath in the court where the trier of fact can observe the witnesses' affect and demeanor. Mental health professionals are not competent to testify whether acts of DV and abuse occurred because they did not observe the events and cannot testify regarding the credibility of the parties. Credibility is for the court to decide.

Moreover, mental health recommendations are feeding judicial misperceptions that DV is not serious, is victim provoked, presents no risk of harm to children, or is fabricated or exaggerated. Some judges base their orders on the recommendations of evaluators, mental health professionals, guardians ad litem, court-appointed special advocates, and mediators (hereafter collectively "evaluators"). Those recommendations determine the extent and conditions of visits by fathers who were abusive to the mothers of their children. Thus, the safety of DV victims and their children may be compromised by the recommendations of evaluators.

Evaluators may lack knowledge of the dynamics of DV and abuse. They fail to recognize the atmosphere of fear created by a single act of violence and dismiss that as "not DV" because there is no "pattern" of repeated violence. When there is no physical violence, but a pattern of humiliation and degradation, evaluators attribute that to "high conflict" between two uncompromising people. This characterization is applied particularly when women demand their legal rights and try to protect their children from emotionally abusive fathers.

There is no legal justification (other than self-defense) for violence against one's partner. The most verbally provocative, nasty partner is not an appropriate target for violent reaction. Physical separation from unpleasant partners is the only alternative, legally. Evaluators ignore or are unaware of the law.

Evaluators may not adopt the statements of offenders denying or minimizing the history of DV and shifting blame to the victims by claiming provocation. Evaluators may not disregard the prior court determinations based on the offenders' subsequent assertions.[20] Prior court findings, judgments, and orders are *res judicata* or law of

---

[18] Hansen, "Feminism and Family Therapy," *supra* note 16, at 78-80.

[19] Id. at 80.

[20] Humphreys & Carter et al., *supra* note 3. This report describes a "four planet" analysis in which the protection order/criminal prosecution, child custody and visitation, child protection, and immigration legal systems ignore each other. In the first, she is a crime victim/witness; in

the case determinations, binding in all future proceedings regarding the same parties. These issues should be raised in cross-examining mental health professionals and evaluators.

DV is not caused by mental illness usually; therefore clinical evaluations are seldom indicated. Mental health evaluations should be opposed in cases in which there are no issues of mental illness, disorder, or incapacity. Mental health evaluations and psychological tests cannot establish that DV occurred or did not occur.[21] There are no diagnoses of violent intimate partner or victim of DV.[22] Mental illness and severe mental disorder rates are about the same among DV offenders as in the general population.[23] Thus, clinical evaluations are often inappropriate, cause delay, and increase litigation costs without providing competent, material, or relevant evidence.[24]

Furthermore, victims of DV may appear less stable than their violent partners because they are suffering from the emotional effects of abuse and fear of losing custody of their children. For these reasons, their test results may not provide accurate assessments of their parental capacity. Abusive partners, by contrast, appear calm and self-assured.[25] The mental health problems experienced by victims of DV may be temporary and resolve when they and their children are safe from violence.[26]

Apparently, there is an assumption among the evaluators working with the courts that visits are to be allowed under all circumstances. The custody evaluators seem to believe they are constrained to recommending the frequency of visits and whether supervision is needed. None of the studies of DV and custody decisions in the special issue on "Child Custody and Domestic Violence" of *Violence Against Women*, mention the possibility of recommending that the court order no contact by violent offenders with their children.[27] This is so despite the risk of harm, which appears to be addressed only by the type of supervision required. Thus, thorough cross-examination of the custody evaluators must be used to discredit their qualifications, methods, and conclusions.

WHEN MENTAL HEALTH EVALUATIONS ARE NEEDED

In those few cases in which the DV offenders suffer from mental illnesses or mental disorders, mental health evaluations by forensic experts may prove the

---

the second, she is an "unfriendly parent"; in the third, she is a mother who fails to protect her child from the violent father; and in the fourth, she is an illegal alien.

[21] Nancy S. Erickson, "Use of the MMPI-2 in Child Custody Evaluations Involving Battered Women: What Does Psychological Research Tell Us?" 39 *Fam. L.Q.* 87, 88 (Spring 2005).

[22] American Psychiatric Association, *Diagnostic and Statistical Manual of Mental Disorders-IV-TR* (4th ed. text revision 2000).

[23] Edward W. Gondolf, "MCMI-III Results for Batterer Program Participants in Four Cities: Less 'Pathological' Than Expected," 14(1) *J. Fam. Violence* 1 (1999).

[24] *See Report of the Matrimonial Commission* 46-54 (New York State Office of Court Administration, Feb. 2006).

[25] Erickson, *supra* note 21, at 87-89, 108; Bancroft & Silverman, *supra* note 17, at 115-20.

[26] Kernic, Holt, Stoner, Wolf & Rivara, *supra* note 2.

[27] "Child Custody and Domestic Violence," 11 *Violence Against Women* (Special Issue 2005).

evidence of the risks posed by a DV offender. When a DV victim's parental capacity is placed in issue by a DV offender, a mental health evaluator may establish that the mother's parental capacity is not compromised by her diagnosis and she is medication compliant, or that there are no bases for the allegations regarding her mental condition.

DOMESTIC VIOLENCE IS CRIMINAL BEHAVIOR AGAINST WOMEN

So pervasive is our tendency to ignore that DV is criminal conduct directed against women primarily, that even the critics of family systems theory as applied to cases of DV commit the error of describing "violent families" and "families in which violence occurs"[28] Use of the intransitive verb, "occur," is misleading. Violence does not "occur" in families. "Violence," unlike weather and earthquakes, which occur, is intentional action taken by a person or persons against others. The intransitive verb hides that the actions are intentional, violent crimes.[29]

Those characterizations obscure the gendered nature of DV and relieve offenders of responsibility for their violent acts. The studies in the special issue of *Violence Against Women* devoted to DV and custody determinations showed that DV is male violence against women.[30] U.S. Department of Justice data for both intimate partner homicide and intimate partner assault show women are the primary victims, and their male intimate partners are the primary offenders.[31] "An estimated 876,340 violent victimization against women by intimate partners occurred during 1998. . . . men were the victims of about 160,000 violent crimes by an intimate partner."[32]

The United Nations, the Council of Europe, and American scholars define DV as a human rights violation because the state is complicit in this criminal conduct. The state supports the rights of offenders, while failing to enforce laws for the protection of victims of crimes by their intimate male partners.[33] Lawyers may present these human rights issues to the courts.

---

[28] Hansen & Harway, "Intervening With Violent Families: Directions for Future Generations of Therapists," *supra* note 16, at 227, 237.

[29] Peter Jaffe, "Foreword," in Bancroft & Silverman, *supra* note 17, at ix.

[30] *See supra* note 27.

[31] Bureau of Justice Statistics, U.S. Dept of Justice—Office of Justice Programs, *Homicide Trends in the U.S., Intimate Homicide* (2006), http://www.ojp.usdoj.gov/bjs/homicide/intimates.htm.

[32] Callie Marie Rennison & Sarah Welchans, "One-Third of All Murdered Females Were Killed by Partner," at 1 (Bureau of Justice Statistics, U.S. Dept of Justice, May 17, 2000), http://www.ojp.gov/bjs/pub/press/IP violence.pr.

[33] Evan Stark, *Coercive Control* 219-21 (2007); UN Commission on the Status of Women, *Violence Against Women in the Family* (1989); Convention on the Elimination of all forms of Discrimination Against Women (CEDAW) (1979); CEDAW General Recommendations 19 para. 24 (1992); UN Conference on Human Rights (Vienna, 1993); UN Conference on Women (Beijing, 1995); M.E. Beasley & D.Q. Thomas, "Domestic Violence as a Human Rights Issue," in M. Fineman & R. Mykitiuk eds., *The Public Nature of Private Violence* 323-48 (1994).

DOMESTIC VIOLENCE OFFENDERS ARE RECIDIVISTS

DV is criminal behavior for which the offender is responsible.[34] Lawyers and custody evaluators should consider the studies showing that men who commit DV often commit other types of crimes and present this evidence in court cases.[35] Usually, these men are serial offenders who commit multiple crimes within a single relationship and with multiple victims.[36] The term "batterers" therefore hides their status as criminal offenders.

PARENT COORDINATORS

Parent coordinators, like many mental health professionals or volunteers, are appointed by judges to mediate and supervise court-ordered custody and visitation. Parent coordinators are inappropriate for DV cases. They receive training from the court system as a prerequisite for being included on the court list. That training, however, is a few hours and concentrates on "high-conflict" cases. Although DV cases are "high conflict," in the literal sense, that label is a disparaging term applied most often to cases in which the parties are engaging in petty acts of financial misconduct to vindicate anger, not violence, control, and abuse. Thus, applying the "high-conflict" designation disregards the psychological and physical injuries suffered in DV and abuse cases.

One cannot risk the safety of clients and their children by agreeing to supervision by parent coordinators whose knowledge of DV may be minimal. Moreover, parent coordinators are given broad authority to resolve parental disputes regarding medical care, religious observances, education, contact with extended family members and parents' significant others, and times and duration of parental visits. Parent coordinators, however, lack enforcement powers and rely on voluntary compliance, or the parties must seek relief from a judge.

A commentator suggested that the scope of parent coordinators' powers violates the due process protections required in family court proceedings by the decision in *In re Gault*.[37] The U.S. Supreme Court held in *Gault* that family courts may not use informal procedures that deny the right to notice and an opportunity to be heard, or the right to counsel and to confront witnesses, on the assertion that family courts do not punish but help accused children and parents. One might add that when judges grant parent coordinators the authority to resolve disputes and impose solutions on parents who cannot reach a compromise, this authority may be an unconstitutional delegation of judicial authority and violates the First Amendment right of access to court for redress of grievances.

---

[34] *See* the penal and criminal laws of every state.

[35] M. Labriola, M. Rempel & R. Davis, *Testing the Effectiveness of Batterer Programs and Judicial Monitoring, "Offender Profiles"* at 32, *available at* http://www.courtinnovation.org (Center for Court Innovation, NY, 2005, NIJ grant study); David M. Kennedy, "Rethinking Law Enforcement Strategies to Prevent Intimate Partner Violence," 8 *Networks* (Spring/Summer 2004); Nancy E. Jones et al., "Men Who Batter: Profile From a Restraining Order Database," 3 *Archives of Fam. Med.* 52 (1994); Jeffrey Fagan et al., "Violent Men or Violent Husbands? Background Factors and Situational Correlates of Domestic and Extra-Intimate Partner Violence," in David Finkelhor et al., eds., *The Dark Side of Families* (1983).

[36] Kennedy, *supra* note 35.

[37] 387 U.S. 1 (1967).

HEAVY BURDEN OF PROOF

Most DV is emotional abuse, degradation, and humiliation, not broken bones and black eyes. A 2007 film, *Waitress*,[38] portrays this type of coercive control. For the reasons discussed in Chapters 2 and 11 in this volume, it is difficult to convince judges to grant protection when the abuse is intangible and causes overwhelming emotional pain. The following discussion addresses how to represent women in divorces for cruel and inhuman treatment[39] and civil protection orders.

The statutory burden of proof is a preponderance of the evidence in divorce cases and civil protection order and custody proceedings. One must prepare, however, as though the burden of proof were higher because of the issues discussed above and in Chapters 5 and 18 in this volume.[40]

SAFETY PLANNING

The first task of lawyers for DV victims is to assure they have information to keep their clients and themselves safe throughout the court process and after. Each client needs a safety plan tailored to her case. The following guidelines are generic.

Planning for the Client's Safety Before She Leaves a Violent Partner

A *safety plan* is a plan of action, with lists of resources, places of safety, trusted people, and essential documents that a woman makes for herself.

- What are the warning signs that tell the client it is time to leave?

- What would prevent her from leaving?

- Will her partner take her car keys? Her car? Her credit cards? Her cash? Put crazy glue in the car door locks? Remove the telephone? Cut the telephone line? Take her mobile (cell) phone?

- How can she get away when these last-minute problems arise?

- Plan ways to exit the home in an emergency, a safe destination, and an alternative destination with multiple, safe routes to each destination.

- Find a secure, accessible location for items needed for quick escape such as car keys, house keys, cash, credit card, driver's license, car registration, passport, green card, and some clothing.

---

[38] *Waitress* (Night and Day Pictures 2007).

[39] New York Domestic Relations Law § 170(1). New York case law holds that the violence must cause suffering (lost appetite, sleeplessness, posttraumatic stress disorder, headache, physical injury, or leaving home in fear for one's safety) and, in long marriages, must be substantial. Rios v. Rios, 29 N.Y.2d 840 (1971); Hessen v. Hessen, 33 N.Y.2d 406 (1974); but see Echevarria v. Echevarria, 40 N.Y.2d 262 (1974), which held that two *beatings* separated by five years are sufficient to satisfy the statutory standard in Domestic Relations Law § 170(1).

[40] See particularly Shockome v. Shockome, 30 A.D.3d 528 (2d Dep't 2006), where the court applied a certainty standard against the protective mother.

- Decide on a person who can be told of the violence and given instructions to call the police when suspicious noises are heard or actions observed in the home.

- Instruct the children regarding when and how to call the police.

- Instruct the children where to go, and how to get to a safe place and get help.

- When an argument may start, pick a safe room to move to: away from the kitchen, bathroom, and garage—a room where no weapons are kept and that has a door to the street.

- Act to avoid the danger. When is violence about to start? Is it time to leave?

- In a dangerous situation, give in so that the anger is diffused. Agree with the partner. Do not challenge or dispute what the partner says. Do not criticize him. Do what is necessary to appease the partner until it is safe to get away after the violent partner leaves or falls asleep.

- Leave duplicate keys, and *copies* of important documents, credit card and bank account statements (belonging to both partners), tax returns, financial records, and house deed or apartment lease, with a trusted person, or get a safe deposit box in a bank unknown to the partner and leave the key with a trusted person. Put jewelry or other valued, small things that will not be missed by the partner in the safe deposit box, or leave them with a trusted person.

- Open a separate bank account using an address different from the shared home, and leave the documents with a trusted person.

- Memorize the local DV telephone hotline number. Call it from a pay telephone or the home of a trusted person to inquire regarding their services. Do not call from a cell phone or any telephone in the shared home: the phone may be bugged, and the number may appear on the bill received by the partner.

- Do not use a cell phone or telephone credit card. The numbers called will appear on bills that the partner may see.

- Have coins for pay telephones available at all times.

- Leave clothing with a trusted person.

- Review and revise this safety plan at scheduled intervals, and review it with the children, if that is safe to do.

- Use an Internet cafe, Internet store, or copy shop for e-mail, Internet access, and making copies. Never use the home computer or the computer in an office shared with the partner for working on this plan, Do *not* use Internet banking or set up or monitor a bank or securities account on the Internet.

- Change all passwords and PINs.

- Determine how to be safe at work and traveling to and from work. Advise the supervisor and coworkers that the partner is abusive and may come to the workplace. Give them copies of the protection order. Is there an employee assistance plan at the workplace? Does the employer have a written "domestic violence" or "workplace violence" policy? If so, obtain copies.

Safety After the Client Separates From a Violent Partner

There are additional steps to take *after the client leaves* the abusive partner or when her partner has left the home. Safety planning continues with ways to secure the home; obtain and enforce a protection order; be cautious in public and at work, school, or church; and seeking emotional support.

- Install new locks on doors and windows.

- Add locks with poles that wedge into a metal slot in the floor to all street doors or apartment doors.

- Replace thin outside doors with heavy wood or metal doors, or cover doors that have glass windows with sturdy metal grills or bars.

- Install bars or metal grills over street level and accessible windows.

- Get folding escape ladders for second-story windows. Escape ladders must have extensions behind every step to keep the steps away from the building wall.

- Make an escape plan with the children—locate all possible exits.

- Have fire extinguishers and smoke and carbon monoxide alarms on every floor. (These are basic fire safety precautions for every home.)

- Install outside lighting systems that turn on when someone approaches (motion sensing) the home.

- Get a burglar alarm system connected to the local police, if available where she lives.

- Program police and fire emergency numbers into land-line and cell phones.

The client should change her routine in public places:

- Vary her route to and from work. Switch between car and public transportation when possible.

- Change her hours at work if possible.

- Request a change of shift, starting hour, or location at work, if these are possible.

- Change her parking space at work: switch with a coworker of the opposite sex. Tell her employer of her security concerns, and request a parking space close to a building exit.

- Give her employer and supervisor copies of her protection order.

- Change the exit that she uses from her workplace.

- Shop at different stores or during different hours.

- Change bank branches or banks or hours when she goes to the bank.

- Change every part of her routine that is possible to change.

- Give child care providers (in her home and at day care or after-school centers) and all schools a list of people who may pick up the children, and the name of any persons who may not take the children out or enter her home. (If she has a protection order or a restraining order, provide a copy of the order to the day care and after-school center managers, school principal, and home child care providers.)

- Inform trusted neighbors and the landlord, if she has one, to call the police if her former partner comes to her home or if they hear disturbing sounds from her home. (Be cautious of informing landlords who are known in the community to evict DV victims for fear of property damage or liability from injury caused by violent partners trying to harm the clients.)

- Devise a code number or word for the client to use with her lawyer, her friends, and her children to signal them to call the police.

- Tell the client to teach her children how to call the police, if they are mature enough.

- Tell the client to teach her children how to make a collect call to her or another trusted person if they are abducted by her former partner or anyone else they fear.

SEEKING A PROTECTION ORDER OR RESTRAINING ORDER

Protection orders and restraining orders work: most offenders obey these orders and stay away from the protected person. The police are required to make arrests for violations of protection orders and restraining orders in most states. Thus, protection orders and restraining orders improve police protection.

One must also consider the likelihood of success in court. Is the evidence strong? Is the judge presiding in the court one who grants protection orders or one who usually denies them? The lawyer does not want to risk losing in court. The offender will be emboldened and may retaliate to show he is still in control. In addition, the offender will get free discovery of the legal theory and evidence if there is a hearing or during oral argument.

Most states have central registries where all the protection orders and restraining orders are filed by the courts, so the police can check the terms of the orders and their duration, if a copy is lost or destroyed. There is a national registry, also, where one can research for orders against the client's partner in other states with different protected parties.

Protection orders and restraining orders from all states are enforced in every other state (given "full faith and credit") when the protected person files the order with the court in the state to which she has relocated. She can get better protection with the order if the following steps are taken:

- Advise the client to keep a copy of the order with her at all times and leave a copy with a trusted family member or friend, in her workplace, and with her employer or supervisor, and her employer's security chief, if they are supportive.

- File a copy of the order with the local police stations where she lives, works, and goes to school; where her children go to school, attend day care, and after-school programs; where she attends religious observances, visits relatives, and receives regular medical care; and where the children receive medical care.

- Keep additional, certified copies of all orders in her lawyer's office.

- If the police do not respond or fail to arrest the client's partner for a violation of her order, the lawyer should call their command and report this. Lawyers should be collegial with the police supervisors: their cooperation is essential to the client's safety and the safety of future clients. Lawyers should send letters to commanders praising protective police officers. These are appreciated by the officers and their commanders, and will enhance the lawyer's credibility when he or she complains.

- File a violation petition in the civil court that granted the original protection order if the evidence is good. If the evidence is weak, teach the client how to gather evidence: tape record telephone conversations; take photographs of property damage with date and time stamps for the future.

Violating a protection order or restraining order is a separate crime in addition to any other crime committed, such as assault or harassment, that may be charged in many states. If there is a criminal case, the lawyer should consult the prosecutor and share evidence; ask the prosecutor to request a protection order in the criminal case, if state law has this relief, as a condition of the defendant's pretrial release; and request high cash bail.

The client should avoid alcohol and mood altering drugs because they impair her judgment and dull her sense of danger, which puts her at risk of harm. She needs to be alert to protect herself if her former partner finds her or stalks her.

GATHERING INFORMATION

Gathering information should be done consistently in all cases, using a system that will enable the building of the case for court in a logical and compelling way.

- Obtain addresses, telephone numbers, and contact information for the client, the opposing party and lawyer, and relatives and friends of the client.

- Obtain alternative contact names, numbers, and addresses for the client.

- Discuss safety planning and prepare a safety plan with the client.

- Ask regarding both parties:
  - Ages
  - Heights
  - Weights
  - Physical health conditions and treatment histories
  - Physical disabilities or limitations
  - Drug and alcohol abuse and treatment histories
  - Employment histories
  - Mental health

    - Treatment
    - Diagnoses
    - Hospitalizations
    - Suicide threats or attempts by either party

  - Criminal convictions.

- Obtain first-hand knowledge of the following or the other party's statements about himself (threats made and admissions against penal or pecuniary interests) to the client; photos in home or shown by other party; medals, awards he has shown the client (not what client heard from friends or family):

  o Military service
  o Military training, skills, and assignments (combat duty; weapons)
  o Martial arts training and experience
  o Physical fitness: weight training

  ☐ Workout routines
  ☐ Endurance training work done requiring strength or endurance:

  - demolition or construction laborer
  - furniture moving
  - heavy equipment operator.

  o Alcohol use:

  ☐ frequency
  ☐ amounts
  ☐ types
  ☐ times of day

  o Controlled substances (drugs) used

  ☐ types
  ☐ frequency.

  o Guns in home/access elsewhere: rifles, shot guns, air guns, and hand guns (public records check will disclose licenses for hunting and hand guns).
  o Hunting knives, machetes or other hunting weapons (such as bows and arrows, and sling shots).

- Get all of the above information regarding the client, also.

ORGANIZING THE DOMESTIC VIOLENCE AND ABUSE HISTORY

DV offenders are inventive; therefore, the following are examples only. Lawyers should inquire about "other actions or events that made the client uncomfortable or fearful."

First event

- Threat with weapons, objects, dog, or to harm the client or the client's loved ones or pets or property

- Property damage

- Choking

- Arm-twisting

- Imprisoning

- Course of mental cruelty or humiliation
- Physical contact
- Shoving
- Pushing
- Crowding
- Punching
- Head banging against floor or wall
- Slapping
- Any contact
- Weapons
- Reckless driving with client or children in car
- Moving violations on driver's license, or driver's license suspension or revocation (These can be corroborated by driver's license search of public records.)
- Driving car toward pedestrian-client.

Specificity is required in pleadings to give notice to the opposing party:

- Date or holiday or memorable event, birthday, anniversary when above occurred
- Time of day
- Place: address, and room of building, outside location
- Others present (names and current contact details)
- Medical treatment: where; name of physician or nurse
- Injuries
    - Types
    - Pain
    - Incapacity
    - Duration
    - Prevented or delayed from getting medical treatment
    - Work or school missed
    - Child care prevented or impaired as result of injuries.

Worst event

- Date
- Time
- Place
- Others present (names and current contact details)
- Medical treatment

- Injuries

  o Types
  o Pain
  o Incapacity
  o Duration
  o Prevented or delayed from getting medical treatment
  o Work missed
  o Child care prevented or impaired as result of injuries.

Latest (most recent) event in pleadings (same as above).

Typical abusive acts and statements

- Describe: withholding money; not allowing contact by the client with her family or friends; refusing to allow the client to earn money or attend school; forbidding the client to go out of the home without him; preventing the client from comforting their crying infant or child.

- Usual or common location for this

- Frequency

- Others present (children, relatives, neighbors, waits until there is no one else present).

Children

- Abuse of the children: direct, inadvertent, psychological, sexual, financial

- For all of the above DV and abuse:

  o Where was child during each event?

    ☐ Same room: see and hear acts against mother
    ☐ Another room: line of sight: see from doorway or down hall

  o Hear noises and shouting and cries of pain or pleading to stop
  o Size of home

DV victims may want to believe that children "were unaware of the violence or abuse" because the children were asleep in another room. Thus, the issue of location of the children should be explored in preparation for testimony by a DV victim. Even when children were out of the house during an attack, they may have seen broken furniture, dishes, or glass, or bruises on their mother when they returned home.

All of the above must be pleaded, but the evidence should not be pleaded. Sufficient information to provide notice of the occurrence must be pleaded. The lawyer should not plead more than can be proven or clutter the pleadings with too many incidents.

In establishing the effects of DV on the children—the literature for the spectrum of potential ill effects and consequences should be examined; expert testimony, however, is needed to prove the emotional effects on the *specific* children in the case or the likely effects on them later. One may establish fear without expert witnesses when fact witnesses (the client or other people) saw the children crying, running out of the home, or hiding in a closet.

THEORY OF THE CASE

The client has no bruises or broken bones: this is a case of persistent, imminent threat of physical abuse by the physically larger and stronger man against his wife. The husband cut off her escape opportunities by depriving her of money and transportation. He isolated her from potential support by her family and friends. This is the theory or theme of the case. The current incident that precipitated legal action for a protection order or a divorce may appear insignificant, unless it is put in the context of this relationship.

The case must be presented so that the judge sees what happened and why. The petitioner's testimony must be plausible and paint a picture for the judge. The judge will grant a protection order only if the judge believes the client's fear and psychic trauma, and identifies with her. The judge must like the client and want to protect her.

Lawyers should take a skeptical view of their own cases. Strengths and weaknesses should be examined; contradictions and how they will be viewed by the judge who will decide the case should be considered.

The presiding judge's prior decisions should be researched. If this is a judge before whom the lawyer has not appeared previously, the judge should be observed hearing other cases. Other lawyers should be consulted on how this judge decides DV and abuse cases. What testimony is the judge likely to believe? What testimony should be corroborated, and what kind of corroboration will convince this judge the testimony is true?

Presentation of the case should start and finish with the strongest evidence and legal arguments. The facts should build the case without characterizing them for the judge. The lawyer should not take extreme positions, and he or she should avoid unconvincing and weak arguments and facts. Lawyers should always be aware of the strengths and weaknesses of the opponent's case and witnesses and correct for them in advance. Written and oral arguments should be factual and compelling, never argumentative.

Direct, factual arguments convince the judge. Hyperbole undermines credibility. Adjectives and adverbs should be eschewed. The use of pronouns should be limited: they may be ambiguous. The lawyer should be concise and to the point.

Legal argument should state the principle of law on which the case relies. Exceptions to that principle should not be mentioned, unless the exceptions are related to the case.

Lawyers should always maintain a calm demeanor. Self-control and a modulated voice impress the judge. Politeness and respect for the court will cause the judge to listen. When confronted with a raging opposing counsel, replying slowly in a modulated, controlled voice forces the opponent to lower his or her voice, too.

MARSHALING EXHIBITS AND WITNESSES

All possible types of documentary and physical evidence and expert witnesses to prove the case should be reviewed:

- Medical records: authenticate and establish business records exception to hearsay through facility's medical records supervisor or manager; follow local rules of evidence.

- X-rays and CT scans: radiologist to authenticate and interpret injuries.

- Photographs of injuries and property damage: client or anyone who saw client at the time the photograph was taken can testify that the photo is an accurate representation of the client's appearance (neighbor, family member, friend, does not need to be person who took photograph).
- Torn or blood-stained clothing.
- Clothing damaged by chemicals thrown at client.
- Broken furniture, dishes, objects, and computers.
- Damaged files, documents, and papers.
- Stalking and cyberstalking evidence: letters; e-mail messages, phone answering machine tapes; CCTV tapes; video tape and photographs of stalker in locations near client (get street signs in photos or videos).
- Eye witnesses and other fact witnesses (including police officers and 911 tapes).
- Expert witnesses: MD, RN, and/or forensic pathologist (medical examiner can testify to etiology of injuries in living people—not limited to deceased people), physical therapist, and/or rehabilitation expert.
- Client's psychotherapists, psychologists, or other counselors for victim (and/or children).
- Clinical social workers.
- Clergy.

(Note: Privileged communication will be waived by presentation of medical, mental health, and clergy witnesses.)

DISCOVERY BUILDS THE CASE

Discovery wins cases and leads to favorable settlements. Discovery has multiple uses. It is a way to obtain evidence from the opposition, assess the opposition witnesses, and find the weaknesses in the opposing case. Discovery provides the opportunity to demonstrate the strength of one's case to the opposing lawyer and the opposing party.

Questioning in discovery is not limited by the rules of evidence. Ask fact witnesses for opinions, reasons, hearsay, and rumors. None of these questions may lead to admissible answers, but they may provide background that leads to new witnesses and admissible evidence. If depositions are unaffordable, or when some questions in a deposition are forgotten, try serving interrogatories, or expected answers can be drafted and served in a request to admit.[41]

When safety is a concern for the client and her lawyer, the lawyer should request that the depositions be held at the court house with a court officer present.

PRELIMINARY STRATEGIC PLANNING FOR COURT

Opposing Mediation

Mediation should be avoided in DV cases. Arguments against a mediation referral by the court should be prepared. The statutes and court rules regarding mediation in cases

---

[41] Fed. R. Civ. Proc. 36 or the state equivalent.

in which there is DV should be reviewed. Many states prohibit mediation in DV cases. Furthermore, there are no data showing that mediated agreements in DV cases produce better results for mothers or children. In addition, the following arguments may be used.

Mediation proscribes discussion of past violence, psychological abuse, and coercive control. It is designed to guide the parties to reach voluntary agreement for future cooperation, only. Mediation, therefore, is dangerous for victims of DV because they are unable to assert their safety needs or seek court protection for themselves and their children.[42] Also, DV victims risk retaliation if they disclose abuse in the presence of the offenders during mediation sessions.

By contrast, in court proceedings, judges have the power to set limits on offender behavior and impose penalties for violations of court orders. The victims are not responsible for the offenders not succeeding because judges make the orders and shift the power from the offenders to the court. Robust court response protects victims.[43]

Thus, it is essential to insist on a trial or hearing when settlement offers leave women and their children at continued risk of harm.[44] When one goes to trial, the evidence must be organized to paint a picture of the parties, their relationship, the abuse, and the effect of spouse abuse on the victim and the children. Corroborating evidence must be presented to overcome the special problems in DV cases, without cluttering the record with too many incidents, cumulative evidence, or extraneous matter.

Opposing Mental Health Evaluation

When there are no mental health issues, it should be argued that mental health evaluations do not provide evidence establishing or rebutting allegations of DV or abuse. Thus, mental health evaluations delay trial without providing competent evidence and increase the cost of litigation. Only the court can determine the facts by taking testimony; therefore, a prompt commencement of the trial is the most appropriate procedure.

EARLY CASE ASSESSMENT PREPARATION

After the lawyer has marshaled the evidence, he or she will be ready to prepare an offer of proof listing documentary and real evidence, fact and expert witnesses, with a brief statement of what each will establish. This will demonstrate that the case is a DV or abuse case in which the *facts* should be heard by the court. At this point in the case, showing evidence may move the offender's lawyer to talk reasonable settlement.

Custody and visitation issues should be tried first and early, as soon as possible after the preliminary conference, and before appointment of neutral, forensic mental health evaluators and financial disclosure begins. This procedure gives the children the security of knowing promptly what the residence and visiting arrangements will be. Delay in determining custody and visitation causes anxiety for children,

Deciding custody first removes the children issues from the financial bargaining process. It provides the opportunity to present the effect of DV and abuse on the children

---

[42] Laura Nadler, "Controlling Processes in the Practice of Law: Hierarchy and Pacification in the Movement to Reform Dispute Ideology," 9 *Ohio St. J. Dispute Res.* 1 (1993); Trina Grillo, "The Mediation Alternative: Process Dangers for Women," 100(6) *Yale L.J.* 1545 (1991).

[43] Dugan, Nagin & Rosenfeld, *supra* note 11.

[44] *See In re* Gault, 387 U.S. 1 (1967), holding due process applies in Family Court.

and show the judge that protection is needed for the children and the mother. This may be the only opportunity to present the DV evidence in states with no-fault divorce.

The lawyer should show that the case is not a "high-conflict" revenge fight, using the children as weapons to avenge marital misconduct, and not a case with mental health issues. The "high-conflict" label will make the client appear unreasonable and irrational. ("Women want to cause pain in divorces,"[45] whereas men are practical and want to settle the finances rationally: these are the myths that must be overcome.)

DAMAGE CONTROL FOR MENTAL HEALTH EVALUATIONS

If a mental health evaluation is required, the lawyer should request that the judge specify the following information in an order:

- Issues to be assessed by the mental health professional;

- Maximum hourly fee to be charged;

- Total fee that may be charged without prior approval of the court for an increase;

- Who is to pay the fee of the mental health professional;

- Date when the report is to be completed;

- Where the report is to be filed in the court;

- Whether all lawyers are to receive copies of the report on the day it is filed with the court;

- If the judge will not see the report until it is received in evidence or upon stipulation of all the lawyers;

- Mental health professional is to speak the language of the parties, and interpreters will not be used for interviews with non-English speaking parties and collaterals;

- Mental health professional is to have expertise in the culture of the parties;

- Substance abuse issues are to be assessed through repeated, random, surprised, directly observed provision of samples and laboratory testing.

The lawyer can offer to draw the order for the court and serve it on the other lawyers before submitting the order for the judge's signature.

PREPARING THE CLIENT FOR THE MENTAL HEALTH EVALUATION

When the court orders a mental health evaluation because there are mental issues or despite claims that there are no mental health issues, the lawyer must prepare his

---

[45] Statement by a woman lawyer in response to question by the presenter during a continuing legal education program on negotiation skills at the New York City Bar Association in September 2007. The audience members laughed.

or her client for the interview. The client should be prepared to tell the truth. (If she tells the truth, as the saying goes, she does not need to remember anything.) The client should be alerted to the following:

- She should not be defensive.

- She should not take responsibility for all that went wrong in her marriage.

- She may admit her faults.

- She should not apologize or make excuses for her spouse's bad behavior, violence, verbal abuse, and degrading and humiliating behavior toward her.

- She may acknowledge her spouse's positive attributes but not to the extent that this is inconsistent with her claims of his abuse or poor parental capacity. (If she says he is a great father, who takes good care of his children and would never harm them, then she can expect that the judge will grant the father equal time with his children, and without supervision.)

- If the father loves the children, she may acknowledge that.

- If the father is at risk of harming the children intentionally or through negligence, then she must state what he did in the past that is the basis for her fear that he may harm her and the children in the future.

- She must be specific; vague or conclusory allegations are not credible.

SUBSTANCE ABUSE ASSESSMENT

When substance abuse allegations are made, courts often order mental health evaluations. These are ineffective unless the parties admit their substance abuse. The way to prove or rebut substance abuse allegations is to seek a court order that testing for controlled substances be done by random, surprise, directly observed laboratory samples. The order should specify the laboratory, the total number of tests to be performed, and the person responsible for notifying the party when to appear at the laboratory for the tests and reporting the test results to the court and all lawyers, and the party responsible to pay for the tests should be designated.

PREPARING FOR EXAMINATIONS OF EXPERT WITNESSES

First, comply with the civil practice law notice requirements when the lawyer intends to call an expert witness. These may include a time period in advance of the trial within which the notice must be given. The expert's curriculum vitae and a list of the expert's conclusions. The scholarly literature and theories on which the expert relies may be required also. The lawyer should review the curriculum vitae of every expert and read the scholarly literature to prepare for the examinations and cross-examinations.

There are two types of expert witness examination preparations: for examination of the client's expert and for examination of the court-appointed neutral expert and the opponent's expert witness. The client's expert should be asked to assist in preparing questions to be posed to him or her and questions to ask the other experts. The client's expert must review the reports of the other experts to criticize their theories, the literature on which they relied, and their methods, and rebut their conclusions. Your expert may attend the depositions of the other experts.

These are the goals of the examinations:

- Lay the foundation for qualification of the client's expert: education, training and experience, articles written, professional affiliations, and professional licenses; knowledge of DV, foreign language and cultural issues, and other special issues in the case; scholarly literature consulted or relied on. Request the court to qualify the witness as an expert.

- Before the court rules on the opposing expert's qualifications, request to cross-examine opponent's experts regarding their education, training, and experience; professional affiliations, and professional licenses; biases; for which parties they have testified in the past (victims or accused) and how many times; knowledge of DV, foreign language, cultural issues, and other special issues in the case; theories, scholarly literature consulted or relied on, and methods. Then, consent or state any objections to qualifying the opposing witness as an expert.

When court-ordered mental health evaluation reports are inaccurate and prejudicial to their clients, lawyers should object to the reports being admitted in evidence, request examination of the makers of the reports, and advance copies of the evaluator's interview notes and raw test results. These should be reviewed by the client's expert who will help prepare questions to ask the evaluator.

- If the court-appointed mental health expert is to be impeached, cross-examine him or her on the same issues as the opponent's expert; otherwise consent to the qualification of the court-appointed expert.

- On direct and cross-examination, ask experts to identify and explain

  o theoretical bases of their opinions, conclusions, and recommendations,
  o scholarly literature upon which they rely,
  o sources of factual information,
  o extent of reliance on self-report by the parties and multilevel hearsay,
  o collateral sources interviewed and documents reviewed,
  o views of the reliability of the parties' descriptions of events and the reasons for those views,
  o explanations of internal inconsistencies in their reports and discrepancies between raw data, test results, and their opinions in the reports and testimony;
  o knowledge and understanding of other pending court cases between the parties and prior court cases and orders or criminal convictions.

PRESENTING FACT EVIDENCE AT TRIAL

Eye witnesses—police, neighbors, family members, friends, and former partners—should be presented to corroborate the victim's descriptions of events and their aftermath, and the offender's intent to harm based on a history of the same acts against the victim and other women, and as rebuttal witnesses if the offender testifies denying prior DV. Other potential fact witnesses and evidence include the following:

- Teachers;

- Day care center staff;

- School nurse;

- School social worker (regarding changes in children's academic performance, attention, and behavior);

- Public records (certified copies only);

- Criminal convictions (databases);

- Criminal history evidence including police records (DV incident reports (DIR))

  o Weapons used: sticks, belts, kitchen implements, firearms, dogs, vehicles,
  o Probation or parole record (although confidential—court can get access),
  o Warrants for arrest;

- Protection orders;

- Weapons permits;

- Hunting licenses;

- Driving while intoxicated convictions

  o Moving violations,
  o Points on license (shows recklessness—corroborates an allegation of endangering and frightening family members if they were in the car).

Chain of custody must be maintained for all real evidence: items should be stored in a locked office safe or bank safety deposit box, to which only the witness or the lawyer has access.

FACT WITNESS PREPARATION

The client and other fact witnesses should be provided with advance notice of the questions that will be asked and what they can expect in court. The appropriate demeanor for witnesses should be explained as well. Lawyers should provide an opportunity for the witnesses to ask questions. The witnesses should never be told what to testify. They should be warned to answer truthfully when asked if they discussed their testimony with anyone. The truthful answer is, "Yes, [name of the lawyer]." The next question will be, "What did she tell you?" Answer, "To tell the truth." Lawyers should advise witnesses of the following:

- Tell the truth.

- Answer questions directly, without hesitation, and without looking at the judge (to gauge his or her reaction).

- Look at the person asking questions; maintain eye contact with the questioner.

- Cry when appropriate to the content of the testimony.

- No anger.

- No shouting at the other party.

- No looking at the other party.

- No volunteering.

- No embellishing.

- No minimizing.

- No defensiveness.

- No excusing the other party's abuse or violence ("he was upset; tired; lost job; reacting to family loss").

- No boot-strapping testimony by reference to the statements of others ("my neighbor said I should get a divorce"; "mother said I should have called police") or actions of nonparties or statements made to others out of court, such as "I told my mother."

- Describing the actions of others is permitted in these circumstances: "police put handcuffs on and took him away"; "child called police"; "child ran out of home"; "doctor gave me an injection, admitted me to the hospital, and took X-rays."

Lawyer should be aware of hearsay issues and check their state court decisions following recent U.S. Supreme Court decisions.[46]

EXAMINING PARTY REQUESTING PROTECTION ORDER AND CUSTODY

The purpose of this examination is to give the court the facts in a way that paints a picture of the parties and their relationship so the court understands how the victim suffered from abuse:

- Married to other party? When? Where?

- Children in common with other party? Dates of birth? Where residing at time of incidents and at time of testimony?

- Related to other party (spouse; unmarried partner; brother; cousin; mother)?

- What is being requested of the court?

- Why (frightened, injured, threatened)?

- Why frightened by threats (ability and inclination of the other party to carry out threats)?

- Where other party lives?

- Height of both parties?

---

[46] Crawford v. Washington, 541 U.S. 36 (2004); Davis v. Washington and Hammon v. Indiana, 126 S. Ct. 2266 (2006) (decided in a single opinion).

- Weight of both parties?

- Military service (of both parties and for the following questions also)?

- Military training, skills, and assignments (combat duty, weapons)?

- Martial arts training and experience?

- Physical fitness? Weight training? Workout routine? Endurance training? Employment (construction, other physically demanding job)?

- Alcohol use? Frequency? Amounts? Types?

- Driving while intoxicated (certified copies of criminal dispositions)?

- Motor vehicle records, license suspension or revocation?

- Controlled substances (drugs) used? Types? Frequency?

- Drug possession/sales convictions (certified copies of dispositions)? (This creates risk to children from drugs in the home and from drug dealers and purchasers coming to the home with weapons, disputes over payment, violence.).

- Weapons possession conviction?

- Guns in home/access elsewhere: long guns and hand guns?

- Concealed weapon/hand gun license?

- Hunting license?

- Hunting knives or other hunting weapons?

- Employment (other party unemployed: around home all the time or travels out of office to job sites with opportunity to stalk during work hours)?

- Employer discipline or termination (reasons stated by DV offender to the client may be admissions against penal or pecuniary interest of declarant, therefore admissible)?

When custody is in issue, some statutes provide that there is not a right to confidential mental health records. Developing the victim's mental health problems to show she suffered as a result of the abuse could have a negative impact on the custody decision by showing plaintiff's parental capacity is compromised as a result of suffering DV or abuse.

Testimony by plaintiff's treating mental health professional can show that when DV stopped—when the defendant was out of the home and stayed away—plaintiff recovered from anxiety, posttraumatic stress disorder, other problems, and that parental capacity is restored. The lawyer should be prepared to ascertain the following concerning the client:

- Treatment?

- Diagnoses?

- Hospitalizations?

- Medications?

- Suicide threats or attempts by DV offender? (Lawyer should get expert testimony regarding heightened risk of homicide by suicidal person; this is not common knowledge.)

- Ever injured?

  o By whom?
  o Date?
  o Time?
  o Place?
  o Injuries (describe)?
  o Types

    ☐ Pain,
    ☐ Incapacity,
    ☐ Duration?

  o Prevented or delayed from getting medical treatment?
  o Medical treatment: Where? By whom—name of doctor or nurse; clinic or hospital—admitted for inpatient treatment, or in doctor's office?
  o Who was present during assault or immediately after?
  o Photos taken?
  o Work missed?
  o Child care prevented or impaired as result of injuries?

- Children in home during attack?

  o Sound insulation of home (hear everything in next room or from below or above on another floor)?
  o Child's reaction

    ☐ Crying,
    ☐ Running out of home,
    ☐ Calling police, neighbors, grandparents, and or other relatives,
    ☐ Hiding; where?

REQUESTING PROVISIONS IN PROTECTION ORDERS

If the judge makes findings of fact and concludes that the client is entitled to a protection order, the lawyer should ask for provisions in the protection order that meet the specific needs of the client and her children. Stay-away provisions should include all locations frequented by the client and the children: day care centers; home child care providers; schools; workplaces; homes of family members and friends visited; places of medical treatment; places of worship. Lawyers should be creative and expansive. The lawyer and his or her client are the experts regarding the client's activities and movements. The judge must be educated regarding the client's needs.

If allowed in the statutes of the client's state, custody of the children should be requested along with denial of visits by the respondent, or supervised visits, specifying the supervisor, time, and location, and transfer provisions should be requested. (Police stations should be avoided: they are not safe places for the children, and the officers will not supervise the exchange. They will be attending to prisoners and the public.)

When the client receives possession of the shared home and the respondent is excluded, a date and time by which the respondent is to leave the home should be specified in the order, and the police should be directed to be present to keep the peace. A list of the items respondent is to be allowed to remove and the date and time for him to remove those items should also be requested, and, again, the police should be directed to attend to keep the peace.

If the client is leaving the joint home, have her prepare an inventory before the court date while she is in the home and can look around. The order should list all the items she may take with her including the clothing, beds, bedding, books, toys, dressers, and computers of the children, if she is taking the children. All the items of hers that she may take should be listed: her clothing, tools, computers, financial records, legal documents, books, selected furniture, clothes washer and dryer (for the children), television, VCR/DVD player, and anything else she needs or bought. The date and time at which she can remove the items should be specified in the order, and, again, the police should be directed to attend and keep the peace.

Vehicles are special problems because the registration may control who gets possession of them. Vehicles are essential where public transportation is inadequate, and DV offenders damage and take vehicles to isolate their victims and prevent them from earning income.

VIOLATION OF PROTECTION ORDER HEARING

The violation hearings begin with documentary evidence: a certified copy of the protection order and proof of service. Then follows the examination of the protected party to establish the factual basis of the violation claim and how the client was injured by the violation. The injury may be fear, financial loss, lost employment, eviction, moving to a new home, and, for safety reasons, hiding and losing contact with family and friends. Then, other fact witnesses and expert witnesses are presented.

If incarceration for civil contempt of court is a remedy in the client's jurisdiction, the burden of proof may be beyond a reasonable doubt or clear and convincing evidence, not preponderance of the evidence. In some states, violations of protection orders are also crimes that may be prosecuted by the state. In those jurisdictions, the lawyer for the protected party/complainant should assist the prosecutor with evidence and client preparation for testimony.

1. A court certified copy of the order alleged to have been violated should be introduced, or the court should be asked to take judicial notice of the original order in the court file that is before the judge. (The original order and whole case file must be in courtroom for a civil protection order violation proceeding. This should be checked in advance with the clerk or by serving a subpoena "so ordered" by the trial judge or clerk's office in another court to have the file sent to the court where the violation proceeding is being heard.)

2. The affidavit of service of the order must be introduced, or the restrained party's signature on the original in the court file, which is acknowledgement that the restrained party received a copy in the court room on the day the order was made should be mentioned, or the court should be asked to take judicial notice of the court record or file showing that the restrained party was in the courtroom when the order was made and therefore knew the contents of the order, even though he left court without waiting to receive a copy. Actual knowledge is sufficient for a contempt finding even when there is no proof of service of the signed order, or the restrained party left the court before receiving a copy of the order. (Check your state's civil contempt statutory and case law.)

3. Event(s) that violated the order of protection should be described:

   a. Dates, locations, others present, child issues from above;

   b. No communication orders: flowers sent, other gifts, cards, all communications received by protected party from the restrained party;

   c. No contact: at door; in hallway of apartment building, at work place or school; on porch or steps of house or building; in front of home standing on public sidewalk or sitting in car on street or—any sighting;

   d. Stalking;

   e. Other (specific) details about what the restrained party did (not what protected person did and not what other people did—omit "my neighbor called the police" testimony).

CONCLUSION

Representing victims of DV and abuse is saving lives, physically and emotionally. Every protection order, divorce judgment, and custody order with no contact or limited contact by the offender is a homicide prevented. Lawyers should prepare and try each case with this responsibility in mind.

Lawyers are teachers. Our role is to educate judges: to teach them the realities of our cases—one case at a time. We must put a human being at the center of a picture of humiliation, degradation, and pain. Judicial seminars cannot accomplish this. Seminars may provide tools for judges, but those tools will be applied *only* when the lawyer proves the facts.

Although judicial seminars include presentations by survivors of DV, those presentations are of insufficient duration to present complete portraits of their lives. The survivors who speak in public are recovering and able to tell their stories. They look and sound strong. They are not the women the judges see making applications for protection orders or in custody and divorce trials.

Everyday in court, judges hear testimony from women who are still in the grip of the offenders and are uncertain if the judges will believe them and grant them protection. The women are in reasonable fear of retaliation and may give hesitant, incomplete testimony. It is *not* by relying on "trained" judges, but rather through *thorough preparation of cases* that lawyers can overcome these obstacles to protection for their clients.

Chapter 20

Fighting False Allegations of Parental Alienation Raised as Defenses to Valid Claims of Abuse

by Nancy S. Erickson, J.D., L.L.M., M.A.

[E]mphasis on child safety must be a much larger focus and much more attention must be paid to the gender bias that has led to the widespread acceptance
of myths that mothers are more likely to make false allegations and that
children who resist visitation have [Parental Alienation Syndrome or parental
alienation].[1]

INTRODUCTION

Frightening numbers of good parents—usually mothers—have lost legal and/
or residential custody[2] of their children on the theory that they have been guilty of
Parental Alienation Syndrome (PAS), parental alienation, or some similar term. Often
the mother also has lost all visitation rights with the children or is permitted only
supervised visitation. In many, if not most, of these cases, the father accused the
mother of alienation in retaliation against a valid accusation that he was abusive to the
children (sometimes sexual abuse) or exposed the children to the domestic violence
(DV) that he perpetrated on the mother.[3]

Once a PAS or parental alienation accusation is made, it is often given credence
by attorneys, judges, and mental health professionals despite a lack of factual evidence
to back it up.[4] There are strong reasons to believe that the concept of PAS gained
credibility because of the sex stereotypes about women that pervade our society.[5]

---

[1] Geraldine B. Stahly, "Domestic Violence and Child Custody: A Critique of Recent
[*Journal of Child Custody*] Articles," 4(3/4) *J. Child Custody* 1, 11 (2007).

[2] Legal custody is the authority to make decisions regarding the child, such as decisions
concerning education, religion, medical care, etc. Residential custody is physical custody (i.e.,
the residential custody determination decides with whom the child will live). If legal custody
is joint and the parents do not agree, then one parent may have to go back to court to get a ruling on the disputed issue. Sometimes a court order states that residential custody is "joint" or
"shared," which simply means that the child spends some time with one parent and some time
with the other parent. However, in situations in which one parent has sole residential custody
and the other has overnight visitation, it could be said that they are "sharing" residential custody, so the term "shared" or "joint" residential custody may be really meaningless, except that
the noncustodial parent may prefer the label of "shared" or "joint" custody.

[3] Many protective parent mothers who lost custody on an alienation theory filed a petition
against the United States with the Inter-American Commission on Human Rights in May 2007.
The petition and supporting documentation is available on the Stop Family Violence Web site,
http://www.stopfamilyviolence.org.

[4] See many of the cases cited *supra* note 3, which were taken to the Inter-American
Commission on Human Rights. See also cases discussed in Lenore E.A. Walker, Kristi L.
Brantley & Justin A. Rigsbee, "A Critical Analysis of Parental Alienation Syndrome and Its
Admissibility in the Family Court," 1(2) *J. Child Custody* 47 (2004), especially *Hanson v.
Spolnik,* 685 N.E.2d 71 (Ind. Ct. App. 1997), discussed on page 68.

[5] *See, e.g.,* Michele A. Adams, "Framing Contests in Child Custody Disputes: Parental
Alienation Syndrome, Child Abuse, Gender, and Fathers' Rights," 40 *Fam. L.Q.* 315 (2006).

The mother is viewed as guilty until she proves she is innocent, custody is transferred to the father, and the mother is allowed only supervised visitation (if she is allowed any visitation at all) on the theory that if she is not supervised, she will continue to engage in alienation. In other words, currently there appears to be a strong presumption that mothers claiming abuse are lying and are actually alienating their children, especially if the children express fear or concern about contact with the other parent. The result for the child in a situation such as this is that the child often is placed with a parent who is an abuser, and if the child is abused by him, he/she has no one to tell—he/she is being kept from her protective parent.

Some children do favor one parent over the other. Some children even disfavor one parent (or both) to the extent that they do not want to be with that parent (or both parents) and may not even want to visit that parent (or parents). However, antipathy shown by a child to a parent usually is not a result of anything the other parent has done or said. Often such a child has valid reasons for his/her fear or dislike of a parent (e.g., abuse, neglect, or abandonment by the parent, or DV by the parent witnessed by the child).[6]

There is a kernel of truth behind the theory of parental alienation. Parents sometimes do badmouth each other, even during an ongoing marriage. During a divorce, the badmouthing may escalate, as the trust and love the parents presumably had for each other earlier in their relationship is broken down. This should be no surprise to anyone—divorce does not bring out the best in people. One or both parents may even intentionally attempt to get the children on their side by unloading on the children a litany of complaints against the other parent. Again, this should be no surprise to anyone—it is very common in divorces. It is wrong. It is not good for children to be put in the middle of the parents' disputes. But it happens. Usually it fades away after the litigation is over.

However, when one parent accuses the other parent of "alienating" the children, this is usually an accusation of something more vicious than badmouthing, namely, intentionally and maliciously lying to the children about the other parent in order to brainwash the children into believing that the other parent is evil and must be totally shunned by the children—to the point where the children parrot back to other adults the lies the parent has planted in the children's brains.

While badmouthing is all too common, attempting to "alienate" the children (as defined above) is rare.[7] Yet, abusers would have us believe that it is not rare—that mothers do it all the time—and that often the particular "lies" a mother tries to brainwash the children into believing (and parroting back to other adults) are that the father has abused the mother and/or the children.

Another possible reason why judges might favor fathers in these situations is the assumption that the relationship between a mother and child is stronger than that between a father and child, so the court is unconsciously and unfairly compensating by favoring the father.

[6] *See, e.g.,* Janet R. Johnston, "Parental Alignments and Rejection: An Empirical Study of Alienation in Children of Divorce," 31 *J. Am. Acad. Psychiatry & L.* 158 (2003).

[7] Joan S. Meier, *Getting Real About Abuse and Alienation: A Response to Drozd and Olesen* (forthcoming 2009) (manuscript at 15-16, on file with author) [hereinafter Meier 2009a]; Joan B. Kelly & Janet R. Johnston, "The Alienated Child: A Reformulation of Parent Alienation Syndrome," 39 *Fam. Ct. Rev.* 249 (2001). Some mental health professionals who are PAs adherents continue to claim that PAS occurs often. *See, e.g.,* Daniel J. Rybicki, *Parental Alienation and Enmeshment Issues in Child Custody Cases*, http://www.forenpsychservices.com/PAS.html.

Unlike parental alienation, spousal abuse and child abuse are very common.[8] Although many people believe that mothers often fabricate stories of DV or child abuse in order to "get the upper hand" in divorce or custody cases, research has shown that this is a myth.[9] Mothers generally allege DV and/or child abuse because it has occurred, and they are seeking protection for themselves and their children. In fact, they often keep silent about the father's abuse, particularly while divorce or custody litigation is going on, for fear of retaliation from the abuser.

In short, most accusations of alienation are false. They are attempts by abusers to defend themselves against valid accusations of abuse by diverting the attention of judges and others involved in the legal system away from their wrongdoing and focusing instead on their victims' behavior, which they falsely label as "alienating." So-called fathers' rights Web sites are full of materials suggesting that fathers should use the parental alienation tactic to get custody.[10]

This chapter will deal with false alienation accusations that arise in the context described above, where an abusive father claims the mother is attempting to alienate the children against him, when actually she is simply trying to protect the children and herself against the abuser. We will call that parent the "protective parent." The protective parent will be referred to as the mother, because statistically speaking the

---

[8] Several studies suggest that over two-thirds of custody disputes include allegations of partner violence and abuse. *See* Janet R. Johnston, "High-Conflict Divorce," 4 *Future of Children* 165 (1994); Janet R. Johnston & Linda E.G. Campbell, *Impasses of Divorce: The Dynamics and Resolution of Family Conflict* (1988), *cited in* Geraldine B. Stahly, "Domestic Violence and Child Custody: A Critique of Recent JCC [*Journal of Child Custody*] Articles," 4(3/4) *J. Child Custody* 1, 5 (2007). See also statistics cited in Chapter 1 in this volume.

[9] *See, e.g.,* Stephanie Dallam & Joyanna Silberg, "Myths That Place Children at Risk During Custody Disputes," 9(3) *Sexual Assault Rep.* 33 (2006). In a research article published by the Department of Justice Canada, Nicholas M.C. Bala et al. summarized several research studies of abuse allegations and indicated that the authors of at least three studies specifi-cally concluded that false allegations were rare: David P.H. Jones & J. Melbourne McGraw, "Reliable and Fictitious Accounts of Sexual Abuse to Children," 2 *J. Interpersonal Violence* 27 (1987) (study of 576 reported cases of child sexual abuse in Denver, Colorado); Thea Brown et al. "Problems and Solutions in the Management of Child Abuse Allegations in Custody and Access Disputes in the Family Court," 36 *Fam. & Conciliation Cts. Rev.* 431 (1998) (study of 200 cases in Australia); L.J. Hlady & E.J. Gunter, "Brief Communication: Alleged Child Abuse in Custody Access Disputes," 14 *Child Abuse & Neglect* 591 (1990) (study of 370 children—forty-one of whom were the subject of custody and access disputes—in British Columbia's Children's Hospital, Canada). The latter two studies dealt specifically with child abuse allegations in custody cases. Nicholas M.C. Bala et al., *Allegations of Child Abuse in the Context of Parental Separation: A Discussion Paper* 27-28 (2001), *available at* http://www. justice.gc.ca/eng/pi/pad-rpad/rep-rap/2001_4.html. Now that many abusive fathers are getting custody by using PAS as a defense or for other reasons, if a mother who has heard of this trend (and many have) ever considers making allegations of abuse against a father—even valid allega-tions—she will certainly be fearful that by so doing she will trigger a loss of custody. Therefore, the argument that abusers make that mothers make false allegations in order to get a benefit in custody cases will not have any validity at all—in fact, mothers will be afraid to reveal the abuse at all for fear that they will be branded "alienators" and lose custody to the abusers. There still are women who think that truth and justice will win out, and the court will protect children, but they often find out that they were naïve, and the children are given to the abusers.

[10] Putting the search terms "father" and "custody" into Google brings up huge numbers of father-supremacist sites promoting PAS and parental alienation. Some have names and descrip-tions that disguise their father-supremacist purposes. *See, e.g.,* Children's Rights Council, http://www.crckids.org. See Chapter 4 in this volume.

overwhelming number of abusers are fathers and most protective parents are mothers (however, the roles could be reversed).

Ironically, when a parent actually does try to alienate the children from the other parent, the alienating parent is quite often the abusive parent.[11] A father's attempts to alienate the children are part of his abuse. If he does not get custody, he uses his visitations with the children to attempt to alienate them from their mother.[12] If he manages to manipulate the court into giving him custody by claiming that the mother is alienating the children, he then tries to do the very thing he has accused her of doing—destroying the relationship between the parent and the children. Sometimes he succeeds. Yet, when the mother looks to the court to protect the children against this real parental alienation, the court often turns away. The children remain with the abuser unless and until the children escape from him,[13]

---

[11] *See, e.g.,* Janet R. Johnston & Joan B. Kelly, "Commentary on Walker, Brantley, and Rigsbee's (2004) 'A Critical Analysis of Parental Alienation Syndrome and Its Admissibility in the Family Court,'" 1(4) *J. Child Custody* 77, 81 (2004). An abuser often seeks custody as a tactic to force his victim to return to him or to punish her for leaving him. Thus, it should be no surprise when an abusive father tries to alienate the children from their mother—if he gets custody, that is not enough, because he wants to force her either to return to him (and the children) or to suffer total deprivation of their company. And if he does not get custody (vengeance) from the court, he will try to get it outside of court. One common tactic of an abuser who gets custody is to schedule fun activities at times when the mother is supposed to have visitation, so that if the mother insists on her visitation, the children will be angry at her for depriving them of the fun activity the father has planned. If she does not insist on her visitation, then she misses out on time with them. Thus, she cannot win, unless she can get make-up visitation, which the abuser usually refuses. This is a tactic that actually interferes with her visitation, as opposed to an occasional negative statement that a parent might make. Occasionally, of course, special events come up that would justify a one-time interference with the noncustodial parent's visitation, but abusers make it a practice to try to interfere with the mothers' visitations. Dr. Joyana Silberg used the term "domestic violence by proxy" to refer to those tactics of abusers. Silberg points out that these are conscious strategies involving abuse, coercion, and threats that abusers use to drive a wedge between children and their preferred parents. Presentation by Dr. Joyanna Silberg at the Fourteenth International Conference on Violence, Abuse and Trauma, San Diego, CA (Sept. 25, 2009).

[12] *See, e.g.,* the Staten Island Family Court case (unreported) of *Vanjak v. Pesa,* in New York County Lawyers' Association (NYCLA), *Interdisciplinary Forum: Effective Legal and Therapeutic Responses to Alienated Children in Divorce and Custody Settings* 8-1 (2007). This book was prepared in connection with a course presented at NYCLA on February 28, 2007. At the course, the mother in *Vanjak v. Pesa,* Tatjana Vanjak, spoke about her case. She reported that the noncustodial father, Emil Pesa, had succeeded in alienating their three children from her by, among other things, forcing them to play a game in which they got points if they demonstrated their hatred and disdain for their mother and had points taken away if they showed her any affection or respect. High numbers of points were rewarded with gifts and privileges. The children competed with each other and tattled on each other, so that, for example, if one child saw another child hug their mother, she would report it to the father and get points. Ms. Vanjak did manage to get the father's contacts with the children restricted by the court. With therapy, the children were brought back to a semblance of normality. However, the litigation was enormously expensive and could not have been successful if the mother and her new husband had not devoted all of their substantial resources to the case. This case illustrates how abusers try to alienate their children from the mothers but also illustrates why mothers, who are usually the lower-income parent, are at a disadvantage in court.

[13] See some of the cases described on the Courageous Kids (CK) Network Web site, http://www.courageouskids.net. One child simply left his abusive father's home and hid with various friends until he could get to the town where his mother lived, and then he sought the assistance of child protective services (CPS) in that town, and CPS assisted him. The Web site states that many of the children who are part of the CK Network were placed in the custody of their abusive fathers by the courts and that their own attorneys and the custody evaluators did not believe them and did not help them even when they cried out for help.

grow up and leave him,[14] or are saved by some extraordinary piece of good luck or skillful litigation.[15]

The final part of this chapter will suggest ways for a parent whose children have been abused by the other parent or who themselves have been abused by the other parent to fight false allegations of parental alienation in custody cases. Alienation arguments have also been used by noncustodial parents to prevent custodial parents from getting child support or to terminate child support;[16] however, this chapter will be limited to the custody context. These suggestions will be tentative, because, to date, there has been no concerted effort to collect, explore, and test such suggestions to see how successful they may prove to be.

DEFINING PARENTAL ALIENATION

When the abuser cries parental alienation (or PAS), he rarely defines his accusation. PAS and parental alienation are not recognized medical or psychological syndromes or symptoms or diagnoses, so their definitions cannot be found in any reputable medical source.[17] The father accusing the mother of parental alienation usually just claims the mother is alienating the children from him. He may state the children are reluctant to visit with him, tell him they do not want to see him, or otherwise express fear or dislike of him. His reports of the children's feelings may or may not be true. However, even if the children are, in fact, expressing those

---

[14] At the Battered Mothers Custody Conference (BMCC) on January 6, 2006, at Siena College in Loudenville, NY (near Albany), Sarah Schottenstein told her story of being held virtually hostage by her father, who had obtained custody of her and her younger sister, of the abuse she suffered at his hands, and of how she left his home the day she turned eighteen and went to live with her protective mother. Sarah's father is a wealthy Ohio businessman, whose name is known throughout the state.

[15] Some examples of such pieces of good luck are situations when (1) a new spouse of the abuser reports his abuse of her or of the children, (2) the abuser gets remarried and the new spouse does not want to take on the responsibility of caring for her new husband's child, (3) the abuser is arrested and convicted of a crime. In no case mentioned on the CK Network Website (see *supra* note 13) did the courts take action when the abuser cut off the visitation of the mother. She had been demonized to the extent that the court would not listen to her or to the children.

[16] Noncustodial parents are assisted in their attempts to get out of paying child support by statutes or cases in some states that permit a court to terminate child support if a custodial parent interferes with the noncustodial parent's visitation or if the child refuses to visit the noncustodial parent, without justification. See Alan D. Scheinkman, "Practice Commentaries to D.R.L. Section 241," in 14 *McKinney's Consolidated Laws of New York Annotated* (1999), and cases cited therein. It is important to note that there are no laws authorizing a court to terminate visitation if a noncustodial parent who is able to pay child support fails to do so. This makes it very difficult for an attorney (such as this author) to explain to a custodial parent why she should obey the court's orders regarding visitation when the noncustodial parent has virtually no sanctions against him (except for a judgment for the arrears) for failure to pay child support. Courts rarely order a noncustodial parent in contempt of court for failure to pay child support.

[17] The American Psychiatric Association publishes the *Diagnostic and Statistical Manual of Mental Disorders* (DSM), which is now in its fourth edition, with a text revision [hereinafter DSM-IV-TR]. American Psychiatric Association, *Diagnostic and Statistical Manual of Mental Disorders* (4th ed. text rev., 2000). The DSM is widely used by all mental health professionals—psychiatrists, psychologists, and social workers—to categorize a patient's mental disorder. Neither parental alienation nor PAS is listed in the DSM-IV-TR.

feelings, he expects the court to make a leap of logic from the children's feelings of antagonism toward him to a conclusion that the mother has *caused* the antagonism, which is then labeled "alienation."

Alternatively, if the children are not reluctant to visit the father, he may claim the mother is *trying* to alienate the children from him, stating (with or without proof other than his own words) the mother has said things about him that are less than glowing.

An abuser typically uses one or more of three terms when accusing the protective parent of parental alienation: "Parental Alienation Syndrome," "parental alienation," or "unfriendly parent." Each of these terms and the concepts to which they are applied will be discussed.

There is, in fact, no real entity called Parental Alienation Syndrome (PAS). This fact has been discussed in many publications, including some of the chapters in this book.[18] The term PAS was invented in the mid-1980s by Richard Gardner, a psychiatrist. He claimed PAS exists and that it is a psychological "syndrome" primarily exhibited by children whose mothers falsely claim their children have been sexually abused by their fathers. He defined it as follows:

> The parental alienation syndrome . . . is a disorder that arises in child custody disputes in which a child will view one parent as all good and another as all bad. . . . Most often, these children have been programmed by their mothers to hate their father and to subject him to a campaign of denigration, but the children themselves often contribute their own scenarios of hostility. It is this *combination* of both the parent's and the child's contributions that warrant the term *parental alienation* syndrome.[19]

In Gardner's view, mothers often make false allegations of child sexual abuse:

> A sex-abuse allegation can often be a part of this package. It is a powerful weapon in the campaign and can be a very attractive accusation for a parent who wishes to wreak vengeance upon and/or exclude a hated spouse. The child complies with the programming parent's coaching and provides the sex-abuse scenarios.[20]

It has been pointed out that Gardner's

> proposition as to the causes of PAS is rendered tautological by the following kind of circular reasoning: an alienated child (who is supposedly distinct from an abused child) has by definition a brainwashing parent; hence, if a child is alienated, then a brainwashing parent exists and is the sole cause.[21]

Gardner opined that when a mother is guilty of PAS, the children should be put in the father's custody and should be kept away from the mother entirely, with the possible

---

[18] Chapters 1, 12, 16, and 25 in this volume include discussions of PAS, parental alienation, and "unfriendly parent," which are related concepts.

[19] Richard Gardner, *True and False Allegations of Child Sex Abuse* 159-60 (1992) (emphasis in original).

[20] Id.

[21] Janet R. Johnston & Joan B. Kelly, "Commentary on Walker, Brantley, and Rigsbee's (2004) 'A Critical Analysis of Parental Alienation Syndrome and Its Admissibility in the Family Court,'" 1 *J. Child Custody* 77, 78 (2004).

exception of rare instances of very short-term visitation supervised in order to prevent her from continuing to make false statements to the children regarding their father.[22]

Gardner was given significant amounts in fees for testifying on behalf of parents (usually fathers) who made PAS claims in custody cases. He was usually hired and paid by those parents, although he was sometimes a court-appointed expert. Many mental health professionals came to accept his theories and testified against protective parents in custody cases—sometimes as expert witnesses for the fathers and sometimes even as court-appointed experts. Many judges used the PAS theory to place children in the custody of their abusive fathers and deprive the children of unsupervised visitation or of all contact with their protective mothers.[23]

Some mental health professionals, attorneys, and judges were suspicious of PAS, however, so Gardner's claims began to unravel. No scientific basis for PAS could be established. Clearly, if parental alienation exists at all, it is not a syndrome. The definition of a syndrome is "a cluster of symptoms that occur together and can be taken as indicative of a particular disease or other abnormality."[24] Thus, for a syndrome to exist, there needs to be a disease or other abnormality plus a group of symptoms that correlate with that disease. Parental alienation is not a recognized disease or abnormality. As Jennifer Hoult has demonstrated in an excellent article, PAS does not meet the definition of a syndrome.[25]

It also began to be clear that virtually all PAS allegations were not factually valid but were a tactic used primarily by abusers against protective parents. Additionally, information concerning Gardner began to surface that made professionals question whether PAS was part of a perverse agenda on Gardner's part. For example, researchers discovered that Gardner believed pedophilia had evolutionary benefits, that Western society is "excessively moralistic and punitive toward pedophiles," and children may initiate sexual encounters with adults and then turn around and blame the adults.[26] By the beginning of the twenty-first century, a significant amount of evidence had piled up against Gardner and his PAS theory. Courts were beginning to reject the theory.[27]

On May 25, 2003, Gardner committed suicide in a most bizarre manner.[28] This led many to question his PAS theory further. Was it the creation of a sick mind? Or was he sane enough to see that his huge income from testifying about PAS was going to dry up, and he was going to be totally discredited? His son Andrew stated that Gardner was suffering from a painful disease,[29] but many people live with pain and disability and do not kill themselves. The truth probably will never be known.

---

[22] See discussions of Gardner's views in Chapters 1 and 12 in this volume. Some PAS adherents still advocate for these extreme actions. *See* Daniel J. Rybicki, *Parental Alienation and Enmeshment Issues in Child Custody Cases* (2001), http://www.forenpsychservices.com/PAS.

[23] Many of the cases cited *supra* note 3 involved PAS. See also cases discussed in Cheri Wood, "The Parental Alienation Syndrome: A Dangerous Aura of Reliability," 27 *Loy. L.A. L. Rev.* 1367 (1994).

[24] Arthur S. Reber & Emily Reber, *The Penguin Dictionary of Psychology* 732 (3d ed. 2001).

[25] Jennifer Hoult, "The Evidentiary Admissibility of Parental Alienation Syndrome: Science, Law, and Policy," 26(1) *Child. Legal Rts. J.* 6 (Spring 2006).

[26] *See* Stephanie J. Dallam, "Dr. Richard Gardner: A Review of His Theories and Opinions on Atypical Sexuality, Pedophilia, and Treatment Issues," 8(1) *Treating Abuse Today* 15, 16 1998) quoting *Richard Gardner, Sex Abuse Hysteria: Salem Witch Trial Revisited* 118 (1991).

[27] *See, e.g.,* People v. Fortin, 184 Misc. 2d 10 (Nassau County Ct. 2000), *aff'd,* 289 A.D.2d 590, 735 N.Y.S.2d 819 (2d Dep't 2001); People v. Loomis, 172 Misc. 2d 265, 658 N.Y.S.2d 787 (Suffolk County Ct. 1997), and other cases cited in Hoult, *supra* note 25.

[28] The autopsy report can be found at http://cincinnatipas.com/dr-richardgardnerautopsy.html.

[29] See excerpts from the *N.Y. Times* obituary of Richard Gardner, at http://cincinnatipas. com/dr-richardgardnerautopsy.html.

What we do know is that there is no scientific evidence of PAS. Consequently, all courts should reject any claim that PAS exists and should refuse to admit any testimony regarding it. This does not mean that PAS claims are no longer made and that all judges and mental health professionals have rejected the concept. Later in this chapter we will discuss how to fight PAS claims if they are asserted in a case.

Parental Alienation Syndrome or Parental Alienation

When PAS began to be discredited, some of its proponents started to drop the word syndrome and claim that although parental alienation may not be a syndrome, parental alienation exists, and parents guilty of parental alienation should be treated in the same way as those previously accused of PAS—namely, by loss of custody and often even visitation. Some proponents of parental alienation softened their stance a bit, advocating only that an alienator should be deprived of custody, not all visitation rights.

Unfortunately, this version and other variations of parental alienation continue to be claimed, and continue to be believed by many judges, despite the fact that there is no more scientific evidence for this version of parental alienation than for PAS. Proponents of PAS, using the term "parental alienation" or other words and phrases, such as "Malicious Mother Syndrome" (later changed to "Malicious Parent Syndrome"[30]) and "maternal gate-keeping," continue to argue that many mothers, consciously or unconsciously, try to alienate children from their fathers and make false allegations of abuse. These parental alienation proponents continue to ignore the fact that there are many valid reasons (such as abuse) why a child would be reluctant to have contact with one or more parents, and they continue to urge the courts to take drastic steps to "remedy" what they claim is alienation, without any empirical evidence that such remedies are needed or effective or that they do less damage than the alleged alienation.

Headway is being made, however, by researchers and writers who are debunking the myth that false allegations of DV and child sexual abuse are weapons used by women to gain advantages in court over their husbands. Additionally, evidence continues to mount showing that fathers—especially abusive fathers—are far more likely than mothers to make intentionally false allegations of abuse.[31]

Reputable researchers, who understand that abusers often use allegations of PAS or parental alienation as smokescreens for their abuse, are trying to educate judges, attorneys, mental health professionals, and the public about abuse and allegations of parental alienation. However, some of them are still giving the concept of parental alienation

---

[30] *See* Chapter 1 in this volume.

[31] *See* Nicholas M.C. Bala et al., *Allegations of Child Abuse in the Context of Parental Separation: A Discussion Paper*, *available at* http://www.justice.gc.ca/eng/pi/pad-rpad/rep-rap/2001_4.html. This research article, which was published by the Department of Justice Canada, summarizes several research studies of abuse allegations. One study, the Ontario Incidence Study (OIS), found that fathers are many times more likely than mothers to make maliciously fabricated allegations of child sexual abuse. The OIS surveyed child protective workers on a sample of 2,447 children whose cases were investigated as a result of allegations of abuse or neglect. One of the OIS findings was that only 1.3 percent of allegations by custodial mothers against noncustodial fathers were deemed malicious, intentionally false allegations, while 21.3 percent of allegations by noncustodial fathers against custodial mothers were deemed malicious and intentionally false. In other words, fathers made intentionally false allegations sixteen times more than mothers did. Id. at 29-32.

too much attention and credibility.[32] As Joan Meier points out, this has the effect of elevating the importance of alienation allegations and demoting the importance of abuse allegations.[33] Abuse and alienation are not equally important. Abuse is a safety issue—sometimes even a life or death matter. Safety should always be of utmost importance. If abuse is occurring, then by definition what the protective parent is doing when she tries to protect the child against the abuse, by attempting to limit the abuser's interactions with the child, is not alienating behavior, but rather protective behavior.

Parental Alienation Syndrome/Parental Alienation Language and Labels

PAS and parental alienation adherents have come to use certain terms in their conversations. Unfortunately, those terms have caught on and are often used without regard to whether they really apply in particular circumstances. We will attempt to avoid the use of these terms inappropriately.

PAS and parental alienation adherents typically use the term "alienating parent" to refer to a parent who is claimed to be damaging the relationship between the other parent and the child. Those who use this term often believe that an alienating parent may either consciously or unconsciously be damaging the parent/child relationship. It is unclear how it could be proved that a parent is unconsciously damaging the parent/child relationship and, if it could be proved, whether such a parent should be blamed or penalized for unconscious behavior. Be that as it may, when the term "alienating parent" is used it is often unclear whether the claim is that the alienating parent is consciously, maliciously, attempting to damage the parent/child relationship or whether the alienating parent is somehow unconsciously damaging that relationship. Usually the label is placed on the parent who is preferred by the child, without any real evidence that that parent has wrongfully caused the child to prefer that parent. We will refer to the preferred parent as the "preferred parent," without specifying why the child prefers that parent.

The term "alienating parent" is sometimes used to describe a parent even if the child has expressed no preference as between the parents; in that situation, the accusation embodied in the term is that the parent is attempting to damage the parent/child relationship with the other parent but has not yet succeeded. If a parent (usually the mother) indicates that she is trying to protect the child against some danger that she fears is posed by the father, such as DV, child physical abuse, or child sexual abuse, we will call the preferred parent a "protective parent." Protective parents are routinely accused of being alienating parents. Generally in such cases, the reality is precisely the opposite: it is the protective parent who is justifiably concerned about the child's safety with the other (unsafe) parent, and it is the unsafe parent who is attempting to create estrangement between the protective parent and the child.

"Parental alienation" is typically used by PAS and parental alienation adherents to refer to any behavior or speech by a parent accused of being an alienating parent that in any way indicates criticism or dislike of the other parent. Parental alienation carries

---

[32] See discussions of this problem in Chapter 1 in this volume; Carol Bruch, "Parental Alienation Syndrome and Parental Alienation: Getting It Wrong in Child Custody Cases," 35 *Fam. L.Q.* 527, 541-49 (2001); Joan S. Meier, "A Historical Perspective on Parental Alienation Syndrome and Parental Alienation," 5 *J. Child Custody* 232 (2009) [hereinafter Meier 2009b].

[33] Meier 2009a, *supra* note 7, and Geraldine B. Stahly, "Domestic Violence and Child Custody: A Critique of Recent JCC [*Journal of Child Custody*] Articles," 4(3/4) *J. Child Custody* 1 (2007).

with it all the baggage of PAS and will not be used in this chapter unless the behavior or speech is clearly intended to damage the parent/child relationship. For example, let us assume a mother tells the children when their father is picking them up for visitation, "Please don't eat a lot of soda and potato chips—they're not good for you, and if your dad gives you candy bars for lunch, see if there's any food and milk in the house that you can eat instead." That is not parental alienation if he in fact feeds them a lot of junk food (although one court has held that it is[34]). On the other hand, if she says, "Your father says he loves you, but he obviously doesn't because he never takes you anyplace where he would have to spend any money, so he obviously loves money more than he loves you," that could be viewed as attempted parental alienation, because no one can know another person's real feelings, and because spending money on a child during visitation may or may not indicate that the parent loves the child—the mother's statement could be totally untrue.

If a parent is merely making a true (although not necessarily flattering) statement about the other parent to a child (such as the statement about junk food), we will call that a truthful, nonflattering statement—not parental alienation. A truthful, nonflattering statement about the other parent may or may not be a wise thing to say to a child, but it is not parental alienation.

PAS and parental alienation adherents typically use the terms "alienated parent" or "target parent" to refer to a parent who claims that the preferred parent is attempting (consciously or unconsciously) to damage the relationship between him/her and the child. The term "target parent" contains even more innuendo than the term "alienated parent." If there is a target, there must be someone who is aiming at and shooting at the target, so logically if there is a "target parent," there must be someone who is intentionally aiming to damage the parent/child relationship with the target. To avoid these loaded terms, we will generally use the term "less favored parent."

Various terms have been used to describe the child: "alienated," "aligned," and "rejecting child" are the most commonly used. All of these imply that the parent/child relationship is damaged to more or less of an extent. Alienated implies the other parent caused the damage. Aligned or rejecting might or might not have such an implication. We will simply use the term "child who wishes less contact (or no contact) with a parent." Although this phrase is somewhat cumbersome, it does not contain any implication as to what caused the child to want less or no contact with the parent.

The behavior of the allegedly alienating parent has also been given several labels: "alienation," "programming," brainwashing," "poisoning," and "interference" are sometimes used. All of these imply that the so-called alienating parent is attempting to damage the relationship between the parent and the child. We will not use any of these terms unless there is proof of actual intentional, volitional behavior of the parent aimed at damaging the parent/child relationship. Thus, although some parental alienation adherents would claim that courts should act on allegations of "unconscious parental alienation," we reject that claim.

---

[34] The trial court's decision in a custody case between one battered mother and her former husband held that the mother was guilty of parental alienation for, among other things, giving her children this good advice regarding eating healthy food. Instead, the court should have encouraged him to feed the children healthy food. Custody was given to the husband, who has prevented the mother from seeing her children for years. The appellate court affirmed the trial court's decision. Shockome v. Shockome, 30 A.D.3d 528 (2d Dep't 2006). The appellate court's decision does not refer to the details in the trial court's decision.

Finally, the result of the preferred parent's alleged attempts to damage the parent/child relationship is described in various terms, which have various meanings to different authors. "Folie a deux" (a term sometimes used to refer to a shared psychotic disorder) was a favorite of Richard Gardner.[35] Others are "alienation," "alignment," "alliance," and "enmeshment." The term "alienation" is appropriate, in this author's view, only if truly alienating behavior by the preferred parent has been proven and the child wishes less or no contact with the less favored parent because of that alienating behavior (rather than because of other circumstances, such as behavior by the less favored parent).

Friendly Parent Concept

In order to define the "friendly parent concept," it is necessary to discuss the history of child custody laws. Under English common law, imported to the United States by our founders, there was rarely a question of which parent should get custody in case married parents separated—the father was assumed to have the right to custody. By the early to mid twentieth century, the pendulum swung in the other direction—at least for very young children. A presumption developed in the law in many states that for children of "tender years," custody should go to the mother, because maternal custody of young children was presumed to be in the best interests of the child (BIC). By the 1970s or so, the "tender years presumption" was in disfavor and was abolished in virtually all states either by statute or case law. Equality of the sexes became the norm. The standard applied in custody cases became the BIC, without any presumption in favor of either parent.[36]

BIC is a vague concept, which a judge could interpret in many different ways, depending on the judge's particular values and biases. In order to give the court more guidance as to what BIC means, many states' custody statutes list factors for the court to consider when determining the BIC, and often the friendly parent concept is embodied in the factors. For example, factors listed in the Michigan Child Custody Act are as follows:

1. The love, affection and other emotional ties existing between the parties involved and the child.

---

[35] "Folie a deux" has been defined as follows: "French for *insanity in pairs*. Descriptive of instances in which two closely related people (e.g. siblings, husband and wife) display the same mental disorder at the same time. See also INDUCED PSYCHOTIC DISORDER." Arthur S. Reber & Emily Reber, *The Penguin Dictionary of Psychology* 280 (3d ed. 2001). The same source, at page 349, defines "induced psychotic disorder" as "A delusional disorder that develops as a result of close contact with an individual who already manifests prominent delusions. The delusions are usually derived from the common experiences of the individuals who, in the typical case, have been together for a long time relatively isolated from others. Also called *shared paranoid disorder* since the delusions are usually of the paranoid variety. See also FOLIE A DEUX." "Shared Psychotic Disorder" is a diagnosis (Code 297.3) described in the DSM-IV-TR, *supra* note 17, which states at page 333 that it is "rare in clinical settings." *See also* Bruch, *supra* note 32, at 530 n.11, in which Bruch discusses shared psychotic disorders. It should be noted that psychotic disorders are serious maladies that generally would be noticeable to any lay person because "[c]lassic symptoms include delusions, hallucinations, severe regressive behaviors, dramatically inappropriate mood and markedly incoherent speech." Reber & Reber, *supra,* at 587. In other words, the individual is grossly out of touch with reality. Consequently, if a "shared psychotic disorder" existed between a parent and child, both the parent and the child would have to manifest psychotic symptoms not simply a shared opinion.

[36] See Chapter 1 in this volume for further details on the history of custody law in the United States.

2. The capacity and disposition of the parties involved to give the child love, affection and guidance, and to continue the education and raising of the child in his or her religion or creed, if any.

3. The capacity and disposition of the parties involved to provide the child with food, clothing, medical care or other remedial care recognized and permitted under the laws of this state in place of medical care and other material needs.

4. The length of time the child has lived in a stable, satisfactory environment and the desirability of maintaining continuity.

5. The permanence, as a family unit, of the existing or proposed custodial home or homes.

6. The moral fitness of the parties involved.

7. The mental and physical health of the parties involved.

8. The home, school and community record of the child.

9. The reasonable preference of the child if the court considers the child to be of sufficient age to express preference.

10. The willingness and ability of each of the parties to facilitate and encourage a close and continuing parent/child relationship between the child and the other parent or the child and the parents.

11. Domestic violence, regardless of whether the violence was directed against or witnessed by the child.

12. Any other factor considered by the court to be relevant to a particular child custody dispute.[37]

The friendly parent concept is embodied in factor 10 (above): "The willingness . . . of each of the parties to facilitate and encourage a close and continuing parent/child relationship between the child and the other parent." This assumes that "a close and continuing parent/child relationship between the child and the other parent" is always in the BIC. The statute does not even make any exception to this factor in a case where the other parent is dangerous to the child.

It should be noted that the statute does not rank the factors—no one factor is listed as having more weight than any other. Nor does the statute list as a factor child abuse or neglect (other than DV, which is certainly abusive to children), although logically it would seem as though abuse or neglect of the child would be one of the most important factors a court should consider. The weight to be given any factor seems to be left up to the judge. Therefore, a judge could decide to give more weight in a particular case to the friendly parent factor than to brutal DV that was witnessed by the child.

Sometimes a state does not have a list of factors in its custody statutes. The statute simply declares that the standard to be applied is the BIC, without listing factors. Such was the case in New York, for example, until 1996, when a single factor—DV—was added to the custody statute.[38] Even in a state where the statute does not list factors, however, the courts, as they decide cases, tend to develop lists of factors similar to

---

[37] Mich. Comp. L. § 722.23 (1970).
[38] N.Y. Dom. Rel. L. § 240(1)(a) (McKinney's 1999), added by 1996 N.Y. Laws ch. 85.

those of the states with statutory factors. Again using New York as an example, there is some case law in New York indicating that the court should consider which parent is most likely to encourage the child to have a good relationship with the other parent.[39]

However, the only factor actually listed in the New York statute is DV, which logically would lead to the conclusion that DV should be weighted more heavily by courts than allegations of unfriendly parent behavior. Similarly, in all other states where both DV and unfriendly parent behavior are custody factors, the argument should be made that DV is weightier because it is more damaging to the child.

Unproven abuse claims should not automatically be judged to be unfriendly parent behavior. Abuse is often hard to prove for many reasons including the fact that it is usually perpetrated behind closed doors. Nonetheless, many abusers claim—and some courts hold—that a mother is an unfriendly parent simply because she makes allegations of DV or child abuse that she is unable to prove.

The friendly parent concept is similar to parental alienation, although not identical.[40] Yet the friendly parent concept has been viewed by some courts as a factor that is totally separate from PAS or parental alienation, so that a judge sometimes "finds" that a parent—usually the mother—is guilty of being an "unfriendly parent" (or interfering with visitation) and engaging in parental alienation, usually based on the same "evidence."[41] Consequently, even if a judge understands that PAS and parental alienation are not scientifically supportable, that same judge may buy an abuser's argument that his victim should be denied custody because she is, or will be, an unfriendly parent.

The friendly parent concept could be viewed as even more dangerous than parental alienation, because a claim of parental alienation is an allegation that the alleged alienator is doing something to damage the parent/child relationship, while a claim of unfriendly parent could simply be an allegation that that parent is not doing everything in her power to encourage the parent/child relationship.[42] Thus, the alleged unfriendly parent is damned by the fact that she is failing to do something that the court apparently expects her to do, although she may never have been ordered by the court to do it, so she may be unaware that the court expects it. An example of this can be found in the case of *M.W. v. S.W.*,[43] in which the parents had an agreement as to when each parent would have "parenting time" with the children. The mother did not obstruct the father's right to have his court-ordered parenting time with the children, but she did not allow him more time than that. The court held that she had interfered with his

---

[39] *See, e.g.,* Barbato v. Barbato, 264 A.D.2d 792, 695 N.Y.S.2d 580 (App. Div. 2d Dep't 1999), where the court opined that "[i]nterference with the relationship between the child and the noncustodial parent is an act so inconsistent with the best interests of the child as to raise a per se probability that the offending party is unfit to act as a custodial parent."

[40] Joan Zorza states in Chapter 1 in this volume that the friendly parent concept is another of Richard Gardner's theories. *See also* Joan Zorza, "The 'Friendly Parent' Concept—Another Gender Biased Legacy from Richard Gardner," 12(5) *Domestic Violence Rep.* 65 (2007) [hereinafter Zorza, "Friendly Parent's Legacy from Gardner"].

[41] See, for example, *M.W. v. S.W.*, 15 Misc. 3d 1127(a), 841 N.Y.S.2d 219 (N.Y. Sup. Ct. Westchester County 2007), in which the court held that the mother had both interfered with the father's visitation rights (i.e., she had been an unfriendly parent) and had also attempted to "alienate" the children from him.

[42] *See* Zorza, "Friendly Parent's Legacy from Gardner," *supra* note 40, which discusses other major problems with the friendly parent concept.

[43] 15 Misc. 3d 1127(a), 841 N.Y.S.2d 219 (N.Y. Sup. Ct. Westchester County 2007), discussed *supra* note 41.

relationship with the children by, among other things, limiting his contact "strictly to that provided by the Settlement" and by arranging for play dates for the children or having them cared for by a babysitter at times when he was available to care for them, although those times were not his parenting time.[44]

True Parental Alienation

It is certainly the case that one parent could badmouth the other parent to an unusual extent, even sometimes with the intention that the children will become alienated from the other parent. Other behaviors could also be done with intent to alienate a child against a parent. Thus, there can be allegations of behavior that, after a trial, could be substantiated as behavior intended to harm the relationship of the child with the other parent and could be viewed as true parental alienation.

For example, if a mother agreed that she and the father should separate but intentionally, falsely told the children "Your father abandoned us," she would be guilty of lying to the children, and she should know that this lie might drive a wedge between them and the father. Similarly, if a father falsely claimed "Your mother doesn't love you—she just wants custody in order to get child support," he would also be in the wrong, and this could be considered parental alienation. Likewise, a parent who knows full well that the other parent has not been guilty of DV, child sexual abuse, or other child abuse but knowingly and intentionally makes false allegations of such behavior and makes sure those false allegations are communicated to the children, with intent to alienate the children from the other parent, should certainly be viewed as attempting to damage both the children and the other parent. The difficulty with such a situation is that courts sometimes jump to conclusions that mothers knowingly and intentionally have made false allegations simply because they have no third-party corroboration of their abuse allegations. Again, it must be emphasized that it is a myth that mothers frequently make false allegations of abuse.

How much alienating behavior a court would require before it found a parent to be attempting to alienate a child is also an important issue. Unless a court has convincing proof of many truly alienating behaviors, a court should not draw such a conclusion, but many courts have found mothers to be alienators simply because they occasionally cursed at or made unflattering statements about the fathers (and with the court's total disregard of the fathers' curses and unflattering statements).

Mothers are also accused of parental alienation for simply answering their children's questions truthfully. For example, when a child asks a battered mother, "Why did we have to move to grandma's house?" and the mother truthfully answers that the child's father was hitting her, and she is afraid of him, that is definitely not parental alienation. Children raised in a household where the father is abusing the mother almost invariably know what is happening, even if they are not direct spectators—they hear the raised voices, they feel the tension, and they see the injuries. It is important for children to know that no one should put up with abuse and that no spouse should abuse the other spouse. Yet, many abusers have successfully twisted such a statement so as to make it seem as if parental alienation took place.

On the other hand, when a father answers his children's questions truthfully, he is rarely accused of alienation. For example, a father whose wife leaves him for another

---

[44] Id.

man may be asked by the children, "Why did you and mommy split up?" He may say, truthfully, "She decided she wanted to be with Richard, not with me," or "She decided she loves Richard, not me." Arguably that is a thoughtless response, because it is not necessary—and may be harmful—to tell children too much about adult behaviors. It might be better for the father to say something like "It was your mother's decision that she didn't want to be with me anymore, but this has nothing to do with you—she loves you very much and will never stop loving you." However, saying something truthful to a child without thinking enough about its impact on a child is not parental alienation, and a court would rarely hold a truthful statement made by a father to be alienation, whereas courts routinely find mothers guilty of alienation for making truthful statements.

Children ask questions and deserve truthful answers, in words that are appropriate to their ages and levels of understanding. In situations where the whole truth might be harmful or frightening, they deserve at least a partial truth. If the father is in prison because he raped and brutally killed someone, a two-year-old might be told "Your dad did something wrong, and he has to be punished for it." An older child might be told, "Your father killed someone, and to make sure he never kills anyone else, the judge put him in prison for a very long time." An older child who has read the newspaper reports may even have to be told more than that. Yet, when the crime is DV, mothers are often accused of parental alienation for answering truthfully when the children want to know the truth.

Similarly, mothers are sometimes ordered to say things to the children to encourage them to visit with the fathers, even though the mothers do not believe what they have been ordered to say. For example, in a Florida case, the court ordered the mother "to do everything in her power to create in the minds of the children a loving, caring feeling toward the father . . . and to convince the children that it is the mother's desire that they see their father and love their father."[45] That was not her desire at all. Thus, she was being ordered to lie to the children. She challenged this order as a violation of her First Amendment rights, but her challenge was unsuccessful. Whether it violates her First Amendment rights or not, such an order is improper in that it mandates that she lie to the children. As one commentator pointed out, the court did not simply order the mother to encourage the children to go on visits with the father and to telephone him, both of which would not have required her to lie to them.[46] Those requirements would have been supportable, but a requirement of lying to the children is not.

It should be remembered that most abused women and children cannot heal until they name the violence and deal with their anger at the abuser, which is justified and needs to be validated. No knowledgeable mental health professional would recommend silencing a victim of trauma. For example, we would not think of prohibiting a victim of Hurricane Katrina from talking about it as part of the healing process.

Advocates of battered women should always remind the court that a father's abuse of a child's mother by definition is extreme parental alienation, because it tells the child that the mother is not worthy of being treated with respect and that abusing her is acceptable behavior.

---

[45] Schutz v. Schutz, 581 So. 2d 1290, 1292 (Fla. 1991), discussed in Wood, *supra* note 23, at 6.

[46] Wood, *supra* note 23, at 6.

HOW TO FIGHT FALSE ALLEGATIONS OF PARENTAL ALIENATION

In reported custody cases where abusers accused the protective parents of alienation, there is often no indication that the protective parents defended vigorously against the accusations.[47] Below some suggestions are presented as to how to fight an allegation of parental alienation or a related theory such as "unfriendly parent," when the abuser uses it in retaliation for the protective parent's attempt to protect the child.[48] Be aware, however, that even following these suggestions "to a T" will not guarantee success. However, if custody is granted to an abuser who claims parental alienation, an appeal may be necessary, so following these suggestions will at least help to prepare a good record for appeal.

Consider Criminal Charges for the Abuse

In all states, a victim of DV is permitted to file criminal charges against her abuser if his actions constitute a crime. Most (although in some states not all) behaviors for which she can seek a civil order of protection are also crimes. Sometimes a victim is able to obtain a favorable criminal disposition more easily than a civil order of protection, despite the higher burden of proof that is required in a criminal case, because of the gender bias against women that is so common in family courts. Additionally, the victim (called a complainant or a complaining witness in a criminal case) does not need an attorney, because the prosecutor's office brings the case against her abuser. In some locales, the prosecutor's office has a special DV bureau or is otherwise well prepared to prosecute DV perpetrators. If the parent making accusations of parental alienation is convicted of a crime, and the conviction is proven, the judge in the custody case will have to consider that in making the custody decision.

However, a victim of DV should usually proceed with her civil proceeding for an order of protection as well, for many reasons. First, in many states there is no such thing as a criminal order of protection. In some states there are no specific criminal DV laws, and in many states it is not possible to obtain the sentencing terms that the victim would prefer. Second, in no state is the standard of proof easier in a criminal case, which requires proof beyond a reasonable doubt. It is mainly because gender bias is so common in family courts that women sometimes find it easier to get criminal convictions than civil orders of protection for the same behavior. Additionally, in a criminal case, the prosecutor—not the victim—is the one who decides whether or not to bring or drop or settle a case, so the victim will probably not have much control over what happens in a criminal case. Furthermore, if she or her partner is an alien, immigration implications may arise from a criminal case, so the victim probably needs to seek advice from an immigration expert to clarify what the risks are to her and her children.

Create a Paper Trail

The protective parent must be diligent about keeping records of everything significant she says and does, the abuser says and does, and the children say and do. This is

---

[47] Walker, Brantley & Rigsbee, *supra* note 4, at 67.

[48] Undoubtedly there are cases where parental alienation or PAS or the friendly parent concept is alleged by someone who has not been abusive to the mother and/or the children, but that situation is not the focus of this chapter.

difficult because of the amount of time and energy that it requires, but it is essential. The protective parent should keep every item that could be used to demonstrate to the court that the abuser is indeed abusive and that the she is not interfering with the father/child relationship. Whatever system will work for her is fine, but it should be comprehensive.

First, the protective parent should have a calendar on which she writes down the abuser's visitation times and keeps track of what happened on each of his visitation times. For example, if he is supposed to pick up the children at 7 p.m. on Friday, February 1, and he arrives at 9 p.m., without calling to say he is going to be late, she should write that down. If the children were crying and asking why he is always late, write that down. If the father is supposed to let the children call her each day but on Saturday, February 2, she receives no call, write that down. If he is supposed to return the children at 5 p.m. on Sunday, February 3, but he returns them at 10 a.m. saying that they are not behaving so he is not taking them to the amusement park that he promised them, write that down. She should not write down extraneous material that might later be used against her in court.

Second, the mother should have a filing system for her papers concerning the case. For example, she could have file folders labeled "Divorce Summons and Complaint," "Divorce Answer," "Financial Disclosure—Mother," "Financial Disclosure—Father," "Visitation Violations," "Children's School Records," "Children's Medical Records," "Notes on Court Appearances," "Custody Evaluation," etc. It is better to have too many file folders than not enough, so that when she wants to find something, she can. Originals of important documents should be kept in a special folder, such as a folder of a different color than the other folders, and copies of these originals can be kept in the other or both folders.

"Notes on Court Appearances" is particularly helpful. Even if the protective parent can find a friend to go to court with her and take notes, she should always take a pad and pen with her to court. She should make note of who is there, including whether there is a court reporter or a tape recorder taking down what is being said (there should be one or the other). If something important happens, she should jot it down. If the court orders a parent or attorney to do something, she should make a note of it and make sure that there is a written, signed order from the judge embodying the oral order and that it is clear and includes all the terms that it should include. As soon as she gets five minutes after the court appearance, she should go through her notes and write down what she did not have time to write down in court. Then if it is necessary to get a transcript of a court appearance at which certain things were said, she will know which court date that was. Some judges make many notes, either in their own record systems or in the court file. But often they make very few notes, so information gets lost. Even if the judge keeps good records, the case may be heard on a different day by a different judge, who may not have access to the previous judge's notes.

Third, important contacts with the father (and sometimes failure of contacts) should be embodied in a letter to him. For example, if he calls and says that he is unable to pick up the children for his visitation the following weekend, the mother should send him a letter saying "This is to confirm that you phoned today, May 3, 2007, at 7:30 p.m., to tell me that you were not going to pick up the children for visitation this weekend. Therefore, I am making other plans for the children this weekend." She should send a copy to her attorney and keep a copy for her files (File Folder: "Letters to Father Re Visitation"). As another example, if both parents agree that a child can be signed up for soccer, which has games every weekend, the mother should send a letter to the father confirming their agreement so that she is not later accused of scheduling things for the child that interfere with his visitation.[49] Proof of mailing should be obtained if at all possible.

Fourth, full descriptions of critical incidents should be written down and put in the file. For example, if the father calls one evening and wants to speak with the children but they are at a friend's house, and he yells at the mother and calls her names, she should write everything down that he said. She should also have the children call him back when they get home, and make a note of that.

Fifth, the mother should never leave court papers out where the children can see them, or she might be accused of trying to alienate the children by exposing them to her allegations against their father in court documents. Similarly, she should not keep court papers where the father could find and obtain them. Many abusers will break and enter, stalk, or in other ways monitor and search the victim's belongings, including her car.

Finally, the mother should keep not only paper evidence but also phone message tapes, e-mail messages, and anything else that may be helpful later.

Demand That the Abuser Define What He Means by Alienation

Most parents going through divorce or separation badmouth each other to some extent. This is so common that separation agreements and court orders in many jurisdictions routinely include language that the parents shall not denigrate each other in front of the children.[50] Alienation must mean more than a parent occasionally letting a criticism of the other parent slip from his/her lips; if that is all it means, all parents are probably equally guilty of it—even many parents who are happily married!

When an abuser claims the protective parent is alienating the children or is guilty of parental alienation or PAS, the protective parent must insist that the abuser define the behavior that he views as alienation. Otherwise it will be impossible for her to defend against his allegations. It would violate the Constitution's requirement of due process to force someone to defend against unspecified accusations. If the person accused is unknowingly doing or saying something inappropriate or harmful, that person needs to know what that is in order to correct it. If the person accused has not done what she is accused of, then she should have notice of the accusations in order to defend against them. Additionally, it would violate due process for a court to presume, without proof, that just because a child does not want to have contact with one parent, the other parent must have alienated the child. Similarly, it would violate due process for a court to presume, in the absence of evidence, that because a person has certain feelings, she must be expressing those feelings to or in the presence of the children. It is likely that the abuser will be unable to define the behavior that he claims is alienation, because he is using the allegations as a tactic. He may claim that she is saying things to the children with the intent to instill fear or hatred of him; however, he may lack any proof of what he alleges she said to them unless someone other than the children heard what she said.

---

[49] It is interesting that when a father make plans that impinge on the mother's time, that is often ignored. *See, e.g.,* M.W. v. S.W., 5 Misc. 3d 1127(a), 841 N.Y.S.2d 219 (N.Y. Sup. Ct. Westchester County 2007).

[50] Meier 2009b, *supra* note 32.

The abuser may claim that the protective parent says derogatory things about him to relatives or friends. Of course, this would not be relevant unless she knew that the children could hear what she was saying about him or intended that the hearer convey her words to the children. Again, proof of what she said and whether she knew the children could overhear it would be necessary.

The father may claim that the mother has been giving off "vibes"—body language—that indicate she is angry at him, afraid of him, or dislikes him. That cannot validly be considered parental alienation, because people cannot usually control signs of their feelings. In fact, if a parent is afraid of her abuser, the children can often sense her fear of him; thus, if he is blaming her for the fact that the children sense her fear, he is blaming her for something that he himself has caused by his abuse!

In some states, a procedure called "Demand for a Bill of Particulars" could potentially be used to insist that the parent claiming parental alienation define what he claims the other parent has done that constitutes alienating behaviors, when and where he claims she did it, whether any witnesses were present, and, if so, their names, addresses (including e-mail addresses), and telephone numbers. In other states, there may be other possible procedural avenues to gain the same objective.

Once the protective parent finds out what the abuser is accusing her of doing to alienate the children, if there is some truth to anything that he is saying, she should make sure she does not deny what she really cannot deny. For example, if he claims that she once told her cousin, in front of the children, that he did XYZ, and intended by so doing to alienate the children, she should tell the truth—that she did not know the children were there and stopped as soon as she realized they were there. She can remind the court that she has a right to talk with other adults about the problems she is having and about her feelings.

The mother should never use the excuse that she has to speak about things in front of the children because her apartment is too small and the phone is in the kitchen or living room or wherever the children are. Cordless phones are inexpensive, and she can always talk in the bathroom if necessary. She should not give him ammunition against her. In the same vein, battered women also need to oppose any language in a court order that they (or both parties) not denigrate the other party, since this is a set-up for him to use against her later.

Debunk and Counter Parental Alienation Syndrome, Parental Alienation, and the Friendly Parent and Similar Concepts

Allegations of alienation should be debunked and countered as soon as the abuser makes the allegations. The most important point to insist on is that the court rule at an appropriate time that alleging abuse or seeking an order of protection is not alienation. The protective parent has both the right and the obligation to seek protection against abuse for herself and her children. Indeed, she may be accused of failure to protect if she does not.[51] Another important point is that there is nothing abnormal about a child preferring one parent over the other. Nor is there any research to support the

---

[51] *See, e.g.,* Nancy S. Erickson, "Battered Mothers of Battered Children," 1A *Current Perspectives in Psychological, Legal & Ethical Issues* 195 (1991). However, some courts are beginning to recognize that a woman who is abused should not be held liable for the fact that the children are exposed to the abuse. *See* Nicholson v. Scopetta, 3 N.Y.3d 357, 820 N.E.2d 840, 787 N.Y.S.2d 196 (2004) (in a neglect proceeding, evidence that the respondent parent has been the victim of domestic violence, and that the child has been exposed to that violence, without more, is insufficient to find that the child has been neglected).

assumption that children are psychologically harmed by being emotionally closer to one parent than the other.

If the abuser makes the alienation allegations in his pleadings, either in a petition/ complaint or in an answer or cross-complaint, it may be possible to make a motion to dismiss his allegations, and, in the motion papers, the protective parent can start to educate the judge. The burden of proof should be on the parent alleging alienation to both plead it in court papers and prove it at trial. First he must plead and prove alienating behavior on the part of the protective parent. If that behavior is alleged to be discussions between the protective parent and the child in which the protective parent has allegedly tried to brainwash the child against the abuser, the statements must be shown to be false statements made with intent to alienate. Second, he must plead and prove that the child is alienated.[52] Third, he must plead and prove that whatever "cure" he advocates, whether it is a change of custody, temporary foster care, therapy for the child or the protective parent, etc., is in the BIC. Although the motion to dismiss his case may not be successful, the facts concerning the unscientific nature of parental alienation theories can be brought to the attention of the judge so that he/she gradually can be educated on this issue.

Often in family courts the rules of procedure and evidence are not strictly enforced. The protective parent should insist that these rules be enforced, especially if the protective parent has an attorney who can argue on her behalf. For example, if the abuser is seeking custody, he should be required to petition for custody, not just oppose the protective parent's petition for custody. As a matter of due process, he should be required to state, as she has done in her petition, why he believes he should get custody. As another example, if the protective parent has petitioned for custody, the other parent should be required to answer the petition. In many family courts, answers are not routinely expected. Yet, under her state's rules of civil procedure, the protective parent can often make a motion to compel the abuser to answer the petition. Usually allegations in a petition that are not denied are deemed to be admitted, and that could be helpful to the protective parent.

This chapter will not address how to deal with alienation allegations in those few states that have adopted some version of the Protective Parent Reform Act, which is intended to shield protective parents against allegations of alienation.[53] Attorneys and litigants in those states should explore how their Protective Parent Acts have been interpreted by their courts.

Parental Alienation Syndrome. PAS has been totally debunked as having no empirical, scientific basis. Thus, testimony or evidence concerning PAS should not be admissible into evidence. There are many books, articles, and other sources to which the protective parent and her attorney can refer.[54] Many of them are now posted on various Web sites, so that makes it easier to obtain them. For example, Justice for Children

---

[52] This is one element that was missing in the famous New York twins case, *John A. v. Bridget M.,* 791 N.Y.S.2d 421 (1st Dep't 2005) (The decision of the Family Court, New York County, transferring custody of the twins from the mother to the father, was reversed by the Appellate Division, which reasoned that despite the mother's coaching of the twins to make false allegations of sexual abuse against the father, the twins had a good relationship with their father, and it was in the girls' best interests to remain in the custody of the parent who had raised them for their entire lives and was a good mother to them).

[53] The Protective Parent Reform Act has been proposed with various modifications. This act states that a protective parent will not be stripped of custody of a child merely for making a good-faith report of child abuse against the other parent. Information is available online; *see, e.g.,* http://www.taliacarner.com/proposedact.html.

[54] See, for example, sources cited in notes 5-7, 11, 12, 21, 23, 25, 26, and 32 *supra.*

(http://www.jfcadvocacy.org) has a position paper on PAS, called *PAS: A Guide for Attorneys or Pro Se Litigants,* and several *amicus* briefs supporting the position that PAS is not a scientific diagnosis and that testimony regarding PAS should not be admissible in evidence. The Web site also posts an article on PAS by Jennifer Hoult[55] and an important publication by the National Council of Juvenile and Family Court Judges (NCJFCJ),[56] which is also available on the NCJFCJ Web site (http://www.ncjfcj.org). The NCJFCJ publication supports the view that testimony on PAS and parental alienation is unscientific and inadmissible in evidence. The Justice for Children Web site also contains a decision by the Ohio State Board of Psychology suspending the license of Douglas C. Darnall for using the "Parental Alienation Scale" as part of his assessment in a custody case. Darnall has written publications in support of PAS that may be cited by the abuser, but his license suspension should be strong evidence to the court that his views are not accepted in the psychology field. The American Psychological Association (APA) also does not support PAS,[57] and its publications can be found on its Web site (http://www.apa.org).

Another Web site that contains many helpful publications is the Leadership Council on Child Abuse and Interpersonal Violence (http://www.leadershipcouncil.org). These publications include works critiquing PAS, articles on child custody and abuse, and *amicus* briefs.

Parental Alienation. Parental alienation is a little more difficult to attack than PAS because it cannot be denied that there are a small number of parents who try to damage or destroy the relationships that the other parents have with the children. However, parental alienation, like PAS, is not a medical diagnosis. Parental alienation, if it exists in a particular case, can be demonstrated only by proving the behaviors of one parent that are intended to damage the relationship between the other parent and the child. The emphasis must be on the need for actual evidence of alienating behavior, not simply (1) allegations of alienation; (2) proof that the alienator dislikes the other parent; (3) proof that a child is fearful of, dislikes, or otherwise is antagonistic to a parent; or (4) testimony by a mental health professional regarding speculation about the alienator's unconscious motives. Facts, not speculation, are required. If a child does not want to visit or be with a parent, there could be many reasons—it is insupportable to jump to a conclusion that, because the child does not want to be with a parent, the other parent must have done something that caused the alienation. There must be evidence connecting the alienator with the fact that the child desires no contact or less contact with the other parent, and there must be evidence proving causation.

Additionally, the assumed prevalence of parental alienation should be debunked. Attempts by one parent to damage the child's relationship with the other are actually quite rare.[58]

Further, it should be pointed out that the abuser is using parental alienation as a defense to valid claims of DV or child sexual abuse—behaviors that are not rare. Often the abuser states or implies that such claims are concocted for the purpose of damaging the parent/child relationship. Thus, it is important to bring in—through testimony of an

---

[55] Hoult, *supra* note 25.

[56] Clare Dalton, Leslie Drozd & Frances Wong, *Navigating Custody and Visitation in Cases With Domestic Violence: A Judge's Guide* (Rev. ed. 2006).

[57] American Psychological Association, *Violence and the Family: Report of the American Psychological Association Presidential Task Force on Violence and The Family* 40 (1996).

[58] See sources cited in note 7 *supra*.

expert or otherwise—statistics demonstrating that false allegations of domestic violence and child sexual abuse are rare[59] and that claims of widespread false allegations are myths based on bias against mothers.[60]

Friendly Parent Concept. The friendly parent concept is also difficult to deal with, but it can be attacked. First, the parent wrongly accused of "unfriendly" behavior should deny it and insist that if the other parent is making accusations, he needs to prove them, as is the case with any alienating behavior. Second, the parent accused of unfriendly behavior can affirmatively assert that neither she nor most divorced parents can be expected to be "friendly." In the best of all divorces, parents would be friendly toward each other and would be fully cooperative, and supportive of each other, etc., but in most divorces, that is not possible. Consequently, experts have come to recognize that it is unreasonable to expect most divorced parents to engage in friendly, cooperative coparenting with each other. That level of cooperation can be achieved by very few parents. Therefore, all that can reasonably be expected is what the mother is doing—namely, "parallel parenting."[61]

Parallel parenting is ok for kids and is the best solution in many cases. As Maccoby and Mnookin pointed out in 1992,

> There are three basic strategies for dealing with the requirements for post-divorce parenting in families in which the children spend time in both households. Some parents handle their interpersonal conflict by avoidance and practice "parallel" parenting, making little or no effort to coordinate their childrearing with each other. Other parents stay in contact with each other and their conflicts remain active, spilling over into the parenting domain. Still other parents suppress, mitigate, or insulate their conflicts and cooperate actively in their dealings concerning the children.[62]

A cooperative parenting strategy is the ideal, but it is rarely attainable. Certainly we do not want parents to engage in the ongoing conflict strategy for dealing with post-divorce parenting. So we can simply hope that most parents can achieve parallel parenting, sometimes called disengaged parenting. The parents are "disengaged from each other and are not maintaining a co-parental relationship except insofar as the

---

[59] *See* Dallam & Silberg, *supra* note 9, and sources cited therein. *See also* Meier 2009b, *supra* note 32, and Chapter 1 in this volume.

[60] *See* id. and Chapter 5 in this volume.

[61] Frank Furstenberg, Jr. and Andrew J. Cherlin stated in 1991 that parallel parenting is the best that can reasonably be expected:

> [F]ew former spouses really cooperate in raising their children. . . . [M]ost couples engage in parallel parenting. . . . They don't consult much about what the children will be doing when with the other parent. In fact, they communicate as little as possible, pursuing instead parallel tracks of parenting. It is an arrangement that minimizes both consultation and conflict. Most divorced couples simply aren't capable of the kind of continuous, courteous communication that is required if both of them are to play major roles in bringing up the children. The best that we should expect for most couples is parallel parenting.

Frank F. Furstenberg, Jr. & Andrew J. Cherlin, *Divided Families: What Happens to the Children When Parents Part* 112 (1991).

[62] Eleanor Maccoby & Robert Mnookin, *Dividing the Child: Social and Legal Dilemmas of Custody* 233-34 (1992).

children serve as intermediaries."[63] These parents exhibit what Maccoby and Mnookin call "low cooperative communication," which means that they rarely communicate with regard to the children (or anything else). That may not be ideal, but the result is "low discord," which is good for the children.[64]

Mothers who are accused of being unfriendly can assert, for example, "I am not being 'unfriendly.' I am practicing a form of parenting that is recognized by experts as being beneficial for children when there has been a lot of conflict in the parental relationship that threatens to spill over into further conflict later—namely 'disengaged' or 'parallel' parenting. I do not reach out to the father and expect that we will be able to work together with regard to the children as though we were happily married, but neither do I communicate with him in ways that could lead to further conflict, which would not be in the best interests of the child. He is not 'friendly' to me, and I am not 'friendly' to him—I try to keep away from him to keep things peaceful. Perhaps as time goes on we can work together more closely with regard to the children, but only time will tell."

Mother Must Be Perfect Even if Father Is Not

In our legal system as it exists today, women/mothers must be perfect, while men/ fathers only need to be passably decent and halfway credible. Bias against women is still pervasive in our society, including in our courts. Women are routinely held to higher standards than men, although that violates constitutional guarantees of equal protection as well as state statutes mandating equal treatment of parents in custody disputes.[65] Therefore, the protective parent who is a mother must be very careful, both in and out of the courtroom, to appear to be a model parent and a model person. From day one, the mother must try to be perfect. This is unfair and a huge burden, but it is important.

In court, and when the mother is with the children's attorney or a custody evaluator, she should try to be calm and not express her anger at the father, even though she has every right to be angry at his behavior. These participants in the legal system are likely to think that if the mother acts angry at him in court, she may do the same in front of the children and that their perception of her anger will alienate the children against him.

If the mother is pro se (representing herself), she should never show anger toward the judge or imply that the judge is biased against her. For example, if the judge makes a statement, she should never say, "That's a lie." Instead, she should calmly and respectfully say, "Your Honor, it's not accurate to say that because [and explain her reason]." Judges are not immune from the ordinary emotions of the rest of humanity.

Mother Must Never Deny Father Visitation Without Giving a Very Good Reason

Even before there is a temporary order of custody/visitation, the mother should offer a reasonable visitation schedule if she can do that without endangering the children. If she cannot offer the father totally unsupervised visitation, because of safety issues, she should document (in writing—see "Create a Paper Trail") her attempts to

---

[63] Id. at 235.

[64] Id. at 234.

[65] See Chapter 5 in this volume.

offer him visitation that is minimally supervised. If the children are reluctant to go with him alone, and if being with him would not be dangerous for her, she could, for example, invite him to come to the local pizza place to have lunch with the children while she sits in a corner of the restaurant, or she could invite him to her brother's Fourth of July gathering, if he gets along with her brother. If she cannot safely be in his presence, she could take the children to his mother's house for dinner with his family and then pick them up a few hours later. She could suggest that he attend Parents' Day at camp, if all the activities are at the camp, so that the children will be protected. The mother does not even have to tell the father what she is doing (i.e., trying to avoid unsupervised visitation)—she should just do as much as she can to keep the visits in public places or in places where there are other people present who will pay some attention to what he is doing with them.

The mother should seek a temporary order of custody, a temporary order of support, and (if necessary) a temporary order of protection, at the very beginning of the case. When asking for custody, she should suggest that the father get as much visitation as is possible consistent with safety concerns.

If the mother cannot offer much visitation because of possible danger to the children, she needs to make sure she explains that to the judge carefully and calmly, in the way best calculated to show the judge that she is being reasonable. For example, she should not say, "He's a horrible nasty abuser and he shouldn't be near the children." Instead, she should say something like, for example,

> He has a serious problem with his temper, which he himself admits, especially when he is under pressure, and the children are really more than a handful. He is not used to taking care of both children without me being there to help. On many occasions in the past, when he was with the children for long periods of time, he ended up exploding at them and hitting them. For example [give several examples]. So until he is used to having the children for longer periods of time, it would be best if they were with him for two separate days with an overnight break for him, so he can rest up from them. Then when he is ready and the children are ready, visitation can be expanded. I am afraid if we go too fast too soon, the children will not enjoy the visits and will resist going. I want to encourage them to go and to have a good relationship with him.

Everything should be expressed in terms of the BIC. For example, if the father has threatened the mother, so that exchanges of the children need to be supervised or, at minimum, need to be in a public place, such as a fast food restaurant, a post office, or a police station, explain it in terms of both the safety of the mother and the safety and well-being of the children. For example, "It will be best for the children if the exchanges of the children involve no overt hostility between the parents. They shouldn't be put in the middle of anything like that."

The court order for visitation should specify the visitation in detail—exact time and place and manner of pickup and drop off, etc., so the possibilities of disputes will be minimized. For example, if the order says the father gets the last three weekends (Friday night to Sunday night) of the month, clarify what that means when the last day of the month is a Friday—does he get the children that weekend or not? In terms of safety, if he needs to have a car seat for a child, the order should say that if he does not have the car seat, he cannot have the visitation—the mother cannot be expected to give him the car seat from her car. This is standard in some jurisdictions but may need to be insisted on in others. Likewise, if he has a lot of convictions for driving under the influence of alcohol, the order should specify that if he has been drinking anything at all, he cannot pick them up.

The visitation order should also specify how long the mother is required to wait for the father to come before she and the children can make other plans for the day. Similarly, the order might need to state that if he is more than X minutes late returning the children without a valid reason, his next visit will be cut short by that same amount of time.

Specificity is necessary, so that the father cannot validly claim the mother is being uncooperative, if the order requires cooperation. For example, if the mother is supposed to share any information she gets from the children's school with the father, she should make sure she does that routinely and has proof that she did it. E-mails can be helpful in this regard, but only if the e-mails are saved. Printing them out to make sure they do not get erased is recommended. If she is supposed to tell him about every doctor visit, she should do so. If she is supposed to tell him about any medical issues, she should do so even if the illness or injury seems minor to her. He can blow it up into something huge. It would be preferable if the order specified that the mother must advise the school or doctor in writing that the father is to receive all documents that the mother receives from the school/doctor and can have the same access as the mother to all school/medical files. This would make the father and the school and the doctor responsible for his keeping up to date on the child's educational and medical issues, taking the responsibility off the mother.

When seeking an order of visitation that will be acceptable to the mother, it is recommended that she or her attorney write out in advance the order that is sought. Then, if changes need to be made in court, they can sometimes just be made on the prepared order.

If the abuser yells at the mother when he picks up the children, she needs to answer him calmly, without raising her voice. It is sometimes amazing to see how even an abuser wants to hear how the mother responds, even if it is just so that he can yell at her again. Abusers sometimes even lower their own tone of voice. Additionally, his conduct during a visitation exchange could be a trap—he could have a witness or be "wired" to record her statements for court.

If it is possible to have a witness to the pickups and drop-offs, that may be necessary on occasion. Similarly, tape recordings and videos may be important at some times. State laws on whether phone conversations can be taped without letting the other party know should be checked. For example, it is permissible in New York State for a party to a phone conversation to tape it, even without telling the other person. However, a third party may not tape it. So if the mother and father are speaking, either of them can tape it without informing the other. But if the father is speaking with the children, the mother cannot legally tape it, and vice versa. In some other states, however, phone conversations may not be taped without letting the other party know.

With regard to telephone visitation ordered by the court, if the father calls and asks to speak with the kids, the mother should let him, even if it is inconvenient, unless it is impossible. If that is the case, the children should call him back as soon as possible (and make the paper trail). If the mother can afford it, she should get a phone just for the father to call the kids, and she should not give the number to anyone else, so she will know the call is from him for the children. She needs to instruct the children on its use (e.g., "If daddy calls on your number and wants to talk with me, just tell him to call me on my phone."). If she cannot afford a separate phone, she can get something like "ringmate"[66] to use for his calls to the children. Again, she should not give the number to anyone else.

The mother should always be super polite over the phone. No matter how the father provokes her, she should never curse at him or even yell, because someone may hear it, or he may be trying to set her up and then tape her.[67]

Keep the Court's Attention on the Domestic Violence or Child Abuse

The parental alienation accusation is usually a tactic to deflect attention away from the abuser and shine an accusing light on the victim, which will blind the court to what is really going on. Therefore, every attempt should be made to calmly insist that the mother is not alienating the child, that it is the father/abuser who is the wrongdoer, and that he is accusing the mother of parental alienation in an attempt to divert the judge's attention away from his wrongdoing.

The mother can point out to the court that, in their state and in every other state, DV (or child abuse, as the case may be) is viewed as an important reason not to give custody or unsupervised visitation to the abuser because of concerns about the safety of the child (and protective parent). If the mother is asking for a temporary order of protection, the judge may not be inclined to issue it against the father, and may even say something like "He is presumed innocent until proven guilty." The mother can point out that the risks of error are not the same. If she obtains a temporary order of protection against him and it was a mistake, no substantial harm is done either to him or the child. However, if the court denies an order of protection, when an order of protection should have been granted, her life and the lives of the children could be endangered. Thus, the court should consider safety first. It is better to provide safeguards for the short period of time of the temporary order than to risk substantial harm during that period.

Prepare the Best Possible Domestic Violence/Child Abuse Case and Custody Case

If the mother's original petition for custody or for an order of protection is not sufficiently detailed, the mother should file an amended petition giving all the necessary details of the DV or other abuse and other reasons why she should get custody and the protection order.

There are many resources to assist protective parents and their attorneys to prepare a good case. The basis of a custody decision is supposed to be the BIC, after all facts and circumstances have been considered. Thus, courts should be urged to follow the lead of the New York State Appellate Division, in *Appel Meller v. Meller*, which found that the mother had "repeatedly defied orders of the New York courts with respect to

---

[66] "Ringmate" is a service offered by some phone companies, and the cost is only a few dollars a month. The subscriber is given a second telephone number, but there still is only one telephone line. When the ringmate number is called, the ring sounds different from the normal ring, so the subscriber can hear the difference and can know which number is being called.

[67] Taping phone calls after harassing the mother was another tactic used by the ex-husband in the *Shockome* case. See discussion *supra* note 34. The mother in that case did not curse or yell at the father, however.

the father's visitation rights."[68] Further, the court found that the mother "is at least partially responsible for the child's alienation from [the father]."[69] Nonetheless, the court affirmed the trial court's denial of the father's motion to change custody "because the standard in these matters is what serves the best interests of the child."[70]

It is extremely important to prove the abuse. If the mother fails to prove the father's abuse, it may be even worse for her than never mentioning the abuse, because then she will be viewed as having "harassed" the father with "false allegations," even though, obviously, failure to prove that something happened does not mean it did not happen and does not mean she intentionally, maliciously alleged the abuse. She could have been sincerely worried about the possibility of abuse and just wanted it checked out. She will not necessarily be believed even if she testified that she was concerned about the child's safety, but now that it has been checked out, she will not impede the relationship between the child and the father. Once an alienator, always an alienator, in some judges' minds; once "unfriendly," always unfriendly. These assumptions violate due process, because they are irrebuttable presumptions. However, judges sometimes make them.

If the mother reports child sexual abuse or other child abuse and child protective services (CPS) "unfounds" it, some judges take this as an irrebuttable presumption that the abuse never happened when, in fact, it simply means that CPS workers, who often are undereducated, undertrained, overworked, and underpaid, did not find enough evidence of abuse or decided that they did not need to file against the father for some other reason.[71]

The mother should keep a chronology of any current abuse and write a history of the past abuse—what the father did, when, where, witnesses if any (not only to his abuse but the aftereffects), and whether she spoke to anyone about the abuse at the time. The latter is especially important because the abuser often claims that she is just now making up these allegations ("recent fabrication") for purposes of getting an advantage in the divorce or custody matter. Thus, if the mother can show that she made allegations of the abuse at an earlier time, that would be admissible in most states to counter his claims of recent fabrication.[72]

The court may need to be educated to the fact that if the children do want to see the father, this does not prove there was no DV and no abuse, because most children still love and want to see their parents even if their parents abuse them (or abuse the other parent). The court also needs to know and understand that if the children do not want

---

[68] 285 A.D.2d 430, 430, 728 N.Y.S.2d 160, 160 (2001).

[69] Id. at 431.

[70] Id. at 430. The same principle—that the BIC is always the overriding concern—was followed in *John A. v. Bridget M.*, 791 N.Y.S.2d 421 (1st Dep't 2005), discussed *supra* note 52.

[71] For example, CPS could decide not to file an abuse case against the abuser because the mother went to the police, and the prosecutor's office decided not to prosecute. Yet, the prosecutor's office may decide not to prosecute for many reasons having nothing to do with whether the abuse actually occurred, such as the high burden of proof in a criminal case, the young age of the victim, etc. On the other hand, CPS could decide not to proceed because the prosecutor's office did decide to prosecute, although this makes no sense because it is of course possible that a conviction might not result. Similarly, CPS could decide not to file an abuse case against the abuser because there was a custody case going on, and CPS could assume that the matter would be appropriately handled within that proceeding. Again, this does not make sense, because if CPS brings an abuse case, the child's interests are being protected by an agency of the state that has resources that the protective parent does not have.

[72] Each state's rules of evidence should be consulted on this issue.

to see their father, there may be many valid reasons, such as that they were abused and treated unkindly during the parents' marriage or relationship; the children witnessed DV; the father does not treat them well on visitations or even frightens them, such as by telling them he is going to take them away from their mother, and they will never see her again; or they are just bored with the visits.

The mother should not ever ask anyone to lie for her or evade the truth to the court, the police, or anyone else, even if it seems like a small lie. If the court catches her in even the smallest lie, her credibility will be destroyed, and it is only a matter of time until the abuser will get custody. This is part of the sex bias that pervades the courts. If the mother is suspected of lying or doing anything else wrong, she will lose custody, whereas the father can lie about a lot of things, and his lies will usually be overlooked.[73]

Similarly, the mother should not ask someone to testify on her behalf unless she is certain that person will not turn around and lie for the abuser. This is difficult to figure out. If in doubt, that witness should not be called.

The mother should be very careful who she allows into her house, whether a boyfriend or a babysitter or a visitor, because any other person might be persuaded, by money or otherwise, to be a spy and/or lie about her to the court.[74] She should also be wary of ex-husbands and ex-boyfriends who may align themselves with the abuser for their mutual benefit. It is not unheard of, when the mother has children with two different fathers, for the fathers to work together to get all of her children away from her.

Regarding testimony about the DV or other abuse, the mother should testify in detail, giving dates, times, places, descriptions of what the abuser did and the effects on her, etc. If there are no photos of injuries, hospital records, police records, etc., she should testify as to why such documentation is not available. Otherwise, she may be found "lacking in credibility."[75]

The mother should carefully consider whether she should make allegations for which she has no proof at all (e.g. he "keyed her car," but no one saw him, there is no forensic evidence to tie him to the crime, etc.).[76] She could be viewed as paranoid.

If the abuser had others attack or harass the mother, she should either make sure she can tie their actions to him or she should ask for an order of protection against those individuals. She will not get an order of protection against him based on what someone else did to her unless she can prove he was working together with that other person to harm her.

Consider Settlement Carefully

Often a judge will suggest that a family offense case be settled by an order of protection on consent of the accused individual without a determination ("findings") of his wrongdoing. This is similar to a plea bargain in a criminal case except that in a plea

---

[73] In *M.W. v. S. W.,* 15 Misc. 3d 1127(a), 841 N.Y.S.2d 219 (N.Y. Sup. Ct. Westchester County 2007), discussed *supra* note 41, at 6, the court noted that the mother asked the babysitter to lie to the father when he asked to pick up the children after school instead of the babysitter picking up the children. The babysitter was told to tell the father that the children had a play date. The babysitter later turned against the mother (whether she was bribed or what her motive was is not clear) and told the court that the mother had asked her to lie to the father. This was the beginning of the end for the mother, who ultimately lost custody.

[74] Ex-boyfriends have been known to collude with ex-husbands at times, and babysitters have been known to be disloyal to the mothers. See *M.W. v. S.W.,* discussed *supra* note 73.

[75] See the discussion of *M.W. v. S.W., supra* note 73.

[76] Id.

bargain the defendant must admit that he committed an offense (although a less serious offense than the one he was charged with). In contrast, an order of protection "on consent without findings" does not usually require the accused to admit to doing anything; his only risk is that if he violates the order of protection, he will be arrested, and mandatory sentences often apply if he is convicted. If he does not violate the order, no consequences will ensue. Judges like this type of settlement because it immediately gets the case off their calendars, and family court calendars are usually very crowded.

In almost every state, it is not wise for a protective parent to agree to accept an order of protection without findings of the abuser's wrongdoing because, without either his admission of guilt or the judge making findings, it is as though his abuse never existed in the eyes of the law. Therefore, when time comes for the custody case, the mother will not be able to use the fact that the father is an abuser to prevent him from getting custody or extensive visitation (because he is not, officially, an abuser). The protective parent or her attorney could insist on a trial unless the abuser admits to at least one of the allegations in the petition so that there will be a record, in any later case, that he was guilty of abuse. That would truly be the equivalent of a plea bargain. Then the accused would have to decide whether to accept that offer or not. If the protective parent does agree to accept an order of protection without an admission of guilt or a judge's findings, she should keep all of her evidence of the abuse, because she may need it later for a custody proceeding.

If custody has already been decided in the protective parent's favor, if the order of protection is for a long period of time, and if she thinks the abuser will be afraid to violate it,[77] a settlement without an admission of guilt or a finding of wrongdoing may be acceptable. The protective parent should be aware, however, that if the abuser later seeks a change of custody, she will not have a court order determining that he committed DV. Then if he claims she is alienating the children against him, but the real reason the children are reluctant to visit him is because of his past abuse, she will not have any judicial finding that the abuse occurred. She will have to prove his abuse, which by that time would be farther in the past, so evidence may no longer be available.

Even more problematic is the fact that some judges improperly limit proof of abuse to abuse that is "recent" or "not too old," which is defined by the judge as he/she determines. To guard against such an eventuality, it would help if the order of protection stated that it was without prejudice to the mother's right, in any future proceeding where the father's abuse may be relevant, to plead and prove the underlying facts upon which the mother's petition was based. Even better would be language stating that for purposes of any custody proceeding or any other proceeding in which the father's abuse may be relevant, his consent to the order will be conclusive proof that he has committed the acts alleged in her petition.

The mother should be careful of a settlement that requires agreeing to any form of joint custody. Legal custody is the authority to make all major decisions regarding the child, such as decisions concerning education, religion, medical care, etc. Therefore, if the parents had joint legal custody, they would be required to consult and cooperate with each other on all such issues. Consequently, if the mother failed to consult with the father about something, she might be in contempt of court, and he could also claim alienation. Further, if parents with joint legal custody fail to agree on an important issue, such as which school the child will go to, they have to go back to

---

[77] Individuals holding certain positions may be in danger of losing their jobs, being demoted, or losing their licenses if they have criminal convictions or other blots on their records. For that reason, they may be deterred from reoffending.

court. Additionally, under the custody laws of most states, joint custody makes it more difficult for the mother to relocate.

However, sometimes it makes sense to agree to joint custody. Some state laws have a presumption in favor of either joint legal custody or joint residential custody or both, so if the case goes to trial, the mother has the burden of proving that joint custody is not in the BIC. If the father is willing to give her primary residential custody and the issue of joint legal custody is the only thing standing in the way of settlement, and if she has serious questions about whether she will win at trial, agreeing to joint legal custody may be the best of her bad alternatives.

If joint legal custody is ordered and the mother has residential custody, the mother should make sure she consults with the father on all important issues and maintains the paper trail of letters saying, for example, "As we discussed on May 1, 2007, when we talked on the phone, the kindergarten options for Johnny are X School and Y School. For the reasons I stated, I believe X School is better for Johnny. I am aware that you may not fully agree, but the time period for enrollment ends in five days, and he must be enrolled in school, so I am enrolling him in X School." This still allows the abuser to petition the court to reverse her decision, but it prevents a situation where an important decision is left in limbo. Sometimes an agreement or order makes it explicit that one parent has the final decision on matters involving the child if, after consulting with the other parent, no agreement can be reached. This, of course, is preferable to joint legal custody, because if the mother is given the final decision-making power, the abuser cannot successfully petition the court to reverse her decision except under unusual circumstances.

Deal With the Law Guardian, Guardian Ad Litem, or Attorney for the Child

In many states, the court will appoint a representative for the child. An attorney for the child is sometimes called a law guardian. That individual is an attorney and, depending on the jurisdiction, is expected to either (1) act very much like an attorney representing an adult (i.e., following the instructions of the client); (2) advocate for what the attorney feels is in the child's best interests; or (3) both, depending on the maturity of the child and other factors. It has been the experience of many attorneys throughout the country who represent survivors of DV that most attorneys for children do not feel bound to advocate for what the child wants, regardless of the rules in their jurisdictions.

A guardian ad litem (GAL) may be an attorney, a social worker, or anyone else viewed by the court as appropriate to represent the child, and usually a GAL is not bound to advocate for the child's wishes but may advocate for what the GAL deems to be in the BIC. The trend in this country seems to be going in the direction of recognizing that a child has a right to an attorney who will follow the child's wishes, but in some states the representative of the child is free to advocate anything he/she thinks best for the child, and such representatives' opinions often carry much weight with the judge. Terms other than attorney for the child, law guardian, and GAL are also sometimes used to denote a child's representative, such as "Friend of the Court," depending on the state.

It is often dangerous for the child and the protective parent when a court appoints a law guardian, attorney for the child, GAL, or other representative of the child, because if that individual turns against the protective parent, then she has two people against her—the abuser and the child's representative (or three if the custody evaluator is against her!). These individuals usually do not have much, if any, training in either DV or child abuse (especially child sexual abuse), usually hold the same biases against mothers as do others in the general public, and may be enamored of PAS, parental alienation, or the friendly parent concept. They may be manipulated or charmed by abusers. There have even been cases where an abuser has bribed a child's representative. Additionally, in some jurisdictions, the parents must pay the fees of the child's representative, and when a mother can barely afford to pay her own attorney, sharing the cost of the child's representative can destroy her finances.

For these reasons, if the court does not routinely appoint a child's representative, a protective parent should generally try to avoid such an appointment, unless the children are in their teens and will forcefully stand up for themselves (this is rare), or the particular child's representative is known to be knowledgeable about DV and child abuse. Inability to pay for a child's representative might be persuasive when a judge is considering whether to appoint one or not. The judge might also be persuaded that a child's representative would not be necessary because it would be sufficient to speak with the children confidentially. This is sometimes called an *in camera* (in chambers) proceeding. Depending on the state, the parents and their attorneys may or may not be present, and the transcript may be sealed, to be viewed only by a higher court if the custody decision is appealed.

Children's representatives should always be treated with the utmost deference, with the hope that they will come to understand that custody to the protective parent is in the BIC. If they need to be trained on PAS, parental alienation, or the unfriendly parent concept, that may be accomplished informally by giving them materials to read, but often briefs will be necessitated, and the court will have to make a determination. A full discussion of problems with children's representatives is outside the scope of this chapter. There are several good articles that should be consulted on this issue.[78]

Deal With the Child Custody Evaluators

A child custody evaluator—usually a psychiatrist, psychologist, social worker, or other similar professional—is sometimes appointed by the court to investigate the family and render a report to the court to assist the court in determining the BIC. Many judges favor the appointment of a child custody evaluator because custody cases are often very difficult, and judges sometimes feel as though they need the assistance of an "expert." Judges are also aware that, once the child custody evaluator has submitted his/her report, the parents often settle the case—often along the lines suggested by the child custody evaluation. That gets the difficult case off the judge's docket.

As has been discussed with regard to children's representatives, child custody evaluators often pose a danger to children because they are usually not sufficiently trained in DV and child abuse issues, and they may share the same biases against women as are prevalent in the world at large. Many tend to become manipulated by abusers and enamored with the alienation concept. As a result, many child custody evaluators have recommended custody to abusive fathers on the theory that the protective parents were trying to alienate the children from the fathers. If that happens, the protective parent may have three people against her: the father, the children's representative, and the child custody evaluator. A judge would have to be very strong to withstand such

---

[78] *See* Chapter 23 in this volume and sources cited therein; Nancy S. Erickson, "Confusion on the Role of Law Guardians: The Matrimonial Commission's Report and the Need for Change," 8(6) *NY Fam. L. Monthly* 1 Feb. 2007).

an onslaught against the mother.[79] Many judges capitulate and grant custody to the abusive father.

There are undoubtedly some mental health professionals who support the PAS or parental alienation concept because they are fathers' rights activists themselves or because—like Gardner—they can make a very good living by testifying on behalf of fathers, who generally have more funds than do mothers to hire "experts." There are surely many more mental health professionals who accept PAS or parental alienation theories and truly believe they have validity, despite the lack of empirical evidence. It is difficult to determine whether a particular mental health professional falls into one category or the other without knowing what he/she has recommended in custody cases in the past. Some seem to be fairly strongly supportive of PAS.[80] Others support the concept of parental alienation but not PAS and present a range of views on the subject.[81] Organizations of mental health professionals hold conferences, or have workshops at conferences, on PAS or parental alienation. Some of these organizations, such as the Association of Family and Conciliation Courts, undoubtedly have members who hold a whole range of views on the subject, while other organizations, such as Canadian Symposium for Parental Alienation Syndrome, clearly indicate their support of PAS.[82]

For all of the reasons above, the appointment of a child custody evaluator should generally be avoided if at all possible. The appointment of a child custody evaluator can sometimes be avoided on the ground of the finances of the parents, since the child custody evaluator usually must be paid for by the parents. The costs can be enormous,

---

[79] Fortunately, some judges know enough about DV to recognize the red flags and are strong enough to reject the recommendations of an "expert." In *Vinciguerra v. Vinciguerra,* 294 A.D.2d 565 (2d Dep't 2002), the custody evaluator in the trial court recommended custody to the father, opining that he was not capable of violence and that the mother lacked credibility. However, the mother testified about the father's controlling behavior, including but not limited to physical abuse. He called her names, would not allow her to breastfeed, to speak Spanish to the child, to teach the child any religion, to take the child to visit her parents in Brooklyn, or to have anything to do with her parents. These are clear signs of an abuser's typical coercive control. The judge ordered custody to the mother, stating that he did not have to accept the recommendation of the evaluator when it was belied by all the other evidence in the case. The Appellate Division, Second Department, affirmed.

[80] *See, e.g.,* Moisy Shopper, "Parental Alienation: The Creation of a False Reality," in *A Handbook of Divorce and Custody: Forensic, Developmental, and Clinical Perspectives* (Linda Gunsberg & Paul Hymowitz eds., 2005); Chaim Steinberger, "Father? What Father? Parental Alienation and Its Effect on Children," 38(1) *NYSBA Fam. L. Rev.* 10 (Spring 2006) and 38(2) *NYSBA Fam. L. Rev.* 9 (Fall 2006).

[81] *See, e.g.,* Jonathan Gould, C*onducting Scientifically Crafted Child Custody Evaluations* 210-24 (2d ed. 2006). But note that Gould states that "alienation dynamics" (undefined) show themselves "frequently." Id. at 217. If he is referring to situations in which children are actually alienated from a parent, such situations are not frequent. However, if he is referring to a wide range of behaviors and feelings, there are no known statistics on the relative frequency of such behaviors and feelings.

[82] The list of speakers at the CS-PAS conference in Toronto, Canada, is interesting because it includes so many Americans: Douglas Darnell (whose psychology license was suspended for, among other things, testifying about PAS—see discussion in *infra* note 89); Randy and Dierdre Rand; Dean Tong (who has built a career as an expert on false DV and child sexual abuse accusations and was arrested for DV against his second wife on January 21, 2008, according to an article by S.I. Rosenbaum in the *St. Petersburg Times* on January 30, 2008, *available at* http://www.tampabay.com/2008/01/30/Hillsborough/Self_styled_false_abu.shtml; other articles have indicated that he was previously arrested for burglary and for DV against his first wife); Daniel Rybicki; J. Michael Bone; and many other Americans who appear to be PAS advocates. It appears that PAS theories are flowing out from the United States to other countries.

and many abusers who can afford it use the tactic of "keep fighting until she runs out of money, and then you can flatten her." Custody evaluations, whether well intentioned or not, often help the abuser to do this. However, sometimes a cost argument will not prevail, because the court has a mental health clinic or private practitioners that perform child custody evaluations for the courts at government expense.

If a parent is seeking a child custody evaluation on the ground that the other parent is guilty of alienation, then the ground for opposition to appointment of a child custody evaluator could be that neither PAS nor any other type of alienation is a valid psychological or psychiatric diagnosis or a mental health condition for which the "expert opinion" of a mental health professional would be relevant.[83] In other words, because any alleged alienating behaviors would have to be behaviors, not mental conditions, the way to prove alienation is by evidence at a hearing, not by means of testimony of a mental health professional. Additionally, because it lacks a scientific basis, alienation would not meet the relevant admissibility standards for scientific evidence.[84]

Furthermore, there is very little research on the many different reasons why a child might not want contact with a parent. Thus, no one could be a sufficient expert on this issue so as to be of assistance to the court. In fact, courts may want to stay out of this controversy altogether, for some of the same reasons as courts and state legislatures decided that courts should get out of the business of adjudicating allegations of "alienation of affections" of a spouse. The primary reason is the extreme difficulty in determining causation.[85] A child may be loathe to have contact with a parent for so many reasons that it would be close to impossible to determine with any degree of certainty that the mother caused the child to want no contact (or less contact) with the father and that the child's decision did not result from a different cause.

Sometimes the appointment of a child custody evaluator cannot be avoided. In that case, the protective parent should insist that any child custody evaluator appointed to the case have special expertise in the issues to be investigated. For example, if there are DV or child abuse issues, the child custody evaluator should be an expert in those areas.[86]

---

[83] PAS advocates might argue that an alienating parent and his/her child might have a "shared psychotic disorder," which is a DSM-IV diagnosis. However, the definition of this disorder requires that the "inducer" already has a "psychotic disorder with prominent delusions," which would have to be proven, and then it would need to be established that the other individual (the child) has the same psychotic delusion. *See supra* note 35. This disorder is so rare that PAS advocates certainly would not want to limit their definition of PAS to parents and children suffering from a "shared psychotic disorder."

[84] Some states use the standard set forth in *Frye v. United States,* 293 F. 1013 (D.C. Cir. 1923). Other states and the federal courts use the standard from *Daubert v. Merrell-Dow Pharmaceuticals*, 509 U.S. 579 (1993). *See* Hoult, *supra* note 25.

[85] Wood, *supra* note 23, at text accompanying n.154, *available at* http://www.gate.net/~liz/clwood.txt.

[86] These guidelines specifically state in Part II 5 c:

> In the course of conducting child custody evaluations, allegations of child abuse, neglect, family violence, or other issues may occur that are not necessarily within the scope of a particular evaluator's expertise. If this is so, the psychologist seeks additional consultation, supervision, and/or specialized knowledge, training, or experience in child abuse, neglect, and family violence to address these complex issues. The psychologist is familiar with the laws of this or her state addressing child abuse, neglect, and family violence and acts accordingly.

This language was changed in the February 2009 revision of the guidelines, now called "Guidelines for Child Custody Evaluations in Family Law Proceedings," which are available at http://www.apa.org/practice/guidelines-evaluation-child-custody-family-law.pdf. The new

Although DV and child abuse are not mental health diagnoses, the psychological effects of DV on the direct and indirect (children) victims have been researched by psychologists, psychiatrists, and social workers for many years, and there is a strong empirical database on those psychological effects, which may include posttraumatic stress disorder, depression, or other disorders. This is to be contrasted to the issue of parental alienation, which has virtually no empirical database to which mental health professionals can refer.

The protective parent may want to ask that the court direct the child custody evaluator not to give an opinion on the "ultimate issue"(i.e., which parent should get custody and what visitation (access) provisions would be best). States and courts differ regarding whether the child custody evaluator should be permitted to give an opinion on the ultimate issue. In a growing number of jurisdictions, the child custody evaluator is asked only to report on what his/her investigation has revealed and not to give an ultimate issue opinion.[87] Then the child custody evaluator's report would include the family history, the education, employment, physical and mental health history of each parent, the education and physical and mental health history of each child, and also the results of collateral contacts with doctors, teachers, family members, neighbors, etc. The child custody evaluator would not, however, make any recommendations regarding custody or visitation. The judge would use the information provided by the child custody evaluator to help him/her to decide the ultimate issue of custody and of visitation specifics.

There is a heated debate on whether a child custody evaluator should render an opinion to the court on the ultimate issue. The majority of child custody evaluators are psychologists, and the APA is divided on whether psychologists should render ultimate issue opinions in custody cases.[88] From a legal viewpoint, it can be argued that the correct view must be against ultimate issue opinions in custody cases because the decision as to which parent should get custody is an issue that the legislature has determined should be made by a judge, and a judge may not delegate his/her role to anyone else. Furthermore, even if the opinion of a child custody evaluator is viewed as a mere recommendation, it must meet the legal rules on expert witness testimony. The judge is not permitted to admit into evidence the opinion of any person off the street—only the opinions of experts can be admitted into evidence and only if the standards for expert witness opinion are met. Hundreds of books and articles have been written on the complex question of expert witness testimony, and attorneys representing protective parents should familiarize themselves with this literature.[89]

---

language, which is now in Part II 4, reads as follows: "Should complex issues arise that are outside psychologists' scope of expertise, they seek to obtain the consultation and supervision necessary to address such concerns." "Complex Issues" thus would include child abuse, neglect, and family violence but might also encompass other complex issues such as substance abuse. American Psychological Association, "Guidelines for Child Custody Evaluations in Divorce Proceedings," 49 A*m. Psychologist* 677 (1994).

[87] New York State courts, at least in the New York City area, seem to be leaning toward the "no opinion on the ultimate issue" rule. Judges are now often making orders for custody evaluators that specifically state that the evaluator is not to give an opinion on which parent should get custody. This may be a result of the criticism levied at custody evaluators during the hearings held by the New York State Matrimonial Commission. *See Matrimonial Commission Report to the Chief Judge of the State of New York*, at 46-53 (Feb. 2006), http://www.courts.state.ny.us/ip/matrimonial-commission.

[88] The 1994 APA guidelines for child custody evaluations, *supra* note 86, do not take a stand on that issue, stating that there is no consensus. The 2007 draft making changes to the guidelines still leaves that issue open.

[89] *See, e.g.,* Timothy Tippins & Jeffrey Wittman, "Empirical and Ethical Problems With Custody Recommendations: A Call for Clinical Humility and Judicial Vigilance," 43 *Fam. Ct.*

If the report of the child custody evaluator indicates that it is based even in part on a PAS theory, the protective parent should ask the court to reject the report in its entirety on the ground that PAS is not a recognized mental health diagnosis and that the court should either appoint another child custody evaluator or proceed without one. It has become public record that at least three psychologists have been disciplined by their licensing boards for giving testimony in custody cases regarding PAS.[90] If licensing boards of mental health professionals would take the step of disciplining a licensee for using PAS in an evaluation, then PAS obviously cannot be said to be accepted in the psychological profession and thus should not be admissible into evidence.

If the custody case goes to trial and the child custody evaluator's report is not good for the protective parent, an attempt should be made to keep it from being introduced into evidence. Instead, the custody evaluator can and should be called as a witness. The report is usually full of hearsay and irrelevant material, which is inadmissible as evidence.[91] If the report is unfavorable for the protective parent and the protective

---

Rev. 193 (2005); Tim Tippins wrote a series of articles in the *New York Law Journal* (http://www.NYLJ.com). They appeared on the following dates: March 17, 2009, January 8, 2009, November 4, 2008, September 5, 2008, July 3, 2008, May 1, 2008, March 6, 2008, January 2, 2008, November 1, 2007, September 10, 2007, September 6, 2007, July 12, 2007, May 1, 2007, March 9, 2007, January 2, 2007, November 3, 2006, October 4, 2006, September 11, 2006, September 1, 2006, July 7, 2006, May 5, 2006, March 3, 2006, January 6, 2006, November 3, 2005, September 1, 2005, July 1, 2005, May 5, 2005, March 3, 2005, January 7, 2005, November 5, 2004, September 2, 2004, July 15, 2004, May 1, 2004, March 16, 2004, January 15, 2004, November 6, 2003, September 4, 2003, September 2, 2003, and July 15, 2003. *See also* Lundy Bancroft & Jay G. Silverman, *The Batterer as Parent: Addressing the Impact of Domestic Violence on Family Dynamics* (2002); Robert Geffner, Kari Geiss & Brenda Aranda, "Family Violence Allegations in Child Custody Evaluations: The Overlap of Family and Forensic Psychology," 22 *Fam. Psychologist* 9 (Spring 2006); Stuart A. Greenberg & Daniel W. Shuman, "Irreconcilable Conflict Between Therapeutic and Forensic Roles," 28 *Prof. Psychol.: Res. & Prac.* 50 (1997); Daniel Krause & Bruce Sales, "Legal Standards, Expertise, and Experts in the Resolution of Contested Child Custody Cases," 6 *Psychol., Pub. Pol'y & L.* 1076 (2000); Thomas Litwack, Gwen Gerber & Abraham Fenster, "The Proper Role of Psychology in Child Custody Disputes," 18 *J. Fam. L.* 269 (1979-80); Gary Melton et al., *Psychological Evaluations for The Courts: A Handbook for Mental Health Professionals and Lawyers* (3d ed. 2007); Lynn Hecht Schafran, "Evaluating the Evaluators: Problems With Outside Neutrals," 42 *Judge's J.* 10 (2003). Kenneth Pope's Web site also provides helpful resources, http://www.kpope.com.

[90] Douglas C. Darnall was disciplined by the Ohio State Board of Psychology, which suspended his license. *See* "Parental Alienation Syndrome" in the section entitled "Debunk and Counter Parental Alienation Syndrome, Parental Alienation, and the Friendly Parent and Similar Concepts" above. One of the protective mothers (known as K.A.) in the international complaint filed against the United States to the Inter-American Commission on Human Rights on behalf of abused mothers and children (see *supra* note 3) reported in the international complaint that the custody evaluator, Larry Leatham, who recommended removal of the children from her custody (charging her with PAS), and placement of the children in the custody of the abuser was fined by the California Board of Psychology and had his license to practice psychology revoked for his conduct in her case (and for performing a grossly negligent evaluation in another case). More recently it was reported that an Australian psychologist, William Wrigley, was disciplined by the Psychologists Board of Queensland, which stated that he acted unprofessionally in giving evidence about PAS to the court. A mother who lost custody of her two children because of his evidence in her custody case brought the complaint against Wrigley that resulted in the suspension of his license. Tony Koch, "Ruling Debunks Custody Diagnosis," *Australian,* Apr. 7, 2008, *available at* http://www.theaustralian.news.com.au/story/0,25197,23495760-2702,00.html.

[91] State law should be consulted on this issue.

parent can keep it or the damaging parts from being admitted into evidence, the judge will never read those damaging statements.

The issue of child custody evaluators in DV and child abuse cases is beyond the scope of this chapter, but there is much that can be done to challenge the custody evaluator's testimony if he/she is called as a witness. For example, the results of any tests administered to family members can and usually should be questioned.[92] Books and articles on cross-examination of custody evaluators should be consulted,[93] as well as case law on the admissibility and weight to be given to child custody evaluators.[94]

Obtain an Expert Witness for the Protective Parent

An expert witness for the protective parent could be helpful not only to counter the court-appointed evaluator's testimony, but also to testify more broadly about child abuse and DV, including the effects of DV on children even if they are not direct witnesses to it. Each case is different, so it is difficult to generalize concerning what specifically the protective parent would need her expert to testify about.

Individuals can be qualified as experts based on their education, training, experience, or any combination of those. Each state's rules on qualifications of experts should be consulted. If possible, an expert witness for the protective parent should be at least as well qualified as the experts relied upon by the abuser, so if he is relying on a Ph.D. psychologist, the protective parent should attempt to obtain the assistance of at least one Ph.D. psychologist or someone equally qualified. In addition, she may wish to obtain the testimony of individuals who have gained expertise on DV through experience, such as counselors at DV shelters.

Usually expert witnesses charge hourly or daily rates for their preparation and testimony, and this could be out of the range of the protective parent's budget. She can try to get experts through the local battered women's shelters, university faculties, and professional organizations such as state affiliates of the APA and the National Association of Social Workers, or other sources.

Relocation: Do Not Ask Unless It Is Necessary and Victory Is Very Likely

A protective parent should not relocate or even ask to relocate to any place more inconvenient for the abuser than where she has been living, unless the court is clearly on her side and it is absolutely necessary (e.g., the mother was laid off from her job and can show that she cannot get an equivalent one nearby). Relocation without court permission is often viewed by a judge as an attempt to interfere with the other parent's visitation.[95]

---

[92] *See, e.g.,* Chapter 21 in this volume. *See also* David Brodzinsky, "On the Use and Misuse of Professional Testing in Child Custody Evaluations," 24 *Prof. Psychol.: Res. & Prac.* 213 (1993); Nancy S. Erickson, "Use of the MMPI-2 in Custody Evaluations Involving Domestic Violence," 39 *Fam. L.Q.* 87 (2005).

[93] *See, e.g.,* David A. Martindale, "Cross-Examining Mental Health Experts in Child Custody Litigation," *J. Psychiatry & L.* 483 (2001).

[94] See, for example, *Vinciguerra v. Vinciguerra,* 294 A.D.2d 565 (2d Dep't 2000), discussed *supra* note 79, where the trial court rejected the recommendations of the custody evaluator.

[95] *See, e.g.,* M.W. v. S.W., 15 Misc. 3d 1127(a), 841 N.Y.S.2d 219 (N.Y. Sup. Ct. Westchester County 2007), discussed *supra* note 73.

This is unfair, especially if the father has not even exercised the visitation to which he was entitled. Each state's laws differ on whether the protective parent will ultimately be permitted to move, but, in the meantime, she should be very cautious in order to avoid angering the judge. For example, if the protective parent has a strong need to relocate (e.g., because of the requirement of a new partner's job), she should ask permission from the court and try to find a home somewhere midway between the new job and the old location, if possible, to show that she is trying to preserve the father's access to the children. This is another area of law on which much has been written, and attorneys should know the laws and cases in their states.[96]

CONCLUSION

The context in which most allegations of alienation arise is in custody cases where a protective parent is attempting to shield her children against the harm threatened or already perpetrated by the other parent. The abusive parent then seeks custody, alleging that the protective parent is alienating the children from him. He asks the court to give custody to him and to prohibit the mother from even visiting or speaking with the children so that they can be "deprogrammed" from her alienation.

This tactic has been very successful in thousands of cases throughout the United States and, increasingly, throughout the world. The abuser often bases his claims on the works of Richard Gardner, who invented the theory of PAS that, despite its total lack of scientific basis, has been alluring to many mental health professionals and judges and is a favorite tactic of father supremacy advocates.[97] PAS and its siblings—parental alienation, alienation, and the unfriendly parent concept—result in children being given into the custody of abusers, where the damage they do is incalculable.

The tide seems to be turning a bit away from the theory of parental alienation. A few child custody evaluators have been disciplined by their licensing boards for using the PAS theory in their custody evaluations, and courts have been increasingly holding that testimony on PAS is inadmissible.

Protective parents and their advocates should challenge abusers who attempt to introduce testimony on alienation. Where alienation theories have been vigorously opposed—in criminal cases—testimony on alienation has been ruled inadmissible. In custody cases, it appears that these theories generally have not been opposed, so in some cases the court has been allowing testimony on these theories to be admitted, to the detriment of children. Protective parents and their advocates also must document all the facts in their cases, must carefully litigate their custody and family offense cases, and must be aware of all the snares that abusers set and the pitfalls that exist.

---

[96] *See, e.g.,* Carol Bruch, "Sound Research or Wishful Thinking in Child Custody Cases? Lessons From Relocation Law," 40 *Fam. L.Q.* 281 (2005); Joan Zorza, "How Abused Women Can Use the Law to Help Protect Their Children," in *Ending the Cycle of Violence: Community Responses to Children of Battered Women* 147-69 (Einat Peled, Peter G. Jaffe & Jeffrey L. Edleson eds., 1995), *available at* http://zorza.net//scanned/doc04201252_0.pdf.

[97] I agree with Barry Goldstein (see Chapter 18 in this volume), Jan Kurth (see Chapter 4 in this volume), and others who state that the term "fathers' rights" is inappropriate for these individuals and the groups they form, because they do not appear to be in favor of equal rights of mothers and fathers but advocate for superior paternal rights.

Chapter 21

Urgent Need for Quality Control in Child Custody Psychological Evaluations

by Robin Yeamans, J.D.

INTRODUCTION

In child custody battles between divorcing parents, the courts often rely on mental health professionals to evaluate the parents and children. Because there are no quality controls over either the evaluation processes or the evaluations themselves, judges sometimes inadvertently end up using horribly flawed evaluations. The result? Children in domestic violence (DV) and abuse cases are at risk of being placed with the wrong parent.

How Could a Psychologist Be So Wrong?

A psychologist who was highly regarded by the local court had completed her personality-assessment test[1] results of a mother in a divorce, after the mother had claimed the father was molesting their daughter. The psychologist concluded as follows:

> [Her] suspiciousness goes to the extent of paranoid thinking, particularly in regard to her husband's action.[2]
>
> [I]t appears that most of her speculations about her husband's possible sexualized attitudes toward their daughter are not based upon documented or reality-based evidence.[3]

The court saw the psychologist's report cited above as credible, which enabled the accused father to obtain physical custody of the parties' two children, a daughter and a son. The father is now serving a twenty-three year prison term for the rape of his daughter.

How could a respected psychologist be so wrong? Is this a rare aberration, or is it typical of the work of psychologists in cases involving DV and/or abuse? If this case is not unusual, then why is this problem occurring in our courts, and what can be done to remedy it?

Expert testimony has become commonplace in many types of legal proceedings, including mental disability[4] and child custody cases.[5] As a certified family law specialist in California for the past twenty-eight years, I witnessed a dramatic upsurge in the use of forensic mental health experts beginning in 1992, when the "custody wars" first broke out,[6] and the courts began ordering parties with no known history of mental problems to undergo psychological evaluations.[7] The ostensible value of the evaluations was their use as a predictive tool. As lawyers, we had to look at the evaluations as if they were predictions of a parent's future conduct and then argue about the validity of the evaluators' prognostications. Given that the "future" they predicted is now in the past, it seems to me that one of the most relevant and compelling

---

[1] The psychologist administered the Minnesota Multiphasic Personality Inventory-2 (MMPI-2), a true and false test typically scored by computer. For more information, see James N. Butcher et al., *Minnesota Multiphasic Personality Inventory-2 Manual for Administration, Scoring and Interpretation* (rev. ed. 2001).

[2] Report by Dr. MQ, July 24, 1999, at 7. Reviews of the record of this and other cases discussed in this chapter were conducted by the author, and any inquiries should be directed to the author. The case citations are not reported in full to protect confidentiality of the parties.

[3] Id.

[4] *See, e.g.*, M. Perlin, *The Hidden Prejudice: Mental Disability on Trial* (2000).

[5] *See, e.g.*, D.R. Baerger et al., "A Methodology for Reviewing the Reliability and Relevance of Child Custody Evaluations," 18 *Child Custody Evaluations* 35 (2002), *available at* http://www.aaml.org/tasks/sites/default/assets/File/docs/journal/Journal_vol_18-1-3_Child_Custody_Evaluations.pdf.

[6] This was a response to federal laws compelling all states to raise child support and effectively enforce child support awards.

[7] In New York, the overuse of psychologists in matrimonial proceedings was an issue brought to the attention of public officials at public hearings in 2004, according to an official state report, *available at* http://www.nycourts.gov/reports/matrimonialcommissionreport.pdf (2006).

questions to answer at this juncture is the following: did the real-life experience of divorced families, especially their children, who went through custody evaluations match the predictions made by the evaluators? Looking back over the evaluators' predictions about family outcomes and then comparing those predictions with the real-life experiences of those same families would be a good test of the validity of those predictions. If custody evaluations rest on valid science, they should withstand such a critique.

In reviewing the cases I handled as a family law attorney, I discovered that, in many cases, the evaluators' predictions were not accurate. This means that the evaluations did not accomplish what they were supposed to do: predict future parenting behavior and outcomes for children. Yet these evaluations, which I discovered to be especially deficient in custody cases involving allegations of abuse, continue to be standard fare in this nation's family court system. They are not useful in helping judges with the most crucial issue of all: determining the abuser and the abused. Further, what occurred in the cases I present here should not be regarded as mere anomalies; rather, they exemplify widespread and serious systemic problems.

The cases I present here were selected because (1) sufficient details about the case were collected and preserved and (2) sufficient time has elapsed to reveal the evaluations' lack of predictive value to the courts that ordered them. In nearly all the abuse cases for which I served either as counsel of record or as an advisor, the "experts" virtually never saw through the tactics of the abuser.

In the cases where I may or may not have served as attorney, I was in a position to track what happened to the family after judicial determinations had been issued. For example, in the case introduced above, after the father obtained physical custody of the parties' two children, he remarried. With the help of the children's attorney the father was permitted to take the children from Silicon Valley and move with them to a mountain county. In his new home, he permitted the son to attend school, but to ensure that what he was doing to the daughter remained a secret, she was "home schooled." I personally interviewed the daughter, who told me how her father pierced not only her nipples but also her clitoris—without any anesthetic. Her childhood was an unbelievable nightmare: to get her father's permission to go out with friends, she would have to argue and bargain with him, finally agreeing to do something like performing fellatio on her father. She now refuses to go to a gynecologist to find out what damage may have been done to her. She is unable to keep a job or maintain a stable residence, even with a roommate. After the rape was revealed, her brother revealed physical and sexual abuse by the father as well. Dr. MQ (above), whose report was the basis of the custody order, had characterized the mother's fear that the father would sexually abuse the children as almost delusional.

Organization of the Chapter

Following my presentation of the details and outcomes of the cases (see "Case Presentations"), I highlight the seriously flawed methodologies of the forensic evaluations performed in these cases, methodologies that have nonetheless been accepted by the California courts (see "Flawed Methodology"). A discussion of this methodology held up to the bright light of scrutiny will show how and where these evaluations go awry. There is a special problem with evaluators using probabilities to assess behavior. As it turns out, often the statistical probabilities are so low that they offer about the same chance of predictability as a flip of a coin. In other words, they were completely useless as a diagnostic tool. Following the methodology section, I take a brief look at the scope of the problem and possible root causes (see "Scope of the Problem"). Lastly, the solutions section (see "How Can This Situation Be Changed") seeks to provide direction for marshaling support for reforms, with a call for litigants and advocates to lead the way.

CASE PRESENTATIONS

How Accurate Were the Psychologists?

In questioning whether a test is "valid," what you are really asking is whether the test measures what it claims to measure. Keep that definition of validity in mind while you read the following illustrations, which I drew from cases I handled in California.

Dr. UK was considered one of the leading psychologists in the Silicon Valley. She did a great deal of the training of other forensic psychologists who practice in this geographic region. How accurate were her evaluation reports in the following cases?

Case #1: Dr. UK and RT. Dr. UK was brought into the case when RT's ex-husband succeeded in having her convicted of contempt of court. What horrible thing did RT do to warrant a conviction of contempt of court? After a visit, Z told RT, her mother, that her paternal uncle had molested her. The molestation had occurred at her paternal grandmother's house. Therefore, Z did not want to be picked up by her paternal grandmother for her next visit with her father, since Z was afraid of ending up at her paternal grandmother's house, where her father often took her during his custodial time. RT immediately contacted Z's father and informed him that Z wanted him, not the grandmother, to pick her up for the visit. The father refused to believe that his brother had molested Z or even that she had been molested at all, so despite RT's request on behalf of Z, he sent his mother to pick up the child. At the designated exchange location, when Z saw her grandmother arrive to pick her up, Z became hysterical and refused to get out of her mother's car. Z's mother attempted to calm Z by reassuring her that her grandmother would take her to see her father. Z continued to cry hysterically, refusing to go with her grandmother. RT explained to the grandmother that Z was not feeling well and did not want to go with her but that she would contact the father to make different arrangements for the exchange. RT immediately called the father and left him a voice mail message explaining what had happened. In her message, she offered to drive Z to the exchange location in the father's city, which was forty miles away. The father did not respond to RT's message; instead, he showed up later that night at RT's home, accompanied by the police. He forced Z to get out of bed and go with him. The father then filed contempt charges against RT for not forcing the child to go with his mother (Z's grandmother) earlier that evening. At trial, RT was found guilty of contempt for not forcing the child to go with the grandmother, even though a therapist working with the child testified that she believed that the molestation had taken place at Z's grandmother's home. The judge then ordered psychological testing of the parties and told the father to go file a motion to modify custody, which the father promptly did, thus turning the case into a custody proceeding. The mother was given a five-day suspended jail sentence and placed on two years' probation.

When Dr. UK's report was done in March 1996, RT's ex-husband had two DV convictions on his record, dating from 1993, due to his violence against the mother, RT.[8] Dr. UK not only entirely ignored the molestation, but also minimized the significance of the two DV convictions and blamed the victim for both:

> The Court also has asked if [father's] anger is appropriate or unjustified. In this situation, it is very predictable that [father] would react with anger to [RT's] passive aggressive behavior, in that his characterlogical [sic] response to pressure and frustration is not depression or withdrawal, but anger. The anger may be more intense or more unpredictable than would appear warranted on first glance, and in fact, there have been times when [father's] impulse controls have been broached [sic] and his behavior has been admittedly inappropriate, but it is important to note that there is a continual subtle provocation occurring.
>
> This is a beautiful, sensitive, strong, intelligent child who deserves two parents, and exposure to the cultural and ethnic differences in her parents' worlds. Unfortunately, it appears that she also needs the protection of the Court from the emotional excesses that occur when either parent acts out. The expressions of anger may be more obvious, but may be much less destructive than the hostility expressed by the maternal grandmother and the subtle passive hostility expressed by [RT].[9]

It is particularly distressing to realize that the psychologist who blamed the victim for "continual subtle provocation" of DV was the same person who headed up the first DV training in Santa Clara County Family Court Services, after such training had become mandatory. She continued in this same role for many years afterward, thereby influencing the thinking *vel non* of psychologists in this area.

How accurate did Dr. UK's report in RT's case turn out to be? Custody of the daughter, Z, was awarded to the father when Z was seven years old. A few months later, he obtained the court's permission to move with the child to New Jersey, far from RT's residence in California. Z became depressed and gained an additional fifty pounds in a short period of time. The father made it extremely difficult for RT to have contact with Z. In order to have visitation with Z, RT had to travel to New Jersey at her own expense and find lodging for herself and Z. She had to borrow money in order to have visitation, as she had no income at the time; the father, however, made a substantial six-figure income. The father attempted to interfere with RT's New Jersey visitation on several occasions, including on Mother's Day, when he informed her not to come (even though it was her court-ordered visitation time) because he had made plans for Z to spend Mother's Day with himself and his mother. On another occasion, he had RT served with a New Jersey Temporary Restraining Order (TRO), so she was compelled to go to court with Z, during her visitation time, to defend herself against the father's allegations that she had harassed him. The case was dismissed after a hearing, and the New Jersey judge made a finding that the father had perpetrated DV against the mother. Unfortunately, RT and Z had to spend the entire day in court fighting the TRO instead of enjoying the New York musical they had planned to attend together to celebrate RT's birthday.

---

[8] Case Nos. A9266111 and C9207098.
[9] Report by Dr. UK, Mar. 18, 1996, at 6-7.

Let us return to Dr. UK's comment about "ethnic differences in her parents' worlds": What were those differences? Was one parent from the United States and the other one from a different country? Was one parent white and the other African American? No, both parties were African American, but RT was biracial and therefore had lighter skin color than the father. This seems to have led Dr. UK to make false assumptions about RT. The trial judge, James Stewart (now deceased), issued a ruling that amounted to a finding that RT was not "black enough" to raise her own daughter. If you were to measure skin color and compare Z's skin to her (darker) father and to her (lighter) mother, you would find that Z's skin color was slightly closer to her father's. On this basis, apparently, RT had to defend herself against accusations of not being sufficiently focused on her African American heritage. In fact, RT had informed Dr. UK about her strong identification with her African American heritage, including the time she spent living in a black theme house with African American students, the fact that she had minored in African American studies in college and had organized the first Malcolm X Day on her campus. However, most of what she told Dr. UK about this was not written down, and the psychologist misrepresented RT's statements to the court.

A friend who testified on behalf of RT was grilled, over the objections of RT's attorney, over whether or not RT had sported an afro hairdo in college:

Q.   And at that time [twenty years ago in college], did [RT] have the same hairdo as she has today?
A.   No.

[RT's attorney]: Objection. I wouldn't know what the relevance of that question is.
The Court: Overruled.

Q.   [Father's attorney]: What kind of hairdo did [RT] have at that time?
A.   She didn't have an afro.[10]

Who would expect to have to defend how they wore their hair twenty years prior, more than a decade before the child at issue was even born?

Eventually, when Z was eleven years old, she came back to live with her mother due to a stipulation between the parents. After Z returned to living with her mother, her father set up a situation enabling him to stop his contact with Z while blaming Z and RT for the cessation of contact. The father told Z that if she ever asked for a change in the visitation schedule after she came to live with RT, he would no longer have any contact with Z at all. When Z's middle-school class in California was going to visit New York, where the father lived, Z tried to change the schedule to accommodate a visit with him (even giving him an extra day) while still going on the class trip. The father has never spoken to or had contact with his daughter since then. He arranged the situation so that Z would likely blame herself for being cut off by her father. (It is assumed that a child would suffer a major psychological blow upon a parent suddenly rejecting and cutting off the relationship with that child.)

Like many other abusive parents whom I have observed during my legal practice, Z's father seemed to have very low self-esteem. Z's love for both her parents was threatening to him, as he apparently believed that if his child, Z, loved her mother, RT, then Z could not possibly also love him.

---

[10] Transcript, page 163, line 17 to page 164, line 3.

Let us hark back to Dr. UK's statement that the father's anger was less of a problem than RT's supposed "provocation" of that anger. Ironically, it was his anger that became the major contributing factor to the breakdown in his relationship with his daughter.

Many abused parents, when faced with the type of report that Dr. UK wrote regarding RT, jump to the easy conclusion that the evaluator was simply gender biased. Often, this explanation is too simplistic. Usually they are not aware of any other case like their own. So when they see how inaccurately the evaluator's report depicts them, they conclude that the evaluator must be gender biased. Based on my experience, issues of money, power, control, smooth manipulativeness, and the psychologist's knowledge of the result the judge prefers are often determinative rather than simply gender.[11] This is not to say that gender bias does not operate in some cases; in fact, later on in this chapter (see "Case #3: Dr. NK and BD"), I will provide striking examples that attest to this problem. However, there also are a number of nonlegal factors that might account for irrational, baseless judicial determinations. These nonlegal factors sometimes override the rule of law.

In fact, the legal theory known as "legal realism" is founded on the very premise that nonlegal factors play a significant role in determining judicial outcomes.[12] Consider the case of former Justice Gerald Garson, who presided over divorce and custody cases at the Brooklyn State Supreme Court in New York. I attended part of his criminal trial in 2007, at the end of which a jury convicted him of bribery and of two lesser charges. The jury found that, in exchange for meals, drinks, and an expensive box of cigars from a law guardian/lawyer, Garson had manipulated outcomes of divorce proceedings, according to published reports.[13]

According to an interview with a writer, one of the mothers who believed that Justice Garson had victimized her stated that she thought he hated her because he screamed at her in court.[14] Was Justice Garson's alleged screaming incident simply a reflection of gender bias? When this mother started to hand over wads of cash to an alleged Garson middleman (which was actually marked money from the Brooklyn D.A.'s office)[15] she noticed that the judge started to treat her better when she appeared in his courtroom. He no longer yelled at her, she said, and she also began to get more favorable rulings from him. What nonlegal factors were at work here?

---

[11] *See, e.g.,* K. Winner, *Divorced From Justice: The Abuse of Women and Children by Divorce Lawyers and Judges* (1996).

[12] Legal realism is defined as "the theory that law is based, not on formal rules or principles, but instead on judicial decisions that should derive from social interests and public policy." *Black's Law Dictionary* 728 (Bryan A. Garner ed., 7th abridged ed. 2000). For another take on legal realism, see http://fredrodell.com.

[13] Daniel Wise, "Ex-Judge Gets 3 to 10 Years for Bribery, Taking Favors, by Daniel Wise, *N.Y.L.J.,* June 6, 2007.

[14] Interview by Karen Winner for the story of Frieda Hanimov (series of interviews in June and July 2003). Hanimov had gone undercover for the Brooklyn District Attorney's (D.A.'s) office after she told the D.A.'s office that she believed that her ex-husband, who was trying to obtain custody of one of their three children, had paid off Justice Gerald Garson.

[15] Id. Hanimov's husband was never charged with bribery, and it is not known if he was investigated by the D.A.'s office. Hanimov's husband is innocent of any such charges. Garson was found guilty of bribery and of manipulating other cases. More information is available at http://www.cbsnews.com/stories/2005/02/18/48hours/main674950.shtml and http://www.nydailynews.com/news/ny_crime/2007/04/22/2007-04-22_stole_our_kids_our_hope_.html.

While a discussion of legal realism and all of the nonlegal factors that may determine rulings lies beyond the scope of this chapter, the Garson case alone suggests the plausibility of any number of nonlegal factors playing a role in judicial rulings.

Case #2: Dr. UK and TM. Turning again to psychologist UK, it is instructive to look at the case of TM. In TM's case, his wife punched him in the face in the presence of their child, breaking his nose.[16] TM insisted that the police not arrest his wife, although they were willing to do so. Dr. UK reported, "These two people show some remarkably similar psychological characteristics." TM was requesting 50/50 visitation—a modest claim for a victim of DV. The judge awarded full custody to the mother, upon Dr. UK's recommendation.

Routine practice, along with the following statement, written by a former presiding judge of the San Jose, California, Family Court system, supports the contention that judges rubber-stamp psychologists' recommendations:

> Who Is the Most Important Person to Persuade in a Court Custody Dispute?
>
> It is not the judge. The judge will make the ultimate decision, of course, but the recommendation of a court-appointed neutral evaluator is adopted by the judge without substantial change in the vast majority of cases—perhaps as high as 85 percent.[17]

In professional psychological journals, experts debate whether psychologists should make recommendations on the ultimate issues of custody and visitation. However, in Santa Clara County, California, psychologists not only make recommendations on the ultimate issues but also often prepare a detailed order, so that there is nothing left for the judge to do but sign on the dotted line.

In the case of TM, when it was a male who was the victim of DV, Dr. UK sided with the abusive female, recommending that she be awarded full custody:

> [The child] needs the opportunity to develop friends in his school and neighborhood environment. To accede to [TM's] request for 50-50 custody would continue to subject [the child] to conflict over everything from therapy to school placement to which parent is good and which is bad. Further, it would have a negative impact on his sense of security and predictability. Therefore, it is my opinion that this situation requires a sole legal custody arrangement with mother's residence as primary, and with father having frequent structured time with his son[18]

Dr. UK additionally recommended that the "mother should have the decision-making authority with regard to medical, psychological and educational matters."[19]

One of the more pathetic items I saw was a page from the diary of the child involved in that case. The entry speaks for itself:

---

[16] Campbell Police Dep't Event Report, Case No. 93–339x, Report ID 6703x.xx, 7/_/93.

[17] J.W. Stewart, *The Child Custody Book—How to Protect Your Children and Win Your Case* 12 (2000). Note that this author's citation to this book is not intended as an endorsement.

[18] Report by Dr. UK, Jan. 6, 1995, at 6.

[19] Id. at 7.

My mom slapped my arm. I cried. She slapped me because I threw-up when I tried Lentels. Actually she forced me to eat lentels. She said I had to eat my throw-up But I didn't. [Mom's boyfriend] yells at me more than mom. If the judge tells mom this, mom will get mad at me.[20]

Of course, at the time, the events the child described could be dismissed as the effects of brainwashing, or it could be argued that TM got the child to write these things down in order to manufacture evidence.

How did his life in the mother's custody turn out for this child? Rather than change her own behavior, the mother took the child for mental health counseling and had him put on the antidepressant Prozac. The child did not need Prozac. To prevent his child from being medicated, TM had to intervene by pointing out that it was the stress the mother inflicted on the child that needed to change, not the child himself. The mother remarried twice after her divorce from TM. Both of those marriages ended in divorce, and at the time of the respective separations, both husbands had to call law enforcement on the mother, unfortunately exposing the child not only to both of the divorces, but also to three instances of police involvement.

A family dynamic is stronger than a court order. If a child is older than, say, the age of five, the relationship ties within the family will likely end up overriding the directives of the court order, unless one parent is wildly and effectively controlling. In the case of TM, he remained committed to protecting his child's well-being while the mother became busy with her job. This family eventually evolved into what was effectively a 50-50 time-sharing situation between the parents. TM told me that he sometimes thought to himself, "Would it be better for our son if I just drop out of this and accept alternating weekends?" The son, now an adult, tells TM that he appreciates that his father stayed in there, fighting to maximize contact with him.

Can the Psychologists' Backgrounds Affect the Evaluation?

When examining the personal lives of the psychologists, it was not particularly unusual to find that they had some pretty severe problems of their own.

For example, Dr. MF, practicing in the Santa Clara–San Mateo County areas of California, turned out to be a stalker, in spite of being fairly elderly. In 1995, a San Jose judge[21] issued a restraining order to stop him—a married psychologist—from stalking a woman who was not his wife and with whom he had never had a personal relationship. The state of California tried unsuccessfully to take his license, and, in the process, they filed a psychological evaluation of this psychologist with the court. The evaluation reported that Dr. MF's mother had died when he was a young child and that he therefore felt that one can survive happily without a mother—a sentiment echoed by many psychologists doing psychological evaluations in custody cases.

Given that Dr. MF was a stalker, and that he harbored warped feelings about the importance of mothers, how would abused mothers be expected to fare under his scrutiny of their psyches? Is it realistic to expect him to detach his unconscious from his evaluations?

---

[20] On file with author.
[21] Case No. 1-95-FL-0535xx.

Another psychologist, Dr. NK, had Tourette's Syndrome, an official disorder, according to the *Diagnostic and Statistical Manual of Mental Disorders.*[22] Dr. NK was doing psychological evaluations in San Jose at the same time he was himself going through a divorce.[23] He filed a very interesting declaration (a sworn-to written statement of factual assertions to the court) right around the time he was recommending taking custody from many mothers and even subjecting them to supervised visitation:

> During past separations, my wife has always insisted that she be able to control the visitation I am to have with our children. In order to "keep the peace" I oftentimes let her do this to me.[24]

How would one suppose Dr. NK is likely to react when separated or divorced fathers voice this same complaint to him (valid or not)? The declaration also says,

> Our middle child, [X], has dyslexia and is hyperactive. . . .

> Our youngest child, [Y], is an autistic child who requires twenty-four hour a day special care. He will need to be eventually institutionalized.[25]

At a time when he was doing custody evaluations in complex cases, Dr. NK swore as follows:

> I suffer from Tourette's Syndrome. Stress affects my ability to cope with this condition and the stress of this dissolution of marriage has had an effect on my ability to perform my professional services for all of my clients.[26]

While regretting the personal suffering Dr. NK must have endured, one must wonder if, given the circumstances, this psychologist was capable of objectively assessing the fitness and skills of other parents. Is it merely a coincidence that he engaged in discernible gender bias, as discussed in the following section?

Case #3: Dr. NK and BD. Dr. NK did a psychological report, dated May 31, 1995, on a mother, BD, in which he declared that she "could alienate the children[27] from their father—a high risk factor in this case."[28] This was in the heyday of the theory known as Parental Alienation Syndrome (PAS). In 1992, federal law directed all of the states to raise and enforce child support awards. In that same year Dr. Richard A. Gardner published *Parental Alienation Syndrome.*[29] This book proved to be the main ideological weapon of abusive parents who want to avoid paying child support by grabbing custody of the child.[30] When a child would say that a parent (usually, but not always, the father)

---

[22] American Psychiatric Association, *Diagnostic and Statistical Manual of Mental Disorders* (4th ed. text rev. 2000).

[23] 1-96-FL06196xx.

[24] Declaration of Dr. NK, ca. 1996 or 1997, at 1.

[25] Id.

[26] Id. at 2.

[27] There was only one child.

[28] Report by Dr. NK, May 31, 1995, at 9.

[29] R. Gardner, *The Parental Alienation Syndrome* (1992).

[30] This is not to deny that alienation of a child by a parent in the divorce context occurs, but it is meant to put this particular book into context.

was hurting him/her, this was taken as proof that the other parent (usually the mother) was brainwashing the child, so that the more the child complained, the more the court came to the rescue of the "targeted" parent. Dr. Gardner's book was his own personal opinion, not the result of scientifically published, peer-reviewed studies.[31]

In BD's case, Dr. NK did not allow this lack of scientific justification to keep him from opining that, although BD had not in the past alienated the father from their daughter, there was a possibility that she might do so in the future, and, therefore, the father should have full custody. There were no studies of any sort to serve as a basis for Dr. NK's claim that there was a "high risk" of BD alienating the daughter from the father at some point in the future. Thus, Dr. NK negated the father's 1995 criminal conviction for drunk driving in favor of his own personal theory of "future alienation." The child was handed into the father's custody at the age of seven. What was living with her father like for her?

First, he did his utmost to cut off BD's contact with the daughter entirely. I represented BD pro bono, but I prepared a bill so I could keep track of my time. By the time my fees reached $70,000, I had to resign from the case, as I could not contribute those types of funds to anyone. What had I done during the time I worked on this case? Mainly, I responded to highly aggressive Orders to Show Cause (OSCs) by the father's attorney and by the so-called attorney for the child (who functioned as the father's de facto second attorney). In one week, the father's legal team flooded us with four OSCs. Due to an error by the court clerk, the last OSC went to the judge for signature so quickly that we could not get our response to the court before the judge signed the papers, ordering a complete cessation of contact between the daughter and BD. By this point, the contact had been supervised, but even that did not satisfy the father's desire to cut BD completely out of her daughter's life. In a cruel irony, the very next week, the judge who cut off BD's contact with her daughter spoke at a conference in support of victims of DV.

All of BD's visits were supervised by a licensed mental health professional. What horrible behavior could she have engaged in that resulted in her losing all contact with her seven-year-old child? The allegation was that BD had used her supervised visits as evidence-gathering sessions by, for example, having the daughter draw pictures to be used in court. However, the evidence that BD brought to court to demonstrate what had actually gone on during her visits consisted of a velveteen poster with the word "Love" colored in by her daughter.

What does this action say about the father's intentions toward BD (and their daughter)? What does it say about the accuracy of the psychologist's opinion regarding which parent was likely to engage in future alienation? What does it say about the court's handling of this case, especially when it was clear that the father was obviously interfering with BD's relationship with their daughter? Why did this development have no impact on the court's decision, which originally had been based on the prediction of BD's "future alienation?"

At the hearing of one of the father's OSCs, the daughter's therapist came to court. However, the judge refused to hear her testimony. She and I were trying to explain to the court that, when you give full custody to a parent who does not have good intentions or enough maturity, it will destroy that parent's relationship with the child. This

---

[31] *See* S.J. Dallam, *The Parental Alienation Syndrome: Is It Scientific?* (1999), *available at* http://www.leadershipcouncil.org/1/res/dallam/3.html; E. St. Charles & L. Crook eds., *Exposé: The Failure of Family Courts to Protect Children From Abuse in Custody Disputes* (2000). *See also* Chapter 20 in this volume.

is precisely what happened in this case: Custody had been given to an abusive person with low self-esteem who had recently had a drunken driving conviction. He might have been able to handle a little visitation or supervised visits, but giving him full custody destroyed his relationship with his daughter. She is now eighteen years old and lives with BD. This young woman had periods of time when she refused to have any contact with her father—not because BD alienated her, but because she was angry about what she had gone through.

How did the judge interpret the facts of this case? He saw it as a case of "high conflict." But, in fact, the father was doing everything he could to push BD entirely out of the daughter's life. Even allowing BD only nine hours of supervised visitation a month was too generous for this father. He wanted BD out of their daughter's life entirely. BD had no choice but to fight back, if she wanted to remain in her daughter's life. How could the judge construe this scenario as mutual "high conflict"?

That is how abuse looks from the bench. Trying to make a factual determination of who did what and whether someone is violent or abusive is not always easy. It is more convenient to decide that both parties are engaging in high conflict. Unfortunately, when these cases are wrongly decided, they show up in court again and again. Therefore, in the long run, a judge who tries to duck the hard work by slapping on the high-conflict label does not actually clean up his/her calendar.

Case #4: Dr. NT and GF. A psychologist's long list of credentials and all the peer accolades in the world unfortunately say nothing about his/her competence or complaint history. Consider one of the local psychologists, NT, well-known among the members of the Association of Family and Conciliation Courts. This psychologist had first given national presentations on the subject of parental alienation (earlier, when it was in vogue) and now spoke about more current topics, such as parent coordinators.

The American Psychological Association (APA) disciplined him for his conduct in GF's case, although this information is not available anywhere on the APA site. On July 7, 1993, Dr. NT had GF take a version of the MCMI (Millon Clinical Multiaxial Inventory) psychological test.[32] Although she took that test only one time, his billing statement when examined, included an entry stating that he had spent 1.5 hours with her a week later, having her retake the same test. In the discovery process, he produced two answer sheets that he claimed were both hers; on one, GF had written her name, and on the other Dr. NT had written a name similar to hers, although the spelling of the first name was different, and he included only the last initial. He also produced two computer printouts of the test results. The two printouts were so different that it should have been obvious that they referred to two different individuals. Because of his clerical error, Dr. NT misdiagnosed her, stating that her inconsistencies in the two tests he gave revealed pathology.

Dr. NT diagnosed GF as having Antisocial Personality Disorder.[33] According to the then-current *Diagnostic and Statistical Manual of Mental Disorders,*[34] the criteria include the person having "Evidence of a Conduct Disorder with onset before age 15, as indicated by a history of *three* or more of the following" and then it lists certain behaviors: "was often truant," "often initiated physical fights," etc.

---

[32] T. Millon, with C. Millon, R. Davis. & S. Grossman, *Millon Clinical Multiaxial Inventory-III* (2d ed. 1997).

[33] Report by Dr. NT, Oct. 25, 1993, at 13.

[34] American Psychiartric Association, *Diagnostic and Statistical Manual of Mental Disorders*, at 344 (3d ed. rev. 1987).

At his deposition, Dr. NT was asked whether GF met the criteria for Conduct Disorder. He responded that he did not have information about her behavior prior to the age of fifteen. Dr. NT was subsequently disciplined for not having the information on which to base a diagnosis as well as for poor record keeping.

What happened to GF's son as a result of Dr. NT's flawed psychological evaluation? The father was permitted to move the boy to another state, where his grades plummeted. When GF obtained copies of the father's credit cards records for a motion to modify child support, it became evident that he still spent half of his time in the California town where GF lives—a fact he carefully concealed from the court. This father's motivation was not to have his son live with him; it was to take the son away from GF. The son then was left adrift, barely graduating from high school and then being convicted of drunken driving shortly afterward. He drifts from job to job. Once the son became an adult and therefore no longer required child support, the father left him to his own devices. Of course, the forensic experts would claim that all of this resulted from the son having parents who went through a "high-conflict" divorce. But if the facts of this case are examined, the differences between GF and her stable life versus the father's irresponsibility, bankruptcy, and abusiveness, it strains credulity to claim that giving custody of the son to his father had no deleterious effects.

How could a prestigious psychologist like Dr. NT make such horrible mistakes? This brings us to the following questions: What could even the best of psychologists do under the conditions presented in family court? Why do we use psychologists and mental health personnel at all, as opposed to, say, judges?

FLAWED METHODOLOGY

Psychologists' training is based, in part, on research studies and on generalizations drawn from those studies. Research on tests that measure personality traits typically rests on the following assumption: if persons respond in x way to y test, they tend to exhibit z behavior or mental characteristic. The way these tests are used in the family court system, however, is not nearly as straightforward or objective as, say, using a thermometer to take a person's temperature. The results of the tests that many forensic psychologists use in matrimonial cases are based on probabilities. In other words, if a given person responds in a certain manner to this particular psychological test, there is a certain probability that the person has a particular mental characteristic. Unfortunately, the psychologists are usually not found at the courthouse telling the judge exactly what that probability is.

Theodore Millon, the author of the MCMI-III test, stated in his book,

[W]e find that the MCMI reports prove to be on the mark in about 55% to 65% of patients to whom it is administered.[35]

If the psychological test, properly given and interpreted, accurately describes the subject in only 55 percent of the cases, how much better is it than flipping a coin? If the test has only a 55 percent likelihood of correctly describing the subject, how can you justify telling a judge that this test score means that the person may have this

---

[35] Theodore Millon & Caryl Bloom, *The Millon Inventories: A Practioner's Guide to Personalized Clinical Assessment* 76 (2008).

particular characteristic (e.g., a mental disorder)? With the MCMI-III, there is, after all, a 45 percent probability that the person does not have that characteristic.

It should also be noted that Dr. Millon refers to "patients" not to "test subjects." because he was not using a representative sample of the population. Dr. Millon makes it clear that the "MCMI-III is not a general personality instrument to be used for 'normal' populations"[36] He goes on to say, "Those who wish to appraise the psychological attributes and traits of non-clinical (i.e., normal) adults may wish to utilize the Millon Index of Personality Styles, also termed the MIPS."[37]

Dr. Millon indicated that his test is not entirely inaccurate in cases where it fails to accurately describe the subject:

> [There are] partial misjudgments in about another 25% to 30% of cases; and they appear off target, that is, appreciably in error, about 10% to 15% of the time.[38]

Yes, but how is a judge to know whether the tests results in the custody evaluation report he/she is reading fall in the category of being accurate 55 to 65 percent of the time, or in the group containing partial misjudgments 25 to 30 percent of the time, or are among those appreciably in error 10 to 15 percent of the time? Hopefully, the psychologist would not use the data if it fell into the latter category. But how should the judge view this evidence? Does it accurately fit the party before the court, or not?

One could argue that the Minnesota Multiphasic Personality Inventory (MMPI-2)[39] is more widely used and is more suited to judging parental fitness, in comparison with MCMI-III. Commenting on the original MMPI (which is not fundamentally different from the MMPI-2 in this regard), Jay Ziskin, Ph.D., stated as follows:

> According to reviewers in Buros' *Fifth Mental Measurements Yearbook* (1959), the MMPI has modest validity for distinguishing one kind of *group* from another in terms of pathology. As its manual states, "A high score on a scale has been found to predict positively the corresponding final clinical diagnosis or estimate in more than 60% of new psychiatric admissions." Simple arithmetic tells us, then, that it obviously fails to predict in close to 40% of the cases.[40]

Psychological Evaluations for the Courts points out that one legal scholar concluded that "for the most part, the law should bar evidence expressed in mathematical probabilities."[41] What should a judge do if presented with evidence that has a 75 percent probability of applying to the person in the case, which means there is a 25 percent probability that it has absolutely nothing to do with that person? Certainly, by the time the probability is up to 75 or 85 percent, the strong temptation is to conclude

[36] Theodore Millon, *The Millon Inventories: Clinical and Personality Assessment* 35 (1997).

[37] Millon, *supra* note 32, at 35.

[38] Id. at 3.

[39] Butcher et al., *supra* note 1.

[40] 2 Jay Ziskin, *Coping With Psychiatric and Psychological Testimony* 785 (1995).

[41] Gary Melton et al., *Psychological Evaluations for the Courts—A Handbook for Mental Health Professionals and Lawyers* 13 (2d ed. 1997).

that this evidence describes this individual with 100 percent accuracy. But what if the person is in the 15 to 25 percent of subjects who are not accurately described? What if the judge is not informed that the evidence is probabilistic? This is frequently what happens with psychological evaluations. It is, obviously, a serious problem that needs to be addressed.[42]

Problems With Computer Scoring

One of the more problematic developments is the computer scoring of most psychological tests. True-false answer sheets for the world's most widely used psychological test, the MMPI-2, for example, are usually sent through the Internet to a computer scoring service, or the psychologists themselves may purchase the scoring program. The result is a computer printout. The computer prints out sentences that purport to describe the tested subject. Very few psychologists are familiar with the computer formulas that result in the computer-generated interpretation of test scores; as stated in a superb study of the validity of sentences printed out by various computer-based test interpretations (C.B.T.I.s):

> [T]he scientific basis for the C.B.T.I., namely the decision rules which codify the rationale and the evidence used to produce the computer interpretations, may wind up locked in a black box, inaccessible to test users.[43]

This one sentence summarizes one of the most problematic and pervasive practices of today's forensic evaluators. When their assessments are based on psychological testing, most use paraphrased or verbatim-copied text that the computerized interpretation program spits out onto its printouts. The psychologists give the test, send the answer sheet to the computer company, get the printout, and largely copy the printout into the purported psychological evaluation without making clear that the sentences are copied into their reports. In the meantime, the psychologists ("test users") have no understanding of the rules that resulted in the computerized interpretation. Knowing these rules is entirely different from a general knowledge of the MMPI-2 and its clinical scales. Based on what I have seen in my years of practice, most matrimonial forensic psychologists have no clue about the actual lines of program that result in the sentences that purport to describe the person and how those sentences are, or are not, actually connected to the MMPI-2.

---

[42] *See* Judge W.J. Giovan, *Admitting Expert Child Custody Evaluations Under Newly Amended MRE 703 & 1101,* Sept. 3, 2003, *available at* http://www.courts.michigan.gov/mji/webcast/090303/ExpertChildCustodyOutline.pdf. Judge Giovan was quoting Melvin Guyer, Ph.D., J.D., "The Expert in Custody Evaluations (Out of the Frye Pan and Into the Tire)," *Mich. Fam. L.J.* 49-51 (special ed. 2000): "Adversary expert child custody reports have questionable value: We do know from scientific research relating to clinical decision making that clinical predictions, which are the essential (though sometimes unexpressed) underpinnings of custody evaluations, are, in a number of forensic areas, quite unreliable and often have only a modicum of predictive validity. In some spheres of clinical prediction the validity/reliability measures associated with those predictions are so low as to render clinical judgments a usefulness little better (and sometimes worse), than chance."

[43] Terry B. Gutkin & Steven L. Wise, *The Computer and the Decision-Making Process* 75 (1991).

Debunking a Popular Computerized Test Interpretation Program

In the San Jose, California, area, by the mid 1990s the computerized program with the Behaviordyne/Behaviordata trade name had become popular with certain psychologists, including, especially, its owners, MF (Dr. MF is the stalker described above (see "Can the Psychologists' Background Affect the Evaluation?") and EF, who were often selected to examine police officers after a shooting. As explained in *The Computer and the Decision-Making Process,* the printed interpretations produced by this computer program's printout were of highly questionable validity. Although the MMPI-2 has been validated for various purposes with particular populations, the specific computer-scoring program used by Behaviordyne/Behaviordata was never validated.[44] When subpoenaed, the owners, Drs. MF and EF, produced a 300-item bibliography. But when it was subjected to expert scrutiny, the proffered bibliography did not list a single validation study. I obtained access to parts of the computer program itself. The written formula that generated the statements below looked like this:

statement no. = 178 -2 (if PdK >= 70) -1 (if Mfm <= 30) + .1 x (PdK - Mfm)

===

00175

the way @H1 @V1 behaves toward men is very feminine indeed, but it's also spiteful and hateful. @H1 may or may not be aware of it, but @H1 @V1 nurses a deep grudge against men.

00176

the way @H1 @V1 behaves toward men is very feminine, but it's also spiteful and hateful. @H1 may or may not be aware of it, but @H1 @V1 nurses a deep grudge against men.

00177

the way @H1 @V1 behaves toward men is very feminine indeed, but it's also spiteful. @H1 may or may not be aware of it, but @H1 @V1 harbors a grudge against men.

00178

the way @H1 @V1 behaves toward men is very feminine, but it's also spiteful. @H1 may or may not be aware of it, but @H1 @V1 harbors a grudge against men.

---

[44] Id.

Given a certain pattern of test scores, the Behaviordyne/Behaviordata computerized scoring program would generate such sentences as those above for female test-takers only but not for male test-takers. For example, if a female received unusual scores on Scales 1, 3, and 4, the scoring program would interpret this pattern of scores as indicative of, say, Borderline Personality Disorder. However, if a male received the very same pattern of scores, the program would *not* identify him as having Borderline Personality Disorder.

Under oath, Dr. EF falsely testified that if the gender of the tested subject was changed, only the pronouns in the printout would change. Although absolutely false, such testimony made it very difficult for attorneys to prove that the psychologists were misusing these tests. One would have to dig down to the very lines of the computer program language to expose the extreme gender bias embedded in it.

Consider the effect the following computerized interpretation would have on a mother's chances of obtaining custody of her son. "The way she behaves toward men is very feminine indeed, but it's also spiteful and hateful. She may or may not be aware of it, but she nurses a deep grudge against men." Bandying about interpretive statements based on wrongful attributions toward a mother is like tossing a hand grenade into the middle of a family picnic.

In addition, the MMPI-2 manual[45] makes it clear that Scale Five (Masculinity/Femininity) should not be used for forensic (court) work at all. The scale was originally developed to assist clinicians who were trying to "cure" homosexual men; it was then applied, in reverse, to female test-takers, making the scale itself highly questionable. Nonetheless, Behaviordyne/Behaviordata used the score on Scale Five in its computerized test interpretation protocol. This brings us back to the fact that without thorough research, the psychologist who uses the computer scoring service has no way of knowing how the program comes up with its interpretations—interpretations, it must be noted, that may be cited as a basis for removing children from the custody of their mothers.[46]

Not only is every single sentence in the computerized printout probabilistic (as opposed to determinative), but the probability that each sentence describes a given subject also varies. To be fair to the judge, a psychological report really should provide information on the probability that each statement actually applies or does not apply to the tested subject. In reality, the psychologist cannot provide this information to the judge because the psychologist does not know this probability. If you ask a psychologist giving testimony about such matters, he/she is likely to say something like, "I'm not a psychometrician." Such a statement means that the psychologist does not know all of the details of the test in question. But if they do not know the details, what do they know? Further, how can they use tests that they themselves do not understand?

In summary, although the MMPI-2 may be highly regarded within some circles and has been validated for some purposes, the wholesale or, especially, verbatim use by forensic evaluators of defective computerized interpretations turns MMPI-2 test results into useless if not harmful garbage. This practice, needless to say, goes completely against established professional rules.

Using additional tests along with the MMPI-2 provides little improvement. A test is "valid" if it actually measures what it claims to measure. Even to nonpsychologists,

---

[45] Butcher et al., *supra* note 1.

[46] The author always considers abuse from the point of view of both genders, but this printout had such sentences only for women.

it should be fairly obvious that if you use a group of tests that are not valid for a specific purpose (such as, in a custody case, tests that do not test parental fitness or any other characteristic relevant to child custody), your accuracy will be no better than if you had used only one invalid test.

In fact, experiments described by Ziskin indicate that when clinical psychologists were asked to differentiate normal subjects from patients, the psychologists who used more than one test often did worse at the task than those using only one test.[47]

So, in our domestic relations courts, we have a situation in which judges are deferring to experts who rely on tests that are about as accurate as flipping a coin. It would be a lot faster, cheaper, and more honest for a judge to simply flip a coin to decide who gets custody, particularly since forensic evaluators charge anywhere from $5,000 to $60,000 per case.

Possible Explanations

In seeking possible explanations for the use of flawed psychological evaluations in domestic relations cases, some scholars have posited that the baggage the expert witnesses themselves bring into the process undermines objectivity, thereby tainting results. In the words of New York Law Professor Michael Perlin, "[there] is a robust body of evidence showing that expert decision making is positively correlated with the witness' underlying political ideology, that a witness' unconscious identification with one side of a legal battle may distort his or her testimony, and that much expert testimony is *not* a matter of scientific expertise, but a matter of social policy."[48]

For abuse victims seeking help through custody and divorce proceedings in domestic relations courts, the overriding social policy seems to be to ignore the abuse. Consider the work of the evaluator Dr. MQ (see "How Could a Psychologist Be So Wrong?"). I learned that she has a pattern of not finding any abuse and of labeling the nonabusive parent as the problem. She is not just your average psychological practitioner. In Silicon Valley today, if you are looking for a forensic psychologist to investigate issues of child sexual abuse in the divorce context, it is quite likely you will be referred to Dr. MQ. Judges have come and gone over the years, but she remains in practice. Why do they choose her to evaluate these cases when she has clearly demonstrated that she cannot see abuse that is otherwise abundantly clear? The answer is in the very question: the court prefers to appoint a psychologist who will declare that there is no abuse. If it were to be determined that a case did involve, for example, sexual abuse, that would create a big problem for the judge. After all, if the sexual abuse is declared nonexistent, whichever parent (usually the mother) reported it can be simply labeled as a false accuser and/or potential alienator.

---

[47] 2 Ziskin, *supra* note 40, at 708.

[48] Michael Perlin, *The Hidden Prejudice: Mental Disability on Trial* 84 (2000). Professor Perlin's statement is drawn from the following: Robert J. Hormant & Daniel B. Kennedy, "Judgment of Legal Insanity as a Function of Attitude Toward the Insanity Defense," 8 *Int'l J.L. & Psychiatry* 67 (1986); Robert J. Hormant & Daniel B. Kennedy "Subjective Factors in the Judgment of Insanity," 14 *Crim. Just. & Behav.* 38 (1987); Robert J. Hormant & Daniel B. Kennedy, "Definitions of Mental Illness as a Factor in Expert Witnesses: Judgments of Insanity," 31 *Corrective & Soc. Psychol. J. Behav. Tech, Methods & Therapy* 125 (1985). Professor Perlin quoted Bernard Diamond, author of "The Fallacy of the Impartial Expert," 3 *Archives Crim. Psychodynamics* 221, 222 (1959), *quoted in* Robert Lloyd Goldstein, "Hiring the Hired Guns: Lawyers and Their Psychiatric Experts," 11 *Leg. Stud. F.* 41 (1987); Ben Bursten, *Beyond Psychiatric Expertise* 167 (1984).

The million-dollar question is, why does the court never do anything to check on the accuracy of psychologists' findings and recommendations? The answer is because the court is not in the business of creating huge problems for itself. This could explain the continued irrational use of highly questionable science by otherwise responsible judges.

SCOPE OF THE PROBLEM

One might ask, "Wasn't this weird computer scoring system used only in Santa Clara County?" or "How do we know that custody evaluators aren't more effective in other state courts?" Or further, "Isn't the data in this article merely anecdotal?"

Unfortunately, there is little hard information available regarding the practices of forensic evaluators. Besides those based on self-reports, only one research study has been conducted of custody evaluation practices by mental health experts, according to the authors of an article published by the American Psychological Society.[49] The numerous self-reports given by the examiners themselves are helpful but raise questions of accuracy, according to the authors.[50]

Despite the curious lack of hard investigation of this issue, there is a widespread perception among legal and mental health professionals that the forensic work done in custody proceedings is of low quality. The authors of the psychological research journal cited above put it this way: "We are dubious about many child custody evaluation practices, because of the absence of solid psychological science and of clear criteria to be predicted by psychological science."[51]

In another article, published by the American Academy of Matrimonial Lawyers (an elite, national trade group of matrimonial lawyers), the authors note that the problem of low-quality forensic evaluations has caused such concern that certain commentators have recommended abolishing child custody evaluations altogether in private divorce and custody proceedings.[52]

I am constantly contacted by people from across the United States who are embroiled in cases similar to those I just described. Given the near-total absence of objective data on the usefulness of evaluations, it seems inconceivable that the courts would continue to routinely, blithely order forensic examinations in custody cases.

I would, therefore, like to offer a proposal: The professional psychological associations are invited to conduct studies to demonstrate that the probability of the accuracy of forensic evaluators' descriptions of tested subjects exceeds 50 percent. As an alternative, the psychological associations are invited to provide empirical evidence regarding which of their practices have been proven successful in determining the abuser from the abused in the context of custody proceedings.

---

[49] Robert E. Emery, R.K. Otto & W.T. O'Donohue, "A Critical Assessment of Child Custody Evaluations," 6(1) *Psychol. Sci. in the Pub. Int.* 6 (2005), *available at* http://www.psychologicalscience.org/journals/index.cfm?journal=pspidcontent=pspi/6-1. The publisher, Association for Psychological Science (previously the American Psychological Society) states that it is a nonprofit organization dedicated to the advancement of scientific psychology and its representation at the national and international level. More information is available at http://www.psychologicalscience.org/about/.

[50] Id. at 6.

[51] Id. at 7.

[52] Baerger et al. *supra* note 5.

We may have only "anecdotal" information, but there is enough of it—especially in the absence of any proof to the contrary—to suggest a serious need for quality control of the products of forensic psychological evaluations.

HOW CAN THIS SITUATION BE CHANGED?

Retrospective studies of the accuracy of the predictions/statements made in the family court context by forensic psychological evaluators are what is really needed. Given the horror stories that abound, such studies are urgently called for. Researchers could examine the reports of the psychologists most frequently employed by the court and then contact the affected family members, especially the children, to see how the evaluator's recommendations worked out a decade after they had been made. In addition, the following steps should be taken:

1. Judges need to take responsibility for their own decisions rather than taking the easy road by, for example, sending the litigants to a psychological evaluator and then rubber-stamping whatever the evaluator says.

2. Judges must avoid labeling custody litigants, in a knee-jerk manner, as "high conflict." Somehow, judges have come to assume that psychologists operate according to scientific objectivity while parents are overly emotional and self-interested. However, considering the financial incentives for psychologists in these cases, and given that parents are in the best position to know their own children, when numerous litigants are all claiming the same thing—that a custody evaluation report does not describe them accurately—their complaints should be given serious consideration.

3. Litigants should find one another and group their psychological reports together to determine if there is a problematic pattern. Unfortunately, many local court rules direct parents not to reveal their reports to anyone else. The state of California has recently passed legislation that gags parents by restricting access to evaluations to parents, their attorneys, and the court personnel only.[53] However, the U.S. Constitution, permits one to prepare his/her case, and gathering databanks of psychological evaluations for information purposes on the evaluators certainly counts as preparation of a case. So the validity of the local rules may be questioned on constitutional grounds. Furthermore, this legislation might run afoul of the First Amendment guarantee of free speech. In any event, such rules function not to protect children, but to protect a system that has gone completely out of control. It might be possible to have one attorney in a given geographical area serve as a clearinghouse for information from litigants.

4. Lawyers must look at psychological reports critically and do adequate discovery to analyze them. Adequate discovery means, at the very least, obtaining full copies of the reports on both parties and the children as well as all of the underlying data. Because the legal standard is the "best interests of the child(ren)," a comparative standard, lawyers must have information on both

---

[53] California Assembly Bill 1877 amends California Family Code Section 3111 by adding subsection (d), which becomes operative on January 1, 2010. The legislation creates monetary sanctions on a party for making unwarranted disclosure of written confidential child custody evaluations if it is done "recklessly or maliciously" and is not in child's best interest.

parties, not just on their own client. The basic guideline for lawyers who cross-examine experts in any field is to learn more than the expert knows on the topics about which the cross-examination will be conducted. Evaluations cannot be demonstrated as faulty merely through the use of questions based on logic. Extensive reading and research are also necessary, or else the lawyer must hire a consultant.

The professional psychological associations and state licensing boards need to function more effectively. Currently, they turn a deaf ear to complaints arising out of family court litigation, which is precisely where the worst work is being done. Immunity laws prevent parents from suing "experts" for malpractice, so slovenly work is common. When parents complain to official agencies, those agencies should function as they are meant to, meaning they should work to protect the consumer-litigant.

Finally, no changes will be forthcoming until parents, both men and women, come together to make it happen. In family courts across the United States, each gender tends to see the other gender as the problem. In the meantime, the faulty system continues to steamroll over mothers, fathers, and children while enriching the pocketbooks of the "experts." It is a perfect example of divide and conquer, and, in that regard, it has been functioning perfectly.

Author's Note

For more information on the topic of this chapter, see "Dissecting Custody Psychological Evaluations," a 2004 lecture on DVD by this author. The DVD contains information based on original research by the author that she has used to win her cases. The information in the DVD is applicable nationwide and is especially helpful to lawyers in challenging custody evaluations that purport to be based on psychological evaluations. The DVD is available at http://www.divorcecal.com.

The author wishes to thank Karen Winner for her editing of an earlier draft of this chapter. Karen Winner, Esq., is author of *Divorced From Justice: The Abuse of Women and Children by Divorce Lawyers and Judges* (1996). In 1992, Ms. Winner, then a policy analyst with the New York City Department of Consumer Affairs, wrote *Women in Divorce: Lawyers, Ethics Fees and Fairness,* a report that uncovered the problem of the routine financial abuse of women by their divorce attorneys. The Consumer Affairs' report prompted statewide public hearings and is widely credited with galvanizing reforms to better protect legal consumers from predatory practices by divorce lawyers. On May 4, 1993, in New York State, the Committee to Examine Lawyer Conduct in Matrimonial Actions (known as the Milonas Commission), headed by Appellate Justice E. Leo Milonas (retired) issued its report. This report called for, among other things, a ban on nonrefundable retainers and on the practice of lawyers of foreclosing on their clients' homes for unpaid legal fees. Then-Chief Judge Judith Kay promulgated these reforms, and more, in 1993.

Chapter 22

Factoring in the Effects of Children's Exposure to Domestic Violence in Determining Appropriate Postseparation Parenting Plans

by Claire V. Crooks, Ph.D., C. Psych., Peter G. Jaffe, P.h.D., C. Psych., and Nicholas Bala, J.D.

INTRODUCTION

Over the past thirty years, children's exposure to domestic violence (DV) has gone from being an overlooked phenomenon to a topic of considerable research and debate. As understanding of the detrimental impacts of DV has grown, it has become increasingly clear that DV is not a matter that solely affects adults, but rather can have an enormous impact on children's development. As a result, researchers and practitioners have been challenged to apply this understanding to child custody determinations. Although there are significant gaps in the research literature, the existing studies show that as a group, children who have been raised in families where there has been violence between the adult intimate partners fare worse than their peers across a range of social, behavioral, and learning outcomes. Unfortunately, much of this research on children's functioning has focused exclusively on the identification of specific pathologies, reducing children's adjustment to the presence or absence of particular behavior problems and disorders. Questions of resilience and vulnerabilities of children have received little attention in the research.

In this chapter we highlight the need for understanding and assessing the impact of exposure to DV on individual children within a developmental framework—that is, in light of the specific developmental tasks of each childhood stage. From this perspective, exposure to DV is likely to interfere with different aspects of development for infants and toddlers, preschoolers, school-aged children, and adolescents. In the second half of the chapter, we identify a set of principles to use when considering competing priorities in developing child-focused parenting plans in cases affected by DV. Finally, we discuss a number of examples of specific dilemmas faced by judges, custody evaluators, and other advocates and advisors in establishing what constitutes the best interests of children who have been exposed to DV.

CHILDREN EXPOSED TO DOMESTIC VIOLENCE: THE BIG PICTURE

In considering the big picture of children's exposure to DV, there are two provisos that need to be kept in mind. First, the phrase itself—*children exposed to domestic violence*—is really a euphemism for a range of damaging experiences. The label originally applied to children of mothers who were battered by a partner, as child "witnesses" of DV. However, the terminology evolved with the recognition that the destructive effects arise even if children do not directly observe intimate partner violence and, further, that children's experiences are often more active than implied by the term "witnessing." In a large four-city study utilizing phone interviews with children, "exposure" was found to include a wide range of circumstances, including hearing a violent event, visually witnessing the event, intervening, or being directly involved in the violent event (e.g., being used as a shield against abusive actions), and experiencing the aftermath of a violent event.[1]

Another study used police-collected data over the course of a year to investigate the patterns of DV to which children are exposed.[2] Police officers used a standard, validated protocol to collect data on all substantiated DV within a large municipality. When analyzed, police protocols revealed that almost half of all events had children present, and 81 percent of these incidents involved children being directly exposed to the violence. Young children (under age six) were at particular risk for exposure. In addition, children were disproportionately exposed to the most unstable and dangerous profiles of DV, including those involving weapon use, mutual assault, and substance abuse.

Even if a child does not directly observe spousal abuse, living in a home where there is spousal abuse can have serious negative effects. One researcher observes the following:

> Hiding in their bedrooms out of fear, the children may hear reported threats of injury, verbal assaults on their mother's character, objects hurled across the room, suicide attempts, beatings, and threats to kill. Such exposure will arouse a mixture of intense feelings in the children. These feelings include a fear that the mother will be killed, guilt that they did not stop the violence, divided loyalties, and anger to the mother for not leaving.[3]

Beyond the role(s) that children may play or the experiences that they have in witnessing the abuse of their mothers, there are other contextual layers that add to the heterogeneity of the experience for different children. The relationship of the perpetrator to the victim parent and to the child, the severity and frequency of the violence, and the age of the child when he/she experiences familial violence are examples of contextual factors that can vary widely from case to case. It is essential to keep this heterogeneity in mind and not assume uniform characteristics or experiences for children who have been exposed to violence perpetrated against their mothers.

Second, most existing research has focused on extreme cases of DV (i.e., battering). A pattern of repeated incidents of battering of a female partner by her abusive male partner is the most frequently studied, and typically the most destructive and dangerous, pattern of intimate partner violence, but it is only one among several.[4] Compared to other forms of DV that may be perpetrated on a more equal basis between partners or may be limited to a short period around the dissolution of a relationship, battering is an ongoing use of threat, force, emotional abuse, and other coercive means to dominate one partner and induce fear, submission, and compliance. In studies of shelter and criminal court samples, men are almost always the offenders, and women are victims in cases of this type.

---

[1] J.L. Edleson, "Children's Witnessing of Adult Domestic Violence," 14(8) *J. Interpersonal Violence* 839 (1999).

[2] J.W. Fantuzzo & R.A. Fusco, "Children's Direct Exposure to Types of Domestic Violence Crime: A Population-Based Investigation, 22 *J. Fam. Violence* 543 (2007).

[3] D.G. Saunders, "Child Custody Decisions in Families Experiencing Woman Abuse," 39 *Social Work* 51, 54 (1994).

[4] M.P. Johnson, "Patriarchal Terrorism and Common Couple Violence: Two Forms of Violence Against Women," 57 *J. Marriage & Fam.* 283 (1995).

As we have argued elsewhere, it is important not to apply policies and procedures developed with respect to male batterers indiscriminately to all cases of DV.[5] Failure to differentiate among different types of violence can, on one hand, lead to inefficient usage of scarce resources by conceptualizing any incident of violence as battering (e.g., termination of visitation or requiring supervised visitation when not necessary) and can harm a positive parent-child relationship. On the other hand, minimizing battering as "couples conflict" can result in a failure to institute the proper safeguards for women and children. Given the scope of this volume, this chapter addresses the needs of children who have been exposed to the battering of their mother by a male partner, rather than providing an exhaustive analysis of all forms and combinations of violence perpetrated within intimate relationships (i.e., female-to-male violence, mutual abuse, and violence within same-sex male and female relationships).

With these two provisos in mind, the extant literature has documented a range of negative impacts for children exposed to the abuse of their mothers by a male partner. These outcomes include numerous behavioral and psychological difficulties that have been identified in a number of reviews and meta-analyses.[6] Most notably, research indicates that children exposed to DV are more likely than other children to be aggressive and have behavioral problems,[7] have different physiological presentations,[8] exhibit higher rates of posttraumatic stress disorder symptomatology,[9] and may also develop a "traumatic bond" (a longing for kindness, leading to confusion between love and abuse) with the perpetrator.[10] An additional concern for children exposed to abuse of their mothers is not an outcome per se, but rather the significant overlap with child maltreatment. It is estimated that in families where a male partner is violent towards his spouse, children are themselves directly the victims of violence in approximately 30 to 60 percent of cases.[11]

The overlap between woman abuse and child abuse is particularly concerning because there is growing evidence that there is a strong dosage effect with respect to the

---

[5] P.G. Jaffe, C.V. Crooks & N. Bala, *Making Appropriate Parenting Arrangements in Family Violence Cases: Applying the Literature to Promising Practices* (Ottawa, ON: Department of Justice. Report 2005-FCY-3E, 2005); P.G. Jaffe et al., "Custody Disputes Involving Allegations of Domestic Violence: The Need for Differentiated Approaches to Parenting Plans," 46 *Fam. Ct. Rev.* 500 (2008).

[6] J.L. Edleson, *Problems Associated With Children's Witnessing of Domestic Violence* (1999), a*vailable at* http://www.vaw.umn.edu/documents/vawnet/witness/witness.html; K.M. Kitzmann et al., "Child Witnesses to Domestic Violence: A Meta-Analytic Review," 71(2) *J. Consulting & Clinical Psychol.* 339 (2003); D.A. Wolfe et al., "The Effects of Children's Exposure to Domestic Violence: A Meta-Analysis and Critique," 6 *Clinical Child & Fam. Psychol. Rev.* 171 (2003).

[7] S.A. Graham-Bermann, "The Impact of Woman Abuse on Children's Social Development: Research and Theoretical Perspectives," in *Children Exposed to Marital Violence: Theory, Research, and Applied Issues* 21-54 (G. Holden, R. Geffner & E. Jouriles eds., 1998).

[8] K.M. Saltzman, G.W. Holden & C.J. Holahan, "The Psychobiology of Children Exposed to Marital Violence,," 34(1) *J. Clinical Child & Adolescent Psychol.* 129 (2005).

[9] K.L. Kilpatrick,M. Litt & M. Williams, "Post-Traumatic Stress Disorder in Child Witnesses to Domestic Violence," 67 *Am. J. Orthopsychiatry* 639 (1997); G. Margolin & K.A. Vickerman, "Posttraumatic Stress in Children and Adolescents Eposed to Family Violence I. Overview and Assues," 38 *Prof. Psychol.: Res. & Prac.* 613 (2007).

[10] L. Bancroft & J.G. Silverman, *The Batterer as Parent: Addressing the Impact of Domestic Violence on Family Dynamics* (2002).

[11] J.E. Edleson, "The Overlap Between Child Maltreatment and Woman Battering," 5 *Violence Against Women* 134 (1999).

number of negative childhood experiences encountered by a child. The Adverse Childhood Experiences Study (ACES)[12] of the Centers for Disease Control and Prevention has collected data on over 8,500 adults from a large primary health care provider. Within this sample, researchers documented that it is not any one specific childhood experience that determines negative outcomes, but rather the cumulative impact of those types of experiences. The ACES has demonstrated that this dosage effect is evident for a wide range of physical and mental health outcomes among adolescents and adults. In a study undertaken by the first author of this chapter, it was found that each cumulative form of child maltreatment (e.g., physical child abuse, sexual child abuse, exposure to DV) added significant risk for negative adolescent outcomes. Specifically, each additional form of abuse was associated with a 124 percent increase in the likelihood of an adolescent exhibiting violent delinquency by the time they were in grade nine.[13]

Although the serious implications for children who are exposed to DV have been well documented, there are a number of studies which indicate that not all children who directly and indirectly experience family violence later develop severe emotional and behavioral problems.[14] Cunningham and Baker caution against making assumptions that (1) all children are negatively affected by DV, (2) all children are affected in the same way, and (3) DV should be the sole focus of interventions (in light of the overlap with other forms of abuse and adverse experiences).[15] Outcomes of individual cases vary widely and are affected by a combination of factors, including the child's age and developmental status when the abuse or neglect occurred, the types of the child abuse (physical abuse, neglect, sexual abuse, etc.), the frequency, duration, and severity of the spousal violence, and the relationship between the child and the abuser.[16] These varying outcomes can be seen in families where children have similar risk factors and exposure experiences but have very different short-term and long-term outcomes.

In addition to variability among risk factors, children may have access to different protective factors that help buffer the impact of exposure to DV. A supportive relationship with a nonabusive adult, connection to community supports, and some child characteristics have been associated with more positive outcomes for children who experience a range of violence.[17] Due to the variability in outcomes among children who have been exposed to DV and/or abused themselves, presence or absence of particular behaviors is neither sufficient nor necessary grounds for verifying the DV.

---

[12] V. Fellitti, R. Anda, D. Nordenberg, D. Williamson, A. Spitz, V. Edwards, M., Koss & J. Marks., "Relationship of Childhood Abuse and Household Dysfunction to Many of the Leading Causes of Death in Adults: The Adverse Childhood Experiences (ACE) Study," 14 *Am. J. Preventive Med.* 245 (1998).

[13] C.V. Crooks et al., "Understanding the Link Between Childhood Maltreatment and Violent Delinquency: What Do Schools Have to Add?" 12 *Child Maltreatment* 269 (2007).

[14] National Clearinghouse on Child Abuse and Neglect Information, *Long-term Consequences of Child Abuse and Neglect* (2004), *available at* http://nccanch.acf.hhs.gov/pubs/factsheets/long_term_consequences.pdf.

[15] A. Cunningham & A. Baker, W*hat About Me! Seeking to Understand the Child's View of Volence in the Family* (2004), *available at* http://www.lfcc.on.ca/what_abut_me.pdf.

[16] R. Chalk, A. Gibbons & H.J. Scarupa, *The Multiple Dimensions of Child Abuse And Neglect: New Insights Into an Old Problem* (2002), *available at* http://www.childtrends.org/files/ChildAbuseRB.pdf.

[17] A.H. Gewirtz & J.E. Edleson, "Young Children's Exposure to Intimate Partner Violence: Towards a Developmental Risk and Resilience Framework for Research and Intervention," 22 *J. Fam. Violence* 151 (2007).

Although there is a general dosage effect for violence, some children exhibit resilience in the face of significant and multiple forms of violence. Thus, children's symptomatology is not a litmus test for whether abuse occurred.

MOVING BEYOND PATHOLOGY: UNDERSTANDING THE IMPACT OF DOMESTIC VIOLENCE WITHIN A DEVELOPMENTAL FRAMEWORK

We are only beginning to move beyond an epidemiological emphasis (i.e., measuring rates of particular problems) to an understanding of the broader picture as it relates to children's exposure to DV. A developmental framework is an important starting point for understanding the myriad ways in which exposure to violence affects children's adjustment and growth towards maturity.[18] A developmental framework highlights the major tasks and characteristics for each childhood stage, with a focus on the experiences necessary for children to achieve optimal adjustment and health. Another important tenet of a developmental framework is that development unfolds in a sequential manner: Interference with a developmental task at one stage of childhood can undermine the achievement of future developmental milestones. Ongoing exposure to any form of violence can interfere with the attainment of important developmental tasks, leading to specific difficulties depending on the age of the child. A developmental psychopathology perspective of abuse views the emergence of maladaptive behaviors, such as peer aggression, school failure, and delinquency, within a longitudinal and multidimensional framework.[19] The discussion that follows identifies the developmental features and tasks of the four stages of childhood—infancy and toddlerhood, preschool age, school age, and adolescence—and the specific ways in which DV jeopardizes these processes.

Infancy and Toddlerhood

There has been much publicity about the importance of children's experiences from birth to age three, and for good reason: the first few years of children's lives provide a critical foundation for their subsequent social, emotional, and intellectual functioning. The most important developmental task during the first year in particular is the development of an organized pattern of attachment. Attachment refers to the systematic manner in which an infant comes to relate to his/her primary caregiver (typically the mother). The field of attachment has identified the parent and child behaviors, some of which are innate, that provide the basis for a secure relationship. Infants are "preadapted" to engage in relationship-enhancing behaviors, such as orienting, smiling, crying, clinging, signaling, and, as they learn to move about, proximity seeking. Infant survival depends on becoming attached to a specific person who is available and responsive to the child's needs. Adults are similarly equipped

---

[18] L.L. Baker, P.G. Jaffe & K. Moore, *Understanding the Effects of Domestic Violence: A Handbook for Early Childhood Educators* (London, ON: Centre for Children and Families in the Justice System of the London Family Court Clinic, 2001); Gewirtz & Edleson, *supra* note 17.

[19] D. Cicchetti, S.L. Toth & A. Maughan, "An Ecological-Transactional Model of Child Maltreatment, in *Handbook of Developmental Psychopathology* 689-722 (A.J. Sameroff, M. Lewis & S.M. Miller eds., 2d ed. 2000).

with attachment-promoting behaviors to respond to infants' needs. These behaviors complement those of the infant—smiling, touching, holding, and rocking. Thus, what begin as instinctive behaviors follow an organized pattern through learning and feedback, primarily from caregivers.[20] Attachment is predominantly determined by the extent to which a child's basic needs are met in a consistent and timely fashion. Simply stated, infants who are fed when they are hungry, comforted when they are upset or startled, and changed when they are wet or uncomfortable tend to develop an organized attachment style. The extent to which a caregiver is able to reflect an infant's feelings back to the child is another important component of developing a secure attachment style and helps the child to form his/her earliest understanding of emotions.[21] The child's attachment style then serves as a prototype for all future relationships and is instrumental in a child's earliest view of the world and the extent to which the world is seen as safe and predictable.[22]

The other defining developmental characteristic of this early stage is the explosive neurological development taking place. Newborns actually have far more brain cells than full grown adults, but their brains are much smaller because these neurons have not yet been connected to each other. During the first few years, and to a lesser extent all the way through childhood and adolescence, brain cells are being connected and pathways are being formed, while other cells are being "pruned" and die off.[23] This hardwiring of the brain is a "use it or lose it" phenomenon. Pathways that are used frequently become strengthened, and as the number of connections increase, the speed with which these pathways can be accessed also increases.[24] Thus, if within the context of consistent and nurturing caregiving an infant is repeatedly soothed when upset, these calming experiences will usually provide the basis for the child to develop the ability to self-soothe. Conversely, an infant who is repeatedly subjected to loud noise and chaos, and who is inconsistently comforted when upset, will tend to strengthen the fight-or-flight pathways of the brain, largely through overactivation of the hypothalamic-pituitary-adrenal (HPA) axis. Studies with maltreated children and adults with a history of childhood abuse show long-term alterations in the HPA axis and norepinephrine systems, which have a pronounced effect on one's responsiveness to stress.[25] These rapid brain development and attachment processes in turn serve as the basis for the emotional regulation that develops over the course of childhood.

---

[20] L.A. Sroufe, "Early Relationships and the Development of Children," 21 *Infant Mental Health J.* 67 (2000).

[21] J. Cassidy, "Emotion Regulation: Influences of Attachment Relationships," 59(2/3) *Monographs of the Soc'y for Res. in Child Dev.* 228 (1994).

[22] C.M. Parkes, J. Stevenson-Hinde & P. Marris eds., *Attachment Across the Life Cycle* (1996); M. Rutter & L.A. Sroufe, " Developmental Psychopathology: Concepts and Challenges," 12 *Dev. & Psychopathology* 265 (2000).

[23] J.P. Shonkoff & P.C. Marshall, "The Biology of Developmental Vulnerability," in *Handbook of Early Childhood Intervention* 35-53 (J. Shonkoff & S. Meisels eds., 2d ed. 2000).

[24] B.D. Perry, *Maltreatment and the Developing Child: How Early Childhood Experience Shapes Child and Culture* (2004). Presentation summarized by A. Cunningham, *available at* http://www.lfcc.on.ca/mccain/perry.pdf.

[25] J.D. Bremner, "Long-Term Effects of Childhood Abuse on Brain and Neurobiology," 12 *Child & Adolescent Psychiatric Clinics of N. Am.,* 271 (2003); C.B. Nemeroff, "Neurobiological Consequences of Childhood Trauma," 65(Supp. 1) *J. Clinical Psychiatry* 18 (2004).

The abuse of an infant or toddler's mother interferes with attachment and ulti-mately influences the rapid brain development taking place. Any form of violence exposes the child to loud and overwhelming stimuli, and the abuse of the infant's mother interferes with the child's primary source of comfort and emotional regulation. It is very difficult for a woman who is being victimized by her partner to attend to her child's needs in a consistent manner. Concomitantly, the infant's brain is developing in such a way that the capacity for self-soothing may be underdeveloped while the speed with which the child becomes aroused to perceived threat may be overdeveloped, essentially hardwiring the infants brain differently than would be the case for infants not exposed to such violence. Indeed, infants under the age of one have been shown to exhibit symptoms of posttraumatic stress disorder when exposed to severe violence towards their mothers.[26] Furthermore, exposure to violence between adults predicts adjustment difficulties for children aged one to three over and above difficulties pre-dicted by angry adult conflict.[27]

Preschool-Aged Children

One of the most important developmental tasks for preschool-aged children (age three to six) is to develop basic social skills, such as cooperation, turn-taking, and negotiation. Simultaneously, they are learning to express emotions in acceptable ways. Where a toddler will understandably throw a tantrum when frustrated, a preschooler is expected to have more control over how frustration is expressed.

One of the most longstanding and robust psychological theories explaining the pro-cess by which these social skills are acquired is Social Learning Theory.[28] According to this theory, much social skill and emotional development takes place through observation of others: How do others react in particular situations, and what are the consequences of their actions? How do people apologize when they are in the wrong? What does it mean to be friends? How do people who love each other show that they are angry? A critical tenet of Social Learning Theory is the salience of perceived contingencies and reinforce-ment with respect to learning from observing others' behavior. That is, young children do not simply imitate those around them; rather, they are more likely to imitate and acquire behaviors that they perceive to lead to positive outcomes. Thus, they are particularly vulnerable to learning that violence has an instrumental value to the perpetrator and that it is an acceptable way to have one's personal needs met. All of these lessons are being learned continuously from their observation and experience of relationships. As the fam-ily unit is still the major arena of socialization for this age group, being exposed to DV puts preschoolers at high risk for acquiring aggressive behaviors and failing to develop more appropriate means of problem solving.

In addition, preschoolers tend to have rigid ideas about gender roles. Because there is so much information for them to process, the use of male and female as organiz-ing concepts is a useful way for them to categorize. As a result, this is the age when

---

[26] G.A. Bogat, GE. DeJonghe, A.A. Levendosky, W.S. Davidson, W. S. & A. von Eye, "Trauma Symptoms Among Infants Exposed to Intimate Partner Violence," 30 *Child Abuse & Neglect* 109 (2006).

[27] R. McDonald et al., "Violence Toward a Family Member, Angry Adult Conflict, and Child Adjustment Difficulties: Relations in Families With 1- to 3-Year-Old Children," 21 *J. Fam. Psychol.* 176 (2007).

[28] A. Bandura, *Social Learning Theory* (1977).

many things are classified as male or female (e.g., girl vs. boy toys and activities, male vs. female occupations) with a strong tendency to overgeneralize.[29] For example, preschoolers may hold fast to the notion that all doctors are male and all nurses are female, even when presented with an exception to that rule.

In light of their rapid development of social skills and emotional regulation, as well as their highly gendered worldview, preschoolers are very susceptible to learning negative ideas about what it means to be a man or a woman, if they are experiencing the gender-based abuse of their mothers. One of the most important messages that preschoolers should receive is about the unacceptability of violence and the need to find alternate ways to solve problems or express anger. Where displays of aggression are expected and somewhat accepted among infants and toddlers, a chief developmental task of the preschool period is to learn to inhibit these impulses toward aggression.[30] Preschoolers who are exposed to DV receive powerful and mixed messages in this regard and, not surprisingly, show higher levels of aggression than their peers. Remembering that development is sequential, children who have been exposed to violence since infancy may be attempting to navigate these developmental tasks in the preschool years with preexisting vulnerabilities.

School-Aged Children

During the school-age development period (ages six to twelve), children place great significance on things being fair and rule based. The preference for rules and order is reflected in their play; this is the age when children can develop elaborate games with each other that have complex rules and regulations. Children this age can understand intent, and they are largely committed to a "just world hypothesis" (i.e., a "good things happen to good people" worldview). As a result, they are prone to explanations of events that are logical and just. In cases where children have experienced the abuse of their mothers, they may try to make sense of the violence by attributing blame to their mother. For example, when asked if it is ever okay for a man to hit a woman, school-aged children whose mothers have been battered will typically say no, but they may add a proviso for extenuating circumstances (e.g., "No . . . unless she is disrespecting her husband").[31] In their attempts to rationalize the gender-based violence to which they are exposed, they may develop negative attitudes about the acceptability of violence and the roles of women and men in relationships.

Another relevant feature of school-aged children is that they develop increased identification with their same-sex parent. They also tend to play in gender-segregated groups that differ in their styles of interaction. Thus, school-aged children who experience the abuse of their mother by a male partner may have different responses and vulnerabilities based on gender, with boys being more likely than girls to develop externalizing aggressive behavioral problems. In one study that analyzed children's responses to various conflict scenarios, abusers' sons who had been excluded by peers were found to show the most violent responses of the children included. In this study, boys and girls exposed

---

[29] L.A. Serbin, K.K. Powlishta & J. Gulko, "The Development of Sex Typing in Middle Childhood," 58 *Monographs of the Soc'y for Res. in Child Dev.* 5 (1983).

[30] R.H. Baillargeon et al., "The Evolution of Problem and Social Competence Behaviors During Toddlerhood: A Prospective Population-Based Cohort Study," 28 *Infant Mental Health J.* 12 (2007).

[31] P.G. Jaffe, D.A. Wolfe & S.K. Wilson, *Children of Battered Women* (1990).

to DV were significantly more violent in conflicts involving aggression and exclusion compared to their nonexposed counterparts.[32] Both boys and girls are developing important social skills and gender roles for relating, and there is a potential to learn negative lessons from witnessing gender-based violence perpetration.

The most important developmental task for this age group is successful engagement at school: developing the intellectual, physical, social, behavioral, intellectual, and physical skills to function effectively with their peers and teachers. In this age group, children's sense of self-esteem and competence tends to be tied to their performance and engagement at school. Children who live with a male perpetrator of violence may experience many barriers to school success. They may be tired from inadequate sleep and unable to focus in class, or they may have sporadic attendance. Even if they attend regularly, it is difficult for children in this age group to focus on their schoolwork when they may be worrying about their mother or father. These children may not have a consistently quiet and orderly place to do their homework. They may not have access to a parent who is in the right frame of mind to help them with their homework.

Socially, children exposed to various forms of violence often develop relationships with their peers and teachers that mirror the relationship models they know best. Instead of a healthy sense of autonomy and self-respect, their models of relationships have elements of being both a victim and a victimizer—those who rule and those who submit—and during interactions with peers, maltreated children may alternate between being the aggressor and being the victim.[33] The strategies that may have worked while the child was living with an unpredictable perpetrator of violence, such as hypervigilance and fear, evolve to become highly responsive to threatening or dangerous situations. These strategies are in conflict, however, with the new challenges of school and peer groups. As a result, children with histories of abuse and neglect may be more distracted by aggressive stimuli and misread the intentions of their peers and teachers as being more hostile than they actually are. These children's aggressive behaviors, along with their tendency to overreact to perceived hostility from others, make it difficult for them to establish positive relationships with peers and teachers. Rejection by pro-social peers, in turn, raises the likelihood of these children associating with other deviant and rejected children. Such peer groups, in turn, raise the risk of antisocial behavior as these children enter adolescence.

It may be difficult to redress the social skills problems of exposed children in that these deficits may be based on problematic emotional regulation. In a longitudinal study of children's development, exposure to DV at age 5 predicted emotional dysregulation at age 9.5, which in turn predicting problems with friendships, peer group interactions, and externalizing and internalizing behavior problems at age 11.[34] This study provides a clear example of how interference with developmental tasks at one age (in this case, developing emotional regulation) later undermines functioning in a range of areas (such as friendships, peer groups, and emotional well-being). Clearly, exposure to violence at home presents myriad challenges for school success in both the academic and social realms.

---

[32] B. Ballif-Spanvill, C.J. Clayton & S.B. Hendrix, "Witness and Nonwitness Children's Violent and Peaceful Behavior in Different Types of Simulated Conflict With Peers," 77 *Am. J. Orthopsychiatry* 206 (2007).

[33] K.A. Dodge, G.S. Pettit & J.E. Bates, "Socialization Mediators of the Relation Between Socioeconomic Status and Child Conduct Problems," 65 *Child Dev.* 649 (1994).

[34] L.F. Katz, D.M. Hessler & A. Annest, "Domestic Violence, Emotional Competence, and Child Adjustment," 16 *Soc. Dev.* 513 (2007).

Adolescence

Adolescence (over the age of twelve) is a time of rapid change and development for children. In a relatively short period of time, they are expected to mature from being children to be being prepared for the demands of adult roles. There are two major developmental tasks undertaken during this period. The first has to do with increased autonomy and differentiation from the family of origin. Essentially, adolescents need to develop an adult identity, and one of the ways they accomplish that is to develop an understanding of how they are similar and different from the other members of their families. There is significant boundary-testing during this phase as adolescents experiment with adult behaviors.

The other set of developmental tasks has to do with the rapidly changing relationship patterns of adolescence.[35] Peer relationships become much more intense than previously, replacing the family as the primary socializing force in children's lives. Romantic relationships become a major focus for adolescents and evolve from group-based dating experiences in early adolescence to dyadic relationships that are more similar to adult relationships by mid- to late adolescence.[36] Parallel to the emergence of intimate dating relationships, youths need to navigate the development of a sexual identity, all within the rapidly occurring physical changes of puberty.

Youths who are exposed to the abuse of their mothers are hindered in these tasks in a number of important ways. These children may not have a solid foundation with their parents from which to navigate the separation that occurs during adolescence. They may be more prone to engage in violence in their own dating relationships, as that is the behavior that has been modeled. In particular, boys may be at increased risk for perpetrating violence in their intimate relationships, and girls may be at increased risk of remaining in a relationship with an abusive partner. Alternatively, adolescent boys may begin to perpetrate violence within their own families, typically directed towards their mothers and siblings. Although boys are the perpetrators in the majority of adolescent-to-parent violence, adolescent girls also may become assaultive with their mothers in an attempt to show that they are not "weak" or vulnerable like their mothers.[37] Furthermore, in an attempt to establish their adult identities without the secure foundation of healthy family relationships, they may be more likely to engage in risk-taking behaviors and to abuse drugs or alcohol.

Summary

A child's exposure to the abuse of his/her mother by a male partner causes interference with normal developmental processes, resulting in a range of subtle and not-so-subtle difficulties in emotional regulation and the development of positive and healthy relationships, as well as affecting the child's behavior. Understanding a child's developmental stage and needs is essential for developing appropriate plans and interventions. Within such a framework, sometimes children who appear to be coping well may be not attaining their optimal developmental trajectories.

---

[35] D.A. Wolfe, P.G. Jaffe & C.V. Crooks, *Adolescent Risk Behavior: Why Teens Experiment and Strategies to Keep Them Safe* (2006).

[36] W. Furman & D. Buhrmester, (1992). Age and Sex-Differences in Perceptions of Networks of Personal Relationships," 63 *Child Dev.* 103 (1992).

[37] B. Cottrell & P. Monk, "Adolescent-to-Parent Abuse: A Qualitative Overview of Common Themes," 25 *J. Fam. Issues* 1072 (2004).

A classic example of this superficial robustness is the "parentified child" who has been inappropriately burdened with adult matters and responsibilities and who assumes an adult role within the family. Although parentified children may appear responsible, polite, and even more mature than their peers, this pseudomaturity comes at a cost.[38] Developmentally, they are not being allowed the chance to be children and to achieve their developmental tasks, which might in turn lead to difficulties down the road. For example, an adolescent who takes on the responsibilities of running the house and trying to appease the adults may seem pleasant, but she is not establishing the autonomy or relationships with peers that are an integral part of adolescence and that provide important stepping stones toward becoming an independent adult. If there has been DV prior to the parents' separation, prioritization of the child's needs in the context of a custody dispute requires an understanding of the developmental tasks and characteristics of the child at each stage. From this vantage point, the negative impacts on the child of exposure to a mother's abuse is critical, regardless of whether a child meets diagnostic criteria for a particular psychological disorder.

DEVELOPMENTAL FRAMEWORK FOR PARENTING PLANS

There is increasing recognition that perpetrators of DV are not appropriate candidates for custody or joint custody in most cases.[39] In many jurisdictions, this recognition has been codified as a statutory rebuttable presumption against custody for a perpetrator of DV. As courts become better at implementing these standards in cases where the mother has been victimized by a male partner, disputes about visitation occur more frequently than genuine disputes over custody. These problems with visitation can continue for many years, whereas disputes over custody are usually resolved "once and for all."

Visitation can be very problematic for victims of abuse and their children, as it is difficult to have it legally terminated. The continuing contact with an abusive ex-partner that visitation requires can be stressful and create risks for abused mothers and their children. Abusive ex-partners may use visitation to try to denigrate and undermine children's respect for the custodial parent, encouraging the children to behave in destructive or defiant ways when they return home.

It must also be appreciated, however, that many children want to see their noncustodial parents, even if these parents have abused their partners. In many cases, children "may benefit from such contact, as long as safety measures are provided, the contact is not overly extensive, and the abuser is not permitted to cause setbacks in the child's healing process."[40] In cases where actual custody is not at stake, the options for structuring visitation include supervised exchange, supervised visitation, and termination of access.

Supervised Exchange

Supervised exchange involves transferring children from one parent to the other under the supervision of a third party. The supervision can be informal, for example,

---

[38] Bancroft & Silverman, *supra* note 10.

[39] National Council of Juvenile and Family Court Judges, *Model Code for Family Violence* (1994), *available at* http://www.ncjfcj.org/dept/fvd/publications/main.cfm?Action=PUBGET&Filename=new_modelcode.pdf.

[40] Bancroft & Silverman, *supra* note 10.

by a family member, neighbor, or volunteer, or through the use of a public venue for the exchange, such as the parking lot of a police station. The supervision can also be formalized through a supervised access center or by using a designated professional, such as a child care worker or a social worker. The underlying premise is that by having third-party witnesses, the parents will be on their best behavior; by staggering their arrival and departure times, they will not come into physical contact. Supervised exchange provides a buffer in cases where the ongoing conflict cannot be contained by the parents at transitions, exposing the children to high levels of conflict. It is also useful in cases where there has been an historical pattern of DV, and the victim experiences distress or trauma coming into contact with the other parent. However, supervised exchanges do not mitigate the risk of violence to a spouse if there are ongoing concerns about safety of children and their primary caretaker.

In our experience, supervised exchanges are sometimes inappropriately utilized to create a sense of safety when a more restrictive measure (such as supervised visitation) is warranted. As well, informal third-party exchanges may be well intended but inadequate; supervision may require a knowledgeable professional to monitor safety and detect inappropriate behaviors. For example, some parents may be involved in more subtle behaviors that are emotionally abusive, undermine the other parent, or signal threats to the other parent. These more insidious transgressions are difficult for lay people or family members aligned with the perpetrator to identify.

Supervision may be especially appropriate during an initial period after separation when the risk of violence or parental conflict may be higher than after some time has passed. Exchange supervision is less costly, intrusive, and restrictive than visitation supervision but should be contemplated only if there is no significant risk of direct harm to the children or victim from the perpetrator. Any red flags with respect to escalating violence or lethality would contraindicate the use of supervised exchange to protect the well-being of the children and their mother.

Supervised Visitation

Supervised visitation is a parenting arrangement designed to promote safe contact with a parent who is deemed to be a risk due to behaviors ranging from physical abuse to abduction of the child. It may also be appropriate where a child fears a parent, for example, because of having witnessed that parent perpetrate abuse or because of having been abused by that parent. Although supervised visitation is a long-accepted practice in the child protection field, it has emerged more recently in the parental separation context. More serious concerns demand specialized centers and well-trained staff, as opposed to volunteers; in reality, shortage of supervised visitation programs remains a significant challenge for most communities. In more extreme cases, the safety offered by the supervisor is not appropriate for the degree of risk, and, therefore, no contact may be a more appropriate plan. Supervision is intrusive and often expensive. It should usually be considered only for a transition period during which the parent proves that the supervision may not be required or, conversely, that visitation should be terminated.

There is great variability among supervised visitation centers as far as the training of staff and mandates for their programs. Some parents may require extensive assistance during visitation to say and do appropriate things that match their children's needs and stage of development. In some cases, there may be a strained relationship due to historical events, the anxiety of the custodial parent, and the lengthy disruption of any meaningful parent-child relationship. In these circumstances parents may require more than a safe place; significant interventions by a trained professional may be necessary to promote healing and enhance parenting. There are situations where the demands on the supervisor outstrip his/her skills or mandate. There are also special considerations about refusing cases after intake due to the assessment of excessive risk or terminating visits in midstream due to inappropriate parental behavior and/or children's refusal to attend.

Supervised visits cannot be a substitute for a comprehensive evaluation by a qualified mental health professional. Without a proper custody evaluation, a court may draw inappropriate conclusions about the meaning of successful and unsuccessful supervised visits out of context of the larger picture. Too often supervision is dropped (i.e., visits are no longer supervised) after a period of time where nothing overly negative has occurred. We would argue that before supervision is ended, the onus is on a perpetrator of the violence to show that he has made significant changes and is taking responsibility for past transgressions, not merely that he can contain inappropriate behavior under close scrutiny.[41]

It has long been recognized in child protection cases that it is important for there to be clear expectations and contracts (between supervisor and court, counsel, and parents) for supervision. More recently, supervised visitation centers that work with families who have experienced DV are moving towards similarly articulated guidelines and contracts. These contracts have many benefits. Supervised parties have clear boundaries about acceptable and unacceptable behaviors; supervisors know what behaviors they are monitoring; court personnel have records and information upon which to base subsequent decisions; and there is clear agreement among parties of the state of affairs (versus an informal arrangement where the supervisor and supervised party may both see the supervised party as a "victim"). The Supervised Visitation Network in the United States has excellent standards and guidelines, as well as sample contracts available on their Web site.[42]

Termination of Visitation to an Abusive Partner

Although legislation and case law effectively create a presumption that continued contact between a noncustodial parent and child is in the child's best interests, if there are significant concerns about DV, it may be appropriate to terminate visitation, especially if there is ongoing battering that involves some form of postseparation spousal abuse or threats.

If a court has initial concerns about visitation and therefore orders supervised visitation, the court may consider abusive conduct or a failure to regularly visit as a reason for terminating supervised visits. Similarly, if it is acknowledged at the time of the original visitation order that the father has an anger problem and must take part in counseling, his failure to complete a program, or his completion of a program while continuing his harassment and threats against the mother, will justify termination of all visits.

The unhappiness of a custodial parent about visitation, or her sense of anger or hatred towards the noncustodial parent, does not in itself justify a termination of visitation. However, where there is a history of abuse of the custodial parent during, and especially

---

[41] For extensive discussion, see Bancroft & Silverman, *supra* note 10.

[42] Supervised Visitation Network (2003), *available at* http://www.svnetwork.net/ StandardsAndGuidelines.html.

after, the end of the period of cohabitation, the custodial parent's fear may legitimately be an important factor in terminating visitation. Consideration of threats to the safety of the custodial parent is important in any decision about visitation; no parent should be placed in a position of danger to facilitate contact between a child and an abusive parent.

If visitation has been terminated due to significant concerns about spousal violence and its effects upon a child, in order to resume visitation the parent with a history of abuse should bear the onus of demonstrating that he recognizes the effect that his conduct had on the children, has taken significant steps to change his behavior, and that it would be in his children's best interests to see him. Evidence that it could help the father's psychological state or meet his needs should not be persuasive in any visitation application, especially when visitation had been limited or terminated due to his abusiveness. Parents who have lost visitation rights due to their abusive conduct (almost always fathers) generally have very significant histories of abuse. Therefore, it should not be surprising that, in practice, these men rarely succeed in persuading a court to reinstate visitation.

Principles for Making Parenting Arrangements and Resolving Conflicting Priorities

In choosing among the preceding options, there are generally multiple factors to consider as far as developing a plan that promotes the best interests of any children involved. The case has been made for a risk-benefit analysis of different kinds of parenting plans that are in the best interests of the particular child and family.[43] What are some guiding principles for undertaking this kind of analysis? Together with our colleague Janet Johnston, we have developed a set of priorities for making decisions about the care of children in cases where DV is present:[44]

1. Priority #1 is to protect children directly from violent, abusive, and neglectful environments.

2. Priority #2 is to provide the support and safety required to ensure the well-being of parents who are victims of abuse (with the assumption that they will then be better able to protect their child).

3. Priority #3 is to respect and empower victim parents to make their own decisions and to direct their own lives (thereby recognizing the state's limitations in the role of *loco parentis*).

4. Priority #4 is to hold perpetrators accountable for their past and future actions (i.e., in the context of family proceedings, have them acknowledge their responsibility and take measures to correct abusive behavior).

5. Priority #5 is to allow and promote the least restrictive plan for parent-child visitation *that benefits the child*, along with parents' reciprocal rights.

Premised on the notion that the goal of protecting children must never be compromised, the strategy is to begin with the aim of achieving all five goals but abandoning the lower priorities when essential to resolving conflicts. This approach provides a

---

[43] C. Sturge & D. Glaser, "Contact and Domestic Violence—The Experts' Court Report," *Fam. L.* 615 (Sept. 2000).

[44] Jaffe et al., *supra* note 5.

child-focused pathway to just and consistent resolution of many common dilemmas. For example, in principle, if a parent denies engaging in substantiated violence and does not comply with court-ordered treatment, Priority #5 should be dropped or modified by suspending or supervising visitation. If the perpetrator is not taking responsibility for his actions, then in order to ensure that violence does not recur, the victim should be allowed to relocate upon request (Priorities #1 to #3 taking precedence over Priorities #4 and #5). Note that Priority #5, as stated, requires that visitation be suspended in some cases, even though a violent parent has sought and benefited from corrective treatment (e.g. if a child, traumatized by a the parent's past abusive conduct, continues to be highly distressed and resistant to supervised visits despite reasonable efforts to alleviate that distress).

Applied to children of women who have been battered by a partner, the first two priorities identify the need to protect children from violence; in many cases, supporting women who have been battered may be the best way to achieve the first priority. However, if a victim leaves one abusive relationship and subsequently establishes a relationship with another abusive partner, these principles require an alternative safe place for the child to live. This may be achieved by offering the mother a choice: "Live with your violent mate, or continue to have your child in your care and custody." This type of case may require involuntary removal of a child from a mother's care by child protection services. (Here, Priorities #3, #4, and #5 are dropped, and Priority #2 may have to be dropped as well.)

SPECIFIC DILEMMAS IN IDENTIFYING BEST INTERESTS OF CHILDREN

Within the context of a developmental understanding of children's exposure to DV and in light of these aforementioned principles, we now turn to four specific dilemmas that custody evaluators and decision makers may encounter in identifying appropriate parenting plans. For each dilemma, we provide some general considerations, a case example, and a brief analysis of the example.

Dilemma #1: Child Expresses Strong Wish to Live With Father Who Has Perpetrated Violence Against Child's Mother

A letter to a judge from a child pleading to live with his/her father can be emotionally compelling evidence in a custody dispute; most jurisdictions identify children's views and preferences as a factor to consider in determining their best interests. To what extent is it important to consider children's expressed wishes when making access arrangements that are feasible and safe? In general, it is important to be responsive to their need for age-appropriate input as well as to respect the requests and fears of a child who is rejecting a violent parent. However, the stated preferences of children who have been abused or witnessed violence should be interpreted with caution, optimally with the help of a child therapist. Some children can be intensely angry at an abusive parent but do not feel safe enough to verbally resist or refuse visitation, or even minimal contact within the safe confines of supervision, until long after the parents' separation. In other cases, children who have witnessed or sustained abuse become aligned with the more powerful perpetrator and reject the parent who was victimized. This alignment with the abusive parent may reflect fear of that person or identification with the more powerful parent. In some cases, abusive husbands have a "princess-like" relationship with their daughters. Other factors, such as not wanting to move away from friends, leave familiar surroundings, or change schools may play an important role in shaping children's expressed wishes. Children also may claim to want visits with an abusive father because they think they might be able to protect their mother by appeasing their father. More commonly, youngsters from abusive homes grieve the loss of a parent who does not visit them; they imagine that they have been abandoned, blame themselves for the parent's absence, and worry greatly about that parent's welfare. All of these possible motivations for the child's expressed preferences need to be considered in a given case.

Sometimes individuals who abuse their partners present very well. In such cases, the abuser is highly manipulative and able to con assessors, especially those who may not be familiar with patterns of abuse or who are impressed by the children's wishes and their apparently close relationship with the abuser. This may be challenging for the counsel of an abused spouse to counteract, but it is possible to do so, especially by introducing independent evidence of abuse as well as by having mental health professionals testify on the effects of DV on children.

> ***Example #1***: Hector, age thirteen, has witnessed the verbal and physical abuse of his mother (Carla) by his father, Joseph, over a period of five years. Carla describes the abuse as mostly verbal and emotional, taking the form of insults and humiliation, although there were also a number of physical assaults. On two occasions, Carla fled to a women's shelter with Hector and his fifteen-year-old sister, Luisa, but on both occasions she returned due to concerns about being able to provide for the children and because Joseph had expressed contrition. Carla has been concerned for a long time about the impact of Joseph's behavior on their children, particularly Hector, who has exhibited significant aggression. During the past year, Hector's behavior has escalated into physical assaults towards his sister and, most recently, a classmate. Carla separated from Joseph following Hector's incident at school. She and the children have been staying with extended family, as Joseph is still in the family home. Carla was shocked and dismayed when she overheard Hector telling a cousin that he plans to return to live with Joseph as soon as he gets a chance to tell his side of the story to the social worker who has been appointed to the case.

> *Case Analysis*: As children age, their wishes are generally given increasing weight by judges and lawyers. It is hard to tell a thirteen-year-old boy like Hector that he cannot do what he wants. Judges may feel that children of that age "will vote with their feet," in any event. Hector's wishes are not surprising, since boys may identify with their father and see him as the source of power and influence in the family. They also may have come to devalue their mother's role and feel that there is no future in choosing the "weaker" and more vulnerable parent. Because he is heading into adolescence, and therefore peer groups and friendships are becoming more important, he also simply may not want to be out of his home and away from his friends.

> Given Hector's adjustment difficulties and concerns about his behavior toward women, especially as he grows closer to the stage in which he will develop

romantic partnerships, his developmental needs are unlikely to be met by staying with a male parent who has neither sought treatment nor taken responsibility for his own abusive behavior. As a result, Hector's wishes are not synonymous with his best interests, even though he is old enough to express those wishes clearly. Furthermore, given the duration of the violence he witnessed and the behaviors he has demonstrated in response to that violence, it is unlikely that his behavior will improve simply because his parents have separated and the violence is no longer overt. Therefore, in addition to a parenting plan that gives custody to Carla and limits unsupervised visitation with Joseph, Hector's mother will need some supports to help her son develop more appropriate attitudes and ways of expressing conflict. Ideally, any parenting plan will be complemented by specialized counseling for Hector on the impact of exposure to DV. The case will likely require ongoing judicial case management, so that the outcome is predicated on Joseph's taking responsibility for his violence and completing a batterer intervention program. A comprehensive plan for the family would likely also require provision of services and support to Luisa, who has had to contend not only with having observed the victimization of her mother by her father, but also having experienced the direct aggression of her brother.

Dilemma #2: Different Children From Same Family Have Experienced Different Levels of Exposure and Therefore Have Conflicting Wishes

Not all children who are exposed to DV suffer the same consequences or experience similar adjustment problems. This reality is especially striking when observed in members of the same family; younger children and adolescents may exhibit a range of reactions, depending on age, gender, sibling order, and temperament as well as the parent with whom they more closely identify.

Even children residing in the same home may have had vastly different experiences and varying exposure level to the abuse of their mother. For example, older adolescents may absent themselves from the home and observe less actual violence than younger children; conversely, older children may also be more involved in direct attempts to intervene. Extremely young children may be more unaware of the violence (although consciously unaware is not the same as unaffected). Favoritism towards a particular child by a perpetrator of violence might also change the individual experiences of children within the same family. These situations pose dilemmas for the court in developing parenting plans, since children are generally seen as a "package deal," and there are practical impediments to developing different plans for different siblings.

Example #2: During his marriage to Nina, Steve was emotionally abusive and controlling, and he threatened her numerous times, but Nina never called the police; she reports that these threats occurred when the children were asleep. Steve was also emotionally abusive to their son, Jeremy (age twelve). In addition, Steve was physically aggressive to Jeremy on numerous occasions, in circumstances that Steve characterized as discipline and as an attempt to "make a man" of Jeremy. When Nina tried to intervene in these situations, Steve would deride her for making a "sissy" of their son. Jeremy, a soft-spoken boy who looks younger than his age, experiences significant anxiety and has few friends at school. In comparison to his harsh treatment of Jeremy, Steve clearly favored their daughter, Caley (age nine), whom he referred to as his "little princess." Since separating from Nina, Steve has shown little interest in seeing Jeremy but has purchased numerous gifts for Caley, including some age-inappropriate clothing. He also tends to confide in Caley about the problems he and Nina had in their marriage. Although Jeremy does not want to have visitation with his father, Caley has expressed clear wishes to have regular visits, including overnights, with her father. Steve also wants access to the baby (Maya, now age two), who was born shortly after the couple separated. His argument in this regard is that since she was not even born when the conflict ensued, she could not have any negative feelings towards her father unless she had been brainwashed in this regard by her mother.

Case Analysis: In considering the needs of these children, it is important to look at their exposure to direct and indirect violence. In addition to being exposed to the abuse of his mother, Jeremy himself is a victim of child maltreatment. There is clear research evidence that children exposed to DV and direct child maltreatment fare worse as a group than those exposed to either DV or maltreatment alone.

However, there is less research on siblings who have observed the abuse of another child in the family. Although few studies have been done in this area, it seems likely that witnessing a sibling being abused by a parent figure threatens the emotional security a child experiences.[45] That is, the child may have a secure relationship with the parent, but the experience of seeing a sibling victimized by that parent may profoundly shape a child's view of the world and relationships. In such circumstances, the child may be physically safe but be suffering from anxiety related to the possibility that he/she might be a future victim or may even be feeling guilty over being spared.

In cases such as the one outlined here, it might be tempting for a custody evaluator or judge to view the children as very different and allow or require access to the two girls, since they have not been directly victimized. There are a number of potential problems caused by such an approach. First, that plan makes the son a "problem child" and a symptom-bearer for the violence in the family. The daughters may not have any immediate fear of their father, but questions have to be raised about him as a suitable parent in regards to the behavior he has modeled and the fear engendered in other family members. In addition, there may be evidence to justify worrying about the father's boundaries with his older daughter. Finally, simply because the youngest child may not have a memory of the abuse her mother experienced does not mean she is unaffected. In this case, safety and rehabilitation efforts must be in place before the father can have unsupervised contact with the children. It may be a question of time before the girls experience his wrath or become pawns in punishing their mother for separation.

---

[45] E.M. Cummings & P.T. Davies, "Emotional Security as a Regulatory Process in Normal Development and the Development of Psychopathology," 8 *Dev. & Psychopathology* 123 (1996); P.T. Davies et al., "Child Emotional Security and Interparental Conflict," 67 *Monographs of Soc'y for Res. in Child Dev.* 1 (2002).

Dilemma #3: Father Has Ceased His Violence Toward Children's Mother but Continues to Minimize Impact of His Behavior on His Children

Even when there is evidence of DV, it is often naively assumed that separation puts an end to the violence and emotional trauma. Separation may end the violence in many cases, but in other cases the perpetrator may escalate his violence. Separation is the most dangerous period in terms of repeated or lethal violence. Differentiating between these two trajectories (i.e., cessation of violence versus escalation of violence following separation) is a critical task for all professionals involved with the courts, and there is a growing body of risk assessment factors in this regard.[46] Separation in itself is not a therapeutic intervention, and often no substantial change can be expected in the perpetrator without his taking responsibility and getting involved in an appropriate intervention program. Further, even if the physical violence towards the mother and children stop upon separation, emotionally abusive patterns of behavior may continue.

The question of appropriate intervention is a tricky one in that the extent to which batterer intervention programs in general are effective is somewhat unclear.[47] The reality is that well-developed programs work for some men and not for others; it somewhat depends on which criteria are considered as constituting success and the timeframe being considered. Drop-out rates are high, and some men may cease physical violence while maintaining or increasing other forms of power and control. Furthermore, research suggests that it is not the nature or length of a program alone that determines outcomes; rather, the extent to which programs are encompassed within a responsive criminal justice system appears to be critical.[48] Programs that are nested in systems that respond quickly and consistently to transgressions (such as absenteeism at sessions) tend to achieve better results.

However, even with a program that achieves reasonable results, there will always be significant variation among individual participants' progress. As a result, completion of a batterer intervention program alone should not be considered evidence that a perpetrator of DV has taken responsibility for past abuse and has made a commitment to not use violence in the future. Perpetrators with severe violence histories especially require some form of ongoing monitoring or follow-up to assess progress. The use of collateral information (in addition to perpetrators' self-reports) is also essential. It is critical that decision makers not rely on their own "gut feeling" or character assessment in determining whether or not a batterer has reformed his behavior, as these impressionistic assessments are highly unreliable.

In some cases, a perpetrator of DV may have ceased his violence but continues his attempts to control and harass his former partner through legal tactics.[49] A common tactic is the filing for custody by a previously uninvolved father for the purpose of punishing his partner for leaving or pressuring her to return. If an abuser has replaced physical assault with excessive litigation, use of superior financial resources, claims

---

[46] J.C. Campbell, *Assessing Dangerousness: Violence by Batterers and Child Abusers* (2007).

[47] J.C. Babcock, C.E. Green & C. Robie, "Does Batterers' Treatment Work? A Meta-Analytic Review of Domestic Violence Treatment," 23 *Clinical Psychol. Rev.* 1023 (2004).

[48] E.W. Gondolf, *Batterer Intervention Systems: Issues, Outcomes, and Recommendations* (2002).

[49] P.G. Jaffe, C.V. Crooks & S.E. Poisson, "Common Misperceptions in Addressing Domestic Violence in Child Custody Disputes," 54 *Juv. & Fam. Ct. J.* 57 (2003).

of parental alienation, use of phone calls and exchanges as a means of having access to his victim, and other similar tactics, there is no reason to believe he has essentially changed. Conversely, a perpetrator who has truly changed and has come to understand the impact of his former behavior might be willing to defer his claims to visitation in order to allow his victims time to heal and rebuild trust.

The question of what constitutes appropriate intervention for batterers vis-á-vis their parenting is also a subject of some debate. Interventions range from add-on modules included at the completion of a general batterer intervention program to specific parenting interventions for batterers. Nonetheless, interventions designed to address the parenting deficits of men who batter their partners are critical for comprehensively addressing the needs of children who have been exposed to this violence.[50] The Caring Dads program, for example, is seventeen-week program that has been designed for fathers who have abused their children and/or exposed their children to woman abuse. The program is based on principles emerging from the literature on batterer intervention, working with resistant clients, and child abuse.[51] Any intervention for fathers who have been abusive should be coordinated with other community service providers to avoid unintended negative consequences (such as reduced monitoring regardless of actual progress in the program).[52] In addition to research on interventions with fathers who perpetrate abuse, there is emerging literature on analyzing whether a batterer has changed as a parent. Such an analysis includes examining the extent to which he makes a full acknowledgement of his violence, takes responsibility for the behavior rather than project blame, articulates the impact of his behavior on his partner and children, develops new relationship skills, and makes proper amends or restitution.[53]

> ***Example # 3:*** After years of Sean engaging in belittling and controlling behavior, Alycia decided to end their relationship following an altercation that escalated to a physical assault. Because the police responded to the physical assault, Sean was ordered to attend a batterer intervention program, which he did reluctantly. Subsequent to the separation, there has been very little contact between the parties and no further violence. Alycia was initially comfortable with Sean having unsupervised visitation with their seven-year-old daughter, McKayla, because he had previously been quite an involved father, and McKayla did not witness the physical assault. However, Alycia has become increasingly concerned about McKayla's behavior following visits with her father. McKayla is very belligerent and defiant following these visits and has made comments to the effect that "Daddy has no furniture in his apartment because he has to give mommy all his money." McKayla has also stated that her father says she does not have to listen to her mother. As a result of observing these behaviors, Alycia has made a motion for Sean's visitation to be supervised. For his part, Sean strongly contests the need for supervised visitation and argues that Alycia is trying to alienate his

---

[50] K.L. Scott & C.V. Crooks, "Intervention for Abusive Fathers: Promising Practices in Court and Community Responses," 57 *Juv. & Fam. Ct. J.* 29 (2006).

[51] K.L. Scott et al., *Caring Dads: Helping Fathers Value Their Children* (2006); K.L. Scott & C.V. Crooks, "Preliminary Evaluation of an Intervention Program for Maltreating Fathers," 7 *Brief Treatment & Crisis Intervention* 224 (2007); C.V. Crooks et al., "Eliciting Change in Maltreating Fathers: Goals, Processes, and Desired Outcomes," 13 *Cognitive & Behav. Prac.* 71 (2006).

[52] K.L. Scott et al., "Accountability Guidelines for Intervention With Abusive Fathers," in *Parenting by Men Who Batter* 102-17 (O. Williams & J. Edleson eds., 2006).

[53] O. Williams & J.L. Edleson eds., *Parenting by Men Who Batter* (2006).

daughter from him. Furthermore, he notes that he has attended a positive parenting course (on the advice of his lawyer), which is more than his ex has done to improve her parenting.

Case Analysis: In this case, the violence ended with the separation, but the domestic abuse continued, although in a different form. In cases like this one, it may be tempting for professionals to accept the abuser's version of his actions, to minimize the abuse, and fail to recognize this behavior as part of the pattern of abuse perpetrated during the marriage. There are worrisome signs that the ongoing behavior is intended to demean and belittle Alycia. Any treatment program has clearly failed if abusive behaviors continue, and Sean's continuing abuse does not speak well to his role and responsibilities as a parent. Visits should be limited and supervised until Sean completes another session of group treatment or enters a specialized program for abusive parents. Clearly, the bar needs to be set higher than mere completion of a parenting program. Indeed, attendance at a regular parenting-after-separation program can do more harm than good in these cases in that the core problems are not addressed. At these programs, communication between parents is emphasized over personal responsibility for behavior; child discipline is emphasized over parents' attitudes towards children, and leaders typically convey great empathy for the challenges of child rearing, all of which can increase an abusive father's sense of entitlement or of being the wronged party.[54] Indicators for unsupervised parenting have to include a full acknowledgement of the inappropriate behavior and a commitment to developing alternative skills. Unless Sean understands the harm his behavior causes McKayla (presumably through appropriate, targeted intervention), he is not qualified to parent without supervision.

Dilemma #4: Father Has Benefited From Treatment, Changed His Behavior, and Taken Responsibility for Past Abuse, but Children's Mother Does Not Want to Acknowledge These Changes and Allow Visitation

There is a legal presumption that absent a proof of real risk of physical or emotional harm, it is in the best interests of a child to have significant contact with each parent. There are cases where a parent with a history of abuse has undertaken all the requirements of a court order and followed a counselor's suggestions, but the victimized parent is still concerned about child safety issues and does not want visitation to occur. These cases pose a dilemma since there is an implied (or explicit) promise from the court that completing and benefiting from required programs will be rewarded by parental contact. A previously victimized parent who does not recognize the progress may be stuck in the past or not be willing to ever forgive the other parent for past misconduct. In these cases, the court and custody evaluators have to distinguish between the parent who is so traumatized by the past that she cannot move forward and the parent who is simply bitter and unwilling to accept personal improvement in an ex-partner, even when it is genuine.

---

[54] K.L. Scott & C.V. Crooks, "Effecting Change in Maltreating Fathers: Critical Principles for Intervention Planning," 11 *Clinical Psychol: Sci & Prac.* 95 (2004).

Example #4: Max and Joanne both describe their marriage as a tumultuous one, with frequent arguments and poor communication and problem solving. On several occasions prior to the final separation, Max stormed out of the house during arguments and went to stay with his brother for a few days. According to Max, he "lost it" during a final confrontation, punched a hole in the wall, and pushed Joanne on his way out the door. Joanne called the police, and Max was required to attend a group treatment program as part of an early intervention initiative that resulted in all charges being dropped. Although initially furious that he had to attend a batterers program, Max found the material useful and came to realize the harmful impact of his previous behavior on Joanne and the children. The program Max attended had a module about parenting, and Max was especially affected by the realization that the yelling and name-calling to which he subjected the children was harmful to them. He and Joanne have had virtually no face-to-face contact since the separation. Max has a new partner but remains committed to playing an active role with his children. There are particular roles that Max would like to maintain in this regard. As a teacher, he feels he would be able to help their ten-year-old daughter, Samantha, who has been diagnosed with a mild reading disability. In addition, Max has coached his son Jason's soccer team for the past four years and would like to continue in that capacity. Although Max has taken responsibility for his past behavior, Joanne sees him as an abusive and manipulative person who will turn the children against her. When asked to clarify her concerns, Joanne raises arguments that she and Max had in the past but is not able to identify any current behaviors. She is unwilling to consider any unsupervised access between Max and the children.

Case Analysis: Max has taken important steps toward reestablishing his relationship with his children. While he was emotionally abusive towards his spouse and children, there was only one incident of physical violence towards his partner at the time of separation. He has taken responsibility and has much to offer his children based on his past parenting. He needs a chance to parent; the challenge is to try to counsel Joanne to see the benefits of this. Smaller steps can be taken to keep the adults apart through supervised exchanges and building towards longer visits. A planned third-party review (such as by a custody evaluator) may be an important safeguard in making decisions based on desirable behavior that has emerged only recently. The notion of monitoring or reevaluation is particularly important, because only time will tell whether the changes Max has shown are lasting; many perpetrators of DV are able to appear remorseful and sincere about changing their behavior in the short term but revert to old patterns once the eyes of the court are no longer focused on them. If Max is indeed able to continue a pattern of positive interaction with his children and noninterference with his ex-partner, Joanne will have to accept the court's granting Max significant contact with his children. In these complicated cases, deliberate undermining of the father-child relationship by the mother or her refusal to follow court orders could eventually trigger a referral to a protective services agency, due to the potential for emotional harm to the child.

SYSTEMIC CHALLENGES

In this chapter, we have argued that legal and mental health professionals need to be guided by the five priorities discussed above (see "Principles for Making Parenting Arrangements and Resolving Conflicting Priorities"), giving precedence to the safety of the children and the nonoffending parent before considering the needs or wishes of abusive adults. For professionals to make sound decisions that promote the best interests of children, they must understand the relevance of DV to parenting as well as have insight into children at different stages of development. Further, they must be able to translate this understanding into practice.

To make any of our recommendations or analysis meaningful, there must be access to good service providers and a coordinated and collaborative approach to DV. The lack of services and coordination remain concerns in many communities. Shortage of supervised visitation centers, parenting programs for batterers, and access to a range of culturally relevant services remain serious roadblocks to the implementation of comprehensive parenting plans following separation.

In the custody-evaluation arena, two research papers present very different pictures of the extent to which the field has changed. Bow and Boxer surveyed custody evaluators across the United States and found that the vast majority reported that they recognized DV as a critical factor in their work.[55] These practitioners indicated that they considered utilizing specialized assessment resources and made differential custody and visitation recommendations when DV was identified. In contrast, studies in the Louisville, Kentucky, courts found that DV was often overlooked in court assessments. This group of studies was particularly compelling because they were based on actual court documents as opposed to the self-report of practitioners. This analysis of custody evaluation reports suggests that DV was not a factor in the recommendations made, even when DV was identified in the same report.[56] Furthermore, an analysis of court records found that court settlement methods (e.g., mediation, adjudication) did not vary for families with and without DV histories. Parents with a history of DV were as likely to be steered into mediation as those without, despite the inappropriateness of mediation in cases involving DV. In addition, custody outcomes did not differ between families with and without this history.[57] Thus, although evaluators may believe they have a good grasp of the dynamics of woman abuse and may feel confident that they are able to assess for this kind of abuse, as a group they may not be applying this framework in making their recommendations.

CONCLUSIONS

In this chapter we highlighted the literature in the field of children's exposure to DV and outlined the importance of using a developmental framework to consider the consequences of this experience. We offered four sample case scenarios to illustrate some of the dilemmas faced by the courts and custody evaluators in sorting

---

[55] J.N. Bow & P. Boxer, "Assessing Allegations of Domestic Violence in Child Custody Evaluations," 18 *J. Interpersonal Violence* 1394 (2003).

[56] L.S. Horvath, T.K. Logan & R. Walker, "Child Custody Cases: A Content Analysis of Evaluations in Practice," 33 *Prof. Psychol.: Res. & Prac.* 557 (2002).

[57] T.K. Logan et al., "Child Custody Evaluations and Domestic Violence: Case Comparisons," 17 *Violence & Victims* 719 (2002).

through the host of factors relevant to children's best interests when formulating parenting plans.

Although we provided the case scenarios to help identify important issues, it is not our intention to oversimplify the complex clinical and legal issues that are raised in these cases. None of the scenarios include enough detailed information to declare that a former perpetrator of DV is truly safe. Rather, the scenarios were meant to demonstrate how the range of pertinent issues can be analyzed from the standpoint of children's developmental needs.

Clearly, the impact of DV on children is a significant factor to consider in developing parenting plans after separation. Although courts and community services have begun to recognize the potential harm of children's exposure to this violence, no simple analysis exists for creating a recipe for parenting plans. The impact of DV may vary according to a host of variables, such as the severity and frequency of the violence and the risk of its recurrence, as well as child characteristics such as age, gender, sibling order, and additional challenges in the child's life.

Beyond the characteristics of the children, there is significant variability among patterns of violence as well as among profiles of perpetrators. Some DV represents an ongoing pattern of abuse and control; in other cases, acts of violence may be isolated and out of character and may not create fear in the victim. A pattern of violence that is abusive and controlling may suggest an individual who is unfit to parent or even have unsupervised visits with the child. Some DV perpetrators may be remorseful and respond to appropriate treatment programs that address their adult relationships and parenting skills. Thus, a history of DV raises questions about parenting but provides no simple answers. Similarly, knowing that DV has ended cannot be equated with emotional safety for children. A developmental framework is an important step toward putting the needs of children back at the forefront of postseparation parenting plans in cases where children have been exposed to violence towards their mother by a male perpetrator.

Chapter 23

Court-Appointed Parenting Evaluators and Guardians Ad Litem: Practical Realities and an Argument for Abolition

by Margaret K. Dore, J.D.

INTRODUCTION

This chapter describes the practical realities of child custody recommendations by court-appointed parenting evaluators and guardians ad litem (GALs). It argues that given these realities, the role of such persons should be abolished from child custody practice. Only with this course will the problems with their use be eliminated. Children will be better protected by the courts.

© 2006 by Margaret K. Dore, Esq.

EVALUATION PROCESS

Parenting evaluators and GALs investigate custody arrangements and report back to the court with their recommendations.[1] In some states, the GAL does not make a "recommendation," but instead provides his position via a brief.[2]

Evaluators and GALs are also known as custody investigators, forensic experts, and law guardians.[3] Evaluators are usually psychologists or social workers; GALs are often lawyers. Sometimes GALs are lay persons, for example, in the CASA program.[4] Many, if not most, of these persons are hardworking and conscientious.

Appointment

It is not uncommon for an evaluator/GAL to be appointed via nomination or suggestion.[5] With this situation, attorneys can and do advocate for the appointment of evaluators/GALs whose views are compatible to their cases. For example, if a father claims that the mother is alienating him from the child, the father's attorney might suggest evaluators known to find alienation determinative.

In some courts, it is permissible for attorneys to contact evaluators/GALs prior to appointment. Such contact can be ostensibly used to verify availability. Its real purpose may be to "test the waters" regarding one's case. If the reaction is favorable, the attorney will move forward to advocate appointment. If the reaction is unfavorable, the attorney may look elsewhere. Certain attorneys also tend to work with certain evaluators/GALs. In other words, they develop business relationships. With these circumstances, the person appointed can be prealigned to one side.

Investigation

Once appointment is made, the lobbying campaign continues. Each side provides the evaluator/GAL with information including multiple level hearsay. Evaluators/GALs also typically meet with the parents and the children. Evaluators/GALs may contact third parties. They may also conduct or commission psychological (profile) testing for the parents or the children.[6]

---

[1] *See, e.g., In re* Guardianship of Stamm, 91 P.3d 126, 130 (Wash. Ct. App. 2004). ("In both guardianship and custody cases, the role of the GAL is the same: to investigate and supply information and recommendations to the court.").

[2] *See* Raven C. Lidman & Betsy R. Hollingsworth, "The Guardian ad Litem in Child Custody Cases: The Contours of Our Judicial System Stretched Beyond Recognition," 6 *Geo. Mason L. Rev.* 255, 271, and 277 n.106 (1998) (describing the GAL's role in Wisconsin as a lawyer for the child, "they can make arguments and file briefs, but they cannot testify themselves nor offer new factual material in reports").

[3] *See, e.g.*, id. at 255 n.2.

[4] The Court Appointed Special Advocate Program (CASA) was founded by a Seattle judge. *See* http://www.nationalcasa.org/htm/about.htm. There are more than 900 CASA programs in operation throughout the country, which are also known as Volunteer Guardian ad Litem Programs. Id.

[5] *See, e.g.* Wash. Rev. Code § 26.12.177(2)(a) (2005) ("The parties may make a joint recommendation for the appointment of a "guardian ad litem.").

[6] *Cf.* Margaret A. Hagen, *Whores of the Court: The Fraud of Psychiatric Testimony and the Rape of American Justice* ch. 8 (1997); Higginbotham v. Higginbotham, 857 So. 2d 341, 342 (Fla. Dist. Ct. App. 2003) (fourteen psychological tests performed on parents, seven psychological tests performed on children).

Report

The results of the investigation, any psychological testing, and recommendations of the evaluator/GAL are typically summarized in a report filed with the court.[7] In these reports the evaluator/GAL may or may not rely on applicable law. This phenomenon has been documented in at least one reported decision.[8]

Evaluators/GALs may also rely on their own personal, social, or cultural values. Paul S. Appelbaum, M.D. states:

> When an evaluator recommends [a child's placement] we are learning not about the relative capacities of the parties but, instead, about the relative values of the evaluators.[9]

Trial

By the time of trial, the evaluator/GAL is in the position of defending his report and recommendations. In states where the GAL files a brief, he is in the position of defending the brief.

Factors encouraging this phenomenon include the need of the evaluator/GAL to maintain his reputation, to thereby gain more appointments.[10] He may also be concerned that the judge will reduce fees if the recommendation or brief does not prevail.[11]

At this point, the evaluator/GAL's recommendations can become more strongly stated, (i.e., more "black and white"). The recommended parent may thus be portrayed as more clearly "good" and the other as more clearly "bad." But the reality may be in the middle (i.e., that like all of us, neither parent is perfect).

At trial, the evaluator/GAL typically testifies regarding his report and recommendations. This testimony typically includes hearsay previously provided by the parties.[12] Repeated yet again, its substance can become grossly distorted—like a story repeated multiple times as part of a child's "telephone game."[13]

---

[7] Lidman & Hollingsworth, *supra* at note 2, at 278.

[8] *See* Gilbert v. Gilbert, 664 A.2d 239, 242 at n.2 (Vt. 1995) (describing survey results). A similar issue is reported in the comments to the Washington State Superior Court Guardian ad Litem Rules, as follows: "Apparently GALs are not following statutory requirements, nor are the courts consistent in enforcing them." Superior Court Guardian ad Litem Rules (GALR) 2, Washington State Bar Association Comment, § (p).

[9] Paul S. Appelbaum, "The Medicalization of Judicial Decision-Making," 10(7) *Elder L. Rep.* 3 (Feb. 1999).

[10] Richard Ducote, "Guardians ad Litem in Private Custody Litigation: The Case of Abolition," 3 *Loy. J. Pub. Int'l L.* 106, 146 (2002): "One of the particularly stealthy problems of GALs is the conflict of interest issue. This most commonly occurs when a GAL fights to keep a child in the custody of a parent previously endorsed and exonerated by the GAL, despite mounting proof that the parent is indeed abusive and the GAL erred. . . . In such instances, GALs have forcefully opposed the introduction of new abuse evidence and instead have increased the blame on the non-abusive parent. . . . [T]he GAL hopes to avoid any judicial finding that suggests his or her incompetence and jeopardizes future lucrative GAL appointments."

[11] Professors Raven Lidman and Betsy Hollingsworth make a similar point. Lidman & Hollingsworth, *supra* note 2, at 3022. *See also* Hagen, *supra* note 6, at 207-08.

[12] *Cf.* Lidman & Hollingsworth, *supra* note 2, at 279.

[13] *Cf.* Gilbert v. Gilbert, 664 A.2d 239, 243 (Vt. 1995) (describing the GAL's facts as "double or triple hearsay when reported").

Evaluator/GAL testimony can also include opinions on credibility.[14] The author has seen, as a basis for such opinions, a parent's psychological profile, for example, that a parent has an "elevated lie scale." The author has observed such testimony to be extremely prejudicial.[15]

The above situation is quite different from the admission of an investigator's testimony in other contexts. For example, an investigator in a criminal trial would not be allowed to testify as to his recommendations regarding conviction, as to hearsay, or as to his opinion on witness credibility.[16]

JUDICIAL RELIANCE ON EVALUATORS/GUARDIANS AD LITEM

Most judges perceive evaluators/GALs as neutral investigators or advisors.[17] Evaluator-psychologists can be held in especially high esteem.

With this status, the reports and recommendations of an evaluator/GAL can become perceived as the factual and legal standard for trial. The burden of the non-recommended party is thus to disprove a factual and legal standard. The burden of the recommended party is merely to provide corroboration for the standard. In *Gilbert*, the Supreme Court of Vermont found such burden shifting so unfair as to require reversal.[18]

A related problem is the legitimization of improper evidence through the evaluator/GAL. In one record reviewed by this author, the evaluator testified that the mother's family was "manipulative" and dishonest. On cross-examination, the evaluator conceded that as a basis for her opinion, she was relying on unsigned written statements provided by the father. Had the father sought to admit these statements through himself, they would have been viewed as hearsay, lacking authenticity, and self-serving. But admitted as they were through the evaluator, their thrust (manipulative/dishonest) was instead perceived as fact. Such "fact" was then incorporated into the court's decision; the child was removed from the mother's primary care.

With the perceived neutrality of evaluators/GALs, their positions are often determinative.[19] But as described above, evaluators/GALs are not neutral. Once they make their recommendations, they are in the position of defending them; they have conflicts of interest including concerns about their future appointments and fees.

---

[14] Id.

[15] *Cf.* Marriage of Luckey, 868 P.2d 189, 194 (Wash. Ct. App. 1994) ("the use of profile testimony is unfairly prejudicial"). *See also* State v. Carlson, 906 P.2d 999, 1002–03 (Wash. Ct. App. 1995): "[No] witness may give an opinion on another witness' credibility . . . An expert opinion [on credibility] will not "assist the trier of fact" . . . because there is no scientific basis for such an opinion, save the polygraph, and the polygraph is not generally accepted as a scientifically reliable technique [footnotes omitted]."

[16] Lidman & Hollingsworth, *supra* note 2, at 279.

[17] *Cf.* *In re* Guardianship of Stamm, 91 P.3d 126, 129 (Wash. Ct. App. 2004), quoting Fernando v. Nieswandt, 940 P.2d 1380 (Wash. Ct. App. 1997) (the GAL acts as a "neutral advisor to the court").

[18] Gilbert v. Gilbert, 664 A.2d 239, 242, sec. C (Vt. 1995)

[19] *See* Lidman & Hollingsworth, *supra* note 2, at 297 ("[m]ore often, . . . [t]he judge merely confirms the guardian ad litem's decision").

REFORMS

The poor quality of custody evaluations has been reported in the literature.[20] Proposed reforms have ranged from making changes designed to improve their quality, to their complete elimination.[21]

Perhaps the most common approach has been to establish evaluation standards. In Washington State, for example, there are now court rules that require GALs to maintain documentation that substantiates their recommendations.[22] Minimum standards have also been imposed through case law.[23]

Another approach has been to redefine the role of the GAL as a lawyer for the child. With this approach, the GAL does not make a recommendation, but instead provides his position via a brief. As noted above, this approach is already used in some states. It is also promoted by the American Bar Association's (ABA's) "Standards of Practice for Lawyers Representing Children in Custody Cases," which call for the appointment of a "Best Interests Attorney."[24] The Best Interests Attorney does not act as a witness or make reports and recommendations.[25] He files briefs and makes arguments.[26]

In Wisconsin, GALs have this role.[27] Professors Raven Lidman and Betsy Hollingsworth report that these persons nonetheless function like traditional GALs

---

[20] *See, e.g.*, Dana Royce Baerger et al., "A Methodology for Reviewing the Reliability and Relevance of Child Custody Evaluations," 18 *J. Am. Acad. Matrimonial L.* 35, 36 ("Concern regarding the generally poor qualify of [child custody evaluations] has prompted some commentators to suggest an end to the use of [evaluations] in divorce proceedings."); Timothy M. Tippins, "Custody Evaluations-Part I: Expertise by Default?" *N.Y.L.J.,* July 15, 2003, at 3, col. 1 ("If the custody recommendation is little more than a personal value, judgment, intuition, or an educated guess, rather than a conclusion compelled by reliable and valid scientific research, it should not be received"); and Lidman & Hollingsworth, *supra* note 2, at 301 ("Soon thereafter . . . [the parents] learn that this *guardian ad litem* is a mere mortal getting information from here and there, frequently not verifying anything.").

[21] *See, e.g.*, *Matrimonial Commission Report to the Chief Judge of the State of New York,* Hon. Sondra Miller, Chairperson (Feb. 2006), http://www.courts.state.ny.us/reports/matrimonialcommissionreport.pdf, at 46 ("Proposed reforms from many different sources have ranged from eliminating the use of forensics altogether to instituting changes that will insure the quality and proper use of the reports."); and Ducote, *supra* note 10, at 115 ("Guardians ad litem must be abolished in private custody cases.").

[22] The Superior Court GALRs were adopted by the Washington State Supreme Court in 2001. *See* GALR § 2(p) and http://www.courts.wa.gov/court_rules/?fa=court_rules.list&group=sup&set=GALR.

[23] *See, e.g.,* Patel v. Patel, 555 S.E.2d 386, 390 (S.C. 2001). *See also In re* Guardianship of Stamm, 91 P.3d 126, 130 (Wash. Ct. App. 2004) (limiting the admissibility of GAL testimony to that which is helpful under ER 702); Heistand v. Heistand, 673 N.W.2d 531, 311–12 (Neb. 2004) (reversing because the GAL had been allowed to testify as an expert).

[24] The "Best Interests Attorney" is defined as a "lawyer who provides independent legal services for the purpose of protecting a child's best interests, without being bound by the child's directives or objectives." *American Bar Association Section of Family Law Standards of Practice for Lawyers Representing Children in Custody Cases,* at 2, § II.B (Aug. 2003), http://www.afccnet.org/pdfs/aba.standards.pdf#search='ABA%20Standards%20of%20Practice%20for%20Lawyers%20Representing%20Children'.

[25] Id. at 3, § III.B.

[26] Id. at 6, § III.G.

[27] Lidman & Hollingsworth, *supra* note 2, at 271, and 277 n.106 (describing the GAL's role in Wisconsin as a lawyer for the child, "they can make arguments and file briefs, but they cannot testify themselves nor offer new factual material in reports").

(i.e., they in effect give reports and recommendations).[28] A similar phenomenon has been noted in New York. There is a "recurring problem" involving the court's expectation of the attorney for the child to give a recommendation.[29]

The concept of the Best Interests Attorney is, regardless, flawed. He represents the child's best interests, which is the ultimate issue before the court. There is the potential for the court to be usurped, or to at least not consider the evidence as carefully because he has already made the best interests determination.[30]

The conflicts of interest described above also continue to exist. As with a traditional GAL, the Best Interests Attorney also has concerns about his future appointment and fees. Once the brief is submitted, he is in the position of defending it. There are also problems with the evidence. As with a traditional GAL, the Best Interests Attorney relies on hearsay.[31]

EVALUATORS/GUARDIANS AD LITEM SHOULD BE ELIMINATED FROM CHILD CUSTODY PROCEEDINGS

Another way to look at the use of evaluators/GALs is that they act as a filter or prism between the court and the evidence.[32] They are like "spin doctors." They tell the court what it sees, which can make a difference as to the court's perception.[33] The court's normal decision-making function is distorted; children are harmed. Attorney Richard Ducote states:

> [I]n domestic violence and abuse cases, where courts are even more eager to appoint GALs, children are frequently ending up in the custody of the abusers and separated from their protecting parents. This tragedy does not happen in spite of the GALs, but rather because of the GALs [footnote omitted].[34]

---

[28] Lidman and Hollingsworth state: "The Wisconsin courts' opinions have an exasperated tone as they repeatedly reiterate that these guardians ad litem must perform lawyer-like functions: they can examine and cross-examine witnesses, and they can make arguments and file briefs, but they cannot testify themselves nor offer new factual material in reports. Trial courts, parents' attorneys, and guardian ad litem-lawyers have been chastised for 'lapses' such as: . . . permitting the guardian ad litem to file a 'report' twenty days after the close of trial; or allowing the guardian ad litem to file a preliminary report and make an oral report to the court after closing arguments. But Wisconsin appellate courts do not reverse for these lapses. Instead the reviewing courts characterize preliminary reports as briefs and oral reports as arguments [footnotes omitted]." Lidman & Hollingsworth, *supra* note 2, at 271.

[29] *Matrimonial Commission Report, supra* note 21, at 43.

[30] *Cf.* C.W. v. K.A.W., 774 A.2d 745, 749 (Pa. 2001) (the trial court's reliance on the GAL constituted "egregious examples of the trial court delegating its judicial power to a non-judicial officer"); Hastings v. Rigsbee, 875 So. 2d 772, 777 (Fla. Dist. Ct. App. 2d 2004) ("The overarching problem in this case is that the trial court effectively delegated its judicial authority to the parenting coordinator.").

[31] *See, e.g., ABA Standards of Practice, supra* note 24, at § V.E.

[32] *Cf. Small Justice: Little Justice in America's Family Courts*, Education Supplement, at 6 (2001) (describing evaluators and guardians ad litem as a filter). *See also* http://www.intermedia-inc.com/title.asp?sku=SM03&subcatID=29.

[33] Id.

[34] Ducote, *supra* note 10, at 135–36.

Richard Wexler, the executive director of the National Coalition for Child Protection Reform, makes a similar point regarding the CASA program:

> [W]e conclude that the only real accomplishment of CASA is to encourage the needless removal of children from their homes.[35]

The distortion of the court's decision-making ability cannot be rectified by reforms that leave the filter of the evaluator/GAL in place. The only reform that will eliminate the problem of the filter is the elimination of the filter itself. Evaluators/GALs must be eliminated from child custody practice.

CONCLUSION

Evaluators/GALs are often hard working and conscientious. There are, however, problems with their role. They cause the court's normal decision-making function to be distorted. Wrong decisions are made.

Court-appointed evaluators/GALs must be eliminated from child custody practice—for the sake of the children.

---

[35] National Coalition for Child Protection Reform, Press Release, at 1, *available at* http://www.law.capital.edu/adoption/news_cases/documents/NATIONAL_COALITION_response.pdf#search='Caliber%20%26%20Wexler%20%26%20CASA%20%26%202122006'; *see also* http://www.nccpr.org/.

Chapter 24

American Law Institute Principles: A Tool for Accessing Justice for Battered Mothers and Children

by Erika A. Sussman, J.D., LL.M.

INTRODUCTION

While legislatures and the general public have come to recognize domestic violence (DV) as a private and public wrong, family courts throughout the nation continue to inflict enormous injustices upon battered women and their children. In the name of "gender equity" and "fatherhood rights," custody courts often render decisions that ignore the substantial risks posed by battering parents, thereby jeopardizing the physical safety of survivors and their children. The epidemic proportions of the problem were poignantly illustrated by the testimony of sixteen women who appeared before the Truth Commission at the Fourth Battered Mothers Custody Conference (BMCC), held in Albany, New York in January of 2007.[1] Advocates for battered women and their children must contend with these injustices on various levels—through systems advocacy, policy making, judicial education, and, of course, litigation.

Depending upon the strengths and weaknesses of a particular state's statute as well as the specific facts of a case, the American Law Institute's (ALI's) *Principles of the Law of Family Dissolution* (ALI Principles)[2] may provide judges and advocates with a tool to access justice in custody cases involving DV.

A mainstream, highly regarded source, the ALI offers promising guidelines for attorneys representing primary caretakers and protective parents. In fact, in the years since their issuance, the ALI Principles have been cited by various trial and appellate courts throughout the nation.[3] West Virginia, previously one of two states with a "primary caretaker presumption," has adopted the ALI Principles as its amended custody statute. Indeed, the "approximation standard" promulgated by the ALI was one of the many proposed recommendations put forth in the BMCC Truth Commission report. Both the approximation standard and the DV specific protections embody the recommendations that are being advocated by protective parent reform initiatives throughout the nation.

This chapter explores the potential uses of the ALI custody provisions as a mechanism for accessing justice for battered mothers. First, the chapter examines the challenges of litigating custody cases on behalf of battered mothers, with a focus upon judicial misunderstandings of the impact of battering on parenting. Next it explores the common statutory frameworks, highlighting the gender bias implicit in the prevailing best interests of the child (BIC) standard as well as the resulting dangers for battered women and children. With this as backdrop, the chapter goes on to examine the ALI custody recommendations and to suggest strategies for utilizing the ALI as a tool for justice in custody courts. Given the social scientific evidence of the importance of caretaking as well as the common deficits of battering parents, this chapter argues that the ALI Principles' "approximation of prior caretaking" standard should be used to restrict custodial access of battering parents. It also asserts that courts and attorneys should use the DV-specific provisions of the ALI to craft safety strategies that incorporate the specific needs of survivors.

---

[1] See Chapter 8 in this volume for its discussion about the formation of the Truth Commission and the report issued by the Commission in response to testimony given by battered mothers at the Fourth Battered Mothers Custody Conference, Albany, New York, in January 2007.

[2] American Law Institute, *Principles of the Law of Family Dissolution* (2002), *available at* http://www.ali.org.

[3] At the time this chapter was written, a search revealed seventy-five reported cases alone, touching upon a range of family law topics.

JUDICIAL MISUNDERSTANDING OF THE IMPACT OF BATTERING ON PARENTING

Judicial misunderstandings of DV, particularly as it applies to batterers as parents, play a critical role in the decision-making process. While lawmakers can provide structures for rendering justice, the application of those laws to the concrete details of individuals' lives often opens up opportunities for judges to inject their thoughts about what constitutes "good parenting." Thus, custody laws that are substantive rules (i.e., laws that promote a particular value) are more likely to achieve that value than laws that provide a formal structure but are silent on substantive criteria. Custody laws that require courts to protect children from their abusive parents are more likely to meet that goal than are laws that simply leave the child's best interests to the discretion of the court. Thus, zealous advocates for protective parents can focus their efforts on educating judges under the current legal framework and offering alternative or supplemental frameworks that are most likely to meet the goal of safety for women and children.

There are several misunderstandings that commonly result in negative custody outcomes for battered women and their children.

Separation Increases the Risk of Violence to Battered Women and Children

One common misperception among courts is that custodial access need not be limited at divorce because the separation of the parents will put an end to the violence. "As a culture, we believe that if women leave, they will be safe, as will their children."[4] In fact, the opposite is true. Battering is a method of exerting power and control. Custody is often an additional opportunity for batterers to attempt to maintain contact with or regain access to battered women. Batterers often perceive their partner's decision to pursue custody through the courts as a major affront to their authority. Both of these factors lead battering fathers to increase their use and threats of violence during and following custody actions.[5]

> Abuse of children by a batterer is more likely when the relationship is dissolving, the couple has separated, and the father is highly committed to continued dominance and control of the mother and children. Since woman and child abuse by husbands and fathers is instrumental, directed at subjugating, controlling, and isolating, when a woman has separated from her batterer and is seeking to establish autonomy and independence from him, his struggle to control and dominate her may increase. He may also turn to abuse and subjugation of the children as a tactic of dominance and control of their mother.[6]

The most dangerous time for battered women is when they attempt to separate from their abusers. Martha Mahoney coined the term "separation assault," which is

---

[4] Barbara J. Hart, *Children of Domestic Violence: Risks and Remedies* (1992).

[5] *See* Barbara J. Hart, *Safety and Accountability: The Underpinnings of a Just Justice System* (1998).

[6] Hart, *supra* note 4 (citing Lee H. Bowker, Michelle Arbitell & Richard McFerron, "On the Relationship Between Wife Beating and Child Abuse," in *Feminist Perspectives on Wife Abuse* (Kersti Yllo & Michelle Bograd, eds., 1988); Evan Stark & Anne Flitcraft, "Women and Children at Risk: A Feminist Perspective on Child Abuse, 18(1) *Int'l J. Health Services* 97 (1988).

defined as an attack that occurs at or after the moment a battered woman decides to separate from her batterer. "Separation assault is the attack on the woman's body and volition in which her partner seeks to prevent her from leaving, retaliate for the separation, or force her to return. It aims at overbearing her will as to where and with whom she will live, coercing her in order to enforce connection in a relationship."[7] Research confirms that battering men often escalate violence to recapture battered women and children who have sought safety in separation. It is shown that when victims of DV leave their abusive partners, the risk of physical harm increases by 75 percent. Battered women seek medical attention for injuries sustained as a consequence of DV significantly more often after separation than during cohabitation; as many as 75 percent of the visits to emergency rooms by battered women occur after separation.[8]

Given what we know about the risks attendant to separation, the period following a survivor's decision to invoke the justice system may very well be the most dangerous time for her. Simply leaving does not protect battered women and children. Safety is assured only by legal and community protections aimed at addressing the particular risks posed by the batterer's access to the protective parent and children.

Perhaps the most recent notorious case of retaliatory child abuse is that which the U.S. Supreme Court considered in *Castle Rock v. Gonzales*.[9] A month after Ms. Gonzales had sought and obtained a protection order against her husband, Mr. Gonzales, he abducted their three daughters as they were playing outside of the family home. Early the following morning, Mr. Gonzales arrived at the police station and opened fire with a semiautomatic handgun he had bought. The police found the bodies of all three daughters in the cab of his pickup truck. This case was the first and only U.S. Supreme Court case to address the legal issue of a police department's failure to enforce a protection order; however, the factual circumstances of a batterer retaliating with lethal violence is not at all unique.

Batterers Are Dangerous Parents

Apart from the blatant physical risks associated with custodial access postseparation, many emotional consequences arise when children are exposed to battering parents. Lundy Bancroft and Jay Silverman have documented the detrimental ways in which batterers perpetrate harm, both during and after separation, on battered mothers and children.[10] Batterers tend to be rigid, authoritarian parents who expect their commands to be obeyed without question and who are intolerant of their children's resistance. In addition to being authoritarian parents, batterers tend to be underinvolved and neglectful parents and less physically affectionate with their children than nonbattering parents. Thus, while batterers deem children to be within their domain of authority, *they consider caretaking to be the responsibility of the protective parent*. They often consider children as a hindrance or annoyance and so create reasons to justify their absence from the home in order to escape parenting duties. Their underinvolvement often translates into lack of knowledge related to their child's daily activities and needs. For example, batterers often do not know the names of their children's schoolteachers or daycare

---

[7] Bowker, Arbitell & McFerron, *supra* note 6.

[8] Stark & Flitcraft, *supra* note 6.

[9] 545 U.S. 748 (2005).

[10] Lundy Bancroft & Jay G. Silverman, *The Batterer as Parent: Addressing the Impact of Domestic Violence on Family Dynamics* (2002).

providers, the details of their medical conditions, or the names of their doctors. They may be unable to articulate their children's interests, strengths, or ambitions. Due to their underinvolvement, batterers often hold distorted views related to the maturity of their children, expecting them to behave in a manner that is not appropriate for their age.

Indeed, the primary instances where batterers express any interest in their children tend to be in circumstances where it boosts their public image as a good parent. For example, Bancroft and Silverman recount one client who, though rarely available to assist his child with homework, boasted of the academic award he won despite his inattention. Another who actively criticized his child for her lack of athletic prowess was found jumping up and down on the soccer field when she did perform well and telling the other parents "I've always told her she could do it if she'd just keep working at it."

Thus, "a batterer's level of commitment to his children cannot be assessed on the basis of his statements or his expressions of emotions," because such displays are more likely illustrations of their "manipulativeness and self centeredness rather than of genuine connection to the child."[11] Just as batterers are known for their promises to be better partners, so too are they known for their promises to become more involved parents. Yet, these promises are rarely fulfilled. For these reasons, Bancroft and Silverman state, "assessment of a batterer's potential as a parent therefore needs to rely largely on what this *actual past performance* has been, which varies considerably from batterer to batterer."[12]

> A logical corollary of his neglectfulness as parent is the batterer's self-centered relationship with his children. Battering parents tend to be selfish and self referential in relationship to their children. The batterer is often unwilling to adjust his lifestyle to meet the needs of his children, and often fails to connect with the children's feelings. Often this manifests as a batterer's expressing violent behavior in response to crying babies. At its most extreme, this self-centeredness results in a role reversal in which the children are expected to take care of their abusive father.[13]

In a recent study, researchers found a gap between fathers' professed concerns about their children being exposed to intimate partner violence and their intentions of changing their abusive behaviors.[14] The study compared biological and social fathers (stepfathers) with regard to their perceptions of the effect of their intimate partner violence on their children. It found that the majority of battering men believed that their physical and verbal abuses negatively impacted the children in their lives and expressed worry about the long-term effects on the children. Biological fathers were more likely than social fathers to report (1) awareness of the negative effects of intimate partner violence exposure on their children, (2) that they were worried about the long-term impact of that abuse, and (3) awareness that their abuses negatively affected their partners' ability to parent. However, this awareness did not translate into increased likelihood of intending to take actions to end the children's exposure to violence.[15] The authors noted that these findings, if supported by future research,

---

[11] Id. at 33.

[12] Id. (emphasis added).

[13] Id. at 34-35.

[14] Emily F. Rothman, David G. Mandel & Jay G. Silverman, "Abusers' Perceptions of the Effect of Their Intimate Partner Violence on Children," 13(11) *Violence Against Women: An Interdisciplinary J.* 1179 (Nov. 2007).

[15] Id. at 1184-87.

could have significant implications for child custody decision making: unsupervised visitation or physical custody of children should be granted only on demonstration of nonviolent behavior over an extended period of time.

As this study shows, batterers' expressions of regret are not enough to keep battered women and children safe in the future. Custody determinations based on hypothetical parenting skills are likely to expose children to violence, despite promises to the contrary. Thus, attorneys and courts seeking to protect children from DV should rely upon *past caretaking* behaviors as the most predictable measure of parenting.

The social science literature related to batterers as parents illustrates that there are several common and dangerous parenting deficits among batterers, whether or not they inflict physical violence against their children. Such findings are particularly startling in light of the general social scientific evidence regarding the importance of caretaking. As will be discussed later in this chapter (see "Importance of Caretaking: Social Science on Attachment Theory"), attachment theory posits that caretaking is critical for the long-term health of children. Taken together, these two knowledge bases require that courts craft custodial arrangements that limit the potential harm caused by battering parents. As noted below this chapter argues that the ALI approximation standard provides authoritative support for that goal.

CUSTODY LAW FRAMEWORK: GENDER BIAS TRANSLATES INTO DANGER FOR BATTERED WOMEN AND CHILDREN

A meaningful exploration of the current state of custody law for battered mothers and their children requires an examination of the history of custody law in general as well as the specific treatment of custody cases involving DV.

Evolution Toward Best Interests of the Child Standard

The tender years presumption did not become an established part of American law until the early 1900s. At common law, fathers were entitled to their children upon separation or divorce. It was not until the Industrial Revolution, which caused the value of children to decline, that custody awards to mothers became more common. While fathers' rights (FRs) advocates argued that this discriminated against men, some feminists argued that such a gender-based standard reified gender stereotypes, precluding any opportunity for a shift in gender roles vis-á-vis child caretaking. Thus, the so-called neutral BIC standard came into being.[16]

The BIC standard is the prevailing legal standard in most states throughout the nation.[17] Pursuant to the statute, courts are to consider a list of enumerated factors in determining which custodial arrangement meets the BIC. Common statutory factors include the preferences of the child and the parents; the mental and physical health of all parties; the child's relationship with each parent; and the circumstances of the

---

[16] *See* Joan Zorza, "Custody Issue, Guest Editors' Introduction," 11(8) *Violence Against Women J.* 983 (Aug. 2005); Laura Sack, "Women and Children First; A Feminist Analysis of the Primary Caretaker Standard in Child Custody Cases," 4 *Yale J.L. & Feminism* 291 (1992).

[17] *See* Barbara J. Hart, Jennifer White & Lisa Matukaitis, "Child Custody," in *The Impact of Domestic Violence on Your Legal Practice, American Bar Association Commission on Domestic Violence* 234–35 (2d ed. 2004).

home, school, and community of the child. Few statutes designate the weight that one factor is to have versus the others.

Practitioners and scholars alike have criticized the best interests standard as indeterminate, vague, highly subjective, and subject to gender bias.[18] Under the BIC standard, primary caretaking—of critical importance to the well-being of children— has been devalued.[19] In its place, courts have placed greater weight on criteria that put women at a disadvantage. Such factors include economic superiority, employment stability, and remarriage.[20] In addition, judges often use a gender-biased perspective when evaluating the best interests factors, leading to injustices for women and children. A judge's gender-biased viewpoint is reflected by (1) evaluating the impact of a mother's employment on her parenting without evaluating the corollary impact of a father's employment, (2) measuring a mother's parenting against a standard that expects her to provide all child care while measuring a father's parenting against a standard that expects him to provide little or no child care, and (3) judging a mother's nonmarital sexual conduct more harshly than a father's conduct.[21]

Custody Laws Involving Domestic Violence

Until the 1970s, with the advent of no-fault divorce statutes, wife abuse was an integral factor to consider in custody decisions throughout the United States. Such conduct was evidence of fault.[22] With the shift from fault to no-fault regimes, DV was no longer considered relevant to the custody determination. Aided by the BIC standard, judges were trained to assess the custodial arrangement prospectively, to exclude evidence of past misdeeds, and to consider the parents as equally qualified to be custodians of the children. However, the emphasis on no-fault divorce created a backdrop for courts to refuse to consider DV as a relevant factor in custody decisions unless the child was also physically abused.[23]

As of 2005, every state has adopted laws that require judges to consider DV when making custody determinations.[24] The types of statutes fall into three general categories: (1) those in which courts are to consider DV as one factor among many in their best interests determination, (2) those in which DV creates a presumption against awarding joint custody or sole custody to the batterer, and (3) those in which there is both a presumption against awarding joint or sole custody to batterers and the inclusion of DV as a factor to be considered in the best interests determination.

---

[18] *See* Martha Fineman, "Dominant Discourse, Professional Language, and Legal Change in Child Custody Decisionmaking," 101 *Harv. L. Rev.* 727, 770–74 (1988); Penelope E. Bryan, "Symposium on Unfinished Feminist Business: Re-asking the Woman Question at Divorce," 75 *Chi-Kent L. Rev.* 713 n.67 (2000)

[19] *See* Nancy D. Polikoff, "Developing the Primary Caretaker Theory in Custody Cases," 7(2) *Women's Advoc.: Newsletter of the Nat'l Center on Women and Fam. L.* (May 1983).

[20] *See* id.; Nancy D. Polikoff, "Why Are Mothers Losing: A Brief Analysis of Criteria Used in Child Custody Determinations," 14 *Women's Rts. L. Rep.* 175 (1992).

[21] Polikoff, *supra* note 19.

[22] *See* Nancy K.D. Lemon, "Statutes Creating Rebuttable Presumptions Against Custody to Batterers: How Effective Are They?" 28 *Wm. Mitchell L. Rev.* 601, 603–04 (2001).

[23] *See* id.

[24] *See* American Bar Association (ABA) Commission on Domestic Violence, *Child Custody and Domestic Violence by State* (Feb. 2008), http://www.abanet.org/domviol.

The efficacy of these laws varies depending upon the specifics of the statutory language, the case law interpreting the standards, as well as the other statutory provisions related to custody. Where DV is a factor to be considered in determining the best interests, statutes and case law typically do not provide guidance as to the weight that DV should be afforded in relation to the statute's other enumerated factors.[25] The presumption statutes vary greatly in terms of (1) whether the presumption applies to all types of custody or only to joint custody; (2) how DV is defined, that is, what type of evidence is required to trigger the presumption; (3) what evidentiary standard is required to trigger the presumption; and (4) what type of evidence is required to rebut the presumption.[26]

One study evaluated the effectiveness of statutes mandating a presumption against custody to a perpetrator of DV. The authors examined 393 custody orders across six states in circumstances where the father perpetrated DV against the mother; they surveyed sixty judges who entered the orders.[27] The study found that in states with the presumption, orders gave legal and physical custody to the battered mother and imposed a structured schedule and restrictive visitation schedule, except for instances in which there was also a "friendly parent" provision and a presumption for joint custody.[28]

"Equality" Rhetoric: Joint Custody, Shared Parenting, and Cooperation

A concomitant result of the FRs movement's push for a so-called gender-neutral custody standard has been the emergence of joint custody preferences and presumptions—that is, the sharing of parental rights and responsibilities post-separation.[29]

Friendly parent preferences and parental alienation claims are outgrowths of this coequal parenting ideal.[30] The negative implications of these standards for battered women and children are clear: friendly parent provisions directing courts to award custody to the parent who best encourages a relationship between the child and the other parent simultaneously endanger battered women seeking to protect themselves and their children.[31] Most states with friendly parenting provisions or joint or shared custody presumptions fail to specify the weight that should be given by courts in cases where one parent has perpetrated violence against another. Therefore, even in states

---

[25] *See* Hart, White & Matukaitis, *supra* note 17, at 234–35.

[26] Lemon, *supra* note 22.

[27] Allison C. Morrill et al., "Child Custody and Visitation Decisions When the Father Has Perpetrated Violence Against the Mother," 11(8) *Violence Against Women* 1076, 1107 (2005).

[28] Id.

[29] *See generally* Barbara J. Hart, "State Codes on Domestic Violence: Analysis, Commentary and Recommendations," 43 *Juv. & Fam. Ct. J.* 34 (1992); Joan Zorza, "Protecting the Children in Custody Disputes When One Parent Abuses the Other," 29 *Clearinghouse Rev.* 1113, 1122–23 (1996).

[30] *See* Margaret K. Dore, "The 'Friendly Parent' Concept: A Flawed Factor for Child Custody," 6 *Loy. J. Pub. Int. L.* 41 (2004); Joan Zorza, "Friendly Parent Provisions in Custody Determinations," 26 *Clearinghouse Rev.* 921, 923 (1992).

[31] *See* Joan S. Meier, "Domestic Violence, Child Custody, and Child Protection: Understanding Judicial Resistance and Imagining the Solutions," 11 *Am. U.J. Gender Soc. Pol'y & L.* 657, 678–79 (2003).

with provisions against DV, when joint custody or friendly parent provisions are also in place, the DV is often given lower or no weight.[32]

The BIC standard has led to negative results for caretaking mothers generally and battered women in particular. Given batterers' tendency to be neglectful parents, custodial statutes that undervalue caretaking are likely to harm the children of abusive parents. While many states have adopted statutory provisions that require courts to take DV into account, the strength of those statutes varies, depending upon the language of the particular provisions and the accompanying provisions within the overall custody statutory scheme. As such, attorneys for survivors and their children may wish to draw from alternative authorities, such as the ALI, to encourage the court to order custodial arrangements that responsibly meet the needs of battered mothers and children.

AMERICAN LAW INSTITUTE PRINCIPLES: ACCESSING JUSTICE FOR BATTERED MOTHERS AND CHILDREN

The ALI was established in 1923 by a group of prominent American judges, lawyers, and legal academics to simplify uncertainties in the law and "to promote those changes which will tend to better adapt the law to the needs of life."[33] For decades, the ALI has promulgated restatements of the law, model codes, and other proposals for reform in a wide variety of legal arenas. For many judges, lawyers, and legislators, ALI "authorship" serves a legitimating function.

This chapter does not propose the ALI provisions as "ideal" standards in custody cases. Rather, it suggests that lawyers use the ALI as a credible tool for increasing safety for survivors of DV in custody proceedings. Unlike most other ALI principles, the ALI Principles strive to provide "best practices" rather than restate the prevailing law.[34] Indeed, advocates and judges can use the ALI Principles to influence the law in several ways:

1. State legislatures might be persuaded to adopt particular provisions of the ALI Principles, integrating them into their state's existing family law system;[35]

2. Where state statutes are either silent or open for broad interpretation, lawyers for protective parents can urge judges to incorporate the custody provisions of the ALI;[36] and

3. Judges searching for safety-promoting custody guidelines that are otherwise absent within their statutory framework might rely upon the ALI as an authoritative source in their decision making.

---

[32] Morrill et al., *supra* note 27.

[33] *See* John P. Frank, "The American Law Institute, 1923–1998," 26 *Hofstra L. Rev.* 615, 617–20 (1998).

[34] *See* Katherine T. Bartlett, "U.S. Custody Law and Trends in the Context of the ALI Principles of the Law of Family Dissolution," 10 *Va. J. Soc. Pol'y & L.* 5, 6 (2002).

[35] *See* Geoffrey C. Hazard, "The American Law Institute Is Alive and Well," 26 *Hofstra L. Rev.* 661, 665 (1998).

[36] *Cf.* Ira Mark Ellman, "Inventing Family Law," 32 *U.C. Davis L. Rev.* 855, 875–76 (1999) (Chief reporter of the ALI Principles describing a major goal of the ALI Principles as being to provide clear rules to replace high levels of trial court discretion); Mary Coombs, "Insiders and Outsiders: What the American Law Institute Has Done for Gay and Lesbian Families," 8 *Duke J. Gender L. & Pol'y* 87, 88–89 (2001).

The goal of the ALI Principles is to achieve "greater determinacy" in family law while preserving the autonomy of partners and parents to make their own decisions about the terms under which relationships are dissolved.[37] The family dissolution project began in 1989, and its final draft was not complete until 2002. Chapter 2 of the ALI Principles provides guidelines to govern allocation of custodial responsibility (physical custody and visitation) and decision-making responsibility (legal custody).[38] The stated primary objective of Chapter 2 is to serve the BIC by facilitating parental planning, continuity of preexisting attachments, meaningful contact between the child and each parent, caretaking relationships, security from exposure to violence, and predictable decision making.[39] The secondary objective is fairness between the parents.[40]

As discussed in the following sections, the ALI Principles advocate for an "approximation of prior caretaking" standard, which allocates custodial responsibility based upon the caretaking patterns that existed prior to the parents' separation. Although not equivalent to a primary caretaker presumption leading to sole custody for the primary caretaker, it does place significant weight on caretaking history. In addition, the ALI Principles are replete with references to DV in custody decision making. The ALI Principles recognize that, when DV has occurred, the court is to implement limitations that are designed to protect the custodial parent, children, and household members from harm, requiring written findings to that effect. Other provisions reflect a heightened awareness of the importance of considering DV in custody determinations. For these reasons, the ALI Principles provide extremely helpful tools for attorneys representing battered women in custody cases.

Approximation of Prior Caretaking Standard

The ALI Principles focus predominantly on past caretaking patterns in the family to determine the allocation of responsibility for children postseparation. To achieve this, the ALI Principles adopt an "approximation" principle. Section 2.08 provides as follows:

> Unless otherwise resolved by agreement of the parents under 2.06, the court should allocate custodial responsibility so that the proportion of custodial time the child spends with each parent approximates the proportion of time each parent spent performing caretaking functions for the child prior to the parents' separation or, if the parents never lived together, before the filing of the action.[41]

This approximation of prior caretaking standard is subject to a limited number of qualifications that justify alteration of the formula when needed to achieve one of the following objectives: (1) to permit the child to have a relationship with the parent, (2) to accommodate the preferences of a child, (3) to keep siblings

---

[37] See Bartlett, *supra* note 34.
[38] See ALI, *Principles of the Law of Family Dissolution, supra* note 2, at §§ 2.01–2.19.
[39] See id., § 2.02(1).
[40] See id. § 2.02(2).
[41] See id., § 2.08(1).

together when doing so is necessary to their welfare, (4) to protect the child when the presumptive allocation would harm the child due to a disparity in the quality of emotional attachment or the ability of the parent to meet the child's needs, (5) to account for any prior agreement, (6) to avoid impracticalities or factors that would lead to instability, (7) to allow parental relocation principles as provided for in another section, and (8) to avoid substantial and almost certain harm to the child.[42]

The comments to Section 2.08 assert that the approximation of prior caretaking standard is intended to achieve the BIC while avoiding the unpredictable results of the traditional best interests test. Section 2.08, Comment b explains the rationale underlying the approximation formula:

> The ideal standard for determining a child's custodial arrangements is one that both yields predictable and easily adjudicated results and also consistently serves the child's best interests. While the best-interests-of-the-child test may appear well suited to this objective, the test is too subjective to produce predictable results. . . . The indeterminacy of the test also draws the court into comparisons between parenting styles and values that are matters of parental autonomy not appropriate for judicial resolution.[43]

The comment goes on to explain that the past caretaking standard is preferable to the traditional best interests test because past caretaking functions "encompass specific tasks and responsibilities about which concrete evidence is available," thereby offering greater determinacy than the best interests test, which is qualitative, future-oriented, and highly subjective.[44]

Section 2.03(5) defines caretaking functions as "tasks that involve interaction with the child or that direct, arrange, and supervise the interaction and care provided by others." They include but are not limited to the following:

(a) satisfying the nutritional needs of a child, managing the child's bedtime and wake-up routines, caring for the child when sick or injured; being attentive to the child's personal hygiene needs, including washing, grooming, and dressing, playing with the child and arranging for recreation, protecting the child's physical safety, and providing transportation;

(b) directing the child's various developmental needs, including the acquisition of motor and language skills, toilet training, self-confidence and maturation;

(c) providing discipline, giving instruction in manners, assigning and supervising chores, and performing other tasks that attend to a child's needs for behavioral control and self-restraint;

(d) arranging for the child's education, including remedial or special services appropriate to the child's needs and interests, communicating with teachers and counselors, and supervising homework;

---

[42] *See* id., § 2.08(1)(a) through (h).

[43] Id., § 2.08, cmt. b.

[44] Id.

(e) helping the child to develop and maintain appropriate interpersonal relationships with peers, siblings, and other family members;

(f) arranging for health-care providers, medical follow-up and home health care;

(g) providing moral and ethical guidance; and

(h) arranging alternative care by a family member, babysitter, or other child-care provider or facility, including investigation of alternatives, communication with providers, and supervision of care.[45]

Unlike the prevailing BIC standard, the approximation of prior caretaking approach prioritizes what social science has long demonstrated: stability of primary attachments are important to the health and well-being of children.

Importance of Caretaking: Social Science on Attachment Theory. Research overwhelmingly supports the fact that past caretaking is critical to the long-term psychological health of children. Attachment theory asserts that a child's ability to form and maintain healthy intimate relationships across the life span depends upon having had a close and consistent relationship with a caretaker during infancy and early childhood.

John Bowlby, a key theorist in attachment literature, identified the intimate relationship between a responsive caregiver and a dependant infant as the context in which we experience all future relationships.[46] The connection between caregiver and child is a survival mechanism that initially ensures that the two will remain close to one another physically. It is the security of this intimate relationship that creates the confidence the child needs to explore the world with a sense of autonomy. When a child is "securely attached" to its caregiver, he/she is able to use that person as a "base of operations" from which to explore.[47]

In her famous "Strange Situation" study, Mary Ainsworth identified different patterns of attachment between infants and their primary caretakers.[48] She conducted a lab experiment in which the interaction between mothers and infants was observed prior to, during, and after a brief period of separation. She found that securely attached children protested when the mother left, sought her out while she was gone, greeted her excitedly when she returned, and engaged in exploratory behavior when the mother was present. Children demonstrating "anxious attachment" were distressed when the mother left, experienced little relief when they were reunited, were highly anxious before, during, and after separation, and were hesitant to explore when the mother was present. In contrast, children with "avoidant attachment" were indifferent to their mother's presence or absence, rarely cried when she left, showed little positive response upon her return, and had exploratory behavior that was unaffected by their mother's presence.

---

[45] Id., § 2.03(5).

[46] See Inge Bretherton, "The Origins of Attachment Theory: John Bowlby and Mary Ainsworth," 28 Developmental Psychol. 759 (1992).

[47] See Eleanor Willemsen & Kristen Marcel, Attachment 101 for Attorneys: Implications for Infant Placement Decisions, http://www.scu.edu/ethics/publications/other/lawreview/attachment101.html.

[48] See Bretherton, supra note 46; Mary S. Ainsworth, Patterns of Attachment: A Psychological Study of the Strange Situation (1978).

This study, along with other work by Ainsworth, demonstrated that responsive caregivers—those who give physical care, emotional communication, and affection to children in relation to their signals of need—promote secure attachment. Securely attached children are better situated for future development.[49] "Sensitive responsiveness" is a caregiver's ability to read emotional signals accurately and to respond in an appropriate manner.[50] "Attachment in infancy gives the individual a base of operations from which to venture forth to learn about the world, connect to other people in it, and acquire a firm sense of one's self and one's place in that world."[51]

Research has shown that early attachment experiences provide the framework in which individuals learn to relate to other people.[52] Infants form a "mental representation" of the experience of being loved and cared for in an intimate context.[53] This representation remains with adults, offering a system of beliefs, images, and emotions about intimate relationships. Once a child has developed a clear mental representation of the self and the caregiver in the relationship, they no longer need the physical reassurance that younger children need. Instead, they internalize the emotional bond, which facilitates independence and serves as the foundation for their capacity to form, sustain, and commit to close relationships. As individuals develop intimate relationships, they develop the skills necessary for such relationships (e.g., attending to other's thoughts and feelings), which in turn facilitates their ability to establish better social relationships across the lifespan.

Of course, the corollary of attachment theory is that, when children experience disruption of their primary caretaking relationship, they develop difficulties in entering new intimate relationships to use as secure bases for exploration, risk taking, and independence, all of which leads to less developed social skills, lower levels of communication skills, and less mature cognitive development. Indeed, the importance of attachment and the "irreparable harm" likely to result from state interruption of parent/child attachment have led many researchers to recommend "attachment centered" custody policies.[54]

We know from attachment theory that caretaking and the resulting parent/infant attachment is critical to the developmental health of children. We also know from research on batterers as parents that batterers are, by definition, not nurturing caretaking parents. Rather than being responsive to their children's needs, batterers use their children to satisfy their own needs. Taken together, these two areas of social science knowledge suggest that judicial determinations

---

[49] *See* Nicola Atwool, *Attachment as a Context for Development: Challenges and Issues, Quality Contexts for Children's Development,* Children's Issues Seminar, Invercargill, Mar. 12, 1997, at 3–4, http://www.thelizlibrary.org/liz/attachment/html.

[50] *See* Joan Stevenson-Hinde, "Attachment Theory and John Bowlby: Some Reflections," 9(4) *Attachment & Hum. Dev.* 3372 (Dec. 2007).

[51] *See* Willemsen & Marcel, *supra* note 47.

[52] *See* Stevenson-Hinde, *supra* note 50.

[53] *See* Willemsen & Marcel, *supra* note 47; *see also* Raphaele Miljkovitch et al., "Associations Between Parental and Child Attachment Representations," 6(3) *Attachment & Hum. Dev.* 305 (Sept. 2004).

[54] *See* Willemsen & Marcel, *supra* note 47 (arguing that "[b]abies are at great risks when their intimate relationships with caregiving parents are disrupted. When we allow the courts to sever a child's most important relationships while disregarding the attachment literature, we are tolerating a moral wrong").

around custody should place a great deal of weight on caretaking and attachment. When custody proceedings prioritize caretaking, battered mothers and children are more likely to be protected from future harm. The ALI approximation of prior caretaking standard offers an authoritative legal source for courts to apply this knowledge.

Incorporation of Attachment Theory Into the Law. As support for the incorporation of the approximation standard, attorneys and judges may rely upon substantial precedent related to primary caretaking, which was adopted in response to the attachment research cited above.

Social science research on attachment and the importance of primary caretaking has significantly influenced state child custody laws. West Virginia was the first state to adopt a presumption in favor of primary caretaking.[55] In *Garska v. McCoy*, the West Virginia State Supreme Court held that it was in the child's best interests to grant custody to his/her primary caretaker. The presumption required that the primary caretaker be awarded custody unless the other parent was able to show that the primary caretaker was unfit or failed to provide emotional support, routine cleanliness, or nourishing food.[56] West Virginia's law was based on the assumption that children develop a unique attachment with their primary caretaker, which "is an essential cornerstone of a child's sense of security and healthy emotional development."[57] The primary caretaker presumption applied only to children of "tender years." In 1985, Minnesota was the second state to adopt a primary caretaker presumption in *Pikula v. Pikula*.[58] Actually, *Pikula* reversed a trial court decision that had granted custody of the children to a father who verbally and physically abused his wife in his daughters' presence and had threatened to take the children away. The Minnesota court adopted a primary caretaker standard to avoid the indeterminacy of the best interests analysis. Subsequently, the Minnesota legislature replaced the rule with legislation providing that primary caretaker status is a factor to be considered by the court in determining the BIC. In 2000, West Virginia replaced its primary caretaker rule with a rule that mirrors the ALI's approximation standard.[59]

Apart from a presumptive standard of caretaking, many states across the nation have required, through statutory and case law, that substantial weight be given to past caretaking. For example, Vermont expresses this in terms of whether one parent has acted as primary caretaker, requiring consideration of "the quality of the child's relationship with the primary care provider, if appropriate given the child's age and development."[60] Many courts have prioritized primary caretaking in assessing the BIC. For example, in *Jordan v. Jordan,* the Pennsylvania court held that courts must bestow "positive consideration" upon the primary caretaker and that "continued presence of a fit parent who through daily affection, guidance, companionship, and discipline fulfills the child's psychological and physical needs is crucial to the child's emotional

---

[55] *See* Sack, *supra* note 16, at 300.

[56] Garska v. McCoy, 278 S.E.2d 357, 363 n.9 (W. Va. 1981).

[57] David M. v. Margaret M., 385 S.E.2d 912, 917 (W. Va. 1989).

[58] 374 N.W.2d 705, 712 (Minn. 1985).

[59] W. Va. Code Ann. § 48–11–206 (2001).

[60] Vt. Stat. Ann. tit. 15, § 665(b)(6) (2001).

well-being."[61] Surely, the courts' rationale in these cases can be borrowed by attorneys and by judges to support the caretaking ALI's approximation standard.

Determinacy: Easily Applied in Court. The ALI's approximation of prior caretaking standard puts less strain on courts, by reducing the amount of evidence required, decreasing the need for social science experts, and decreasing the need to litigate.

In fact, in the *Garska* case, one of the court's main rationales for adopting a primary caretaker presumption was the "establishment of certainty." In particular, the court noted the negative impact of uncertain standards of primary caretaking parents, particularly those who are economically disadvantaged. "[The] uncertainty of outcome is very destructive of the position of the primary caretaker parent because he or she will be willing to sacrifice everything else in order to avoid the terrible prospect of losing the child in the unpredictable process of litigation." This position is exacerbated by the fact that the primary caretaker often has less financial security and is therefore unable to sustain the expense of custody litigation. The court adopted a standard based on caretaking to avoid "counter-productive litigation which a procedure inviting exhaustive evidence will inevitably create."[62] The injustice of bargaining away rights is more likely to befall women because they "tend to be less well-off economically than their husbands, and . . . cannot afford" drawn out custody proceedings.[63]

The approximation standard promises to reduce the common onslaught of social science experts and evaluators. Use of such experts has been particularly damaging in the context of DV where unfounded psychological theories (such as parental alienation, etc.) often replace judicial decision making and result in custody awards to batterers. Indeed, the *Pikula* court based its primary caretaking rule, in part, on the fact that "legal rules governing custody awards have generally incorporated evaluations of parental fitness replete with *ad hoc* judgments on the beliefs, lifestyles, and perceived credibility of the proposed custodian."[64]

---

[61] Commonwealth ex rel. Jordan v. Jordan, 448 A.2d 1113, 1115 (Pa. Super. Ct. 1982); *see also* Foreng v. Foreng, 509 NW.2d 40 (N.D. 1993) (holding that the trial court did not err in focusing on the mother's primary caretaker status); Wheeler v. Mazur, 793 A.2d 929 (Pa. Super. Ct. 2002) (holding that when both parents are otherwise fit, one parent's role as primary caretaker may be given weight as determining factor in child custody determination); Patel v. Patel, 599 S.E.2d 114 (S.C. 2004) (recognizing that, although there is no rule of law requiring custody be awarded to the primary caretaker, there is an assumption that custody will be awarded to the primary caretaker); Fuerstenberg v. Fuerstenberg, 591 N.W.2d 798 (S.D. 1999) (holding that consideration of which parent has served as child's primary caretaker is important in determining child custody award, not by reason of any preference it might accord, but because it is a fair indicator of which parent has been more responsible to the child in the past); *see generally* Women's Legal Defense Fund, *Representing Primary Caretaker Parents in Custody Disputes: A Manual for Attorneys* (1984).

[62] Garska v. McCoy, 278 S.E.2d 357, 362 (W. Va. 1981).

[63] Fineman, supra note 18.

[64] Pikula v. Pikula, 374 N.W.2d 705, 712 (Minn. 1985); indeed many scholars have highlighted the difference between most forms of court litigation that require factual findings about the past and custody hearings that require prospective predictions about the future. *See, e.g.,* Fobert H. Mnookin, "Child-Custody Adjudication: Judicial Functions in the Fact of Indeterminacy," 39 *Law & Contemp. Probs.* 226, 251–52 (1975).

Elizabeth Scott, the original proponent of the approximation standard, asserts that the approach promises much greater judicial efficiency than the prevailing best interests standard. "A custody decision rule that seeks to approximate past patterns of care will demand a narrower, more quantitative inquiry than the best interests standard requires."[65] The court will only consider factual evidence relating to parental participation in the child's life prior to separation (e.g., amount of time spent with the child, extent to which the parent engaged in tasks that contributed to the child's care and development, and participation in decision making), as opposed to inquiring into the hypothetical potential of each party's ability to parent. The potential for error in applying the approximation rule is substantially less than under a best interests analysis because a best interests assessment is retrospective. An approach that attempts to reorder custody is inherently unreliable because it requires "speculative prediction of future parental performance."[66] The approximation is more easily applied, because it involves past fact finding, an inquiry that is traditionally a function of the judiciary. The predictability of the outcome will likely reduce the need for litigation. Given the frequency with which batterers use litigation to further their abuse, the approximation standard may remove that particular tool from their arsenal.

Past Caretaking Reduces Gender Bias. The prevailing BIC standard has provided courts with the opportunity to inject gender bias and consequently has led to unjust case outcomes for women and their children. Based on these trends, scholars and policy makers have advocated a custody theory that elevates caretaking above and beyond all other factors. While the tender years maternal presumption "reflected a move away from the concept of children as property and recognized the child's paramount need for care and nurturance,"[67] it was discriminatory and had the tendency to reify gender stereotypes. However, as scholars such as Nancy Polikoff have argued, we need not reject the value of caretaking in an attempt to achieve gender neutrality. Rather, a gender-neutral standard that examines who performed prior caretaking of the child (regardless of gender) honors that goal and thereby achieves the BIC.[68]

FRs groups argue that a joint custody presumption is more likely to achieve gender equality than a primary caretaker presumption. However, while such a standard may appear equal in the abstract, it is based on ideal visions of shared parenting, furthers the interests of noncaretaking fathers, and is against the interests of caretaking mothers and the developmental interests of their children.

---

[65] Elizabeth S. Scott, "Pluralism, Parental Preference, and Child Custody," 80 *Cal. L. Rev.* 615 (1992).

[66] Id. at 638.

[67] Polikoff, *supra* note 20, at 183.

[68] At a workshop, Nancy Polikoff noted, "The primary caretaker presumption died on a belief that it was really just a tender years presumption, though I disagreed. . . . They saw it as sex discrimination, which is a position people could have only in a profoundly gendered world." Woodrow Wilson International Center for Scholars, Workshop on the American Law Institute's Principles of the Law of Family Dissolution Analysis and Recommendations, May 20, 2003, at 26, *available at* http://www.wilsoncenter.org/topics/docs/ALI%20at%20WWIC%20-%20 Transcript.doc.

Presumptions favoring joint custody upon divorce, regardless of who has provided care and nurturance during the marriage, actually discourage co-parenting during marriage by sending a clear message to fathers that they have a right to intimate involvement of their children upon divorce—if they choose to exercise it—no matter how detached they are from the ongoing care of their children during the marriage.[69]

Joint custody poses acute problems in cases of DV.

The approximation of prior caretaking standard goes further in achieving gender equity by basing custody, not on a maternal or paternal preference, nor on aspirational parenting, but on historical facts that illustrate prior caretaking. The approximation standard awards custody to whichever parent, regardless of gender, performed the important caretaking functions that are critical to children's long-term development.

The approximation standard is not a primary caretaker presumption.[70] Rather, caretaking is to be allocated in proportion to that which it was prior to separation. Thus, this standard can present substantial dangers for cases involving DV where the batterer participated in caretaking. Where one parent has perpetrated DV against another, shared custodial responsibility without protective measures would be an inappropriate arrangement. Thus, where the parties have presented DV, and there is evidence that the abusive parent engaged in caretaking prior to separation, courts should instead employ the specific DV provisions found in Chapter 2 of the ALI Principles, discussed further below.

Utility of the Approximation Principle for Attorneys Representing Protective Parents. Attorneys for battered mothers can bolster their advocacy on behalf of DV survivors by persuading courts to consider prior caretaking as a presumptive measure of the BIC. The ALI's approximation standard offers authority that caretaking is the most important factor to be considered in determining the BIC, with the exception of a few circumstances, including among them the presence of DV. Courts that place primary reliance on caretaking are likely to award custody to protective parents. Characteristically underinvolved, batterers leave primary caretaking responsibilities to their partners. Unable to provide the names of their children's doctors or teachers and out of touch with their daily habits, batterers will present in a comparatively negative light insofar as caretaking is concerned. Apart from the "ordinary" ways in which caretaking parents nurture their children, battered mothers care for their children by shielding them from their fathers' physical and emotional abuses. Attorneys for protective parents might highlight the specific ways in which their clients took steps to plan for their daily safety (e.g., putting the child to bed before the batterers were due to return home).

Research on batterers' unwillingness to take steps to change further supports the approximation standard's reliance upon past caretaking. Custodial arrangements based upon "what is possible" contradict the research that shows that abusive parents are unlikely to change their caretaking patterns. Awards of custody without evidence of actual changes in behavior are unlikely to be met with success. While the ALI's approximation language excludes instances in which there is a finding of DV, the

---

[69] Nancy D. Polikoff, "Why Are Mothers Losing: A Brief Analysis of Criteria Used in Child Custody Determinations," 7(3) *Women's Rts. L. Rep.* 235 (1987).

[70] Nancy Polikoff noted as follows: "What the ALI has done has, in some ways, represented a compromise." Woodrow Wilson International Center for Scholars, *supra* note 68.

ALI's definition of "domestic violence" only includes physical violence. Thus, protective parents who are unable to evidence DV under the ALI's definition or under their own state's statute would benefit from the approximation of prior caretaking standard. Similarly, those victims who, for fear of retaliatory violence, are unwilling to reveal the fact that their partners perpetrated abuse against them, might rely upon past caretaking as their primary litigation strategy.

Indeed, several state courts have incorporated the ALI's approximation principle as authority for their custody decisions. In *In re Custody of Kali*, the Massachusetts court relied upon the ALI in holding that the BIC can best be achieved by preserving the current placement with a parent, assuming it is a satisfactory one, and continuity with the child's primary caregiver.[71] The Massachusetts statute required that the judge award custody "as may be appropriate to the best interests of the child," and further provided that the judge (1) preserve the relationship between the child and primary caregiver, (2) consider who the child resided with within the past six months preceding the action, and (3) consider whether either parent has established a personal and parental relationship with the child.[72] The court explored the relationship between the BIC standard, set forth in the first paragraph of the statute, and the three requirements set forth in the second.[73] The court held that the Massachusetts statute was consistent with the ALI and offered direction by "evincing a general intent on the part of the Legislature to maintain the bonds between the child and her caregiver."[74] In short, the court reasoned that caretaking stability is in the BIC.

The ALI Principles were also cited by the Florida appellate court in *Young v. Hector*, though not ultimately followed.[75] In this case, the Florida court of appeal reversed the trial court's decision to grant custody to the father where it had failed to allocate physical custody based on prior caretaking roles, citing to the ALI Principles illustration of the fact that caretaking, not fairness, should dictate the allocation of custody. Facts that constituted primary caretaking included the following: (1) the parent was available after school, (2) the parent took the children to doctor and dentist appointments, and (3) the parent actively participated in the children's school and after school activities. Although the guardian ad litem (GAL) recommended custody based on the father's economic resources, the court held that "the fact that one parent is the primary caretaker should always outweigh the fact that the other parent is more financially stable."[76] On rehearing, the appeals court reversed the prior panel's decision, holding that the trial court's discretion should prevail.[77] A dissenting judge relied on the ALI for the proposition that primary caretaking should carry great weight.

The Iowa Supreme Court relied upon the ALI Principles in *In re Marriage of Hansen* to reject a district court's award of joint legal custody and joint physical custody. The court cited to the ALI in *In re Marriage of Hansen*, holding that the approximation principle is "a factor to be considered by courts in determining whether to grant joint physical care."[78] The court emphasized "stability" and "continuity" as two important

---

[71] *In re* Custody of Kali, 792 N.E.2d 635 (Mass. 2003).

[72] *See In re* Custody of Kali, 792 N.E.2d 635, 639 (Mass. 2003) (citing Mass. Gen. L. Ann. Ch. 209C, § 10(a) (1986)).

[73] Id.

[74] Id. at 641 (citing Custody of Zia, 736 N.E.2d 449 (Mass. App. Ct. 2000)).

[75] Young v. Hector, 740 So. 2d 1153 (Fla. Dist. Ct. App. 1999).

[76] Id. at 1157.

[77] Id. at 1164.

[78] *See In re* Marriage of Hansen, 733 N.W.2d 683 (Iowa 2007).

factors to consider in custody determinations and dismissed the notion that there was a presumption of joint custody. Instead, the court held, "by focusing on historic patterns of caregiving, the approximation rule provides a relatively objective factor for the court to consider . . . it tends to ensure that any decision to grant joint physical care is firmly rooted in the past practices of the individual family."[79] Specifically, the Iowa court rejected a joint custody arrangement where one spouse had been the primary caregiver, and there was evidence of *high conflict* in the marriage. The court noted that "evidence of controlling behavior by a spouse" weighed against a grant of joint custody.[80] This case did not include DV in the record, but surely given that this case involved a high-conflict marriage (less severe than DV), the court's opinion would ipso facto seem to support an argument against awarding joint custody where one parent perpetrated abuse against the other who served as the primary caregiver.

Apart from the cases that have specifically cited to the ALI Principles, attorneys and courts interested in adopting the ALI approximation of prior caretaking standard can draw upon the substantial precedent (case law and statutory law) that has developed over the past thirty years, which holds that (1) primary caretaking should be weighed heavily in making child custody determinations and (2) stability and continuity are major factors to be considered in determining the BIC.

Assuming that courts accept the ALI Principles' approximation standard, attorneys will need to elicit detailed testimony from their clients and from third-party witnesses to illustrate prior caretaking. Judges may themselves be unfamiliar with the nature and extent of activities required for the caretaking of children. Thus, attorneys will need to paint a vivid and rich picture of the tasks involved in childrearing and the prior efforts expended by their clients. Section 2.03(5) of the ALI Principles explicitly sets out factors to consider in assessing caretaking.[81] To satisfy the approximation standard, attorneys must therefore use the testimony of their clients, teachers, doctors, clergy, or others who have observed their clients with their children to illustrate one or more of those factors. Attorneys and courts may rely upon primary caretaking case law and cases that emphasize "stability" to further identify facts that support this standard. For examples of direct examination questions, practitioners may refer to *Representing Primary Caretaker Parents in Custody Disputes: A Manual for Attorneys,* a packet compiled by what was the Women's Legal Defense Fund.[82]

Domestic Violence Provisions

Discussion of DV permeates the ALI Principles. Such attention reflects the recognition that DV has a profound impact upon custodial parents and the welfare of their children. The usefulness of the ALI Principles depends upon the strengths and weaknesses of a particular state's DV and custody statutes, as well as the specific facts of the case. Given the breadth of variation, the following merely outlines the main ALI provisions related to DV, in hopes that attorneys and courts will use the provisions to optimize safety and agency for survivors.

---

[79] Id. at 697.

[80] Id. at 698.

[81] *See* "Approximation of Prior Caretaking Standard."

[82] Women's Legal Defense Fund, *supra* note 61, at 56-68, reprinting Nancy D. Polikoff, "Evidentiary Concerns in Proving Primary Caretaking," 4(3) *Women's Advoc., Newsletter of the Nat'l Center on Women & Fam. L.* (July 1983).

Definition of Domestic Violence.   The ALI Principles define DV as "the infliction of physical injury, or the creation of a reasonable fear thereof, by a parent or a present or former member of the child's household, against the child or another member of the household."[83] The comments to that section explain that "the definition does not include emotional abuse," however, "[t]aking advantage of the emotional vulnerability of a parent . . . may be a reason for the court to decide that a parental agreement is not voluntary, and thus not entitled to deference."[84] Although on its face, the ALI Principles' definition of DV fails to encompass the wide range of abusive behaviors that batterers utilize to exert power and control, zealous advocates and well-intended courts would be wise to interpret the language liberally, acknowledging how a wide range of nonphysical behaviors are often utilized to invoke fear of physical violence.[85]

The ALI Principles provide that, for purposes of custody determinations, "reasonable action taken by an individual for self-protection, or the protection of another individual, is not DV."[86] Furthermore, the ALI Principles state, "[I]n situations of mutual domestic abuse, when one parents aggression is substantially more extreme or dangerous than the other's, it may be appropriate for the court to impose limits on the primary aggressor but not on the primary victim."[87] This language is, of course, critical to distinguishing between survivors and perpetrators; indeed simplistic applications of an incident-based definition of DV can and have, historically, led to unintended consequences for survivors. Unfortunately, as one author has noted elsewhere, the ALI Principles' primary aggressor language becomes relevant only at the stage of crafting the limitation and not for determining whether abuse exists.[88]

Limitations on the Allocation of Responsibility Based on Domestic Violence.   Under Section 2.06 of the ALI Principles, the court is to order the provisions of a parenting plan, unless the agreement "(a) is not knowing or voluntary, or (b) would be harmful to the child." If credible information of DV is presented, the court is required to hold a hearing. If the court finds that DV has occurred, it should order appropriate measures under ALI Principle Section 2.11.

Section 2.11(1)(b) provides that, if the court finds that one of the parents has inflicted DV, then the court is to "impose limits that are reasonably calculated to protect the child, child's parent, or other member of the household from harm." Limitations include the following:

(a) an adjustment, including a reduction or the elimination, of the custodial responsibility of a parent;

[83] *Principles of the Law of Family Dissolution, supra* note 2, at § 2.03(7).

[84] Id., § 2.03, cmt. h.

[85] *See* Evan Stark, *Coercive Control: How Men Entrap Women in Personal Life,* at 83–111 (2007).

[86] *Principles of the Law of Family Dissolution, supra* note 2, at § 2.03(7).

[87] Id., § 2.11, cmt. c.

[88] Merle Weiner, "Domestic Violence and Custody: Importing the American Law Institute's Principles of the Law of Family Dissolution Into Oregon Law," 35 *Williamette L. Rev.* 643, 673 (1999).

(b) supervision of the custodial time between a parent and the child;

(c) exchange of the child between parents through an intermediary, or in a protected setting;

(d) restraints on a parent's communication with or proximity to the other parent or the child;

(e) a requirement that a parent abstain from possession or consumption of alcohol or nonprescribed drugs while exercising custodial responsibility and within a specified period immediately preceding such exercise;

(f) denial of overnight custodial responsibility;

(g) restrictions on the presence of specific persons while a parent is with the child;

(h) a requirement that a parent post a bond to secure return of the child following a period in which the parent is exercising custodial responsibility or to secure other performance required by the court;

(i) a requirement that a parent complete a treatment program for perpetrators of domestic violence, for drug or alcohol abuse, or for other behavior addressed in this section;

(j) any other constraints or conditions that the court deems necessary to provide for the safety of the child, a child's parent, or any other person whose safety immediately affects the child's welfare.[89]

In ordering a measure designed to protect the parent or child, "courts should recognize that abusers often use access to the child as a way to continue abusive behavior against a parent."[90] The comment further recognizes that "[p]rotection of the safety and welfare of an abused parent is consistent with the primary objective of furthering the safety and welfare of the child."[91]

If the court determines that DV has occurred, it should not allocate custodial or decision-making responsibility to that parent without making "special written findings."[92] The written findings should articulate that the "child, other parent, or other household member can be adequately protected from harm" by the limitations imposed by the court. Moreover, the batterer has the burden of proving that an allocation of custodial or decision-making responsibility to him "will not endanger the child, other parent, or other household member."[93]

The findings required by paragraph (3) "should be sufficiently specific to permit meaningful judicial review." Such findings "should include both the circumstances giving rise to the [finding of DV] and the specific factors that give assurance that those circumstances will not recur."[94] It further provides that "The mere passage of time without a recurrence following serious acts of violence ordinarily is not sufficient to

---

[89] *Principles of the Law of Family Dissolution, supra* note 2, at § 2.11(2).

[90] *See* id., § 2.11, cmt. c.

[91] Id.

[92] *See* id., § 2.11, cmt. g.

[93] Id., § 2.11(3).

[94] Id., § 2.11, cmt. g.

warrant unsupervised visitation, nor is attendance in a treatment program."[95] However, "completion of a treatment program and cessation of abusive behavior for a year or more . . . may be sufficient."[96]

Other Sections Addressing Domestic Violence. Apart from the above, a number of provisions throughout the ALI Principles address DV in custody determinations. First, parties seeking custody or visitation must file a parenting plan, which includes, among other things, information on whether a party has inflicted DV in the past, as well as the existence of any restraining orders.[97] The court should maintain the confidentiality of this information if the individual "demonstrates a reasonable fear of . . . DV and disclosure of the information would increase safety risks."[98] Second, the court is required to provide a screening process to identify cases in which DV has occurred.[99] The screening process is to assist victims with complying with the parenting plan and to provide referrals to shelter, counseling, safety planning, information regarding the potential impact of DV on children, and information regarding civil and criminal remedies for DV.[100] Third, when substantial allegations of DV have been made or when there is credible information that DV has occurred, the court should order an investigation or appoint a GAL, unless the court is satisfied that the information is adequate.[101] In addition, the ALI Principles require that a mediator screen for DV. If the mediator finds that DV is present, the mediation should not occur unless reasonable steps are taken "(a) to ensure meaningful consent of each party to participate in the mediation and to any results reached through the mediation process; and (b) to protect the safety of the victim."[102]

The ALI Principles provide promising practices for relocating parents, particularly those who are relocating for safety reasons. If relocation significantly impairs the other parent's rights, "the court should revise the parenting plan to accommodate the relocation without changing the proportion of custodial responsibilities each parent is exercising."[103] But, if the relocation renders it impossible to maintain the same proportion of custodial responsibility, and the relocating party has the significant majority of custodial responsibility, then the court should allow relocation as long as the parent requesting relocation "shows that the relocation is for a valid purpose, in good faith, and to a location that is reasonable in light of the purpose."[104] The ALI Principles further state that a relocation is valid if it is "to protect the safety of the child or another member of the child's household from a significant risk of harm."[105] Numerous state courts have relied upon the ALI Principles relocation provisions in upholding the relocation of protective parents.[106]

---

[95] Id.
[96] Id.
[97] See id. § 2.05(2)(f).
[98] See id., § 2.05(2).
[99] See id., § 2.05(3).
[100] See id.
[101] See id., § 2.13(4).
[102] See id., § 2.07(2).
[103] See id., § 2.17(3).
[104] See id., § 2.17(4)(a).
[105] See id., § 2.17(4)(a)(ii).
[106] See, e.g., J.F. v. J.F., 894 N.E.2d 617, 626 (Mass. 2008); Rogers v. Parrish, 923 A.2d 607, 612 (Vt. 2007); Mason v. Coleman, 850 N.E.2d 513, 518–19 (Mass. 2006); Hawkes v. Spence,

Application of the Domestic Violence Provisions. All of the above DV-related provisions of the ALI Principles are potentially helpful for attorneys and judges seeking to protect battered mothers and their children from future harm. Most important is the explicit recognition that (1) abusers often use the custody proceedings as an arena to further their abuse and (2) protective parents' and the children's safety interests are aligned. However, one cautionary note is in order: given the variability in battered women's needs, the ALI provisions are best applied with flexibility in mind, contingent upon the particular case at stake and context of the custody issue in that case.[107] No single custody formula exists that can protect survivors and their children. By failing to consider the particular risks and knowledge by individual battered women, "cookie cutter" solutions jeopardize the short- and long-term safety of women and children.[108] Instead, family court judges and attorneys for protective parents should use the ALI provisions as guidelines to assist in tailoring a custodial arrangement that meets the individual and comprehensive needs of survivors and their children. In essence, the ALI provisions related to DV should engage the court in safety planning. Courts are to "impose limits that are reasonably calculated to protect the child, child's parent, or other member of the household from harm." From the judicial perspective, this means listening carefully to the individual circumstances and needs of survivors and ordering arrangements that meet those circumstances and needs. From the attorney perspective, this means developing relationships with clients that enable a better understanding of their safety assessments, presenting evidence to the court that illustrates the particular risks at stake, and drawing upon the ALI and precedent to support relief that meets the self-defined and particular needs of survivors and their children.

---

878 A.2d 273, 278–82 (Vt. 2005); Dupre v. Dupre, 857 A.2d 242, 255–59 (R.I. 2004); Hayes v. Gallacher, 972 P.2d 1138, 1140–41 (Nev. 1999).

[107] *See* Nicole E. Allen, Deborah I. Bybee & Cris M. Sullivan, "Battered Women's Multitude of Needs: Evidence Supporting the Need for Comprehensive Advocacy," 10(9) *Violence Against Women J.* 1015 (Sept. 2004).

[108] *See* Jill Davies, Eleanor Lyon & Diane Monti-Catania, *Safety Planning With Battered Women: Complex Lives/Difficult Choices* (1998).

Chapter 25

Covering the Crisis in the Custody Courts

by Anne Grant, M.A., M.Div.

INTRODUCTION

Why would anyone want to write about the crisis in this nation's custody courts? I stumbled into this horrifying hidden world while serving as executive director of the Women's Center of Rhode Island, the state's oldest and largest shelter for battered women and their children. We planned a capital campaign and wanted to publicize our work. I asked the deputy executive editor of our only statewide daily, the *Providence Journal*, if I could write a column called "Overcoming Abuse." He welcomed the idea. Battered mothers and shelter staff helped me comprehend issues that I described in the column.

A year earlier, a family court magistrate had ordered a woman at the shelter to let her children visit their father. The magistrate had no idea how violent her husband was, but we knew. The smashed hulk of her car sat outside the shelter for weeks after he demolished it there. She managed to find another car and an apartment. She enrolled her children in new schools and worked to exhaustion earning her certificate as a nursing assistant.

Shortly before Christmas, her husband called and said he could not come for the children. He asked her to bring them to him. Her sister warned her not to, but she feared violating the court order. She left the car running outside his house and walked the children to his door. Within seconds, he drew her inside, where he raped, sodomized, and stabbed her to death.

No-fault divorce makes it easy for people to end marriages without revealing any sordid details of domestic violence (DV). Judges automatically award joint custody to both parents, even if one is a documented batterer. That decision sends children and protective parents who escaped the terror back to ground zero.

Judges who overlook the record of assaults, restraining orders, and residence in shelters typically believe that both of the parents who are fighting over custody and visitation are self-centered litigants. Nothing could be further from the truth.

TRUTH BECOMES A CASUALTY

As in any war, truth is the first casualty. Most news editors consider custody cases confidential, too time-consuming for regular reporters, and fraught with the danger of lawsuits. When mayhem results, editors often assume both parents are fighting for selfish reasons. Many fail to notice that intractable custody cases[1] are often campaigns of terror against parents who are trying to protect their children.

Professor Richard Gelles, whose research has been distorted to suggest women and men are equally guilty of battering their intimate partners, insists

> Research shows that nearly 90 percent of battering victims are women and only about ten percent are men. . . . There are very few women who stalk male partners or kill them and then their children in a cataclysmic act of familicide. The most brutal, terrorizing, and continuing pattern of harmful intimate violence is carried out primarily by men.[2]

---

[1] Rhode Island Family Court Judge Laureen D'Ambra and attorney Christine D'Ambra write that "about ten per cent of domestic cases nationally" are not suitable for mediation due to "the emotional battle that one party generally initiates to keep the divorce alive," in "Is Mediation a Solution To the Family Court's Burgeoning Domestic Caseload?" 15(56) *Rhode Island B.J.* 16 (Jan./Feb. 2008).

[2] Richard J. Gelles, *Not an Even Playing Field*, http://thesafetyzone.org/everyone/gelles.html.

Editors might doubt that I could write objectively about these cases when I was the director of a battered women's shelter, as if I automatically believed what mothers and children told me without considering the fathers' points of view. Responsible journalists generally try to include opposing points of view in their stories, but once litigation takes over, the court file is full of fiction, and corroboration must be sought elsewhere. The fact that children's records are usually sealed, and their statements frequently distrusted, complicates the task. Meanwhile abusive and controlling parents spread rumors and hire lawyers skilled at confusing the evidence.

Fathers' rights activists can commandeer well-intentioned programs that encourage men to become more involved as parents. Vocal, sometimes violent men may demand equal time raising children merely because it is a way to avoid paying child support, even as it throws their children's daily lives into unmanageable chaos.[3] Adamant fathers divest their assets and misrepresent their income to convince courts that they are suddenly impoverished. Their obsession can produce years of court-sustained, custody-related torment, while children grow up in poverty and mothers juggle low-paying jobs.

Those of us who write and speak about these cases have to learn the art of dispassion from good lawyers, even though we may be tempted to despise the ruthlessness of many in their profession. This lesson has been a hard one for me. My writing has ranged from fierce narratives that won few new friends to a carefully footnoted report that convinced one attorney to write an appeal to Rhode Island's Supreme Court, arguing my constitutional right to blog on the Internet about controversial subjects like Parental Alienation Syndrome (PAS).[4]

WRITING AS A TOOL FOR CHANGE

Writing reports, correspondence, and fund-raising proposals helped to expand our shelter and advocacy programs.[5] We printed posters and fliers in multiple languages,

---

[3] One of the most famous of these terrorist campaigns was the Beltway Sniper, John Allen Muhammad, who drove east in October 2002 on a killing spree to find his ex-wife and children on the advice of a lawyer in a Tacoma, Washington, fathers' program that was funded by the federal Department of Health and Human Services Office for Child Support Enforcement (OCSE). Liz Richards writes that these federal funds "provide non-custodial fathers with free attorneys to litigate for custody" and "Both former OCSE Commissioner David Gray Ross and current Assistant HHS Secretary Wade Horn have turned the department into a father custody agency through 'Access/Visitation Enforcement' and 'Responsible Fatherhood' programs incorporating the Gardner methodologies," in *Program Produces Motherless Kids* (Nov. 6, 2003), http://sisyphe.org/article.php3?id_article=754.

[4] As described in several other chapters in this volume (see Chapters 1, 12, and 20), psychiatrist Richard Gardner devised PAS. From the mid-1980s until his suicide in 2003, Gardner published books and articles and served as an expert witness promoting his theories on PAS in contested child custody cases, especially those involving abuse allegations. The scientific community generally views Gardner's theory and opinions as "junk science," since his ideas are based primarily on his own clinical observations, and most of his published writings did not undergo standard peer-review process. See further resources at http://www.leadershipcouncil.org/1/pas/1.html.

[5] Humorist Garrison Keillor gently mocks his tribe of English majors. But stories touch the heart in ways that statistics never can. Those in the social sciences may seem more scientific when they use abstractions, multisyllabic words, passive verbs, and Latinized nouns, but their academic objectivity may lull readers to sleep. In contrast, English majors get trained to use

produced newsletters, radio and TV spots, a short video, and a full-length public television program. We convened a major conference using tightly written case studies to help people grasp the complexity of the social web that entangles battered mothers and children.

Given press scruples and the necessary shield of confidentiality, could we use writing to create public awareness and to generate political consensus? My "Overcoming Abuse" columns seldom named litigants, but one batterer recognized himself and threatened to sue the paper. Another tried unsuccessfully to bring the shelter and me to court as third parties in his custody case.

Under increasing pressure, both organizations went on the defense: the newspaper stopped me from writing about family court cases, and in 1996, the Women's Center board fired me as executive director after eight successful years of expanding our property and program. Some board members felt my public advocacy had become a liability.

Perhaps they had no choice. In 1993, we had started a support group named after Phyllis Chesler's ground-breaking book, *Mothers on Trial*.[6] Group members helped me understand the patterns emerging in their court cases. I saw this knowledge as essential to our agency's long-range plans. In pursuing our mission to help battered women and their children, we could not be satisfied merely to provide social services. We had to take on the risky business of social change.

During these years, a revealing shift occurred in the battered women's movement. When I arrived at the shelter in 1988, I asked our assistant director what word staff used for the women who lived there. She laughed and replied, "We call them 'women'."

That was before federal funding forced service providers to describe their services in self-aggrandizing terms. Women and children who once lived together like a small village got labeled as "clients," thus deriving their entire identities from the professionals who were presumed to manage their lives. For a while, we sought to distinguish between funders' terminology and our own political understanding of how power corrupts. In staff meetings, we kept a can and fined ourselves a quarter each time we called a woman a "client."[7]

Eventually, our effort failed. We had been the first shelter in the state to bring in a clinical therapist while other agencies derided that profession by splitting the word in two: "the rapist." Before leaving the agency, I asked our counselor, who excelled at her work, why she persisted in calling the women "clients." She responded that it was a prerogative of the profession she had worked so hard to enter. As a woman, didn't she deserve this mark of professional distinction?

By 1996, I saw that the momentum to change custody courts probably would not come from our agency or our statewide Coalition Against Domestic Violence, which relied heavily on state and federal funding for legal advocacy programs.[8]

---

fewer words, precisely chosen for accuracy, vibrant verbs, and Anglo-Saxon nouns that appeal to the senses while telling stories that intrigue, inform, and spur readers to action.

[6] Phyllis Chesler, *Mothers on Trial: The Battle for Children and Custody* (1985).

[7] I learned this strategy from batterers' reeducation programs that require participants to hold a stuffed donkey and to pay a fine when they refer to women in derogatory terms or as an extension of themselves (for example, calling a woman "my ball-and-chain" or always calling her "my wife" instead of using her name with respect for her independent identity).

[8] The patronage in this system was immediately clear when Rhode Island legislative leaders dispensed funds to DV programs for seven new court advocates in 1989 and required that two of those new employees must be people they sent to us.

EDITOR PUBLISHES THE WHOLE STORY

I left the agency and the coalition, relieved to know that Lisa Prevost, an outstanding editor at a weekly alternative newspaper, the *Providence Phoenix,* had decided to investigate the family courts. She had conducted an in-depth inquiry into a case in which a police officer won custody of his daughter and kept having his ex-wife arrested on false charges. It took Prevost a year of research, reading court files, interviewing all parties, and writing a lengthy report and sidebars to produce her series in February 1997. Finally, I thought, the truth has come out. Once those in authority see the chicanery, the smoke and mirrors of adversarial litigation in custody cases, then justice will roll down.

Prevost's reports validated the mother's story and provided credible documentation in her defense whenever her ex-husband tried to malign her. But their daughter endured six more years with him before realizing, at age fourteen, that her mother had never been a drug addict. The teenager successfully appealed to a judge who let her return to her mother. For the girl, this meant leaving behind two cherished half-sisters, whom her father still forbids her to see six years later. She has spent the intervening years strengthened by her mother and stepfather but still struggling to grow beyond a lifetime of rage and guilt as she continues to find her way through emotional landmines.

Prevost's detailed series brought no official response and no investigation by any branch of government. The family court's chief judge saw the *Phoenix* series, but when I asked him about it a decade later, he brushed it off, saying, "I never read it." Then he added, "But she's gone back to her mother now," as if that assuaged the years of psychic damage he had caused when he ignored compelling evidence that this mother was no drug addict.[9]

I finally understood that the court system distrusts outsiders and has a vested interest in hearing no criticism. By itself, writing could not change our custody courts.

BUILDING A SUPPORT SYSTEM TO CONFRONT A CABAL

Once free of responsibilities as executive director, I hoped that grassroots activism by those outside the system could change the court. So I sought help from the church. My husband, Phil West, and I are both ordained ministers in the United Methodist Church. While our children were growing up, we were pastors of congregations in New York City and Connecticut.

In 1988, after I began work at the Rhode Island shelter, Phil became executive director of the state's chapter of Common Cause, a national citizens' lobby for government reform. Rhode Island, with just over one million citizens, had earned its reputation as one of the most corrupt states. Phil's first project at Common Cause was to draft an ethics complaint against Governor Edward DiPrete for steering contracts to large campaign contributors. DiPrete eventually went to prison, but the investigation never touched his former executive counsel, Jeremiah S. Jeremiah, Jr., whom the governor had appointed to the family court in 1986 and, less than a year later, elevated to becoming its chief. DiPrete called Chief Judge Jeremiah "my closest friend."[10]

---

[9] Ironically, the same chief judge, Jeremiah S. Jeremiah, later won considerable praise for establishing an expensive specialty court with limited success that allowed drug-addicted mothers to keep their children. *See infra* note 14.

[10] "When Jeremiah S. Jeremiah, Jr., was appointed chief judge of the Rhode Island Family Court in 1987, he probably knew more about politics than he did about family law," wrote Lisa Prevost, "Love in Ruins," *Providence Phoenix,* Feb. 7, 1997, at 13.

Both men rose to power in the small city of Cranston, where DiPrete was mayor. Jeremiah chaired the city's Republican Party and served as city solicitor until they advanced together to the statehouse after DiPrete's gubernatorial election in 1984.

In 1996, we formed the Parenting Project at Mathewson Street United Methodist Church a few blocks from the Providence family court. The pastor and congregation were committed to social justice and supported our volunteer work with battered mothers and their children. As a nonprofit sponsor, they provided us with clerical help and a safe space for meetings. At first, we organized a board and recruited volunteers to provide art therapy and supervised visits. We also briefly ran a pilot court-watch project with law school interns.

My first attempt to secure government funds for the Parenting Project failed. Later, we learned how much influence Chief Judge Jeremiah held over funding decisions: he awarded money to a group of police who paid it back to him as tenants of his Cranston office building.[11]

Lawyers who had worked in the DiPrete City Hall or rented space in Jeremiah's building also found their way to the family court bench and bar. The Mothers on Trial support group called them the "Cranston cabal" and tracked the ways they assisted each other in case after case.

CLOSE TEXTUAL ANALYSIS

Research into these cases often required close textual analysis. In one transcript, I found the judge specifying the dates and times for a child's visits with his father. The father's lawyer wrote up the order and sent it to the mother's lawyer before getting the judge's signature. Once signed, an order has the weight of law, and police will enforce it.

I discovered years later, after matching up the transcript with its resulting order, that the father's lawyer had added three small letters, "ren," thereby changing "child" to "children." When the mother received the signed order, she discovered that both her children were ordered to visit their father. That tiny, deceptive edit swept away the larger matter before the court, which was to protect the daughter from a father who had been indicated by a child protective investigator for sexually molesting her.

On the day the mother received the order, no transcript was available; she had only her memory of the judge issuing orders about her son (but not her daughter). If the father appeared at their door with a police escort and the signed order for both children, there was no way she could prevent the visit.

Studying the documents of these cases years later reminds me how some lawyers took delight in creating a constant state of panic, setting up ambushes to wear down the other side in an unending war of attrition. Neither truth nor justice was served, and court officers seemed to know it. Some of the most decent lawyers left family court.

When the process of adversarial litigation grinds up the evidence, a close reading of the documents may reveal how this happens. It took months to pore over horrific transcripts of the case that Prevost was researching for her *Phoenix* series. Despite evidence of DV and perjury and two years of state motions against the police officer for failing to pay child support, Chief Judge Jeremiah awarded him possession of his two-year-old daughter and with it, license to spread rumors that the child's mother was an addict.

---

[11] Jonathan Saltzman, "Judge Jeremiah Voted for Grant for Group That Rents From Him," *Providence J.,* Aug. 1, 1998, at A3.

Chief Judge Jeremiah freely acknowledged his affinity for police and the political connections that won his lifetime appointment to the bench. When I interviewed him in 1993, he admitted amiably, "I think we all got here because of politics."[12]

WRITING PUBLIC TESTIMONY

In 1994, my husband, Phil West, and other Rhode Island reformers tempered that reality by successfully lobbying to establish the Judicial Nominating Commission, which held public interviews and hearings on the qualifications of candidates for judgeships. Six years later, in 2000, Phil showed me a news article. The Judicial Nominating Commission had scheduled hearings to consider nominees for chief justice of the Rhode Island Supreme Court. Rumor had it that family court Chief Judge Jeremiah S. Jeremiah was the odds-on favorite. Phil suggested that I testify against him. Reformers had always intended that the judicial nominating process would expose the truth.

Public hearings on nominee qualifications sometimes drone on with endless praise from power brokers, court friends, fawning lawyers, and cronies. Anyone can offer public testimony about the qualifications of any judicial nominee. I sent the commission a letter saying that I planned to testify against Judge Jeremiah. I urged the commissioners to seek access to a confidential sixty-four-page report of findings by staff at the state Ethics Commission.

In 1999, staff investigators of the ethics agency were troubled when the full commission narrowly dismissed a complaint against Jeremiah. At that stage, the proceedings were closed, as they would be in a grand jury. But a *Providence Journal* reporter learned of the dropped complaint. I enclosed his article[13] about an unprecedented conflict between commissioners and staff, which was all the public knew about charges that Jeremiah had awarded public funds to police who also were tenants in his building. I went to the Judicial Nominating Commission and presented detailed testimony about shortfalls in Jeremiah's handling of custody cases. The room full of lawyers and judges fell silent as I challenged his fitness to serve on the Rhode Island Supreme Court. *Providence Journal* reporters followed up with a lengthy article that identified other concerns, forever shattering Jeremiah's dream of moving up.[14]

I later testified against another family court judge, a woman who had ignored the findings of a psychiatric evaluation ordered by a prior judge in a custody case. She, too, lost her bid to advance. I hoped judges would get the message that they should pay

---

[12] Anne Grant, "R.I. Court System Further Victimizes Battered Families," *Providence Sunday J.,* July 18, 1993, at E7.

[13] Jonathan Saltzman, "Ethics Panel Dismisses Case Against Jeremiah," *Providence J.,* Mar. 10, 1999, at B1.

[14] National Council of Juvenile and Family Court Judges press release, July 22, 2005, http://www.ncjfcj.org/content/view/468/379/. Chief Judge Jeremiah proved open to some kinds of change, as evidenced when The National Council of Juvenile and Family Court Judges named him its "Judge of the Year" in 2005. Its annual award recognizes "leadership, dedication, fairness and innovation" in juvenile or family court systems and praised Jeremiah for working "to improve the lives of Rhode Island's children and families" by establishing "nationally recognized specialty courts, including family and juvenile drug treatment courts, truancy court, and DV court, which have been emulated throughout the country," Critics have countered that these specialty courts allowed Chief Judge Jeremiah to reward political allies by making them magistrates on a par with judges while circumventing the legal process for judicial selection.

closer attention to these custody scams and no longer let their courts be used to harass victims of DV. But my efforts felt like spitting at the ocean.

COMING OF AGE IN FAMILY COURT

I retired from parish ministry in 2003, the year that three children from our original Mothers on Trial group were finally old enough to convince judges to let them return to their mothers. Another teen had gone back to his mother after his father abandoned him.

Two more children who had grown up under the shadow of family court custody rulings, died in their twenties: A son shot himself. His younger sister succumbed to a drug-related death. Their heartbroken mother, who still carries a bullet in her head from her husband's earlier violence, blamed herself for letting their wealthy father raise them. She urged other mothers never to give up protecting their children from abusers and from the court.

Some of the women in the group stayed in touch with each other. Friendships waxed and waned. Traumatized children, ongoing legal harassment, menial jobs, illness, poverty, depression, and exhaustion took their toll. While these mothers suffered, I benefited from a husband who affirmed me and shared my concern for these families. Phil West exuded hope and kept me from descending into despair and rage against all men. From him, I learned the importance of intentionally nurturing a personal support system that will last over the long haul.

I retired, returned to Mathewson Street Church, and pulled out the old Parenting Project stationery. I finally had time to read cartons full of documents, sit through hearings, and update my knowledge of family court. The virus of custody court abuse had spread, infecting lawyers, clinicians, and visitation supervisors. News coverage about the legal plight of battered mothers and their children had lost ground.

WRITING OPINION PIECES

Since my "Overcoming Abuse" columns, a Texas media conglomerate had bought the *Providence Journal,* monitored its editorials, and featured wire stories. Few opportunities remained for local columns. If I could get anything published, it would be an op-ed of about 800 words, with clear opinions, published opposite the editorials.

Day and night, my mind kept circling around this conundrum: How could the very people legally charged with protecting children behave with such disregard for their well-being? How could our child protective systems and family courts become instruments of such enduring damage? How could I explain cases that were hidden from public view, supposedly for the good of children, whom lawyers and clinicians exploited for billable hours? How was it that lawyers, clinicians, and judges could be as brutal agents of abuse as the batterers themselves? Books sometimes gave me pieces to the puzzle. Jon Krakauer's *Under the Banner of Heaven: A Story of Violent Faith,*[15] about Fundamentalist Mormons in the American West, first showed me the role of narcissistic personality disorder. That psychiatric term and the behavior it described eerily matched many documented batterers who were winning custody of their children in Rhode Island.

---

[15] Jon Krakauer, *Under the Banner of Heaven: A Story of Violent Faith* (2003).

I wrote about narcissistic personality disorder and praised one family court judge who recognized the psychological games being played by a batterer. I diplomatically called the op-ed "Signs of Hope in Family Court."[16] However, my optimism displayed my ignorance, for the judge not only failed to order child support when he returned the children to their mother, but also removed himself from the case, saying he was no longer impartial. He sent the tormented family to its twelfth judge in eleven years, knowing that both children already suffered severe emotional problems.

I phoned him and asked, "Does this mean our adversarial system is not able to handle these cases?"

"Yes," he said. "And if we think it can, we're fooling ourselves."[17] What hope is left when even judges who see the dysfunction from within cannot change the system?

FINDING PARADIGMS: THE RHETORIC OF WAR

At home, in the car, and while doing chores, I always keep a radio nearby tuned to Rhode Island's National Public Radio station, WRNI. I draw hope from the quality of discourse and mull over insights that shed light on child protection and parental rights. Often those insights come from metaphoric language, such as the rhetoric of war. Elaborate lies about uranium yellowcake from Niger sounded like the rumors and innuendos that occupy costly hours of custody court hearings. Iraqi weapons of mass destruction were no more real than the wild accusations that gain currency under the junk psychological theory called "parental alienation." Like many battered families, sanctions had weakened Iraq long before American forces invaded with our brazen display of shock and awe. The costs of war have depleted our nation, sunk the dollar, and left domestic needs unmet, just like the custody court reduces families to financial ruin. Even when analysts agree that this war is a fiasco, vital information to examine the disaster remains classified, like the secrecy that shrouds family court.

In the Iraq war, no-bid contracts have gone to insiders, and profiteers have made fortunes without being held accountable for their failed missions. So, too, in family court guardians ad litem (GALs), lawyers, and clinicians demand huge payouts while putting children at ever greater risk. Parents are pressed to raise hundreds of thousands of dollars in their desperate effort to rescue children held hostage by our child protective system.

Who dreamed up this idea that adversarial litigation could help troubled families? I wrote an op-ed telling how batterers often reward or punish children according to the value of intelligence they deliver against the other parent. Like tortured hostages and prisoners of war, children learn to lie. They also suffer an abiding sense of guilt.[18]

Every op-ed brought phone calls, e-mails, and new cases to study, each with anguished children, distraught parents, and surreal courtroom scenes. I searched court files and poured coins into the copier. At home, I studied documents, writing dates in the upper corner, punching holes, organizing them chronologically in notebooks, and coaxing myself to delve into excruciating stories of official malfeasance.

I struggled to make sense of the cruelty of ordinary professionals in our court and child protection systems. I knew they were not so different from me. What could explain it? What was it about this institutional culture that brought out the worst in people?

---

[16] Anne Grant, "Signs of Hope in Family Court," *Providence J.,* Dec. 27, 2003, at B7.

[17] Id.

[18] Anne Grant, "Extracting Intelligence From Children," *Providence J.,* June 21, 2004, at A11.

The personal lives of some family court judges, lawyers, and clinicians were riddled with red flags. One judge lost his seat on the bench to a gambling habit, but the lawyers who bankrolled him were hardly reprimanded; one even ascended to the bench himself. Sexual harassment charges against another judge mysteriously disappeared. Complaints we wanted to file made no sense when we found out that the judges in question sat on the Judicial Tenure and Discipline Commission.

Fear reigned. In a small state where judges hold lifetime tenure and politically connected lawyers quickly vault over each other, expediency rules. Principles are expendable.

BATTERER'S ABCS

I knew nothing about Dr. Richard Gardner or the PAS he created in 1985, until Eileen King, at Justice for Children in Washington, DC, read one of my articles and invited me to the Second Annual Battered Mothers Custody Conference (BMCC) at Siena College in Albany, New York, in January 2005.

Listening to the discussion of these issues by conference participants from across the nation, I heard everything we had been learning in Rhode Island. Pieces of the puzzle that confounded me started to snap into place.

Psychologists use the term "projection" to describe the way people deny their own destructive behavior by blaming someone else for it. Like a film projector, these people "project" their motives and trickery onto others.

For some, such as we saw in the shelter, projection works like preemptive war. Often the first woman who complained of a theft proved to be the one who had begun stealing from others. New to the shelter, she thought this kind of behavior went on all the time. She assumed her accusation would place her above suspicion.

Many batterers project obsessively onto members of their own families. Clinicians and court officers validate this projective narcissism, using the same words in their reports. The three accusations became so common, I began calling them the "Batterer's ABCs":

- *Alienation:* Even as he accuses their mother of alienating the children against him, the abuser forbids them to have a picture of her or to communicate privately with her. Meanwhile, the custody court stops her from having normal parental contact with, or information about, her children.

- *Brainwashing:* The abuser blames her for brainwashing the children as he pours out endless criticism and ridicule of her. In the same way, officers of the custody court function as prosecutors, spreading prejudicial rumors against her to other court personnel and witnesses.

- *Coaching:* He says she coaches the children even as he drills them in what they are permitted to say to others. This is also the way GALs seek out experts and other witnesses who will assert the guardians' biased point of view.

At the BMCC, producer Garland Waller (see Chapter 15) played segments of an interview she did with New Jersey psychiatrist Richard Gardner, who devised his parental alienation theory much like the common law tort action called alienation of affections, when a deserted spouse blames some third party for contributing to the failure of the marriage. Publishing his ideas without subjecting them to peer review, he portrayed PAS as a psychological disorder in children whose mothers had turned them against their fathers. The American Psychiatric Association steadfastly excluded PAS from its definitive *Diagnostic and Statistical Manual of Mental Disorders* (DSM-IV).[19] Nevertheless, Gardner's testimony impressed judges, who freed fathers from paying child support and sometimes awarded pedophiles sole custody of their children. Waller's video, *Small Justice*,[20] documented the crisis of children who are taken from protective mothers and forced by courts to live with abusive fathers.

WOUNDED MEN YEARN FOR GOOD MOTHERS

Well aware of my own deficits as a parent, I have never assumed that all mothers are good. At the shelter, we saw a wide range of mothering styles. Some women resisted our rules against verbal abuse and corporal punishment. If a mother persisted in abusing her children, we were obligated to report her to the authorities. Staff and shelter guests had no qualms about confronting bad attitudes of women who claimed to be abused but who justified their own objectionable behavior.

Women who came to the shelter were not naïve about motherhood. Several had suffered under violent mothers who burned them and broke their bones during an era when doctors did not report child abuse. One mother in our group had sought her first restraining order against her own mother and left home while still in high school. The Mothers on Trial support group did not take child abuse lightly.

Yet, despite what they had endured as children, many support group members were extraordinarily good mothers. Creative, funny, and wise, they were the ones to whom children at the shelter would naturally gravitate. Their playful spontaneity seemed magical to me. These mothers modeled parenting skills that I had lacked when our own children were young.

But I also saw the downside of this gift. Empathy for children can make a good mother stay too long with an immature man who has yearned all his life for a good mother. She recognizes the wounded child within him and tries to draw it out.

The men who abused these women were, themselves, often emotionally scarred survivors of violence, which sometimes included childhood sexual abuse. They hid behind tough, aggressive denial. Few admitted the humiliations they suffered as children; their wives learned of it through relatives who let the secret slip.

When their babies were born, these men resented the extraordinary bond that formed between mother and child. They felt excluded, even as they themselves withdrew from parenting. They seethed with anger, drifted from the family, and refused to pay child support. The mothers lived for their children; their abusers knew that. There was no more gratifying way to punish these good mothers than through their children.

Court personnel viewed the parents from another perspective. They saw solemn, carefully controlled fathers on one side and frantic mothers on the other.

Rarely did judges learn how to speak to children or how to recognize signs that a child might be suffering from coercion, intimidation, or an imbalance of power between parents. One therapist wrote to a judge:

---

[19] American Psychological Association, *The Diagnostic and Statistical Manual of Mental Disorders* (4th ed. 1994).

[20] *Small Justice: Little Justice in America's Family Courts,* http://www.intermedia-inc.com/title.asp?sku=SM03&subcatID=29.

There is no indication that [this mother's] emotional condition has had any effect on her ability to parent. She is currently struggling with symptoms of depression and anxiety, neither of which was significant until the onset of her on-going custody issues. At the present time I see her as coping as well as could be expected in the face of her fears for her son's safety and well-being.[21]

Despite the boy's evident terror and phone calls from complete strangers reporting the father's violence at sports events, two women lawyers convinced the judge to let the man enter the mother's home and remove the boy from his bedroom, where he had barricaded himself. An excellent student, he had refused to attend school, saying he feared his father would kidnap him and kill his mother. Two police officers accompanied the father when he carried the screaming nine-year-old over his shoulder like a trophy for his new wife, who sat outside in a truck. According to the father's medical records, this would have been the easiest way for his new wife to have his child. His first wife had endured two miscarriages and three difficult cycles of *in vitro* fertilization to give birth. This boy was the sole survivor of fetal triplets.

That part of the back-story probably never reached the judge, who simply witnessed the boy's real mother emotionally collapsing in the courtroom. The father's attorney and the GAL, two women working in unison, subjected the mother to cruel assaults in verbal and written harangues, saying she was turning her son into a "mama's boy."[22]

By 2003, the marble corridors and courtrooms were no longer an "old boys club." Women lawyers and judges had come into their own, proving they could be as ruthless as any man.

Batterers have often used women to fight for them, recruiting mothers, aunts, girlfriends, and policewomen to assault their wives.[23] I was not surprised to find abusive men favoring women attorneys, whose gender brought extra credibility to these clients' contention that wives were "vindictive," "gold-digging," or otherwise "unfit" to raise children they had "brainwashed" against their fathers.[24]

COURT GETS A RESIDENT EXPERT

In 2004, Chief Judge Jeremiah's right-hand man, David Tassoni, told me he had found a licensed clinical psychologist, who "understood parental alienation." Lori Meyerson moved from a cramped country office to a posh suite at the Regency Plaza, a few blocks from the courthouse, where she became the court's custody

---

[21] Various unpublished court documents cited throughout this chapter are on file with the author. Letter from Lesley Landau, Ph.D., to Attorney Schreiber, July 14, 2005.

[22] Letter from Sandra H. Smith to Timothy J. Robenhymer, Apr. 21, 2003. *See supra* note 21.

[23] Wives sometimes recognized how they had been used to harass a former wife and that they were then harassed in turn by the next girlfriend. We also found that when prostitutes came to the shelter to escape the mob, they would be followed a day or two later by another woman sent to spy on them. We learned that the first one must move out quickly to a safer location.

[24] I wondered whether some of the harshest women lawyers, often childless themselves, were acting out of personal resentment of an oppressive "cult" of motherhood or perhaps working out hostility to their own mothers. They also enhanced their professional standing and reaped obvious financial rewards by representing the wealthier parent. The prejudice against mothers would be demonstrated in the online essays of Department of Children, Youth and Families (DCYF) hearing officer Norbara Octeau, *infra* notes 37 and 38.

expert. She made her debut on the case of a deputy sheriff who once kept order in the court. He also repaired plumbing and lawn sprinklers for judges and other court personnel on the side.

Cranston police knew him well. They had taken the precaution of removing a truck full of firearms and ammunition from his home before he was served with divorce papers. When his ex-wife later sought a restraining order against him, seven judges declined to hear the petition. Finally, a Cranston police detective met with the chief judge and demanded action.

Jeremiah sent the case to his nemesis, General Magistrate John O'Brien, in the same courtroom where the man once sat as deputy sheriff in a swivel chair at the door. He took his old seat and smirked when his ex-wife entered the courtroom. There he pressed his demand for custody of their ten-year-old daughter, who was already being medicated by her pediatrician for stress from court-ordered visits.

While Tassoni was recruiting Meyerson to be pro bono GAL in this case, police in neighboring Warwick arrested the deputy sheriff for felony DV against his live-in girlfriend, who had her own lengthy record of drug charges. This was an inconvenient time for him to get arrested, with his custody motion pending. But delays can be arranged. Before Meyerson submitted her report nearly a year later, state funds earmarked for victims of crime provided reconstructive surgery for the girlfriend. To the consternation of Warwick police, she stopped coming to testify against her alleged assailant, leading Superior Court Judge Melanie Thunberg to suspend the felony charges against the deputy sheriff.[25]

Psychologist Meyerson ignored the lengthy police and court records, the photos of the girlfriend's injuries, and her surgical repairs, all fully documented in superior court files. On the witness stand in family court, Meyerson reported that the father's lawyer had assured her that no charges remained against this man. She added that she had "never known a lawyer to lie," and coughing erupted in the courtroom, for laughing outright is forbidden.

Her GAL report noted the man's "tendency to engage in verbal arguments with romantic partners,"[26] but Meyerson affirmed his description of himself as "typically a happy, calm, and 'level' person."[27] She did not visit either parent's home or offer reasons why the school had devised a five-point safety plan for the girl's protection. She discredited concerns raised by the child's therapist and pediatrician and persuaded the magistrate to suspend their work with the girl.[28]

The psychologist repeatedly cited her own "hypothesis," of parental alienation, condemning the mother for behavior that she, as a clinician, should have recognized as symptomatic of posttraumatic stress. After a total of three hours interviewing the father in her office, Meyerson recommended placing the girl in his "sole physical care"[29] and allowing the mother only one supervised visit a week.

Chief Judge Jeremiah knew this situation well enough to see the danger of the GAL's recommendations. General Master John O'Brien briefly left the bench to confer with the

---

[25] Previously, I had written to Rhode Island Supreme Court Chief Justice Frank Williams about the problems in DV custody cases. He referred me to Judge Thunberg, whom he had assigned to report on concerns about the judiciary's handling of these cases. I met with her, provided resources, and later requested her final report, but received no reply. Warwick police and the assistant attorney general both expressed dismay at her decision on this case.

[26] Lori Meyerson, Ph.D., "Report of the Guardian ad Litem." (Family Court FC NO.: P01-2766) Sept. 10, 2005, at 44. *See supra* note 21.

[27] Id. at 12.

[28] Id. at 35.

[29] Id. at 46.

chief and returned to announce that the child would remain with her mother. But the magistrate also heralded the psychologist's "outstanding report" and said this example was "as close as you can get to parental alienation." Though the father paid no child support, O'Brien still warned the mother "to cease and desist from interfering with this man's rights."[30]

WRITING COMPLAINTS AGAINST COURT PROFESSIONALS

Although the *Providence Journal* does not assign news staff to family court cases, it did report the arrest and felony charges against the father. Reporters covered each superior court hearing until Judge Thunberg dismissed the case. Back in family court, the GAL's densely written report defied reason as she condemned not only the mother but also the girl's counselor and pediatrician. Meyerson urged that her own report become the basis for all future therapy and evaluation.

Dismayed by this clinician's performance, I filed two complaints against her: one with the Ethics Committee of the Rhode Island Psychological Association and one using the state's downloaded complaint form for their Office of Health Professionals Regulation. That office sent my concerns to Meyerson, received her explanation, and ruled that my complaint was unfounded. I had not provided enough documentation, in part because I feared it might lead to retaliation against the mother and daughter.

Since that first case, when Meyerson distributed her freshly printed business cards to lawyers who gathered around her at each recess, her role in the custody court has been secured. Judges routinely refer litigants to her for expensive court-ordered evaluations and classes in coparenting, a concept that requires two parents to work together regardless of dangerous power imbalances between them.

But progress is coming in other places. The Psychologists Board of Queensland, Australia, made history with their March 3, 2008, response after a mother complained to them. The board disciplined prominent Brisbane clinical psychologist, William Wrigley, for unprofessional behavior because he reported PAS three years earlier, prompting the court to remove the mother's two children. The board voted unanimously that this constituted "professional conduct that demonstrates incompetence or a lack of adequate knowledge, skill, judgment or care."[31]

They advised Wrigley that "referring to an unrecognized syndrome in his reports"[32] violated their code of ethics. Scores of Queensland custody cases may now be challenged because of similar violations by other clinicians. While protecting the safety of children, the board's censure may also help to restore the integrity of their own profession.

CASE PRESENTATION

Sausage Games

In 2006, people in a seaside town read my op-ed on PAS[33] and recognized the same pattern in an astounding case when the Rhode Island Department of Children, Youth

---

[30] Anne Grant, Courtroom Notes (Family Court FC NO.: P01-2766), Nov. 21, 2005. *See supra* note 21.

[31] Tony Koch, "Ruling Debunks Custody Diagnosis," *Australian,* Apr. 7, 2008, http://www.theaustralian.news.com.au/story/0,25197,23495760-2702,00.html.

[32] Id.

[33] Anne Grant, "Family Court Devastation: Discredited 'Parental Alienation Syndrome'," *Providence J.,* June 27, 2006, at B5.

and Families (DCYF) removed two young girls from an excellent mother and ignored the community outcry.

The case began more than two years earlier, after three-year-old "Molly"[34] angrily protested the "sausage games" she said her father played while her mother was at work and her older sister at school. She said her father took off his clothes and rubbed his sausage until it got big, then sprayed her face with sausage juice. The mother, a research scientist, knew she must be cautious. She took her daughter to the pediatrician, where a nurse practitioner called the child abuse hotline. DCYF sent an investigator and indicated the father for sexual molestation.

The father moved out of their home, hired lawyers, and appealed the finding against him. His brother, a divorce lawyer who specializes in sex abuse cases, came from Europe to meet with DCYF. The girls remained with their mother for more than two years until April 7, 2006, when DCYF took them into temporary custody, claiming it was for psychiatric evaluation.

Without producing evidence against their mother, DCYF sent the sisters, then five and nine years old, into its archipelago of foster homes and shelter care, costing tax payers $60,000 a year in addition to countless hours poured into the case by agency and court personnel. The damage to the girls has been incalculable.

Robbed of their mother's inspired parenting, they also were torn from a world full of their friends, school, church, science, robotics, animals, crafts, piano, ballet, gardening, hiking, swimming, biking, and cooking. Transported into the domain of television and profanity, they began displaying behavior and using words that appalled their mother.

Years ago, I developed a procedure for investigating custody cases, which I did at no charge, to help me determine which parents are genuinely protective. Before I agree to research a case, I request documents, photographs, school papers, police and medical records, and anything else that can help me understand the history of the children and their parents. Sometimes parents who want my help give me only those materials that are favorable to them. Since litigation is under way, it is usually impossible to speak to the other parent. I need to discern the truth: is either parent motivated by self-aggrandizement, revenge, or a desire to use children for retribution or personal gratification?

This mother passed the test. She immediately provided the full range of documents, including those not favorable to her. She was eager to do anything to protect her children. I interviewed people who knew the family. We photographed their home. Based on all the information, I felt confident that the mother was not merely a good parent but an outstanding one. She loved her work, but her top priority was her children.

How the Department of Children, Youth and Families Hearing Officer Flipped the Case

I organized documents from the mother with pages from the court file and traced the father's allegations that his wife had alienated the girls against him. In 2004, the father had appealed the finding of sexual molestation. DCYF contracted with attorney Norbara Octeau to serve as adiministrative hearing officer. She wrote that the father blamed "influences of what he termed Parental Alienation Syndrome."[35]

---

[34] Names have been changed to protect confidentiality.

[35] Norbara L. Octeau, "Decision," DCYF Administrative Hearing AH/04-55 (stamped Dec. 20, 2004), at 14. *See supra* note 21.

DCYF gave Octeau no exhibits, not even its original report indicating the father for sexual molestation. Agency staff held *ex parte* meetings with the father, his brother, and his criminal defense attorney. They never notified the mother of these meetings or of the hearing.

Hearing officer Octeau wrote that she knew further evidence existed. She could have insisted on seeing it, but she did not. She expressed concern only for the father's defense and not for the children's. She flipped the case from a finding of sexual molestation against the father to a charge of parental alienation against the mother, which is neither a crime nor a provable allegation. Though she never met the mother nor heard from other witnesses who might challenge the father's testimony, she labeled the mother's "behavior and conduct . . . highly unorthodox and rather suspicious." She stated, "This maternal behavior casts a shadow over the reliability of the child's statements."[36]

Clinicians and court officers, including the GAL, Lise Iwon, later repeated Octeau's opinions as if they were findings of fact. The children were clearly in no danger with their mother. They remained with her for sixteen more months as the father's legal team built its case to remove them and to give the younger girl to him.

I did not recognize the hearing officer's name, Norbara Octeau. In April 2007, one year after the state took the girls into custody, I found an online essay she had written to attract fathers to her private law practice. "It is amazing," Octeau wrote, "in today's modern society that many women revert to touting their traditional roles of cooking, cleaning, laundry and being the tender hands of motherhood to elevate their argument to a pedestal of holy motherhood."[37] In a later article she mocked, "the pedestal which still elicits a knee-jerk reaction to the hallowed image of mother and child."[38]

I sent a letter to the director of DCYF, Patricia Martinez, with a copy to the state's child advocate, asking how DCYF had appointed a hearing officer who was so evidently biased against mothers to rule on a finding of sexual molestation. I did not realize that Rhode Island's child advocate, Jametta Alston, was already preparing a class action suit against DCYF for failure to protect abused children. Her lawsuit prompted state Senator Rhoda Perry to convene hearings into the performance of DCYF by the Senate Health and Human Services Committee.

As I wrote testimony for the Senate committee, I knew there would be no time to give details about this case, which so dramatically illustrates abuses by both the executive branch (DCYF) and the judicial branch (family court) of government. I also knew that lawmakers might not let me testify about a pending case. But if I left obvious questions hanging, they would ignore the harm being done to these children. I decided to mount a blog that legislators and the public could read outside of the committee hearing.

---

[36] Id. at 20.

[37] Norbara L. Octeau & Christopher A. Pearsall, *Rhode Island Divorce Lawyer Tips for You—Are the Rhode Island Family Courts against Fathers?* http://www.rhodeislanddivorce-tips.com/2007/02/rhode_islanddi_12.html. After my letter to DCYF, Mr. Pearsall's name was removed from this posting, and another article by Octeau was substituted. Both articles reveal similar hostility to mothers.

[38] Norbara L. Octeau, DCYF Children Abuse/Are the Rhode Island Courts against fathers? (Feb. 20, 2007), http://rhodeislanddivorcetips.typepad.com/dcyf_children_abuse/2007/02/are_the_rhode_i.html.

Writing a Blog: *Custody Scam*

Night after night, I scanned photos and documents, which the mother had already given me. I uploaded these and told the story as simply as possible without using the family's names. Once I knew this mother's commitment to telling the truth, I dared to do this without consulting her. If she were implicated in any way, it could hurt her children.

After the second Senate hearing, when I referred legislators to the blog, DCYF retaliated by asking the judge to seal the parents' divorce file along with the DCYF files and to impose a gag order that prevented the mother from telling anyone about daily proceedings. By then, I understood what was happening and the urgency of exposing the truth about DCYF's treatment of these girls, who had been held in state custody for 497 days.

People often resist hearing about cases like this. Eyes shift to the side as if looking for a way to escape.

The blog gave readers time to absorb the facts at their own pace.

Some friends were horrified that I would put photos of actual children on line. But by then, DCYF's plans were clear: Their staff revealed that they were being told "Molly" had recanted. DCYF was actively trying to separate her from her older sister, "Sara," and reunite Molly with the only person she had ever identified as her molester. The photographs of her embracing her sister made these children come alive for readers of the blog. The girls' drawings and handwritten notes let them speak eloquently for themselves.

Sara was nine when police went with a social worker to her school and took her to a foster home. Always an organizer, Sara worked out a plan: She would write a journal.

Once a week the girls were allowed a two-hour visit with their *Mami* (which means and sounds the same as "Mommy"), who had been writing and illustrating a personal journal for each daughter since birth. Now Sara began keeping her own journal and told Mami to buy a notebook just like hers and to follow her instructions: Mother and daughter must write messages to each other and exchange their notebooks every week to read what the other had written and to write their own responses. Sara mixed her birth languages, English and Swiss-German, which the girls had learned from their mother.[39]

"Mami, I asked Alice [their foster mother] why I am a foster child," Sara wrote in Swiss-German." She said that the father is 'not guilty.' Then she said that you have 'mental problems.' I can't believe it." Mami wrote to reassure Sara, decorating the page with hearts, a smiling sun and flower: "Alice has never seen me, has never talked to me, she has no idea what happened in our family. Forget about what she said, don't worry. I am normal," Mami wrote in Swiss-German. "I am simpler, more fun to be around than most people. If I were sick in my head, I would not have so many friends, and all those friends would have noticed a long time ago."

Those hand-written pages gave a sense of immediacy to the blog, which became an effective way to report what was happening to children in custody court. The format mixed photographs, documents, writing, and drawings with narrative that moved smoothly from story telling to textual analysis and scholarly research.

---

[39] Their father called Swiss-German their "mother tongue" and complained that they did not speak his preferred language, French. He accused his wife of using Swiss-German to malign him. When the girls lapsed into Swiss-German with their mother in medical exams, visits, or even prayers, it led to punishment and retaliatory court orders.

Gardner's Signs of Genuine Sexual Abuse

If these children had impartial juries deciding their fate, how many jurors could look at Molly's drawing of her father (see Figure 25.1) and still believe that her mother was the one who put this image into her mind?

The *CustodyScam* blog allowed me to show photos and quotes of Richard Gardner's self-published books and to document the numerous ways in which his work actually validates this case as a genuine instance of child sex abuse, as opposed to one that had been fabricated.

Molly fit Gardner's list of criteria matching children who have actually experienced sexual abuse. Here are only a few examples. Gardner wrote that sexually abused children

1. "Have a fairly clear visual image of the experience";

2. "Will usually provide specific details, and they will be consistently the same on subsequent interviews";[40]

3. "Will describe settings that are likely and reasonable";

4. "Provide a credible description of the ejaculate"[41]

5. Are "fearful of the perpetrator. This fear may result in the child's making every attempt to be away from home as much as possible, especially when alone with the offender";[42]

6. Are "often depressed";

7. Suffer "sleep disturbances"; and

8. "Prefer more a fantasy world that is safe and free from the traumas of their real life."[43]

Some of the characteristics that Gardner described as fitting fathers who sexually abuse their children also applied to Molly's father, including the following:

1. They show a "tendency to regress in stressful situations, especially hetero-sexual disappointment. They then regress to sexuality with a child—the less threatening sexual experience";[44]

2. "Sexually abusing fathers are more likely to be social isolates";[45] and

3. They are "rigid and controlling."[46]

In addition, Gardner described characteristics of the drawings of sexually abused children that closely resemble Molly and Sara's drawings:

---

[40] Richard Gardner, *The Parental Alienation Syndrome and the Differentiation Between Fabricated and Genuine Child Sex Abuse* 110 (1987).

[41] Id. at 111. Molly correctly noted the "clear" color of ejaculate, in contrast to children who are uncertain and think it must be yellow like urine.

[42] Id. at 115-16.

[43] Id. at 118.

[44] Id. at. 136.

[45] Id. at 137.

[46] Id. at 138.

Figure 25.1
Sausage Games

1. "Shading in or covering" sexual parts and drawing; and

2. "Attenuated hands and fingers" that "may relate to the manual fondling that these children have been exposed to."[47]

Molly's older sister, Sara, drew their father (see Figure 25.2).

---

[47] Id. at 155–56.

Figure 25.2
Father: "I Hate You"

Molly and Sara's family also possessed a characteristic viewed by Gardner as a strong indicator of genuine sexual abuse: their father and his siblings had all been molested by their own father, who was twice imprisoned for sexual abuse of children outside his family. This fact was known and admitted by the hearing officer, the GAL, and clinicians, who nevertheless reported that the father "did not present with the profile of a sexual offender."[48]

According to Richard Gardner's own criteria, Molly's case was not "fabricated." The evidence easily meets Gardner's standards to show that she suffered "genuine" sexual abuse by her father. Her case reveals how custody evaluators paid by the father could selectively report only those parts of Gardner's parental alienation paradigm that blames mothers in order to justify removing children from mothers and giving them to fathers. The blog allowed me to compare psychological evaluations, which are not considered confidential in custody cases.[49]

Defendant's Rights Versus Victim's Rights

While mothers, minorities, and marginalized people are likely to bear the brunt of blame, American jurisprudence goes to great lengths to presume the innocence of other defendants. In this case, the father's criminal defense attorney, Lise Gescheidt, hired a private investigator, Patricia Azarian, who produced a report that quoted the father's handpicked informants. Court officers and clinicians then quoted the Azarian report, piling hearsay upon hearsay.

For example, on September 15, 2004, licensed clinical psychologist John Parsons spoke on the phone with an elderly daycare owner who described the girls' mother as "a very odd person" and said the mother was "at times jealous that [Molly] was closer to her father."[50] Three pages later, he repeated this from the Azarian report: "[Day care owner] says that [mother] was resentful and jealous of the fact that [Molly] was much closer to her father than to her mother."[51]

Parsons repeated this on the next page, quoting the DCYF hearing officer's report, who appeared to be referencing the Azarian report: "The child's daycare provider was interviewed and stated that [mother] was jealous of the loving and warm relationship between [father] and his children."[52] Later, virtually the same words came from the father himself, who told the psychologist, "[my wife] was just jealous of me and resentful that [Molly] was close to me. She was also envious that I made more money than her and got to present workshops all over the world."[53] The psychologist did not seem to pick up the fact that the father's exact words, "jealous" and "resentful," are those used by the daycare provider and repeated in other reports. He did not question whether the father is "coaching" the day care provider.

Providence is a small city, and it was not hard for me to locate members of this woman's family who also knew Molly's family. Seeking an independent reality check,

---

[48] Psychologist John P. Parsons' report cites and concurs with another psychologist, John Wincze, in John P. Parsons, "Psychological Assessment/Sexual Offender Evaluation," Jan. 8, 2005 (incorrectly dated 2004), at 43. *See supra* note 21.

[49] State employees, such as DCYF staff, are still bound by rules of confidentiality. But lawyers openly spread the most persistent lies, rumors, and innuendos in the courtroom and the community, while blaming each other for this professional lapse.

[50] Id. at 5.

[51] Id. at 8.

[52] Id. at 9. The passive voice often makes court reports muddled and imprecise.

[53] Id. at 15.

I met with them separately and showed each the quotes attributed to their elderly relative. Each one independently stated that she probably said these words, but that the quotes did not accurately describe Molly, Sara, or the girls' reactions to their parents.

Each relative told me that the girls relied emotionally on their mother and avoided their father. They credited the mother with these girls' extraordinary brightness and creativity. One of the relatives wept openly when I told him that Molly and Sara were in a state shelter.

"That's unbelievable!" he said repeatedly, affirming that the girls' mother is "unusual," but "she is a very good mother." The relatives each told me that the girls' father constantly visited this woman, whose unsubstantiated opinion became critical to the case. In the end, the father's defense team may have realized that her testimony could not hold up in court, for they never called her as a witness.

But the harm had been done. The psychologist not only believed her but placed her support for the father at the top of his list of reasons for concluding "To a reasonable degree of psychological certainty, [the father] did not sexually or physically abuse [Molly and Sara] and that [their mother] coached the children to make negative and false statements against their father."[54]

Amazingly, the psychologist assigned greater credibility to a simple phone conversation with the day care owner than to the detailed reports of trained therapists who met with the girls for dozens of sessions at the Sexual Assault and Trauma Resource Center, later renamed Day One. He noted that these therapists "are firmly convinced that [Molly] was sexually assaulted by her father and that [Sara] was physically abused. They do not feel that [the mother] coached the children."[55] Parsons stopped these therapists from meeting with the girls during his evaluation, even though he admitted the possibility that Molly's paternal grandfather, who lived openly as a pedophile in the Philippines, may have molested her.

Truth-Telling: Children Versus the Expert

The psychologist reported that both girls told him disturbing things that he later discounted, as when he quotes Molly, age four: "My dad bumped my head on the floor because he don't love me."[56] His report further states that "When [Molly] was asked why her father does not live with her, she made the following statement: 'He made bad stuff to us like sausage game, and I did not like it at all'."[57] "[Molly] was asked to draw a picture of the sausage game, and she drew a 4-inch long oval shape. In the middle of the oval, she drew scribbling lines. She described the oval as a sausage and the scribbling lines as the hand of her father, but refused to elaborate."[58] "When [Molly] was asked if she had bad dreams, she replied, 'About the sausage game'."[59]

Parsons asked Molly to show the sausage game on an anatomically correct drawing of a male figure, and she marked the penis. When he asked her to show the sausage game on a female figure, she was "not responsive" and soon complained that he was

[54] Id. at 43.
[55] Id. at 45.
[56] Id. at 32.
[57] Id. at 33.
[58] Id.
[59] Id.

Figure 25.3
Masks

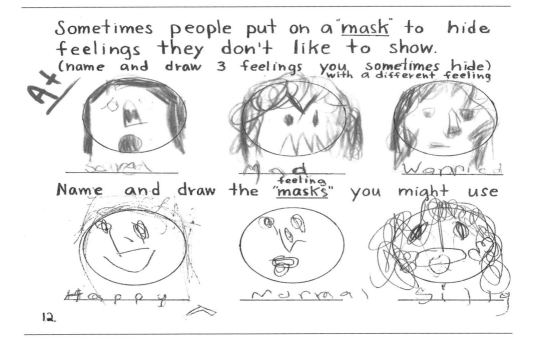

asking her "too many questions."[60] In her last session, the psychologist asked her again about the sausage game, and Molly replied, "My dad does the sausage game and he touches." Parsons continued, "As she made this statement, she touched her vagina and the vagina of a doll. She laughed and giggled and showed no sign of alarm, but refused to discuss the issue further."[61]

The psychologist failed to recognize the giggle and laughter as a likely sign of embarrassment for a four-year-old girl to say these things when she was alone with a grown man who may have a sausage of his own. Instead, he discounted all her disclosures, because Molly "never seemed frightened or upset. She always smiled and was positive."[62] Parsons described Sara the same way: "She told me she had never had a positive experience with her father, but said this with a smile on her face. She did not appear to be distressed, anxious, or concerned."[63]

The psychologist did not seem to grasp what the girls themselves knew. Sara tried to help her troubled little sister by pretending she was a teacher. She gave Molly an assignment from a workbook about feelings. She asked Molly to draw feelings that she sometimes hides under a mask. Molly understood the assignment. She identified the feelings she does not like to show: scared, mad, and worried. She saw herself replacing them with these masks: happy, normal, and silly. Like a good teacher, her big sister affirmed her work with an A+. It does not require a Ph.D. in psychology to comprehend these things (see Figure 25.3).

---

[60] Id.
[61] Id. at 34.
[62] Id. at 45.
[63] Id.

Figure 25.4
Girls With Father, Sun

Nor does it take higher learning to see Molly's authentic feelings about her parents. In July 2005, she drew herself and Sara with their father. Everyone, even the sun above, is miserable (see Figure 25.4).

Figure 25.5
Mami-Visit

A year later, in July 2006, after three months living in state custody and with every reason to be forlorn, Molly drew their utter delight at their "Mami-visit." A joyous balloon with the Swiss symbol dances in mid-air. Molly wrote, "I am having a wonderful Mami-visit" (see Figure 25.5).

Sara, too, adored their mother and wrote it in her journal, "Good night, Mami. You are the best! See you tomorrow in my diary. You are the best Mami in the whole world."

For a few critical weeks, the *CustodyScam* blog proved to be an effective way to let the girls speak for themselves through their writings and drawings, to show in photos the quality of their lives in their mother's care, and to document professional improprieties by clinicians and officers of the court. The blog also helped to inform neighbors of the bewildering legal morass that had swallowed these children. This, in turn, gave rise to a surge of new letters from people in the United States and Europe written to government officials.

When I mounted the *CustodyScam* blog, some people warned that if I posted children's photos on the Internet, predators in cyberspace might find them. This concern made the truth absurdly ironic: DCYF claimed that Molly had recanted and then forced her into unsupervised visits with the only person she had ever identified as sexually abusing her—her father. She had consistently named him, drawn him, and reenacted him masturbating.

Clinician "Reunites" Daughter and Father

The GAL, Lise Iwon, had worked closely with Haven Miles, a clinician contracted by DCYF to reunite the younger girl with her father. This licensed clinical social worker wrote, "It does not seem possible . . . to make a determination of whether and/ or how there was sexual abuse."[64] Nevertheless, Miles' report shows her taking Molly, by then five years old, into a room alone with her father. The girl was horrified. She turned her back on him and screamed "for 20 or 30 minutes." Exhausted, the child accepted a glass of water from Miles, who soothed her feverish face with a wet cloth and began talking quietly. Miles got Molly to enter into a conversation with her father about "small topics."[65] Exactly the same procedure might be used to groom a child for molestation. After another visit with her father, Molly portrayed herself as handless, helpless, and bereft (see Figure 25.6).

The *CustodyScam* blog also published scholarly observations about the trauma of sexual abuse. For example, the blog describes Sigmund Freud's supression of evidence of incest as a fundamental failure of psychoanalysis:

> Jeffrey Moussaieff Masson stumbled onto secrets that Anna Freud urged him to forget. She had given the young psychoanalyst and researcher free run of her father's final home. There, he found letters and notes showing that

---

[64] Haven Miles, MSW, LICSW, "Summary of Contacts, Parent-Child Assessment," Nov. 28, 2005, at 5. *See supra* note 21.

[65] Id. at 4. Lawyers use clinicians in these cases with evident cynicism, cherry-picking their reports for exactly the phrase that is needed to convince a judge. PAS legal strategies are not a search for truth. The father's legal team, including the GAL, completely ignores some of Miles' advice, such as "The emotional complexities of this situation are so overwhelming as to be crushing. Each person involved will be dramatically impaired if progress through this is not achieved. The youngest participant will be the most damaged. Every effort should be made to support her staying connected with her relationships in a way which will insure her own safety"; id. at 6. DCYF first removed this child from her mother, did not permit her to eat, sleep, or speak privately with her sister at the shelter, and finally placed her alone with her father.

Figure 25.6
Molly Weeping

Sigmund Freud, father of modern psychoanalysis, harbored misgivings about some of his most famous conclusions. In 1984, Masson documented this history in his ground-breaking book, *The Assault on Truth: Freud's Suppression of the Seduction Theory*."[66]

> [Masson] expresses dismay that "sexual abuse of one form or another was the core trauma of many women's lives, yet there was total silence about it. There was no taboo on the commission of incest, only a taboo on speaking about incest."[67]

The silence around incest had begun with Freud, himself. The father of psychoanalysis knew the truth, but he also knew it would destroy his career if he spoke it.

Suppressing the Blog

The *CustodyScam* blog caused problems for DCYF. Midway through the Senate hearings, DCYF attorney Martha Kelly secured a strangely worded order advising me to remove it. Although I was not subject to family court orders, I complied, following all the legal advice I could get. Later, a subpoena arrived from the father's civil attorney, Deborah Tate, commanding me to bring "any and all photographs, writings, documents, records, etc., in your possession concerning any of the parties or the children of the parties in this matter."[68] Delivering these copies afforded me a fascinating front-row seat in this closed-door hearing and confirmed what I had sensed from outside the door of dysfunction within the courtroom. Sitting in the witness stand, I saw the court documents coming to life before me: the father sat tightly flanked by a team of four women lawyers: his criminal defense attorney Gescheidt, civil attorney Tate, DCYF attorney Kelly, and the supposedly neutral GAL, Iwon, who clung to the corner farthest from the girls' mother.

When I had tried to get legal representation, Iwon had warned at least one prominent attorney not to get involved. They were good friends, he explained to me, as did several other lawyers I consulted. None would represent me.[69] Many of them volunteered with the Rhode Island affiliate of the American Civil Liberties Union (ACLU),

---

[66] Anne Grant, "9. Protecting Freud," *Custody Scam,* Aug. 3, 2007, http://custodyscam. blogspot.com, republished under "Freud Knew About It but Protected His Career," http://little-hostages.blogspot.com/2008_05_01_archive.html#5645063201966153534.

[67] Id., quoting Jeffrey Moussaieff Masson, *Final Analysis: The Making and Unmaking of a Psychoanalyst* 176 (2003),.

[68] Subpoena from Deborah M. Tate to Anne Grant, Aug. 31, 2007. *See supra* note 21.

[69] Enormously influential as a champion of progressive causes and president of an agency that serves victims of DV, Lise Iwon had been lionized as a GAL in the *Rhode Island Monthly* (Oct. 2003). She had long been a feminist hero of mine until I studied the documents in this case and saw her efforts to remove these children. Her GAL's report, much of it hearsay, was my first indication that this case was a custody scam. Iwon had not portrayed the children's home accurately. She never interviewed the family's priest, local police, or dozens of neighbors who had known these girls all their lives. I wondered if part of her predisposition came from the fact that a conservative church was heavily involved in supporting the mother. Iwon publicly expressed her disdain for religious opponents of progressive causes. By April 2007, she had received about $12,000 from the girls' father and eventually threatened the mother with prison unless she paid the GAL thousands more. Much of her itemized bill included hours seeking clinicians who would support her attack on the mother. She spent very little time meeting with the children, whose best interests she claimed to represent.

which likewise refused to defend my right to blog about family court custody cases. Ironically, the ACLU Web site reports that its Massachusetts affiliate's support for the pro-pedophile group, North American Man/Boy Love Association (NAMBLA), was based on a "robust freedom of speech for everyone."[70]

In August 2007, the state of Rhode Island moved Molly, age seven, from its shelter into her father's sole care in another state and sent Sara to yet another foster home.

Writing an Access to Public Records Act Report

Feeling forced to remove most of the *CustodyScam* blog, I sent a letter to the director of DCYF invoking our state version of the federal Freedom of Information Act,[71] known in Rhode Island as the Access to Public Records Act (APRA).[72] Months earlier, I had written to her twice but received no reply. I needed to confirm a fact she had privately admitted: DCYF does not track findings of sexual molestation. If that were the case, there would be no way to determine whether certain staff and contractors were inclined to dismiss these findings. I sent her a formal request.[73] I asked a series of detailed questions about what policies and procedures they have in place to track findings of child molestation. Under APRA, her agency must respond within ten business days, or I could file a formal complaint with the attorney general.

The response came in the form of a letter and computer disk with documents about their policies and procedures. We combed through the documents. I spent the next week hammering out a report on the inadequacies of the procedures being used to protect children and to ensure that hearing officers were qualified and objective.[74] In contrast to the blog, this report needed a reserved tone and careful documentation of the evidence. After we released the report, the media had no idea what to do with it, given the delicacy of the subject of incest and the interminable litigation going on behind closed doors.[75]

On the basis of the APRA report, Thomas R. Bender, an appellate attorney, wrote pro bono a "Memorandum of Law" and a "Petition for Writ of Certiorari" to the Rhode Island Supreme Court. But the high court refused to hear the matter, probably because, as DCYF admitted, the family court had no authority over me to begin with. Bender said it was worth filing the petition "because it raised public awareness about the First Amendment and the internet and, more importantly, about the use of parental alienation syndrome in custody matters by the family court."[76]

---

[70] *See* http://www.aclu.org/freespeech/protest/11289prs20000831.html.

[71] 5 U.S.C. § 552.

[72] R.I. Gen. L. § 38-2. For federal and state open records laws, see http://www.spj.org/foi.asp.

[73] The text of this letter and the resulting report are available at http://littlehostages.blogspot.com.

[74] Parenting Project, "Parenting Project Report Describes the Failure of DCYF and Family Court to Protect Children, Especially in Sexual Molestation Cases," Oct. 11, 2007, http://www.thelizlibrary.org/liz/therapeutic-jurisprudence-in-Rhode-Island.pdf.

[75] One editor tried repeatedly to get my op-ed, "Should We Legalize Incest?" into print and finally acknowledged the difficulty getting it past his censors: "It's in bad taste." The comment reminded me of Jeffrey Moussaieff Masson's dismay that "There was no taboo on the commission of incest, only a taboo on speaking about incest." Jeffrey Moussaieff Masson, *Final Analysis: The Making and Unmaking of a Psychoanalyst* 176–77 (1990).

[76] Edward Fitzpatrick, "Supreme Court Won't Hear Case of Minister's Custody Blog," *Providence J.,* Jan. 19, 2008, at B1, *available at.* http://www.projo.com/news/courts/content/anne_grant_denied_01-19-08_J48M3F7_v28.27a3382.html.

Securing Strategic Litigation Against Public Participation Suit Protection

In addition to APRA, another state law can advance the cause of custody court reform. In 1995, Rhode Island reformers secured Strategic Litigation Against Public Participation (SLAPP) suit legislation, which served as a powerful tool for civil rights and environmental issues.[77] SLAPP signifies how retaliatory lawsuits can have a chilling effect on citizens' right to petition their government, due to the fear of enormously expensive legal costs to defend oneself in court.

In order to avail myself of this legal protection, I frame my writing in terms of the need for government reform. I make sure my work is well-researched, accurate, and not maliciously motivated, as set forth in Rhode Island's anti-SLAPP suit law. Then, if I become the target of a SLAPP suit, I can petition the judge for a declaratory judgment that the suit is invalid and that the litigator must pay the costs of my legal defense.

Daunting Truths

The *CustodyScam* blog and newspaper coverage of our petition to the Supreme Court brought more phone messages and e-mails with similar stories—about children who came home from visits to their fathers and acted out sexually, sometimes asking their mothers questions that would have led even Richard Gardner to suspect genuine abuse. Responses also came from fathers: Some worried about children getting abused by their mothers' boyfriends or new husbands. One father described his anguish at feeling falsely accused.

In a culture saturated with drugs, sex, and narcissism, children contend with daunting truths about the people who wield power in their lives. Limited by their specialties, the experts often fail to see the whole picture and rely on officers of the court to help them interpret cases. Few want to cause offense that will cost them jobs or professional standing in a tenuous economy. Consequently programs that are intended to protect children are not independent, but rather are highly susceptible to influential clinicians and attorneys, especially GALs, who have built-in conflicts of interest. Although assigned to advocate for children's "best interests," GALs are paid by whichever parent can afford their high price.

Their itemized bills tell that story. At $200 an hour, GAL Lise Iwon had charged $1,000 for her only home visit, including $400 for the hours in her car.[78]

Iwon communicated closely with the doctor at the Child Protection Program (CPP) of Hasbro Children's Hospital, where staff are able to document evidence of child rape, but too often, in our experience, miss the far greater prevalence of adults forcing children to undress and to participate in adult masturbation. Since this leaves no physical signs, it can be detected only through a child's words, behavior, and emotional preoccupation.

---

[77] R.I. Gen. Laws § 9-33, *available at* http://www.rilin.state.ri.us/Statutes/TITLE9/9-33/INDEX.HTM. The Rhode Island Supreme Court has affirmed the state's SLAPP-suit law as constitutional and has awarded damages to those who were targeted for trying to petition the government. (I may have been one of the first to use this protection when a batterer tried to name me and the Women's Center of Rhode Island as third parties in his custody case. The judge recognized that his suit was a reprisal for our work assisting his wife and would not allow it to go forward.) To learn which states offer this protection, see http://www.casp.net/.

[78] *See supra* note 69.

In Molly's case, a CPP fellow, Dr. Nancy Harper, stepped far beyond her scientific role. Her narrative included one page of medical information, then added ten more pages of hearsay, pounding out the father's drumbeat against the mother in a circle of allegations from Norbara Octeau, Lise Iwon, Haven Miles, and John Parsons.[79] Harper's report, never signed by her supervisor, went directly to Iwon, then immediately to court, and secured the order that removed the girls from their mother. It would take sixteen more months to give Molly to her father.

As a GAL, Iwon removed three clinicians from the case who strongly disagreed with her position against the mother. She then recruited more support from Massachusetts General Hospital, where clinical psychologist Bernice Kelly wrote that Iwon had suggested parental alienation to her.[80] In her report to the court, Kelly proceeded to list the "eight primary symptoms"[81] set forth by Gardner. She clearly was unaware that his theory has been discredited as junk science and is considered legally inadmissible under nationally recognized rules of evidence.

WRITING VERBATIMS

Even though Gardner himself described many genuine signs of child sexual abuse, it has become dangerous for protective parents to report such evidence. Abusers and their attorneys retaliate, bombarding clinicians with phone calls and e-mails alleging "parental alienation." They create a litigious climate that frightens professionals. Doctors become circumspect and distance themselves from protective parents, usually mothers, who feel abandoned by those they turned to for help. The mothers' increasingly frantic behavior appears bizarre and self-incriminating. This happened at Hasbro Hospital, where the physician grossly misjudged Molly's mother.

I encourage protective parents caught in this Kafkaesque predicament to record conversations electronically[82] or to write "verbatims" as soon as possible after each conversation. First, they must learn the difficult skill of listening to children, clinicians, and lawyers without visibly reacting. Then they must quickly write the words that were spoken from memory (placing gestures and actions in parentheses). Later they should add the date, place, time, circumstance, and names. Here is an outline for a verbatim:

DATE:
PLACE:
TIME:
CIRCUMSTANCE:
AB [initials of person] = NAME
BC = NAME
DE = NAME

AB: What happened when you . . .?

---

[79] Nancy Harper, M.D., "Child Safe/Child Protection Clinic," 1676-86-32 AC 000119896231 (Mar. 21, 2006). *See supra* note 21.

[80] Bernice Kelly, Psy.D., M.S., R.N., "Status Report (N20040106)," Jan. 11, 2007, at 2. *See supra* note 21.

[81] Id. at 6.

[82] For more about state laws on secret recording of conversations, see http://www.abanet.org/cpr/ethicsearch/record.html.

BC: I did thus and so . . .
AB: Did so and so speak to you?
DE: (etc.)

With caution, this verbatim format can document conversations with children, as long as parents remember that the court typically forbids them to talk with children about alleged abuse. Good parents know they should respond to children's concerns, but a litigator might use this as evidence that a parent is "alienating, brainwashing, and coaching" a child. Sometimes the best a parent can do is to keep a record without responding to the child's comments. This record may someday help to discern the truth. Here is one mother's short verbatim:

DATE: xx-xx-xx
TIME: 7:15 p.m.
PLACE: DB's bathtub
CIRCUMSTANCES: DB playing with her My Little Pony in the tub.

DB: (trying to put My Little Pony in her vaginal area) Daddy does this. He puts things here and I have to put them in his bottom (staring and thinking) but his bottom has hair, not like my bottom. It doesn't have hair.

Writing verbatims is a valuable way to record evidence that may never be safe to use in court, but may one day help children in therapy to retrieve the truth of their earliest years. Sensory motor psychotherapy is especially helpful to trauma survivors and far superior to court-ordered talk therapy that often compounds the ordeal.[83]

WRITING AS PUNISHMENT, THERAPY, AND STRATEGY

Children who suffer from DV or legal abuse often express themselves and seek validation through writing: letters to judges, diaries, e-mails, and text messages. If they try to communicate with protective parents after being removed for court-ordered deprogramming,[84] judges frequently respond punitively by imposing gag orders and penalizing the protective parent. Ironically, judges often err on the other side: trying to induce reunification with an abusive parent by coercing children to write letters.

In one clumsy attempt at family engineering, a judge incorrectly blamed the mother when her daughter refused to write court-ordered letters to her father. But he also accused that mother of creating the illustrated short story her fourteen-year-old son had produced independently about the children's ordeal with their father. Ironically this judge accused the children of being "manipulative" as if he, himself, were not.

In his story, the boy told how he, his sister, mother, and other relatives hastily escaped for a water park outing in 2000, when he was eleven and his sister was ten, before their father, armed with a court order, hauled the children back to Rhode Island: "We were running away, just for the weekend because it was the only way to get our

---

[83] For examples of sensorimotor psychotherapy, see http://www.traumacenter.org/ and http://www.sensorimotorpsychotherapy.org/home/index.html.

[84] The court "reunifies" children with rejected parents by methods similar to those used to kidnap and deprogram cult members in the 1970s.

last time together."[85] Like many children trapped in these cases, he described his father as the "Monster" who "has no feeling or emotion for others" and "can't be stopped." At the police station the "Monster" "tried to use its mask to hide itself, trying to pretend it was a sugary sweet man."

> It came toward me and opened its arms for a hug. I screamed at it. Suddenly that mask popped off and the Monster snapped over and grabbed me. He was grumbling his evil grumble. . . . I couldn't stop at my house to gather things . . . I couldn't even get my coat out of my mother's car. The Monster grabbed my sister and me and headed to the door.[86]

The boy tries to run away, but fails. Police threaten him with juvenile detention, call him a "girl" for crying, promise it will all work out, tell him lies. The children languish for twenty-nine months in the "Kingdom of the Monster," and the boy hints at suicide: "the lifeline of my mother was slipping away."[87] He comes home one day to find something is wrong. The "Monster" is screaming on the phone. His sister whispers in the boy's ear. He starts to cry, but he is also laughing: "We won, we won, we won won won."[88]

CONCLUDING QUESTIONS

So has all this writing made any difference? Can writing help us keep our sanity, speak truth to power, create public awareness, and build political consensus? As horrific as these truths remain, knowing them compels us to write, speak, sing, choreograph, produce films, and creatively communicate the truth as we have witnessed it.

Someday Sara and Molly (see "Case Presentation") will read all that is being written to protest the violations against them. They will see their mother's journals, their teachers' and neighbors' letters, the petitions, testimony, transcripts, blogs, articles, books, and films. We will finally hear what Molly and Sara say about being forcibly removed from their home, mother, and each other during these irreplaceable years.

I hope that those who have spoken and written truth to power, especially Molly, who dared to disclose abuse in the first place, will see the ways she inspired us to break the silence about sexual abuse, clinical abuse, and judicial abuse of children.

---

[85] Christopher DiRuggiero, "The Boy, the Monster, and the Life That Never Was," at 6 (2003).
[86] Id. at 7.
[87] Id. at 20.
[88] Id. at 21.

Afterword

by Rita Smith, B.A.

Thank you for reading this important and critical book. The focus of this piece was on men's violence against women, as that is the majority of violence committed between intimate partners. It is true, of course, that some women abuse their male partners, some abuse their female partners, and some men abuse their male partners. Regardless, whenever a case may involve intimate partner violence, a careful assessment of the tactics used by the abuser must be made, in order to ensure the safety of the family.

In over thirty years of work to end men's violence against women, the question of who gets custody has consistently been a huge problem for victims of battering and abuse. In the early days of our work in the domestic violence (DV) movement, very little action was taken by law enforcement when a woman was assaulted by an intimate partner. It was difficult to get the police or sheriff's deputy to respond to a call for help, much less arrest someone at the scene.

After many years of work by DV advocates with the criminal justice system and legislative bodies around the country, this is no longer the case. In most states, when one parent assaults the other, an arrest is made as long as probable cause exists. This signifies good progress toward the goal of keeping families and communities safer.

However, the handling of child custody matters after these parents separate is another matter. In many cases, the mother's safety is greatly compromised, and deaths of a mother and/or children are all too often the tragic outcome of the unwillingness of our civil court system to fully examine the complex issues presented by these cases.

Every day, DV advocates work with women who have taken the courageous step of leaving their abuser. If they have children, they feel a tremendous responsibility to protect not only themselves but also their children from the violence. Throughout this book, there have been many examples of how the systems designed to protect mothers and children have failed to fulfill that responsibility. In communities all across the United States, battered mothers encounter child protection workers, attorneys, and judges who refuse to believe women's reports of abuse and violence. Even with medical or other documentary proof to support these mothers' claims, judges routinely award unsupervised visitation or even full or joint custody to alleged abusers.

The good news is that most separating couples with children in the United States are able to come to an agreement about custody on their own. Studies indicate that about 95 percent of custody cases are not contested in court. For the 5 percent of cases that are contested, most include allegations of abuse and violence. The National Coalition Against Domestic Violence (NCADV) and many other organizations have worked to educate local community advocates about the issues facing women who file for divorce and custody orders. As advocates, our job is to be prepared to challenge the abuser's attempts to continue to control the mother through access to the children.

A story about one woman's struggle to separate from her abuser illustrates some of the typical tactics used in these cases. This woman was staying in a shelter for battered women but was still in contact with her abuser. He begged her to allow him to see the children. He persisted in crying and pleading with her to let him see them. She finally decided that he must truly miss his children, so she relented, meeting him in a public place where he could spend time with their children. When she got back to the shelter, she spoke sadly about how the abuser had spent the entire time focused on her instead of talking to his children. His goal was to get access to her so that he could try to get her back under his control. He was fully willing to use the children as a tool for that purpose.

Abusers are very good at manipulating people. They are obsessed with getting their way and will use any means, including violence, to control the person they claim to love. They will use the civil court system to harass, abuse, and financially devastate their victim long after she has gained her physical freedom. Leaving the abuser does not make a victim safe. It might allow her to find a place that her abuser does not have constant access to, but it does not mean that he will stop trying to control and abuse her. If she has a job, he can shift his efforts toward contacting her at her workplace. He can follow her home to find out where she is living, or, if the children attend school, he can gain access to their records to discover her location.

The control tactics used by abusers have a negative impact upon their immediate family, friends, neighbors, and the communities in which they live. The mother must constantly be on alert to monitor any signs that his abuse is escalating. Other family members may get drawn into the effort by the abuser to manipulate her and regain control of her. In the most tragic of cases, those in which the mother and/or children are murdered by the abuser, an entire community may be devastated.

It is imperative that we educate ourselves and others about this issue. We must challenge our systems to develop strategies that focus on the safety of the family as the first and most important goal when making custody decisions. If we do not make such critical changes, we will continue to see these kinds of tragedies befall children and their mothers—something we simply cannot allow to happen.

This book took a multidisciplinary approach to the problem of DV and child custody by using up-to-date research from leading experts in their fields, including judges, lawyers, psychiatrists, psychologists, sociologists, journalists, and DV advocates. This research confirms what the NCADV has been concerned about for many years: thousands of children are being sent to live with abusive fathers while safe, protective mothers are denied a meaningful relationship with their children. The experts who wrote chapters for this book provide the information and practices necessary to prevent these tragedies. With the publication of this book, any professional who persists in using the misguided practices that have ruined the lives of so many children might be considered guilty of malpractice.

Protective mothers have been telling DV advocates for years that they were afraid to leave, because their abusers threatened to seek custody of the children. It is the courts' own mistakes that have allowed abusers to make good on these threats. When courts begin to set a high priority on preventing abusers from winning custody, they will finally be fulfilling their assigned and critical role in the quest to end DV.

Appendix A

Organizations and Online Resources

Listed below are organizations and Web sites that might be useful to readers. This list is not intended to be exhaustive, but rather it is a starting point for those seeking additional information. Some of these organizations are national in focus, while others are limited to a state or local area. Please be aware that URLs change frequently, so it is possible that some of these Web-based organizations may not still be available.

Battered Mothers Custody Conference
URL: http://www.batteredmotherscustodyconference.org

Barry Goldstein
URL: http://www.barrygoldstein.net

National Coalition Against Domestic Violence (NCADV)
1120 Lincoln Street, Suite #1603
Denver, CO 80203
Phone: (303) 839-1852
URL: /http://www.ncadv.org
URL for information on state coalitions:
http://http://www.ncadv.org/resources/StateCoalitionList_73.html
E-mail: mainoffice@ncadv.org

The Leadership Council
191 Presidential Boulevard
Suite C-132
Bala Cynwyd, PA 19004
URL: http://www.leadershipcouncil.org
E-mail: desk1@leadershipcouncil.org

National Council of Juvenile and Family Court Judges (NCJFCJ)
P.O. Box 8970
Reno, NV 89507
Phone: (775) 784-6012
URL: http://www.ncjfcj.org
E-mail: staff@ncjfcj.org

National Organization for Women (NOW)
1100 H. Street NW 3rd Floor
Washington, DC 20005
Phone: (202) 628-8669
URL: http://www.now.org

ABA Commission on Domestic Violence
740 15th St. NW
Washington, DC 20005
(202) 662-1720
URL: http://www.abanet.org/domviol/home.html

ABA Center on Children and the Law
740 15th St., NW
Washington, DC 20005
Phone: (202) 662-1720 or (800) 285-2221 (Service Center)
URL: http://www.abanet.org/child
E-mail: http://www.ctrchildlaw@abanet.org

ABA Child Custody Pro Bono Project
740 15th St. NW
Washington, DC 20005
Phone: (202) 662-1720
URL: http://www.abanet.org/legalservices/probono/childcustody.html

American Domestic Violence Crisis Line
Phone: (866) 879-6626
URL: http://www.866uswomen.org

American Professional Society on the Abuse of Children (APSAC)
407 South Dearborn St., Suite 1300
Chicago , IL60605
Phone: (312) 554-0166
FAX: (312) 554-0919
URL: http://www.apsac.org/mc/page.do

Asian & Pacific Islander Institute on Domestic Violence
450 Sutter St. Suite 600
San Francisco, CA. 94108
Phone: (415) 954-9988
URL: http://www.apiahf.org/index.php/programs/domestic-violence.html

Association for Children for Enforcement of Support (ACES)
3474 Raymond Blvd. 2nd Floor
University Heights, Ohio 44118
Phone: (800) 738-2337
URL: http://www.childsupport-aces.org

Lundy Bancroft
URL: http://www.lundybancroft.com

Battered Women's Justice Project
1801 Nicollet Avenue South # 102
Minneapolis, MN 55403
Phone: (612) 824-8768 or (800) 903-0111, ext 1
URL: http://www.bwjp.org

California Protective Parents Association
PO Box 15284
Sacramento CA 95851-0284
Phone: (866) 874.9815
URL: http://www.protectiveparents.com
E-mail: cppa001@aol.com

Talia Carner
URL: http://www.Taliacarner.com

Center for Research & Education
On Violence Against Women and Children
1137 Western Road Room 1118
Faculty of Education Building
The University of Western Ontario
London, Ontario, Canada N6G 1G7
(519) 661-4040
URL: http://www.crvawc.ca/section-contact/index.htm

The Center for Survivor Agency and Justice (Erika Sussman)
2001 S. St. NW Suite 400
Washington, DC 20009
Phone: (202) 552-8304
URL: http://www.csaj.org

Children Against Court Appointed Child Abuse
URL: http://www.ca3cacaca.blogspot.com/

Civic Research Institute
P. O. Box 585
Kingston, NJ 08528
Phone: 609-683-4450
URL: http://www.civicresearchinstitute.com

Courageous Kids Network
URL: http://www.courageouskids.net

Custody Prep for Moms
URL: http://www.custodyprepformoms.org/index.php

The Custody Scam Blogspot (Anne Grant)
URL: http://www.custodyscam.blogspot.com

Margaret Dore
URL: http://www.margaretdore.com

Molly Dragiewicz
URL: http://www.mollydragiewicz.com

Illinois Coalition for Family Court Reform
URL: http://www.Icfcr.org

Institute on Domestic Violence in the African American Community
290 Peters Hall
1404 Gortner Avenue
St. Paul, MN. 55108
Phone: (612) 624-5357
URL: http://www.idvaac.org

Justice for Children
2600 Southwest Freeway, Suite 806
Houston, TX 77098
Phone: (800) 733-0059
URL: http://www.justiceforchildren.org

Legal Momentum
395 Hudson Street
New York, NY 10014
Phone: (212) 925-6635
URL: http://www.Legalmomentum.org

The Legal Project
Stuyvescent Plaza
1475 Western Avenue
Albany, NY 12203
Phone: (518) 435-1770
URL: http://www.Legalproject.org

Legal Resource Center on Violence Against Women
6930 Carroll Ave. #400
Takoma Park, MD. 20912
Phone: (301) 270-1550 or (800) 556-4053
URL: http://www.lrcvaw.org

Michael Lesher
URL: http://www.michaellesher.com

The Liz Library (Elizabeth J. Kates)
URL: http://www.thelizlibrary.org/index

National Center for Victims of Crime
2000 M. Street NW #480
Washington, DC 20005
Phone: (202) 467-8700
URL: http://www.ncvc.org/NCVC/Main.Aspx

National Center on Domestic and Sexual Violence
4612 Shoal Creek Blvd.
Austin, TX 78756
Phone: (512) 407-9020
URL: http://www.ncdsv.org

National Domestic Violence Hotline
Phone: (800) 799-7233
URL: http://www.ndvh.org

National Family Court Watch Project
510 Highland Ave. # 414
Milford MI. 48381
Phone: 248-752-8623
URL: http://www.nationalfamilycourtwatchproject.org

National Latino Alliance for the Elimination of Domestic Violence (Alianza)
P.O. Box 672 Triborough Station
New York, NY 10035
Phone: (646) 672-1404
URL: http://www.dvalianza.org

National Organization for Women Foundation
URL: http://www.nowfoundation.org

National Network to End Domestic Violence (NNEDV)
National Domestic Violence Hotline: 1-800-799-SAFE (7233) or 1-800-787-3224 (TTY).
2001 S Street NW, Suite 400
Washington, DC 20009
Phone: (202) 543-5566
URL: http://www.nnedv.org

National Online Resource Center on Violence Against Women
6400 Flank Dr. Suite 1300
Harrisburg, PA. 17112
Phone: (717) 545-6400 or (800) 537-2238
URL: http://www.vawnet.org

National Organization of Men Against Sexism (NOMAS)
P.O. Box 455
Louisville, CO 80027
Phone: (303) 666-7043
URL: http://www.nomas.org

National Resource Center on Domestic Violence
6400 Flank Dr. Suite 1300
Harrisburg, PA. 17112
Phone: (717) 545-6400 or (800) 932-4632
URL: http://www.pcadv.org/About-Contact/National-Projects/National-Resource-
Center-on-Domestic-Violence.asp

New York Model Batterer Program
VCS Community Change Project
77 South Main Street
New City, NY 10956
Phone: (845) 634-5729
URL: http://www.nymbp.org

Office on Violence Against Women (USDOJ)
950 Pennsylvania Avenue NW
Washington, DC 20530
Phone: (202) 514-2000
URL: http://www.ovw.usdoj.gov/

Rights for Mothers
URL: http://www.rightsformothers.com

Sheila Wellstone Institute
2446 University Avenue W Suite 170
St. Paul, MN. 55114
Phone: (651) 645-3939
URL: http://www.wellstone.org/our-programs/sheila-wellstone-institute

Small Justice (Garland Waller)
URL: http://www.smalljustice.com

Stop Family Violence
URL: http://www.stopfamilyviolence.org

Violence Against Women Online Resources
URL: http://www.vaw.umn.edu/library/ccp/

Women of Color Network
6400 Flank Drive Suite 1300
Harrisburg, PA 17112
Phone: (800) 537-2238
URL: http://www.womenofcolornetwork.org

Robin Yeamans
URL: http://www.divorcecal.com

Joan Zorza
URL: http://www.zorza.net

Appendix B

Books

For readers who want more information about the topics in this book, we recommend the following books and publications:

Goldstein, B., *Scared to Leave Afraid to Stay: Paths from Family Violence to Safety* (Robert D. Reed Publishers 2002)

Bancroft, L., & Silverman, J., *The Batterer as Parent: Addressing the Impact of Domestic Violence on Family Dynamics* (Sage Publications 2002).

Bancroft, L., *Why Does He Do That: Inside the Minds of Angry and Controlling Men.* (Berkeley Publishing Group 2002).

Bancroft, L., *When Dad Hurts Mom: Helping Your Children Heal the Wounds of Witnessing Abuse* (Penquin Group 2002).

Bass, E., & Davis, L., *The Courage to Heal: A Guide for Women Survivors of Child Sexual Abuse; 20th Anniversary Edition* (Harper Paperbacks 2008).

Chesler, P., *Mothers on Trial: The Battle for Children and Custody* (Harcourt 1991).

Evans, P., *The Verbally Abusive Relationship: How to Recognize It and How to Respond* (Adams Media 2003).

Jaffe, P.G., Baker, L.L. & Cunningham, A.J., *Protecting Children From Domestic Violence Strategies for Community Intervention* (Guilford Press 2004).

Jaffe, P., Lemon, N. , & Poisson, S., *Child Custody and Domestic Violence: A Call for Safety and Accountability* (Sage Publications 2002).

Lemon, N.K.D., *Domestic Violence Law* (West, 3d ed. 2009).

Muhammad, M., *Scared Silent* (Streban Books 2009).

Myers, J.E.B., *A Mother's Nightmare—Incest: A Practical Legal Guide for Parents and Professionals* (Interpersonal Violence: The Practice Series) (Sage Publications 1997).

Neustein, A., & Lesher, M., *From Madness to Mutiny: Why Mothers Are Running From the Family Courts—And What Can Be Done About It?* (University of New England Press 2005).

Ptacek, J., *Battered Women in the Courtroom: The Power of Judicial Responses* (Northeastern University Press 1999).

Stark, E., *Coercive Control: How Men Entrap Women in Personal Life* (Oxford University Press 2007).

Stark, E., & Flitcraft, A., *Women at Risk: Domestic Violence and Women's Health* (Sage Publications 1996).

Titelman, W., *Let My Children Go: A Mother's Journal* (Kinderlex Books (2003).

Winner, K., *Divorced From Justice: The Abuse of Women and Children by Divorce Lawyers and Judges* (Regan Books 1996).

Zorza, J., ed., *Violence Against Woman* (3 volumes) (Civic Research Institute 2002, 2004, 2006).

Appendix C

List of Abbreviations and Acronyms

ABA   American Bar Association
APA   American Psychological Association
BIC   best interests of the child(ren)
BMCC   Battered Mothers Custody Conference
CDC   Centers for Disease Control
CK   Courageous Kids
CPPA   California Protective Parents Association
CPS   child protective services
DV   domestic violence
FRs   fathers' rights
GAL   guardian ad litem
NCADV   National Coalition Against Domestic Violence
NCJFCJ   National Council of Juvenile and Family Court Judges
NOW   National Organization for Women
PAS   Parental Alienation Syndrome

Table of Cases

[References are to pages.]

Index

[References are to pages.]